Elements

of

Programming

Interviews

The Insiders' Guide

Adnan Aziz

Tsung-Hsien Lee

Amit Prakash

ElementsOfProgrammingInterviews.com

Adnan Aziz is a professor at the Department of Electrical and Computer Engineering at The University of Texas at Austin, where he conducts research and teaches classes in applied algorithms. He received his Ph.D. from The University of California at Berkeley; his undergraduate degree is from Indian Institutes of Technology Kanpur. He has worked at Google, Qualcomm, IBM, and several software startups. When not designing algorithms, he plays with his children, Laila, Imran, and Omar.

Tsung-Hsien Lee is a Software Engineer at Google. Previously, he worked as a Software Engineer Intern at Facebook. He received both his M.S. and undergraduate degrees from National Tsing Hua University. He has a passion for designing and implementing algorithms. He likes to apply algorithms to every aspect of his life. He takes special pride in helping to organize Google Code Jam 2014 and 2015.

Amit Prakash is a co-founder and CTO of ThoughtSpot, a Silicon Valley startup. Previously, he was a Member of the Technical Staff at Google, where he worked primarily on machine learning problems that arise in the context of online advertising. Before that he worked at Microsoft in the web search team. He received his Ph.D. from The University of Texas at Austin; his undergraduate degree is from Indian Institutes of Technology Kanpur. When he is not improving business intelligence, he indulges in his passion for puzzles, movies, travel, and adventures with Nidhi and Aanya.

Elements of Programming Interviews: The Insiders' Guide
by Adnan Aziz, Tsung-Hsien Lee, and Amit Prakash

We typeset this book using LATEX and the Memoir class. We used TikZ to draw figures. Allan Ytac created the cover, based on a design brief we provided.

The companion website for the book includes contact information and a list of known errors for each version of the book. If you come across an error or an improvement, please let us know.

Version 1.5.9

Website: http://elementsofprogramminginterviews.com

To my father, Ishrat Aziz,
for giving me my lifelong love of learning

Adnan Aziz

To my parents, Hsien-Kuo Lee and Tseng-Hsia Li,
for the everlasting support and love they give me

Tsung-Hsien Lee

To my parents, Manju Shree and Arun Prakash,
the most loving parents I can imagine

Amit Prakash

Table of Contents

Introduction

> And it ought to be remembered that there is nothing more
> difficult to take in hand, more perilous to conduct, or
> more uncertain in its success, than to take the lead in the
> introduction of a new order of things.

— N. MACHIAVELLI, 1513

Elements of Programming Interviews (EPI) aims to help engineers interviewing for software development positions. The primary focus of EPI is data structures, algorithms, system design, and problem solving. The material is largely presented through questions.

An interview problem

Let's begin with Figure 1 below. It depicts movements in the share price of a company over 40 days. Specifically, for each day, the chart shows the daily high and low, and the price at the opening bell (denoted by the white square). Suppose you were asked in an interview to design an algorithm that determines the maximum profit that could have been made by buying and then selling a single share over a given day range, subject to the constraint that the buy and the sell have to take place at the start of the day. (This algorithm may be needed to backtest a trading strategy.)

You may want to stop reading now, and attempt this problem on your own.

First clarify the problem. For example, you should ask for the input format. Let's say the input consists of three arrays L, H, and S, of nonnegative floating point numbers, representing the low, high, and starting prices for each day. The constraint

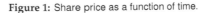

| Day 0 | Day 5 | Day 10 | Day 15 | Day 20 | Day 25 | Day 30 | Day 35 | Day 40 |

Figure 1: Share price as a function of time.

1

that the purchase and sale have to take place at the start of the day means that it suffices to consider S. You may be tempted to simply return the difference of the minimum and maximum elements in S. If you try a few test cases, you will see that the minimum can occur after the maximum, which violates the requirement in the problem statement—you have to buy before you can sell.

At this point, a brute-force algorithm would be appropriate. For each pair of indices i and $j > i$, if $S[j] - S[i]$ is greater than the largest difference seen so far, update the largest difference to $S[j] - S[i]$. You should be able to code this algorithm using a pair of nested for-loops and test it in a matter of a few minutes. You should also derive its time complexity as a function of the length n of the input array. The outer loop is invoked $n - 1$ times, and the ith iteration processes $n - 1 - i$ elements. Processing an element entails computing a difference, performing a compare, and possibly updating a variable, all of which take constant time. Hence, the run time is proportional to $\sum_{i=0}^{n-2}(n - 1 - i) = \frac{(n-1)(n)}{2}$, i.e., the time complexity of the brute-force algorithm is $O(n^2)$. You should also consider the space complexity, i.e., how much memory your algorithm uses. The array itself takes memory proportional to n, and the additional memory used by the brute-force algorithm is a constant independent of n—a couple of iterators and one floating point variable.

Once you have a working algorithm, try to improve upon it. Specifically, an $O(n^2)$ algorithm is usually not acceptable when faced with large arrays. You may have heard of an algorithm design pattern called divide-and-conquer. It yields the following algorithm for this problem. Split S into two subarrays, $S[0 : \lfloor\frac{n}{2}\rfloor]$ and $S[\lfloor\frac{n}{2}\rfloor + 1 : n - 1]$; compute the best result for the first and second subarrays; and combine these results. In the combine step we take the better of the results for the two subarrays. However, we also need to consider the case where the optimum buy and sell take place in separate subarrays. When this is the case, the buy must be in the first subarray, and the sell in the second subarray, since the buy must happen before the sell. If the optimum buy and sell are in different subarrays, the optimum buy price is the minimum price in the first subarray, and the optimum sell price is in the maximum price in the second subarray. We can compute these prices in $O(n)$ time with a single pass over each subarray. Therefore, the time complexity $T(n)$ for the divide-and-conquer algorithm satisfies the recurrence relation $T(n) = 2T(\frac{n}{2}) + O(n)$, which solves to $O(n \log n)$.

The divide-and-conquer algorithm is elegant and fast. Its implementation entails some corner cases, e.g., an empty subarray, subarrays of length one, and an array in which the price decreases monotonically, but it can still be written and tested by a good developer in 20–30 minutes.

Looking carefully at the combine step of the divide-and-conquer algorithm, you may have a flash of insight. Specifically, you may notice that the maximum profit that can be made by selling on a specific day is determined by the minimum of the

2

stock prices over the previous days. Since the maximum profit corresponds to selling on *some* day, the following algorithm correctly computes the maximum profit. Iterate through S, keeping track of the minimum element m seen thus far. If the difference of the current element and m is greater than the maximum profit recorded so far, update the maximum profit. This algorithm performs a constant amount of work per array element, leading to an $O(n)$ time complexity. It uses two float-valued variables (the minimum element and the maximum profit recorded so far) and an iterator, i.e., $O(1)$ additional space. It is considerably simpler to implement than the divide-and-conquer algorithm—a few minutes should suffice to write and test it. Working code is presented in Solution 6.7 on Page 67.

If in a 45–60 minutes interview, you can develop the algorithm described above, implement and test it, and analyze its complexity, you would have had a very successful interview. In particular, you would have demonstrated to your interviewer that you possess several key skills:

- The ability to rigorously formulate real-world problems.
- The skills to solve problems and design algorithms.
- The tools to go from an algorithm to a tested program.
- The analytical techniques required to determine the computational complexity of your solution.

Book organization

Interviewing successfully is about more than being able to intelligently select data structures and design algorithms quickly. For example, you also need to know how to identify suitable companies, pitch yourself, ask for help when you are stuck on an interview problem, and convey your enthusiasm. These aspects of interviewing are the subject of Chapters 1–3, and are summarized in Table 1.1 on Page 8.

Chapter 1 is specifically concerned with preparation. Chapter 2 discusses how you should conduct yourself at the interview itself. Chapter 3 describes interviewing from the interviewer's perspective. The latter is important for candidates too, because of the insights it offers into the decision making process. Chapter 4 reviews problem solving.

Since not everyone will have the time to work through EPI in its entirety, we have prepared a study guide (Table 1.2 on Page 9) to problems you should solve, based on the amount of time you have available.

The problem chapters are organized as follows. Chapters 5–15 are concerned with basic data structures, such as arrays and binary search trees, and basic algorithms, such as binary search and quicksort. In our experience, this is the material that most interview questions are based on. Chapters 16–19 cover advanced algorithm design principles, such as dynamic programming and heuristics, as well as graphs. Chapters 20–21 focus on distributed and parallel programming, and design problems.

Each chapter begins with a summary of key concepts, followed by problems. Broadly speaking, problems are ordered by subtopic, with more commonly asked problems appearing first. Chapter 22 is a collection of more challenging problems.

The notation, specifically the symbols we use for describing algorithms, e.g., $\sum_{i=0}^{n-1} i^2, [a, b), \langle 2, 3, 5, 7 \rangle, A[i : j], \lceil x \rceil, (1011)_2, n!, \{x \mid x^2 > 2\}$, etc., is summarized starting on Page 493. It should be familiar to anyone with a technical undergraduate degree, but we still request you to review it carefully before getting into the book, and whenever you have doubts about the meaning of a symbol. Terms, e.g., BFS and dequeue, are indexed starting on Page 496.

The EPI editorial style

Solutions are based on basic concepts, such as arrays, hash tables, and binary search, used in clever ways. Some solutions use relatively advanced machinery, e.g., Dijkstra's shortest path algorithm. You will encounter such problems in an interview only if you have a graduate degree or claim specialized knowledge.

Most solutions include code snippets. These are primarily written in C++, and use C++11 features. Programs concerned with concurrency are in Java. In Chapter III on Page 495 we discuss C++ and C++11 features germane to EPI. We also give a guide to reading C++ programs for Java developers. Source code, which includes randomized and directed test cases, can be found at the book website. Java equivalents for all C++ programs are available at the same site. System design problems are conceptual and not meant to be coded; a few algorithm design problems are also in this spirit.

One of our key design goals for EPI was to make learning easier by establishing a uniform way in which to describe problems and solutions. We refer to our exposition style as the EPI Editorial Style.

Problems are specified as follows:

(1.) We establish **context**, e.g., a real-world scenario, an example, etc.

(2.) We **state the problem** to be solved. Unlike a textbook, but as is true for an interview, we do not give formal specifications, e.g., we do not specify the detailed input format or say what to do on illegal inputs. As a general rule, avoid writing code that parses input. See Page 14 for an elaboration.

(3.) We give a **short hint**—you should read this only if you get stuck. (The hint is similar to what an interviewer will give you if you do not make progress.)

Solutions are developed as follows:

(1.) We begin a **simple brute-force solution**.

(2.) We then **analyze** the brute-force approach and try to get **intuition** for why it is **inefficient** and where we can **improve upon it**, possibly by looking at concrete examples, related algorithms, etc.

(3.) Based on these insights, we develop a **more efficient** algorithm, and describe it in prose.

4

(4.) We **apply** the program to a concrete input.

(5.) We give **code** for the key steps.

(6.) We analyze time and space **complexity**.

(7.) We outline **variants**—problems whose formulation or solution is similar to the solved problem. Use variants for practice, and to test your understanding of the solution.

Note that exceptions exists to this style—for example a brute-force solution may not be meaningful, e.g., if it entails enumerating all double-precision floating point numbers in some range. For the chapters at the end of the book, which correspond to more advanced topics, such as Dynamic Programming, and Graph Algorithms, we use more parsimonious presentations, e.g., we forgo examples of applying the derived algorithm to a concrete example.

Level and prerequisites

We expect readers to be familiar with data structures and algorithms taught at the undergraduate level. The chapters on concurrency and system design require knowledge of locks, distributed systems, operating systems (OS), and insight into commonly used applications. Some of the material in the later chapters, specifically dynamic programming, graphs, and greedy algorithms, is more advanced and geared towards candidates with graduate degrees or specialized knowledge.

The review at the start of each chapter is not meant to be comprehensive and if you are not familiar with the material, you should first study it in an algorithms textbook. There are dozens of such texts and our preference is to master one or two good books rather than superficially sample many. *Algorithms* by Dasgupta, *et al.* is succinct and beautifully written; *Introduction to Algorithms* by Cormen, *et al.* is an amazing reference.

Reader engagement

Many of the best ideas in EPI came from readers like you. The study guide, ninja notation, and hints, are a few examples of many improvements that were brought about by our readers. The companion website, elementsofprogramminginterviews.com, includes a Stack Overflow-style discussion forum, and links to our social media presence. It also has links blog postings, code, and bug reports. You can always communicate with us directly—our contact information is on the website.

Part I

The Interview

1

Getting Ready

Before everything else, getting ready is the secret of success.

— H. FORD

The most important part of interview preparation is knowing the material and practicing problem solving. However, the nontechnical aspects of interviewing are also very important, and often overlooked. Chapters 1–3 are concerned with the nontechnical aspects of interviewing, ranging from résumé preparation to how hiring decisions are made. These aspects of interviewing are summarized in Table 1.1 on the following page

Study guide

Ideally, you would prepare for an interview by solving all the problems in EPI. This is doable over 12 months if you solve a problem a day, where solving entails writing a program and getting it to work on some test cases.

Since different candidates have different time constraints, we have outlined several study scenarios, and recommended a subset of problems for each scenario. This information is summarized in Table 1.2 on Page 9. The preparation scenarios we consider are Hackathon (a weekend entirely devoted to preparation), finals cram (one week, 3–4 hours per day), term project (four weeks, 1.5–2.5 hours per day), and algorithms class (3–4 months, 1 hour per day).

The problems in EPI are meant to be representative of the problems you will encounter in an interview. If you need a data structure and algorithms refresher, take a look at the EPI website, which includes a collection of review problems that will get you ready for EPI more quickly that a textbook would.

A large majority of the interview questions at Google, Amazon, Microsoft, and similar companies are drawn from the topics in Chapters 5–15. Exercise common sense when using Table 1.2, e.g., if you are interviewing for a position with a financial firm, do more problems related to probability.

Although an interviewer may occasionally ask a question directly from EPI, you should not base your preparation on memorizing solutions. Rote learning will likely lead to your giving a perfect solution to the wrong problem.

Table 1.1: A summary of nontechnical aspects of interviewing

The Interview Lifecycle, on the current page	At the Interview, on Page 12
<ul><li>Identify companies, contacts</li><li>Résumé preparation<ul><li>Basic principles</li><li>Website with links to projects</li><li>LinkedIn profile & recommendations</li></ul></li><li>Résumé submission</li><li>Mock interview practice</li><li>Phone/campus screening</li><li>On-site interview</li><li>Negotiating an offer</li></ul>	<ul><li>Don't solve the wrong problem</li><li>Get specs & requirements</li><li>Construct sample input/output</li><li>Work on concrete examples first</li><li>Spell out the brute-force solution</li><li>Think out loud</li><li>Apply patterns</li><li>Assume valid inputs</li><li>Test for corner-cases</li><li>Use proper syntax</li><li>Manage the whiteboard</li><li>Be aware of memory management</li><li>Get function signatures right</li></ul>
General Advice, on Page 16<ul><li>Know the company & interviewers</li><li>Communicate clearly</li><li>Be passionate</li><li>Be honest</li><li>Stay positive</li><li>Don't apologize</li><li>Leave perks and money out</li><li>Be well-groomed</li><li>Mind your body language</li><li>Be ready for a stress interview</li><li>Learn from bad outcomes</li><li>Negotiate the best offer</li></ul>	**Conducting an Interview, on Page 19**<ul><li>Don't be indecisive</li><li>Create a brand ambassador</li><li>Coordinate with other interviewers<ul><li>know what to test on</li><li>look for patterns of mistakes</li></ul></li><li>Characteristics of a good problem:<ul><li>no single point of failure</li><li>has multiple solutions</li><li>covers multiple areas</li><li>is calibrated on colleagues</li><li>does not require unnecessary domain knowledge</li></ul></li><li>Control the conversation<ul><li>draw out quiet candidates</li><li>manage verbose/overconfident candidates</li></ul></li><li>Use a process for recording & scoring</li><li>Determine what training is needed</li><li>Apply the litmus test</li></ul>

Chapter 22 contains a diverse collection of challenging questions. Use them to hone your problem solving skills, but go to them only after you have made major inroads into the earlier chapters. If you have a graduate degree, or claim specialized knowledge, you should definitely solve some problems from Chapter 22.

The interview lifecycle

Generally speaking, interviewing takes place in the following steps:

(1.) Identify companies that you are interested in, and, ideally, find people you know at these companies.

(2.) Prepare your résumé using the guidelines on Page 10, and submit it via a personal contact (preferred), or through an online submission process or a campus career fair.

Table 1.2: First read Chapter 4. For each chapter, first read its introductory text. Use reference only. Unless a problem is italicized, it entails writing code. For Scenario i, write for the problems in Columns 0 to $i - 1$, and pseudo-code for the problems in Column i.

Scenario 1 Hackathon 3 days		Scenario 2 Finals cram 7 days	Scenario 3 Term project 1 month	Scenario 4 Algorithms class 4 months
C0	C1	C2	C3	C4
5.1	5.7	5.8	5.3, 5.11	5.9
6.1, 6.7	6.12, 6.18	6.2, 6.17	6.6, 6.9	6.3, 6.10, 6.15
7.1	7.2, 7.4	7.5, 7.6	7.7, 7.8	7.9, 7.13
8.1	8.2, 8.4	8.5, 8.8	8.11	8.12
9.1	9.9	9.2, 9.10	9.3, 9.11	9.4
10.1	10.4	10.2, 10.10	10.9	10.11, 10.14
11.1	11.4	11.3	11.5	11.7
12.1	12.5, 12.9	12.4, 12.11	12.6, 12.12	12.7, 12.8
13.1	13.3, 13.4	13.2, 13.7	13.5, 13.8	13.11
14.1	14.2	14.3, 14.5	14.7, 14.10	14.8
15.1	15.3, 15.4	15.5, *15.9*	15.6, 15.10	15.8, 15.11
16.1	16.2	16.3	16.4, 16.9	16.6, 16.10
17.1	17.2	17.3, 17.6	17.5, 17.7	17.12
18.5	18.7	18.6, 18.8	18.9	18.1
19.1	19.7	19.2	19.3	19.10
20.3	20.7	*20.6*	*20.9*	*20.10*
21.11	*21.13*	*21.14*	*21.1*	*21.2*

(3.) Perform an initial phone screening, which often consists of a question-answer session over the phone or video chat with an engineer. You may be asked to submit code via a shared document or an online coding site such as ideone.com, collabedit.com, or coderpad.io. Don't take the screening casually—it can be extremely challenging.

(4.) Go for an on-site interview—this consists of a series of one-on-one interviews with engineers and managers, and a conversation with your Human Resources (HR) contact.

(5.) Receive offers—these are usually a starting point for negotiations.

Note that there may be variations—e.g., a company may contact you, or you may submit via your college's career placement center. The screening may involve a homework assignment to be done before or after the conversation. The on-site interview may be conducted over a video chat session. Most on-sites are half a day, but others may last the entire day. For anything involving interaction over a network, be absolutely sure to work out logistics (a quiet place to talk with a landline rather than a mobile, familiarity with the coding website and chat software, etc.) well in advance.

We recommend that you interview at as many places as you can without it taking away from your job or classes. The experience will help you feel more comfortable with interviewing and you may discover you really like a company that you did not know much about.

It always astonishes us to see candidates who've worked hard for at least four years in school, and often many more in the workplace, spend 30 minutes jotting down random factoids about themselves and calling the result a résumé.

A résumé needs to address HR staff, the individuals interviewing you, and the hiring manager. The HR staff, who typically first review your résumé, look for keywords, so you need to be sure you have those covered. The people interviewing you and the hiring manager need to know what you've done that makes you special, so you need to differentiate yourself.

Here are some key points to keep in mind when writing a résumé:

(1.) Have a clear statement of your objective; in particular, make sure that you tailor your résumé for a given employer.

E.g., "My outstanding ability is developing solutions to computationally challenging problems; communicating them in written and oral form; and working with teams to implement them. I would like to apply these abilities at XYZ."

(2.) The most important points—the ones that differentiate you from everyone else—should come first. People reading your résumé proceed in sequential order, so you want to impress them with what makes you special early on. (Maintaining a logical flow, though desirable, is secondary compared to this principle.)

As a consequence, you should not list your programming languages, coursework, etc. early on, since these are likely common to everyone. You should list significant class projects (this also helps with keywords for HR.), as well as talks/papers you've presented, and even standardized test scores, if truly exceptional.

(3.) The résumé should be of a high-quality: no spelling mistakes; consistent spacings, capitalizations, numberings; and correct grammar and punctuation. Use few fonts. Portable Document Format (PDF) is preferred, since it renders well across platforms.

(4.) Include contact information, a LinkedIn profile, and, ideally, a URL to a personal homepage with examples of your work. These samples may be class projects, a thesis, and links to companies and products you've worked on. Include design documents as well as a link to your version control repository.

(5.) If you can work at the company without requiring any special processing (e.g., if you have a Green Card, and are applying for a job in the US), make a note of that.

(6.) Have friends review your résumé; they are certain to find problems with it that you missed. It is better to get something written up quickly, and then refine it based on feedback.

(7.) A résumé does not have to be one page long—two pages are perfectly appropriate. (Over two pages is probably not a good idea.)

(8.) As a rule, we prefer not to see a list of hobbies/extracurricular activities (e.g., "reading books", "watching TV", "organizing tea party activities") unless they are really different (e.g., "Olympic rower") and not controversial.

Whenever possible, have a friend or professional acquaintance at the company route your résumé to the appropriate manager/HR contact—the odds of it reaching the right hands are much higher. At one company whose practices we are familiar with, a résumé submitted through a contact is 50 times more likely to result in a hire than one submitted online. Don't worry about wasting your contact's time—employees often receive a referral bonus, and being responsible for bringing in stars is also viewed positively.

Mock interviews

Mock interviews are a great way of preparing for an interview. Get a friend to ask you questions (from EPI or any other source) and solve them on a whiteboard, with pen and paper, or on a shared document. Have your friend take notes and give you feedback, both positive and negative. Make a video recording of the interview. You will cringe as you watch it, but it is better to learn of your mannerisms beforehand. Ask your friend to give hints when you get stuck. In addition to sharpening your problem solving and presentation skills, the experience will help reduce anxiety at the actual interview setting. If you cannot find a friend, you can still go through the same process, recording yourself.

Strategies For A Great Interview

The essence of strategy is choosing what not to do.

— M. E. PORTER

A typical one hour interview with a single interviewer consists of five minutes of introductions and questions about the candidate's résumé. This is followed by five to fifteen minutes of questioning on basic programming concepts. The core of the interview is one or two detailed design questions where the candidate is expected to present a detailed solution on a whiteboard, paper, or integrated development environments (IDEs). Depending on the interviewer and the question, the solution may be required to include syntactically correct code and tests.

Approaching the problem

No matter how clever and well prepared you are, the solution to an interview problem may not occur to you immediately. Here are some things to keep in mind when this happens.

Clarify the question: This may seem obvious but it is amazing how many interviews go badly because the candidate spends most of his time trying to solve the wrong problem. If a question seems exceptionally hard, you may have misunderstood it.

A good way of clarifying the question is to state a concrete instance of the problem. For example, if the question is "find the first occurrence of a number greater than k in a sorted array", you could ask "if the input array is $\langle 2, 20, 30 \rangle$ and k is 3, then are you supposed to return 1, the index of 20?" These questions can be formalized as unit tests.

Feel free to ask the interviewer what time and space complexity he would like in your solution. If you are told to implement an $O(n)$ algorithm or use $O(1)$ space, it can simplify your life considerably. It is possible that he will refuse to specify these, or be vague about complexity requirements, but there is no harm in asking. Even if they are evasive, you may get some clues.

Work on concrete examples: Consider the problem of determining which of the 500 doors are open described on Page 30. This problem may seem difficult at first. However, if you start working out which doors are going to be open up to the fifth door, you will see that only Door 1 and Door 4 are open. This may suggest to you that the door is open only if its index is of the form n^2 for some integer n. Once you have this epiphany, the proof of its correctness is straightforward. (Keep in mind this approach will not work for all problems you encounter.)

Spell out the brute-force solution: Problems that are put to you in an interview tend to have an obvious brute-force solution that has a high time complexity compared to more sophisticated solutions. For example, instead of trying to work out a DP solution for a problem (e.g., for Problem 17.7 on Page 316), try all the possible configurations. Advantages to this approach include: (1.) it helps you explore opportunities for optimization and hence reach a better solution, (2.) it gives you an opportunity to demonstrate some problem solving and coding skills, and (3.) it establishes that both you and the interviewer are thinking about the same problem. Be warned that this strategy can sometimes be detrimental if it takes a long time to describe the brute-force approach.

Think out loud: One of the worst things you can do in an interview is to freeze up when solving the problem. It is always a good idea to think out loud and stay engaged. On the one hand, this increases your chances of finding the right solution because it forces you to put your thoughts in a coherent manner. On the other hand, this helps the interviewer guide your thought process in the right direction. Even if you are not able to reach the solution, the interviewer will form some impression of your intellectual ability.

Apply patterns: Patterns—general reusable solutions to commonly occurring problems—can be a good way to approach a baffling problem. Examples include finding a good data structure, seeing if your problem is a good fit for a general algorithmic technique, e.g., divide-and-conquer, recursion, or dynamic programming, and mapping the problem to a graph. Patterns are described in Chapter 4.

Presenting the solution

Once you have an algorithm, it is important to present it in a clear manner. Your solution will be much simpler if you take advantage of libraries such as Java Collections or C++ Boost. However, it is far more important that you use the language you are most comfortable with. Here are some things to keep in mind when presenting a solution.

Libraries: Do not reinvent the wheel (unless asked to invent it). In particular, master the libraries, especially the data structures. For example, do not waste time and lose credibility trying to remember how to pass an explicit comparator to a BST constructor. Remember that a hash function should use exactly those fields which are used in the equality check. A comparison function should be transitive.

Focus on the top-level algorithm: It's OK to use functions that you will implement later. This will let you focus on the main part of the algorithm, will penalize you less if you don't complete the algorithm. (Hash, equals, and compare functions are good candidates for deferred implementation.) Specify that you will handle main algorithm first, then corner cases. Add TODO comments for portions that you want to come back to.

Manage the whiteboard: You will likely use more of the board than you expect, so start at the top-left corner. Make use of functions—skip implementing anything that's trivial (e.g., finding the maximum of an array) or standard (e.g., a thread pool). Best practices for coding on a whiteboard are very different from best practices for coding on a production project. For example, don't worry about skipping documentation, or using the right indentation. Writing on a whiteboard is much slower than on a keyboard, so keeping your identifiers short (our recommendation is no more than 7 characters) but recognizable is a best practice. Have a convention for identifiers, e.g., i,j,k for array indices, A,B,C for arrays, hm for HashMaps, s for a String, sb for a StringBuilder, etc.

Assume valid inputs: In a production environment, it is good practice to check if inputs are valid, e.g., that a string purporting to represent a nonnegative integer actually consists solely of numeric characters, no flight in a timetable arrives before it departs, etc. Unless they are part of the problem statement, in an interview setting, such checks are inappropriate: they take time to code, and distract from the core problem. (You should clarify this assumption with the interviewer.)

Test for corner cases: For many problems, your general idea may work for most valid inputs but there may be pathological valid inputs where your algorithm (or your implementation of it) fails. For example, your binary search code may crash if the input is an empty array; or you may do arithmetic without considering the possibility of overflow. It is important to systematically consider these possibilities. If there is time, write unit tests. Small, extreme, or random inputs make for good stimuli. Don't forget to add code for checking the result. Occasionally, the code to handle obscure corner cases may be too complicated to implement in an interview setting. If so, you should mention to the interviewer that you are aware of these problems, and could address them if required.

Syntax: Interviewers rarely penalize you for small syntax errors since modern IDE excel at handling these details. However, lots of bad syntax may result in the impression that you have limited coding experience. Once you are done writing your program, make a pass through it to fix any obvious syntax errors before claiming you are done. We use the Google coding style standards in this book, and advise you to become proficient with them. They are available at code.google.com/p/google-styleguide

Candidates often tend to get function signatures wrong and it reflects poorly on them. For example, it would be an error to write a function in C that returns an array but not its size. In C++ it is important to know whether to pass parameters by value or by reference. Use const as appropriate.

Memory management: Generally speaking, it is best to avoid memory management operations altogether. In C++, if you are using dynamic allocation consider using scoped pointers. The run time environment will automatically deallocate the object a scoped pointer points to when it goes out of scope. If you explicitly allocate memory, ensure that in every execution path, this memory is de-allocated. See if you can reuse space. For example, some linked list problems can be solved with $O(1)$ additional space by reusing existing nodes.

Your Interviewer Is Not Alan Turing: Interviewers are not capable of analyzing long programs, particularly on a whiteboard or paper. Therefore, they ask questions whose solutions use short programs. A good tip is that if your solution takes more than 50-70 lines to code, it's a sign that you are on the wrong track, and you should reconsider your approach.

Know your interviewers & the company

It can help you a great deal if the company can share with you the background of your interviewers in advance. You should use search and social networks to learn more about the people interviewing you. Letting your interviewers know that you have researched them helps break the ice and forms the impression that you are enthusiastic and will go the extra mile. For fresh graduates, it is also important to think from the perspective of the interviewers as described in Chapter 3.

Once you ace your interviews and have an offer, you have an important decision to make—is this the organization where you want to work? Interviews are a great time to collect this information. Interviews usually end with the interviewers letting the candidates ask questions. You should make the best use of this time by getting the information you would need and communicating to the interviewer that you are genuinely interested in the job. Based on your interaction with the interviewers, you may get a good idea of their intellect, passion, and fairness. This extends to the team and company.

In addition to knowing your interviewers, you should know about the company vision, history, organization, products, and technology. You should be ready to talk about what specifically appeals to you, and to ask intelligent questions about the company and the job. Prepare a list of questions in advance; it gets you helpful information as well as shows your knowledge and enthusiasm for the organization. You may also want to think of some concrete ideas around things you could do for the company; be careful not to come across as a pushy know-it-all.

All companies want bright and motivated engineers. However, companies differ greatly in their culture and organization. Here is a brief classification.

Startup, e.g., Quora: values engineers who take initiative and develop products on their own. Such companies do not have time to train new hires, and tend to hire candidates who are very fast learners or are already familiar with their technology stack, e.g., their web application framework, machine learning system, etc.

Mature consumer-facing company, e.g., Google: wants candidates who understand emerging technologies from the user's perspective. Such companies have a deeper technology stack, much of which is developed in-house. They have the resources and the time to train a new hire.

Enterprise-oriented company, e.g., Oracle: looks for developers familiar with how large projects are organized, e.g., engineers who are familiar with reviews, documentation, and rigorous testing.

Government contractor, e.g., Lockheed-Martin: values knowledge of specifications and testing, and looks for engineers who are familiar with government-mandated processes.

Embedded systems/chip design company, e.g., National Instruments: wants software engineers who know enough about hardware to interface with the hardware engineers. The tool chain and development practices at such companies tend to be very mature.

General conversation

Often interviewers will ask you questions about your past projects, such as a senior design project or an internship. The point of this conversation is to answer the following questions:

Can the candidate clearly communicate a complex idea? This is one of the most important skills for working in an engineering team. If you have a grand idea to redesign a big system, can you communicate it to your colleagues and bring them on board? It is crucial to practice how you will present your best work. Being precise, clear, and having concrete examples can go a long way here. Candidates communicating in a language that is not their first language, should take extra care to speak slowly and make more use of the whiteboard to augment their words.

Is the candidate passionate about his work? We always want our colleagues to be excited, energetic, and inspiring to work with. If you feel passionately about your work, and your eyes light up when describing what you've done, it goes a long way in establishing you as a great colleague. Hence, when you are asked to describe a project from the past, it is best to pick something that you are passionate about rather than a project that was complex but did not interest you.

Is there a potential interest match with some project? The interviewer may gauge areas of strengths for a potential project match. If you know the requirements of the job, you may want to steer the conversation in that direction. Keep in mind that because technology changes so fast many teams prefer a strong generalist, so don't pigeonhole yourself.

Other advice

A bad mental and physical attitude can lead to a negative outcome. Don't let these simple mistakes lead to your years of preparation going to waste.

Be honest: Nobody wants a colleague who falsely claims to have tested code or done a code review. Dishonesty in an interview is a fast pass to an early exit.

Remember, nothing breaks the truth more than stretching it—you should be ready to defend anything you claim on your résumé. If your knowledge of Python extends only as far as having cut-and-paste sample code, do not add Python to your résumé.

Similarly, if you have seen a problem before, you should say so. (Be sure that it really is the same problem, and bear in mind you should describe a correct solution quickly if you claim to have solved it before.) Interviewers have been known to collude to ask the same question of a candidate to see if he tells the second interviewer about the first instance. An interviewer may feign ignorance on a topic he knows in depth to see if a candidate pretends to know it.

Keep a positive spirit: A cheerful and optimistic attitude can go a long way. Absolutely nothing is to be gained, and much can be lost, by complaining how difficult your journey was, how you are not a morning person, how inconsiderate the airline/hotel/HR staff were, etc.

Don't apologize: Candidates sometimes apologize in advance for a weak GPA, rusty coding skills, or not knowing the technology stack. Their logic is that by being proactive they will somehow benefit from lowered expectations. Nothing can be further from the truth. It focuses attention on shortcomings. More generally, if you do not believe in yourself, you cannot expect others to believe in you.

Keep money and perks out of the interview: Money is a big element in any job but it is best left discussed with the HR division after an offer is made. The same is true for vacation time, day care support, and funding for conference travel.

Appearance: Most software companies have a relaxed dress-code, and new graduates may wonder if they will look foolish by overdressing. The damage done when you are too casual is greater than the minor embarrassment you may feel at being overdressed. It is always a good idea to err on the side of caution and dress formally for your interviews. At the minimum, be clean and well-groomed.

Be aware of your body language: Think of a friend or coworker slouched all the time or absentmindedly doing things that may offend others. Work on your posture, eye contact and handshake, and remember to smile.

Stress interviews

Some companies, primarily in the finance industry, make a practice of having one of the interviewers create a stressful situation for the candidate. The stress may be injected technically, e.g., via a ninja problem, or through behavioral means, e.g., the interviewer rejecting a correct answer or ridiculing the candidate. The goal is to see how a candidate reacts to such situations—does he fall apart, become belligerent, or get swayed easily. The guidelines in the previous section should help you through a stress interview. (Bear in mind you will not know *a priori* if a particular interviewer will be conducting a stress interview.)

Learning from bad outcomes

The reality is that not every interview results in a job offer. There are many reasons for not getting a particular job. Some are technical: you may have missed that key flash of insight, e.g., the key to solving the maximum-profit on Page 1 in linear time. If this is the case, go back and solve that problem, as well as related problems.

Often, your interviewer may have spent a few minutes looking at your résumé—this is a depressingly common practice. This can lead to your being asked questions on topics outside of the area of expertise you claimed on your résumé, e.g., routing protocols or Structured Query Language (SQL). If so, make sure your résumé is accurate, and brush up on that topic for the future.

You can fail an interview for nontechnical reasons, e.g., you came across as uninterested, or you did not communicate clearly. The company may have decided not to hire in your area, or another candidate with similar ability but more relevant experience was hired.

You will not get any feedback from a bad outcome, so it is your responsibility to try and piece together the causes. Remember the only mistakes are the ones you don't learn from.

Negotiating an offer

An offer is not an offer till it is on paper, with all the details filled in. All offers are negotiable. We have seen compensation packages bargained up to twice the initial offer, but 10–20% is more typical. When negotiating, remember there is nothing to be gained, and much to lose, by being rude. (Being firm is not the same as being rude.)

To get the best possible offer, get multiple offers, and be flexible about the form of your compensation. For example, base salary is less flexible than stock options, sign-on bonus, relocation expenses, and Immigration and Naturalization Service (INS) filing costs. Be concrete—instead of just asking for more money, ask for a $P\%$ higher salary. Otherwise the recruiter will simply come back with a small increase in the sign-on bonus and claim to have met your request.

Your HR contact is a professional negotiator, whose fiduciary duty is to the company. He will know and use negotiating techniques such as reciprocity, getting consensus, putting words in your mouth ("don't you think that's reasonable?"), as well as threats, to get the best possible deal for the company. (This is what recruiters themselves are evaluated on internally.) The Wikipedia article on negotiation lays bare many tricks we have seen recruiters employ.

One suggestion: stick to email, where it is harder for someone to paint you into a corner. If you are asked for something (such as a copy of a competing offer), get something in return. Often it is better to bypass the HR contact and speak directly with the hiring manager.

At the end of the day, remember your long term career is what counts, and joining a company that has a brighter future (social-mobile vs. legacy enterprise), or offers a position that has more opportunities to rise (developer vs. tester) is much more important than a 10–20% difference in compensation.

3

Conducting An Interview

知己知彼，百戰不殆。
Translated—"If you know both yourself and your enemy, you can win numerous battles without jeopardy."

— *"The Art of War,"*
SUN TZU, 515 B.C.

In this chapter we review practices that help interviewers identify a top hire. We strongly recommend interviewees read it—knowing what an interviewer is looking for will help you present yourself better and increase the likelihood of a successful outcome.

For someone at the beginning of their career, interviewing may feel like a huge responsibility. Hiring a bad candidate is expensive for the organization, not just because the hire is unproductive, but also because he is a drain on the productivity of his mentors and managers, and sets a bad example. Firing someone is extremely painful as well as bad for to the morale of the team. On the other hand, discarding good candidates is problematic for a rapidly growing organization. Interviewers also have a moral responsibility not to unfairly crush the interviewee's dreams and aspirations.

Objective

The ultimate goal of any interview is to determine the odds that a candidate will be a successful employee of the company. The ideal candidate is smart, dedicated, articulate, collegial, and gets things done quickly, both as an individual and in a team. Ideally, your interviews should be designed such that a good candidate scores 1.0 and a bad candidate scores 0.0.

One mistake, frequently made by novice interviewers, is to be indecisive. Unless the candidate walks on water or completely disappoints, the interviewer tries not to make a decision and scores the candidate somewhere in the middle. This means that the interview was a wasted effort.

A secondary objective of the interview process is to turn the candidate into a brand ambassador for the recruiting organization. Even if a candidate is not a good fit for the organization, he may know others who would be. It is important for the candidate to have an overall positive experience during the process. It seems obvious that it is a bad idea for an interviewer to check email while the candidate is talking or insult the candidate over a mistake he made, but such behavior is depressingly common. Outside of a stress interview, the interviewer should work on making the candidate feel positively about the experience, and, by extension, the position and the company.

What to ask

One important question you should ask yourself as an interviewer is how much training time your work environment allows. For a startup it is important that a new hire is productive from the first week, whereas a larger organization can budget for several months of training. Consequently, in a startup it is important to test the candidate on the specific technologies that he will use, in addition to his general abilities.

For a larger organization, it is reasonable not to emphasize domain knowledge and instead test candidates on data structures, algorithms, system design skills, and problem solving techniques. The justification for this is as follows. Algorithms, data structures, and system design underlie all software. Algorithms and data structure code is usually a small component of a system dominated by the user interface (UI), input/output (I/O), and format conversion. It is often hidden in library calls. However, such code is usually the crucial component in terms of performance and correctness, and often serves to differentiate products. Furthermore, platforms and programming languages change quickly but a firm grasp of data structures, algorithms, and system design principles, will always be a foundational part of any successful software endeavor. Finally, many of the most successful software companies have hired based on ability and potential rather than experience or knowledge of specifics, underlying the effectiveness of this approach to selecting candidates.

Most big organizations have a structured interview process where designated interviewers are responsible for probing specific areas. For example, you may be asked to evaluate the candidate on their coding skills, algorithm knowledge, critical thinking, or the ability to design complex systems. This book gives interviewers access to a fairly large collection of problems to choose from. When selecting a problem keep the following in mind:

No single point of failure—if you are going to ask just one question, you should not pick a problem where the candidate passes the interview if and only if he gets one particular insight. The best candidate may miss a simple insight, and a mediocre candidate may stumble across the right idea. There should be at least two or three opportunities for the candidates to redeem themselves. For example, problems that can be solved by dynamic programming can almost always be solved through a greedy algorithm that is fast but suboptimum or a brute-force algorithm that is slow but optimum. In such cases, even if the candidate cannot get the key insight, he can still demonstrate some problem solving abilities. Problem 6.7 on Page 67 exemplifies this type of question.

Multiple possible solutions—if a given problem has multiple solutions, the chances of a good candidate coming up with a solution increases. It also gives the interviewer more freedom to steer the candidate. A great candidate may finish with one solution quickly enough to discuss other approaches and the trade-offs between them. For example, Problem 12.11 on Page 198 can be solved using a hash table or a bit array; the best solution makes use of binary search.

Cover multiple areas—even if you are responsible for testing the candidate on algorithms, you could easily pick a problem that also exposes some aspects of design and software development. For example, Problem 20.6 on Page 377 tests candidates on concurrency as well as data structures. Problem 6.16 on Page 81 requires knowledge of both probability and binary search.

Calibrate on colleagues—interviewers often have an incorrect notion of how difficult a problem is for a thirty minute or one hour interview. It is a good idea to check the appropriateness of a problem by asking one of your colleagues to solve it and seeing how much difficulty they have with it.

No unnecessary domain knowledge—it is not a good idea to quiz a candidate on advanced graph algorithms if the job does not require it and the candidate does not claim any special knowledge of the field. (The exception to this rule is if you want to test the candidate's response to stress.)

Conducting the interview

Conducting a good interview is akin to juggling. At a high level, you want to ask your questions and evaluate the candidate's responses. Many things can happen in an interview that could help you reach a decision, so it is important to take notes. At the same time, it is important to keep a conversation going with the candidate and help him out if he gets stuck. Ideally, have a series of hints worked out beforehand, which can then be provided progressively as needed. Coming up with the right set of hints may require some thinking. You do not want to give away the problem, yet find a way for the candidate to make progress. Here are situations that may throw you off:

A candidate that gets stuck and shuts up: Some candidates get intimidated by the problem, the process, or the interviewer, and just shut up. In such situations, a candidate's performance does not reflect his true caliber. It is important to put the candidate at ease, e.g., by beginning with a straightforward question, mentioning that a problem is tough, or asking them to think out loud.

A verbose candidate: Candidates who go off on tangents and keep on talking without making progress render an interview ineffective. Again, it is important to take control of the conversation. For example you could assert that a particular path will not make progress.

An overconfident candidate: It is common to meet candidates who weaken their case by defending an incorrect answer. To give the candidate a fair chance, it is important to demonstrate to him that he is making a mistake, and allow him to correct it. Often the best way of doing this is to construct a test case where the candidate's solution breaks down.

Scoring and reporting

At the end of an interview, the interviewers usually have a good idea of how the candidate scored. However, it is important to keep notes and revisit them before making a final decision. Whiteboard snapshots and samples of any code that the candidate wrote should also be recorded. You should standardize scoring based on which hints were given, how many questions the candidate was able to get to, etc. Although isolated minor mistakes can be ignored, sometimes when you look at all the mistakes together, clear signs of weakness in certain areas may emerge, such as a lack of attention to detail and unfamiliarity with a language.

When the right choice is not clear, wait for the next candidate instead of possibly making a bad hiring decision. The litmus test is to see if you would react positively to the candidate replacing a valuable member of your team.

4

Problem Solving

It's not that I'm so smart, it's just that I stay with problems longer.

— A. EINSTEIN

In this chapter we describe approaches to solving programming problems that can help you when you are faced with a tricky interview problem. Specifically, we cover key data structures in Section 4.1, we present algorithm patterns in Section 4.2 on Page 29, we describe ideas and notation from complexity theory in Section 4.3 on Page 40, and we discuss strategies for coping with computationally intractable problems in Section 4.4 on Page 40.

Bear in mind developing problem solving skills is like learning to play a musical instrument—books and teachers can point you in the right direction, but only your hard work will take you there. Just as a musician, you need to know underlying concepts, but theory is no substitute for practice. It is precisely for this reason that EPI focuses on problems.

4.1 DATA STRUCTURE REVIEW

A data structure is a particular way of storing and organizing related data items so that they can be manipulated efficiently. Usually, the correct selection of data structures is key to designing a good algorithm. Different data structures are suited to different applications; some are highly specialized. For example, heaps are particularly well-suited for algorithms that merge sorted data streams, while compiler implementations usually use hash tables to lookup identifiers.

The data structures described in this chapter are the ones commonly used. Other data structures, such as skip lists, treaps, Fibonacci heaps, tries, and disjoint-set data structures, have more specialized applications.

Solutions often require a combination of data structures. For example, tracking the most visited pages on a website involves a combination of a heap, a queue, a binary search tree, and a hash table. See Solution 22.25 on Page 441 for details.

PRIMITIVE TYPES

You should be comfortable with the basic types (chars, integers, doubles, etc.), their variants (unsigned, long, etc.), and operations on them (bitwise operators, comparison, etc.). Don't forget that the basic types differ among programming languages.

Table 4.1: Data structures.

Data structure	Key points
Primitive types	Know how int, char, double, etc. are represented in memory and the primitive operations on them.
Arrays	Fast access for element at an index, slow lookups (unless sorted) and insertions. Be comfortable with notions of iteration, resizing, partitioning, merging, etc.
Strings	Know how strings are represented in memory. Understand basic operators such as comparison, copying, matching, joining, splitting, etc.
Lists	Understand trade-offs with respect to arrays. Be comfortable with iteration, insertion, and deletion within singly and doubly linked lists. Know how to implement a list with dynamic allocation, and with arrays.
Stacks and queues	Recognize where last-in first-out (stack) and first-in first-out (queue) semantics are applicable. Know array and linked list implementations.
Binary trees	Use for representing hierarchical data. Know about depth, height, leaves, search path, traversal sequences, successor/predecessor operations.
Heaps	Key benefit: $O(1)$ lookup find-max, $O(\log n)$ insertion, and $O(\log n)$ deletion of max. Node and array representations. Min-heap variant.
Hash tables	Key benefit: $O(1)$ insertions, deletions and lookups. Key disadvantages: not suitable for order-related queries; need for resizing; poor worst-case performance. Understand implementation using array of buckets and collision chains. Know hash functions for integers, strings, objects.
Binary search trees	Key benefit: $O(\log n)$ insertions, deletions, lookups, find-min, find-max, successor, predecessor when tree is balanced. Understand node fields, pointer implementation. Be familiar with notion of balance, and operations maintaining balance.

For example, Java has no unsigned integers, and the integer width is compiler- and machine-dependent in C.

A common problem related to basic types is computing the number of bits set to 1 in an integer-valued variable x. To solve this problem you need to know how to manipulate individual bits in an integer. One straightforward approach is to iteratively test individual bits using the value 1 as a bitmask. Specifically, we iteratively identify bits of x that are set to 1 by examining the bitwise-AND of x with the bitmask, shifting x right one bit at a time. The overall complexity is $O(n)$ where n is the length of the integer.

Another approach, which may run faster on some inputs, is based on computing $y = x$ & $\sim(x-1)$, where & is the bitwise-AND operator and $\sim$ is the bitwise complement operator. The variable y is 1 at exactly the lowest bit of x that is 1; all other bits in y are 0. For example, if $x = (00101100)_2$, then $x - 1 = (00101011)_2$, $\sim(x - 1) = (11010100)_2$, and $y = (00101100)_2$ & $(11010100)_2 = (00000100)_2$. This calculation is robust—it is correct for unsigned and two's-complement representations. Consequently, this bit may be removed from x by computing $x \oplus y$, where $\oplus$ is the bitwise-XOR function. The time complexity is $O(s)$, where s is the number of bits set to 1 in x.

The fact that x & $\sim(x - 1)$ isolates the lowest bit that is 1 in x is important enough that you should memorize it. However, it is also fairly easy to derive. First, suppose x is not 0, i.e., it has has a bit that is one. Subtracting one from x changes the rightmost bit to zero and sets all the lower bits to one (if you add one now, you get the original value back). The effect is to mask out the rightmost one. Therefore x & $\sim(x - 1)$ has a single bit set to one, namely, the rightmost 1 in x. Now suppose x is 0. Subtracting one from x underflows, resulting in a word in which all bits are set to one. Again, x & $\sim(x - 1)$ is 0.

A similar derivation shows that x &$(x - 1)$ replaces the lowest bit that is 1 with 0. For example, if $x = (00101100)_2$, then $x - 1 = (00101011)_2$, so x &$(x - 1) = (00101100)_2$&$(00101011)_2 = (00101000)_2$. This fact can also be very useful.

Consider sharpening your bit manipulation skills by writing expressions that use bitwise operators, equality checks, and Boolean operators to do the following.

- Right propagate the rightmost set bit in x, e.g., turns $(01010000)_2$ to $(01011111)_2$.
- Compute x modulo a power of two, e.g., returns 13 for 77 mod 64.
- Test if x is a power of 2, i.e., evaluates to true for $x = 1, 2, 4, 8, \ldots$, false for all other values.

In practice, if the computation is done repeatedly, the most efficient approach would be to create a lookup table. In this case, we could use a 65536 entry integer-valued array P, such that $P[i]$ is the number of bits set to 1 in i. If x is 64 bits, the result can be computed by decomposing x into 4 disjoint 16-bit words, $h3, h2, h1$, and $h0$. The 16-bit words are computed using bitmasks and shifting, e.g., $h1$ is $(x \gg 16$ & $(1111111111111111)_2)$. The final result is $P[h3] + P[h2] + P[h1] + P[h0]$. Computing the parity of an integer is closely related to counting the number of bits set to 1, and we present a detailed analysis of the parity problem in Solution 5.1 on Page 43.

Problems involving manipulation of bit-level data are often asked in interviews. It is easy to introduce errors in code that manipulates bit-level data; as the saying goes, when you play with bits, expect to get bitten.

ARRAYS

Conceptually, an array maps integers in the range $[0, n - 1]$ to objects of a given type, where n is the number of objects in this array. Array lookup and insertion are fast, making arrays suitable for a variety of applications. Reading past the last element of an array is a common error, invariably with catastrophic consequences.

The following problem arises when optimizing quicksort: given an array A whose elements are comparable, and an index i, reorder the elements of A so that the initial elements are all less than $A[i]$, and are followed by elements equal to $A[i]$, which in turn are followed by elements greater than $A[i]$, using $O(1)$ space.

The key to the solution is to maintain two regions on opposite sides of the array that meet the requirements, and expand these regions one element at a time. Details are given in Solution 6.1 on Page 58.

Strings

A string can be viewed as a special kind of array, namely one made out of characters. We treat strings separately from arrays because certain operations which are commonly applied to strings—for example, comparison, joining, splitting, searching for substrings, replacing one string by another, parsing, etc.—do not make sense for general arrays.

Our solution to the look-and-say problem illustrates operations on strings. The look-and-say sequence begins with 1; the subsequent integers describe the digits appearing in the previous number in the sequence. The first eight integers in the look-and-say sequence are $\langle 1, 11, 21, 1211, 111221, 312211, 13112221, 1113213211 \rangle$. The look-and-say problem entails computing the nth integer in this sequence. Although the problem is cast in terms of integers, the string representation is far more convenient for counting digits. Details are given in Solution 7.8 on Page 100.

Lists

A list implements an ordered collection of values, which may include repetitions. In the context of this book we view a list as a sequence of nodes where each node has a link to the next node in the sequence. In a doubly linked list each node also has a link to the prior node.

A list is similar to an array in that it contains objects in a linear order. The key differences are that inserting and deleting elements in a list has time complexity $O(1)$. On the other hand, obtaining the kth element in a list is expensive, having $O(n)$ time complexity. Lists are usually building blocks of more complex data structures. However, they can be the subject of tricky problems in their own right, as illustrated by the following:

Let L be a singly linked list. Assume its nodes are numbered starting at 0. Define the zip of L to be the list consisting of the interleaving of the nodes numbered $0, 1, 2, \ldots$ with the nodes numbered $n - 1, n - 2, n - 3, \ldots$, where n is the number of nodes in the list.

Suppose you were asked to write a program that computes the zip of a list, with the constraint that it uses $O(1)$ space. The operation of this program is illustrated in Figure 4.1 on the facing page.

The solution is based on an appropriate iteration combined with "pointer swapping", i.e., updating next field for each node. Refer to Solution 22.10 on Page 416 for details.

26

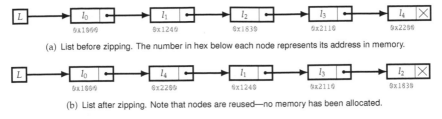

(a) List before zipping. The number in hex below each node represents its address in memory.

(b) List after zipping. Note that nodes are reused—no memory has been allocated.

Figure 4.1: Zipping a list.

STACKS AND QUEUES

Stacks support last-in, first-out semantics for inserts and deletes, whereas queues are first-in, first-out. Both are commonly implemented using linked lists or arrays. Similar to lists, stacks and queues are usually building blocks in a solution to a complex problem, but can make for interesting problems in their own right.

As an example consider the problem of evaluating Reverse Polish notation expressions, i.e., expressions of the form "$3, 4, \times, 1, 2, +, +$", "$1, 1, +, -2, \times$", or "$4, 6, /, 2, /$". A stack is ideal for this purpose—operands are pushed on the stack, and popped as operators are processed, with intermediate results being pushed back onto the stack. Details are given in Solution 9.2 on Page 131.

BINARY TREES

A binary tree is a data structure that is used to represent hierarchical relationships. Binary trees are the subject of Chapter 10. Binary trees most commonly occur in the context of binary search trees, wherein keys are stored in a sorted fashion. However, there are many other applications of binary trees. Consider a set of resources organized as nodes in a binary tree. Processes need to lock resource nodes. A node may be locked if and only if none of its descendants and ancestors are locked. Your task is to design and implement an application programming interface (API) for locking.

A reasonable API is one with a method for checking if a node is locked, and methods for locking and unlocking a node. Naively implemented, the time complexity for these methods is $O(n)$, where n is the number of nodes. However, these can be made to run in time $O(1)$, $O(h)$, and $O(h)$, respectively, where h is the height of the tree, if nodes have a parent field. Details are given in Solution 10.15 on Page 167.

HEAPS

A heap is a data structure based on a binary tree. It efficiently implements the priority queue API. A priority queue resembles a queue, with one difference: each element has a "priority" associated with it, and deletion removes the element with the highest priority.

Let's say you are given a set of files, each containing stock trade information. Each trade appears as a separate line containing information about that trade. Lines begin with an integer-valued timestamp, and lines within a file are sorted in increasing order of timestamp. Suppose you were asked to design an algorithm that combines the set of files into a single file R in which trades are sorted by timestamp.

This problem can be solved by a multistage merge process, but there is a trivial solution based on a min-heap data structure. Entries are trade-file pairs and are ordered by the timestamp of the trade. Initially, the min-heap contains the first trade from each file. Iteratively delete the minimum entry $e = (t, f)$ from the min-heap, write t to R, and add in the next entry in the file f. Details are given in Solution 11.1 on Page 171.

Hash tables

A hash table is a data structure used to store keys, optionally, with corresponding values. Inserts, deletes and lookups run in $O(1)$ time on average. One caveat is that these operations require a good hash function—a mapping from the set of all possible keys to the integers which is similar to a uniform random assignment. Another caveat is that if the number of keys that is to be stored is not known in advance then the hash table needs to be periodically resized, which, depending on how the resizing is implemented, can lead to some updates having $O(n)$ complexity.

Suppose you were asked to write a program which takes a string s as input, and returns true if the characters in s can be permuted to form a string that is palindromic, i.e., reads the same backwards as forwards. For example, your program should return true for "GATTAACAG", since "GATACATAG" is a permutation of this string and is palindromic. Working through examples, you should see that a string is palindromic if and only if each character appears an even number of times, with possibly a single exception, since this allows for pairing characters in the first and second halves.

A hash table makes performing this test trivial. We build a hash table H whose keys are characters, and corresponding values are the number of occurrences for that character. The hash table H is created with a single pass over the string. After computing the number of occurrences, we iterate over the key-value pairs in H. If more than one character has an odd count, we return false; otherwise, we return true. Details are given in Solution 13.2 on Page 206.

Suppose you were asked to write an application that compares n programs for plagiarism. Specifically, your application is to break every program into overlapping character strings, each of length 100, and report on the number of strings that appear in each pair of programs. A hash table can be used to perform this check very efficiently if the right hash function is used. Details are given in Solution 21.3 on Page 388.

Binary search trees

Binary search trees (BSTs) are used to store objects that are comparable. BSTs are the subject of Chapter 15. The underlying idea is to organize the objects in a binary tree

28

in which the nodes satisfy the BST property on Page 250. Insertion and deletion can be implemented so that the height of the BST is $O(\log n)$, leading to fast ($O(\log n)$) lookup and update times. AVL trees and red-black trees are BST implementations that support this form of insertion and deletion.

BSTs are a workhorse of data structures and can be used to solve almost every data structures problem reasonably efficiently. It is common to augment the BST to make it possible to manipulate more complicated data, e.g., intervals, and efficiently support more complex queries, e.g., the number of elements in a range.

As an example application of BSTs, consider the following problem. You are given a set of line segments. Each segment is a closed interval $[l_i, r_i]$ of the X-axis, a color, and a height. For simplicity assume no two segments whose intervals overlap have the same height. When the X-axis is viewed from above the color at point x on the X-axis is the color of the highest segment that includes x. (If no segment contains x, the color is blank.) You are to implement a function that computes the sequence of colors as seen from the top.

The key idea is to sort the endpoints of the line segments and do a scan from left-to-right. As we do the scan, we maintain a list of line segments that intersect the current position as well as the highest line and its color. To quickly lookup the highest line in a set of intersecting lines we keep the current set in a BST, with the interval's height as its key. Details are given in Solution 22.30 on Page 448.

4.2 ALGORITHM PATTERNS

We describe algorithm design patterns that we have found to be helpful in solving interview problems. These patterns fall into two categories—analysis patterns, summarized in Table 4.2, which yield insight into the problem, and algorithm design patterns, summarized in Table 4.3 on the following page, which provide skeletal code. Keep in mind that you may have to use a combination of approaches to solve a problem.

Table 4.2: Analysis patterns.

Analysis principle	Key points
Concrete examples	Manually solve concrete instances of the problem and then build a general solution.
Case analysis	Split the input/execution into a number of cases and solve each case in isolation.
Iterative refinement	Most problems can be solved using a brute-force approach. Find such a solution and improve upon it.
Reduction	Use a well-known solution to some other problem as a subroutine.
Graph modeling	Describe the problem using a graph and solve it using an existing algorithm.

Table 4.3: Algorithm design patterns.

Technique	Key points
Sorting	Uncover some structure by sorting the input.
Recursion	If the structure of the input is defined in a recursive manner, design a recursive algorithm that follows the input definition.
Divide-and-conquer	Divide the problem into two or more smaller independent subproblems and solve the original problem using solutions to the subproblems.
Dynamic programming	Compute solutions for smaller instances of a given problem and use these solutions to construct a solution to the problem. Cache for performance.
Greedy algorithms	Compute a solution in stages, making choices that are locally optimum at step; these choices are never undone.
Invariants	Identify an invariant and use it to rule out potential solutions that are suboptimal/dominated by other solutions.

CONCRETE EXAMPLES

Problems that seem difficult to solve in the abstract can become much more tractable when you examine concrete instances. Specifically, the following types of inputs can offer tremendous insight:

- small inputs, such as an array or a BST containing 5–7 elements.
- extreme/specialized inputs, e.g., binary values, nonoverlapping intervals, sorted arrays, connected graphs, etc.

Problems 22.24 on Page 439 and 16.1 on Page 278 are illustrative of small inputs, and Problems 22.1 on Page 403, 7.4 on Page 95, 12.9 on Page 195, and 22.34 on Page 458 are illustrative of extreme/specialized inputs.

Consider the following problem. Five hundred closed doors along a corridor are numbered from 1 to 500. A person walks through the corridor and opens each door. Another person walks through the corridor and closes every alternate door. Continuing in this manner, the ith person comes and toggles the state (open or closed) of every ith door starting from Door i. You must determine exactly how many doors are open after the 500th person has walked through the corridor.

It is difficult to solve this problem using an abstract approach, e.g., introducing Boolean variables for the state of each door and a state update function. However, if you try the same problem with 1, 2, 3, 4, 10, and 20 doors, it takes a short time to see that the doors that remain open are 1, 4, 9, 16, ..., regardless of the total number of doors. The 10 doors case is illustrated in Figure 4.2 on the next page. Now the pattern is obvious—the doors that remain open are those corresponding to the squares of integers. Hence, the total number of open doors is $\lfloor \sqrt{500} \rfloor = 22$.

Here is a rigorous justification. If the number of times a door's state changes is odd, it will be open; otherwise it is closed. Therefore, the number of times door k's state changes equals the number of divisors of k. The concrete example analysis suggests that the number of divisors of k is odd exactly when k is a perfect square, i.e., the square of a number.

Elaborating, if d divides k, then k/d also divides k. Therefore, we can uniquely pair off all divisors of k, except for $\sqrt{k}$ (if it is an integer), so k has an even number of divisors if and only if it is a perfect square. For example, the divisors of 24 are $1, 2, 3, 4, 6, 8, 12, 24$, which can be paired of as follows—$(1, 24), (2, 12), (3, 8), (4, 6)$ so 24 has an even number of divisors. On the other hand, the divisors of 36, which is a perfect square, are $1, 2, 3, 4, 6, 9, 12, 18, 36$, which pair off as follows— $(1, 36), (2, 18), (3, 12), (4, 9), (6, 6)$. Since 6 is paired with itself, the number of divisors is odd.

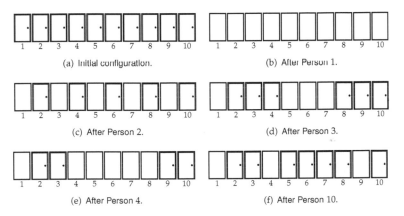

(a) Initial configuration.

(b) After Person 1.

(c) After Person 2.

(d) After Person 3.

(e) After Person 4.

(f) After Person 10.

Figure 4.2: Progressive updates to 10 doors.

The smallest nonconstructible change problem 22.24 on Page 439, the Towers of Hanoi 16.1 on Page 278 problem, the Levenshtein distance problem 17.2 on Page 304, and the maximum water that is trappable problem 22.42 on Page 475 are further examples of problems whose solution benefits from use of the concrete example pattern.

CASE ANALYSIS

In case analysis, a problem is divided into a number of separate cases, and analyzing each such case individually suffices to solve the initial problem. Cases do not have to be mutually exclusive; however, they must be exhaustive, that is cover all possibilities. For example, to prove that for all n, n^3 mod 9 is 0, 1, or 8, we can consider the cases $n = 3m$, $n = 3m + 1$, and $n = 3m + 2$. These cases are individually easy to prove, and are exhaustive. Case analysis is commonly used in mathematics and games of strategy. Here we consider an application of case analysis to algorithm design.

Suppose you are given a set S of 25 distinct integers and a CPU that has a special instruction, SORT5, that can sort five integers in one cycle. Your task is to identify the

31

largest, second-largest, and third-largest integers in S using SORT5 to compare and sort subsets of S; furthermore, you must minimize the number of calls to SORT5.

If all we had to compute was the largest integer in the set, the optimum approach would be to form five disjoint subsets $S_1, \ldots, S_5$ of S, sort each subset, and then sort $\{\max S_1, \ldots, \max S_5\}$. This takes six calls to SORT5 but leaves ambiguity about the second and third largest integers.

It may seem like many additional calls to SORT5 are still needed. However, if you do a careful case analysis and eliminate all $x \in S$ for which there are at least three integers in S larger than x, only five integers remain and hence just one more call to SORT5 is needed to compute the result.

The solutions to Problems 22.1 on Page 403, 22.4 on Page 406, and 14.7 on Page 240, among many others, also illustrate the case analysis pattern.

ITERATIVE REFINEMENT OF A BRUTE-FORCE SOLUTION

Many problems can be solved optimally by a simple algorithm that has a high time/space complexity—this is sometimes referred to as a brute-force solution. Other terms are *exhaustive search* and *generate-and-test*. Often this algorithm can be refined to one that is faster. At the very least it may offer hints into the nature of the problem.

As an example, suppose you were asked to write a program that takes an array A of n numbers, and rearranges A's elements to get a new array B having the property that $B[0] \leq B[1] \geq B[2] \leq B[3] \geq B[4] \leq B[5] \geq \cdots$.

One straightforward solution is to sort A and interleave the bottom and top halves of the sorted array. Alternatively, we could sort A and then swap the elements at the pairs $(A[1], A[2]), (A[3], A[4]), \ldots$. Both these approaches have the same time complexity as sorting, namely $O(n \log n)$.

You will soon realize that it is not necessary to sort A to achieve the desired configuration—you could simply rearrange the elements around the median, and then perform the interleaving. Median finding can be performed in time almost certain $O(n)$, as per Solution 12.9 on Page 195, which is the overall time complexity of this approach.

Finally, you may notice that the desired ordering is very local, and realize that it is not necessary to find the median. Iterating through the array and swapping $A[i]$ and $A[i+1]$ when i is even and $A[i] > A[i+1]$ or i is odd and $A[i] < A[i+1]$ achieves the desired configuration. In code:

```
void Rearrange(vector<int>* A_ptr) {
  vector<int>& A = *A_ptr;
  for (size_t i = 1; i < A.size(); ++i) {
    if ((!(i % 2) && A[i - 1] < A[i]) || ((i % 2) && A[i - 1] > A[i])) {
      swap(A[i - 1], A[i]);
    }
  }
}
```

This approach has time complexity $O(n)$, which is the same as the approach based on median finding. However, it is much easier to implement and operates in an online fashion, i.e., it never needs to store more than two elements in memory or read a previous element.

As another example of iterative refinement, consider the problem of string search: given two strings s (search string) and t (text), find all occurrences of s in t. Since s can occur at any offset in t, the brute-force solution is to test for a match at every offset. This algorithm is perfectly correct; its time complexity is $O(nm)$, where n and m are the lengths of s and t. See Solution 7.14 on Page 107 for details.

After trying some examples you may see that there are several ways to improve the time complexity of the brute-force algorithm. As an example, if the character $t[i]$ is not present in s you can skip past $t[i]$. Furthermore, this skipping works better if we match the search string from its end and work backwards. These refinements will make the algorithm very fast (linear time) on random text and search strings; however, the worst-case complexity remains $O(nm)$.

You can make the additional observation that a partial match of s that does not result in a full match implies other offsets that cannot lead to full matches. If $s = abdabcabc$ and if, starting backwards, we have a partial match up to $abcabc$ that does not result in a full match, we know that the next possible matching offset has to be at least three positions ahead (where we can match the second abc from the partial match).

By putting together these refinements you will have arrived at the famous Boyer-Moore string search algorithm—its worst-case time complexity is $O(n + m)$ (which is the best possible from a theoretical perspective); it is also one of the fastest string search algorithms in practice.

As another example, the brute-force solution to computing the maximum subarray sum for an integer array of length n is to compute the sum of all subarrays, which has $O(n^3)$ time complexity. This can be improved to $O(n^2)$ by precomputing the sums of all the prefixes of the given arrays; this allows the sum of a subarray to be computed in $O(1)$ time. The natural divide-and-conquer algorithm has an $O(n \log n)$ time complexity. Finally, one can observe that a maximum subarray must end at one of n indices, and the maximum subarray sum for a subarray ending at index i can be computed from previous maximum subarray sums, which leads to an $O(n)$ algorithm. Details are presented on Page 300.

Many more sophisticated algorithms can be developed in this fashion. See Solutions 5.1 on Page 43, 22.4 on Page 406, 22.5 on Page 408, and 22.13 on Page 420 for examples.

REDUCTION

Consider the problem of determining if one string is a rotation of the other, e.g., "car" and "arc" are rotations of each other. A natural approach may be to rotate the first string by every possible offset and then compare it with the second string. This algorithm would have quadratic time complexity.

You may notice that this problem is quite similar to string search, which can be done in linear time, albeit using a somewhat complex algorithm. Therefore, it is natural to try to reduce this problem to string search. Indeed, if we concatenate the second string with itself and search for the first string in the resulting string, we will find a match if and only if the two original strings are rotations of each other. This reduction yields a linear time algorithm for our problem.

The reduction principle is also illustrated in the solutions to converting between different base representations (Problem 7.2 on Page 93), computing all permutations (Problem 16.3 on Page 282), checking whether a road network is resilient in the presence of blockages (Problem 22.47 on Page 484), and finding the minimum number of pictures needed to photograph a set of teams (Problem 19.9 on Page 365).

Usually, you try to reduce the given problem to an easier problem. Sometimes, however, you need to reduce a problem known to be difficult to the given problem. This shows that the given problem is difficult, which justifies heuristics and approximate solutions.

Graph modeling

Drawing pictures is a great way to brainstorm for a potential solution. If the relationships in a given problem can be represented using a graph, quite often the problem can be reduced to a well-known graph problem. For example, suppose you are given a set of exchange rates among currencies and you want to determine if an arbitrage exists, i.e., there is a way by which you can start with one unit of some currency C and perform a series of barters which results in having more than one unit of C.

Table 4.4 shows a representative example. An arbitrage is possible for this set of exchange rates: $1 \text{ USD} \rightarrow 1 \times 0.8123 = 0.8123 \text{ EUR} \rightarrow 0.8123 \times 1.2010 = 0.9755723 \text{ CHF} \rightarrow 0.9755723 \times 80.39 = 78.426257197 \text{ JPY} \rightarrow 78.426257197 \times 0.0128 = 1.00385609212 \text{ USD}$.

Table 4.4: Exchange rates for seven major currencies.

Symbol	USD	EUR	GBP	JPY	CHF	CAD	AUD
USD	1	0.8123	0.6404	78.125	0.9784	0.9924	0.9465
EUR	1.2275	1	0.7860	96.55	1.2010	1.2182	1.1616
GBP	1.5617	1.2724	1	122.83	1.5280	1.5498	1.4778
JPY	0.0128	0.0104	0.0081	1	1.2442	0.0126	0.0120
CHF	1.0219	0.8327	0.6546	80.39	1	1.0142	0.9672
CAD	1.0076	0.8206	0.6453	79.26	0.9859	1	0.9535
AUD	1.0567	0.8609	0.6767	83.12	1.0339	1.0487	1

We can model the problem with a graph where currencies correspond to vertices, exchanges correspond to edges, and the edge weight is set to the logarithm of the exchange rate. If we can find a cycle in the graph with a positive weight, we would

34

have found such a series of exchanges. Such a cycle can be solved using the Bellman-Ford algorithm. This is described in Solution 22.50 on Page 489. The solutions to the problems of painting a Boolean matrix (Problem 19.2 on Page 353), string transformation (Problem 19.7 on Page 361), and wiring a circuit (Problem 19.6 on Page 359) also illustrate modeling with graphs.

Sorting

Certain problems become easier to understand, as well as solve, when the input is sorted. The solution to the calendar rendering problem (Problem 14.5 on Page 236) entails taking a set of intervals and computing the maximum number of intervals whose intersection is nonempty. Naive strategies yield quadratic run times. However, once the interval endpoints have been sorted, it is easy to see that a point of maximum overlap can be determined by a linear time iteration through the endpoints.

Often it is not obvious what to sort on—for example, we could have sorted the intervals on starting points rather than endpoints. This sort sequence, which in some respects is more natural, does not work. However, some experimentation with it will, in all likelihood, lead to the correct criterion.

Sorting is not appropriate when an $O(n)$ (or better) algorithm is possible. For example, the kth largest element in an array can be computed in almost certain $O(n)$ time (Solution 12.9 on Page 195). Another good example of a problem where a total ordering is not required is the problem of rearranging elements in an array described on Page 32. Furthermore, sorting can obfuscate the problem. For example, given an array A of numbers, if we are to determine the maximum of $A[i] - A[j]$, for $i < j$, sorting destroys the order and complicates the problem.

Recursion

A recursive function consists of base cases and calls to the same function with different arguments. A recursive algorithm is often appropriate when the input is expressed using recursive rules, such as a computer grammar. More generally, searching, enumeration, divide-and-conquer, and decomposing a complex problem into a set of similar smaller instances are all scenarios where recursion may be suitable.

String matching exemplifies the use of recursion. Suppose you were asked to write a Boolean-valued function which takes a string and a matching expression, and returns true if and only if the matching expression "matches" the string. Specifically, the matching expression is itself a string, and could be

- x, where x is a character, for simplicity assumed to be a lowercase letter (matches the string "x").
- . (matches any string of length 1).
- $x*$ (matches the string consisting of zero or more occurrences of the character x).
- .* (matches the string consisting of zero or more of any characters).

35

- $r_1 r_2$, where r_1 and r_2 are regular expressions of the given form (matches any string that is the concatenation of strings s_1 and s_2, where r_1 matches s_1 and r_2 matches s_2).

This problem can be solved by checking a number of cases based on the first one or two characters of the matching expression, and recursively matching the rest of the string. Details are given in Solution 22.32 on Page 453.

DIVIDE-AND-CONQUER

A divide-and-conquer algorithm works by decomposing a problem into two or more smaller independent subproblems until it gets to instances that are simple enough to be solved directly; the results from the subproblems are then combined. More details and examples are given in Chapter 18; we illustrate the basic idea below.

A triomino is formed by joining three unit-sized squares in an L-shape. A mutilated chessboard (henceforth 8×8 Mboard) is made up of 64 unit-sized squares arranged in an 8×8 square, minus the top-left square, as depicted in Figure 4.3(a). Suppose you are asked to design an algorithm that computes a placement of 21 triominoes that covers the 8×8 Mboard. Since the 8×8 Mboard contains 63 squares, and we have 21 triominoes, a valid placement cannot have overlapping triominoes or triominoes which extend out of the 8×8 Mboard.

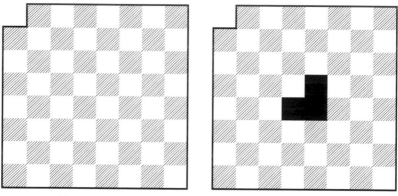

 (a) An 8×8 Mboard.  (b) Four 4×4 Mboards.

Figure 4.3: Mutilated chessboards.

Divide-and-conquer is a good strategy for this problem. Instead of the 8×8 Mboard, let's consider an $n \times n$ Mboard. A 2×2 Mboard can be covered with one triomino since it is of the same exact shape. You may hypothesize that a triomino placement for an $n \times n$ Mboard with the top-left square missing can be used to compute a placement for an $(n + 1) \times (n + 1)$ Mboard. However, you will quickly see that this line of reasoning does not lead you anywhere.

Another hypothesis is that if a placement exists for an $n \times n$ Mboard, then one also exists for a $2n \times 2n$ Mboard. Now we can apply divide-and-conquer. Take four $n \times n$

Mboards and arrange them to form a $2n \times 2n$ square in such a way that three of the Mboards have their missing square set towards the center and one Mboard has its missing square outward to coincide with the missing corner of a $2n \times 2n$ Mboard, as shown in Figure 4.3(b) on the facing page. The gap in the center can be covered with a triomino and, by hypothesis, we can cover the four $n \times n$ Mboards with triominoes as well. Hence, a placement exists for any n that is a power of 2. In particular, a placement exists for the $2^3 \times 2^3$ Mboard; the recursion used in the proof directly yields the placement.

Divide-and-conquer is usually implemented using recursion. However, the two concepts are not synonymous. Recursion is more general—subproblems do not have to be of the same form.

In addition to divide-and-conquer, we used the generalization principle above. The idea behind generalization is to find a problem that subsumes the given problem and is easier to solve. We used it to go from the 8×8 Mboard to the $2^n \times 2^n$ Mboard.

Other examples of divide-and-conquer include solving the number of pairs of elements in an array that are out of sorted order (Problem 22.34 on Page 458) and computing the closest pair of points (Problem 22.36 on Page 463) in a set of points in the plane.

DYNAMIC PROGRAMMING

Dynamic programming (DP) is applicable when the problem has the "optimal substructure" property, that is, it is possible to reconstruct a solution to the given instance from solutions to subinstances of smaller problems of the same kind. A key aspect of DP is maintaining a cache of solutions to subinstances. DP can be implemented recursively (in which case the cache is typically a dynamic data structure such as a hash table or a BST), or iteratively (in which case the cache is usually a one- or multi-dimensional array). It is most natural to design a DP algorithm using recursion. Usually, but not always, it is more efficient to implement it using iteration.

As an example of the power of DP, consider the problem of determining the number of combinations of 2, 3, and 7 point plays that can generate a score of 222. Let $C(s)$ be the number of combinations that can generate a score of s. Then $C(222) = C(222-7) + C(222-3) + C(222-2)$, since a combination ending with a 2 point play is different from the one ending with a 3 point play, and a combination ending with a 3 point play is different from the one ending with a 7 point play, etc.

The recursion ends at small scores, specifically, when (1.) $s < 0 \Rightarrow C(s) = 0$, and (2.) $s = 0 \Rightarrow C(s) = 1$.

Implementing the recursion naively results in multiple calls to the same subinstance. Let $C(a) \rightarrow C(b)$ indicate that a call to C with input a directly calls C with input b. Then $C(222)$ will be called in the order $C(222) \rightarrow C(222-7) \rightarrow C((222-7)-2)$, as well as $C(222) \rightarrow C(222-3) \rightarrow C((222-3)-3) \rightarrow C(((222-3)-3)-3)$.

This phenomenon results in the run time increasing exponentially with the size of the input. The solution is to store previously computed values of C in an array of length 223. Details are given in Solution 17.1 on Page 302.

Dynamic programming is the subject of Chapter 17. The solutions to problems 17.2 on Page 304, 17.3 on Page 307, and 17.6 on Page 313 are good illustrations of the principles of dynamic programming.

GREEDY ALGORITHMS

A greedy algorithm is one which makes decisions that are locally optimum and never changes them. This strategy does not always yield the optimum solution. Furthermore, there may be multiple greedy algorithms for a given problem, and only some of them are optimum.

For example, consider $2n$ cities on a line, half of which are white, and the other half are black. We want to map white to black cities in a one-to-one fashion so that the total length of the road sections required to connect paired cities is minimized. Multiple pairs of cities may share a single section of road, e.g., if we have the pairing $(0, 4)$ and $(1, 2)$ then the section of road between Cities 0 and 4 can be used by Cities 1 and 2.

The most straightforward greedy algorithm for this problem is to scan through the white cities, and, for each white city, pair it with the closest unpaired black city. This algorithm leads to suboptimum results. Consider the case where white cities are at 0 and at 3 and black cities are at 2 and at 5. If the straightforward greedy algorithm processes the white city at 3 first, it pairs it with 2, forcing the cities at 0 and 5 to pair up, leading to a road length of 5, whereas the pairing of cities at 0 and 2, and 3 and 5 leads to a road length of 4.

However, a slightly more sophisticated greedy algorithm does lead to optimum results: iterate through all the cities in left-to-right order, pairing each city with the nearest unpaired city of opposite color. More succinctly, let W and B be the arrays of white and black city coordinates. Sort W and B, and pair $W[i]$ with $B[i]$. We can prove this leads to an optimum pairing by induction. The idea is that the pairing for the first city must be optimum, since if it were to be paired with any other city, we could always change its pairing to be with the nearest black city without adding any road.

Chapter 18 contains a number of problems whose solutions employ greedy algorithms. The solutions to Problems 18.1 on Page 329 and 18.3 on Page 333 are especially representative. Several problems in other chapters also use a greedy algorithm as a key subroutine.

INVARIANTS

One common approach to designing an efficient algorithm is to use invariants. Briefly, an invariant is a condition that is true during execution of a program. This condition may be on the values of the variables of the program, or on the control logic. A well-chosen invariant can be used to rule out potential solutions that are suboptimal or dominated by other solutions.

An invariant can also be used to analyze a given algorithm, e.g., to prove its correctness, or analyze its time complexity. Here our focus is on designing algorithms with invariants, not analyzing them.

As an example, consider the 2-sum problem. We are given an array A of sorted integers, and a target value K. We want to know if there exist entries i and j in A such that $A[i] + A[j] = K$.

The brute-force algorithm for the 2-sum problem consists of a pair of nested for loops. Its complexity is $O(n^2)$, where n is the length of A. A faster approach is to add each element of A to a hash H, and test for each i if $K - A[i]$ is present in H. While reducing time complexity to $O(n)$, this approach requires $O(n)$ additional storage for H.

We want to compute i and j such that $A[i] + A[j] = K$. Without loss of generality, we can take $i \le j$. We know that $0 \le i$, and $j \le n - 1$. A natural approach then is to initialize i to 0, and j to $n - 1$, and then update i and j preserving the following invariant:

- no $i' < i$ can ever be paired with any j' such that $A[i'] + A[j'] = K$, and
- no $j' > j$ can ever be paired with any i' such that $A[i'] + A[j'] = K$.

The invariant is certainly true at initialization, since there are no $i' < 0$ and $j' > n - 1$. To show how i and j can be updated while ensuring the invariant continues to hold, consider $A[i] + A[j]$. If $A[i] + A[j] = K$, we are done. Otherwise, consider the case $A[i] + A[j] < K$. We know from the invariant that for no $j' > j$ is there a solution in which the element with the larger index is j'. The element at i cannot be paired with any element at an index j' smaller than j—because A is sorted, $A[i] + A[j'] \le A[i] + A[j] < K$. Therefore, we can increment i, and preserve the invariant. Similarly, in the case $A[i] + A[j] > K$, we can decrement j and preserve the invariant.

We terminate when either $A[i] + A[j] = K$ (success) or $i > j$ (failure). At each step, we increment or decrement i or j. Since there are at most n steps, and each takes $O(1)$ time, the time complexity is $O(n)$. Correctness follows from the fact that the invariant never discards a value for i or j which could possibly be the index of an element which sums with another element to K.

Identifying the right invariant is an art. Usually, it is arrived at by studying concrete examples and then making an educated guess. Often the first invariant is too strong, i.e., it does not hold as the program executes, or too weak, i.e., it holds throughout the program execution but cannot be used to infer the result.

The solutions to Problems 18.5 on Page 337 and 22.44 on Page 478 make use of invariants to solve generalizations of the 2-sum problem. Binary search, which we study in Chapter 12, uses an invariant to design an $O(\log n)$ algorithm for searching in a sorted array. Solution 12.6 on Page 191, which uses elimination in conjunction with an invariant to compute the square root of a real number, is especially instructive. Other examples of problems whose solutions make use of invariants are finding the longest subarray containing all entries (Problem 13.10 on Page 219), enumerating numbers of the form $a + b\sqrt{2}$ (Problem 15.8 on Page 263), and finding the majority element (Problem 18.6 on Page 339).

4.3 Complexity Analysis

The run time of an algorithm depends on the size of its input. A common approach to capture the run time dependency is by expressing asymptotic bounds on the worst-case run time as a function of the input size. Specifically, the run time of an algorithm on an input of size n is $O(f(n))$ if, for sufficiently large n, the run time is not more than $f(n)$ times a constant. The big-O notation indicates an upper bound on running time.

As an example, searching an unsorted array of integers of length n, for a given integer, has an asymptotic complexity of $O(n)$ since in the worst-case, the given integer may not be present. Similarly, consider the naive algorithm for testing primality that tries all numbers from 2 to the square root of the input number n. What is its complexity? In the best-case, n is divisible by 2. However, in the worst-case, the input may be a prime, so the algorithm performs $\sqrt{n}$ iterations.

Complexity theory is applied in a similar manner when analyzing the space requirements of an algorithm. The space needed to read in an instance is not included; otherwise, every algorithm would have $O(n)$ space complexity. Several of our problems call for an algorithm that uses $O(1)$ space. Specifically, it should be possible to implement the algorithm without dynamic memory allocation (explicitly, or indirectly, e.g., through library routines). Furthermore, the maximum depth of the function call stack should also be a constant, independent of the input. The standard algorithm for depth-first search of a graph is an example of an algorithm that does not perform any dynamic allocation, but uses the function call stack for implicit storage—its space complexity is not $O(1)$.

A streaming algorithm is one in which the input is presented as a sequence of items and is examined in only a few passes (typically just one). These algorithms have limited memory available to them (much less than the input size) and also limited processing time per item. Algorithms for computing summary statistics on log file data often fall into this category.

Many authors, ourselves included, will refer to the time complexity of an algorithm as its complexity without the time qualification. The space complexity is always qualified as such.

4.4 Intractability

In real-world settings you will often encounter problems that can be solved using efficient algorithms such as binary search and shortest paths. As we will see in the coming chapters, it is often difficult to identify such problems because the algorithmic core is obscured by details. Sometimes, you may encounter problems which can be

Figure 4.4: Traveling Salesman Problem by xkcd.

transformed into equivalent problems that have an efficient textbook algorithm, or problems that can be solved efficiently using meta-algorithms such as DP.

Occasionally, the problem you are given is intractable—i.e., there may not exist an efficient algorithm for the problem. Complexity theory addresses these problems. Some have been proved to not have an efficient solution but the vast majority are only conjectured to be intractable. The conjunctive normal form satisfiability (CNF-SAT) problem is an example of a problem that is conjectured to be intractable. Specifically, the CNF-SAT problem belongs to the complexity class NP—problems for which a candidate solution can be efficiently checked—and is conjectured to be the hardest problem in this class.

When faced with a problem P that appears to be intractable, the first thing to do is to prove intractability. This is usually done by taking a problem which is known to be intractable and showing how it can be efficiently reduced to P. Often this reduction gives insight into the cause of intractability.

Unless you are a complexity theorist, proving a problem to be intractable is only the starting point. Remember something is a problem only if it has a solution. There are a number of approaches to solving intractable problems:

- brute-force solutions, including dynamic programming, which have exponential time complexity, may be acceptable, if the instances encountered are small, or if the specific parameter that the complexity is exponential in is small;
- search algorithms, such as backtracking, branch-and-bound, and hill-climbing, which prune much of the complexity of a brute-force search;
- approximation algorithms which return a solution that is provably close to optimum;
- heuristics based on insight, common case analysis, and careful tuning that may solve the problem reasonably well;
- parallel algorithms, wherein a large number of computers can work on subparts simultaneously.

Solutions 19.8 on Page 363, 13.15 on Page 226, 16.9 on Page 292, 22.33 on Page 456, 17.6 on Page 313, 22.37 on Page 466, and 20.10 on Page 382 illustrate the use of some of these techniques.

Don't forget it may be possible to dramatically change the problem formulation while still achieving the higher level goal, as illustrated in Figure 4.4.

Part II

Problems

5

Primitive Types

Representation is the essence of programming.

— *"The Mythical Man Month,"*
F. P. BROOKS, 1975

A program updates variables in memory according to its instructions. Variables come in types—a type is a classification of data that spells out possible values for that type and the operations that can be performed on it.

A type can be provided by the language or defined by the programmer. Many languages provide types for Boolean, integer, character and floating point data. Often, there are multiple integer and floating point types, depending on signedness and precision. The width of these types is the number of bits of storage a corresponding variable takes in memory. For example, most implementations of C++ use 32 or 64 bits for an int. In Java an int is always 32 bits.

5.1 COMPUTING THE PARITY OF A WORD

The parity of a binary word is 1 if the number of 1s in the word is odd; otherwise, it is 0. For example, the parity of 1011 is 1, and the parity of 10001000 is 0. Parity checks are used to detect single bit errors in data storage and communication. It is fairly straightforward to write code that computes the parity of a single 64-bit word.

How would you compute the parity of a very large number of 64-bit words?

Hint: Use a lookup table, but don't use 2^{64} entries!

Solution: The brute-force algorithm iteratively tests the value of each bit while tracking the number of 1s seen so far. Since we only care if the number of 1s is even or odd, we can store the number modulo 2.

```
short Parity(unsigned long x) {
  short result = 0;
  while (x) {
    result += (x & 1);
    x >>= 1;
  }
  return result % 2;
}
```

The time complexity is $O(n)$, where n is the word size.

On Page 24 we showed how to erase the lowest set bit in a word in a single operation. This can be used to improve performance in the best- and average-cases.

```
short Parity(unsigned long x) {
  short result = 0;
  while (x) {
    result ^= 1;
    x &= (x - 1);  // Drops the lowest set bit of x.
  }
  return result;
}
```

Let k be the number of bits set to 1 in a particular word. (For example, for 10001010, $k = 3$.) Then time complexity of the algorithm above is $O(k)$.

The problem statement refers to computing the parity for a very large number of words. When you have to perform a large number of parity computations, and, more generally, any kind of bit fiddling computations, two keys to performance are processing multiple bits at a time and caching results in an array-based lookup table.

First we demonstrate caching. Clearly, we cannot cache the parity of every 64-bit integer—we would need 2^{64} bits of storage, which is of the order of ten trillion exabytes. However, when computing the parity of a collection of bits, it does not matter how we group those bits, i.e., the computation is associative. Therefore, we can compute the parity of a 64-bit integer by grouping its bits into four nonoverlapping 16 bit subwords, computing the parity of each subwords, and then computing the parity of these four subresults. We choose 16 since $2^{16} = 65536$ is relatively small, which makes it feasible to cache the parity of all 16-bit words using an array. Furthermore, since 16 evenly divides 64, the code is simpler than if we were, for example, to use 10 bit subwords.

We illustrate the approach with a lookup table for 2-bit words. The cache is $\langle 0, 1, 1, 0 \rangle$—these are the parities of $(00), (01), (10), (11)$, respectively. To compute the parity of (11001010) we would compute the parities of $(11), (00), (10), (10)$. By table lookup we see these are $0, 0, 1, 1$, respectively, so the final result is the parity of $0, 0, 1, 1$ which is 0.

To lookup the parity of the first two bits in (11101010), we right shift by 6, to get (00000011), and use this as an index into the cache. To lookup the parity of the next two bits, i.e., (10), we right shift by 4, to get (10) in the two least-significant bit places. The right shift does not remove the leading (11)—it results in (00001110). We cannot index the cache with this, it leads to an out-of-bounds access. To get the last two bits after the right shift by 4, we bitwise-AND (00001110) with (00000011) (this is the "mask" used to extract the last 2 bits). The result is (00000010). Similar masking is needed for the two other 2-bit lookups.

```
short Parity(unsigned long x) {
  const int kWordSize = 16;
  const int kBitMask = 0xFFFF;
  return precomputed_parity[x >> (3 * kWordSize)] ^
         precomputed_parity[(x >> (2 * kWordSize)) & kBitMask] ^
```

```
    precomputed_parity[(x >> kWordSize) & kBitMask] ^
    precomputed_parity[x & kBitMask];
}
```

The time complexity is a function of the size of the keys used to index the lookup table. Let L be the width of the words for which we cache the results, and n the word size. Since there are n/L terms, the time complexity is $O(n/L)$, assuming word-level operations, such as shifting, take $O(1)$ time. (This does not include the time for initialization of the lookup table.)

The XOR of two bits is 0 if both bits are 0 or both bits are 1; otherwise it is 1. XOR has the property of being associative (as previously described), as well as commutative, i.e., the order in which we perform the XORs does not change the result. The XOR of a group of bits is its parity. We can exploit this fact to use the CPU's word-level XOR instruction to process multiple bits at a time.

For example, the parity of $\langle b_{63}, b_{62}, \ldots, b_3, b_2, b_1, b_0 \rangle$ equals the parity of the XOR of $\langle b_{63}, b_{62}, \ldots, b_{32} \rangle$ and $\langle b_{31}, b_{30}, \ldots, b_0 \rangle$. The XOR of these two 32-bit values can be computed with a single shift and a single 32-bit XOR instruction. We repeat the same operation on 32-, 16-, 8-, 4-, 2-, and 1-bit operands to get the final result. Note that the leading bits are not meaningful, and we have to explicitly extract the result from the least-significant bit.

We illustrate the approach with an 8-bit word. The parity of (11010111) is the same as the parity of (1101) XORed with (0111), i.e., of (1010). This in turn is the same as the parity of (10) XORed with (10), i.e., of (00). The final result is the XOR of (0) with (0), i.e., 0. Note that the first XOR yields (11011010), and only the last 4 bits are relevant going forward. The second XOR yields (11101100), and only the last 2 bits are relevant. The third XOR yields (10011010). The last bit is the result, and to extract it we have to bitwise-AND with (00000001).

```
short Parity(unsigned long x) {
  x ^= x >> 32;
  x ^= x >> 16;
  x ^= x >> 8;
  x ^= x >> 4;
  x ^= x >> 2;
  x ^= x >> 1;
  return x & 0x1;
}
```

The time complexity is $O(\log n)$, where n is the word size.

Note that we could have combined caching with word-level operations, e.g., by doing a lookup once we get to 16 bits. The actual runtimes depend on the input data, e.g., the refinement of the brute-force algorithm is very fast on sparse inputs. However, for random inputs, the refinement of the brute-force is roughly 20% faster than the brute-force algorithm. The table-based approach is four times faster still, and using associativity reduces run time by another factor of two.

There are a number of ways in which bit manipulations can be accelerated. For example, as described on Page 24, the expression $x \& (x - 1)$ clears the lowest set bit in x, and $x \& \sim(x - 1)$ extracts the lowest set bit of x. Here are a few examples: $16\&(16-1) = 0, 11\&(11-1) = 10, 20\&(20-1) = 16, 16\&\sim(16-1) = 16, 11\&\sim(11-1) = 1$, and $20\&\sim(20 - 1) = 4$.

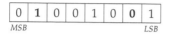

(a) The 8-bit integer 73 can be viewed as array of bits, with the LSB being at index 0.

(b) The result of swapping the bits at indices 1 and 6, with the LSB being at index 0. The corresponding integer is 11.

Figure 5.1: Example of swapping a pair of bits.

A 64-bit integer can be viewed as an array of 64 bits, with the bit at index 0 corresponding to the least significant bit (LSB), and the bit at index 63 corresponding to the most significant bit (MSB). Implement code that takes as input a 64-bit integer and swaps the bits at indices i and j. Figure 5.1 illustrates bit swapping for an 8-bit integer.

Hint: When is the swap necessary?

Solution: A brute-force approach would be to use bitmasks to extract the ith and jth bits, saving them to local variables. Consequently, write the saved jth bit to index i and the saved ith bit to index j, using a combination of bitmasks and bitwise operations.

The brute-force approach works generally, e.g., if we were swapping objects stored in an array. However, since a bit can only take two values, we can do a little better. Specifically, we first test if the bits to be swapped differ. If they do not, the swap does not change the integer. If the bits are different, swapping them is the same as flipping their individual values. For example in Figure 5.1, since the bits at Index 1 and Index 6 differ, flipping each bit has the effect of a swap.

In the code below we use standard bit-fiddling idioms for testing and flipping bits. Overall, the resulting code is slightly more succinct and efficient than the brute force approach.

```
long SwapBits(long x, int i, int j) {
  // Extract the i-th and j-th bits, and see if they differ.
  if (((x >> i) & 1) != ((x >> j) & 1)) {
    // i-th and j-th bits differ. We will swap them by flipping their values.
    // Select the bits to flip with bitMask. Since x^1 = 0 when x = 1 and 1
    // when x = 0, we can perform the flip XOR.
    unsigned long bit_mask = (1L << i) | (1L << j);
    x ^= bit_mask;
  }
  return x;
```

}

The time complexity is $O(1)$, independent of the word size.

5.3 REVERSE BITS

Write a program that takes a 64-bit word and returns the 64-bit word consisting of the bits of the input word in reverse order. For example, if the input is alternating 1s and 0s, i.e., $(1010\ldots10)$, the output should be alternating 0s and 1s, i.e., $(0101\ldots01)$.

Hint: Use a lookup table.

Solution: If we need to perform this operation just once, there is a simple brute-force algorithm: iterate through the 32 least significant bits of the input, and swap each with the corresponding most significant bit, using, for example, the approach in Solution 5.2 on the preceding page.

To implement reverse when the operation is to be performed repeatedly, we look more carefully at the structure of the input, with an eye towards using a cache. Let the input consist of the four 16-bit words y_3, y_2, y_1, y_0, with y_3 holding the most significant bits. Then the 16 least significant bits in the reverse come from y_3. To be precise, these bits appear in the reverse order in which they do in y_3. For example, if y_3 is (1110000000000001), then the 16 LSBs of the result are (1000000000000111).

Similar to computing parity (Problem 5.1 on Page 43), a very fast way to reverse bits for 16-bit words when we are performing many reverses is to build an array-based lookup-table A such that for every 16-bit number y, $A[y]$ holds the bit-reversal of y. We can then form the reverse of x with the reverse of y_0 in the most significant bit positions, followed by the reverse of y_1, followed by the reverse of y_2, followed by the reverse of y_3.

We illustrate the approach with 8-bit words and 2-bit lookup table keys. The table is rev $= \langle(00),(10),(01),(11)\rangle$. If the input is (10010011), its reverse is rev(11), rev(00), rev(01), rev(10), i.e., (11001001).

```
long ReverseBits(long x) {
  const int kWordSize = 16;
  const int kBitMask = 0xFFFF;
  return precomputed_reverse[x & kBitMask] << (3 * kWordSize) |
         precomputed_reverse[(x >> kWordSize) & kBitMask] << (2 * kWordSize) |
         precomputed_reverse[(x >> (2 * kWordSize)) & kBitMask] << kWordSize |
         precomputed_reverse[(x >> (3 * kWordSize)) & kBitMask];
}
```

The time complexity is identical to that for Solution 5.1 on Page 43, i.e., $O(n/L)$, for n-bit integers and L-bit cache keys.

Define the *weight* of a nonnegative integer x to be the number of bits that are set to 1 in its binary representation. For example, since 92 in base-2 equals $(1011100)_2$, the weight of 92 is 4.

Write a program which takes as input a nonnegative integer x and returns a number y which is not equal to x, but has the same weight as x and their difference, $|y - x|$, is as small as possible. You can assume x is not 0, or all 1s. For example, if $x = 6$, you should return 5.

Hint: Start with the least significant bit.

Solution: A brute-force approach might be to try all integers $x-1, x+1, x-2, x+2, \ldots$, stopping as soon as we encounter one with the same weight at x. This performs very poorly on some inputs. One way to see this is to consider the case where $x = 2^3 = 8$. The only numbers with a weight of 1 are powers of 2. Thus, the algorithm will try the following sequence: $7, 9, 6, 10, 5, 11, 4$, stopping at 4 (since its weight is the same as 8's weight). The algorithm tries 2^{3-1} numbers smaller than 8, namely, $7, 6, 5, 4$, and $2^{3-1} - 1$ numbers greater than 8, namely, $9, 10, 11$. This example generalizes. Suppose $x = 2^{30}$. The power of 2 nearest to 2^{30} is 2^{29}. Therefore this computation will evaluate the weight of all integers between 2^{30} and 2^{29} and between 2^{30} and $2^{30} + 2^{29} - 1$, i.e., over one billion integers.

Heuristically, it is natural to focus on the LSB of the input, specifically, to swap the LSB with rightmost bit that differs from it. This yields the correct result for some inputs, e.g., for $(10)_2$ it returns $(01)_2$, which is the closest possible. However, more experimentation shows this heuristic does not work generally. For example, for $(111)_2$ (7 in decimal) it returns $(1110)_2$ which is 14 in decimal; however, $(1011)_2$ (11 in decimal) has the same weight, and is closer to $(111)_2$.

A little math leads to the correct approach. Suppose we flip the bit at index $k1$ and flip the bit at index $k2$, $k1 > k2$. Then the absolute value of the difference between the original integer and the new one is $2^{k1} - 2^{k2}$. To minimize this, we should make $k1$ as small as possible and $k2$ as close to $k1$.

Since we must preserve the weight, the bit at index $k1$ has to be different from the bit in $k2$, otherwise the flips lead to an integer with different weight. This means the smallest $k1$ can be is the rightmost bit that's different from the LSB, and $k2$ must be the very next bit. In summary, the correct approach is to swap the two rightmost consecutive bits that differ.

```
const int kNumUnsignBits = 64;

unsigned long ClosestIntSameBitCount(unsigned long x) {
  for (int i = 0; i < kNumUnsignBits - 1; ++i) {
    if (((x >> i) & 1) != ((x >> (i + 1)) & 1)) {
      x ^= (1UL << i) | (1UL << (i + 1));  // Swaps bit-i and bit-(i + 1).
      return x;
    }
  }
}
```

```
    // Throw error if all bits of x are 0 or 1.
    throw invalid_argument("All bits are 0 or 1");
}
```

The time complexity is $O(n)$, where n is the integer width.

5.5 COMPUTE $x \times y$ WITHOUT ARITHMETICAL OPERATORS

Sometimes the processors used in ultra low-power devices such as hearing aids do not have dedicated hardware for performing multiplication. A program that needs to perform multiplication must do so explicitly using lower-level primitives.

Write a program that multiplies two nonnegative integers. The only operators you are allowed to use are

- assignment,
- the bitwise operators », «, |, &, ~, ^ and
- equality checks and Boolean combinations thereof.

You may use loops and functions that you write yourself. These constraints imply, for example, that you cannot use increment or decrement, or test if $x < y$.

Hint: Add using bitwise operations; multiply using shift-and-add.

Solution: A brute-force approach would be to perform repeated addition, i.e., initialize the result to 0 and then add x to it y times. For example, to form 5×3, we would start with 0 and repeatedly add 5, i.e., form $0 + 5, 5 + 5, 10 + 5$. The time complexity is very high—as much as $O(2^n)$, where n is the number of bits in the input, and it still leaves open the problem of adding numbers without the presence of an add instruction.

The algorithm taught in grade-school for decimal multiplication does not use repeated addition—it uses shift and add to achieve a much better time complexity. We can do the same with binary numbers—to multiply x and y we initialize the result to 0 and iterate through the bits of x, adding $2^k y$ to the result if the kth bit of x is 1.

The value $2^k y$ can be computed by left-shifting y by k. Since we cannot use add directly, we must implement it. We apply the grade-school algorithm for addition to the binary case, i.e., compute the sum bit-by-bit, and "rippling" the carry along.

As an example, we show how to multiply $13 = (1101)_2$ and $9 = (1001)_2$ using the algorithm described above. In the first iteration, since the LSB of 13 is 1, we set the result to $(1001)_2$. The second bit of $(1101)_2$ is 0, so we move on to the third bit. This bit is 1, so we shift $(1001)_2$ to the left by 2 to obtain $(100100)_2$, which we add to $(1001)_2$ to get $(101101)_2$. The fourth and final bit of $(1101)_2$ is 1, so we shift $(1001)_2$ to the left by 3 to obtain $(1001000)_2$, which we add to $(101101)_2$ to get $(1110101)_2 = 117$.

Each addition is itself performed bit-by-bit. For example, when adding $(101101)_2$ and $(1001000)_2$, the LSB of the result is 1 (since exactly one of the two LSBs of the operands is 1). The next bit is 0 (since both the next bits of the operands are 0). The next bit is 1 (since exactly one of the next bits of the operands is 1). The next bit is

0 (since both the next bits of the operands are 1). We also "carry" a 1 to the next position. The next bit is 1 (since the carry-in is 1 and both the next bits of the operands are 0). The remaining bits are assigned similarly.

```
unsigned Multiply(unsigned x, unsigned y) {
  unsigned sum = 0;
  while (x) {
    // Examines each bit of x.
    if (x & 1) {
      sum = Add(sum, y);
    }
    x >>= 1, y <<= 1;
  }
  return sum;
}

unsigned Add(unsigned a, unsigned b) {
  unsigned sum = 0, carryin = 0, k = 1, temp_a = a, temp_b = b;
  while (temp_a || temp_b) {
    unsigned ak = a & k, bk = b & k;
    unsigned carryout = (ak & bk) | (ak & carryin) | (bk & carryin);
    sum |= (ak ^ bk ^ carryin);
    carryin = carryout << 1, k <<= 1, temp_a >>= 1, temp_b >>= 1;
  }
  return sum | carryin;
}
```

The time complexity of addition is $O(n)$, where n is the width of the operands. Since we do n additions to perform a single multiplication, the total time complexity is $O(n^2)$.

5.6 COMPUTE x/y

Given two positive integers, compute their quotient, using only the addition, subtraction, and shifting operators.

Hint: Relate x/y to $(x - y)/y$.

Solution: A brute-force approach is to iteratively subtract y from x until what remains is less than y. The number of such subtractions is exactly the quotient, x/y, and the remainder is the term that's less than y. The complexity of the brute-force approach is very high, e.g., when $y = 1$ and $x = 2^{31} - 1$, it will take $2^{31} - 1$ iterations.

A better approach is to try and get more work done in each iteration. For example, we can compute the largest k such that $2^k y \leq x$, subtract $2^k y$ from x, and add 2^k to the quotient. For example, if $x = (1011)_2$ and $y = (10)_2$, then $k = 2$, since $2 \times 2^2 \leq 11$ and $2 \times 2^3 > 11$. We subtract $(1000)_2$ from $(1011)_2$ to get $(11)_2$, add $2^k = 2^2 = (100)_2$ to the quotient, and continue by updating x to $(11)_2$.

The advantage of using $2^k y$ is that it can be computed very efficiently using shifting, and x is at least halved in each iteration. If it takes n bits to represent x/y, there are

50

$O(n)$ iterations. If the largest k such that $2^k y \leq x$ is computed by iterating through k, each iteration has time complexity $O(n)$. This leads to an $O(n^2)$ algorithm.

A better way to find the largest k in each iteration is to recognize that it keeps decreasing. Therefore, instead of testing in each iteration whether $2^0 y, 2^1 y, 2^2 y, \ldots$ is less than or equal to x, after we initially find the largest k such that $2^k y \leq x$, in subsequent iterations we test $2^{k-1} y, 2^{k-2} y, 2^{k-3} y, \ldots$ with x.

For the example given earlier, after setting the quotient to $(100)_2$ we continue with $(11)_2$. Now the largest k such that $2^k y \leq (11)_2$ is 0, so we add $2^0 = (1)_2$ to the quotient, which is now $(101)_2$. We continue with $(11)_2 - (10)_2 = (1)_2$. Since $(1)_2 < y$, we are done—the quotient is $(101)_2$ and the remainder is $(1)_2$.

```
unsigned Divide(unsigned x, unsigned y) {
  unsigned result = 0;
  int power = 32;
  unsigned long long y_power = static_cast<unsigned long long>(y) << power;
  while (x >= y) {
    while (y_power > x) {
      y_power >>= 1;
      --power;
    }

    result += 1U << power;
    x -= y_power;
  }
  return result;
}
```

In essence, the program applies the grade-school division algorithm to binary numbers. With each iteration, we process an additional bit. Therefore, assuming individual shift and add operations take $O(1)$ time, the time complexity is $O(n)$.

5.7 COMPUTE x^y

Write a program that takes a double x and an integer y and returns x^y. You can ignore overflow and underflow.

Hint: Exploit mathematical properties of exponentiation.

Solution: First, assume y is nonnegative. The brute-force algorithm is to form $x^2 = x \times x$, then $x^3 = x^2 \times x$, and so on. This approach takes $y - 1$ multiplications, which is $O(2^n)$, where n is number of bits in the integer type.

The key to efficiency is to try and get more work done with each multiplication, thereby using fewer multiplications to accomplish the same result. For example, to compute 1.1^{21}, instead of starting with 1.1 and multiplying by 1.1 20 times, we could multiply 1.1 by $1.1^2 = 1.21$ 10 times for a total of 11 multiplications (one to compute 1.1^2, and 10 additional multiplications by 1.21). We can do still better by computing $1.1^3, 1.1^4$, etc.

When y is a power of 2, the approach that uses fewest multiplications is iterated squaring, i.e., forming $x, x^2, (x^2)^2 = x^4, (x^4)^2 = x^8, \ldots$. To develop an algorithm that works for general y, it is instructive to look at the binary representation of y, as well as properties of exponentiation, specifically $x^{y_0+y_1} = x^{y_0} \cdot x^{y_1}$.

We begin with some small concrete instances, first assuming that y is nonnegative. For example, $x^{(1010)_2} = x^{(101)_2+(101)_2} = x^{(101)_2} \times x^{(101)_2}$. Similarly, $x^{(101)_2} = x^{(100)_2+(1)_2} = x^{(100)_2} \times x = x^{(10)_2} \times x^{(10)_2} \times x$.

Generalizing, if the least significant bit of y is 0, the result is $(x^{y/2})^2$; otherwise, it is $x \times (x^{y/2})^2$. This gives us a recursive algorithm for computing x^y when y is nonnegative.

The only change when y is negative is replacing x by $1/x$ and y by $-y$. In the implementation below we replace the recursion with a while loop to avoid the overhead of function calls.

```
double Power(double x, int y) {
    double result = 1.0;
    long long power = y;
    if (y < 0) {
        power = -power, x = 1.0 / x;
    }
    while (power) {
        if (power & 1) {
            result *= x;
        }
        x *= x, power >>= 1;
    }
    return result;
}
```

The number of multiplications is at most twice the index of y's MSB, implying an $O(n)$ time complexity.

5.8 REVERSE DIGITS

Write a program which takes an integer and returns the integer corresponding to the digits of the input written in reverse order. For example, the reverse of 42 is 24, and the reverse of -314 is -413.

Hint: How would you solve the same problem if the input is presented as a string?

Solution: The brute-force approach is to convert the input to a string, and then compute the reverse from the string by traversing it from back to front. For example, $(1100)_2$ is the decimal number 12, and the answer for $(1100)_2$ can be computed by traversing the string "12" in reverse order.

Closer analysis shows that we can avoid having to form a string. Consider the input 1132. The first digit of the result is 2, which we can obtain by taking the input modulo 10. The remaining digits of the result are the reverse of $1132/10 = 113$. Generalizing, let the input be k. If $k \geq 0$, then $k \bmod 10$ is the most significant digit of the result and the subsequent digits are the reverse of $\frac{k}{10}$. Continuing with the example, we iteratively update the result and the input as 2 and 113, then 23 and 11, then 231 and 1, then 2311.

For general k, we record its sign, solve the problem for $|k|$, and apply the sign to the result.

```
long Reverse(int x) {
  bool is_negative = x < 0;
  long result = 0, x_remaining = abs(x);
  while (x_remaining) {
    result = result * 10 + x_remaining % 10;
    x_remaining /= 10;
  }
  return is_negative ? -result : result;
}
```

The time complexity is $O(n)$, where n is the number of digits in k.

5.9 CHECK IF A DECIMAL INTEGER IS A PALINDROME

A palindromic string is one which reads the same forwards and backwards, e.g., "redivider". In this problem, you are to write a program which determines if the decimal representation of an integer is a palindromic string. For example, your program should return true for the inputs $0, 1, 7, 11, 121, 333$, and 2147447412, and false for the inputs $-1, 12, 100$, and 2147483647.

Write a program that takes an integer and determines if that integer's representation as a decimal string is a palindrome.

Hint: It's easy to come up with a simple expression that extracts the least significant digit. Can you find a simple expression for the most significant digit?

Solution: First note that if the input is negative, then its representation as a decimal string cannot be palindromic, since it begins with a −.

A brute-force approach would be to convert the input to a string and then iterate through the string, pairwise comparing digits starting from the least significant digit and the most significant digit, and working inwards, stopping if there is a mismatch. The time and space complexity are $O(n)$, where n is the number of digits in the input.

We can avoid the $O(n)$ space complexity used by the string representation by directly extracting the digits from the input. The number of digits, n, in the input's string representation is the log (base 10) of the input value, x. To be precise, $n = \lfloor \log_{10} x \rfloor + 1$. Therefore, the least significant digit is $x \bmod 10$, and the most significant digit is $x/10^{n-1}$. In the program below, we iteratively compare the most and least significant digits, and then remove them from the input. For example, if the input is 151751, we would compare the leading and trailing digits, 1 and 1. Since these are equal, we update the value to 5175. The leading and trailing digits are equal, so we update to 17. Now the leading and trailing are unequal, so we return false. If instead the number was 157751, the final compare would be of 7 with 7, so we would return true.

```
bool IsPalindromeNumber(int x) {
```

```
if (x < 0) {
  return false;
} else if (x == 0) {
  return true;
}

const int num_digits = static_cast<int>(floor(log10(x))) + 1;
int msd_mask = static_cast<int>(pow(10, num_digits - 1));
for (int i = 0; i < (num_digits / 2); ++i) {
  if (x / msd_mask != x % 10) {
    return false;
  }
  x %= msd_mask;  // Remove the most significant digit of x.
  x /= 10;        // Remove the least significant digit of x.
  msd_mask /= 100;
}
return true;
}
```

The time complexity is $O(n)$, and the space complexity is $O(1)$. Alternatively, we could use Solution 5.8 on Page 52 to reverse the digits in the number and see if it is unchanged.

5.10 GENERATE UNIFORM RANDOM NUMBERS

This problem is motivated by the following scenario. Six friends have to select a designated driver using a single unbiased coin. The process should be fair to everyone.

How would you implement a random number generator that generates a random integer i between a and b, inclusive, given a random number generator that produces zero or one with equal probability? All values in $[a, b]$ should be equally likely?

Hint: How would you mimic a three-sided coin with a two-sided coin?

Solution: Note that it is easy to produce a random integer between 0 and $2^i - 1$, inclusive: concatenate i bits produced by the random number generator. For example, two calls to the random number generator will produce one of $(00)_2, (01)_2, (10)_2, (11)_2$. These four possible outcomes encode the four integers $0, 1, 2, 3$, and all of them are equally likely.

For the general case, first note that it is equivalent to produce a random integer between 0 and $b - a$, inclusive, since we can simply add a to the result. If $b - a$ is equal to $2^i - 1$, for some i, then we can use the approach in the previous paragraph.

If $b - a$ is not of the form $2^i - 1$, we find the smallest number of the form $2^i - 1$ that is greater than $b - a$. We generate an i-bit number as before. This i-bit number may or may not lie between 0 and $b - a$, inclusive. If it is within the range, we return it—all such numbers are equally likely. If it is not within the range, we try again with i new random bits. We keep trying until we get a number within the range.

54

For example, to generate a random number corresponding to a dice roll, i.e., a number between 1 and 6, we begin by making three calls to the random number generator (since $2^2 - 1 < (6 - 1) \le 2^3 - 1$). If this yields one of $(000)_2, (001)_2, (010)_2, (011)_2, (100)_2, (101)_2$, we return 1 plus the corresponding value. Observe that all six values between 1 and 6, inclusive, are equally likely to be returned. If the three calls yields one of $(110)_2, (111)_2$, we make three more calls. Note that the probability of having to try again is 2/8, which is less than half. Since successive calls are independent, the probability that we require many attempts diminishes very rapidly, e.g., the probability of not getting a result in 10 attempts is $(2/8)^{10}$ which is less than one-in-a-million.

```
int UniformRandom(int lower_bound, int upper_bound) {
  int number_of_outcomes = upper_bound - lower_bound + 1, result;
  do {
    result = 0;
    for (int i = 0; (1 << i) < number_of_outcomes; ++i) {
      // ZeroOneRandom() is the provided random number generator.
      result = (result << 1) | ZeroOneRandom();
    }
  } while (result >= number_of_outcomes);
  return result + lower_bound;
}
```

To analyze the time complexity, let $t = b - a + 1$. The probability that we succeed in the first try is $t/2^i$. Since 2^i is the smallest power of 2 greater than or equal to t, it must be less than $2t$. (An easy way to see this is to consider the binary representation of t and $2t$.) This implies that $t/2^i > t/2t = (1/2)$. Hence the probability that we do not succeed on the first try is $1 - t/2^i < 1/2$. Since successive tries are independent, the probability that more than k tries are needed is less than or equal to $1/2^k$. Hence, the expected number of tries is not more than $1 + 2(1/2)^1 + 3(1/2)^2 + \ldots$. The series converges, so the number of tries is $O(1)$. Each try makes $\lceil \lg(b - a + 1) \rceil$ calls to the 0/1-valued random number generator. Assuming the 0/1-valued random number generator takes $O(1)$ time, the time complexity is $O(\lg(b - a + 1))$.

5.11 RECTANGLE INTERSECTION

This problem is concerned with rectangles whose sides are parallel to the X-axis and Y-axis. See Figure 5.2 for examples.

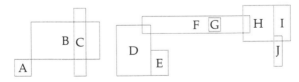

Figure 5.2: Examples of XY-aligned rectangles.

Write a program which tests if two rectangles have a nonempty intersection. If the intersection is nonempty, return the rectangle formed by their intersection.

Hint: Think of the X and Y dimensions independently.

Solution: Since the problem leaves it unspecified, we will treat the boundary as part of the rectangle. This implies, for example, rectangles A and B in Figure 5.2 on the preceding page intersect.

There are many qualitatively different ways in which rectangles can intersect, e.g., they have partial overlap (D and F), one contains the other (F and G), they share a common side (D and E), they share a common corner (A and B), they form a cross (B and C), they form a tee (F and H), etc. The case analysis is quite tricky.

A better approach is to focus on conditions under which it can be guaranteed that the rectangles do *not* intersect. For example, the rectangle with left-most lower point $(1, 2)$, width 3, and height 4 cannot possibly intersect with the rectangle with left-most lower point $(5, 3)$, width 2, and height 4, since the X-values of the first rectangle range from 1 to $1 + 3 = 4$, inclusive, and the X-values of the second rectangle range from 5 to $5 + 2 = 7$, inclusive.

Similarly, if the Y-values of the first rectangle do not intersect with the Y-values of the second rectangle, the two rectangles cannot intersect.

Equivalently, if the set of X-values for the rectangles intersect and the set of Y-values for the rectangles intersect, then all points with those X- and Y-values are common to the two rectangles, so there is a nonempty intersection.

```
struct Rectangle {
  int x, y, width, height;
};


Rectangle IntersectRectangle(const Rectangle& R1, const Rectangle& R2) {
  if (IsIntersect(R1, R2)) {
    return {max(R1.x, R2.x), max(R1.y, R2.y),
            min(R1.x + R1.width, R2.x + R2.width) - max(R1.x, R2.x),
            min(R1.y + R1.height, R2.y + R2.height) - max(R1.y, R2.y)};
  }
  return {0, 0, -1, -1};  // No intersection.
}


bool IsIntersect(const Rectangle& R1, const Rectangle& R2) {
  return R1.x <= R2.x + R2.width && R1.x + R1.width >= R2.x &&
         R1.y <= R2.y + R2.height && R1.y + R1.height >= R2.y;
}
```

The time complexity is $O(1)$, since the number of operations is constant.

Variant: Given four points in the plane, how would you check if they are the vertices of a rectangle?

Variant: How would you check if two rectangles, not necessarily aligned with the X and Y axes, intersect?

6

Arrays

The machine can alter the scanned symbol and its behavior is in part determined by that symbol, but the symbols on the tape elsewhere do not affect the behavior of the machine.

— *"Intelligent Machinery,"*
A. M. TURING, 1948

The simplest data structure is the *array*, which is a contiguous block of memory. It is usually used to represent sequences. Given an array A, $A[i]$ denotes the $(i+1)$th object stored in the array. Retrieving and updating $A[i]$ takes $O(1)$ time. Insertion into a full array can be handled by resizing, i.e., allocating a new array with additional memory and copying over the entries from the original array. This increases the worst-case time of insertion, but if the new array has, for example, a constant factor larger than the original array, the average time for insertion is constant since resizing is infrequent. Deleting an element from an array entails moving all successive elements one over to the left to fill the vacated space. For example, if the array is $\langle 2,3,5,7,9,11,13,17 \rangle$, then deleting the element at index 4 results in the array $\langle 2,3,5,7,11,13,17,0 \rangle$. (We do not care about the last value.) The time complexity to delete the element at index i from an array of length n is $O(n-i)$.

6.1 THE DUTCH NATIONAL FLAG PROBLEM

The quicksort algorithm for sorting arrays proceeds recursively—it selects an element (the "pivot"), reorders the array to make all the elements less than or equal to the pivot appear first, followed by all the elements greater than the pivot. The two subarrays are then sorted recursively.

Implemented naively, quicksort has large run times and deep function call stacks on arrays with many duplicates because the subarrays may differ greatly in size. One solution is to reorder the array so that all elements less than the pivot appear first, followed by elements equal to the pivot, followed by elements greater than the pivot. This is known as Dutch national flag partitioning, because the Dutch national flag consists of three horizontal bands, each in a different color.

As an example, assuming that black precedes white and white precedes gray, Figure 6.1(b) on the next page is a valid partitioning for Figure 6.1(a) on the following page. If gray precedes black and black precedes white, Figure 6.1(c) on the next page is a valid partitioning for Figure 6.1(a) on the following page.

(a) Before partitioning.

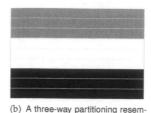
(b) A three-way partitioning resembling the Dutch national flag.

(c) Another three-way partitioning: the Russian national flag.

Figure 6.1: Illustrating the Dutch national flag problem.

Write a program that takes an array A and an index i into A, and rearranges the elements such that all elements less than $A[i]$ (the "pivot") appear first, followed by elements equal to the pivot, followed by elements greater than the pivot.

Hint: Think about the partition step in quicksort.

Solution: The problem is trivial to solve with $O(n)$ additional space, where n is the length of A. We form three lists, namely, elements less than the pivot, elements equal to the pivot, and elements greater than the pivot. Consequently, we write these values into A. The time complexity is $O(n)$.

We can avoid using $O(n)$ additional space at the cost of increased time complexity as follows. In the first stage, we iterate through A starting from index 0, then index 1, etc. In each iteration, we seek an element smaller than the pivot—as soon as we find it, we move it to the subarray of smaller elements via an exchange. This moves all the elements less than the pivot to the start of the array. The second stage is similar to the first one, the difference being that we move elements greater than the pivot to the end of the array. Code illustrating this approach is shown below.

```
typedef enum { RED, WHITE, BLUE } Color;

void DutchFlagPartition(int pivot_index, vector<Color>* A_ptr) {
  vector<Color>& A = *A_ptr;
  Color pivot = A[pivot_index];
  // First pass: group elements smaller than pivot.
  for (int i = 0; i < A.size(); ++i) {
    // Look for a smaller element.
    for (int j = i + 1; j < A.size(); ++j) {
      if (A[j] < pivot) {
        swap(A[i], A[j]);
        break;
      }
    }
  }
  // Second pass: group elements larger than pivot.
  for (int i = A.size() - 1; i >= 0 && A[i] >= pivot; --i) {
    // Look for a larger element. Stop when we reach an element less
    // than pivot, since first pass has moved them to the start of A.
    for (int j = i - 1; j >= 0 && A[j] >= pivot; --j) {
```

```
        if (A[j] > pivot) {
          swap(A[i], A[j]);
          break;
        }
      }
    }
  }
}
```

The additional space complexity is now $O(1)$, but the time complexity is $O(n^2)$, e.g., if $i = n/2$ and all elements before i are greater than $A[i]$, and all elements after i are less than $A[i]$. Intuitively, this approach has bad time complexity because in the first pass when searching for each additional element smaller than the pivot we start from the beginning. However, there is no reason to start from so far back—we can begin from the last location we advanced to. (Similar comments hold for the second pass.)

To improve time complexity, we make a single pass and move all the elements less than the pivot to the beginning, In the second pass we move the larger elements to the end. It is easy to perform each pass in a single iteration, moving out-of-place elements as soon as they are discovered.

```
typedef enum { RED, WHITE, BLUE } Color;

void DutchFlagPartition(int pivot_index, vector<Color>* A_ptr) {
  vector<Color>& A = *A_ptr;
  Color pivot = A[pivot_index];
  // First pass: group elements smaller than pivot.
  int smaller = 0;
  for (int i = 0; i < A.size(); ++i) {
    if (A[i] < pivot) {
      swap(A[i], A[smaller++]);
    }
  }
  // Second pass: group elements larger than pivot.
  int larger = A.size() - 1;
  for (int i = A.size() - 1; i >= 0 && A[i] >= pivot; --i) {
    if (A[i] > pivot) {
      swap(A[i], A[larger--]);
    }
  }
}
```

The time complexity is $O(n)$ and the space complexity is $O(1)$.

The algorithm we now present is similar to the one sketched above. The main difference is that it performs classification into elements less than, equal to, and greater than the pivot in a single pass. This reduces runtime, at the cost of a trickier implementation. We do this by maintaining four subarrays: *bottom* (elements less than pivot), *middle* (elements equal to pivot), *unclassified*, and *top* (elements greater than pivot). Initially, all elements are in *unclassified*. We iterate through elements in *unclassified,* and move elements into one of *bottom, middle,* and *top* groups according to the relative order between the incoming unclassified element and the pivot.

As a concrete example, suppose the array is currently $A = \langle -3, 0, -1, 1, 1, ?, ?, ?, 4, 2 \rangle$, where the pivot is 1 and ? denotes unclassified elements. There are three possibilities for the first unclassified element, $A[5]$.

- $A[5]$ is less than the pivot, e.g., $A[5] = -5$. We exchange it with the first 1, i.e., the new array is $\langle -3, 0, -1, -5, 1, 1, ?, ?, 4, 2 \rangle$.
- $A[5]$ is equal to the pivot, i.e., $A[5] = 1$. We do not need to move it, we just advance to the next unclassified element, i.e., the array is $\langle -3, 0, -1, 1, 1, 1, ?, ?, 4, 2 \rangle$.
- $A[5]$ is greater than the pivot, e.g., $A[5] = 3$. We exchange it with the last unclassified element, i.e., the new array is $\langle -3, 0, -1, 1, 1, ?, ?, 3, 4, 2 \rangle$.

Note how the number of unclassified elements reduces by one in each case.

```cpp
typedef enum { RED, WHITE, BLUE } Color;

void DutchFlagPartition(int pivot_index, vector<Color>* A_ptr) {
  vector<Color>& A = *A_ptr;
  Color pivot = A[pivot_index];
  /**
   * Keep the following invariants during partitioning:
   * bottom group: A[0 : smaller - 1].
   * middle group: A[smaller : equal - 1].
   * unclassified group: A[equal : larger - 1].
   * top group: A[larger : A.size() - 1].
   */
  int smaller = 0, equal = 0, larger = A.size();
  // Keep iterating as long as there is an unclassified element.
  while (equal < larger) {
    // A[equal] is the incoming unclassified element.
    if (A[equal] < pivot) {
      swap(A[smaller++], A[equal++]);
    } else if (A[equal] == pivot) {
      ++equal;
    } else {  // A[equal] > pivot.
      swap(A[equal], A[--larger]);
    }
  }
}
```

Each iteration decreases the size of *unclassified* by 1, and the time spent within each iteration is $O(1)$, implying the time complexity is $O(n)$. The space complexity is clearly $O(1)$.

Variant: Assuming that keys take one of three values, reorder the array so that all objects with the same key appear together. The order of the subarrays is not important. For example, both Figures 6.1(b) and 6.1(c) on Page 58 are valid answers for Figure 6.1(a) on Page 58. Use $O(1)$ additional space and $O(n)$ time.

Variant: Given an array A of n objects with keys that takes one of four values, reorder the array so that all objects that have the same key appear together. Use $O(1)$ additional space and $O(n)$ time.

Variant: Given an array A of n objects with Boolean-valued keys, reorder the array so that objects that have the key false appear first. Use $O(1)$ additional space and $O(n)$ time.

Variant: Given an array A of n objects with Boolean-valued keys, reorder the array so that objects that have the key false appear first. The relative ordering of objects with key true should not change. Use $O(1)$ additional space and $O(n)$ time.

6.2 INCREMENT AN ARBITRARY-PRECISION INTEGER

Write a program which takes as input an array of digits encoding a decimal number D and updates the array to represent the number $D + 1$. For example, if the input is $\langle 1, 2, 9 \rangle$ then you should update the array to $\langle 1, 3, 0 \rangle$. Your algorithm should work even if it is implemented in a language that has finite-precision arithmetic.

Hint: Experiment with concrete examples.

Solution: A brute-force approach might be to convert the array of digits to the equivalent integer, increment that, and then convert the resulting value back to an array of digits. For example, if the array is $\langle 1, 2, 9 \rangle$, we would derive the integer 129, add one to get 130, then extract its digits to form $\langle 1, 3, 0 \rangle$. When implemented in a language that imposes a limit on the range of values an integer type can take, this approach will fail on inputs that encode integers outside of that range.

We can avoid overflow issues by operating directly on the array of digits. Specifically, we mimic the grade-school algorithm for adding numbers, which entails adding digits starting from the least significant digit, and propagate carries. If the result has an additional digit, e.g., $99 + 1 = 100$, all digits have to be moved to the right by one.

For the given example, we would update 9 to 0 with a carry-out of 1. We update 2 to 3 (because of the carry-in). There is no carry-out, so we stop—the result is $\langle 1, 3, 0 \rangle$.

```
vector<int> PlusOne(vector<int> A) {
  ++A.back();
  for (int i = A.size() - 1; i > 0 && A[i] == 10; --i) {
    A[i] = 0, ++A[i - 1];
  }
  if (A[0] == 10) {
    // Need additional digit as the most significant digit (i.e., A[0]) has a
    // carry-out.
    A[0] = 0;
    A.insert(A.begin(), 1);
  }
  return A;
}
```

The time complexity is $O(n)$, where n is the length of A.

Variant: Write a program which takes as input two strings s and t of bits encoding binary numbers B_s and B_t, respectively, and returns a new string of bits representing the number $B_s + B_t$.

6.3 MULTIPLY TWO ARBITRARY-PRECISION INTEGERS

Certain applications require arbitrary precision arithmetic. One way to achieve this is to use arrays to represent integers, e.g., with one digit per array entry, with the most significant digit appearing first, and a negative leading digit denoting a negative integer. For example, $\langle 1, 9, 3, 7, 0, 7, 7, 2, 1 \rangle$ represents 193707721 and $\langle -7, 6, 1, 8, 3, 8, 2, 5, 7, 2, 8, 7 \rangle$ represents −761838257287.

Write a program that takes two arrays representing integers, and returns an integer representing their product. For example, since $193707721 \times -761838257287 = -147573952589676412927$, if the inputs are $\langle 1, 9, 3, 7, 0, 7, 7, 2, 1 \rangle$ and $\langle -7, 6, 1, 8, 3, 8, 2, 5, 7, 2, 8, 7 \rangle$, your function should return $\langle -1, 4, 7, 5, 7, 3, 9, 5, 2, 5, 8, 9, 6, 7, 6, 4, 1, 2, 9, 2, 7 \rangle$.

Hint: Use arrays to simulate the grade-school multiplication algorithm.

Solution: As in Solution 6.2 on the previous page, the possibility of overflow precludes us from converting to the integer type.

Instead we can use the grade-school algorithm for multiplication which consists of multiplying the first number by each digit of the second, and then adding all the resulting terms.

From a space perspective, it is better to incrementally add the terms rather than compute all of them individually and then add them up. The number of digits required for the product is at most $n + m$ for n and m digit operands, so we use an array of size $n + m$ for the result. Indexing into the arrays is simplified if we reverse them—the first entry becomes the least significant digit.

For example, when multiplying 123 with 987, we would form $7 \times 123 = 861$, then we would form $8 \times 123 \times 10 = 9840$, which we would add to 861 to get 10701. Then we would form $9 \times 123 \times 100 = 110700$, which we would add to 10701 to get the final result 121401. (All numbers shown are represented using arrays of digits.)

```
vector<int> Multiply(vector<int> num1, vector<int> num2) {
  bool is_negative = (num1.front() < 0 && num2.front() >= 0) ||
                     (num1.front() >= 0 && num2.front() < 0);
  num1.front() = abs(num1.front()), num2.front() = abs(num2.front());

  // Reverses num1 and num2 to make multiplication easier.
  reverse(num1.begin(), num1.end());
  reverse(num2.begin(), num2.end());
  vector<int> result(num1.size() + num2.size(), 0);
  for (int i = 0; i < num1.size(); ++i) {
    for (int j = 0; j < num2.size(); ++j) {
```

```
        result[i + j] += num1[i] * num2[j];
        result[i + j + 1] += result[i + j] / 10;
        result[i + j] %= 10;
    }
}

// Skips the leading 0s and keeps one 0 if all are 0s.
while (result.size() != 1 && result.back() == 0) {
    result.pop_back();
}
// Reverses result to get the most significant digit as the start of array.
reverse(result.begin(), result.end());
if (is_negative) {
    result.front() *= -1;
}
return result;
}
```

There are m partial products, each with at most $n + 1$ digits. We perform $O(1)$ operations on each digit in each partial product, so the time complexity is $O(nm)$.

Variant: Solve the same problem when numbers are represented as lists of digits.

6.4 ADVANCING THROUGH AN ARRAY

In a particular board game, a player has to try to advance through a sequence of positions. Each position has a nonnegative integer associated with it, representing the maximum you can advance from that position in one move. You begin at the first position, and win by getting to the last position. For example, let $A = \langle 3, 3, 1, 0, 2, 0, 1 \rangle$ represent the board game, i.e., the ith entry in A is the maximum we can advance from i. Then the game can be won by the following sequence of advances through A: take 1 step from $A[0]$ to $A[1]$, then 3 steps from $A[1]$ to $A[4]$, then 2 steps from $A[4]$ to $A[6]$, which is the last position. Note that $A[0] = 3 \geq 1$, $A[1] = 3 \geq 3$, and $A[4] = 2 \geq 2$, so all moves are valid. If A instead was $\langle 3, 2, 0, 0, 2, 0, 1 \rangle$, it would not possible to advance past position 3, so the game cannot be won.

Write a program which takes an array of n integers, where $A[i]$ denotes the maximum you can advance from index i, and returns whether it is possible to advance to the last index starting from the beginning of the array.

Hint: Analyze each location, starting from the beginning.

Solution: It is natural to try advancing as far as possible in each step. This approach does not always work, because it potentially skips indices containing large entries. For example, if $A = \langle 2, 4, 1, 1, 0, 2, 3 \rangle$, then it advances to index 2, which contains a 1, which leads to index 3, after which it cannot progress. However, advancing to index 1, which contains a 4 lets us proceed to index 5, from which we can advance to index 6.

The above example suggests iterating through all entries in A. As we iterate through the array, we track the furthest index we know we can advance to. The furthest we can advance from index i is $i + A[i]$. If, for some i before the end of the array, i is the furthest index that we have demonstrated that we can advance to, we cannot reach the last index. Otherwise, we reach the end.

For example, if $A = \langle 3, 3, 1, 0, 2, 0, 1 \rangle$, we iteratively compute the furthest we can advance to as $0, 3, 4, 4, 4, 6, 6, 7$, which reaches the last index, 6. If $A = \langle 3, 2, 0, 0, 2, 0, 1 \rangle$, we iteratively update the furthest we can advance to as $0, 3, 3, 3, 3$, after which we cannot advance, so it is not possible to reach the last index.

The code below implements this algorithm. Note that it is robust with respect to negative entries, since we track the maximum of how far we proved we can advance to and $i + A[i]$.

```
bool CanReachEnd(const vector<int>& max_advance_steps) {
  int furthest_reach_so_far = 0, last_index = max_advance_steps.size() - 1;
  for (int i = 0;
       i <= furthest_reach_so_far && furthest_reach_so_far < last_index; ++i) {
    furthest_reach_so_far =
        max(furthest_reach_so_far, max_advance_steps[i] + i);
  }
  return furthest_reach_so_far >= last_index;
}
```

The time complexity is $O(n)$, and the additional space complexity (beyond what is used for A) is three integer variables, i.e., $O(1)$.

Variant: Write a program to compute the minimum number of steps needed to advance to the last location.

6.5 DELETE A KEY FROM AN ARRAY

This problem is concerned with writing a remove function for arrays. For example, if the array is $\langle 5, 3, 7, 11, 2, 3, 13, 5, 7 \rangle$ and the key to remove is 3, then $\langle 5, 7, 11, 2, 13, 5, 7, 0, 0 \rangle$ is an acceptable update to the array. (The last two entries are not important—$\langle 5, 7, 11, 2, 13, 5, 7, 5, 7 \rangle$ would also be acceptable.) Many languages have library functions for performing this operation. You cannot use these functions.

Implement a function which takes as input an array and a key, and updates the array so that all occurrences of the input key have been removed and the remaining elements have been shifted left to fill the emptied indices. Return the number of remaining elements. There are no requirements as to the values stored beyond the last valid element.

Hint: Don't delete entries one-at-a-time.

Solution: A brute-force approach might be to traverse the input array, storing entries not equal to the key into a new array, and then copying the entries of the new array back over to the input array. The time and space complexity are both $O(n)$, where n is the length of the input array.

We can avoid the additional space complexity with an increased time complexity by traversing the array, and every time an entry equals the key, moving all subsequent entries one entry to the left. This approach performs poorly when the key appears frequently, since subarrays are repeatedly shifted left. The time complexity is $O(n^2)$, where n is the length of the array. For example, when all entries are equal to the key, the number of shifts is $(n-1) + (n-2) + \cdots + 2 + 1$.

The key to improving time complexity while sticking to $O(1)$ space is avoiding wasted copies. Note that if we iterate forward through the array, any element not equal to the key that we move left never needs to be moved again. At a top level, our algorithm skips over elements equal to the key, and tracks the location the next value not equal to the key should be written to.

For the given example, we would iterate to the first 3, which is at index 1. We would then write subsequent elements one to the left till we get to the next 3. At this point the array would be $\langle 5, 7, 11, 2, 2, 3, 13, 5, 7 \rangle$. To skip the next 3 we write subsequent elements two to the left. We continue till the end of the array, which is now $\langle 5, 7, 11, 2, 13, 5, 7, 5, 7 \rangle$. Since we are not required to reset the invalid entries, we simply return 7, the index of the next entry to write to, which is also the number of valid elements.

```
// Returns the number of valid entries after deletion.
size_t DeleteKey(int key, vector<int>* A_ptr) {
  auto& A = *A_ptr;
  size_t write_idx = 0;
  for (size_t i = 0; i < A.size(); ++i) {
    if (A[i] != key) {
      A[write_idx++] = A[i];
    }
  }
  return write_idx;
}
```

The time complexity is $O(n)$, where n is the length of the array. The additional space complexity is $O(1)$.

6.6 DELETE DUPLICATES FROM A SORTED ARRAY

This problem is concerned with deleting repeated elements from a sorted array. For example, for the array $\langle 2, 3, 5, 5, 7, 11, 11, 11, 13 \rangle$, then after deletion, the array is $\langle 2, 3, 5, 7, 11, 13, 0, 0, 0 \rangle$. After deleting repeated elements, there are 6 valid entries. There are no requirements as to the values stored beyond the last valid element.

Write a program which takes as input a sorted array and updates it so that all duplicates have been removed and the remaining elements have been shifted left to fill the emptied indices. Return the number of valid elements. Many languages have library functions for performing this operation—you cannot use these functions.

Hint: There is an $O(n)$ time and $O(1)$ space solution.

Solution: Let A be the array and n its length. If we allow ourselves $O(n)$ additional space, we can solve the problem by iterating through A and recording values that have not appeared previously into a hash table. (The hash table is used to determine if a value is new.) New values are also written to a list. The list is then copied back into A.

Here is a brute-force algorithm that uses $O(1)$ additional space—iterate through A, testing if $A[i]$ equals $A[i + 1]$, and, if so, shift all elements at and after $i + 2$ to the left by one. As in Solution 6.5 on Page 64, the same worst-case input demonstrates the time complexity is $O(n^2)$, where n is the length of the array.

The intuition behind achieving a better time complexity is to reduce the amount of shifting. Since the array is sorted, repeated elements must appear one-after-another, so we do not need an auxiliary data structure to check if an element has appeared already. We move just one element, rather than an entire subarray, and ensure that we move it just once.

For the given example, $\langle 2, 3, 5, 5, 7, 11, 11, 11, 13 \rangle$, when processing the $A[3]$, since we already have a 5 (which we know by comparing $A[3]$ with $A[2]$), we advance to $A[4]$. Since this is a new value, we move it to the first vacant entry, namely $A[3]$. Now the array is $\langle 2, 3, 5, 7, 7, 11, 11, 11, 13 \rangle$, and the first vacant entry is $A[4]$. We continue from $A[5]$.

```
// Returns the number of valid entries after deletion.
int DeleteDuplicates(vector<int>* A_ptr) {
  vector<int>& A = *A_ptr;
  if (A.empty()) {
    return 0;
  }

  int write_index = 1;
  for (int i = 1; i < A.size(); ++i) {
    if (A[write_index - 1] != A[i]) {
      A[write_index++] = A[i];
    }
  }
  return write_index;
}
```

The time complexity is $O(n)$, and the space complexity is $O(1)$, since all that is needed is the two additional variables.

Variant: Write a program which takes as input a sorted array A of integers and a positive integer m, and updates A so that if x appears m times in A it appears exactly $\min(2, m)$ times in A. The update to A should be performed in one pass, and no additional storage may be allocated.

This problem is concerned with the problem of optimally buying and selling a stock once, as described on Page 2. As an example, consider the following sequence of stock prices: ⟨310, 315, 275, 295, 260, 270, 290, 230, 255, 250⟩. The maximum profit that can be made with one buy and one sell is 30—buy at 260 and sell at 290. Note that 260 is not the lowest price, nor 290 the highest price.

Write a program that takes an array denoting the daily stock price, and returns the maximum profit that could be made by buying and then selling one share of that stock.

Hint: Identifying the minimum and maximum is not enough since the minimum may appear after the maximum height. Focus on valid differences.

Solution: We developed several algorithms for this problem in the introduction. Specifically, on Page 2 we showed how to compute the maximum profit by computing the difference of the current entry with the minimum value seen so far as we iterate through the array.

For example, the array of minimum values seen so far for the given example is ⟨310, 310, 275, 275, 260, 260, 260, 230, 230, 230⟩. The maximum profit that can be made by selling on each specific day is the difference of the current price and the minimum seen so far, i.e., ⟨0, 5, 0, 20, 0, 10, 30, 0, 25, 20⟩. The maximum profit overall is 30, corresponding to buying 260 and selling for 290.

```cpp
double BuyAndSellStockOnce(const vector<double>& prices) {
  double min_price_so_far = numeric_limits<double>::max(), max_profit = 0;
  for (const double& price : prices) {
    double max_profit_sell_today = price - min_price_so_far;
    max_profit = max(max_profit, max_profit_sell_today);
    min_price_so_far = min(min_price_so_far, price);
  }
  return max_profit;
}
```

The time complexity is $O(n)$ and the space complexity is $O(1)$, where n is the length of the array.

Variant: Write a program that takes an array of integers and finds the length of a longest subarray all of whose entries are equal.

6.8 BUY AND SELL A STOCK TWICE

The max difference problem, introduced on Page 1, formalizes the maximum profit that can be made by buying and then selling a single share over a given day range.

Write a program that computes the maximum profit that can be made by buying and selling a share at most twice. The second buy must be made after the first sale.

Hint: What do you need to know about the first i elements when processing the $(i+1)$th element?

Solution: The brute-force algorithm which examines all possible combinations of buy-sell-buy-sell days has complexity $O(n^4)$. The complexity can be improved to $O(n^2)$ by applying the $O(n)$ algorithm to each pair of subarrays formed by splitting A.

The inefficiency in the above approaches comes from not taking advantage of previous computations. Suppose we record the best solution for $A[0:j]$, j between 1 and $n-1$, inclusive. Now we can do a reverse iteration, computing the best solution for a single buy-and-sell for $A[j:n-1]$, j between 1 and $n-1$, inclusive. For each day, we combine this result with the result from the forward iteration for the previous day—this yields the maximum profit if we buy and sell once before the current day and once at or after the current day.

For example, suppose the input array is $\langle 12, 11, 13, 9, 12, 8, 14, 13, 15\rangle$. Then the most profit that can be made with a single buy and sell by Day i (inclusive) is $F = \langle 0, 0, 2, 2, 3, 3, 6, 6, 7\rangle$. Working backwards, the most profit that can be made with a single buy and sell on or after Day i is $B = \langle 7, 7, 7, 7, 7, 7, 2, 2, 0\rangle$. To combine these two, we compute $M[i] = F[i-1] + B[i]$, where $F[-1]$ is taken to be 0 (since the second buy must happen strictly after the first sell). This yields $M = \langle 7, 7, 7, 9, 9, 10, 5, 8, 6\rangle$, i.e., the maximum profit is 10.

```
double BuyAndSellStockTwice(const vector<double>& prices) {
  double max_total_profit = 0;
  vector<double> first_buy_sell_profits(prices.size(), 0);
  double min_price_so_far = numeric_limits<double>::max();

  // Forward phase. For each day, we record maximum profit if we
  // sell on that day.
  for (int i = 0; i < prices.size(); ++i) {
    min_price_so_far = min(min_price_so_far, prices[i]);
    max_total_profit = max(max_total_profit, prices[i] - min_price_so_far);
    first_buy_sell_profits[i] = max_total_profit;
  }

  // Backward phase. For each day, find the maximum profit if we make
  // the second buy on that day.
  double max_price_so_far = numeric_limits<double>::min();
  for (int i = prices.size() - 1; i > 0; --i) {
    max_price_so_far = max(max_price_so_far, prices[i]);
    max_total_profit =
        max(max_total_profit,
            max_price_so_far - prices[i] + first_buy_sell_profits[i - 1]);
  }
  return max_total_profit;
}
```

The time complexity is $O(n)$, and the additional space complexity is $O(n)$, which is the space used to store the best solutions for the subarrays.

Variant: Solve the same problem in $O(n)$ time and $O(1)$ space.

A natural number is called a prime if it is bigger than 1 and has no divisors other than 1 and itself.

Write a program that takes an integer argument and returns all the primes between 1 and that integer. For example, if the input is 18, you should return $\langle 2, 3, 5, 7, 11, 13, 17 \rangle$.

Hint: Exclude the multiples of primes.

Solution: The natural brute-force algorithm is to iterate over all i from 2 to n, where n is the input to the program. For each i, we test if i is prime; if so we add it to the result. We can use "trial-division" to test if i is prime, i.e., by dividing i by each integer from 2 to the square root of i, and checking if the remainder is 0. (There is no need to test beyond the square root of i, since if i has a divisor other than 1 and itself, it must also have a divisor that is no greater than its square root.) Since each test has time complexity $O(\sqrt{n})$, the time complexity of the entire computation is upper bounded by $O(n \times \sqrt{n})$, i.e., $O(n^{3/2})$.

Intuitively, the brute-force algorithm tests each number from 1 to n independently, and does not exploit the fact that we need to compute *all* primes from 1 to n. Heuristically, a better approach is to compute the primes and when a number is identified as a prime, to "sieve" it, i.e., remove all its multiples from future consideration.

We use a Boolean array to encode the candidates, i.e., if the ith entry in the array is true, then i is potentially a prime. Initially, every number greater than or equal to 2 is a candidate. Whenever we determine a number is a prime, we will add it to the result, which is an array. The first prime is 2. We add it to the result. None of its multiples can be primes, so remove all its multiples from the candidate set by writing false in the corresponding locations. The next location set to true is 3. It must be a prime since nothing smaller than it and greater than 1 is a divisor of it. As before, we add it to result and remove its multiples from the candidate array. We continue till we get to the end of the array of candidates.

As an example, if $n = 10$, the candidate array is initialized to $\langle F, F, T, T, T, T, T, T, T, T \rangle$, where T is true and F is false. (Entries 0 and 1 are false, since 0 and 1 are not primes.) We begin with index 2. Since the corresponding entry is one, we add 2 to the list of primes, and sieve out its multiples. The array is now $\langle F, F, T, T, F, T, F, T, F, T, F \rangle$. The next nonzero entry is 3, so we add it to the list of primes, and sieve out its multiples. The array is now $\langle F, F, T, T, F, T, F, T, F, F, F \rangle$. The next nonzero entries are 5 and 7, and neither of them can be used to sieve out more entries.

```
// Given n, return all primes up to and including n.
vector<int> GeneratePrimes(int n) {
  vector<int> primes;
  // is_prime[p] represents if p is prime or not. Initially, set each to true,
  // excepting 0 and 1. Then use sieving to eliminate nonprimes.
  deque<bool> is_prime(n + 1, true);
  is_prime[0] = is_prime[1] = false;
```

```
      for (int p = 2; p < n; ++p) {
        if (is_prime[p]) {
          primes.emplace_back(p);
          // Sieve p's multiples.
          for (int j = p; j <= n; j += p) {
            is_prime[j] = false;
          }
        }
      }
      return primes;
    }
```

We justified the sifting approach over the trial-division algorithm on heuristic grounds. The time to sift out the multiples of p is proportional to n/p, so the overall time complexity is $O(n/2 + n/3 + n/5 + n/7 + n/11 + \ldots)$. Although not obvious, this sum asymptotically tends to $n \log \log n$, yielding an $O(n \log \log n)$ time bound. The space complexity is dominated by the storage for P, i.e., $O(n)$.

The bound we gave for the trial-division approach, namely $O(n^{3/2})$, is based on an $O(\sqrt{n})$ bound for each individual test. Since most numbers are not prime, the actual time complexity of trial-division is actually lower on average, since the test frequently early-returns false. It is known that the time complexity of the trial-division approach is $O(n^{3/2}/(\log n)^2)$, so sieving is in fact superior to trial-division.

We can improve runtime by sieving p's multiples from p^2 instead of p, since all numbers of the form kp, where $k < p$ have already been sieved out. The storage can be reduced by ignoring even numbers. The code below reflects these optimizations.

```
// Given n, return all primes up to and including n.
vector<int> GeneratePrimes(int n) {
  const int size = floor(0.5 * (n - 3)) + 1;
  vector<int> primes;
  primes.emplace_back(2);
  // is_prime[i] represents whether (2i + 3) is prime or not.
  // Initially, set each to true. Then use sieving to eliminate nonprimes.
  deque<bool> is_prime(size, true);
  for (int i = 0; i < size; ++i) {
    if (is_prime[i]) {
      int p = (i * 2) + 3;
      primes.emplace_back(p);
      // Sieving from p^2, whose value is (4i^2 + 12i + 9). The index in
      // is_prime is (2i^2 + 6i + 3) because is_prime[i] represents 2i + 3.
      //
      // Note that we need to use long for j because p^2 might overflow.
      for (long j =
              ((static_cast<long>(i) * static_cast<long>(i)) * 2) + 6 * i + 3;
           j < size; j += p) {
        is_prime[j] = false;
      }
    }
  }
  return primes;
}
```

The asymptotic time and space complexity are the same as that for the basic sieving approach.

6.10 PERMUTE THE ELEMENTS OF AN ARRAY

A permutation is a rearrangement of members of a sequence into a new sequence. For example, there are 24 permutations of $\langle a, b, c, d \rangle$; some of these are $\langle b, a, d, c \rangle, \langle d, a, b, c \rangle$, and $\langle a, d, b, c \rangle$.

A permutation can be specified by an array P, where $P[i]$ represents the location of the element at i in the permutation. For example, the array $\langle 2, 0, 1, 3 \rangle$ represents the permutation that maps the element at location 0 to location 2, the element at location 1 to location 0, the element at location 2 to location 1, and keep the element at location 3 unchanged. A permutation can be applied to an array to reorder the array. For example, the permutation $\langle 2, 0, 1, 3 \rangle$ applied to $A = \langle a, b, c, d \rangle$ yields the array $\langle b, c, a, d \rangle$.

Given an array A of n elements and a permutation P, apply P to A.

Hint: Any permutation can be viewed as a set of cyclic permutations. For an element in a cycle, how would you identify if it has been permuted?

Solution: It is simple to apply a permutation-array to a given array if additional storage is available to write the resulting array. We allocate a new array B of the same length, set $B[P[i]] = A[i]$ for each i, and then copy B to A. The time complexity is $O(n)$, and the additional space complexity is $O(n)$.

A key insight to improving space complexity is to decompose permutations into simpler structures which can be processed incrementally. For example, consider the permutation $\langle 3, 2, 1, 0 \rangle$. To apply it to an array $A = \langle a, b, c, \delta \rangle$, we move the element at index 0 (a) to index 3 and the element already at index 3 (δ) to index 0. Continuing, we move the element at index 1 (b) to index 2 and the element already at index 2 (c) to index 1. Now all elements have been moved according to the permutation, and the result is $\langle \delta, c, b, a \rangle$.

This example generalizes: every permutation can be represented by a collection of independent permutations, each of which is *cyclic*, that is, it moves all elements by a fixed offset, wrapping around.

This is significant, because a single cyclic permutation can be performed one element at a time, i.e., with constant additional storage. Consequently, if the permutation is described as a set of cyclic permutations, it can easily be applied using a constant amount of additional storage by applying each cyclic permutation one-at-a-time. Therefore, we want to identify the disjoint cycles that constitute the permutation.

To find and apply the cycle that includes entry i we just keep going forward (from i to $P[i]$) till we get back to i. After we are done with that cycle, we need to find another cycle that has not yet been applied. It is trivial to do this by storing a Boolean for each array element.

One way to perform this without explicitly using additional $O(n)$ storage is to use the sign bit in the entries in the permutation-array. Specifically, we subtract n from $P[i]$ after applying it. This means that if an entry in $P[i]$ is negative, we have performed the corresponding move.

For example, to apply $\langle 3, 1, 2, 0 \rangle$, we begin with the first entry, 3. We move $A[0]$ to $A[3]$, first saving the original $A[3]$. We update the permutation to $\langle -1, 1, 2, 0 \rangle$. We move $A[3]$ to $A[0]$. Since $P[0]$ is negative we know we are done with the cycle starting at 0. We also update the permutation to $\langle -1, 1, 2, -4 \rangle$. Now we examine $P[1]$. Since it is not negative, it means the cycle it belongs to cannot have been applied. We continue as before.

```
void ApplyPermutation(vector<int>* perm_ptr, vector<int>* A_ptr) {
  vector<int> &perm = *perm_ptr, &A = *A_ptr;
  for (int i = 0; i < A.size(); ++i) {
    // Check if the element at index i has not been moved by checking if
    // perm[i] is nonnegative.
    int next = i;
    while (perm[next] >= 0) {
      swap(A[i], A[perm[next]]);
      int temp = perm[next];
      // Subtracts perm.size() from an entry in perm to make it negative, which
      // indicates the corresponding move has been performed.
      perm[next] -= perm.size();
      next = temp;
    }
  }

  // Restore perm.
  for_each(perm.begin(), perm.end(), [&](int& x) { x += perm.size(); });
}

} // ApplyPermutation1

#endif // SOLUTIONS_PERMUTATION_ARRAY1_H_
```

The program above will apply the permutation in $O(n)$ time. The space complexity is $O(1)$, assuming we can temporarily modify the sign bit from entries in the permutation array.

If we cannot use the sign bit, we can allocate an array of n Booleans indicating whether the element at index i has been processed. Alternatively, we can avoid using $O(n)$ additional storage by going from left-to-right and applying the cycle only if the current position is the leftmost position in the cycle.

```
void ApplyPermutation(const vector<int>& perm, vector<int>* A_ptr) {
  vector<int>& A = *A_ptr;
  for (int i = 0; i < A.size(); ++i) {
    // Traverses the cycle to see if i is the minimum element.
    bool is_min = true;
```

```
    int j = perm[i];
    while (j != i) {
      if (j < i) {
        is_min = false;
        break;
      }
      j = perm[j];
    }

    if (is_min) {
      CyclicPermutation(i, perm, &A);
    }
  }
}


void CyclicPermutation(int start, const vector<int>& perm,
                       vector<int>* A_ptr) {
  vector<int>& A = *A_ptr;
  int i = start;
  int temp = A[start];
  do {
    int next_i = perm[i];
    int next_temp = A[next_i];
    A[next_i] = temp;
    i = next_i, temp = next_temp;
  } while (i != start);
}
```

Testing whether the current position is the leftmost position entails traversing the cycle once more, which increases the run time to $O(n^2)$.

Variant: Given an array A of integers representing a permutation, update A to represent the inverse permutation using only constant additional storage.

6.11 COMPUTE THE NEXT PERMUTATION

There exist exactly $n!$ permutations of n elements. These can be totally ordered using the *dictionary ordering*—define permutation p to appear before permutation q if in the first place where p and q differ in their array representations, starting from index 0, the corresponding entry for p is less than that for q. For example, $\langle 2, 0, 1 \rangle < \langle 2, 1, 0 \rangle$. Note that the permutation $\langle 0, 1, 2 \rangle$ is the smallest permutation under dictionary ordering, and $\langle 2, 1, 0 \rangle$ is the largest permutation under dictionary ordering.

Write a program that takes as input a permutation, and returns the next permutation under dictionary ordering. If the permutation is the last permutation, return the empty array. For example, if the input is $\langle 1, 0, 3, 2 \rangle$ your function should return $\langle 1, 2, 0, 3 \rangle$. If the input is $\langle 3, 2, 1, 0 \rangle$, return $\langle \rangle$.

Hint: Study concrete examples.

Solution: A brute-force approach might be to find all permutations whose length equals that of the input array, sort them according to the dictionary order, then find the successor of the input permutation in that ordering. Apart from the enormous space and time complexity this entails, simply computing all permutations of length n is a nontrivial problem; see Problem 16.3 on Page 282 for details.

The key insight is that we want to increase the permutation by as little as possible. The loose analogy is how a car's odometer increments; the difference is that we cannot change values, only reorder them. We will use the permutation $\langle 6,2,1,5,4,3,0 \rangle$ to develop this approach.

Specifically, we start from the right, and look at the longest decreasing suffix, which is $\langle 5,4,3,0 \rangle$ for our example. We cannot get the next permutation just by modifying this suffix, since it is already the maximum it can be.

Instead we look at the entry e that appears just before the longest decreasing suffix, which is 1 in this case. (If there's no such element, i.e., the longest decreasing suffix is the entire permutation, the permutation must be $\langle n-1, n-2, \ldots, 2, 1, 0 \rangle$, for which there is no next permutation.)

Observe that e must be less than some entries in the suffix (since the entry immediately after e is greater than e). Intuitively, we should swap e with the smallest entry s in the suffix which is larger than e so as to minimize the change to the prefix (which is defined to be the part of the sequence that appears before the suffix).

For our example, e is 1 and s is 3. Swapping s and e results in $\langle 6,2,3,5,4,1,0 \rangle$.

We are not done yet—the new prefix is the smallest possible for all permutations greater than the initial permutation, but the new suffix may not be the smallest. We can get the smallest suffix by sorting the entries in the suffix from smallest to largest. For our working example, this yields the suffix $\langle 0,1,4,5 \rangle$.

As an optimization, it is not necessary to call a full blown sorting algorithm on suffix. Since the suffix was initially decreasing, and after replacing s by e it remains decreasing, reversing the suffix has the effect of sorting it from smallest to largest.

The general algorithm for computing the next permutation is as follows:

(1.) Find k such that $p[k] < p[k+1]$ and entries after index k appear in decreasing order.

(2.) Find the smallest $p[l]$ such that $p[l] > p[k]$ (such an l must exist since $p[k] < p[k+1]$).

(3.) Swap $p[l]$ and $p[k]$ (note that the sequence after position k remains in decreasing order).

(4.) Reverse the sequence after position k.

```
vector<int> NextPermutation(vector<int> perm) {
  int k = perm.size() - 2;
  while (k >= 0 && perm[k] >= perm[k + 1]) {
    --k;
  }
  if (k == -1) {
    return {};  // perm is the last permutation.
  }
```

```
// Swap the smallest entry after index k that is greater than perm[k]. We
// exploit the fact that perm[k + 1 : perm.size() - 1] is decreasing so if we
// search in reverse order, the first entry that is greater than perm[k] is
// the smallest such entry.
for (int i = perm.size() - 1; i > k; --i) {
  if (perm[i] > perm[k]) {
    swap(perm[k], perm[i]);
    break;
  }
}

// Since perm[k + 1 : perm.size() - 1] is in decreasing order, we can build
// the smallest dictionary ordering of this subarray by reversing it.
reverse(perm.begin() + k + 1, perm.end());
return perm;
}
```

Each step is an iteration through an array, so the time complexity is $O(n)$. All that we use are a few local variables, so the additional space complexity is $O(1)$.

Variant: Compute the kth permutation under dictionary ordering, starting from the identity permutation (which is the first permutation in dictionary ordering).

Variant: Given a permutation p, return the permutation corresponding to the *previous* permutation of p under dictionary ordering.

6.12 SAMPLE OFFLINE DATA

This problem is motivated by the need for a company to select a random subset of its customers to roll out a new feature to. For example, a social networking company may want to see the effect of a new UI on page visit duration without taking the chance of alienating all its users if the rollout is unsuccessful.

Implement an algorithm that takes as input an array of distinct elements and a size, and returns a subset of the given size of the array elements. All subsets should be equally likely. Return the result in input array itself.

Hint: How would you construct a random subset of size $k + 1$ given a random subset of size k?

Solution: Let the input array be A, its length n, and the specified size k. A naive approach is to iterate through the input array, selecting entries with probability k/n. Although the average number of selected entries is k, we may select more or less than k entries in this way.

Another approach is to enumerate all subsets of size k and then select one at random from these. Since there are $\binom{n}{k}$ subsets of size k, the time and space complexity are huge. Furthermore, enumerating all subsets of size k is nontrivial (Problem 16.5 on Page 286).

The key to efficiently building a random subset of size exactly k is to first build one of size $k - 1$ and then adding one more element, selected randomly from the rest. The problem is trivial when $k = 1$. We make one call to the random number generator, take the returned value mod n (call it r), and swap $A[0]$ with $A[r]$. The entry $A[0]$ now holds the result.

For $k > 1$, we begin by choosing one element at random as above and we now repeat the same process with the $n - 1$ element subarray $A[1 : n - 1]$. Eventually, the random subset occupies the slots $A[0 : k - 1]$ and the remaining elements are in the last $n - k$ slots.

Intuitively, if all subsets of size k are equally likely, then the construction process ensures that the subsets of size $k + 1$ are also equally likely. A formal proof, which we do not present, uses mathematical induction—the induction hypothesis is that every permutation of every size k subset of A is equally likely to be in $A[0 : k - 1]$.

As a concrete example, let the input be $A = \langle 3,7,5,11 \rangle$ and the size be 3. In the first iteration, we use the random number generator to pick a random integer in the interval $[0,3]$. Let the returned random number be 2. We swap $A[0]$ with $A[2]$—now the array is $\langle 5,7,3,11 \rangle$. Now we pick a random integer in the interval $[1,3]$. Let the returned random number be 3. We swap $A[1]$ with $A[3]$—now the resulting array is $\langle 5,11,3,7 \rangle$. Now we pick a random integer in the interval $[2,3]$. Let the returned random number be 2. When we swap $A[2]$ with itself the resulting array is unchanged. The random subset consists of the first three entries, i.e., $\{5,11,3\}$.

```
void RandomSampling(int k, vector<int>* A_ptr) {
  vector<int>& A = *A_ptr;
  default_random_engine seed((random_device())());  // Random num generator.
  for (int i = 0; i < k; ++i) {
    // Generate a random index in [i, A.size() - 1].
    swap(A[i], A[uniform_int_distribution<int>{
                 i, static_cast<int>(A.size()) - 1}(seed)]);
  }
}
```

The algorithm clearly runs in additional $O(1)$ space. The time complexity is $O(k)$ to select the elements.

The algorithm makes k calls to the random number generator. When k is bigger than $\frac{n}{2}$, we can optimize by computing a subset of $n - k$ elements to remove from the set. For example, when $k = n - 1$, this replaces $n - 1$ calls to the random number generator with a single call.

Variant: The rand() function in the standard C library returns a uniformly random number in $[0, \texttt{RAND\_MAX} - 1]$. Does rand() mod n generate a number uniformly distributed in $[0, n - 1]$?

This problem is motivated by the design of a packet sniffer that provides a uniform sample of packets for a network session.

Design a program that takes as input a size k, and reads packets, continuously maintaining a uniform random subset of size k of the read packets.

Hint: Suppose you have a procedure which selects k packets from the first $n \geq k$ packets as specified. How would you deal with the $(n + 1)$th packet?

Solution: A brute force approach would be to store all the packets read so far. After reading in each packet, we apply Solution 6.12 on Page 75 to compute a random subset of k packets. The space complexity is high—$O(n)$, after n packets have been read. The time complexity is also high—$O(nk)$, since each packet read is followed by a call to Solution 6.12 on Page 75.

At first glance it may seem that it is impossible to do better than the brute-force approach, since after reading the nth packet, we need to choose k packets uniformly from this set. However, suppose we have read the first n packets, and have a random subset of k of them. When we read the $(n + 1)$th packet, it should belong to the new subset with probability $k/(n + 1)$. If we choose one of the packets in the existing subset uniformly randomly to remove, the resulting collection will be a random subset of the $n + 1$ packets.

The formal proof that the algorithm works correctly, uses induction on the number of packets that have been read. Specifically, the induction hypothesis is that all k-sized subsets are equally likely after $n \geq k$ packets have been read.

As an example, suppose $k = 2$, and the packets are read in the order p, q, r, t, u, v. We keep the first two packets in the subset, which is $\{p, q\}$. We select the next packet, r, with probability $2/3$. Suppose it is not selected. Then the subset after reading the first three packets is still $\{p, q\}$. We select the next packet, t, with probability $2/4$. Suppose it is selected. Then we choose one of the packets in $\{p, q\}$ uniformly, and replace it with t. Let q be the selected packet—now the subset is $\{p, t\}$. We select the next packet u with probability $2/5$. Suppose it is selected. Then we choose one of the packets in $\{p, t\}$ uniformly, and replace it with u. Let t be the selected packet—now the subset is $\{p, u\}$. We select the next packet v with probability $2/6$. Suppose it is not selected. The random subset remains $\{p, u\}$.

```
// Assumption: there are at least k elements in the stream.
vector<int> OnlineRandomSample(istringstream* sin, int k) {
  int x;
  vector<int> running_sample;
  // Stores the first k elements.
  for (int i = 0; i < k && *sin >> x; ++i) {
    running_sample.emplace_back(x);
  }

  default_random_engine seed((random_device())());  // Random num generator.
```

```
  // Have read the first k elements.
  int num_seen_so_far = k;
  while (*sin >> x) {
    ++num_seen_so_far;
    // Generate a random number in [0, num_seen_so_far - 1], and if this
    // number is in [0, k - 1], we replace that element from the sample with x.
    int idx_to_replace =
        uniform_int_distribution<int>{0, num_seen_so_far - 1}(seed);
    if (idx_to_replace < k) {
      running_sample[idx_to_replace] = x;
    }
  }
  return running_sample;
}
```

The time complexity is proportional to the number of elements in the stream, since we spend $O(1)$ time per element. The space complexity is $O(k)$.

Note that at each iteration, every subset is equally likely. However, the subsets are not independent from iteration to iteration—successive subsets differ in at most one element. In contrast, the subsets computed by brute-force algorithm are independent from iteration to iteration.

6.14 COMPUTE A RANDOM PERMUTATION

Generating random permutations is not as straightforward as it seems. For example, iterating through $\langle 0, 1, \ldots, n - 1 \rangle$ and swapping each element with another randomly selected element does *not* generate all permutations with equal probability. One way to see this is to consider the case $n = 3$. The number of permutations is $3! = 6$. The total number of ways in which we can choose the elements to swap is $3^3 = 27$ and all are equally likely. Since 27 is not divisible by 6, some permutations correspond to more ways than others, so not all permutations are equally likely.

Design an algorithm that creates uniformly random permutations of $\{0, 1, \ldots, n - 1\}$. You are given a random number generator that returns integers in the set $\{0, 1, \ldots, n-1\}$ with equal probability; use as few calls to it as possible.

Hint: If the result is stored in A, how would you proceed once $A[n - 1]$ is assigned correctly?

Solution: A brute-force approach might be to iteratively pick random numbers between 0 and $n - 1$, inclusive. If number repeats, we discard it, and try again. A hash table is a good way to store and test values that have already been picked.

For example, if $n = 4$, we might have the sequence 1, 2, 1 (repeats), 3, 1 (repeats), 2 (repeat), 0 (done, all numbers from 0 to 3 are present). The corresponding permutation is $\langle 1, 2, 3, 0 \rangle$.

It is fairly clear that all permutations are equally likely with this approach. The space complexity beyond that of the result array is $O(n)$ for the hash table. The time complexity is slightly challenging to analyze. Early on, it takes very few iterations to get more new values, but it takes a long time to collect the last few values. Computing the average number of tries to complete the permutation in this way is known as the Coupon Collector's Problem. It is known that the number of tries on average (and hence the average time complexity) is $O(n \log n)$.

Clearly, the way to improve time complexity is to avoid repeats. We can do this by restricting the set we randomly choose the remaining values from. If we apply Solution 6.12 on Page 75 to $\langle 0, 1, 2, \ldots, n-1 \rangle$ with $k = n$, at each iteration the array is partitioned into the partial permutation and remaining values. Although the subset that is returned is unique (it will be $\{0, 1, \ldots, n-1\}$), all $n!$ possible orderings of the elements in the set occur with equal probability. For example, let $n = 4$. We begin with $\langle 0, 1, 2, 3 \rangle$. The first random number is chosen between 0 and 3, inclusive. Suppose it is 1. We update the array to $\langle 1, 0, 2, 3 \rangle$. The second random number is chosen between 1 and 3, inclusive. Suppose it is 3. We update the array to $\langle 1, 3, 0, 2 \rangle$. The third random number is chosen between 2 and 3, inclusive. Suppose it is 3. We update the array to $\langle 1, 3, 2, 0 \rangle$. This is the returned result.

```
vector<int> ComputeRandomPermutation(int n) {
  vector<int> permutation(n);
  // Initializes permutation to 0, 1, 2, ..., n - 1.
  iota(permutation.begin(), permutation.end(), 0);
  RandomSampling(permutation.size(), &permutation);
  return permutation;
}
```

The time complexity is $O(n)$, and, as an added bonus, no storage outside of that needed for the permutation array itself is needed.

6.15 COMPUTE A RANDOM SUBSET

The set $\{0, 1, 2, \ldots, n-1\}$ has $\binom{n}{k} = n!/((n-k)!k!)$ subsets of size k. We seek to design an algorithm that returns any one of these subsets with equal probability.

Write a program that takes as input a positive integer n and a size $k \leq n$, and returns a size-k subset of $\{0, 1, 2, \ldots, n-1\}$. The subset should be represented as an array. All subsets should be equally likely and, in addition, all permutations of elements of the array should be equally likely. You may assume you have a function which takes as input a nonnegative integer t and returns an integer in the set $\{0, 1, \ldots, t-1\}$ with uniform probability.

Hint: Simulate Solution 6.12 on Page 75, using an appropriate data structure to reduce space.

Solution: Similar to the brute-force algorithm presented in Solution 6.14 on the facing page, we could iteratively choose random numbers between 0 and $n-1$ until we get k distinct values. This approach suffers from the same performance degradation when k is close to n, and it also requires $O(k)$ additional space.

We could mimic the offline sampling algorithm described in Solution 6.12 on Page 75, with $A[i] = i$ initially, stopping after k iterations. This requires $O(n)$ space and $O(n)$ time to create the array. After creating $\langle 0, 1, 2, \ldots, n-1 \rangle$, we need $O(k)$ time to produce the subset.

Note that when $k \ll n$, most of the array is untouched, i.e., $A[i] = i$. The key to reducing the space complexity to $O(k)$ is simulating A with a hash table. We do this by only tracking entries whose values are modified by the algorithm—the remainder have the default value, i.e., the value of an entry is its index.

Specifically, we maintain a hash table H whose keys and values are from $\{0, 1, \ldots, n-1\}$. Conceptually, H tracks entries of the array which have been touched in the process of randomization—these are entries $A[i]$ which may not equal i. The hash table H is updated as the algorithm advances.

- If i is in H, then its value in H is the value stored at $A[i]$ in the brute-force algorithm.
- If i is not in H, then this implicitly implies $A[i] = i$.

Since we track no more than k entries, when k is small compared to n, we save time and space over the brute-force approach, which has to initialize and update an array of length n.

Initially, H is empty. We do k iterations of the following. Choose a random integer r in $[0, n-1-i]$, where i is the current iteration count, starting at 0. There are four possibilities, corresponding to whether the two entries in A that are being swapped are already present or not present in H. The desired result is in $A[0 : k-1]$, which can be determined from H.

For example, suppose $n = 100$ and $k = 4$. In the first iteration, suppose we get the random number 28. We update H to $(0, 28), (28, 0)$. This means that $A[0]$ is 28 and $A[28]$ is 0—for all other i, $A[i] = i$. In the second iteration, suppose we get the random number 42. We update H to $(0, 28), (28, 0), (1, 42), (42, 1)$. In the third iteration, suppose we get the random number 28 again. We update H to $(0, 28), (28, 2), (1, 42), (42, 1), (2, 0)$. In the third iteration, suppose we get the random number 64. We update H to $(0, 28), (28, 2), (1, 42), (42, 1), (2, 0), (3, 64), (64, 3)$. The random subset is the 4 elements corresponding to indices $0, 1, 2, 3$, i.e., $\langle 28, 42, 0, 64 \rangle$.

```
// Returns a random k-sized subset of {0, 1, ..., n - 1}.
vector<int> RandomSubset(int n, int k) {
  unordered_map<int, int> changed_elements;
  default_random_engine seed((random_device())());  // Random num generator.
  for (int i = 0; i < k; ++i) {
    // Generate a random index in [i, n - 1].
    int rand_idx = uniform_int_distribution<int>{i, n - 1}(seed);
    auto ptr1 = changed_elements.find(rand_idx),
         ptr2 = changed_elements.find(i);
    if (ptr1 == changed_elements.end() && ptr2 == changed_elements.end()) {
      changed_elements[rand_idx] = i;
      changed_elements[i] = rand_idx;
    } else if (ptr1 == changed_elements.end() &&
               ptr2 != changed_elements.end()) {
      changed_elements[rand_idx] = ptr2->second;
      ptr2->second = rand_idx;
    } else if (ptr1 != changed_elements.end() &&
```

```
                ptr2 == changed_elements.end()) {
        changed_elements[i] = ptr1->second;
        ptr1->second = i;
    } else {
        int temp = ptr2->second;
        changed_elements[i] = ptr1->second;
        changed_elements[rand_idx] = temp;
    }
}

    vector<int> result;
    for (int i = 0; i < k; ++i) {
        result.emplace_back(changed_elements[i]);
    }
    return result;
}
```

The time complexity is $O(k)$, since we perform a bounded number of operations per iteration. The space complexity is also $O(k)$, since H and the result array never contain more than k entries.

6.16 GENERATE NONUNIFORM RANDOM NUMBERS

Suppose you need to write a load test for a server. You have studied the inter-arrival time of requests to the server over a period of one year. From this data you have computed a histogram of the distribution of the inter-arrival time of requests. In the load test you would like to generate requests for the server such that the inter-arrival times come from the same distribution that was observed in the historical data. The following problem formalizes the generation of inter-arrival times.

You are given n numbers as well as probabilities $p_0, p_1, \ldots, p_{n-1}$, which sum up to 1. Given a random number generator that produces values in $[0, 1]$ uniformly, how would you generate one of the n numbers according to the specified probabilities? For example, if the numbers are $3, 5, 7, 11$, and the probabilities are $9/18, 6/18, 2/18, 1/18$, then in 1000000 calls to your program, 3 should appear roughly 500000 times, 5 should appear roughly 333333 times, 7 should appear roughly 111111 times, and 11 should appear roughly 55555 times.

Hint: Look at the graph of the probability that the selected number is less than or equal to α. What do the jumps correspond to?

Solution: First note that actual values of the numbers is immaterial—we want to choose from one of n outcomes with probabilities $p_0, p_1, \ldots, p_{n-1}$. If all probabilities were the same, i.e., $1/n$, we could make a single call to the random number generator, and choose outcome i if the number falls lies between i/n and $(i+1)/n$.

For the case where the probabilities are not the same, we can solve the problem by partitioning the unit interval $[0, 1]$ into n disjoint segments, in a way so that the length of the jth interval is proportional to p_j. Then we select a number uniformly

81

at random in the unit interval, $[0, 1]$, and return the number corresponding to the interval the randomly generated number falls in.

An easy way to create these intervals is to use $p_0, p_0 + p_1, p_0 + p_1 + p_2, \ldots, p_0 + p_1 + p_2 + \cdots + p_{n-1}$ as the endpoints. Using the example given in the problem statement, the four intervals are $[0.0, 0.5), [0.5, 0.833), [0.833, 0.944), [0.944, 1.0]$. Now, for example, if the random number generated uniformly in $[0.0, 1.0]$ is 0.873, since 0.873 lies in $[0.833, 0.944)$, which is the third interval, we return the third number, which is 7.

In general, searching an array of n disjoint intervals for the interval containing a number takes $O(n)$ time. However, we can do better. Since the array $\langle p_0, p_0 + p_1, p_0 + p_1 + p_2, \ldots, p_0 + p_1 + p_2 + \cdots + p_{n-1} \rangle$ is sorted, we can use binary search to find the interval in $O(\log n)$ time.

```cpp
int NonuniformRandomNumberGeneration(const vector<int>& values,
                                     const vector<double>& probabilities) {
  vector<double> prefix_sums_of_probabilities;
  prefix_sums_of_probabilities.emplace_back(0.0);
  // Creating the endpoints for the intervals corresponding to the
  // probabilities.
  partial_sum(probabilities.cbegin(), probabilities.cend(),
              back_inserter(prefix_sums_of_probabilities));

  default_random_engine seed((random_device())());
  double uniform_0_1 =
      generate_canonical<double, numeric_limits<double>::digits>(seed);
  // Find the index of the interval that uniform_0_1 lies in, which is the
  // return value of upper_bound() minus 1.
  int interval_idx =
      distance(prefix_sums_of_probabilities.cbegin(),
               upper_bound(prefix_sums_of_probabilities.cbegin(),
                           prefix_sums_of_probabilities.cend(), uniform_0_1)) -
      1;
  return values[interval_idx];
}
```

The time complexity to compute a single value is $O(n)$, which is the time to create the array of intervals. This array also implies an $O(n)$ space complexity.

Once the array is constructed, computing each additional result entails one call to the uniform random number generator, followed by a binary search, i.e., $O(\log n)$.

Variant: Given a random number generator that produces values in $[0, 1]$ uniformly, how would you generate a value X from T according to a continuous probability distribution, such as the exponential distribution?

Multidimensional arrays

Thus far we have focused our attention in this chapter on one-dimensional arrays. We now turn our attention to multidimensional arrays. A 2D array in an array whose entries are themselves arrays; the concept generalizes naturally to k dimensional arrays.

Multidimensional arrays arise in image processing, board games, graphs, modeling spatial phenomenon, etc. Often, but not always, the arrays that constitute the entries of a 2D array A have the same length, in which case we refer to A as being an $m \times n$ rectangular array (or sometimes just an $m \times n$ array), where m is the number of entries in A, and n the number of entries in $A[0]$. The elements within a 2D array A are often referred to by their *row* and *column* indices i and j, and written as $A[i][j]$.

6.17 THE SUDOKU CHECKER PROBLEM

Sudoku is a popular logic-based combinatorial number placement puzzle. The objective is to fill a 9×9 grid with digits subject to the constraint that each column, each row, and each of the nine 3×3 sub-grids that compose the grid contains unique integers in $[1, 9]$. The grid is initialized with a partial assignment as shown in Figure 6.2(a); a complete solution is shown in Figure 6.2(b).

5	3			7				
6			1	9	5			
	9	8					6	
8				6				3
4			8		3			1
7				2				6
	6					2	8	
			4	1	9			5
				8			7	9

(a) Partial assignment.

5	3	4	6	7	8	9	1	2
6	7	2	1	9	5	3	4	8
1	9	8	3	4	2	5	6	7
8	5	9	7	6	1	4	2	3
4	2	6	8	5	3	7	9	1
7	1	3	9	2	4	8	5	6
9	6	1	5	3	7	2	8	4
2	8	7	4	1	9	6	3	5
3	4	5	2	8	6	1	7	9

(b) A complete solution.

Figure 6.2: Sudoku configurations.

Check whether a 9×9 2D array representing a partially completed Sudoku is valid. Specifically, check that no row, column, or 3×3 2D subarray contains duplicates. A 0-value in the 2D array indicates that entry is blank; every other entry is in $[1, 9]$.

Hint: Directly test the constraints. Use an array to encode sets.

Solution: There is no real scope for algorithm optimization in this problem—it's all about writing clean code.

We need to check nine row constraints, nine column constraints, and nine sub-grid constraints. It is convenient to use bit arrays to test for constraint violations, that is to ensure no number in $[1, 9]$ appears more than once.

```
// Check if a partially filled matrix has any conflicts.
bool IsValidSudoku(const vector<vector<int>>& partial_assignment) {
  // Check row constraints.
  for (int i = 0; i < partial_assignment.size(); ++i) {
    if (HasDuplicate(partial_assignment, i, i + 1, 0,
                     partial_assignment.size())) {
      return false;
```

```cpp
    }
  }

  // Check column constraints.
  for (int j = 0; j < partial_assignment.size(); ++j) {
    if (HasDuplicate(partial_assignment, 0, partial_assignment.size(), j,
                     j + 1)) {
      return false;
    }
  }

  // Check region constraints.
  int region_size = sqrt(partial_assignment.size());
  for (int I = 0; I < region_size; ++I) {
    for (int J = 0; J < region_size; ++J) {
      if (HasDuplicate(partial_assignment, region_size * I,
                       region_size * (I + 1), region_size * J,
                       region_size * (J + 1))) {
        return false;
      }
    }
  }
  return true;
}

// Return true if subarray partial_assignment[start_row : end_row -
// 1][start_col : end_col - 1] contains any duplicates in {1, 2, ...,
// partial_assignment.size()}; otherwise return false.
bool HasDuplicate(const vector<vector<int>>& partial_assignment, int start_row,
                  int end_row, int start_col, int end_col) {
  deque<bool> is_present(partial_assignment.size() + 1, false);
  for (int i = start_row; i < end_row; ++i) {
    for (int j = start_col; j < end_col; ++j) {
      if (partial_assignment[i][j] != 0 &&
          is_present[partial_assignment[i][j]]) {
        return true;
      }
      is_present[partial_assignment[i][j]] = true;
    }
  }
  return false;
}
```

The time complexity of this algorithm for an $n \times n$ Sudoku grid with $\sqrt{n} \times \sqrt{n}$ subgrids is $O(n^2) + O(n^2) + O(n^2/(\sqrt{n})^2 \times (\sqrt{n})^2) = O(n^2)$; the terms correspond to the complexity to check n row constraints, the n column constraints, and the n subgrid constraints, respectively. The memory usage is dominated by the bit array used to check the constraints, so the space complexity is $O(n)$.

Solution 16.9 on Page 292 describes how to solve Sudoku instances.

A 2D array can be written as a sequence in several orders—the most natural ones being row-by-row or column-by-column. In this problem we explore the problem of writing the 2D array in spiral order. For example, the spiral ordering for the 2D array in Figure 6.3(a) is $\langle 1, 2, 3, 6, 9, 8, 7, 4, 5 \rangle$. For Figure 6.3(b), the spiral ordering is $\langle 1, 2, 3, 4, 8, 12, 16, 15, 14, 13, 9, 5, 6, 7, 1, 10 \rangle$.

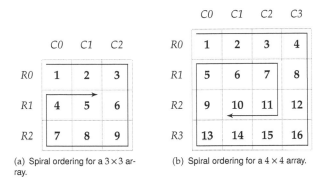

(a) Spiral ordering for a 3×3 array.

(b) Spiral ordering for a 4×4 array.

Figure 6.3: Spiral orderings. Column and row ids are specified above and to the left of the matrix, i.e., 1 is at entry $(0, 0)$.

Write a program which takes an $n \times n$ 2D array and returns the spiral ordering of the array.

Hint: Use case analysis and divide-and-conquer.

Solution: It is natural to solve this problem starting from the outside, and working to the center. The naive approach begins by adding the first row, which consists of n elements. Next we add the $n - 1$ remaining elements of the last column, then the $n - 1$ remaining elements of the last row, and then the $n - 2$ remaining elements of the first column. The lack of uniformity makes it hard to get the code right.

Here is a uniform way of adding the boundary. Add the first $n - 1$ elements of the first row. Then add the first $n - 1$ elements of the last column. Then add the last $n - 1$ elements of the last row in reverse order. Finally, add the last $n - 1$ elements of the first column in reverse order.

After this, we are left with the problem of adding the elements of an $(n-2) \times (n-2)$ 2D array in spiral order. This leads to an iterative algorithm that adds the outermost elements of $n \times n, (n - 2) \times (n - 2), (n - 4) \times (n - 4), \ldots$ 2D arrays. Note that a matrix of odd dimension has a corner-case, namely when we reach its center.

As an example, for the 3×3 array in Figure 6.3(a), we would add $1, 2$ (first two elements of the first row), then $3, 6$ (first two elements of the last column), then $9, 8$ (last two elements of the last row), then $7, 4$ (last two elements of the first column).

We are now left with the 1×1 array, whose sole element is 5. After processing it, all elements are processed.

For the 4×4 array in Figure 6.3(b) on the preceding page, we would add $1, 2, 3$ (first three elements of the first row), then $4, 8, 12$ (first three elements of the last column), then $16, 15, 14$ (last three elements of the last row), then $13, 9, 5$ (last three elements of the first column). We are now left with a 2×2 matrix, which we process similarly in the order $6, 7, 11, 10$, after which all elements are processed.

```
vector<int> MatrixInSpiralOrder(const vector<vector<int>>& square_matrix) {
  vector<int> spiral_ordering;
  for (int offset = 0; offset < ceil(0.5 * square_matrix.size()); ++offset) {
    MatrixLayerInClockwise(square_matrix, offset, &spiral_ordering);
  }
  return spiral_ordering;
}


void MatrixLayerInClockwise(const vector<vector<int>>& square_matrix,
                            int offset, vector<int>* spiral_ordering) {
  if (offset == square_matrix.size() - offset - 1) {
    // square_matrix has odd dimension, and we are at the center of
    // square_matrix.
    spiral_ordering->emplace_back(square_matrix[offset][offset]);
    return;
  }

  for (int j = offset; j < square_matrix.size() - offset - 1; ++j) {
    spiral_ordering->emplace_back(square_matrix[offset][j]);
  }
  for (int i = offset; i < square_matrix.size() - offset - 1; ++i) {
    spiral_ordering->emplace_back(
        square_matrix[i][square_matrix.size() - offset - 1]);
  }
  for (int j = square_matrix.size() - offset - 1; j > offset; --j) {
    spiral_ordering->emplace_back(
        square_matrix[square_matrix.size() - offset - 1][j]);
  }
  for (int i = square_matrix.size() - offset - 1; i > offset; --i) {
    spiral_ordering->emplace_back(square_matrix[i][offset]);
  }
}
```

The time complexity is $O(n^2)$ and the space complexity is $O(1)$.

The above solution uses four iterations which are almost identical. Now we present a solution that uses a single iteration that tracks the next element to process and the direction—left,right,up,down—to advance in. Think of the matrix as laid out on a 2D grid with X- and Y-axes. The pair (i, j) denotes the entry in Column i and Row j. Let (x, y) be the next element to process. Initially we move to the right (incrementing x until $(n-1, 0)$ is processed). Then we move down (incrementing y until $(n-1, n-1)$ is processed). Then we move left (decrementing x until $(0, n-1)$ is processed). Then we move up (decrementing y until $(0, 1)$ is processed). Note that we stop at 1, not 0, since

$(0, 0)$ was already processed. We record that an element has already been processed by setting it to 0, which is assumed to be a value that is not already present in the array. (Any value not in the array works too.) After processing $(0, 1)$ we move to the right till we get to $(n - 2, 1)$ (since $(n - 2, 0)$ was already processed). This method is applied until all elements are processed.

```cpp
vector<int> MatrixInSpiralOrder(vector<vector<int>> square_matrix) {
    const array<array<int, 2>, 4> kShift = {{{0, 1}, {1, 0}, {0, -1}, {-1, 0}}};
    int dir = 0, x = 0, y = 0;
    vector<int> spiral_ordering;

    for (int i = 0; i < square_matrix.size() * square_matrix.size(); ++i) {
        spiral_ordering.emplace_back(square_matrix[x][y]);
        square_matrix[x][y] = 0;
        int next_x = x + kShift[dir][0], next_y = y + kShift[dir][1];
        if (next_x < 0 || next_x >= square_matrix.size() || next_y < 0 ||
            next_y >= square_matrix.size() || square_matrix[next_x][next_y] == 0) {
            dir = (dir + 1) % 4;
            next_x = x + kShift[dir][0], next_y = y + kShift[dir][1];
        }
        x = next_x, y = next_y;
    }
    return spiral_ordering;
}
```

The time complexity is $O(n^2)$ and the space complexity is $O(1)$.

Variant: Given a dimension d, write a program to generate a $d \times d$ 2D array which in spiral order is $\langle 1, 2, 3, \ldots, d^2 \rangle$. For example, if $d = 3$, the result should be

$$A = \begin{bmatrix} 1 & 2 & 3 \\ 8 & 9 & 4 \\ 7 & 6 & 5 \end{bmatrix}.$$

Variant: Given a sequence of integers P, compute a 2D array A whose spiral order is P. (Assume the size of P is n^2 for some integer n.)

Variant: Write a program to enumerate the first n pairs of integers (a, b) in spiral order, starting from $(0, 0)$ followed by $(1, 0)$. For example, if $n = 10$, your output should be $(0, 0), (1, 0), (1, -1), (0, -1), (-1, -1), (-1, 0), (-1, 1), (0, 1), (1, 1), (2, 1)$.

Variant: Compute the spiral order for an $m \times n$ 2D array A.

Variant: Compute the last element in spiral order for an $m \times n$ 2D array A in $O(1)$ time.

Variant: Compute the kth element in spiral order for an $m \times n$ 2D array A in $O(1)$ time.

Image rotation is a fundamental operation in computer graphics. Figure 6.4 illustrates the rotation operation on a 2D array representing a bit-map of an image. Specifically, the image is rotated by 90 degrees clockwise.

1	2	3	4
5	6	7	8
9	10	11	12
13	14	15	16

(a) Initial 4 × 4 2D array.

13	9	5	1
14	10	6	2
15	11	7	3
16	12	8	4

(b) Array rotated by 90 degrees clockwise.

Figure 6.4: Example of 2D array rotation.

Write a function that takes as input an $n \times n$ 2D array, and rotates the array by 90 degrees clockwise.

Hint: Focus on the boundary elements.

Solution: With a little experimentation, it is easy to see that ith column of the rotate matrix is the ith row of the original matrix. For example, the first row, $\langle 13, 14, 15, 16 \rangle$ of the initial array in 6.4 becomes the first column in the rotated version. Therefore, a brute-force approach is to allocate a new $n \times n$ 2D array, write the rotation to it (writing rows of the original matrix into the columns of the new matrix), and then copying the new array back to the original one. The last step is needed since the problem says to update the original array. The time and additional space complexity are both $O(n^2)$.

Since we are not explicitly required to allocate a new array, it is natural to ask if we can perform the rotation in-place, i.e., with $O(1)$ additional storage. The first insight is that we can perform the rotation in a layer-by-layer fashion—different layers can be processed independently. Furthermore, within a layer, we can exchange groups of four elements at a time to perform the rotation, e.g., send 1 to 4's location, 4 to 16's location, 16 to 13's location, and 13 to 1's location, then send 2 to 8's location, 8 to 15's location, 15 to 9's location, and 9 to 2's location, etc. The program below works its way into the center of the array from the outermost layers, performing exchanges within a layer iteratively using the four-way swap just described.

```
void RotateMatrix(vector<vector<int>>* square_matrix_ptr) {
  vector<vector<int>>& square_matrix = *square_matrix_ptr;
  const int matrix_size = square_matrix.size() - 1;
  for (int i = 0; i < (square_matrix.size() / 2); ++i) {
    for (int j = i; j < matrix_size - i; ++j) {
      // Perform a 4-way exchange.
      int temp1 = square_matrix[matrix_size - j][i];
      int temp2 = square_matrix[matrix_size - i][matrix_size - j];
      int temp3 = square_matrix[j][matrix_size - i];
```

```
    int temp4 = square_matrix[i][j];
    square_matrix[i][j] = temp1;
    square_matrix[matrix_size - j][i] = temp2;
    square_matrix[matrix_size - i][matrix_size - j] = temp3;
    square_matrix[j][matrix_size - i] = temp4;
  }
 }
}
```

The time complexity is $O(n^2)$ and the additional space complexity is $O(1)$.

Interestingly, we can get the effect of a rotation with $O(1)$ space and time complexity, albeit with some limitations. Specifically, we return an object r that composes the original matrix A. A read of the element at indices i and j in r is converted into a read from A at index $[n - 1 - j][i]$. Writes are handled similarly. The time to create r is constant, since it simply consists of a reference to A. The time to perform reads and writes is unchanged. This approach breaks when there are clients of the original A object, since writes to r change A. Even if A is not written to, if methods on the stored objects change their state, the system gets corrupted. Copy-on-write can be used to solve these issues.

```
class RotatedMatrix {
 public:
  explicit RotatedMatrix(vector<vector<int>>* square_matrix)
      : square_matrix_(*square_matrix) {}

  int ReadEntry(int i, int j) const {
    return square_matrix_[square_matrix_.size() - 1 - j][i];
  }

  void WriteEntry(int i, int j, int v) {
    square_matrix_[square_matrix_.size() - 1 - j][i] = v;
  }

 private:
  vector<vector<int>>& square_matrix_;
};
```

Variant: Implement an algorithm to reflect A, assumed to be an $n \times n$ 2D array, about the horizontal axis of symmetry. Repeat the same for reflections about the vertical axis, the diagonal from top-left to bottom-right, and the diagonal from top-right to bottom-left.

6.20 COMPUTE ROWS IN PASCAL'S TRIANGLE

Figure 6.5 on the next page shows the first five rows of a graphic that is known as Pascal's triangle. Each row contains one more entry than the previous one. Except for entries in the last row, each entry is adjacent to one or two numbers in the row below it. The first row holds 1. Each entry holds the sum of the numbers in the adjacent entries above it.

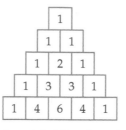

Figure 6.5: A Pascal triangle.

Write a program which takes as input a nonnegative integer n and returns the first n rows of Pascal's triangle.

Hint: Write the given fact as an equation.

Solution: A brute-force approach might be to organize the arrays in memory similar to how they appear in the figure. The challenge is to determine the correct indices to range over and to read from.

A better approach is to keep the arrays left-aligned, that is the first entry is at location 0. Now it is simple: the jth entry in the ith row is 1 if $j = 0$ or $j = i$, otherwise it is the sum of the $(j-1)$th and jth entries in the $(i-1)$th row. The first row R_0 is $\langle 1 \rangle$. The second row R_1 is $\langle 1, 1 \rangle$. The third row R_2 is $\langle 1, R_1[0] + R_1[1] = 2, 1 \rangle$. The fourth row R_3 is $\langle 1, R_2[0] + R_2[1] = 3, R_2[1] + R_2[2] = 3, 1 \rangle$.

```
vector<vector<int>> GeneratePascalTriangle(int num_rows) {
  vector<vector<int>> pascal_triangle;
  for (int i = 0; i < num_rows; ++i) {
    vector<int> curr_row;
    for (int j = 0; j <= i; ++j) {
      // Sets this entry to the sum of the two above adjacent entries if they
      // exist.
      curr_row.emplace_back((0 < j && j < i)
                                ? pascal_triangle.back()[j - 1] +
                                      pascal_triangle.back()[j]
                                : 1);
    }
    pascal_triangle.emplace_back(curr_row);
  }
  return pascal_triangle;
}
```

Since each element takes $O(1)$ time to compute, the time complexity is $O(1+2+\cdots+n) = O(n(n+1)/2) = O(n^2)$. Similarly, the space complexity is $O(n^2)$.

It is a fact that the ith entry in the nth row of Pascal's triangle is $\binom{n}{i}$. This in itself does not trivialize the problem, since computing $\binom{n}{i}$ itself is tricky. (In fact, Pascal's triangle can be used to compute $\binom{n}{i}$.)

Variant: Compute the nth row of Pascal's triangle using $O(n)$ space.

7

Strings

String pattern matching is an important problem that occurs in many areas of science and information processing. In computing, it occurs naturally as part of data processing, text editing, term rewriting, lexical analysis, and information retrieval.

— *"Algorithms For Finding Patterns in Strings,"*
A. V. Aho, 1990

Strings are ubiquitous in programming today—scripting, web development, and bioinformatics all make extensive use of strings. You should know how strings are represented in memory, and understand basic operations on strings such as comparison, copying, joining, splitting, matching, etc. We now present problems on strings which can be solved using elementary techniques. Advanced string processing algorithms often use hash tables (Chapter 13) and dynamic programming (Page 299).

7.1 INTERCONVERT STRINGS AND INTEGERS

A string is a sequence of characters. A string may encode an integer, e.g., "123" encodes 123. In this problem, you are to implement methods that take a string representing an integer and return the corresponding integer, and vice versa. Your code should handle negative integers. You cannot use library functions like `stoi` in C++ and `parseInt` in Java.

Implement string/integer inter-conversion functions.

Hint: Build the result one digit at a time.

Solution: Let's consider the integer to string problem first. If the number to convert is a single digit, i.e., it is between 0 and 9, the result is easy to compute: it is the string consisting of the single character encoding that digit.

If the number has more than one digit, it is natural to perform the conversion digit-by-digit. The key insight is that for any positive integer x, the least significant digit in the decimal representation of x is x mod 10, and the remaining digits are $x/10$. This approach computes the digits in reverse order, e.g., if we begin with 423, we get 3 and are left with 42 to convert. Then we get 2, and are left with 4 to convert. Finally, we get 4 and there are no digits to convert. There are multiple ways in which we can form a string from the reverse order of the digits, but a particularly simple and memory-efficient way is to add the digits to the end of a string, and eventually reverse it.

If x is negative, we record that, negate x, and then add a '-' before reversing. If x is 0, our code breaks out of the iteration without writing any digits, in which case we need to explicitly set a 0.

To convert from a string to an integer we recall the basic working of a positional number system. A base-10 number $d_2 d_1 d_0$ encodes the number $10^2 \times d_2 + 10^1 \times d_1 + d_0$. A brute-force algorithm then is to begin with the rightmost digit, and iteratively add $10^i \times d_i$ to a cumulative sum. The efficient way to compute 10^{i+1} is to use the existing value 10^i and multiply that by 10.

A more elegant solution is to begin from the leftmost digit and with each succeeding digit, multiply the partial result by 10 and add that digit. For example, to convert "314" to an integer, we initial the partial result r to 0. In the first iteration, $r = 3$, in the second iteration $r = 3 \times 10 + 1 = 31$, and in the third iteration $r = 31 \times 10 + 4 = 314$, which is the final result.

Negative numbers are handled by recording the sign and negating the result.

```cpp
string IntToString(int x) {
  bool is_negative = false;
  if (x < 0) {
    x = -x, is_negative = true;
  }

  string s;
  do {
    s += '0' + x % 10;
    x /= 10;
  } while (x);

  if (is_negative) {
    s += '-';  // Adds the negative sign back.
  }
  reverse(s.begin(), s.end());
  return s;
}

int StringToInt(const string& s) {
  bool is_negative = s[0] == '-';
  int result = 0;
  for (int i = s[0] == '-' ? 1 : 0; i < s.size(); ++i) {
    int digit = s[i] - '0';
    result = result * 10 + digit;
  }
  return is_negative ? -result : result;
}
```

In the decimal number system, the position of a digit is used to signify the power of 10 that digit is to be multiplied with. For example, "314" denotes the number $3 \times 100 + 1 \times 10 + 4 \times 1$. The base b number system generalizes the decimal number system: the string "$a_{k-1}a_{k-2} \ldots a_1 a_0$", where $0 \le a_i < b$, denotes in base-b the integer $a_0 \times b^0 + a_1 \times b^1 + a_2 \times b^2 + \cdots + a_{k-1} \times b^{k-1}$.

Write a program that performs base conversion. The input is a string, an integer b_1, and another integer b_2. The string represents be an integer in base b_1. The output should be the string representing the integer in base b_2. Assume $2 \le b_1, b_2 \le 16$. Use "A" to represent 10, "B" for 11, ..., and "F" for 15. (For example, if the string is "615", b_1 is 7 and b_2 is 13, then the result should be "1A7", since $6 \times 7^2 + 1 \times 7 + 5 = 1 \times 13^2 + 10 \times 13 + 7$.)

Hint: What base can you easily convert to and from?

Solution: A brute-force approach might be to convert the input to a unary representation, and then group the 1s as multiples of b_2, b_2^2, b_2^3, etc. For example, $(102)_3 = (1111111111)_1$. To convert to base 4, there are two groups of 4 and with three 1s remaining, so the result is $(23)_4$. This approach is hard to implement, and has terrible time and space complexity.

The insight to a good algorithm is the fact that all languages have an integer type, which supports arithmetical operations like multiply, add, divide, modulus, etc. These operations make the conversion much easier. Specifically, we can convert a string in base b_1 to integer type using a sequence of multiply and adds. Then we convert that integer type to a string in base b_2 using a sequence of modulus and division operations. For example, for the string is "615", $b_1 = 7$ and $b_2 = 13$, then the integer value, expressed in decimal, is 306. The least significant digit of the result is 306 mod 13 = 7, and we continue with 306/13 = 23. The next digit is 23 mod 13 = 10, which we denote by 'A'. We continue with 23/13 = 1. Since 1 mod 13 = 1 and 1/13 = 0, the final digit is 1, and the overall result is "1A7".

```
string ConvertBase(const string& s, int b1, int b2) {
  bool is_negative = s.front() == '-';
  int x = 0;
  for (size_t i = (is_negative == true ? 1 : 0); i < s.size(); ++i) {
    x *= b1;
    x += isdigit(s[i]) ? s[i] - '0' : s[i] - 'A' + 10;
  }

  string result;
  do {
    int remainder = x % b2;
    result.push_back(remainder >= 10 ? 'A' + remainder - 10 : '0' + remainder);
    x /= b2;
  } while (x);
```

```
if (is_negative) {    // s is a negative number.
  result.push_back('-');
}
reverse(result.begin(), result.end());
return result;
}
```

The time complexity is $O(n(1 + \log_{b_2} b_1))$, where n is the length of s. The reasoning is as follows. First, we perform n multiply-and-adds to get x from s. Then we perform $\log_{b_2} x$ multiply and adds to get the result. The value x is upper-bounded by b_1^n, and $\log_{b_2}(b_1^n) = n \log_{b_2} b_1$.

7.3 COMPUTE THE SPREADSHEET COLUMN ENCODING

Spreadsheets often use an alphabetical encoding of the successive columns. Specifically, columns are identified by "A", "B", "C", ..., "X", "Y", "Z", "AA", "AB", ..., "ZZ", "AAA", "AAB", ...

Implement a function that converts a spreadsheet column id to the corresponding integer, with "A" corresponding to 1. For example, you should return 4 for "D", 27 for "AA", 702 for "ZZ", etc. How would you test your code?

Hint: There are 26 characters in ["A", "Z"], and each can be mapped to an integer.

Solution: A brute-force approach could be to enumerate the column ids, stopping when the id equals the input. The logic for getting the successor of "Z", "AZ", etc. is slightly involved. The bigger issue is the time-complexity—it takes 26^6 steps to get to "ZZZZZZ". In general, the time complexity is $O(26^n)$, where n is the length of the string.

We can do better by taking larger jumps. Specifically, this problem is basically the problem of converting a string representing a base-26 number to the corresponding integer, except that "A" corresponds to 1 not 0. We can use the string to integer conversion approach given in Solution 7.1 on Page 91

For example to convert "ZZ", we initialize result to 0. We add 26, multiply by 26, then add 26 again, i.e., the id is $26^2 + 26 = 702$.

Good test cases are around boundaries, e.g., "A", "B", "Y", "Z", "AA", "AB", "ZY", "ZZ", and some random strings, e.g., "M", "BZ", "CCC".

```
int SSDecodeColID(const string& col) {
  int ret = 0;
  for (char c : col) {
    ret = ret * 26 + c - 'A' + 1;
  }
  return ret;
}
```

The time complexity is $O(n)$.

Variant: Solve the same problem with "A" corresponding to 0.

7.4 REPLACE AND REMOVE

Consider the following two rules that are to be applied to an array of characters.
- Replace each 'a' by two 'd's.
- Delete each entry containing a 'b'.

For example, applying these rules to the array $\langle a, c, d, b, b, c, a \rangle$ results in the array $\langle d, d, c, d, c, d, d \rangle$.

Write a program which takes as input an array of characters, and removes each 'b' and replaces each 'a' by two 'd's. Specifically, along with the array, you are provided an integer-valued size. Size denotes the number of entries of the array that the operation is to be applied to. You do not have to worry preserving about subsequent entries. For example, if the array is $\langle a, b, a, c, \_ \rangle$ and the size is 4, then you can return $\langle d, d, d, d, c \rangle$. You can assume there is enough space in the array to hold the final result.

Hint: Consider performing multiples passes on s.

Solution: Library array implementations often have methods for inserting into a specific location (all later entries are shifted right, and the array is resized) and deleting from a specific location (all later entries are shifted left, and the size of the array is decremented). If the input array had such methods, we could apply them—however, the time complexity would be $O(n^2)$, where n is the array's length. The reason is that each insertion and deletion from the array would have $O(n)$ time complexity.

This problem is trivial to solve in $O(n)$ time if we write result to a new array—we skip 'b's, replace 'a's by two 'd's, and copy over all other characters. However, this entails $O(n)$ additional space.

If there are no 'a's, we can implement the function without allocating additional space with one forward iteration by skipping 'b's and copying over the other characters.

If there are no 'b's, we can implement the function without additional space as follows. First, we compute the final length of the resulting string, which is the length of the array plus the number of 'a's. We can then write the result, character by character, starting from the last character, working our way backwards.

For example, suppose the array is $\langle a, c, a, a, \_, \_, \_ \rangle$, and the specified size is 4. Our algorithm updates the array to $\langle a, c, a, a, \_, d, d \rangle$. (Boldface denotes characters that are part of the final result.) The next update is $\langle a, c, a, d, d, d, d \rangle$, followed by $\langle a, c, c, d, d, d, d \rangle$, and finally $\langle d, d, c, d, d, d, d \rangle$.

We can combine these two approaches to get a complete algorithm. First, we delete 'b's and compute the final number of valid characters of the string, with a forward iteration through the string. Then we replace each 'a' by two 'd's, iterating backwards from the end of the resulting string. If there are more 'b's than 'a's, the number of valid entries will decrease, and if there are more 'a's than 'b's the number will increase. In the program below we return the number of valid entries in the final result.

```
int ReplaceAndRemove(int size, char s[]) {
  // Forward iteration: remove "b"s and count the number of "a"s.
  int write_idx = 0, a_count = 0;
  for (int i = 0; i < size; ++i) {
    if (s[i] != 'b') {
      s[write_idx++] = s[i];
    }
    if (s[i] == 'a') {
      ++a_count;
    }
  }

  // Backward iteration: replace "a"s with "dd"s starting from the end.
  int cur_idx = write_idx - 1;
  write_idx = write_idx + a_count - 1;
  int final_size = write_idx + 1;
  while (cur_idx >= 0) {
    if (s[cur_idx] == 'a') {
      s[write_idx--] = 'd';
      s[write_idx--] = 'd';
    } else {
      s[write_idx--] = s[cur_idx];
    }
    --cur_idx;
  }
  return final_size;
}
```

The forward and backward iterations each take $O(n)$ time, so the total time complexity is $O(n)$. No additional space is allocated.

Variant: You have an array C of characters. The characters may be letters, digits, blanks, and punctuation. The telex-encoding of the array C is an array T of characters in which letters, digits, and blanks appear as before, but punctuation marks are spelled out. For example, telex-encoding entails replacing the character "." by the string "DOT", the character "," by "COMMA", the character "?" by "QUESTION MARK", and the character "!" by "EXCLAMATION MARK". Design an algorithm to perform telex-encoding with $O(1)$ space.

Variant: Write a program which merges two sorted arrays of integers, A and B. Specifically, the final result should be a sorted array of length $m + n$, where n and m are the lengths of A and B, respectively. Use $O(1)$ additional storage—assume the result is stored in A, which has sufficient space. These arrays are C-style arrays, i.e., contiguous preallocated blocks of memory.

For the purpose of this problem, define a palindromic string to be a string which when all the nonalphanumeric are removed it reads the same front to back ignoring case. For example, "A man, a plan, a canal, Panama." and "Able was I, ere I saw Elba!" are palindromic, but "Ray a Ray" is not.

Implement a function which takes as input a string *s* and returns true if *s* is a palindromic string.

Hint: Use two indices.

Solution: The naive approach is to create a reversed version of *s*, and compare it with *s*, skipping nonalphanumeric characters. This requires additional space proportional to the length of *s*.

We do not need to create the reverse—rather, we can get the effect of the reverse of *s* by traversing *s* from right to left. Specifically, we use two indices to traverse the string, one forwards, the other backwards, skipping nonalphanumeric characters, performing case-insensitive comparison on the alphanumeric characters. We return false as soon as there is a mismatch. If the indices cross, we have verified palindromicity.

```
bool IsPalindrome(const string& s) {
  // i moves forward, and j moves backward.
  int i = 0, j = s.size() - 1;
  while (i < j) {
    // i and j both skip non-alphanumeric characters.
    while (!isalnum(s[i]) && i < j) {
      ++i;
    }
    while (!isalnum(s[j]) && i < j) {
      --j;
    }
    if (tolower(s[i]) != tolower(s[j])) {
      return false;
    }
    ++i, --j;
  }
  return true;
}
```

We spend $O(1)$ per character, so the time complexity is $O(n)$, where n is the length of *s*.

7.6 REVERSE ALL THE WORDS IN A SENTENCE

Given a string containing a set of words separated by whitespace, we would like to transform it to a string in which the words appear in the reverse order. For example,

"Alice likes Bob" transforms to "Bob likes Alice". We do not need to keep the original string.

Implement a function for reversing the words in a string s.

Hint: It's difficult to solve this with one pass.

Solution: The code for computing the position for each character in the final result in a single pass is intricate.

However, for the special case where each word is a single character, the desired result is simply the reverse of s.

For the general case, reversing s gets the words to their correct relative positions. However, for words that are longer than one character, their letters appear in reverse order. This situation can be corrected by reversing the individual words.

For example, "ram is costly" reversed yields "yltsoc si mar". We obtain the final result by reversing each word to obtain "costly is ram".

```
void ReverseWords(string* s) {
  // Reverses the whole string first.
  reverse(s->begin(), s->end());

  size_t start = 0, end;
  while ((end = s->find(" ", start)) != string::npos) {
    // Reverses each word in the string.
    reverse(s->begin() + start, s->begin() + end);
    start = end + 1;
  }
  // Reverses the last word.
  reverse(s->begin() + start, s->end());
}
```

Since we spend $O(1)$ per character, the time complexity is $O(n)$, where n is the length of s. If strings are mutable, we can perform the computation in place, i.e., the additional space complexity is $O(1)$. If the string cannot be changed, the additional space complexity is $O(n)$, since we need to create a new string of length n.

7.7 COMPUTE ALL MNEMONICS FOR A PHONE NUMBER

Each digit, apart from 0 and 1, in a phone keypad corresponds to one of three or four letters of the alphabet, as shown in Figure 7.1 on the next page. Since words are easier to remember than numbers, it is natural to ask if a 7 or 10-digit phone number can be represented by a word. For example, "2276696" corresponds to "ACRONYM" as well as "ABPOMZN".

Write a program which takes as input a phone number, specified as a string of digits, and returns all possible character sequences that correspond to the phone number. The cell phone keypad is specified by a mapping that takes a digit and returns the

Figure 7.1: Phone keypad.

corresponding set of characters. The character sequences do not have to be legal words or phrases.

Hint: Use recursion.

Solution: For a 7 digit phone number, the brute-force approach is to form 7 ranges of characters, one for each digit. For example, if the number is "2276696" then the ranges are 'A'–'C', 'A'–'C', 'P'–'S', 'M'–'O', 'M'–'O', 'W'–'Z', and 'M'–'O'. We use 7 nested for-loops where the iteration variables correspond to the 7 ranges to enumerate all possible mnemonics. The drawbacks of such an approach are its repetitiveness in code and its inflexibility.

As a general rule, any such enumeration is best computed using recursion. The execution path is very similar to that of the brute-force approach, but the compiler handles the looping.

```
vector<string> PhoneMnemonic(const string& phone_number) {
  string partial_mnemonic(phone_number.size(), 0);
  vector<string> mnemonics;
  PhoneMnemonicHelper(phone_number, 0, &partial_mnemonic, &mnemonics);
  return mnemonics;
}

const int kNumTelDigits = 10;

// The mapping from digit to corresponding characters.
const array<string, kNumTelDigits> kMapping = {
    {"0", "1", "ABC", "DEF", "GHI", "JKL", "MNO", "PQRS", "TUV", "WXYZ"}};

void PhoneMnemonicHelper(const string& phone_number, int digit,
                         string* partial_mnemonic, vector<string>* mnemonics) {
  if (digit == phone_number.size()) {
    // All digits are processed, so add partial_mnemonic to mnemonics.
    // (We add a copy since subsequent calls modify partial_mnemonic.)
    mnemonics->emplace_back(*partial_mnemonic);
  } else {
    // Try all possible characters for this digit.
    for (char c : kMapping[phone_number[digit] - '0']) {
      (*partial_mnemonic)[digit] = c;
```

```
      PhoneMnemonicHelper(phone_number, digit + 1, partial_mnemonic,
                          mnemonics);
    }
  }
}
```

Since there are no more than 4 possible characters for each digit, the number of recursive calls, $T(n)$, satisfies $T(n) \leq 4T(n-1)$, where n is the number of digits in the number. This solves to $T(n) = O(4^n)$. For the function calls that entail recursion, the time spent within the function, not including the recursive calls, is $O(1)$. Each base case entails making a copy of a string and adding it to the result. Since each such string has length n, each base case takes time $O(n)$. Therefore, the time complexity is $O(4^n n)$.

Variant: Solve the same problem without using recursion.

7.8 THE LOOK-AND-SAY PROBLEM

The look-and-say sequence starts with 1. Subsequent numbers are derived by describing the previous number in terms of consecutive digits. Specifically, to generate an entry of the sequence from the previous entry, read off the digits of the previous entry, counting the number of digits in groups of the same digit. For example, 1; one 1; two 1s; one 2 then one 1; one 1, then one 2, then two 1s; three 1s, then two 2s, then one 1. The first eight numbers in the look-and-say sequence are $\langle 1, 11, 21, 1211, 111221, 312211, 13112221, 1113213211 \rangle$.

Write a program that takes as input an integer n and returns the nth integer in the look-and-say sequence. Return the result as a string.

Hint: You need to return the result as a string.

Solution: We compute the nth number by iteratively applying this rule $n-1$ times. Since we are counting digits, it is natural to use strings to represent the integers in the sequence. Specifically, going from the ith number to the $(i+1)$th number entails scanning the digits from most significant to least significant, counting the number of consecutive equal digits, and writing these counts.

```
string LookAndSay(int n) {
  string s = "1";
  for (int i = 1; i < n; ++i) {
    s = NextNumber(s);
  }
  return s;
}

string NextNumber(const string& s) {
  string ret;
```

```
  for (int i = 0; i < s.size(); ++i) {
    int count = 1;
    while (i + 1 < s.size() && s[i] == s[i + 1]) {
      ++i, ++count;
    }
    ret += to_string(count) + s[i];
  }
  return ret;
}
```

The precise time complexity is a function of the lengths of the terms, which is extremely hard to analyze. Each successive number can have at most twice as many digits as the previous number—this happens when all digits are different. This means the maximum length number has length no more than 2^n. Since there are n iterations and the work in each iteration is proportional to the length of the number computed in the iteration, a simple bound on the time complexity is $O(n2^n)$.

7.9 CONVERT FROM ROMAN TO DECIMAL

The Roman numeral representation of positive integers uses the symbols I, V, X, L, C, D, M. Each symbol represents a value, with I being 1, V being 5, X being 10, L being 50, C being 100, D being 500, and M being 1000.

In this problem we give simplified rules for representing numbers in this system. Specifically, define a string over the Roman number symbols to be a valid Roman number string if symbols appear in nonincreasing order, with the following exceptions allowed:

- I can immediately precede V and X.
- X can immediately precede L and C.
- C can immediately precede D and M.

Back-to-back exceptions are not allowed, e.g., IXC is invalid, as is CDM.

A valid complex Roman number string represents the integer which is the sum of the symbols that do not correspond to exceptions; for the exceptions, add the difference of the larger symbol and the smaller symbol.

For example, the strings "XXXXXIIIIIIIII", "LVIIII" and "LIX" are valid Roman number strings representing 59. The shortest valid complex Roman number string corresponding to the integer 59 is "LIX".

Write a program which takes as input a valid Roman number string s and returns the integer it corresponds to.

Hint: Start by solving the problem assuming no exception cases.

Solution: The brute-force approach is to scan s from left to right, adding the value for the corresponding symbol unless the symbol subsequent to the one being considered has a higher value, in which case the pair is one of the six exception cases and the value of the pair is added.

A slightly easier-to-code solution is to start from the right, and if the symbol after the current one is greater than it, we subtract the current symbol. The code below performs the right-to-left iteration. It does not check that when a smaller symbol appears to the left of a larger one that it is one of the six allowed exceptions, so it will, for example, return 99 for "IC".

```cpp
int RomanToInteger(const string& s) {
  unordered_map<char, int> T = {{'I', 1},   {'V', 5},   {'X', 10},   {'L', 50},
                                {'C', 100}, {'D', 500}, {'M', 1000}};

  int sum = T[s.back()];
  for (int i = s.length() - 2; i >= 0; --i) {
    if (T[s[i]] < T[s[i + 1]]) {
      sum -= T[s[i]];
    } else {
      sum += T[s[i]];
    }
  }
  return sum;
}
```

Each character of s is processed in $O(1)$ time, yielding an $O(n)$ overall time complexity, where n is the length of s.

Variant: Write a program that takes as input a string of Roman number symbols and checks whether that string is valid.

Variant: Write a program that takes as input a positive integer n and returns a shortest valid simple Roman number string representing n.

7.10 COMPUTE ALL VALID IP ADDRESSES

A decimal string is a string consisting of digits between 0 and 9. Internet Protocol (IP) addresses can be written as four decimal strings separated by periods, e.g., 192.168.1.201. A careless programmer mangles a string representing an IP address in such a way that all the periods vanish.

Write a program that determines where to add periods to a decimal string so that the resulting string is a valid IP address. There may be more than one valid IP address corresponding to a string, in which case you should print all possibilities.

For example, if the mangled string is "19216811" then two corresponding IP addresses are 192.168.1.1 and 19.216.81.1. (There are seven other possible IP addresses for this string.)

Hint: Use nested loops.

Solution: There are three periods in a valid IP address, so we can enumerate all possible placements of these periods, and check whether all four corresponding substrings are between 0 and 255. We can reduce the number of placements considered by spacing the periods 1 to 3 characters apart. We can also prune by stopping as soon as a substring is not valid.

For example, if the string is "19216811", we could put the first period after "1", "19", and "192". If the first part is "1", the second part could be "9", "92", and "921". Of these, "921" is illegal so we do not continue with it.

```cpp
vector<string> GetValidIPAddress(const string& s) {
  vector<string> result;
  for (size_t i = 1; i < 4 && i < s.size(); ++i) {
    auto first = s.substr(0, i);
    if (IsValidPart(first)) {
      for (size_t j = 1; i + j < s.size() && j < 4; ++j) {
        auto second = s.substr(i, j);
        if (IsValidPart(second)) {
          for (size_t k = 1; i + j + k < s.size() && k < 4; ++k) {
            auto third = s.substr(i + j, k), fourth = s.substr(i + j + k);
            if (IsValidPart(third) && IsValidPart(fourth)) {
              result.emplace_back(first + "." + second + "." + third + "." +
                                  fourth);
            }
          }
        }
      }
    }
  }
  return result;
}

bool IsValidPart(const string& s) {
  if (s.size() > 3) {
    return false;
  }
  // "00", "000", "01", etc. are not valid, but "0" is valid.
  if (s.front() == '0' && s.size() > 1) {
    return false;
  }
  int val = stoi(s);
  return val <= 255 && val >= 0;
}
```

The total number of IP addresses is a constant (2^{32}), implying an $O(1)$ time complexity for the above algorithm.

Variant: Solve the analogous problem when the number of periods is a parameter k and the string length is unbounded.

We illustrate what it means to write a string in sinusoidal fashion by means of an example. The string "Hello␣World!" written in sinusoidal fashion is

```
        e               ␣                   l
  H     l       o       W       r       d           (Here ␣ denotes a blank.)
            l                   o                   !
```

Define the snakestring of s to be the left-right top-to-bottom sequence in which characters appear when s is written in sinusoidal fashion. For example, the snakestring string for "Hello␣World!" is "e␣lHloWrdlo!".

Write a program which takes as input a string s and returns the snakestring of s.

Hint: Try concrete examples, and look for periodicity.

Solution: The brute-force approach is to populate a $3 \times n$ 2D array of characters, initialized to null entries. We then write the string in sinusoidal manner in this array. Finally, we read out the non-null characters in row-major manner.

However, observe that the result begins with the characters $s[1], s[5], s[9], \ldots$, followed by $s[0], s[2], s[4], \ldots$, and then $s[3], s[7], s[11], \ldots$. Therefore, we can create the snakestring directly, with three iterations through s.

```cpp
string SnakeString(const string& s) {
  string result;
  // Outputs the first row, i.e., s[1], s[5], s[9], ...
  for (int i = 1; i < s.size(); i += 4) {
    result += s[i];
  }
  // Outputs the second row, i.e., s[0], s[2], s[4], ...
  for (int i = 0; i < s.size(); i += 2) {
    result += s[i];
  }
  // Outputs the third row, i.e., s[3], s[7], s[11], ...
  for (int i = 3; i < s.size(); i += 4) {
    result += s[i];
  }
  return result;
}
```

Let n be the length of s. Each of the three iterations takes $O(n)$ time, implying an $O(n)$ time complexity.

7.12 Implement run-length encoding

Run-length encoding (RLE) compression offers a fast way to do efficient on-the-fly compression and decompression of strings. The idea is simple—encode successive repeated characters by the repetition count and the character. For example, the RLE of "aaaabcccaa" is "4a1b3c2a". The decoding of "3e4f2e" returns "eeeffffee".

Implement run-length encoding and decoding functions. Assume the string to be encoded consists of letters of the alphabet, with no digits, and the string to be decoded is a valid encoding.

Hint: This is similar to converting between binary and string representations.

Solution: First we consider the decoding function. Every encoded string is a repetition of a string of digits followed by a single character. The string of digits is the decimal representation of a positive integer. To generate the decoded string, we need to convert this sequence of digits into its integer equivalent and then write the character that many times. We do this for each character.

The encoding function requires an integer (the repetition count) to string conversion.

```cpp
string Decoding(const string &s) {
  int count = 0;
  string result;
  for (const char &c : s) {
    if (isdigit(c)) {
      count = count * 10 + c - '0';
    } else {  // c is a letter of alphabet.
      result.append(count, c);  // Appends count copies of c to result.
      count - 0;
    }
  }
  return result;
}

string Encoding(const string &s) {
  string result;
  for (int i = 1, count = 1; i <= s.size(); ++i) {
    if (i == s.size() || s[i] != s[i - 1]) {
      // Found new character so write the count of previous character.
      result += to_string(count) + s[i - 1];
      count = 1;
    } else {  // s[i] == s[i - 1].
      ++count;
    }
  }
  return result;
}
```

The time complexity is $O(n)$, where n is the length of the string.

7.13 IMPLEMENT THE UNIX TAIL COMMAND

The UNIX `tail` command displays the last part of a file. For this problem, assume that `tail` takes two arguments—a filename, and the number of lines, starting from the last line, that are to be printed.

Implement the UNIX `tail` command.

Hint: Don't start at the beginning of the file.

Solution: The natural approach to this problem is to read the input one line at a time. Each line can be stored in a queue. When the queue size is equal to the number of desired lines, each additional line is inserted at the tail, and the line at the head is deleted. The drawback of this approach is that it entails reading the entire file which could be huge.

The OS provides the ability to perform random access on a file, essentially allowing us to treat the file as an array of characters, albeit with much slower access times. In the code below, we use library functions to process the file in reverse order starting the end of the file. We store the characters in a string, stopping when the specified number of lines have been read.

```
string tail(const string& file_name, int N) {
  fstream file_ptr(file_name.c_str());

  file_ptr.seekg(0, ios::end);
  int file_size = file_ptr.tellg(), newline_count = 0;
  string last_N_lines;
  // Reads file in reverse looking for '\n'.
  for (int i = 0; i < file_size; ++i) {
    file_ptr.seekg(-1 - i, ios::end);
    char c;
    file_ptr.get(c);
    if (c == '\n') {
      ++newline_count;
      if (newline_count >= N) {
        break;
      }
    }
    last_N_lines.push_back(c);
  }

  reverse(last_N_lines.begin(), last_N_lines.end());
  return last_N_lines;
}
```

7.14 FIND THE FIRST OCCURRENCE OF A SUBSTRING

A good string search algorithm is fundamental to the performance of many applications. Several clever algorithms have been proposed for string search, each with its own trade-offs. As a result, there is no single perfect answer. If someone asks you this question in an interview, the best way to approach this problem would be to work through one good algorithm in detail and discuss at a high level other algorithms.

Given two strings s (the "search string") and t (the "text"), find the first occurrence of s in t.

Hint: Form a signature from a string.

Solution: The brute-force algorithm uses two nested loops, the first iterates through t, the second tests if s occurs starting at the current index in t. The worst-case complexity is high. If t consists of n 'a's and s is $n/2$ 'a's followed by a 'b', it will perform $n/2$ unsuccessful string compares, each of which entails $n/2 + 1$ character compares, so the brute-force algorithm's time complexity is $O(n^2)$.

Intuitively, the brute-force algorithm is slow because it advances through t one character at a time, and potentially does $O(m)$ computation with each advance, where m is the length of s.

There are three linear time string matching algorithms: KMP, Boyer-Moore, and Rabin-Karp. Of these, Rabin-Karp is by far the simplest to understand and implement.

The Rabin-Karp algorithm is very similar to the brute-force algorithm, but it does not require the second loop. Instead it uses the concept of a "fingerprint". Specifically, let m be the length of s. It computes hash codes of each substring whose length is m—these are the fingerprints. The key to efficiency is using an incremental hash function, such as a function with the property that the hash code of a string is an additive function of each individual character. (Such a hash function is sometimes referred to as a rolling hash.) For such a function, getting the hash code of a sliding window of characters is very fast for each shift.

For example, let the strings consist of letters from $\{A, C, G, T\}$. Suppose t is "GACGCCA" and s is "CGC". Define the code for "A" to be 0, the code for "C" to be 1, etc. Let the hash function be the decimal number formed by the integer codes for the letters mod 31. The hash code of s is 121 mod 31 = 28. The hash code of the first three characters of t, "GAC", is 201 mod 31 = 15, so s cannot be the first three characters of t. Continuing, the next substring of t is "ACG", whose hash code can be computed from 15 by subtracting 200, then multiplying by 10, then adding 2 and finally taking mod 31. This yields 12, so there no match yet. We then reach "CGC" whose hash code, 28, is derived in a similar manner. We are not done yet—there may be a collision. We check explicitly if the substring matches s, which in this case it does.

For the Rabin-Karp algorithm to run in linear time, we need a good hash function, to reduce the likelihood of collisions, which entail potentially time consuming string equality checks.

```
const int kBase = 26, kMod = 997;

// Returns the index of the first character of the substring if found, -1
// otherwise.
int RabinKarp(const string &t, const string &s) {
  if (s.size() > t.size()) {
```

```
    return -1;  // s is not a substring of t.
  }

  int t_hash = 0, s_hash = 0;  // Hash codes for the substring of t and s.
  int power_s = 1;  // The modulo result of kBase^|s|.
  for (int i = 0; i < s.size(); ++i) {
    power_s = i ? power_s * kBase % kMod : 1;
    t_hash = (t_hash * kBase + t[i]) % kMod;
    s_hash = (s_hash * kBase + s[i]) % kMod;
  }

  for (int i = s.size(); i < t.size(); ++i) {
    // Checks the two substrings are actually equal or not, to protect
    // against hash collision.
    if (t_hash == s_hash && !t.compare(i - s.size(), s.size(), s)) {
      return i - s.size();  // Found a match.
    }

    // Uses rolling hash to compute the new hash code.
    t_hash -= (t[i - s.size()] * power_s) % kMod;
    if (t_hash < 0) {
      t_hash += kMod;
    }
    t_hash = (t_hash * kBase + t[i]) % kMod;
  }

  // Tries to match s and t[t.size() - s.size() : t.size() - 1].
  if (t_hash == s_hash && t.compare(t.size() - s.size(), s.size(), s) == 0) {
    return t.size() - s.size();
  }
  return -1;  // s is not a substring of t.
}
```

For a good hash function, the time complexity is $O(m + n)$, independent of the inputs s and t, where m is the length of s and n is the length of t.

Linked Lists

The S-expressions are formed according to the following recursive rules.

1. *The atomic symbols p_1, p_2, etc., are S-expressions.*
2. *A null expression $\wedge$ is also admitted.*
3. *If e is an S-expression so is (e).*
4. *If e_1 and e_2 are S-expressions so is (e_1, e_2).*

— *"Recursive Functions Of Symbolic Expressions,"*
J. McCarthy, 1959

A *singly linked list* is a data structure that contains a sequence of nodes such that each node contains an object and a reference to the next node in the list. The first node is referred to as the *head* and the last node is referred to as the *tail*; the tail's next field is null. The structure of a singly linked list is given in Figure 8.1. There are many variants of linked lists, e.g., in a *doubly linked list*, each node has a link to its predecessor; similarly, a sentinel node or a self-loop can be used instead of null. The structure of a doubly linked list is given in Figure 8.2.

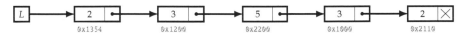

Figure 8.1: Example of a singly linked list. The number in hex below a node indicates the memory address of that node.

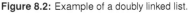

Figure 8.2: Example of a doubly linked list.

For all problems in this chapter, unless otherwise stated, each node has two entries—a data field, and a next field, which points to the next node in the list, with the next field of the last node being null. Its prototype is as follows:

```
template <typename T>
struct ListNode {
  T data;
  shared_ptr<ListNode<T>> next;
};
```

Consider two singly linked lists in which each node holds a number. Assume the lists are sorted, i.e., numbers in the lists appear in ascending order within each list. The *merge* of the two lists is a list consisting of the nodes of the two lists in which numbers appear in ascending order. Merge is illustrated in Figure 8.3.

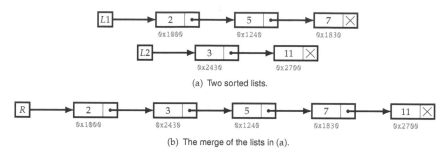

(a) Two sorted lists.

(b) The merge of the lists in (a).

Figure 8.3: Merging sorted lists.

Write a program that takes two lists, assumed to be sorted, and returns their merge. The only field your program can change in a node is its next field.

Hint: Two sorted arrays can be merged using two indices. For lists, take care when one iterator reaches the end.

Solution: A naive approach is to append the two lists together and sort the resulting list. The drawback of this approach is that it does not use the fact that the initial lists are sorted. The time complexity is that of sorting, which is $O((n + m) \log(n + m))$, where n and m are the lengths of each of the two input lists.

A better approach, in terms of time complexity, is to traverse the two lists, always choosing the node containing the smaller key to continue traversing from.

```
shared_ptr<ListNode<int>> MergeTwoSortedLists(shared_ptr<ListNode<int>> L1,
                                              shared_ptr<ListNode<int>> L2) {
  // Creates a placeholder for the result.
  shared_ptr<ListNode<int>> dummy_head(new ListNode<int>);
  auto tail = dummy_head;

  while (L1 && L2) {
    AppendNode(L1->data <= L2->data ? &L1 : &L2, &tail);
  }

  // Appends the remaining nodes of L1 or L2.
  tail->next = L1 ? L1 : L2;
  return dummy_head->next;
}

void AppendNode(shared_ptr<ListNode<int>> *node,
                shared_ptr<ListNode<int>> *tail) {
```

```
  (*tail)->next = *node;
  *tail = *node;  // Updates tail.
  *node = (*node)->next;
}
```

The worst-case, from a runtime perspective, corresponds to the case when the lists are of comparable length, so the time complexity is $O(n + m)$. (In the best-case, one list is much shorter than the other and all its entries appear at the beginning of the merged list.) Since we reuse the existing nodes, the space complexity is $O(1)$.

Variant: Solve the same problem when the lists are doubly linked.

8.2 REVERSE A SINGLY LINKED LIST

Suppose you were given a singly linked list of integers sorted in ascending order and you need to return a list with the elements sorted in descending order. Memory is scarce, but you can reuse nodes in the original list, i.e., your function can change the original list.

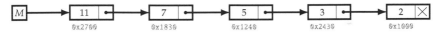

Figure 8.4: The reversed list for the list in Figure 8.3(b) on the facing page. Note that no new nodes have been allocated.

Write a function that reverses a singly linked list. The function should use no more than constant storage beyond that needed for the list itself. The desired transformation is illustrated in Figure 8.4.

Hint: Use a pair of iterators.

Solution: The natural way of implementing the reversal is through recursion. This approach has $O(n)$ time complexity, since $O(1)$ time is spent within each call, and one node is moved to its correct location.

```
shared_ptr<ListNode<int>> ReverseLinkedList(
    const shared_ptr<ListNode<int>>& head) {
  if (!head || !head->next) {
    return head;
  }
  auto new_head = ReverseLinkedList(head->next);
  head->next->next = head;
  head->next = nullptr;
  return new_head;
}
```

However, the recursive approach implicitly uses $O(n)$ space on the stack. The function is not tail recursive, which precludes compilers from automatically converting the function to an iterative one.

111

A common technique for manipulating a singly linked list is to use a temporary variable to hold information about the list that cannot be directly recovered once an update is made. For this problem, we use two pointers, one to traverse the list, and the other to record the next node, which would otherwise be lost on updates.

```
shared_ptr<ListNode<int>> ReverseLinkedList(
    const shared_ptr<ListNode<int>>& head) {
  shared_ptr<ListNode<int>> prev = nullptr, curr = head;
  while (curr) {
    auto next = curr->next;
    curr->next = prev;
    prev = curr;
    curr = next;
  }
  return prev;
}
```

The program uses $O(1)$ additional storage, and has $O(n)$ time complexity.

8.3 REVERSE A SINGLE SUBLIST

This problem is concerned with reversing a sublist within a list. See Figure 8.5 for an example of sublist reversal.

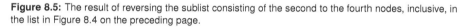

Figure 8.5: The result of reversing the sublist consisting of the second to the fourth nodes, inclusive, in the list in Figure 8.4 on the preceding page.

Write a program which takes a singly linked list L and two integers s and f as arguments, and reverses the order of the nodes from the sth node to fth node, inclusive. The numbering begins at 1, i.e., the head node is the first node. Do not allocate additional nodes.

Hint: Focus on the successor fields which have to be updated.

Solution: The direct approach is to extract the sublist, reverse it, and splice it back in. We can use Solution 8.2 on the previous page to perform the reversal. The drawback for this approach is that it requires two passes over the sublist.

The update can be performed with a single pass by combining the identification of the sublist with its reversal. We identify the start of sublist by using an iteration to get the sth node and its predecessor. Once we reach the sth node, we start the reversing process and keep counting. When we reach the fth node, we stop the reversion process and link the reverted section with the unreverted sections.

```
shared_ptr<ListNode<int>> ReverseSublist(shared_ptr<ListNode<int>> L,
                                          int start, int finish) {
```

```
if (start == finish) {  // No need to reverse since start == finish.
  return L;
}

auto dummy_head = make_shared<ListNode<int>>(ListNode<int>{0, L});
auto sublist_head = dummy_head;
int k = 1;
while (k++ < start) {
  sublist_head = sublist_head->next;
}

// Reverses sublist.
auto sublist_iter = sublist_head->next;
while (start++ < finish) {
  auto temp = sublist_iter->next;
  sublist_iter->next = temp->next;
  temp->next = sublist_head->next;
  sublist_head->next = temp;
}
return dummy_head->next;
}
```

The time complexity is dominated by the search for the fth node, i.e., $O(f)$.

8.4 TEST FOR CYCLICITY

Although a linked list is supposed to be a sequence of nodes ending in null, it is possible to create a cycle in a linked list by making the next field of an element reference to one of the earlier nodes.

Write a program that takes the head of a singly linked list and returns null if there does not exist a cycle, and the node at the start of the cycle, if a cycle is present. (You do not know the length of the list in advance.)

Hint: Consider using two iterators, one fast and one slow.

Solution: This problem has several solutions. If space is not an issue, the simplest approach is to explore nodes via the next field starting from the head and storing visited nodes in a hash table—a cycle exists if and only if we visit a node already in the hash table. If no cycle exists, the search ends at the tail (often represented by having the next field set to null). This solution requires $O(n)$ space, where n is the number of nodes in the list.

A brute-force approach that does not use additional storage and does not modify the list is to traverse the list in two loops—the outer loop traverses the nodes one-by-one, and the inner loop starts from the head, and traverses as many nodes as the outer loop has gone through so far. If the node being visited by the outer loop is visited twice, a loop has been detected. (If the outer loop encounters the end of the list, no cycle exists.) This approach has $O(n^2)$ time complexity.

This idea can be made to work in linear time—use a slow iterator and a fast iterator to traverse the list. In each iteration, advance the slow iterator by one and the fast iterator by two. The list has a cycle if and only if the two iterators meet. The reasoning is as follows: if the fast iterator jumps over the slow iterator, the slow iterator will equal the fast iterator in the next step.

Now, assuming that we have detected a cycle using the above method, we can find the start of the cycle, by first calculating the cycle length C. Once we know there is a cycle, and we have a node on it, it is trivial to compute the cycle length. To find the first node on the cycle, we use two iterators, one of which is C ahead of the other. We advance them in tandem, and when they meet, that node must be the first node on the cycle.

The code to do this traversal is quite simple:

```
shared_ptr<ListNode<int>> HasCycle(const shared_ptr<ListNode<int>>& head) {
  shared_ptr<ListNode<int>> fast = head, slow = head;

  while (fast && fast->next && fast->next->next) {
    slow = slow->next, fast = fast->next->next;
    if (slow == fast) {
      // There is a cycle, so now let's calculate the cycle length.
      int cycle_len = 0;
      do {
        ++cycle_len;
        fast = fast->next;
      } while (slow != fast);

      // Finds the start of the cycle.
      auto cycle_len_advanced_iter = head;
      while (cycle_len--) {
        cycle_len_advanced_iter = cycle_len_advanced_iter->next;
      }

      auto iter = head;
      // Both iterators advance in tandem.
      while (iter != cycle_len_advanced_iter) {
        iter = iter->next;
        cycle_len_advanced_iter = cycle_len_advanced_iter->next;
      }
      return iter;  // iter is the start of cycle.
    }
  }
  return nullptr;  // No cycle.
}
```

Let F be the number of nodes to the start of the cycle, C the number of nodes on the cycle, and n the total number of nodes. Then the time complexity is $O(F) + O(C) = O(n)$—$O(F)$ for both pointers to reach the cycle, and $O(C)$ for them to overlap once the slower one enters the cycle.

Variant: The following program purports to compute the beginning of the cycle without determining the length of the cycle; it has the benefit of being more succinct than the code listed above. Is the program correct?

```
shared_ptr<ListNode<int>> HasCycle(const shared_ptr<ListNode<int>>& head) {
  shared_ptr<ListNode<int>> fast = head, slow = head;

  while (fast && fast->next && fast->next->next) {
    slow = slow->next, fast = fast->next->next;
    if (slow == fast) {   // There is a cycle.
      // Tries to find the start of the cycle.
      slow = head;
      // Both pointers advance at the same time.
      while (slow != fast) {
        slow = slow->next, fast = fast->next;
      }
      return slow;   // slow is the start of cycle.
    }
  }
  return nullptr;   // No cycle.
}
```

8.5 TEST FOR OVERLAPPING LISTS—LISTS ARE CYCLE-FREE

Given two singly linked lists there may be list nodes that are common to both. (This may not be a bug—it may be desirable from the perspective of reducing memory footprint, as in the flyweight pattern, or maintaining a canonical form.) For example, the lists in Figure 8.6 overlap at Node I.

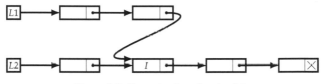

Figure 8.6: Example of overlapping lists.

Write a program that takes two cycle-free singly linked lists, and determines if there exists a node that is common to both lists.

Hint: Solve the simple cases first.

Solution: A brute-force approach is to store one list's nodes in a hash table, and then iterate through the nodes of the other, testing each for presence in the hash table. This takes $O(n)$ time and $O(n)$ space, where n is the total number of nodes.

We can avoid the extra space by using two nested loops, one iterating through the first list, and the other to search the second for the node being processed in the first list. However, the time complexity is $O(n^2)$.

The lists overlap if and only if both have the same tail node: once the lists converge at a node, they cannot diverge at a later node. Therefore, checking for overlap amounts to finding the tail nodes for each list.

To find the first overlapping node, we first compute the length of each list. The first overlapping node is determined by advancing through the longer list by the difference in lengths, and then advancing through both lists in tandem, stopping at the first common node. If we reach the end of a list without finding a common node, the lists do not overlap.

```
shared_ptr<ListNode<int>> OverlappingNoCycleLists(
    shared_ptr<ListNode<int>> L1, shared_ptr<ListNode<int>> L2) {
  int L1_len = Length(L1), L2_len = Length(L2);

  // Advances the longer list to get equal length lists.
  AdvanceListByK(abs(L1_len - L2_len), L1_len > L2_len ? &L1 : &L2);

  while (L1 && L2 && L1 != L2) {
    L1 = L1->next, L2 = L2->next;
  }
  return L1;  // nullptr implies there is no overlap between L1 and L2.
}

int Length(shared_ptr<ListNode<int>> L) {
  int length = 0;
  while (L) {
    ++length, L = L->next;
  }
  return length;
}

// Advances L by k steps.
void AdvanceListByK(int k, shared_ptr<ListNode<int>>* L) {
  while (k--) {
    *L = (*L)->next;
  }
}
```

The time complexity is $O(n)$ and the space complexity is $O(1)$.

8.6 TEST FOR OVERLAPPING LISTS—LISTS MAY HAVE CYCLES

Solve Problem 8.5 on the previous page for the case where the lists may each or both have a cycle. If such a node exists, return a node that appears first when traversing the lists. This node may not be unique—if one node ends in a cycle, the first cycle node encountered when traversing it may be different from the first cycle node encountered when traversing the second list, even though the cycle is the same. In such cases, you may return either of the two nodes.

For example, Figure 8.7 on the facing page shows an example of lists which overlap and have cycles. For this example, both A and B are acceptable answers.

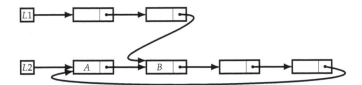

Figure 8.7: Overlapping lists.

Hint: Use case analysis. What if both lists have cycles? What if they end in a common cycle? What if one list has cycle and the other does not?

Solution: This problem is easy to solve using $O(n)$ time and space complexity, where n is the total number of nodes, using the hash table approach in Solution 8.5 on Page 115.

We can improve space complexity by studying different cases. The easiest case is when neither list is cyclic, which we can determine using Solution 8.4 on Page 113. In this case, we can check overlap using the technique in Solution 8.5 on Page 115.

If one list is cyclic, and the other is not, they cannot overlap, so we are done.

This leaves us with the case that both lists are cyclic. In this case, if they overlap, the cycles must be identical.

There are two subcases: the paths to the cycle merge before the cycle, in which case there is a unique first node that is common, or the paths reach the cycle at different nodes on the cycle. For the first case, we can use the approach of Solution 8.5 on Page 115. For the second case, we use the technique in Solution 8.4 on Page 113.

```
shared_ptr<ListNode<int>> OverlappingLists(shared_ptr<ListNode<int>> L1,
                                           shared_ptr<ListNode<int>> L2) {
  // Store the start of cycle if any.
  auto root1 = HasCycle(L1), root2 = HasCycle(L2);

  if (!root1 && !root2) {
    // Both lists don't have cycles.
    return OverlappingNoCycleLists(L1, L2);
  } else if ((root1 && !root2) || (!root1 && root2)) {
    // One list has cycle, and one list has no cycle.
    return nullptr;
  }
  // Both lists have cycles.
  auto temp = root2;
  do {
    temp = temp->next;
  } while (temp != root1 && temp != root2);

  // L1 and L2 do not end in the same cycle.
  if (temp != root1) {
    return nullptr;  // Cycles are disjoint.
  }
```

```
// L1 and L2 end in the same cycle, locate the overlapping node if they
// first overlap before cycle starts.
int stem1_length = Distance(L1, root1), stem2_length = Distance(L2, root2);
AdvanceListByK(abs(stem1_length - stem2_length),
               stem1_length > stem2_length ? &L1 : &L2);
while (L1 != L2 && L1 != root1 && L2 != root2) {
  L1 = L1->next, L2 = L2->next;
}

// If L1 == L2 before reaching root1, it means the overlap first occurs
// before the cycle starts; otherwise, the first overlapping node is not
// unique, so we can return any node on the cycle.
return L1 == L2 ? L1 : root1;
}

// Calculates the distance between a and b.
int Distance(shared_ptr<ListNode<int>> a, shared_ptr<ListNode<int>> b) {
  int dis = 0;
  while (a != b) {
    a = a->next, ++dis;
  }
  return dis;
}
```

The algorithm has time complexity $O(n + m)$, where n and m are the lengths of the input lists, and space complexity $O(1)$.

8.7 DELETE A NODE FROM A SINGLY LINKED LIST

Given a node in a singly linked list, deleting it in $O(1)$ time appears impossible because its predecessor's next field has to be updated. Surprisingly, it can be done with one small caveat—the node to delete cannot be the last one in the list and it is easy to copy the value part of a node.

Write a program which deletes a node in a singly linked list. The input node is guaranteed not to be the tail node.

Hint: Instead of deleting the node, can you delete its successor and still achieve the desired configuration?

Solution: Given the pointer to a node, it is impossible to delete it from the list without modifying its predecessor's next pointer and the only way to get to the predecessor is to traverse the list from head, which requires $O(n)$ time, where n is the number of nodes in the list.

Given a node, it is easy to delete its successor, since this just requires updating the next pointer of the current node. If we copy the value part of the next node to the current node, and then delete the next node, we have effectively deleted the current node. The time complexity is $O(1)$.

118

```
// Assumes node_to_delete is not tail.
void DeletionFromList(const shared_ptr<ListNode<int>>& node_to_delete) {
  node_to_delete->data = node_to_delete->next->data;
  node_to_delete->next = node_to_delete->next->next;
}
```

8.8 REMOVE THE kTH LAST ELEMENT FROM A LIST

Without knowing the length of a linked list, it is not trivial to delete the kth last element in a singly linked list.

Given a singly linked list and an integer k, write a program to remove the kth last element from the list. Your algorithm cannot use more than a few words of storage, regardless of the length of the list. In particular, you cannot assume that it is possible to record the length of the list.

Hint: If you know the length of the list, can you find the kth last node using two iterators?

Solution: A brute-force approach is to compute the length with one pass, and then use that to determine which node to delete in a second pass. A drawback of this approach is that it entails two passes over the data, which is slow, e.g., if traversing the list entails disc accesses.

We use two iterators to traverse the list. The first iterator is advanced by k steps, and then the two iterators advance in tandem. When the first iterator reaches the tail, the second iterator is at the $(k + 1)$th last node, and we can remove the kth node.

```
// Assumes L has at least k nodes, deletes the k-th last node in L.
shared_ptr<ListNode<int>> RemoveKthLast(const shared_ptr<ListNode<int>>& L,
                                        int k) {
  auto dummy_head = make_shared<ListNode<int>>(ListNode<int>{0, L});
  auto first = dummy_head->next;
  while (k--) {
    first = first->next;
  }

  auto second = dummy_head;
  while (first) {
    second = second->next, first = first->next;
  }
  // second points to the (k + 1)-th last node, deletes its successor.
  second->next = second->next->next;
  return dummy_head->next;
}
```

The time complexity is that of list traversal, i.e., $O(n)$, where n is the length of the list. The space complexity is $O(1)$, since there are only two iterators.

Compared to the brute-force approach, if k is small enough that we can keep the set of nodes between the two iterators in memory, but the list is too big to fit in memory, the two-iterator approach halves the number of disc accesses.

8.9 REMOVE DUPLICATES FROM A SORTED LIST

This problem is concerned with removing duplicates from a sorted list of integers. See Figure 8.8 for an example.

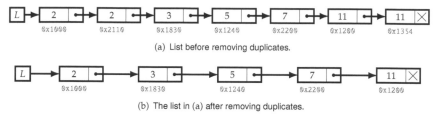

(a) List before removing duplicates.

(b) The list in (a) after removing duplicates.

Figure 8.8: Example of duplicate removal.

Write a program that takes as input a singly linked list of integers in sorted order, and removes duplicates from it. The list should be sorted.

Hint: Focus on the successor fields which have to be updated.

Solution: A brute-force algorithm is to create a new list, using a hash table to test if a value has already been added to the new list. Alternatively, we could search in the new list itself to see if the candidate value already is present. If the length of the list is n, the first approach requires $O(n)$ additional space for the hash table, and the second requires $O(n^2)$ time to perform the lookups. Both allocate n nodes for the new list.

A better approach is to exploit the sorted nature of the list. As we traverse the list, we remove all successive nodes with the same value as the current node.

```
shared_ptr<ListNode<int>> RemoveDuplicates(
    const shared_ptr<ListNode<int>>& L) {
  auto iter = L;
  while (iter) {
    // Uses next_distinct to find the next distinct value.
    auto next_distinct = iter->next;
    while (next_distinct && next_distinct->data == iter->data) {
      next_distinct = next_distinct->next;
    }
    iter->next = next_distinct;
    iter = next_distinct;
  }
  return L;
}
```

Figure 8.9: The result of applying a right cyclic shift by 3 to the list in Figure 8.1 on Page 109. Note that no new nodes have been allocated.

Determining the time complexity requires a little amortized analysis. A single node may take more than $O(1)$ time to process if there are many successive nodes with the same value. A clearer justification for the time complexity is that each link is traversed once, so the time complexity is $O(n)$. The space complexity is $O(1)$.

Variant: Let m be a positive integer and L a sorted singly linked list of integers. For each integer k, if k appears more than m times in L, remove all nodes from L containing k.

8.10 IMPLEMENT CYCLIC RIGHT SHIFT FOR SINGLY LINKED LISTS

This problem is concerned with performing a cyclic right shift on a list.

Write a program that takes as input a singly linked list and a nonnegative integer k, and returns the list cyclically shifted to the right by k. See Figure 8.9 for an example of a cyclic right shift.

Hint: How does this problem differ from rotating an array?

Solution: A brute-force strategy is to right shift the list by one node k times. Each right shift by a single node entails finding the tail, and its predecessor. The tail is prepended to the current head, and its original predecessor's successor is set to null to make it the new tail. The time complexity is $O(kn)$, and the space complexity is $O(1)$, where n is the number of nodes in the list.

Note that k may be larger than n. If so, it is equivalent to shift by $k \bmod n$, so we assume $k < n$. The key to improving upon the brute-force approach is to use the fact that linked lists can be cut and the sublists reassembled very efficiently. First we find the tail node t. Since the successor of the tail is the original head, we update t's successor. The original head is to become the kth node from the start of the new list. Therefore, the new head is the $(n - k)$th node in the initial list.

```
shared_ptr<ListNode<int>> CyclicallyRightShiftList(shared_ptr<ListNode<int>> L,
                                                    int k) {
  if (L == nullptr) {
    return L;
  }

  // Computes the length of L and the tail.
  auto tail = L;
  int n = 1;
  while (tail->next) {
    ++n, tail = tail->next;
```

```
  }
  k %= n;
  if (k == 0) {
    return L;
  }

  tail->next = L;  // Makes a cycle by connecting the tail to the head.
  int steps_to_new_head = n - k;
  auto new_tail = tail;
  while (steps_to_new_head--) {
    new_tail = new_tail->next;
  }
  auto new_head = new_tail->next;
  new_tail->next = nullptr;
  return new_head;
}
```

The time complexity is $O(n)$, and the space complexity is $O(1)$.

8.11 IMPLEMENT EVEN-ODD MERGE

Consider a singly linked list whose nodes are numbered starting at 0. Define the even-odd merge of the list to be the list consisting of the even-numbered nodes followed by the odd-numbered nodes. The even-odd merge is illustrated in Figure 8.10.

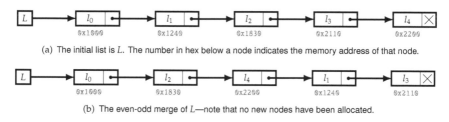

(a) The initial list is L. The number in hex below a node indicates the memory address of that node.

(b) The even-odd merge of L—note that no new nodes have been allocated.

Figure 8.10: Even-odd merge example.

Write a program that computes the even-odd merge.

Hint: Use temporary additional storage.

Solution: The brute-force algorithm is to allocate new nodes and compute two new lists, one for the even and one for the odd nodes. The result is the first list concatenated with the second list. The time and space complexity are both $O(n)$.

However, we can avoid the extra space by reusing the existing list nodes. We do this by iterating through the list, and appending even elements to one list and odd elements to another list. We use an indicator variable to tell us which list to append to. Finally we append the odd list to the even list.

```
shared_ptr<ListNode<int>> EvenOddMerge(const shared_ptr<ListNode<int>>& L) {
    const shared_ptr<ListNode<int>>& L) {
```

```cpp
  if (L == nullptr) {
    return L;
  }

  auto even_dummy_head =
      make_shared<ListNode<int>>(ListNode<int>{0, nullptr}),
      odd_dummy_head =
          make_shared<ListNode<int>>(ListNode<int>{0, nullptr});
  array<shared_ptr<ListNode<int>>, 2> tails = {even_dummy_head,
                                               odd_dummy_head};
  int turn = 0;
  for (auto iter = L; iter; iter = iter->next) {
    tails[turn]->next = iter;
    tails[turn] = tails[turn]->next;
    turn ^= 1;  // Alternate between even and odd.
  }
  tails[1]->next = nullptr;
  tails[0]->next = odd_dummy_head->next;
  return even_dummy_head->next;
}
```

The time complexity is $O(n)$ and the space complexity is $O(1)$.

8.12 TEST WHETHER A SINGLY LINKED LIST IS PALINDROMIC

It is straightforward to check whether the sequence stored in an array is a palindrome. However, if this sequence is stored as a singly linked list, the problem of detecting palindromicity becomes more challenging. See Figure 8.1 on Page 109 for an example of a palindromic singly linked list.

Write a program that tests whether a singly linked list is palindromic.

Hint: It's easy if you can traverse the list forwards and backwards simultaneously.

Solution: A brute-force algorithm is to compare the first and last nodes, then the second and second-to-last nodes, etc. The time complexity is $O(n^2)$, where n is the number of nodes in the list. The space complexity is $O(1)$.

The $O(n^2)$ complexity comes from having to repeatedly traverse the list to identify the last, second-to-last, etc. Getting the first node in a singly linked list is an $O(1)$ time operation. This suggests paying a one-time cost of $O(n)$ time complexity to get the reverse of the second half of the original list, after which testing palindromicity of the original list reduces to testing if the first half and the reversed second half are equal. This approach changes the list passed in, but the reversed sublist can be reversed again to restore the original list.

```cpp
bool IsLinkedListAPalindrome(shared_ptr<ListNode<int>> L) {
  if (L == nullptr) {
    return true;
  }
}
```

```
// Finds the second half of L.
shared_ptr<ListNode<int>> slow = L, fast = L;
while (fast && fast->next) {
  fast = fast->next->next, slow = slow->next;
}

// Compares the first half and the reversed second half lists.
auto first_half_iter = L, second_half_iter = ReverseLinkedList(slow);
while (second_half_iter && first_half_iter) {
  if (second_half_iter->data != first_half_iter->data) {
    return false;
  }
  second_half_iter = second_half_iter->next;
  first_half_iter = first_half_iter->next;
}
return true;
}
```

The time complexity is $O(n)$. The space complexity is $O(1)$.

Variant: Solve the same problem when the list is doubly linked and you have pointers to the head and the tail.

8.13 IMPLEMENT LIST PIVOTING

For any integer k, the pivot of a list of integers with respect to k is that list with its nodes reordered so that all nodes containing keys less than k appear before nodes containing k, and all nodes containing keys greater than k appear after the nodes containing k. See Figure 8.11 for an example of pivoting.

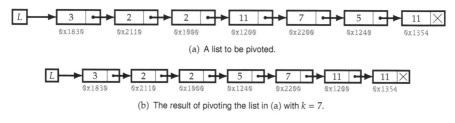

(a) A list to be pivoted.

(b) The result of pivoting the list in (a) with $k = 7$.

Figure 8.11: List pivoting.

Implement a function which takes as input a singly linked list and an integer k and performs a pivot of the list with respect to k. The relative ordering of nodes that appear before k, and after k, must remain unchanged; the same must hold for nodes holding keys equal to k.

Hint: Form the three regions independently.

Solution: A brute-force approach is to form three lists by iterating through the list and writing values into one of the three new lists based on whether the current value is less than, equal to, or greater than k. We then traverse the list from the head, and overwrite values in the original list from the less than, then equal to, and finally greater than lists. The time and space complexity are $O(n)$, where n is the number of nodes in the list.

A key observation is that we do not really need to create new nodes for the three lists. Instead we reorganize the original list nodes into these three lists in a single traversal of the original list. Since the traversal is in order, the individual lists preserve the ordering. We combine these three lists in the final step.

```cpp
shared_ptr<ListNode<int>> ListPivoting(const shared_ptr<ListNode<int>>& L,
                                       int x) {
  shared_ptr<ListNode<int>> less_head(new ListNode<int>),
      equal_head(new ListNode<int>), greater_head(new ListNode<int>);
  shared_ptr<ListNode<int>> less_iter = less_head, equal_iter = equal_head,
                            greater_iter = greater_head;
  // Populates the three lists.
  shared_ptr<ListNode<int>> iter = L;
  while (iter) {
    AppendNode(&iter, iter->data < x ? &less_iter : iter->data == x
                                        ? &equal_iter
                                        : &greater_iter);
  }
  // Combines the three lists.
  greater_iter->next = nullptr;
  equal_iter->next = greater_head->next;
  less_iter->next = equal_head->next;
  return less_head->next;
}
```

The time to compute the three lists is $O(n)$. Combining the lists takes $O(1)$ time, yielding an overall $O(n)$ time complexity. The space complexity is $O(1)$.

8.14   ADD LIST-BASED INTEGERS

A singly linked list whose nodes contain digits can be viewed as an integer, with the least significant digit coming first. Such a representation can be used to represent unbounded integers. This problem is concerned with adding integers represented in this fashion. See Figure 8.12 for an example.

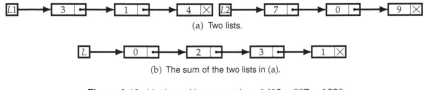

(a) Two lists.

(b) The sum of the two lists in (a).

Figure 8.12: List-based interpretation of $413 + 907 = 1320$.

125

Write a program which takes two singly linked lists of digits, and returns the list corresponding to the sum of the integers they represent. The least significant digit comes first.

Hint: First, solve the problem assuming no pair of corresponding digits sum to more than 9.

Solution: Note that we cannot simply convert the lists to integers, since the integer word length is fixed by the machine architecture, and the lists can be arbitrarily long.

Instead we mimic the grade-school algorithm, i.e., we compute the sum of the digits in corresponding nodes in the two lists. A key nuance of the computation is handling the carry-out from a particular place. Care has to be taken to remember to allocate an additional node if the final carry is nonzero.

```
shared_ptr<ListNode<int>> AddTwoNumbers(shared_ptr<ListNode<int>> L1,
                                        shared_ptr<ListNode<int>> L2) {
  shared_ptr<ListNode<int>> dummy_head(new ListNode<int>);
  auto place_iter = dummy_head;
  int carry = 0;
  while (L1 || L2) {
    int sum = carry;
    if (L1) {
      sum += L1->data;
      L1 = L1->next;
    }
    if (L2) {
      sum += L2->data;
      L2 = L2->next;
    }
    place_iter->next =
        make_shared<ListNode<int>>(ListNode<int>{sum % 10, nullptr});
    carry = sum / 10, place_iter = place_iter->next;
  }
  // carry cannot exceed 1, so we never need to add more than one node.
  if (carry) {
    place_iter->next =
        make_shared<ListNode<int>>(ListNode<int>{carry, nullptr});
  }
  return dummy_head->next;
}
```

The time complexity is $O(n + m)$ and the space complexity is $O(\max(n, m))$, where n and m are the lengths of the two lists.

Variant: Solve the same problem when integers are represented as lists of digits with the most significant digit comes first.

9

Stacks and Queues

*Linear lists in which insertions, deletions, and accesses
to values occur almost always at the first or the last
node are very frequently encountered, and we give
them special names . . .*

— *"The Art of Computer Programming, Volume 1,"*
D. E. KNUTH, 1997

Stacks

A *stack* supports two basic operations—push and pop. Elements are added (pushed)
and removed (popped) in last-in, first-out order, as shown in Figure 9.1. If the stack
is empty, pop typically returns null or throws an exception.

When the stack is implemented using a linked list these operations have $O(1)$
time complexity. If it is implemented using an array, there is maximum number of
entries it can have—push and pop are still $O(1)$. If the array is dynamically resized,
the amortized time for both push and pop is $O(1)$. A stack can support additional
operations such as peek, which returns the top of the stack without popping it.

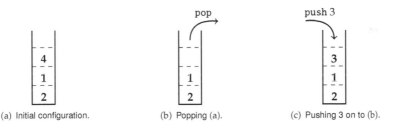

(a) Initial configuration. (b) Popping (a). (c) Pushing 3 on to (b).

Figure 9.1: Operations on a stack.

9.1 IMPLEMENT A STACK WITH MAX API

Design a stack that includes a max operation, in addition to push and pop. The max
method should return the maximum value stored in the stack.

Hint: Use additional storage to track the maximum value.

Solution: The simplest way to implement a max operation is to consider each element
in the stack, e.g., by iterating through the underlying array for an array-based stack.

The time complexity is $O(n)$ and the space complexity is $O(1)$, where n is the number of elements currently in the stack.

The time complexity can be reduced to $O(\log n)$ using auxiliary data structures, specifically, a heap or a BST, and a hash table. The space complexity increases to $O(n)$ and the code is quite complex.

Suppose we use a single auxiliary variable, M, to record the element that is maximum in the stack. Updating M on pushes is easy: $M = \max(M, e)$, where e is the element being pushed. However, updating M on pop is very time consuming. If M is the element being popped, we have no way of knowing what the maximum remaining element is, and are forced to consider all the remaining elements.

We can dramatically improve on the time complexity of popping by caching, in essence, trading time for space. Specifically, for each entry in the stack, we cache the maximum stored at or below that entry. Now when we pop, we evict the corresponding cached value.

```cpp
class Stack {
public:
  bool Empty() const { return element_with_cached_max_.empty(); }

  int Max() const {
    if (Empty()) {
      throw length_error("Max(): empty stack");
    }
    return element_with_cached_max_.top().max;
  }

  int Pop() {
    if (Empty()) {
      throw length_error("Pop(): empty stack");
    }
    int pop_element = element_with_cached_max_.top().element;
    element_with_cached_max_.pop();
    return pop_element;
  }

  void Push(int x) {
    element_with_cached_max_.emplace(
        ElementWithCachedMax{x, max(x, Empty() ? x : Max())});
  }

 private:
  struct ElementWithCachedMax {
    int element, max;
  };
  stack<ElementWithCachedMax> element_with_cached_max_;
};
```

Each of the specified methods has time complexity $O(1)$. The additional space complexity is $O(n)$, regardless of the stored keys.

We can improve on the best-case space needed by observing that if an element e being pushed is smaller than the maximum element already in the stack, then e can never be the maximum, so we do not need to record it. We cannot store the sequence of maximum values in a separate stack because of the possibility of duplicates. We resolve this by additionally recording the number of occurrences of each maximum value. See Figure 9.2 on the next page for an example.

```cpp
class Stack {
 public:
  bool Empty() const { return element_.empty(); }

  int Max() const {
    if (Empty()) {
      throw length_error("Max(): empty stack");
    }
    return cached_max_with_count_.top().max;
  }

  int Pop() {
    if (Empty()) {
      throw length_error("Pop(): empty stack");
    }
    int pop_element = element_.top();
    element_.pop();
    const int current_max = cached_max_with_count_.top().max;
    if (pop_element == current_max) {
      int& max_frequency = cached_max_with_count_.top().count;
      --max_frequency;
      if (max_frequency == 0) {
        cached_max_with_count_.pop();
      }
    }
    return pop_element;
  }

  void Push(int x) {
    element_.emplace(x);
    if (cached_max_with_count_.empty()) {
      cached_max_with_count_.emplace(MaxWithCount{x, 1});
    } else {
      const int current_max = cached_max_with_count_.top().max;
      if (x == current_max) {
        int& max_frequency = cached_max_with_count_.top().count;
        ++max_frequency;
      } else if (x > current_max) {
        cached_max_with_count_.emplace(MaxWithCount{x, 1});
      }
    }
  }

 private:
  stack<int> element_;

  struct MaxWithCount {
    int max, count;
  };
```

129

```
    stack<MaxWithCount> cached_max_with_count_;
};
```

The worst-case additional space complexity is $O(n)$, which occurs when each key pushed is greater than all keys in the primary stack. However, when the number of distinct keys is small, or the maximum changes infrequently, the additional space complexity is less, $O(1)$ in the best-case. The time complexity for each specified method is still $O(1)$.

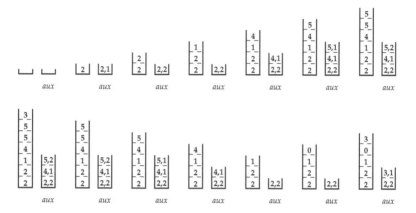

Figure 9.2: The primary and auxiliary stacks for the following operations: push 2, push 2, push 1, push 4, push 5, push 5, push 3, pop, pop, pop, pop, push 0, push 3. Both stacks are initially empty, and their progression is shown from left-to-right, then top-to-bottom. The top of the auxiliary stack holds the maximum element in the stack, and the number of times that element occurs in the stack. The auxiliary stack is denoted by *aux*.

9.2 EVALUATE RPN EXPRESSIONS

A string is said to be an arithmetical expression in Reverse Polish notation (RPN) if:

(1.) It is a single digit or a sequence of digits, prefixed with an option −, e.g., "6", "123", "−42".

(2.) It is of the form "$A, B, \circ$" where A and B are RPN expressions and $\circ$ is one of $+, -, \times, /$.

For example, the following strings satisfy these rules: "1729", "$3, 4, +, 2, \times, 1, +$", "$1, 1, +, -2, \times$", "$-641, 6, /, 28, /$".

An RPN expression can be evaluated uniquely to an integer, which is determined recursively. The base case corresponds to Rule (1.), which is an integer expressed in base-10 positional system. Rule (2.)corresponds to the recursive case, and the RPNs are evaluated in the natural way, e.g., if A evaluates to 2 and B evaluates to 3, then "$A, B, \times$" evaluates to 6.

Write a program that takes an arithmetical expression in RPN and returns the number that the expression evaluates to.

Hint: Process subexpressions, keeping values in a stack. How should operators be handled?

Solution: Let's begin with the RPN example "3, 4, +, 2, ×, 1, + The ordinary form for this is $(3 + 4) \times 2 + 1$. To evaluate this by hand, we would scan from left to right. We record 3, then 4, then applying the + to 3 and 4, and record the result, 7. Note that we never need to examine the 3 and 4 again. Next we multiply by 2, and record the result, 14. Finally, we add 1 to obtain the final result, 15.

Observe that we need to record partial results, and as we encounter operators, we apply them to the partial results. The partial results are added and removed in last-in, first-out order, which makes a stack the natural data structure for evaluating RPN expressions.

```
int Eval(const string& RPN_expression) {
  stack<int> intermediate_results;
  stringstream ss(RPN_expression);
  string token;
  const char kDelimiter = ',';

  while (getline(ss, token, kDelimiter)) {
    if (token == "+" || token == "-" || token == "*" || token == "/") {
      int y = intermediate_results.top();
      intermediate_results.pop();
      int x = intermediate_results.top();
      intermediate_results.pop();
      switch (token.front()) {
        case '+':
          intermediate_results.emplace(x + y);
          break;
        case '-':
          intermediate_results.emplace(x - y);
          break;
        case '*':
          intermediate_results.emplace(x * y);
          break;
        case '/':
          intermediate_results.emplace(x / y);
          break;
      }
    } else {  // token is a number.
      intermediate_results.emplace(stoi(token));
    }
  }
  return intermediate_results.top();
}
```

Since we perform $O(1)$ computation per character of the string, the time complexity is $O(n)$, where n is the length of the string.

Variant: Solve the same problem for expressions in Polish notation, i.e., when $A, B, \circ$ is replaced by $\circ, A, B$ in Rule (2.) on the facing page.

A string over the characters "{,},(,),[,]" is said to be well-formed if the different types of brackets match in the correct order.

For example, "([]){()}" is well-formed, as is "[()[]{()()}]". However, "{)" and "[()[]{()()" are not well-formed,

Write a program that tests if a string made up of the characters '(', ')', '[', ']','{' and'}' is well-formed.

Hint: Which left parenthesis does a right parenthesis match with?

Solution: Let's begin with well-formed strings consisting solely of left and right parentheses, e.g., "()(())". If such a string is well-formed, each right parenthesis must match the closest left parenthesis to its left. Therefore, starting from the left, every time we see a left parenthesis, we store it. Each time we see a right parenthesis, we match it with a stored left parenthesis. Since there are not brackets or braces, we can simply keep a count of the number of unmatched left parentheses.

For the general case, we do the same, except that we need to explicitly store the unmatched left characters, i.e., left parenthesis, left brackets, and left braces. We cannot use three counters, because that will not tell us the last unmatched one. A stack is a perfect option for this application: we use it to record the unmatched left characters, with the most recent one at the top.

If we encounter a right character and the stack is empty or the top of the stack is a different type of left character, the right character is not matched, implying the string is not matched. If all characters have been processed and the stack is nonempty, there are unmatched left characters so the string is not matched.

```cpp
bool IsWellFormed(const string& s) {
  stack<char> left_chars;
  for (size_t i = 0; i < s.size(); ++i) {
    if (s[i] == '(' || s[i] == '{' || s[i] == '[') {
      left_chars.emplace(s[i]);
    } else {
      if (left_chars.empty()) {
        return false;  // Unmatched right char.
      }
      if ((s[i] == ')' && left_chars.top() != '(') ||
          (s[i] == '}' && left_chars.top() != '{') ||
          (s[i] == ']' && left_chars.top() != '[')) {
        return false;  // Mismatched chars.
      }
      left_chars.pop();
    }
  }
  return left_chars.empty();
}
```

The time complexity is $O(n)$ since for each character we perform $O(1)$ operations.

A file or directory can be specified via a string called the pathname. This string may specify an absolute path, starting from the root, e.g., /usr/bin/gcc, or a path relative to the current working directory, e.g., scripts/awkscripts.

The same directory may be specified by multiple directory paths. For example, /usr/lib/../bin/gcc and scripts//./../scripts/awkscripts/././ specify equivalent absolute and relative pathnames.

Write a program which takes a pathname, and returns the shortest equivalent pathname. Assume individual directories and files have names that use only alphanumeric characters. Subdirectory names may be combined using forward slashes (/), the current directory (.), and parent directory (..).

Hint: Trace the cases. How should . and .. be handled? Watch for invalid paths.

Solution: It is natural to process the string from left-to-right, splitting on forward slashes (/s). We record directory and file names. Each time we encounter a .., we delete the most recent name, which corresponds to going up directory hierarchy. Since names are processed in a last-in, first-out order, it is natural to store them in a stack. Individual periods (.s) are skipped.

If the string begins with /, then we cannot go up from it. We record this in the stack. If the stack does not begin with /, we may encounter an empty stack when processing .., which indicates a path that begins with an ancestor of the current working path. We need to record this in order to give the shortest equivalent path. The final state of the stack directly corresponds to the shortest equivalent directory path.

For example, if the string is sc//./../tc/awk/././, the stack progression is as follows: ⟨sc⟩, ⟨⟩, ⟨tc⟩, ⟨tc, awk⟩. Note that we skip three .s and the / after sc/.

```
string ShortestEquivalentPath(const string& path) {
  if (path.empty()) {
    throw invalid_argument("Empty string is not a valid path.");
  }

  vector<string> path_names;  // Uses vector as a stack.
  // Special case: starts with "/", which is an absolute path.
  if (path.front() == '/') {
    path_names.emplace_back("/");
  }

  stringstream ss(path);
  string token;
  while (getline(ss, token, '/')) {
    if (token == "..") {
      if (path_names.empty() || path_names.back() == "..") {
        path_names.emplace_back(token);
      } else {
        if (path_names.back() == "/") {
          throw invalid_argument("Path error");
        }
```

```
      path_names.pop_back();
    }
  } else if (token != "." && token != "") {  // Must be a name.
    path_names.emplace_back(token);
  }
}

string result;
if (!path_names.empty()) {
  result = path_names.front();
  for (int i = 1; i < path_names.size(); ++i) {
    if (i == 1 && result == "/") {  // Avoid starting "//".
      result += path_names[i];
    } else {
      result += "/" + path_names[i];
    }
  }
}
return result;
}
```

The time complexity is $O(n)$, where n is the length of the pathname.

9.5 BST KEYS IN SORT ORDER

BSTs are the subject of Chapter 15. See Page 250 for a definition and an example of a BST.

Given a BST node, compute all the keys at that node and its descendants. The nodes should be returned in sorted order, and you cannot use recursion. For example, for Node I in the BST in Figure 15.1 on Page 251 you should return the sequence $\langle 23, 29, 31, 37, 41, 43, 47, 53 \rangle$.

Hint: In a recursive program for iterating over BST keys in sorted order, the function call stack implicitly hold values—simulate it.

Solution: The recursive solution is trivial—first add the left subtree, then add the root, and finally add the right subtree. This algorithm can be converted into a iterative algorithm by using an explicit stack. Several implementations are possible; the one below is noteworthy in that it pushes the current node, and not its right child. Furthermore, it does not use a visited field.

```
vector<int> BSTInSortedOrder(const unique_ptr<BSTNode<int>>& tree) {
  stack<const BSTNode<int>*> s;
  const auto* curr = tree.get();
  vector<int> result;

  while (!s.empty() || curr) {
    if (curr) {
      s.push(curr);
      // Going left.
      curr = curr->left.get();
```

```
      } else {
        // Going up.
        curr = s.top();
        s.pop();
        result.emplace_back(curr->data);
        // Going right.
        curr = curr->right.get();
      }
  }
  return result;
}
```

For the given example, the stack evolves as follows: $\langle\rangle$, $\langle 43\rangle$, $\langle 43,23\rangle$, $\langle 43\rangle$, $\langle 43,37\rangle$, $\langle 43,37,29\rangle$, $\langle 43,37\rangle$, $\langle 43,37,31\rangle$, $\langle 43,37\rangle$, $\langle 43\rangle$, $\langle 43,41\rangle$, $\langle 43\rangle$, $\langle\rangle$, $\langle 47\rangle$, $\langle\rangle$, $\langle 53\rangle$, $\langle\rangle$.

The time complexity is $O(n)$, since the total time spent on each node is $O(1)$. The space complexity is $O(h)$, where h is the height of the tree. This space is allocated dynamically, specifically it is the maximum depth of the function call stack. See Page 147 for a definition of tree height.

9.6 SEARCH A POSTINGS LIST

A postings list is a singly linked list with an additional "jump" field at each node. The jump field points to any other node. Figure 9.3 illustrates a postings list with four nodes.

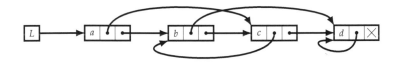

Figure 9.3: A postings list.

One way to enumerate the nodes in a postings list is to iteratively follow the next field. Another is to always first follow the jump field if it leads to a node that has not been explored previously, and then search from the next node. Call the order in which these nodes are traversed the jump-first order.

Write recursive and iterative routines that take a postings list, and compute the jump-first order. Assume each node has an integer-valued field that holds the order, and is initialized to -1.

Hint: Recursion makes the problem trivial. Mimic the recursion with a stack.

Solution: The recursive algorithm directly follows the specification. If the current node is unvisited, update the current node's order, visit its jump node, then visit the next node.

```
void SetJumpOrder(const shared_ptr<PostingListNode>& L) {
  int order = 0;
```

135

```
  SetJumpOrderHelper(L, &order);
}

void SetJumpOrderHelper(const shared_ptr<PostingListNode>& L, int* order) {
  if (L && L->order == -1) {
    L->order = (*order)++;
    SetJumpOrderHelper(L->jump, order);
    SetJumpOrderHelper(L->next, order);
  }
}
```

The iterative solution uses a stack to simulate the recursive algorithm. The key insight is that for every node, we want to visit its next node after visiting its jump node. A stack works well because of its last-in, first-out semantics. Specifically, when processing a node, we push its next node on to the stack and then we push its jump node on to the stack. This way we process the jump node before the next node.

```
void SetJumpOrder(const shared_ptr<PostingListNode>& L) {
  stack<shared_ptr<PostingListNode>> s;
  int order = 0;
  s.emplace(L);
  while (!s.empty()) {
    auto curr = s.top();
    s.pop();
    if (curr && curr->order == -1) {
      curr->order = order++;
      // Stack is last-in, first-out, and we want to process
      // the jump node first, so push next, then push jump.
      s.emplace(curr->next);
      s.emplace(curr->jump);
    }
  }
}
```

Let n denote the number of tree nodes. For both algorithms, the time complexity is $O(n)$, since the total time spent on each node is $O(1)$, and the space complexity is $O(n)$. The recursive implementation has a maximum function call stack depth of n; the iterative implementation has a maximum stack size of n. A worst-case input is one where every node's jump node and next node are equal.

9.7 COMPUTE BUILDINGS WITH A SUNSET VIEW

You are given with a series of buildings that have windows facing west. The buildings are in a straight line, and any building which is to the east of a building of equal or greater height cannot view the sunset.

Design an algorithm that processes buildings in east-to-west order and returns the set of buildings which view the sunset. Each building is specified by its height.

Hint: When does a building not have a sunset view?

136

Solution: A brute-force approach is to store all buildings in an array. We then do a reverse scan of this array, tracking the running maximum. Any building whose height is less than or equal to the running maximum does not have a sunset view.

The time and space complexity are both $O(n)$, where n is the number of buildings.

Note that if a building is to the east of a taller building, it cannot view the sunset. This suggests a way to reduce the space complexity. We record buildings which potentially have a view. Each new building may block views from the existing set. We determine which such buildings are blocked by comparing the new building's height to that of the buildings in the existing set. We can store the existing set as a hash set—this requires us to iterate over all buildings each time a new building is processed.

If a new building is shorter than a building in the current set, then all buildings in the current set which are further to the east cannot be blocked by the new building. This suggests keeping the buildings in a last-in, first-out manner, so that we can terminate earlier.

Specifically, we use a stack to record buildings that have a view. Each time a building b is processed, if it is taller than the building at the top of the stack, we pop the stack until the top of the stack is taller than b—all the buildings thus removed lie to the east of a taller building.

Although some individual steps may require many pops, each building is pushed and popped at most once. Therefore, the run time to process n buildings is $O(n)$, and the stack always holds precisely the buildings which currently have a view.

The memory used is $O(n)$, and the bound is tight, even when only one building has a view—consider the input where the west-most building is the tallest, and the remaining $n - 1$ buildings decrease in height from east to west. However, in the best-case, e.g., when buildings appear in increasing height, we use $O(1)$ space. In contrast, the brute-force approach always uses $O(n)$ space.

```cpp
vector<int> ExamineBuildingsWithSunset(istringstream* sin) {
  int building_idx = 0, building_height;
  struct BuildingWithHeight {
    int id, height;
  };
  stack<BuildingWithHeight> candidates;
  while (*sin >> building_height) {
    while (!candidates.empty() && building_height >= candidates.top().height) {
      candidates.pop();
    }
    candidates.emplace(BuildingWithHeight{building_idx++, building_height});
  }

  vector<int> buildings_with_sunset;
  while (!candidates.empty()) {
    buildings_with_sunset.emplace_back(candidates.top().id);
    candidates.pop();
  }
  return buildings_with_sunset;
}
```

Variant: Solve the problem subject to the same constraints when buildings are presented in west-to-east order.

9.8 SORT A STACK

Design an algorithm to sort a stack in descending order, i.e., the top of the stack holds the largest value. The only operations allowed are push, pop, top (which returns the top of the stack without removing it), and checking if the stack is empty. You cannot explicitly allocate memory outside of a few words.

Hint: Simulate insertion sort.

Solution: The brute-force approach is to allocate a new array made up of the stack elements, sort it, and write it to the stack. However, this entails allocating $O(n)$ space, where n is the number of entries in the stack, which violates the requirement that we do not explicitly allocate memory.

The key idea is to incrementally build up the sorted region of the stack. We do this using recursion—pop the stack and store the result in a variable e, sort the popped stack, then insert e in the right place. The insertion is also done using recursion—if e is greater than or equal to the element at the top of the stack, then push e and return, else pop the stack, storing the popped value in a variable f, insert e in the popped stack, then push f. For both the sort and the insert functions the empty stack is the base case.

```cpp
void Sort(stack<int>* S) {
  if (!S->empty()) {
    int val = S->top();
    S->pop();
    Sort(S);
    Insert(val, S);
  }
}

void Insert(int val, stack<int>* S) {
  if (S->empty() || S->top() <= val) {
    S->push(val);
  } else {
    int f = S->top();
    S->pop();
    Insert(val, S);
    S->push(f);
  }
}
```

The time complexity is $O(n^2)$; the worst-case input is one where the initial stack is sorted in descending order. Note that although the program does not perform any explicit allocation, it uses $O(n)$ storage on the function call stack.

Queues

A *queue* supports two basic operations—enqueue and dequeue. (If the queue is empty, dequeue typically returns null or throws an exception.) Elements are added (enqueued) and removed (dequeued) in first-in, first-out order. The most recently inserted element is referred to as the tail or back element, and the item that was inserted least recently is referred to as the head or front element.

A queue can be implemented using a linked list, in which case these operations have $O(1)$ time complexity. The queue API often includes other operations, e.g., a method that returns the item at the head of the queue without removing it, a method that returns the item at the tail of the queue without removing it, etc. A queue can also be implemented using an array; see Problem 9.10 on Page 141 for details.

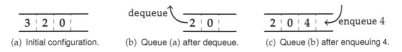

| (a) Initial configuration. | (b) Queue (a) after dequeue. | (c) Queue (b) after enqueuing 4. |

Figure 9.4: Examples of enqueuing and dequeuing.

A *deque*, also sometimes called a double-ended queue, is a doubly linked list in which all insertions and deletions are from one of the two ends of the list, i.e., at the head or the tail. An insertion to the front is commonly called a push, and an insertion to the back is commonly called an inject. A deletion from the front is commonly called a pop, and a deletion from the back is commonly called an eject. (Different languages and libraries may have different nomenclature.)

9.9 COMPUTE BINARY TREE NODES IN ORDER OF INCREASING DEPTH

Binary trees are formally defined in Chapter 10. In particular, each node in a binary tree has a depth, which is its distance from the root.

Given a binary tree, return an array consisting of the keys at the same level. Keys should appear in the order of the corresponding nodes' depths, breaking ties from left to right. For example, you should return $\langle\langle314\rangle, \langle6,6\rangle, \langle271,561,2,271\rangle, \langle28,0,3,1,28\rangle, \langle17,401,257\rangle, \langle641\rangle\rangle$ for the binary tree in Figure 10.1 on Page 146.

Hint: First think about solving this problem with a pair of queues.

Solution: The brute-force approach is to keep an array A of lists. The list at $A[i]$ is the set of nodes at depth i. We initialize $A[0]$ to the root. To get $A[i+1]$ from $A[i]$, we traverse $A[i]$ and add children to $A[i+1]$. The time and space complexities are both $O(n)$, where n is the number of nodes in the tree.

We can improve on the space complexity by recycling space. Specifically, we do not need $A[i]$ after $A[i+1]$ is computed, i.e., two lists suffice.

As an alternative, we can maintain a queue of nodes to process. Specifically the queue contains nodes at depth i followed by nodes at depth $i+1$. After all nodes at depth i are processed, the head of the queue is a node at depth $i+1$; processing this node introduces nodes from depth $i+2$ to the end of the queue.

We use a count to record the number of nodes at the depth of the head of the queue that remain to be processed. When all nodes at depth i are processed, the queue consists of exactly the set of nodes at depth $i + 1$, and the count is updated to the size of the queue.

```
vector<vector<int>> BinaryTreeDepthOrder(
    const unique_ptr<BinaryTreeNode<int>>& tree) {
  queue<BinaryTreeNode<int>*> processing_nodes;
  processing_nodes.emplace(tree.get());
  int num_nodes_to_process_at_current_level = processing_nodes.size();
  vector<vector<int>> result;
  vector<int> one_level;

  while (!processing_nodes.empty()) {
    auto curr = processing_nodes.front();
    processing_nodes.pop();
    --num_nodes_to_process_at_current_level;
    if (curr) {
      one_level.emplace_back(curr->data);

      // Defer the null checks to the null test above.
      processing_nodes.emplace(curr->left.get());
      processing_nodes.emplace(curr->right.get());
    }
    // Done with the nodes at the current depth.
    if (!num_nodes_to_process_at_current_level) {
      num_nodes_to_process_at_current_level = processing_nodes.size();
      if (!one_level.empty()) {
        result.emplace_back(move(one_level));
      }
    }
  }
  return result;
}
```

Since each node is enqueued and dequeued exactly once, the time complexity is $O(n)$. The space complexity is $O(m)$, where m is the maximum number of nodes at any single depth.

Variant: Write a program which takes as input a binary tree and returns the keys in top down, alternating left-to-right and right-to-left order, starting from left-to-right. For example, if the input is the tree in Figure 10.1 on Page 146, your program should return $\langle\langle314\rangle, \langle6,6\rangle, \langle271,561,2,271\rangle, \langle28,1,3,0,28\rangle, \langle17,401,257\rangle, \langle641\rangle\rangle$.

Variant: Write a program which takes as input a binary tree and returns the keys in a bottom up, left-to-right order. For example, if the input is the tree in Figure 10.1 on Page 146, your program should return $\langle\langle641\rangle, \langle17,401,257\rangle, \langle28,0,3,1,28\rangle, \langle271,561,2,271\rangle, \langle6,6\rangle, \langle314\rangle\rangle$.

Variant: Write a program which takes as input a binary tree with integer keys, and returns the average of the keys at each level. For example, if the input is the tree in Figure 10.1 on Page 146, your program should return $\langle314,6,276.25,12,225,641\rangle$.

A queue can be implemented using an array and two additional fields, the beginning and the end indices. This structure is sometimes referred to as a circular queue. Both enqueue and dequeue have $O(1)$ time complexity. If the array is fixed, there is a maximum number of entries that can be stored. If the array is dynamically resized, the total time for m combined enqueue and dequeue operations is $O(m)$.

Implement a queue API using an array for storing elements. Your API should include a constructor function, which takes as argument the initial capacity of the queue, enqueue and dequeue functions, and a function which returns the number of elements stored. Implement dynamic resizing to support storing an arbitrarily large number of elements.

Hint: Track the head and tail. How can you differentiate a full queue from an empty one?

Solution: A brute-force approach is to use an array, with the head always at index 0. An additional variable tracks the index of the tail element. Enqueue has $O(1)$ time complexity. However dequeue's time complexity is $O(n)$, where n is the number of elements in the queue, since every element has to be left-shifted to fill up the space created at index 0.

A better approach is to keep one more variable to track the head. This way, dequeue can also be performed in $O(1)$ time. When performing an enqueue into a full array, we need to resize the array. We cannot only resize, because this results in queue elements not appearing contiguously. For example, if the array is $\langle e, b, c, d \rangle$, with e being the tail and b the head, if we resize to get $\langle e, b, c, d, \_, \_, \_, \_ \rangle$, we cannot enqueue without overwriting or moving elements.

```
class Queue {
 public:
  explicit Queue(size_t capacity) : entries_(capacity) {}

  void Enqueue(int x) {
    if (num_queue_elements == entries_.size()) {  // Needs to resize.
      // Makes the queue elements appear consecutively.
      rotate(entries_.begin(), entries_.begin() + head_, entries_.end());
      head_ = 0, tail_ = num_queue_elements;  // Resets head and tail.
      entries_.resize(entries_.size() * kScaleFactor);
    }

    entries_[tail_] = x;
    tail_ = (tail_ + 1) % entries_.size(), ++num_queue_elements;
  }

  int Dequeue() {
    if (!num_queue_elements) {
      throw length_error("empty queue");
    }
    --num_queue_elements;
    int ret = entries_[head_];
    head_ = (head_ + 1) % entries_.size();
```

```
      return ret;
  }

  size_t size() const { return num_queue_elements; }

 private:
  const int kScaleFactor = 2;
  size_t head_ = 0, tail_ = 0, num_queue_elements = 0;
  vector<int> entries_;
};
```

The time complexity of dequeue is $O(1)$, and the amortized time complexity of enqueue is $O(1)$.

9.11 IMPLEMENT A QUEUE USING STACKS

Queue insertion and deletion follows first-in, first-out semantics; stack insertion and deletion is last-in, first-out.

How would you implement a queue given a library implementing stacks?

Hint: It is impossible to solve this problem with a single stack.

Solution: A straightforward implementation is to enqueue by pushing the element to be enqueued onto one stack. The element to be dequeued is then the element at the bottom of this stack, which can be achieved by first popping all its elements and pushing them to another stack, then popping the top of the second stack (which was the bottom-most element of the first stack), and finally popping the remaining elements back to the first stack.

The primary problem with this approach is that every dequeue takes two pushes and two pops of *every* element, i.e., dequeue has $O(n)$ time complexity, where n is the number of stored elements. (Enqueue takes $O(1)$ time.)

The intuition for improving the time complexity of dequeue is that after we move elements from the first stack to the second stack, any further dequeues are trivial, until the second stack is empty. This is true even if we need to enqueue, as long as we enqueue onto the first stack. When the second stack becomes empty, and we need to perform a dequeue, we simply repeat the process of transferring from the first stack to the second stack. In essence, we are using the first stack for enqueue and the second for dequeue.

```
class Queue {
 public:
  void Enqueue(int x) { enq_.emplace(x); }

  int Dequeue() {
    if (deq_.empty()) {
      // Transfers the elements in enq_ to deq_.
      while (!enq_.empty()) {
        deq_.emplace(enq_.top());
        enq_.pop();
```

```
      }
    }

    if (deq_.empty()) {  // deq_ is still empty!
      throw length_error("empty queue");
    }
    int ret = deq_.top();
    deq_.pop();
    return ret;
  }

 private:
  stack<int> enq_, deq_;
};
```

This approach takes $O(m)$ time for m operations, which can be seen from the fact that each element is pushed no more than twice and popped no more than twice.

9.12 IMPLEMENT A QUEUE WITH MAX API

Implement a queue with enqueue, dequeue, and max operations. The max operation returns the maximum element currently stored in the queue.

Hint: When can an element never be returned by max, regardless of future updates?

Solution: A brute-force approach is to track the current maximum. The current maximum has to be updated on both enqueue and dequeue. Updating the current maximum on enqueue is trivial and fast—just compare the enqueued value with the current maximum. However, updating the current maximum on dequeue is slow— we must examine every single remaining element, which takes $O(n)$ time, where n is the size of the queue.

Consider an element s in the queue that has the property that it entered the queue before a later element, b, which is greater than s. Since s will be dequeued before b, s can never in the future become the maximum element stored in the queue, regardless of the subsequent enqueues and dequeues.

The key to a faster implementation of a queue-with-max is to eliminate elements like s from consideration. We do this by maintaining the set of entries in the queue that have no later entry in the queue greater than them in a separate deque. Elements in the deque will be ordered by their position in the queue, with the candidate closest to the head of the queue appearing first. Since each entry in the deque is greater than or equal to its successors, the largest element in the queue is at the head of the deque.

We now briefly describe how to update the deque on queue updates. If the queue is dequeued, and if the element just dequeued is at the deque's head, we pop the deque from its head; otherwise the deque remains unchanged. When we add an entry to the queue, we iteratively evict from the deque's tail until the element at the tail is greater than or equal to the entry being enqueued, and then add the new entry to the deque's tail. These operations are illustrated in Figure 9.5 on the following page.

Q | 3 | 1 | 3 | 2 | 0 | Q | 3 | 1 | 3 | 2 | 0 | 1 | Q | 1 | 3 | 2 | 0 | 1 | Q | 3 | 2 | 0 | 1 |

D | 3 | 3 | 2 | 0 | D | 3 | 3 | 2 | 1 | D | 3 | 2 | 1 | D | 3 | 2 | 1 |

Q | 3 | 2 | 0 | 1 | 2 | Q | 3 | 2 | 0 | 1 | 2 | 4 | Q | 2 | 0 | 1 | 2 | 4 | Q | 3 | 2 | 0 | 1 | 2 | 4 | 4 |

D | 3 | 2 | 2 | D | 4 | D | 4 | D | 4 | 4 |

Figure 9.5: The queue with max for the following operations: enqueue 1, dequeue, dequeue, enqueue 2, enqueue 4, dequeue, enqueue 4. The queue initially contains 3, 1, 3, 2, and 0 in that order. The deque D corresponding to queue Q is immediately below Q. The progression is shown from left-to-right, then top-to-bottom. The head of each queue and deque is on the left. Observe how the head of the deque holds the maximum element in the queue.

```
template <typename T>
class QueueWithMax {
 public:
  void Enqueue(const T& x) {
    entries_.emplace(x);
    // Eliminate dominated elements in candidates_for_max_.
    while (!candidates_for_max_.empty()) {
      if (candidates_for_max_.back() >= x) {
        break;
      }
      candidates_for_max_.pop_back();
    }
    candidates_for_max_.emplace_back(x);
  }

  T Dequeue() {
    if (!entries_.empty()) {
      T result = entries_.front();
      if (result == candidates_for_max_.front()) {
        candidates_for_max_.pop_front();
      }
      entries_.pop();
      return result;
    }
    throw length_error("empty queue");
  }

  const T& Max() const {
    if (!candidates_for_max_.empty()) {
      return candidates_for_max_.front();
    }
    throw length_error("empty queue");
  }

 private:
  queue<T> entries_;
  deque<T> candidates_for_max_;
};
```

Each dequeue operation has time $O(1)$ complexity. A single enqueue operation may entail many ejections from the deque. However, the amortized time complexity of n enqueues and dequeues is $O(n)$, since an element can be added and removed from the deque no more than once. The max operation is $O(1)$ since it consists of returning the element at the head of the deque.

An alternate solution that is often presented is to use reduction. Specifically, we know how to solve the stack-with-max problem efficiently (Solution 9.1 on Page 127) and we also know how to efficiently model a queue with two stacks (Solution 9.11 on Page 142), so we can solve the queue-with-max design by modeling a queue with two stacks-with-max. This approach feels unnatural compared to the one presented above.

```
class QueueWithMax {
 public:
  void Enqueue(int x) { enqueue_.Push(x); }

  int Dequeue() {
    if (dequeue_.Empty()) {
      while (!enqueue_.Empty()) {
        dequeue_.Push(enqueue_.Pop());
      }
    }
    if (!dequeue_.Empty()) {
      return dequeue_.Pop();
    }
    throw length_error("empty queue");
  }

  int Max() const {
    if (!enqueue_.Empty()) {
      return dequeue_.Empty() ? enqueue_.Max()
                              : max(enqueue_.Max(), dequeue_.Max());
    } else {  // enqueue_.Empty() == true.
      if (!dequeue_.Empty()) {
        return dequeue_.Max();
      }
      throw length_error("empty queue");
    }
  }

 private:
  Stack enqueue_, dequeue_;
};
```

Since the stack-with-max has $O(1)$ amortized time complexity for push, pop, and max, and the queue from two stacks has $O(1)$ amortized time complexity for enqueue and dequeue, this approach has $O(1)$ amortized time complexity for enqueue, dequeue, and max.

10

Binary Trees

The method of solution involves the development of a theory of finite automata operating on infinite trees.

— "Decidability of Second Order Theories and Automata on Trees," M. O. Rabin, 1969

A *binary tree* is a data structure that is useful for representing hierarchy. Formally, a binary tree is either empty, or a *root* node r together with a left binary tree and a right binary tree. The subtrees themselves are binary trees. The left binary tree is sometimes referred to as the *left subtree* of the root, and the right binary tree is referred to as the *right subtree* of the root.

Figure 10.1 gives a graphical representation of a binary tree. Node A is the root. Nodes B and I are the left and right children of A.

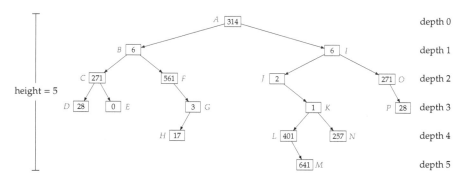

Figure 10.1: Example of a binary tree. The node depths range from 0 to 5. Node M has the highest depth (5) of any node in the tree, implying the height of the tree is 5.

Often the root stores additional data. Its prototype is listed as follows:

```
template <typename T>
struct BinaryTreeNode {
  T data;
  unique_ptr<BinaryTreeNode<T>> left, right;
};
```

Each node, except the root, is itself the root of a left subtree or a right subtree. If l is the root of p's left subtree, we will say l is the *left child* of p, and p is the *parent* of

l; the notion of *right child* is similar. If a node is a left or a right child of p, we say it is a *child* of p. Note that with the exception of the root, every node has a unique parent. Usually, but not universally, the node object definition includes a parent field (which is null for the root). Observe that for any node there exists a unique sequence of nodes from the root to that node with each node in the sequence being a child of the previous node. This sequence is sometimes referred to as the *search path* from the root to the node.

The parent-child relationship defines an ancestor-descendant relationship on nodes in a binary tree. Specifically, a node is an *ancestor* of d if it lies on the search path from the root to d. If a node is an ancestor of d, we say d is a *descendant* of that node. Our convention is that a node is an ancestor and descendant of itself. A node that has no descendants except for itself is called a *leaf*.

The *depth* of a node n is the number of nodes on the search path from the root to n, not including n itself. The *height* of a binary tree is the maximum depth of any node in that tree. A *level* of a tree is all nodes at the same depth. See Figure 10.1 on the facing page for an example of the depth and height concepts.

As concrete examples of these concepts, consider the binary tree in Figure 10.1 on the preceding page. Node I is the parent of J and O. Node G is a descendant of B. The search path to L is $\langle A, I, J, K, L \rangle$. The depth of N is 4. Node M is the node of maximum depth, and hence the height of the tree is 5. The height of the subtree rooted at B is 3. The height of the subtree rooted at H is 0. Nodes D, E, H, M, N, and P are the leaves of the tree.

A *full binary tree* is a binary tree in which every node other than the leaves has two children. A *perfect binary tree* is a full binary tree in which all leaves are at the same depth, and in which every parent has two children. A *complete binary tree* is a binary tree in which every level, except possibly the last, is completely filled, and all nodes are as far left as possible. (This terminology is not universal, e.g., some authors use complete binary tree where we write perfect binary tree.) It is straightforward to prove using induction that the number of nonleaf nodes in a full binary tree is one less than the number of leaves. A perfect binary tree of height h contains exactly $2^{h+1} - 1$ nodes, of which 2^h are leaves. A complete binary tree on n nodes has height $\lfloor \lg n \rfloor$. A left-skewed tree is a tree in which no node has a right child; a right-skewed tree is a tree in which no node has a left child. In either case, we refer to the binary tree as being skewed.

A key computation on a binary tree is *traversing* all the nodes in the tree. (Traversing is also sometimes called *walking*.) Here are some ways in which this visit can be done.

- Traverse the left subtree, visit the root, then traverse the right subtree (an *inorder* traversal). An inorder traversal of the binary tree in Figure 10.1 on the facing page visits the nodes in the following order: $\langle D, C, E, B, F, H, G, A, J, L, M, K, N, I, O, P \rangle$.

- Visit the root, traverse the left subtree, then traverse the right subtree (a *preorder* traversal). A preorder traversal of the binary tree in Figure 10.1 on Page 146 visits the nodes in the following order: $\langle A, B, C, D, E, F, G, H, I, J, K, L, M, N, O, P \rangle$.

- Traverse the left subtree, traverse the right subtree, and then visit the root (a *postorder* traversal). A postorder traversal of the binary tree in Figure 10.1 on Page 146 visits the nodes in the following order: $\langle D, E, C, H, G, F, B, M, L, N, K, J, P, O, I, A \rangle$.

Let T be a binary tree of n nodes, with height h. Implemented recursively, these traversals have $O(n)$ time complexity and $O(h)$ additional space complexity. (The space complexity is dictated by the maximum depth of the function call stack.) If each node has a parent field, the traversals can be done with $O(1)$ additional space complexity.

The term tree is overloaded, which can lead to confusion; see Page 350 for an overview of the common variants.

10.1 TEST IF A BINARY TREE IS BALANCED

A binary tree is said to be balanced if for each node in the tree, the difference in the height of its left and right subtrees is at most one. A perfect binary tree is balanced, as is a complete binary tree. A balanced binary tree does not have to be perfect or complete—see Figure 10.2 for an example.

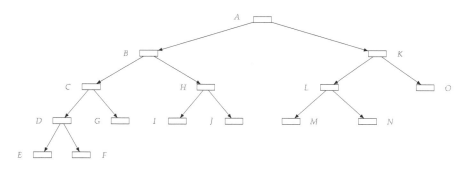

Figure 10.2: A balanced binary tree of height 4.

Write a program that takes as input the root of a binary tree and checks whether the tree is balanced.

Hint: Think of a classic binary tree algorithm.

Solution: Here is a brute-force algorithm. Compute the height for the tree rooted at each node x recursively. The basic computation is to compute the height for each node starting from the leaves, and proceeding upwards. For each node, we check if the difference in heights of the left and right children is greater than one. We can store the heights in a hash table, or in a new field in the nodes. This entails $O(n)$ storage and $O(n)$ time, where n is the number of nodes of the tree.

We can solve this problem using less storage by observing that we do not need to store the heights of all nodes at the same time. Once we are done with a subtree, all we need is whether it is balanced, and if so, what its height is—we do not need any information about descendants of the subtree's root.

```cpp
struct BalancedStatusWithHeight {
  bool balanced;
  int height;
};

bool IsBalanced(const unique_ptr<BinaryTreeNode<int>>& tree) {
  return CheckBalanced(tree).balanced;
}

// First value of the return value indicates if tree is balanced, and if
// balanced the second value of the return value is the height of tree.
BalancedStatusWithHeight CheckBalanced(
    const unique_ptr<BinaryTreeNode<int>>& tree) {
  if (tree == nullptr) {
    return {true, -1};  // Base case.
  }

  auto left_result = CheckBalanced(tree->left);
  if (!left_result.balanced) {
    return {false, 0};  // Left subtree is not balanced.
  }
  auto right_result = CheckBalanced(tree->right);
  if (!right_result.balanced) {
    return {false, 0};  // Right subtree is not balanced.
  }

  bool is_balanced = abs(left_result.height - right_result.height) <= 1;
  int height = max(left_result.height, right_result.height) + 1;
  return {is_balanced, height};
}
```

The program implements a postorder traversal with some calls possibly being eliminated because of early termination. Specifically, if any left subtree is unbalanced we do not need to visit the corresponding right subtree. The function call stack corresponds to a sequence of calls from the root through the unique path to the current node, and the stack height is therefore bounded by the height of the tree, leading to an $O(h)$ space bound. The time complexity is the same as that for a postorder traversal, namely $O(n)$.

Variant: Write a program that returns the size of the largest subtree that is complete.

Variant: Define a node in a binary tree to be k-balanced if the difference in the number of nodes in its left and right subtrees is no more than k. Design an algorithm that takes as input a binary tree and positive integer k, and returns a node in the binary tree such that the node is not k-balanced, but all of its descendants are k-balanced. For example, when applied to the binary tree in Figure 10.1 on Page 146, if $k = 3$, your algorithm should return Node J.

A binary tree is symmetric if you can draw a vertical line through the root and then the left subtree is the mirror image of the right subtree. The concept of a symmetric binary tree is illustrated in Figure 10.3.

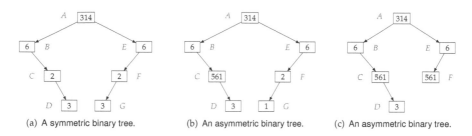

(a) A symmetric binary tree.   (b) An asymmetric binary tree.   (c) An asymmetric binary tree.

Figure 10.3: Symmetric and asymmetric binary trees. The tree in (a) is symmetric. The tree in (b) is structurally symmetric, but not symmetric, because symmetry requires that corresponding nodes have the same keys; here C and F as well as D and G break symmetry. The tree in (c) is asymmetric because there is no node corresponding to D.

Write a program that checks whether a binary tree is symmetric.

Hint: The definition of symmetry is recursive.

Solution: We can test if a tree is symmetric by computing its mirror image and seeing if the mirror image is equal to the original tree. Computing the mirror image of a tree is as simple as swapping the left and right subtrees, and recursively continuing. The time and space complexity are both $O(n)$, where n is the number of nodes in the tree.

The insight to a better algorithm is that we do not need to construct the mirrored subtrees. All that is important is whether a pair of subtrees are mirror images. As soon as a pair fails the test, we can short circuit the check to false. This is shown in the code below.

```
bool IsSymmetric(const unique_ptr<BinaryTreeNode<int>>& tree) {
  return tree == nullptr || CheckSymmetric(tree->left, tree->right);
}

bool CheckSymmetric(const unique_ptr<BinaryTreeNode<int>>& subtree_0,
                    const unique_ptr<BinaryTreeNode<int>>& subtree_1) {
  if (subtree_0 == nullptr && subtree_1 == nullptr) {
    return true;
  } else if (subtree_0 != nullptr && subtree_1 != nullptr) {
    return subtree_0->data == subtree_1->data &&
           CheckSymmetric(subtree_0->left, subtree_1->right) &&
           CheckSymmetric(subtree_0->right, subtree_1->left);
  }
  // One subtree is empty, and the other is not.
  return false;
}
```

The time complexity and space complexity are $O(n)$ and $O(h)$, respectively, where n is the number of nodes in the tree and h is the height of the tree.

10.3 COMPUTE THE LOWEST COMMON ANCESTOR IN A BINARY TREE

Any two nodes in a binary tree have a common ancestor, namely the root. The lowest common ancestor (LCA) of any two nodes in a binary tree is the node furthest from the root that is an ancestor of both nodes. For example, the LCA of M and N in Figure 10.1 on Page 146 is K.

Computing the LCA has important applications. For example, it is an essential calculation when rendering web pages, specifically when computing the Cascading Style Sheet (CSS) that is applicable to a particular Document Object Model (DOM) element.

Design an algorithm for computing the LCA of two nodes in a binary tree in which nodes do not have a parent field.

Hint: When is the root the LCA?

Solution: A brute-force approach is to see if the nodes are in different immediate subtrees of the root, or if one of the nodes is the root. In this case, the root must be the LCA. If both nodes are in the left subtree of the root, or the right subtree of the root, we recurse on that subtree. The time complexity is $O(n^2)$, where n is the number of nodes. The worst-case is a skewed tree with the two nodes at the bottom of the tree.

The insight to a better time complexity is that we do not need to perform multiple passes. If the two nodes are in a subtree, we can compute the LCA directly, instead of simply returning a Boolean indicating that both nodes are in that subtree. The program below returns an object with two fields—the first is an integer indicating how many of the two nodes were present in that subtree, and the second is their LCA, if both nodes were present.

```
BinaryTreeNode<int>* LCA(const unique_ptr<BinaryTreeNode<int>>& tree,
                         const unique_ptr<BinaryTreeNode<int>>& node0,
                         const unique_ptr<BinaryTreeNode<int>>& node1) {
  return LCAHelper(tree, node0, node1).ancestor;
}


// Returns an object consisting of an int and a node. The int field is
// 0, 1, or 2 depending on how many of {node0, node1} are present in
// the tree. If both are present in the tree, when ancestor is
// assigned to a non-null value, it is the LCA.
Status LCAHelper(const unique_ptr<BinaryTreeNode<int>>& tree,
                 const unique_ptr<BinaryTreeNode<int>>& node0,
                 const unique_ptr<BinaryTreeNode<int>>& node1) {
  if (tree == nullptr) {
    return {0, nullptr};
  }

  auto left_result = LCAHelper(tree->left, node0, node1);
```

151

```
if (left_result.num_target_nodes ==
    2) {  // Found both nodes in the left subtree.
  return left_result;
}
auto right_result = LCAHelper(tree->right, node0, node1);
if (right_result.num_target_nodes ==
    2) {  // Found both nodes in the right subtree.
  return right_result;
}
int num_target_nodes = left_result.num_target_nodes +
                       right_result.num_target_nodes + (tree == node0) +
                       (tree == node1);
return {num_target_nodes, num_target_nodes == 2 ? tree.get() : nullptr};
}
```

The algorithm is structurally similar to a recursive postorder traversal, and the complexities are the same. Specifically, the time complexity and space complexity are $O(n)$ and $O(h)$, respectively, where h is the height of the tree.

10.4 Compute the LCA when nodes have parent pointers

Given two nodes in a binary tree, design an algorithm that computes their LCA. Assume that each node has a parent pointer.

Hint: The problem is easy if both nodes are the same distance from the root.

Solution: A brute-force approach is to store the nodes on the search path from the root to one of the nodes in a hash table. This is easily done since we can use the parent field. Then we go up from the second node, stopping as soon as we hit a node in the hash table. The time and space complexity are both $O(h)$, where h is the height of the tree.

We know the two nodes have a common ancestor, namely the root. If the nodes are at the same depth, we can move up the tree in tandem from both nodes, stopping at the first common node, which is the LCA. However, if they are not the same depth, we need to keep the set of traversed nodes to know when we find the first common node. We can circumvent having to store these nodes by ascending from the deeper node to get the same depth as the shallower node, and then performing the tandem upward movement.

For example, for the tree in Figure 10.1 on Page 146, nodes M and P are depths 5 and 3, respectively. Their search paths are $\langle A, I, J, K, L, M \rangle$ and $\langle A, I, O, P \rangle$. If we ascend to depth 3 from M, we get to K. Now when we move upwards in tandem, the first common node is I, which is the LCA of M and P.

Computing the depth is straightforward since we have the parent field—the time complexity is $O(h)$ and the space complexity is $O(1)$. Once we have the depths we can perform the tandem move to get the LCA.

```
BinaryTreeNode<int>* LCA(const unique_ptr<BinaryTreeNode<int>>& node_0,
                         const unique_ptr<BinaryTreeNode<int>>& node_1) {
```

```
  auto *iter_0 = node_0.get(), *iter_1 = node_1.get();
  int depth_0 = GetDepth(iter_0), depth_1 = GetDepth(iter_1);
  // Makes iter_0 as the deeper node in order to simplify the code.
  if (depth_1 > depth_0) {
    swap(iter_0, iter_1);
  }
  // Ascends from the deeper node.
  int depth_diff = abs(depth_0 - depth_1);
  while (depth_diff--) {
    iter_0 = iter_0->parent;
  }

  // Now ascends both nodes until we reach the LCA.
  while (iter_0 != iter_1) {
    iter_0 = iter_0->parent, iter_1 = iter_1->parent;
  }
  return iter_0;
}

int GetDepth(const BinaryTreeNode<int>* node) {
  int depth = 0;
  while (node->parent) {
    ++depth, node = node->parent;
  }
  return depth;
}
```

The time and space complexity are that of computing the depth, namely $O(h)$ and $O(1)$, respectively.

10.5 SUM THE ROOT-TO-LEAF PATHS IN A BINARY TREE

Consider a binary tree in which each node contains a binary digit. A root-to-leaf path can be associated with a binary number—the MSB is at the root. As an example, the binary tree in Figure 10.4 on the next page represents the numbers $(1000)_2, (1001)_2, (10110)_2, (110011)_2, (11000)_2,$ and $(1100)_2$.

Design an algorithm to compute the sum of the binary numbers represented by the root-to-leaf paths.

Hint: Think of an appropriate way of traversing the tree.

Solution: Here is a brute-force algorithm. We compute the leaves, and store the child-parent mapping in a hash table, e.g., via an inorder walk. Afterwards, we traverse from each of the leaves to the root using the child-parent map. Each leaf-to-root path yields a binary integer, with the leaf's bit being the LSB. We sum these integers to obtain the result. The time complexity is $O(Lh)$, where L is the number of root-to-leaf paths (which equals the number of leaves), and h is the tree height. The space complexity is dominated by the hash table, namely $O(n)$, where n is the number of nodes.

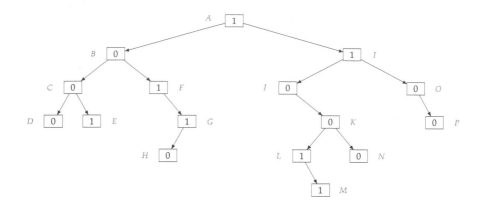

Figure 10.4: Binary tree encoding integers.

The insight to improving complexity is to recognize that paths share nodes and that it is not necessary to repeat computations across the shared nodes. To compute the integer for the path from the root to any node, we take the integer for the node's parent, double it, and add the bit at that node. For example, the integer for the path from A to L is $2 \times (1100)_2 + 1 = (11001)_2$.

Therefore, we can compute the sum of all root to leaf node as follows. Each time we visit a node, we compute the integer it encodes using the number for its parent. If the node is a leaf we return its integer. If it is not a leaf, we return the sum of the results from its left and right children.

```
int SumRootToLeaf(const unique_ptr<BinaryTreeNode<int>>& tree) {
  return SumRootToLeafHelper(tree, 0);
}

int SumRootToLeafHelper(const unique_ptr<BinaryTreeNode<int>>& tree,
                        int partial_path_sum) {
  if (tree == nullptr) {
    return 0;
  }

  partial_path_sum = partial_path_sum * 2 + tree->data;
  if (tree->left == nullptr && tree->right == nullptr) {  // Leaf.
    return partial_path_sum;
  }
  // Non-leaf.
  return SumRootToLeafHelper(tree->left, partial_path_sum) +
         SumRootToLeafHelper(tree->right, partial_path_sum);
}
```

The time complexity and space complexity are $O(n)$ and $O(h)$, respectively.

You are given a binary tree where each node is labeled with an integer. The path weight of a node in such a tree is the sum of the integers on the unique path from the root to that node. For the example shown in Figure 10.1 on Page 146, the path weight of E is 591.

Write a program which takes as input an integer and a binary tree with integer node weights, and checks if there exists a leaf whose path weight equals the given integer.

Hint: What do you need to know about the rest of the tree when checking a specific subtree?

Solution: The brute-force algorithm in Solution 10.5 on Page 153 can be directly applied to this problem, and it has the same time complexity, namely, $O(Lh)$, where L is the number of root-to-leaf paths (which equals the number of leaves), and h is the tree height. The space complexity is dominated by the hash table, namely $O(n)$, where n is the number of nodes.

The inefficiency in the brute-force algorithm stems from the fact that we have overlapping paths, and we do not share the summation computation across those overlaps.

A better approach is to traverse the tree, keeping track of the root-to-node path sum. The first time we encounter a leaf whose weight equals the target weight, we have succeeded at locating a desired leaf. Short circuit evaluation of the check ensures that we do not process additional leaves.

```
bool HasPathSum(const unique_ptr<BinaryTreeNode<int>>& tree, int target_sum) {
  return HasPathSumHelper(tree, 0, target_sum);
}

bool HasPathSumHelper(const unique_ptr<BinaryTreeNode<int>>& node,
                      int partial_path_sum, int target_sum) {
  if (node == nullptr) {
    return false;
  }
  partial_path_sum += node->data;
  if (node->left == nullptr && node->right == nullptr) {  // Leaf.
    return partial_path_sum == target_sum;
  }
  // Non-leaf.
  return HasPathSumHelper(node->left, partial_path_sum, target_sum) ||
         HasPathSumHelper(node->right, partial_path_sum, target_sum);
}
```

The time complexity and space complexity are $O(n)$ and $O(h)$, respectively.

Variant: Write a program which takes the same inputs as in Problem 10.6 on the preceding page and returns all the paths to leaves whose weight equals s. For example, if $s = 619$, you should return $\langle\langle A, B, C, D\rangle, \langle A, I, O, P\rangle\rangle$.

It is trivial to find the kth node that appears in an inorder traversal with $O(n)$ time complexity, where n is the number of nodes. However, with additional information on each node, you can do better.

Write a program that efficiently computes the kth node appearing in an inorder traversal. Assume that each node stores the number of nodes in the subtree rooted at that node.

Hint: Use the divide and conquer principle.

Solution: The brute-force approach is to perform an inorder walk, keeping track of the number of visited nodes, stopping when the node being visited is the kth one. The time complexity is $O(n)$. (Consider for example, a left-skewed tree—to get the first node ($k = 1$) we have to pass through all the nodes.)

Looking carefully at the brute-force algorithm, observe that it does not take advantage of the information present in the node. For example, if k is greater than the number of nodes in the left subtree, the kth node cannot lie in the left subtree. More precisely, if the left subtree has L nodes, then the kth node in the original tree is the $(k - L)$th node when we skip the left subtree. Conversely, if $k \le L$, the desired node lies in the left subtree. For example, the left subtree in Figure 10.1 on Page 146 has seven nodes, so the tenth node cannot in the left subtree. Instead it is the third node if we skip the left subtree. This observation leads to the following program.

```cpp
const BinaryTreeNode<int>* FindKthNodeBinaryTree(
    const unique_ptr<BinaryTreeNode<int>>& tree, int k) {
  const auto* iter = tree.get();
  while (iter != nullptr) {
    int left_size = iter->left ? iter->left->size : 0;
    if (left_size + 1 < k) {  // k-th node must be in right subtree of iter.
      k -= (left_size + 1);
      iter = iter->right.get();
    } else if (left_size == k - 1) {  // k-th is iter itself.
      return iter;
    } else {  // k-th node must be in left subtree of iter.
      iter = iter->left.get();
    }
  }
  // If k is between 1 and the tree size, this line is unreachable.
  return nullptr;
}
```

Since we descend the tree in each iteration, the time complexity is $O(h)$, where h is the height of the tree.

10.8 COMPUTE THE SUCCESSOR

The successor of a node in a binary tree is the node that appears immediately after the given node in an inorder traversal. For example, in Figure 10.1 on Page 146, the successor of *G* is *A*, and the successor of *A* is *J*.

Design an algorithm that computes the successor of a node in a binary tree. Assume that each node stores its parent.

Hint: Study the node's right subtree. What if the node does not have a right subtree?

Solution: The brute-force algorithm is to perform the inorder walk, stopping immediately at the first node to be visited after the given node. The time complexity is that of an inorder walk, namely $O(n)$, where n is the number of nodes.

Looking more carefully at the structure of the tree, observe that if the given node has a nonempty right subtree, its successor must lie in that subtree, and the rest of the nodes are immaterial. For example, in Figure 10.1 on Page 146, regardless of the structure of *A*'s left subtree, *A*'s successor must lie in the subtree rooted at *I*. Similarly, *B*'s successor must lie in the subtree rooted at *F*. Furthermore, when a node has a nonempty right subtree, its successor is the first node visited when performing an inorder traversal on that subtree. This node is the "left-most" node in that subtree, and can be computed by following left children exclusively, stopping when there is no left child to continue from.

The challenge comes when the given node does not have a right subtree, e.g., *H* in Figure 10.1 on Page 146. If the node is its parent's left child, the parent will be the next node we visit, and hence is its successor, e.g., *G* is *H*'s successor. If the node is its parent's right child, e.g., *G*, then we have already visited the parent. We can determine the next visited node by iteratively following parents, stopping when we move up from a left child. For example, from *G* we traverse *F*, then *B*, then *A*. We stop at *A*, since *B* is the left child of *A*—the successor of *G* is *A*.

Note that we may reach the root without ever moving up from a left child. This happens when the given node is the last node visited in an inorder traversal, and hence has no successor. Node *P* in Figure 10.1 on Page 146 illustrates this scenario.

```cpp
BinaryTreeNode<int>* FindSuccessor(
    const unique_ptr<BinaryTreeNode<int>>& node) {
  auto* iter = node.get();
  if (iter->right != nullptr) {
    // Successor is the leftmost element in node's right subtree.
    iter = iter->right.get();
    while (iter->left) {
      iter = iter->left.get();
    }
    return iter;
  }

  // Find the closest ancestor whose left subtree contains node.
  while (iter->parent != nullptr && iter->parent->right.get() == iter) {
    iter = iter->parent;
  }
  // A return value of nullptr means node does not have successor, i.e., it is
  // the rightmost node in the tree.
  return iter->parent;
```

```
}
```

Since the number of edges followed cannot be more than the tree height, the time complexity is $O(h)$, where h is the height of the tree.

10.9 IMPLEMENT AN INORDER TRAVERSAL WITH $O(1)$ SPACE

The direct implementation of an inorder traversal using recursion has $O(h)$ space complexity, where h is the height of the tree. Recursion can be removed with an explicit stack, but the space complexity remains $O(h)$.

Write a nonrecursive program for computing the inorder traversal sequence for a binary tree. Assume nodes have parent fields.

Hint: How can you tell whether a node is a left child or right child of its parent?

Solution: The standard idiom for an inorder traversal is traverse-left, visit-root, traverse-right. When we complete traversing a subtree we need to return to its parent. What we do after that depends on whether the subtree we returned from was the left subtree or right subtree of the parent. In the former, we visit the parent, and then its right subtree; in the latter, we return from the parent itself.

One way to do this traversal without recursion is to record the parent node for each node we begin a traversal from. This can be done with a hash table, and entails $O(n)$ time and space complexity for the hash table, where n is the number of nodes, and h the height of the tree. The space complexity can be reduced to $O(h)$ by evicting a node from the hash table when we complete traversing the subtree rooted at it.

For the given problem, since each node stores its parent, we do not need the hash table, which improves the space complexity to $O(1)$.

To complete this algorithm, we need to know when we return to a parent if the just completed subtree was the parent's left child (in which case we need to visit the parent and then traverse its right subtree) or a right subtree (in which case we have completed traversing the parent). We achieve this by recording the subtree's root before we move to the parent. We can then compare the subtree's root with the parent's left child. For example, for the tree in Figure 10.1 on Page 146, after traversing the subtree rooted at C, when we return to B, we record C. Since C is B's left child, we still need to traverse B's right child. When we return from F to B, we record F. Since F is not B's left child, it must be B's right child, and we are done traversing B.

```
vector<int> InorderTraversal(const unique_ptr<BinaryTreeNode<int>>& tree) {
  BinaryTreeNode<int> *prev = nullptr, *curr = tree.get();
  vector<int> result;

  while (curr != nullptr) {
    BinaryTreeNode<int>* next;
    if (curr->parent == prev) {
      // We came down to curr from prev.
      if (curr->left != nullptr) {  // Keep going left.
```

```
      next = curr->left.get();
    } else {
      result.emplace_back(curr->data);
      // Done with left, so go right if right is not empty.
      // Otherwise, go up.
      next = (curr->right != nullptr) ? curr->right.get() : curr->parent;
    }
  } else if (curr->left.get() == prev) {
    // We came up to curr from its left child.
    result.emplace_back(curr->data);
    // Done with left, so go right if right is not empty. Otherwise, go up.
    next = (curr->right != nullptr) ? curr->right.get() : curr->parent;
  } else {   // Done with both children, so move up.
    next = curr->parent;
  }

  prev = curr;
  curr = next;
  }
  return result;
}
```

The time complexity is $O(n)$ and the additional space complexity is $O(1)$.

Alternatively, since the successor of a node is the node appearing after it in an inorder visit sequence, we could start with the left-most node, and keep calling successor. This enables us to reuse Solution 10.8 on Page 157.

Variant: How would you perform preorder and postorder traversals iteratively using $O(1)$ additional space? Your algorithm cannot modify the tree. Nodes have an explicit parent field.

10.10 RECONSTRUCT A BINARY TREE FROM TRAVERSAL DATA

Many different binary trees yield the same sequence of keys in an inorder, preorder, or postorder traversal. However, given an inorder traversal and one of any two other traversal orders of a binary tree, there exists a unique binary tree that yields those orders, assuming each node holds a distinct key. For example, the unique binary tree whose inorder traversal sequence is $\langle F, B, A, E, H, C, D, I, G \rangle$ and whose preorder traversal sequence is $\langle H, B, F, E, A, C, D, G, I \rangle$ is given in Figure 10.5 on the following page.

Given an inorder traversal sequence and a preorder traversal sequence of a binary tree write a program to reconstruct the tree. Assume each node has a unique key.

Hint: Focus on the root.

Solution: A truly brute-force approach is to enumerate every binary tree on the inorder traversal sequence, and check if the preorder sequence from that tree is the given one. The complexity is enormous.

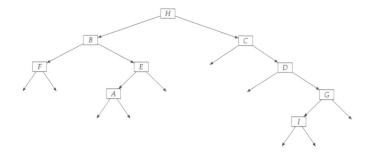

Figure 10.5: A binary tree—edges that do not terminate in nodes denote empty subtrees.

Looking more carefully at the example, the preorder sequence gives us the key of the root node—it is the first node in the sequence. This in turn allows us to split the inorder sequence into an inorder sequence for the left subtree, followed by the root, followed by the right subtree.

The next insight is that we can use the left subtree inorder sequence to compute the preorder sequence for the left subtree from the preorder sequence for the entire tree. A preorder traversal sequence consists of the root, followed by the preorder traversal sequence of the left subtree, followed by the preorder traversal sequence of the right subtree. We know the number k of nodes in the left subtree from the location of the root in the inorder traversal sequence. Therefore, the subsequence of k nodes after the root in the preorder traversal sequence is the preorder traversal sequence for the left subtree.

As a concrete example, for the inorder traversal sequence $\langle F, B, A, E, H, C, D, I, G \rangle$ and preorder traversal sequence $\langle H, B, F, E, A, C, D, G, I \rangle$ (in Figure 10.5) the root is the first node in the preorder traversal sequence, namely H. From the inorder traversal sequence, we know the inorder traversal sequence for the root's left subtree is $\langle F, B, A, E \rangle$. Therefore the sequence $\langle B, F, E, A \rangle$, which is the four nodes after the root, H, in the preorder traversal sequence $\langle H, B, F, E, A, C, D, G, I \rangle$ is the preorder traversal sequence for the root's left subtree. A similar construction applies to the root's right subtree. This construction is continued recursively till we get to the leaves.

Implemented naively, the above algorithm has a time complexity of $O(n^2)$. The worst-case corresponds to a skewed tree. Finding the root within the inorder sequences takes time $O(n)$. We can improve the time complexity to $O(n)$ by initially building a hash table from keys to their positions in the inorder sequence. This is the approach described below.

```
unique_ptr<BinaryTreeNode<int>> BinaryTreeFromPreorderInorder(
    const vector<int>& preorder, const vector<int>& inorder) {
  unordered_map<int, size_t> node_to_inorder_idx;
  for (size_t i = 0; i < inorder.size(); ++i) {
    node_to_inorder_idx.emplace(inorder[i], i);
  }
```

```
  return BinaryTreeFromPreorderInorderHelper(
      preorder, 0, preorder.size(), 0, inorder.size(), node_to_inorder_idx);
}


// Builds the subtree with preorder[preorder_start : preorder_end - 1] and
// inorder[inorder_start : inorder_end - 1].
unique_ptr<BinaryTreeNode<int>> BinaryTreeFromPreorderInorderHelper(
    const vector<int>& preorder, size_t preorder_start, size_t preorder_end,
    size_t inorder_start, size_t inorder_end,
    const unordered_map<int, size_t>& node_to_inorder_idx) {
  if (preorder_end <= preorder_start || inorder_end <= inorder_start) {
    return nullptr;
  }
  size_t root_inorder_idx = node_to_inorder_idx.at(preorder[preorder_start]);
  size_t left_subtree_size = root_inorder_idx - inorder_start;

  return make_unique<BinaryTreeNode<int>>(BinaryTreeNode<int>{
      preorder[preorder_start],
      // Recursively builds the left subtree.
      BinaryTreeFromPreorderInorderHelper(
          preorder, preorder_start + 1, preorder_start + 1 + left_subtree_size,
          inorder_start, root_inorder_idx, node_to_inorder_idx),
      // Recursively builds the right subtree.
      BinaryTreeFromPreorderInorderHelper(
          preorder, preorder_start + 1 + left_subtree_size, preorder_end,
          root_inorder_idx + 1, inorder_end, node_to_inorder_idx)});
}
```

Variant: Solve the same problem with an inorder traversal sequence and a postorder traversal sequence.

Variant: Let A be an array of n distinct integers. Let the index of the maximum element of A be m. Define the max-tree on A to be the binary tree on the entries of A in which the root contains the maximum element of A, the left child is the max-tree on $A[0 : m - 1]$ and the right child is the max-tree on $A[m + 1 : n - 1]$. Design an $O(n)$ algorithm for building the max-tree of A.

10.11 RECONSTRUCT A BINARY TREE FROM A PREORDER TRAVERSAL WITH MARKERS

Many different binary trees have the same preorder traversal sequence.

In this problem, the preorder traversal computation is modified to mark where a left or right child is empty. For example, the binary tree in Figure 10.5 on the facing page yields the following preorder traversal sequence:

$\langle H, B, F, \texttt{null}, \texttt{null}, E, A, \texttt{null}, \texttt{null}, \texttt{null}, C, \texttt{null}, D, \texttt{null}, G, I, \texttt{null}, \texttt{null}, \texttt{null} \rangle$

Design an algorithm for reconstructing a binary tree from a preorder traversal visit sequence that uses null to mark empty children.

Hint: It's difficult to solve this problem by examining the preorder traversal visit sequence from left-to-right.

Solution: One brute-force approach is to enumerate all binary trees and compare the resulting preorder sequence with the given one. This approach will have unacceptable time complexity.

The intuition for a better algorithm is the recognition that the first node in the sequence is the root, and the sequence for the root's left subtree appears before all the nodes in the root's right subtree. It is not easy to see where the left subtree sequence ends. However, if we solve the problem recursively, we can assume that the routine correctly computes the left subtree, which will also tell us where the right subtree begins.

```cpp
unique_ptr<BinaryTreeNode<int>> ReconstructPreorder(
    const vector<int*>& preorder) {
  int subtree_idx_pointer = 0;
  return ReconstructPreorderHelper(preorder, &subtree_idx_pointer);
}

// Reconstructs the subtree that is rooted at subtreeIdx.
unique_ptr<BinaryTreeNode<int>> ReconstructPreorderHelper(
    const vector<int*>& preorder, int* subtree_idx_pointer) {
  int& subtree_idx = *subtree_idx_pointer;
  int* subtree_key = preorder[subtree_idx];
  ++subtree_idx;
  if (subtree_key == nullptr) {
    return nullptr;
  }
  // Note that ReconstructPreorderHelper updates subtree_idx. So the order of
  // following two calls are critical.
  auto left_subtree = ReconstructPreorderHelper(preorder, subtree_idx_pointer);
  auto right_subtree =
      ReconstructPreorderHelper(preorder, subtree_idx_pointer);
  return make_unique<BinaryTreeNode<int>>(BinaryTreeNode<int>{
      *subtree_key, move(left_subtree), move(right_subtree)});
}
```

The time complexity is $O(n)$, where n is the number of nodes in the tree.

Variant: Solve the same problem when the sequence corresponds to a postorder traversal sequence. Is this problem solvable when the sequence corresponds to an inorder traversal sequence?

10.12 FORM A LINKED LIST FROM THE LEAVES OF A BINARY TREE

In some applications of a binary tree, only the leaf nodes contain actual information. For example, the outcomes of matches in a tennis tournament can be represented by a binary tree where leaves are players. The internal nodes correspond to matches, with a single winner advancing. For such a tree, we can link the leaves to get a list of participants.

Given a binary tree, compute a linked list from the leaves of the binary tree. The leaves should appear in left-to-right order. For example, when applied to the binary tree in Figure 10.1 on Page 146, your function should return $\langle D, E, H, M, N, P \rangle$.

Hint: Build the list incrementally—it's easy if the partial list is a global.

Solution: A fairly direct approach is to use two passes—one to compute the leaves, and the other to assign ranks to the leaves, with the left-most leaf getting the lowest rank. The final result is the leaves sorted by ascending order of rank.

In fact, it is not necessary to make two passes—if we process the tree from left to right, the leaves occur in the desired order, so we can incrementally add them to the result. This idea is shown below.

```
list<const unique_ptr<BinaryTreeNode<int>>*> CreateListOfLeaves(
    const unique_ptr<BinaryTreeNode<int>>& tree) {
  list<const unique_ptr<BinaryTreeNode<int>>*> leaves;
  if (tree != nullptr) {
    if (tree->left == nullptr && tree->right == nullptr) {
      leaves.emplace_back(&tree);
    } else {
      // First do the left subtree, and then do the right subtree.
      leaves.splice(leaves.end(), CreateListOfLeaves(tree->left));
      leaves.splice(leaves.end(), CreateListOfLeaves(tree->right));
    }
  }
  return leaves;
}
```

The time complexity is $O(n)$, where n is the number of nodes.

10.13 COMPUTE THE EXTERIOR OF A BINARY TREE

The exterior of a binary tree is the following sequence of nodes: the nodes from the root to the leftmost leaf, followed by the leaves in left-to-right order, followed by the nodes from the rightmost leaf to the root. (By leftmost (rightmost) leaf, we mean the leaf that appears first (last) in an inorder traversal.) For example, the exterior of the binary tree in Figure 10.1 on Page 146 is $\langle A, B, C, D, E, H, M, N, P, O, I \rangle$.

Write a program that computes the exterior of a binary tree.

Hint: Handle the root's left child and right child in mirror fashion.

Solution: A brute-force approach is to use a case analysis. We need the nodes on the path from the root to the leftmost leaf, the nodes on the path from the root to the rightmost leaf, and the leaves in left-to-right order.

We already know how to compute the leaves in left-to-right order (Solution 10.12 on the previous page). The path from root to leftmost leaf is computed by going left if a left child exists, and otherwise going right. When we reach a leaf, it must be the leftmost leaf. A similar computation yields the nodes on the path from the root to

163

the rightmost leaf. The time complexity is $O(h + n + h) = O(n)$, where n and h are the number of nodes and the height of the tree, respectively. The implementation is a little tricky, because some nodes appear in multiple sequences. For example, in Figure 10.1 on Page 146, the path from the root to the leftmost leaf is $\langle A, B, C, D \rangle$, the leaves in left-to-right order are $\langle D, E, H, M, N, P \rangle$, and the path from the root to the rightmost leaf is $\langle A, I, O, P \rangle$. Note the leftmost leaf, D, the rightmost leaf, P, and the root, A, appear in two sequences.

We can simplify the above approach by computing the nodes on the path from the root to the leftmost leaf and the leaves in the left subtree in one traversal. After that, we find the leaves in the right subtree followed by the nodes from the rightmost leaf to the root with another traversal. This is the program shown below. For the tree in Figure 10.1 on Page 146, the first traversal returns $\langle B, C, D, E, H \rangle$, and the second traversal returns $\langle M, N, P, O, I \rangle$. We append the first and then the second sequences to $\langle A \rangle$.

```
list<const unique_ptr<BinaryTreeNode<int>>*> ExteriorBinaryTree(
    const unique_ptr<BinaryTreeNode<int>>& tree) {
  list<const unique_ptr<BinaryTreeNode<int>>*> exterior;
  if (tree != nullptr) {
    exterior.emplace_back(&tree);
    exterior.splice(exterior.end(), LeftBoundaryAndLeaves(tree->left, true));
    exterior.splice(exterior.end(), RightBoundaryAndLeaves(tree->right, true));
  }
  return exterior;
}


// Computes the nodes from the root to the leftmost leaf followed by all the
// leaves in subtree.
list<const unique_ptr<BinaryTreeNode<int>>*> LeftBoundaryAndLeaves(
    const unique_ptr<BinaryTreeNode<int>>& subtree, bool is_boundary) {
  list<const unique_ptr<BinaryTreeNode<int>>*> result;
  if (subtree != nullptr) {
    if (is_boundary || IsLeaf(subtree)) {
      result.emplace_back(&subtree);
    }
    result.splice(result.end(),
                  LeftBoundaryAndLeaves(subtree->left, is_boundary));
    result.splice(result.end(), LeftBoundaryAndLeaves(
                                  subtree->right,
                                  is_boundary && subtree->left == nullptr));
  }
  return result;
}


// Computes the leaves in left-to-right order followed by the rightmost leaf
// to the root path in subtree.
list<const unique_ptr<BinaryTreeNode<int>>*> RightBoundaryAndLeaves(
    const unique_ptr<BinaryTreeNode<int>>& subtree, bool is_boundary) {
  list<const unique_ptr<BinaryTreeNode<int>>*> result;
  if (subtree != nullptr) {
```

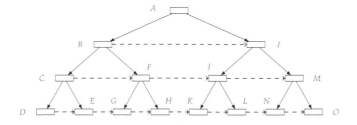

Figure 10.6: Assigning each node's level-next field to its right sibling in a perfect binary tree. A dashed arrow indicates the value held by the level-next field after the update. No dashed arrow is shown for the nodes on the path from the root to the rightmost leaf, i.e., A, I, M, and O, since these nodes have no right siblings.

```
    result.splice(result.end(), RightBoundaryAndLeaves(
                       subtree->left,
                       is_boundary && subtree->right == nullptr));
    result.splice(result.end(),
             RightBoundaryAndLeaves(subtree->right, is_boundary));
    if (is_boundary || IsLeaf(subtree)) {
      result.emplace_back(&subtree);
    }
  }
  return result;
}

bool IsLeaf(const unique_ptr<BinaryTreeNode<int>>& node) {
  return node->left == nullptr && node->right == nullptr;
}
```

The time complexity is $O(n)$.

10.14 COMPUTE THE RIGHT SIBLING TREE

For this problem, assume that each binary tree node has a extra field, call it level-next, that holds a binary tree node (this field is distinct from the fields for the left and right children). The level-next field will be used to compute a map from nodes to their right siblings. The input is assumed to be perfect binary tree. See Figure 10.6 for an example.

Write a program that takes a perfect binary tree, and sets each node's level-next field to the node on its right, if one exists.

Hint: Think of an appropriate traversal order.

Solution: A brute-force approach is to compute the depth of each node, which is stored in a hash table. Next we order nodes at the same depth using inorder visit times. Then we set each node's level-next field according to this order. The time and space complexity are $O(n)$, where n is the number of nodes.

165

The key insight into solving this problem with better space complexity is to use the structure of the tree. Since it is a perfect binary tree, for a node which is a left child, its right sibling is just its parent's right child. For a node which is a right child, its right sibling is its parent's right sibling's left child. For example in Figure 10.6 on the previous page, since C is B's left child, C's right sibling is B's right child, i.e., F. Since Node F is B's right child, F's right sibling is B's right sibling's left child, i.e., J.

For this approach to work, we need to ensure that we process nodes level-by-level, left-to-right. Traversing a level in which the level-next field is set is trivial. As we do the traversal, we set the level-next fields for the nodes on the level below using the principle outlined above. To get to the next level, we record the starting node for each level. When we complete that level, the next level is the starting node's left child.

```
void ConstructRightSibling(BinaryTreeNode<int>* tree) {
  auto left_start = tree;
  while (left_start && left_start->left) {
    PopulateLowerLevelNextField(left_start);
    left_start = left_start->left.get();
  }
}

void PopulateLowerLevelNextField(BinaryTreeNode<int>* start_node) {
  auto iter = start_node;
  while (iter) {
    // Populate left child's next field.
    iter->left->next = iter->right.get();
    // Populate right child's next field if iter is not the last node of this
    // level.
    if (iter->next) {
      iter->right->next = iter->next->left.get();
    }
    iter = iter->next;
  }
}
```

Since we perform $O(1)$ computation per node, the time complexity is $O(n)$. The space complexity is $O(1)$.

Variant: Solve the same problem when there is no level-next field. Your result should be stored in the right child field.

Variant: Solve the same problem for a general binary tree. See Figure 10.7 on the facing page for an example.

10.15 IMPLEMENT LOCKING IN A BINARY TREE

This problem is concerned with the design of an API for setting the state of nodes in a binary tree to lock or unlock. A node's state cannot be set to lock if any of its descendants or ancestors are in lock.

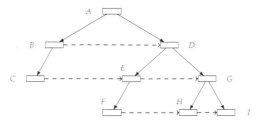

Figure 10.7: Assigning each node's level-next field to its right sibling in a general binary tree. A dashed arrow indicates the value held by the level-next field after the update.

Changing a node's state to lock does not change the state of any other nodes. For example, all leaves may simultaneously be in state lock. (If this is the case, no nonleaf nodes can be in state lock.)

Write the following methods for a binary tree node class:

1. A function to test if the node is locked.
2. A function to lock the node. If the node cannot be locked, return false, otherwise lock it and return true.
3. A function to unlock the node.

Assume that each node has a parent field. The API will be used in a single threaded program, so there is no need for concurrency constructs such as mutexes or synchronization.

Hint: Track the number of locked nodes for each subtree.

Solution: The brute-force approach is to have a Boolean-valued lock variable for each node. Testing if a node is locked is trivial, we simply return that field. Locking is more involved—we must visit all the node's ancestors and descendants to see if any of them are already locked. If so we cannot lock the node. Unlocking is trivial, we simply change the lock variable to false.

The problem with the brute-force approach is that the time complexity to lock is very high—$O(m + d)$, where m is the number of nodes in the node's subtree, and d is the depth of the node. If the node is the root, the time complexity is $O(n)$, where n is the number of nodes.

The insight to improving the time complexity is that we do not actually care which nodes in a node's subtree are locked—all we need to know is whether any node is locked or not. We can achieve this with a little extra book-keeping. Specifically, for each node we have an additional field which counts the number of nodes in that node's subtree that are locked. This makes locking straightforward—to test if any descendant is locked, we just look at the count. Testing if an ancestor is locked is done as before. If lock succeeds, we have to update the lock counts. The only nodes affected are the ones on the path from the root to the given node. Unlocking is slightly more involved than before. Specifically, we must reduce the locked node count for all ancestors.

```cpp
class BinaryTreeNode {
 public:
  bool IsLocked() const { return locked_; }

  bool Lock() {
    // We cannot lock if any of this node's descendants are locked.
    if (numLockedDescendants_ > 0 || locked_) {
      return false;
    }

    // We cannot lock if any of this node's ancestors are locked.
    for (auto iter = parent_; iter != nullptr; iter = iter->parent_) {
      if (iter->locked_) {
        return false;
      }
    }

    // Lock this node and increments all its ancestors's descendant lock
    // counts.
    locked_ = true;
    for (auto iter = parent_; iter != nullptr; iter = iter->parent_) {
      ++iter->numLockedDescendants_;
    }
    return true;
  }

  void Unlock() {
    if (locked_) {
      // Unlocks itself and decrements its ancestors's descendant lock counts.
      locked_ = false;
      for (auto iter = parent_; iter != nullptr; iter = iter->parent_) {
        --iter->numLockedDescendants_;
      }
    }
  }

 private:
  shared_ptr<BinaryTreeNode> left_, right_, parent_;

  bool locked_ = false;
  int numLockedDescendants_ = 0;
};
```

The time complexity for locking and unlocking is bounded by the depth of the node, which, in the worst-case is the tree height, i.e., $O(h)$. The space complexity is $O(n)$ for the count field. The time complexity for checking whether a node is already locked remains $O(h)$.

11

Heaps

Using F-heaps we are able to obtain improved running times for several network optimization algorithms.

— *"Fibonacci heaps and their uses,"*
M. L. FREDMAN AND R. E. TARJAN, 1987

A *heap* is a specialized binary tree, specifically it is a complete binary tree as defined on Page 147. The keys must satisfy the *heap property*—the key at each node is at least as great as the keys stored at its children. See Figure 11.1(a) for an example of a max-heap. A max-heap can be implemented as an array; the children of the node at index i are at indices $2i + 1$ and $2i + 2$. The array representation for the max-heap in Figure 11.1(a) is $\langle 561, 314, 401, 28, 156, 359, 271, 11, 3 \rangle$.

A max-heap supports $O(\log n)$ insertions, $O(1)$ time lookup for the max element, and $O(\log n)$ deletion of the max element. The extract-max operation is defined to delete and return the maximum element. See Figure 11.1(b) for an example of deletion of the max element. Searching for arbitrary keys has $O(n)$ time complexity.

The *min-heap* is a completely symmetric version of the data structure and supports $O(1)$ time lookups for the minimum element.

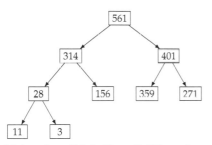

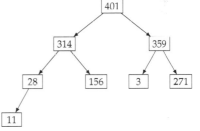

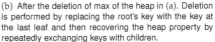

(a) A max-heap. Note that the root hold the maximum key, 561.

(b) After the deletion of max of the heap in (a). Deletion is performed by replacing the root's key with the key at the last leaf and then recovering the heap property by repeatedly exchanging keys with children.

Figure 11.1: A max-heap and deletion on that max-heap.

This problem is motivated by the following scenario. You are given 500 files, each containing stock trade information for an S&P 500 company. Each trade is encoded by a line as follows:

```
1232111,AAPL,30,456.12
```

The first number is the time of the trade expressed as the number of milliseconds since the start of the day's trading. Lines within each file are sorted in increasing order of time. The remaining values are the stock symbol, number of shares, and price. You are to create a single file containing all the trades from the 500 files, sorted in order of increasing trade times. The individual files are of the order of 5–100 megabytes; the combined file will be of the order of five gigabytes. In the abstract, we are trying to solve the following problem.

Write a program that takes as input a set of sorted sequences and computes the union of these sequences as a sorted sequence. For example, if the input is $\langle 3, 5, 7 \rangle$, $\langle 0, 6 \rangle$, and $\langle 0, 6, 28 \rangle$, then the output is $\langle 0, 0, 3, 5, 6, 6, 7, 28 \rangle$.

Hint: Which part of each sequence is significant as the algorithm executes?

Solution: A brute-force approach is to concatenate these sequences into a single array and then sort it. The time complexity is $O(n \log n)$, assuming there are n elements in total.

The brute-force approach does not use the fact that the individual sequences are sorted. We can take advantage of this fact by restricting our attention to the first remaining element in each sequence. Specifically, we repeatedly pick the smallest element amongst the first element of each of the remaining part of each of the sequences.

A min-heap is ideal for maintaining a collection of elements when we need to add arbitrary values and extract the smallest element.

For ease of exposition, we show how to merge sorted arrays, rather than files. As a concrete example, suppose there are three sorted arrays to be merged: $\langle 3, 5, 7 \rangle$, $\langle 0, 6 \rangle$, and $\langle 0, 6, 28 \rangle$. For simplicity, we show the min-heap as containing entries from these three arrays. In practice, we need additional information for each entry, namely the array it is from, and its index in that array. (In the file case we do not need to explicitly maintain an index for next unprocessed element in each sequence—the file I/O library tracks the first unread entry in the file.)

The min-heap is initialized to the first entry of each array, i.e., it is $\{3, 0, 0\}$. We extract the smallest entry, 0, and add it to the output which is $\langle 0 \rangle$. Then we add 6 to the min-heap which is $\{3, 0, 6\}$ now. (We chose the 0 entry corresponding to the third array arbitrarily, it would be a perfectly acceptable to choose from the second array.) Next, extract 0, and add it to the output which is $\langle 0, 0 \rangle$; then add 6 to the min-heap which is $\{3, 6, 6\}$. Next, extract 3, and add it to the output which is $\langle 0, 0, 3 \rangle$; then add 5 to the min-heap which is $\{5, 6, 6\}$. Next, extract 5, and add it to the output which is $\langle 0, 0, 3, 5 \rangle$; then add 7 to the min-heap which is $\{7, 6, 6\}$. Next, extract 6, and add it to the output which is $\langle 0, 0, 3, 5, 6 \rangle$; assuming 6 is selected from the second array, which has no remaining elements, the min-heap is $\{7, 6\}$. Next, extract 6, and add it to the output which is $\langle 0, 0, 3, 5, 6, 6 \rangle$; then add 28 to the min-heap which is $\{7, 28\}$. Next, extract 7, and add it to the output which is $\langle 0, 0, 3, 5, 6, 6, 7 \rangle$; the min-heap is $\{28\}$. Next, extract 28, and add it to the output which is $\langle 0, 0, 3, 5, 6, 6, 7, 28 \rangle$; now, all elements are processed and the output stores the sorted elements.

```cpp
struct IteratorCurrentAndEnd {
  bool operator<(const IteratorCurrentAndEnd& that) const {
    return *current > *that.current;
  }

  vector<int>::const_iterator current;
  vector<int>::const_iterator end;
};

vector<int> MergeSortedArrays(const vector<vector<int>>& sorted_arrays) {
  priority_queue<IteratorCurrentAndEnd, vector<IteratorCurrentAndEnd>>
      min_heap;

  for (const vector<int>& sorted_array : sorted_arrays) {
    if (!sorted_array.empty()) {
      min_heap.emplace(
          IteratorCurrentAndEnd{sorted_array.cbegin(), sorted_array.cend()});
    }
  }

  vector<int> result;
  while (!min_heap.empty()) {
    auto smallest_array = min_heap.top();
    min_heap.pop();
    if (smallest_array.current != smallest_array.end) {
      result.emplace_back(*smallest_array.current);
      min_heap.emplace(IteratorCurrentAndEnd{next(smallest_array.current),
                                             smallest_array.end});
    }
  }
  return result;
}
```

Let k be the number of input sequences. Then there are no more than k elements in the min-heap. Both extract-min and insert take $O(\log k)$ time. Hence, we can do the merge in $O(n \log k)$ time. The space complexity is $O(k)$ beyond the space needed to write the final result. In particular, if the data comes from files and is written to a file, instead of arrays, we would need only $O(k)$ additional storage.

Alternatively, we could recursively merge the k files, two at a time using the merge step from merge sort. We would go from k to $k/2$ then $k/4$, etc. files. There would be $\log k$ stages, and each has time complexity $O(n)$, so the time complexity is the same as that of the heap-based approach, i.e., $O(n \log k)$. The space complexity of any reasonable implementation of merge sort would end up being $O(n)$, which is considerably worse than the heap based approach when $k \ll n$.

11.2 SORT AN INCREASING-DECREASING ARRAY

An array is said to be k-increasing-decreasing if elements repeatedly increase up to a certain index after which they decrease, then again increase, a total of k times. This is illustrated in Figure 11.2.

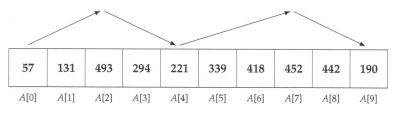

57	131	493	294	221	339	418	452	442	190

$A[0]$ $A[1]$ $A[2]$ $A[3]$ $A[4]$ $A[5]$ $A[6]$ $A[7]$ $A[8]$ $A[9]$

Figure 11.2: A 4-increasing-decreasing array.

Design an efficient algorithm for sorting a k-increasing-decreasing array.

Hint: Can you cast this in terms of combining k sorted arrays?

Solution: The brute-force approach is to sort the array, without taking advantage of the k-increasing-decreasing property. Sorting algorithms run in time $O(n \log n)$, where n is the length of the array.

If k is significantly smaller than n we can do better. For example, if $k = 2$, the input array consists of two subarrays, one increasing, the other decreasing. Reversing the second subarray yields two sorted arrays, and the result is their merge. It is fairly easy to merge two sorted arrays in $O(n)$ time.

Generalizing, we could first reverse the order of each of the decreasing subarrays. For the example in Figure 11.2, we would decompose A into four sorted arrays—$\langle 57, 131, 493 \rangle$, $\langle 221, 294 \rangle$, $\langle 339, 418, 452 \rangle$, and $\langle 190, 442 \rangle$. Now we can use the techniques in Solution 11.1 on Page 171 to merge these.

```cpp
vector<int> SortKIncreasingDecreasingArray(const vector<int>& A) {
  // Decomposes A into a set of sorted arrays.
  vector<vector<int>> sorted_subarrays;
  typedef enum { INCREASING, DECREASING } SubarrayType;
  SubarrayType subarray_type = INCREASING;
  int start_idx = 0;
  for (int i = 1; i <= A.size(); ++i) {
    if (i == A.size() ||  // A is ended. Adds the last subarray.
        (A[i - 1] < A[i] && subarray_type == DECREASING) ||
        (A[i - 1] >= A[i] && subarray_type == INCREASING)) {
      if (subarray_type == INCREASING) {
        sorted_subarrays.emplace_back(A.cbegin() + start_idx, A.cbegin() + i);
      } else {
        sorted_subarrays.emplace_back(A.crbegin() + A.size() - i,
```

```
                        A.crbegin() + A.size() - start_idx);
    }
    start_idx = i;
    subarray_type = (subarray_type == INCREASING ? DECREASING : INCREASING);
  }
}

  return MergeSortedArrays(sorted_subarrays);
}
```

Just as in Solution 11.1 on Page 171, the time complexity is $O(n \log k)$ time.

11.3 SORT AN ALMOST-SORTED ARRAY

Often data is almost-sorted—for example, a server receives timestamped stock quotes and earlier quotes may arrive slightly after later quotes because of differences in server loads and network routes. In this problem we address efficient ways to sort such data.

Write a program which takes as input a very long sequence of numbers and prints the numbers in sorted order. Each number is at most k away from its correctly sorted position. (Such an array is sometimes referred to as being k-sorted.) For example, no number in the sequence $\langle 3, -1, 2, 6, 4, 5, 8 \rangle$ is more than 2 away from its final sorted position.

Hint: How many numbers must you read after reading the *i*th number to be sure you can place it in the correct location?

Solution: The brute-force approach is to put the sequence in an array, sort it, and then print it. The time complexity is $O(n \log n)$, where n is the length of the input sequence. The space complexity is $O(n)$.

   We can do better by taking advantage of the almost-sorted property. Specifically, after we have read $k + 1$ numbers, the smallest number in that group must be smaller than all following numbers. For the given example, after we have read the first 3 numbers, 3, -1, 2, the smallest, -1, must be globally the smallest. This is because the sequence was specified to have the property that every number is at most 2 away from its final sorted location and the smallest number is at index 0 in sorted order. After we read in the 4, the second smallest number must be the minimum of 3, 2, 4, i.e., 2.

   To solve this problem in the general setting, we need to store $k + 1$ numbers and want to be able to efficiently extract the minimum number and add a new number. A min-heap is exactly what we need. We add the first k numbers to a min-heap. Now, we add additional numbers to the min-heap and extract the minimum from the heap. (When the numbers run out, we just perform the extraction.)

```
void SortApproximatelySortedData(istringstream* sequence, int k) {
  priority_queue<int, vector<int>, greater<int>> min_heap;
  // Adds the first k elements into min_heap. Stop if there are fewer than k
  // elements.
```

```
int x;
for (int i = 0; i < k && *sequence >> x; ++i) {
  min_heap.push(x);
}

// For every new element, add it to min_heap and extract the smallest.
while (*sequence >> x) {
  min_heap.push(x);
  cout << min_heap.top() << endl;
  min_heap.pop();
}

// sequence is exhausted, iteratively extracts the remaining elements.
while (!min_heap.empty()) {
  cout << min_heap.top() << endl;
  min_heap.pop();
}
}
```

The time complexity is $O(n \log k)$. The space complexity is $O(k)$.

11.4 COMPUTE THE k CLOSEST STARS

Consider a coordinate system for the Milky Way, in which Earth is at $(0,0,0)$. Model stars as points, and assume distances are in light years. The Milky Way consists of approximately 10^{12} stars, and their coordinates are stored in a file.

How would you compute the k stars which are closest to Earth?

Hint: Suppose you know the k closest stars in the first n stars. If the $(n + 1)$th star is to be added to the set of k closest stars, which element in that set should be evicted?

Solution: If RAM was not a limitation, we could read the data into an array, and compute the k smallest elements using sorting. Alternatively, we could use Solution 12.9 on Page 195 to find the kth smallest element, after which it is easy to find the k smallest elements. For both, the space complexity is $O(n)$, which, for the given dataset, cannot be stored in RAM.

Intuitively, we only care about stars close to Earth. Therefore, we can keep a set of candidates, and iteratively update the candidate set. The candidates are the k closest stars we have seen so far. When we examine a new star, we want to see if it should be added to the candidates. This entails comparing the candidate that is furthest from Earth with the new star. To find this candidate efficiently, we should store the candidates in a container that supports efficiently extracting the maximum and adding a new member.

A max-heap is perfect for this application. Conceptually, we start by adding the first k stars to the max-heap. As we process the stars, each time we encounter a new star that is closer to Earth than the star which is the furthest from Earth among the stars in the max-heap, we delete from the max-heap, and add the new one. Otherwise, we discard the new star and continue. We can simplify the code somewhat by simply adding each star to the max-heap, and discarding the maximum element from the max-heap once it contains $k + 1$ elements.

```
struct Star {
  bool operator<(const Star& that) const {
    return Distance() < that.Distance();
  }

  double Distance() const { return sqrt(x * x + y * y + z * z); }

  double x, y, z;
};

vector<Star> FindClosestKStars(int k, istringstream* stars) {
  // max_heap to store the closest k stars seen so far.
  priority_queue<Star, vector<Star>> max_heap;

  string line;
  while (getline(*stars, line)) {
    stringstream line_stream(line);
    array<double, 3> data;  // stores x, y, and z.
    for (int i = 0; i < 3; ++i) {
      string buf;
      getline(line_stream, buf, ',');
      data[i] = stod(buf);
    }

    // Add each star to the max-heap. If the max-heap size exceeds k,
    // remove the maximum element from the max-heap.
    max_heap.emplace(Star{data[0], data[1], data[2]});
    if (max_heap.size() == k + 1) {
      max_heap.pop();
    }
  }

  // Iteratively extract from the max-heap, which yields the stars
  // sorted according from furthest to closest.
  vector<Star> closest_stars;
  while (!max_heap.empty()) {
    closest_stars.emplace_back(max_heap.top());
    max_heap.pop();
  }
  reverse(closest_stars.begin(), closest_stars.end());
  return closest_stars;
}
```

The time complexity is $O(n \log k)$ and the space complexity is $O(k)$.

Variant: Design an $O(n \log k)$ time algorithm that reads a sequence of n elements and for each element, starting from the kth element, prints the kth largest element read up to that point. The length of the sequence is not known in advance. Your algorithm

175

cannot use more than $O(k)$ additional storage. What are the worst-case inputs for your algorithm?

11.5 COMPUTE THE MEDIAN OF ONLINE DATA

You want to compute the running median of a sequence of numbers. The sequence is presented to you in a streaming fashion—you cannot back up to read an earlier value, and you need to output the median after reading in each new element. For example, if the input is 1, 0, 3, 5, 2, 0, 1 the output is 1, 0.5, 1, 2, 2, 1.5, 1.

Design an algorithm for computing the running median of a sequence.

Hint: Avoid looking at all values each time you read a new value.

Solution: The brute-force approach is to store all the elements seen so far in an array and compute the median using, for example Solution 12.9 on Page 195 for finding the kth smallest entry in an array. This has time complexity $O(n^2)$ for computing the running median for the first n elements.

The shortcoming of the brute-force approach is that it is not incremental, i.e., it does not take advantage of the previous computation. Note that the median of a collection divides the collection into two equal parts. When a new element is added to the collection, the parts can change by at most one element, and the element to be moved is the largest of the smaller half or the smallest of the larger half.

We can use two heaps, a max-heap for the smaller half and a min-heap for the larger half. We will keep these heaps balanced in size. The max-heap has the property that we can efficiently extract the largest element in the smaller part; the min-heap is similar.

For example, let the input values be 1, 0, 3, 5, 2, 0, 1. Let L and H be the contents of the min-heap and the max-heap, respectively. Here is how they progress:
1. Read in 1: $L = [1], H = []$, median is 1.
2. Read in 0: $L = [1], H = [0]$, median is $(1 + 0)/2 = 0.5$.
3. Read in 3: $L = [1, 3], H = [0]$, median is 1.
4. Read in 5: $L = [3, 5], H = [1, 0]$, median is $(3 + 1)/2 = 2$.
5. Read in 2: $L = [2, 3, 5], H = [1, 0]$, median is 2.
6. Read in 0: $L = [2, 3, 5], H = [1, 0, 0]$, median is $(2 + 1)/2 = 1.5$.
7. Read in 1: $L = [1, 2, 3, 5], H = [1, 0, 0]$, median is 1.

```
void OnlineMedian(istringstream* sequence) {
  // min_heap stores the larger half seen so far.
  priority_queue<int, vector<int>, greater<int>> min_heap;
  // max_heap stores the smaller half seen so far.
  priority_queue<int, vector<int>, less<int>> max_heap;

  int x;
  while (*sequence >> x) {
    if (min_heap.empty()) {
      // This is the very first element.
```

```
      min_heap.emplace(x);
    } else {
      if (x >= min_heap.top()) {
        min_heap.emplace(x);
      } else {
        max_heap.emplace(x);
      }
    }
    // Ensure min_heap and max_heap have equal number of elements if
    // an even number of elements is read; otherwise, min_heap must have
    // one more element than max_heap.
    if (min_heap.size() > max_heap.size() + 1) {
      max_heap.emplace(min_heap.top());
      min_heap.pop();
    } else if (max_heap.size() > min_heap.size()) {
      min_heap.emplace(max_heap.top());
      max_heap.pop();
    }

    cout << (min_heap.size() == max_heap.size()
                ? 0.5 * (min_heap.top() + max_heap.top())
                : min_heap.top())
         << endl;
  }
}
```

The time complexity per entry is $O(\log n)$, corresponding to insertion and extraction from a heap.

11.6 COMPUTE THE k LARGEST ELEMENTS IN A MAX-HEAP

A heap contains limited information about the ordering of elements, so unlike a sorted array or a balanced BST, naive algorithms for computing the k largest elements have a time complexity that depends linearly on the number of elements in the collection.

Given a max-heap, represented as an array A, design an algorithm that computes the k largest elements stored in the max-heap. You cannot modify the heap. For example, if the heap is the one shown in Figure 11.1(a) on Page 170, then the array representation is $\langle 561, 314, 401, 28, 156, 359, 271, 11, 3 \rangle$, the four largest elements are $561, 314, 401$, and 359.

Solution: The brute-force algorithm is to perform k extract-max operations. The time complexity is $O(k \log n)$, where n is the number of elements in the heap. Note that this algorithm entails modifying the heap.

Another approach is to use an algorithm for finding the kth smallest element in an array, such as the one described in Solution 12.9 on Page 195. That has time complexity almost certain $O(n)$, and it too modifies the heap.

The following algorithm is based on the insight that the heap has partial order information, specifically, a parent node always stores value greater than or equal to the values stored at its children. Therefore, the root, which is stored in $A[0]$, must be one of the k largest elements—in fact, it is the largest element. The second largest element must be the larger of the root's children, which are $A[1]$ and $A[2]$—this is the index we continue processing from.

The ideal data structure for tracking the index to process next is a data structure which support fast insertions, and fast extract-max, i.e., in a max-heap. So our algorithm is to create a max-heap of candidates, initialized to hold the index 0, which serves as a reference to $A[0]$. The indices in the max-heap are ordered according to corresponding value in A. We then iteratively perform k extract-max operations from the max-heap. Each extraction of an index i is followed by inserting the indices of i's left child, $2i + 1$, and right child, $2i + 2$, to the max-heap, assuming these children exist.

```cpp
vector<int> KLargestInBinaryHeap(const vector<int>& A, int k) {
  if (k <= 0) {
    return {};
  }

  struct HeapEntry {
    int index, value;
  };
  priority_queue<HeapEntry, vector<HeapEntry>,
                 function<bool(HeapEntry, HeapEntry)>>
  candidate_max_heap([](const HeapEntry& a, const HeapEntry& b) -> bool {
    return a.value < b.value;
  });
  // The largest element in A is at index 0.
  candidate_max_heap.emplace(HeapEntry{0, A[0]});
  vector<int> result;
  for (int i = 0; i < k; ++i) {
    int candidate_idx = candidate_max_heap.top().index;
    result.emplace_back(candidate_max_heap.top().value);
    candidate_max_heap.pop();

    int left_child_idx = 2 * candidate_idx + 1;
    if (left_child_idx < A.size()) {
      candidate_max_heap.emplace(HeapEntry{left_child_idx, A[left_child_idx]});
    }
    int right_child_idx = 2 * candidate_idx + 2;
    if (right_child_idx < A.size()) {
      candidate_max_heap.emplace(
          HeapEntry{right_child_idx, A[right_child_idx]});
    }
  }
  return result;
}
```

The total number of insertion and extract-max operations is $O(k)$, yielding an $O(k \log k)$ time complexity, and an $O(k)$ additional space complexity. This algorithm does not modify the original heap.

We discussed the notion of reduction when describing problem solving patterns. Usually, reductions are used to solve a more complex problem using a solution to a simpler problem as a subroutine.

Occasionally it makes sense to go the other way—for example, if we need the functionality of a heap, we can use a BST library, which is more commonly available, with modest performance penalties with respect, for example, to an array-based implementation of a heap.

How would you implement a stack API using a heap?

Hint: Store an additional value with each element that is inserted.

Solution: The key property of a stack is that elements are removed in LIFO order. Since we need to implement this property using a heap, we should look at ways of tracking the insertion order using the heap property.

We can use a global "timestamp" for each element, which we increment on each insert. We use this timestamp to order elements in a max-heap. This way the most recently added element is at the root, which is exactly what we want.

```cpp
class Stack {
 public:
  void Push(int x) { max_heap_.emplace(ValueWithRank{timestamp_++, x}); }

  int Pop() {
    if (max_heap_.empty()) {
      throw length_error("empty stack");
    }
    int val = max_heap_.top().rank;
    max_heap_.pop();
    return val;
  }

  int Peek() const { return max_heap_.top().rank; }

 private:
  int timestamp_ = 0;

  struct ValueWithRank {
    int value, rank;

    bool operator<(const ValueWithRank& that) const {
      return value < that.value;
    }
  };
  priority_queue<ValueWithRank, vector<ValueWithRank>> max_heap_;
};
```

The time complexity for push and pop is that of adding and extracting-max from a max-heap, i.e., $O(\log n)$, where n is the current number of elements.

Variant: How would you implement a queue API using a heap?

12

Searching

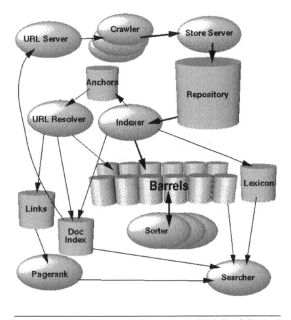

— *"The Anatomy of A Large-Scale Hypertextual Web Search Engine,"*
S. M. BRIN AND L. PAGE, 1998

Search algorithms can be classified in a number of ways. Is the underlying collection static or dynamic, i.e., inserts and deletes are interleaved with searching? Is it worth spending the computational cost to preprocess the data so as to speed up subsequent queries? Are there statistical properties of the data that can be exploited? Should we operate directly on the data or transform it?

In this chapter, our focus is on static data stored in sorted order in an array. Data structures appropriate for dynamic updates are the subject of Chapters 11, 13, and 15.

The first collection of problems in this chapter are related to binary search. The second collection pertains to general search.

Binary search

Given an arbitrary collection of n keys, the only way to determine if a search key is present is by examining each element. This has $O(n)$ time complexity. Fundamentally, binary search is a natural elimination-based strategy for searching a sorted array. The idea is to eliminate half the keys from consideration by keeping the keys in sorted order. If the search key is not equal to the middle element of the array, one of the two sets of keys to the left and to the right of the middle element can be eliminated from further consideration.

Questions based on binary search are ideal from the interviewers perspective: it is a basic technique that every reasonable candidate is supposed to know and it can be implemented in a few lines of code. On the other hand, binary search is much trickier to implement correctly than it appears—you should implement it as well as write corner case tests to ensure you understand it properly.

Many published implementations are incorrect in subtle and not-so-subtle ways—a study reported that it is correctly implemented in only five out of twenty textbooks. Jon Bentley, in his book *"Programming Pearls"* reported that he assigned binary search in a course for professional programmers and found that 90% failed to code it correctly despite having ample time. (Bentley's students would have been gratified to know that his own published implementation of binary search, in a column titled "Writing Correct Programs", contained a bug that remained undetected for over twenty years.)

Binary search can be written in many ways—recursive, iterative, different idioms for conditionals, etc. Here is an iterative implementation adapted from Bentley's book, which includes his bug.

```
int bsearch(int t, const vector<int>& A) {
  int L = 0, U = A.size() - 1;
  while (L <= U) {
    int M = (L + U) / 2;
    if (A[M] < t) {
      L = M + 1;
    } else if (A[M] == t) {
      return M;
    } else {
      U = M - 1;
    }
  }
  return -1;
}
```

The error is in the assignment M = (L + U) / 2 in Line 4, which can lead to overflow. A common solution is to use M = L + (U - L) / 2.

However, even this refinement is problematic in a C-style implementation. *The C Programming Language (2nd ed.)* by Kernighan and Ritchie (Page 100) states: "If one is sure that the elements exist, it is also possible to index backwards in an array; p[-1], p[-2], etc. are syntactically legal, and refer to the elements that immediately precede p[0]." In the expression L + (U - L) / 2, if U is a sufficiently large positive integer and L is a sufficiently large negative integer, (U - L) can overflow, leading to out-of-bounds array access. The problem is illustrated below:

```
#define N 3000000000
char A[N];
char* B = (A + 1500000000);
```

```
int L = -1499000000;
int U = 1499000000;
// On a 32-bit machine (U - L) = -1296967296 because the actual value,
// 2998000000 is larger than 2^31 - 1. Consequently, the bsearch function
// called below sets m to -2147483648 instead of 0, which leads to an
// out-of-bounds access, since the most negative index that can be applied
// to B is -1500000000.
int result = BinarySearch(key, B, L, U);
```

The solution is to check the signs of L and U. If U is positive and L is negative, M = (L + U) / 2 is appropriate, otherwise set M = L + (U - L) / 2.

In our solutions that make use of binary search, L and U are nonnegative and so we use M = L + (U - L) / 2 in the associated programs.

The time complexity of binary search is given by $T(n) = T(n/2) + c$, where c is a constant. This solves to $T(n) = O(\log n)$, which is far superior to the $O(n)$ approach needed when the keys are unsorted. A disadvantage of binary search is that it requires a sorted array and sorting an array takes $O(n \log n)$ time. However, if there are many searches to perform, the time taken to sort is not an issue.

Many variants of searching a sorted array require a little more thinking and create opportunities for missing corner cases.

12.1 SEARCH A SORTED ARRAY FOR FIRST OCCURRENCE OF k

Binary search commonly asks for the index of *any* element of a sorted array that is equal to a specified element. The following problem has a slight twist on this.

-14	-10	2	108	108	243	285	285	285	401
A[0]	A[1]	A[2]	A[3]	A[4]	A[5]	A[6]	A[7]	A[8]	A[9]

Figure 12.1: A sorted array with repeated elements.

Write a method that takes a sorted array and a key and returns the index of the *first* occurrence of that key in the array. For example, when applied to the array in Figure 12.1 your algorithm should return 3 if the given key is 108; if it is 285, your algorithm should return 6.

Hint: What happens when every entry equals k? Don't stop when you first see k.

Solution: A naive approach is to use binary search to find the index of any element equal to the key, k. (If k is not present, we simply return −1.) After finding such an element, we traverse backwards from it to find the first occurrence of that element. The binary search takes time $O(\log n)$, where n is the number of entries in the array. Traversing backwards takes $O(n)$ time in the worst-case—consider the case where entries are equal to k.

The fundamental idea of binary search is to maintain a set of candidate solutions. For the current problem, if we see the element at index i equals k, although we do not know whether i is the first element equal to k, we do know that no subsequent elements can be the first one. Therefore we remove all elements with index $i + 1$ or more from the candidates.

Let's apply the above logic to the given example, with $k = 108$. We start with all indices as candidates, i.e., with $[0,9]$. The midpoint index, 4 contains k. Therefore we can now update the candidate set to $[0,3]$, and record 4 as an occurrence of k. The next midpoint is 1, and this index contains -10. We update the candidate set to $[2,3]$. The value at the midpoint 2 is 2, so we update the candidate set to $[3,3]$. Since the value at this midpoint is 108, we update the first seen occurrence of k to 3. Now the interval is $[3,2]$, which is empty, terminating the search—the result is 3.

```
int SearchFirstOfK(const vector<int>& A, int k) {
  int left = 0, right = A.size() - 1, result = -1;
  // [left : right] is the candidate set.
  while (left <= right) {
    int mid = left + ((right - left) / 2);
    if (A[mid] > k) {
      right = mid - 1;
    } else if (A[mid] == k) {
      result = mid;
      // Nothing to the right of mid can be the first occurrence of k.
      right = mid - 1;
    } else {  // A[mid] < k.
      left = mid + 1;
    }
  }
  return result;
}
```

The complexity bound is still $O(\log n)$—this is because each iteration reduces the size of the candidate set by half.

Variant: Let A be an unsorted array of n integers, with $A[0] \geq A[1]$ and $A[n-2] \leq A[n-1]$. Call an index i a *local minimum* if $A[i]$ is less than or equal to its neighbors. How would you efficiently find a local minimum, if one exists?

Variant: A sequence is said to be ascending if each element is greater than or equal to its predecessor; a descending sequence is one in which each element is less than or equal to its predecessor. A sequence is strictly ascending if each element is greater than its predecessor. Suppose it is known that an array A consists of an ascending sequence followed by a descending sequence. Design an algorithm for finding the maximum element in A. Solve the same problem when A consists of a strictly ascending sequence, followed by a descending sequence.

12.2 SEARCH A SORTED ARRAY FOR THE FIRST ELEMENT GREATER THAN k

Sometimes, we want the first element greater than a given element.

Design an efficient algorithm that takes a sorted array and a key, and finds the index of the *first* occurrence of an element greater than that key. For example, when applied to the array in Figure 12.1 on Page 184 your algorithm should return 9 if the key is 285; if it is −13, your algorithm should return 1.

Hint: Look for the last occurrence of k.

Solution: The brute-force approach is to iterate through the array from the smallest element onward, returning when we first see an element larger than k. (If there is no such element, we return −1.) The time complexity is $O(n)$, where n is the length of the array.

Clearly the above strategy is wasteful—it does not take advantage of the sortedness of the array. A better approach is to maintain a set of candidate indices, and use binary search to eliminate half the candidates at each iteration. If the element at index m is larger than k, we record m, and continue the search in the candidates to the left of m—no element after m can possibly be the result. We must continue the search amongst the candidates to the left of m since we have not ruled out the possibility of those elements being larger than k. If the element at index m is less than or equal to k, we continue searching in the candidates on the right.

Let's apply the above logic to the given example, with $k = 200$. We start with all indices as candidates, i.e., with $[0, 9]$. The midpoint index, 4 contains 108. Therefore we can now update the candidate set to $[5, 9]$. The next midpoint is 7, and this index contains 285. We update the candidate set to $[5, 6]$, and record index 7 as the potential result. The value at the midpoint 5 is 243, so we update the candidate set to $[5, 4]$ and update the potential result to 5. Now the interval is $[5, 4]$, which is empty, so we terminate the search—the result is 5.

```
int SearchFirstLargerOfK(const vector<int>& A, int k) {
  int left = 0, right = A.size() - 1, result = -1;
  // [left : right] is the candidate set.
  while (left <= right) {
    int m = left + ((right - left) / 2);
    if (A[m] > k) {
      result - m;
      right = m - 1;  // Nothing to the right of mid can be solution.
    } else {  // A[m] <= k.
      left = m + 1;
    }
  }
  return result;
}
```

This algorithm, presented above, has an $O(\log n)$ time complexity.

Variant: Write a program which takes a sorted array A of integers, and an integer k, and returns the interval enclosing k, i.e., the pair of integers L and U such that L is the first occurrence of k in A and U is the last occurrence of k in A. If k does not appear in A, return $[-1, -1]$. For example if $A = \langle 1, 2, 2, 4, 4, 4, 7, 11, 11, 13 \rangle$ and $k = 11$, you should return $[7, 8]$.

185

Variant: Write a program which tests if p is a prefix of a string in an array of sorted strings.

12.3 SEARCH A SORTED ARRAY FOR ENTRY EQUAL TO ITS INDEX

Design an efficient algorithm that takes a sorted array of distinct integers, and returns an index i such that the element at index i equals i. For example, when the input is $\langle -2, 0, 2, 3, 6, 7, 9 \rangle$ your algorithm should return 2 or 3.

Hint: Reduce this problem to ordinary binary search.

Solution: A brute-force approach is to iterate through the array, testing whether the ith entry equals i. The time complexity is $O(n)$, where n is the length of the array.

The brute-force approach does not take advantage of the fact that the array (call it A) is sorted and consists of distinct elements. In particular, note that the difference between an entry and its index increases by at least 1 as we iterate through A. Observe that if $A[j] > j$, then no entry after j can satisfy the given criterion. This is because each element in the array is at least 1 greater than the previous element. For the same reason, if $A[j] < j$, no entry before j can satisfy the given criterion.

The above observations can be directly used to create a binary search type algorithm for finding an i such that $A[i] = i$. A slightly simpler approach is to search the secondary array B whose ith entry is $A[i] - i$ for 0, which is just ordinary binary search. We do not need to actually create the secondary array, we can simply use $A[i] - i$ wherever $B[i]$ is referenced.

For the given example, the secondary array B is $\langle -2, -1, 0, 0, 2, 2, 3 \rangle$. Binary search for 0 returns the desired result, i.e., either of index 2 or 3.

```
int SearchEntryEqualToItsIndex(const vector<int>& A) {
  int left = 0, right = A.size() - 1;
  while (left <= right) {
    int mid = left + ((right - left) / 2);
    int difference = A[mid] - mid;
    // A[mid] == mid if and only if difference == 0.
    if (difference == 0) {
      return mid;
    } else if (difference > 0) {
      right = mid - 1;
    } else {  // difference < 0.
      left = mid + 1;
    }
  }
  return -1;
}
```

The time complexity is the same as that for binary search , i.e., $O(\log n)$, where n is the length of A.

Variant: Solve the same problem when A is sorted but may contain duplicates.

An array is said to be cyclically sorted if it is possible to cyclically shift its entries so that it becomes sorted. For example, the array in Figure 12.2 is cyclically sorted—a cyclic left shift by 4 leads to a sorted array.

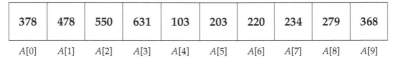

378	478	550	631	103	203	220	234	279	368
$A[0]$	$A[1]$	$A[2]$	$A[3]$	$A[4]$	$A[5]$	$A[6]$	$A[7]$	$A[8]$	$A[9]$

Figure 12.2: A cyclically sorted array.

Design an $O(\log n)$ algorithm for finding the position of the smallest element in a cyclically sorted array. Assume all elements are distinct. For example, for the array in Figure 12.2, your algorithm should return 4.

Hint: Use the divide and conquer principle.

Solution: A brute-force approach is to iterate through the array, comparing the running minimum with the current entry. The time complexity is $O(n)$, where n is the length of the array.

The brute-force approach does not take advantage of the special properties of the array, A. For example, for any m, if $A[m] > A[n-1]$, then the minimum value must be an index in the range $[m+1, n-1]$. Conversely, if $A[m] < A[n-1]$, then no index in the range $[m+1, n-1]$ can be the index of the minimum value. (The minimum value may be at $A[m]$.) Note that it is not possible for $A[m] = A[n-1]$, since it is given that all elements are distinct. These two observations are the basis for a binary search algorithm, described below.

```
int SearchSmallest(const vector<int>& A) {
  int left = 0, right = A.size() - 1;
  while (left < right) {
    int mid = left + ((right - left) / 2);
    if (A[mid] > A[right]) {
      // Minimum must be in [mid + 1 : right].
      left = mid + 1;
    } else {  // A[mid] < A[right].
      // Minimum cannot be in [mid + 1 : right] so it must be in [left : mid].
      right = mid;
    }
  }
  // Loop ends when left == right.
  return left;
}
```

The time complexity is the same as that of binary search, namely $O(\log n)$.

Note that this problem cannot, in general, be solved in less than linear time when elements may be repeated. For example, if A consists of $n-1$ 1s and a single 0, that

0 cannot be detected in the worst-case without inspecting every element. We can perform some pruning of the search as before, e.g., if $A[m] < A[n-1]$, then no index in the range $[m+1, n-1]$ can be the index of the minimum value.

```cpp
int SearchSmallest(const vector<int>& A) {
  return SearchSmallestHelper(A, 0, A.size() - 1);
}

int SearchSmallestHelper(const vector<int>& A, int left, int right) {
  if (left == right) {
    return left;
  }

  int mid = left + ((right - left) / 2);
  if (A[mid] > A[right]) {
    return SearchSmallestHelper(A, mid + 1, right);
  } else if (A[mid] < A[right]) {
    return SearchSmallestHelper(A, left, mid);
  } else {  // A[mid] == A[right].
    // We cannot eliminate either side so we compare the results from both
    // sides.
    int left_result = SearchSmallestHelper(A, left, mid);
    int right_result = SearchSmallestHelper(A, mid + 1, right);
    return A[right_result] < A[left_result] ? right_result : left_result;
  }
}
```

The time complexity is $O(n)$, e.g., for the example given in the above paragraph. If most entries are distinct, the time complexity will tend to $O(\log n)$.

Variant: Design an $O(\log n)$ algorithm for finding the position of an element k in a cyclically sorted array of distinct elements.

12.5 COMPUTE THE INTEGER SQUARE ROOT

Write a program which takes a nonnegative integer and returns the largest integer whose square is less than or equal to the given integer. For example, if the input is 16, return 4; if the input is 300, return 17, since $17^2 = 289 < 300$ and $18^2 = 324 > 300$.

Hint: Look out for a corner-case.

Solution: A brute-force approach is to square each number from 1 to the key, k, stopping as soon as we exceed k. The time complexity is $O(k)$. For a 64 bit integer, at one nanosecond per iteration, this algorithm will take over 500 years.

Looking more carefully at the problem, it should be clear that it is wasteful to take unit-sized increments. For example, if $x^2 < k$, then no number smaller than x can be the result, and if $x^2 > k$, then no number greater than or equal to x can be the result.

This ability to eliminate large sets of possibilities is suggestive of binary search. Specifically, we can maintain an interval consisting of values whose squares are unclassified with respect to k, i.e., might be less than or greater than k.

We initialize the interval to $[0, k]$. We compare the square of $m = \lfloor (l + r)/2 \rfloor$ with k, and use the elimination rule to update the interval. If $m^2 \leq k$, we know all integers less than or equal to m have a square less than or equal to k. Therefore, we update the interval to $[m + 1, r]$. If $m^2 > k$, we know all numbers greater than or equal to m have a square greater than k, so we update the candidate interval to $[l, m - 1]$. The algorithm terminates when the interval is empty, in which case every number less than l has a square less than or equal to k and l's square is greater than k, so the result is $l - 1$.

For example, if $k = 21$, we initialize the interval to $[0, 21]$. The midpoint $m = \lfloor (0 + 21)/2 \rfloor = 10$; since $10^2 > 21$, we update the interval to $[0, 9]$. Now $m = \lfloor (0 + 9)/2 \rfloor = 4$; since $4^2 < 21$, we update the interval to $[5, 9]$. Now $m = \lfloor (5 + 8)/2 \rfloor = 7$; since $7^2 > 21$, we update the interval to $[5, 6]$. Now $m = \lfloor (5 + 6)/2 \rfloor = 5$; since $5^2 > 21$, we update the interval to $[5, 4]$. Now the right endpoint is less than the left endpoint, i.e., the interval is empty, so the result is $5 - 1 = 4$, which is the value returned.

For $k = 25$, the sequence of intervals is $[0, 25], [0, 11], [6, 11], [6, 7], [6, 5]$. The returned value is $6 - 1 = 5$.

```
int SquareRoot(int k) {
  int left = 0, right = k;
  // Candidate interval [left, right] where everything before left has
  // square <= k, and everything after right has square > k.
  while (left <= right) {
    long mid = left + ((right - left) / 2);
    long mid_squared = mid * mid;
    if (mid_squared <= k) {
      left = mid + 1;
    } else {
      right = mid - 1;
    }
  }
  return left - 1;
}
```

The time complexity is that of binary search over the interval $[0, k]$, i.e., $O(\log k)$.

12.6 COMPUTE THE REAL SQUARE ROOT

Square root computations can be implemented using sophisticated numerical techniques involving iterative methods and logarithms. However, if you were asked to implement a square root function, you would not be expected to know these techniques.

Implement a function which takes as input a floating point value and returns its square root.

Hint: Iteratively compute a sequence of intervals, each contained in the previous interval, that contain the result.

Solution: Let x be the input. One approach is to find an integer n such that $n^2 \leq x$ and $(n+1)^2 > x$, using, for example, the approach in Solution 12.5 on Page 189. We can then search within $[n, n+1]$ to find the square root of x to any specified tolerance.

We can avoid decomposing the computation into an integer computation followed by a floating point computation by directly performing binary search. The reason is that if a number is too big to be the square root of x, then any number bigger than that number can be eliminated. Similarly, if a number is too small to be the square root of x, then any number smaller than that number can be eliminated.

Trivial choices for the initial lower bound and upper bound are 0 and the largest floating point number that is representable. The problem with this is that it does not play well with finite precision arithmetic—the first midpoint itself will overflow on squaring.

We cannot start with $[0, x]$ because the square root may be larger than x, e.g., $\sqrt{1/4} = 1/2$. However, if $x \geq 1.0$, we can tighten the lower and upper bounds to 1.0 and x, respectively, since if $1.0 \leq x$ then $x \leq x^2$. On the other hand, if $x < 1.0$, we can use x and 1.0 as the lower and upper bounds respectively, since then the square root of x is greater than x but less than 1.0. Note that the floating point square root problem differs in a fundamental way from the integer square root (Problem 12.5 on Page 189). In that problem, the initial interval containing the solution is always $[0, x]$.

```
typedef enum { SMALLER, EQUAL, LARGER } Ordering;

double SquareRoot(double x) {
  // Decides the search range according to x's value relative to 1.0.
  double left, right;
  if (x < 1.0) {
    left = x, right = 1.0;
  } else {  // x >= 1.0.
    left = 1.0, right = x;
  }

  // Keeps searching as long as left < right, within tolerance.
  while (Compare(left, right) == SMALLER) {
    double mid = left + 0.5 * (right - left);
    double mid_squared = mid * mid;
    if (Compare(mid_squared, x) == EQUAL) {
      return mid;
    } else if (Compare(mid_squared, x) == LARGER) {
      right = mid;
    } else {
      left = mid;
    }
  }
  return left;
}

Ordering Compare(double a, double b) {
  // Uses normalization for precision problem.
  double diff = (a - b) / b;
  return diff < -numeric_limits<double>::epsilon()
```

```
    ? SMALLER
    : diff > numeric_limits<double>::epsilon() ? LARGER : EQUAL;
}
```

The time complexity is $O(\log \frac{x}{s})$, where s is the tolerance.

Variant: Given two positive floating point numbers x and y, how would you compute $\frac{x}{y}$ to within a specified tolerance ϵ if the division operator cannot be used? You cannot use any library functions, such as *log* and *exp*; addition and multiplication are acceptable.

Generalized search

Now we consider a number of search problems that do not use the binary search principle. For example, they focus on tradeoffs between RAM and computation time, avoid wasted comparisons when searching for the minimum and maximum simultaneously, use randomization to perform elimination efficiently, use bit-level manipulations to identify missing elements, etc.

12.7 SEARCH IN A 2D SORTED ARRAY

Call a 2D array sorted if its rows and its columns are nondecreasing. See Figure 12.3 for an example of a 2D sorted array.

	C0	C1	C2	C3	C4
R0	-1	2	4	4	6
R1	1	5	5	9	21
R2	3	6	6	9	22
R3	3	6	8	10	24
R4	6	8	9	12	25
R5	8	10	12	13	40

Figure 12.3: A 2D sorted array.

Design an algorithm that takes a 2D sorted array and a number and checks whether that number appears in the array. For example, if the input is the 2D sorted array in Figure 12.3, and the number is 7, your algorithm should return false; if the number is 8, your algorithm should return true.

Hint: Can you eliminate a row or a column per comparison?

Solution: Let the 2D array be A and the input number be x. We can perform binary search on each row independently, which has a time complexity $O(m \log n)$, where m is the number of rows and n is the number of columns. (If searching on columns, the time complexity is $O(n \log m)$.)

191

Note that the above approach fails to take advantage of the fact that both rows and columns are sorted—it treats separate rows independently of each other. For example, if $x < A[0][0]$ then no row or column can contain x—the sortedness property guarantees that $A[0][0]$ is the smallest element in A.

However, if $x > A[0][0]$, we cannot eliminate the first row or the first column of A. Searching along both rows and columns will lead to a $O(mn)$ solution, which is far worse than the previous solution. The same problem arises if $x < A[m - 1][n - 1]$.

A good rule of design is to look at extremal cases. We have already seen that there is nothing to be gained by comparing with $A[0][0]$ and $A[m-1][n-1]$. However, there are some more extremal cases. For example, suppose we compare x with $A[0][n - 1]$. If $x = A[0][n - 1]$, we have found the desired value. Otherwise:

- $x > A[0][n - 1]$, in which case x is greater than all elements in Row 0.
- $x < A[0][n - 1]$, in which case x is less than all elements in Column $n - 1$.

In either case, we have a 2D array with one fewer row or column to search. The other extremal case, namely comparing with $A[m - 1][0]$ yields a very similar algorithm.

For the example in Figure 12.3 on the preceding page, if the number is 7, our algorithm compares the top-right entry, $A[0][4] = 6$ with 7. Since $7 > 6$, we know 7 cannot be present in Row 0. Now we compare with $A[1][4] = 21$. Since $7 < 21$, we know 7 cannot be present in Column 4. Now we compare with $A[1][3] = 9$. Since $7 < 9$, we know 7 cannot be present in Column 3. Now we compare with $A[1][2] = 5$. Since $7 > 5$, we know 7 cannot be present in Row 1. Now we compare with $A[2][2] = 6$. Since $7 > 6$, we know 7 cannot be present in Row 2. Now we compare with $A[3][2] = 8$. Since $7 < 8$, we know 7 cannot be present in Column 2. Now we compare with $A[3][1] = 6$. Since $7 > 6$, we know 7 cannot be present in Row 3. Now we compare with $A[4][1] = 8$. Since $7 < 8$, we know 7 cannot be present in Column 1. Now we compare with $A[4][0] = 6$. Since $7 > 6$, we know 7 cannot be present in Row 4. Now we compare with $A[5][0] = 8$. Since $7 < 8$, we know 7 cannot be present in Column 0. There are no remaining entries, so we return false.

Now suppose we want to see if 8 is present. Proceeding similarly, we eliminate Row 0, then Column 4, then Row 1, then Column 3, then Row 2. When we compare with $A[3][2]$ we have a match so we return true.

```cpp
bool MatrixSearch(const vector<vector<int>>& A, int x) {
  int row = 0, col = A[0].size() - 1;  // Start from the top-right corner.
  // Keeps searching while there are unclassified rows and columns.
  while (row < A.size() && col >= 0) {
    if (A[row][col] == x) {
      return true;
    } else if (A[row][col] < x) {
      ++row;  // Eliminate this row.
    } else {  // A[row][col] > x.
      --col;  // Eliminate this column.
    }
  }
  return false;
}
```

In each iteration, we remove a row or a column, which means we inspect at most $m + n - 1$ elements, yielding an $O(m + n)$ time complexity.

12.8 FIND THE MIN AND MAX SIMULTANEOUSLY

Given an array of comparable objects, you can find either the *min* or the *max* of the elements in the array with $n - 1$ comparisons, where n is the length of the array.

Comparing elements may be expensive, e.g., a comparison may involve a number of nested calls or the elements being compared may be long strings. Therefore, it is natural to ask if both the min and the max can be computed with less than the $2(n - 1)$ comparisons required to compute the min and the max independently.

Design an algorithm to find the min and max elements in an array. For example, if $A = \langle 3, 2, 5, 1, 2, 4 \rangle$, you should return 1 for the min and 5 for the max.

Hint: Use the fact that $a < b$ and $b < c$ implies $a < c$ to reduce the number of compares used by the brute-force approach.

Solution: The brute-force approach is to compute the min and the max independently, i.e., with $2(n - 1)$ comparisons. We can reduce the number of comparisons by 1 by first computing the min and then skipping the comparison with it when computing the max.

One way to think of this problem is that we are searching for the strongest and weakest players in a group of players, assuming players are totally ordered. There is no point in looking at any player who won a game when we want to find the weakest player. The better approach is to play $n/2$ matches between disjoint pairs of players. The strongest player will come from the $n/2$ winners and the weakest player will come from the $n/2$ losers.

Following the above analogy, we partition the array into min candidates and max candidates by comparing successive pairs—this will give us $n/2$ candidates for min and $n/2$ candidates for max at the cost of $n/2$ comparisons. It takes $n/2 - 1$ comparisons to find the min from the min candidates and $n/2 - 1$ comparisons to find the max from the max candidates, yielding a total of $3n/2 - 2$ comparisons.

Naively implemented, the above algorithm need $O(n)$ storage. However, we can implement it in streaming fashion, by maintaining candidate min and max as we process successive pairs. Note that this entails three comparisons for each pair.

For the given example, we begin by comparing 3 and 2. Since $3 > 2$, we set min to 2 and max to 3. Next we compare 5 and 1. Since $5 > 1$, we compare 5 with the current max, namely 3, and update max to 5. We compare 1 with the current min, namely 2, and update min to 1. Then we compare 2 and 4. Since $4 > 2$, we compare 4 with the current max, namely 5. Since $4 < 5$, we do not update max. We compare 2 with the current min, namely 1 Since $2 > 1$, we do not update min.

```
struct MinMax {
  int min, max;
};
```

```
MinMax FindMinMax(const vector<int>& A) {
  if (A.size() <= 1) {
    return {A.front(), A.front()};
  }

  pair<int, int> global_min_max = minmax(A[0], A[1]);
  // Process two elements at a time.
  for (int i = 2; i + 1 < A.size(); i += 2) {
    pair<int, int> local_min_max = minmax(A[i], A[i + 1]);
    global_min_max = {min(global_min_max.first, local_min_max.first),
                      max(global_min_max.second, local_min_max.second)};
  }
  // If there is odd number of elements in the array, we still
  // need to compare the last element with the existing answer.
  if (A.size() % 2) {
    global_min_max = {min(global_min_max.first, A.back()),
                      max(global_min_max.second, A.back())};
  }
  return {global_min_max.first, global_min_max.second};
}
```

The time complexity is $O(n)$ and the space complexity is $O(1)$.

Variant: What is the least number of comparisons required to find the min and the max in the worst-case?

12.9 FIND THE kTH LARGEST ELEMENT

Many algorithms require as a subroutine the computation of the kth largest element of an array. The first largest element is simply the largest element. The nth largest element is the smallest element, where n is the length of the array.

For example, if the input array $A = \langle 3, 2, 1, 5, 4 \rangle$, then $A[3]$ is the first largest element in A, $A[0]$ is the third largest element in A, and $A[2]$ is the fifth largest element in A.

Design an algorithm for computing the kth largest element in an array. Assume entries are distinct.

Hint: Use divide and conquer in conjunction with randomization.

Solution: The brute-force approach is to sort the input array A in descending order and return the element at index $k - 1$. The time complexity is $O(n \log n)$, where n is the length of A.

Sorting is wasteful, since it does more than what is required. For example, if we want the first largest element, we can compute that with a single iteration, which is $O(n)$.

For general k, we can store a candidate set of k elements in a min-heap, in a fashion analogous to Solution 11.4 on Page 175, which will yield a $O(n \log k)$ time complexity and $O(k)$ space complexity. This approach is faster than sorting but is not in-place.

Additionally, it does more than what's required—it computes the k largest elements in sorted order, but all that's asked for is the kth largest element.

Conceptually, to focus on the kth largest element in-place without completely sorting the array we can select an element at random (the "pivot"), and partition the remaining entries into those greater than the pivot and those less than the pivot. (Since the problem states all elements are distinct, there cannot be any other elements equal to the pivot.) If there are exactly $k - 1$ elements greater than the pivot, the pivot must be the kth largest element. If there are more than $k - 1$ elements greater than the pivot, we can discard elements less than or equal to the pivot—the k-largest element must be greater than the pivot. If there are less than $k - 1$ elements greater than the pivot, we can discard elements greater than or equal to the pivot.

Intuitively, this is a good approach because on average we reduce by half the number of entries to be considered.

Implemented naively, this approach requires $O(n)$ additional memory. However, we can avoid the additional storage by using the array itself to record the partitioning.

```
// The numbering starts from one, i.e., if A = [3,1,-1,2] then
// FindKthLargest(1, A) returns 3, FindKthLargest(2, A) returns 2,
// FindKthLargest(3, A) returns 1, and FindKthLargest(4, A) returns -1.
int FindKthLargest(int k, vector<int>* A_ptr) {
  return FindKth(k, greater<int>(), A_ptr);
}

template <typename Compare>
int FindKth(int k, Compare comp, vector<int>* A_ptr) {
  vector<int>& A = *A_ptr;
  int left = 0, right = A.size() - 1;
  default_random_engine gen((random_device())());
  while (left <= right) {
    // Generates a random integer in [left, right].
    int pivot_idx = uniform_int_distribution<int>{left, right}(gen);
    int new_pivot_idx = PartitionAroundPivot(left, right, pivot_idx, comp, &A);
    if (new_pivot_idx == k - 1) {
      return A[new_pivot_idx];
    } else if (new_pivot_idx > k - 1) {
      right = new_pivot_idx - 1;
    } else {  // new_pivot_idx < k - 1.
      left = new_pivot_idx + 1;
    }
  }
}

// Partition A[left : right] around pivot_idx, returns the new index of the
// pivot, new_pivot_idx, after partition. After partitioning,
// A[left : new_pivot_idx - 1] contains elements that are greater than the
// pivot, and A[new_pivot_idx + 1 : right] contains elements that are less
// than the pivot.
//
// Note: "less than" is defined by the Compare object.
//
// Returns the new index of the pivot element after partition.
```

```
template <typename Compare>
int PartitionAroundPivot(int left, int right, int pivot_idx, Compare comp,
                         vector<int>* A_ptr) {
  vector<int>& A = *A_ptr;
  int pivot_value = A[pivot_idx];
  int new_pivot_idx = left;
  swap(A[pivot_idx], A[right]);
  for (int i = left; i < right; ++i) {
    if (comp(A[i], pivot_value)) {
      swap(A[i], A[new_pivot_idx++]);
    }
  }
  swap(A[right], A[new_pivot_idx]);
  return new_pivot_idx;
}
```

Since we expect to reduce the number of elements to process by roughly half, the average time complexity $T(n)$ satisfies $T(n) = O(n) + T(n/2)$. This solves to $T(n) = O(n)$. The space complexity is $O(1)$. The worst-case time complexity is $O(n^2)$, which occurs the randomly selected pivot is the smallest or largest element in the current subarray. The probability of the worst-case reduces exponentially with the length of the input array, and the worst-case is a nonissue in practice. For this reason, the randomize selection algorithm is sometimes said to have almost certain $O(n)$ time complexity.

Variant: Design an algorithm for finding the kth largest element of A in the presence of duplicates. The kth largest element is defined to be $A[k-1]$ after A has been sorted in a stable manner, i.e., if $A[i] = A[j]$ and $i < j$ then $A[i]$ must appear before $A[j]$ after stable sorting.

12.10 COMPUTE THE OPTIMUM MAILBOX PLACEMENT

A number of apartment buildings are coming up on a new street. The postal service wants to place a single mailbox on the street. Their objective is to minimize the total distance that residents have to walk to collect their mail each day. (Different buildings may have different numbers of residents.)

Devise an algorithm that computes where to place the mailbox so as to minimize the total distance, that residents travel to get to the mailbox. Assume the input is specified as an array of building objects, where each building object has a field indicating the number of residents in that building, and a field indicating the building's distance from the start of the street.

Hint: Process the buildings in sorted order.

Solution: The idea is to place the mailbox close to the middle of the street. Placing it halfway between the first and last buildings may not be optimum if the distribution and placement of buildings is skewed, e.g., if there is a single building with a small number of residents which is far up the street from the rest.

What we want is a point which balances the number of residents on either side of that point—if the mailbox is placed in such a way that more than half the residents are on one side, then by moving the mailbox to the balance point, the number of residents who travel a lesser distance is greater than the number of residents whose travel distance is increased. For both groups, the change in distance traveled per resident is the same.

Sort the buildings according to their distance from the beginning of the street. Suppose the total number of residents is odd, say $2m + 1$. Let the sum of the number of residents in the first i buildings be S_i. Then the optimum location for the mailbox is at the building where S_i first becomes greater than or equal to $m + 1$.

If the number of residents is even, say $2m$, any location between the mth and $(m + 1)$th resident's buildings can be used as the solution. (If they live in the same building, that building will be the optimum location.)

For example, suppose there are buildings at distances 10, 20, 25, and 100 from the start of the street, and the buildings contain 3, 5, 4, and 3 residents, respectively. Then the optimum location for the mailbox is at the second building, since $3 + 5 + 4 + 3 = 15 = 2 \times 7 + 1$, and the $(7 + 1)$th resident resides in the second building. If instead the fourth building had 4 residents, the optimum location would be any location between the second and third buildings.

If the buildings are given sorted by distance from the beginning of the street, the median resident can be found in linear time by iterating through the offsets in increasing order, adding the corresponding resident counts until the count gets to the median. The time complexity is $O(n)$ where n is the number of buildings; it is independent of the number of residents.

If the distances are not sorted, we can sort in $O(n \log n)$, and then find the median. Alternatively, we can extend Solution 12.9 on Page 195 to weighted inputs to achieve almost certain $O(n)$ time.

Variant: Compute a location that minimizes the sum of the squares of the distances traveled by the residents.

Variant: Compute a location that minimizes the maximum distance that any resident travels.

12.11 FIND THE MISSING IP ADDRESS

The storage capacity of hard drives dwarfs that of RAM. This can lead to interesting space-time trade-offs.

Suppose you were given a file containing roughly one billion IP addresses, each of which is a 32-bit quantity. How would you programmatically find an IP address that is not in the file? Assume you have unlimited drive space but only a few megabytes of RAM at your disposal.

Hint: Can you be sure there is an address which is not in the file?

Solution: Since the file can be treated as consisting of 32-bit integers, we can sort the input file and then iterate through it, searching for a gap between values. The time complexity is $O(n \log n)$, where n is number of entries. Furthermore, to keep the RAM usage low, the sort will have to use disk as storage, which in practice is very slow.

Note that we cannot just compute the largest entry and add one to it, since if the largest entry is 255.255.255.255 (the highest possible IP address), adding one to it leads to overflow. The same holds for the smallest entry. (In practice this would be a good heuristic.)

We could add all the IP addresses in the file to a hash table, and then enumerate IP addresses, starting with 0.0.0.0, until we find one not in the hash table. However, a hash table requires considerable overhead—of the order of 10 bytes for each integer, i.e., of the order of 10 gigabytes.

We can reduce the storage requirement by an order of magnitude by using a bit array representation for the set of all possible IP addresses. Specifically, we allocate an array of 2^{32} bits, initialized to 0, and write a 1 at each index that corresponds to an IP address in the file. Then we iterate through the bit array, looking for an entry set to 0. There are $2^{32} \approx 4 \times 10^9$ possible IP addresses, so not all IP addresses appear in the file. The storage is $2^{32}/8$ bytes, is half a gigabyte. This is still well in excess of the storage limit.

Since the input is in a file, we can make multiple passes through it. We can use this to narrow the search down to subsets of the space of all IP addresses as follows. We make a pass through the file to count the number of IP addresses present whose leading bit is a 1, and the number of IP addresses whose leading bit is a 0. At least one IP address must exist which is not present in the file, so at least one of these two counts is below 2^{31}. For example, suppose we have determined using counting that there must be an IP address which begins with 0 and is absent from the file. We can focus our attention on IP addresses in the file that begin with 0, and continue the process of elimination based on the second bit. This entails 32 passes, and uses only two integer-valued count variables as storage.

Since we have more storage, we can count on groups of bits. Specifically, we can count the number of IP addresses in the file that begin with $0, 1, 2, \ldots, 2^{16} - 1$ using an array of 2^{16} 32-bit integers. For every IP address in the file, we take its 16 MSBs to index into this array and increment the count of that number. Since the file contains fewer than 2^{32} numbers, there must be one entry in the array that is less than 2^{16}. This tells us that there is at least one IP address which has those upper bits and is not in the file. In the second pass, we can focus only on the addresses whose leading 16 bits match the one we have found, and use a bit array of size 2^{16} to identify a missing address.

```
int FindMissingElement(ifstream* ifs) {
  const int kNumBucket = 1 << 16;
  vector<size_t> counter(kNumBucket, 0);
  unsigned int x;
  while (*ifs >> x) {
    int upper_part_x = x >> 16;
```

```
    ++counter[upper_part_x];
}


// Look for a bucket that contains less than (1 << 16) elements.
const int kBucketCapacity = 1 << 16;
int candidate_bucket;
for (int i = 0; i < kNumBucket; ++i) {
  if (counter[i] < kBucketCapacity) {
    candidate_bucket = i;
    break;
  }
}


// Finds all IP addresses in the stream whose first 16 bits
// are equal to candidate_bucket.
ifs->clear();
ifs->seekg(0, ios::beg);
bitset<kBucketCapacity> bit_vec;
while (*ifs >> x) {
  int upper_part_x = x >> 16;
  if (candidate_bucket == upper_part_x) {
    // Records the presence of 16 LSB of x.
    int lower_part_x = ((1 << 16) - 1) & x;
    bit_vec.set(lower_part_x);
  }
}
ifs->close();


// At least one of the LSB combinations is absent, find it.
for (int i = 0; i < kBucketCapacity; ++i) {
  if (bit_vec[i] == 0) {
    return (candidate_bucket << 16) | i;
  }
}
}
```

The storage requirement is dominated by the count array, i.e., 2^{16} 4 byte entries, which is a quarter of a megabyte.

12.12 FIND THE DUPLICATE AND MISSING ELEMENTS

If an array contains $n-1$ integers, each between 0 and $n-1$, inclusive, and all numbers in the array are distinct, then it must be the case that exactly one number between 0 and $n-1$ is absent.

We can determine the missing number in $O(n)$ time and $O(1)$ space by computing the sum of the elements in the array. Since the sum of all the numbers from 0 to $n-1$, inclusive, is $\frac{(n-1)n}{2}$, we can subtract the sum of the numbers in the array from $\frac{(n-1)n}{2}$ to get the missing number.

For example, if the array is $\langle 5, 3, 0, 1, 2 \rangle$, then $n = 6$. We subtract $(5+3+0+1+2) = 11$ from $\frac{5(6)}{2} = 15$, and the result, 4, is the missing number.

Similarly, if the array contains $n + 1$ integers, each between 0 and $n - 1$, inclusive, with exactly one element appearing twice, the duplicated integer will be equal to the sum of the elements of the array minus $\frac{(n-1)n}{2}$.

Alternatively, for the first problem, we can compute the missing number by computing the XOR of all the integers from 0 to $n - 1$, inclusive, and XORing that with the XOR of all the elements in the array. Every element in the array, except for the missing element, cancels out with an integer from the first set. Therefore, the resulting XOR equals the missing element. The same approach works for the problem of finding the duplicated element. For example, the array $\langle 5, 3, 0, 1, 2 \rangle$ represented in binary is $\langle (101)_2, (011)_2, (000)_2, (001)_2, (010)_2 \rangle$. The XOR of these entries is $(101)_2$. The XOR of all numbers from 0 to 5, inclusive, is $(001)_2$. The XOR of $(101)_2$ and $(001)_2$ is $(100)_2 = 4$, which is the missing number.

We now turn to a related, though harder, problem.

You are given an array of n integers, each between 0 and $n - 1$, inclusive. Exactly one element appears twice, implying that exactly one number between 0 and $n - 1$ is missing from the array. How would you compute the duplicate and missing numbers?

Hint: Consider performing multiple passes through the array.

Solution: A brute-force approach is to use a hash table to store the entries in the array. The number added twice is the duplicate. After having built the hash table, we can test for the missing element by iterating through the numbers from 0 to $n - 1$, inclusive, stopping when a number is not present in the hash table. The time complexity and space complexity are $O(n)$. We can improve the space complexity to $O(1)$ by sorting the array, subsequent to which finding duplicate and missing values is trivial. However, the time complexity increases to $O(n \log n)$.

We can improve on the space complexity by focusing on a collective property of the numbers in the array, rather than the individual numbers. For example, let t be the element appearing twice, and m be the missing number. The sum of the numbers from 0 to $n - 1$, inclusive, is $\frac{(n-1)n}{2}$, so the sum of the elements in the array is exactly $\frac{(n-1)n}{2} + t - m$. This gives us an equation in t and m, but we need one more independent equation to solve for them.

We could use an equation for the product of the elements in the array, or for the sum of the squares of the elements in the array. Both of these are unsatisfactory because they are prone to overflow.

The introduction to this problem showed how to find a missing number from an array of $n - 2$ distinct numbers between 0 and $n - 1$ using XOR. Applying the same idea to the current problem, i.e., computing the XOR of all the numbers from 0 to $n - 1$, inclusive, and the entries in the array, yields $m \oplus t$. This does not seem very helpful at first glance, since we want m and t. However, since $m \neq t$, there must be some bit in $m \oplus t$ that is set to 1, i.e., m and t differ in that bit. For example, the XOR of $(01101)_2$ and $(11100)_2$ is $(10001)_2$. The 1s in the XOR are exactly the bits where $(01101)_2$ and $(11100)_2$ differ.

This fact allows us to focus on a subset of numbers from 0 to $n - 1$ where we can guarantee exactly one of m and t is present. Suppose we know m and t differ in the kth bit. We compute the XOR of the numbers from 0 to $n - 1$ in which the kth bit is 1, and the entries in the array in which the kth bit is 1. Let this XOR be h—by the logic described in the problem statement, h must be one of m or t. We can make another pass through A to determine if h is the duplicate or the missing element.

For example, for the array $\langle 5, 3, 0, 3, 1, 2 \rangle$, the duplicate entry t is 3 and the missing entry m is 4. Represented in binary the array is $\langle (101)_2, (011)_2, (000)_2, (011)_2, (001)_2, (010)_2 \rangle$. The XOR of these entries is $(110)_2$. The XOR of the numbers from 0 to 5, inclusive, is $(001)_2$. The XOR of $(110)_2$ and $(001)_2$ is $(111)_2$. This tells we can focus our attention on entries where the least significant bit is 1. We compute the XOR of all numbers between 0 and 5 in which this bit is 1, i.e., $(001)_2, (011)_2$, and $(101)_2$, and all entries in the array in which this bit is 1, i.e., $(101)_2, (011)_2, (011)_2$, and $(001)_2$. The XOR of these seven values is $(011)_2$. This implies that $(011)_2 = 3$ is either the missing or the duplicate entry. Another pass through the array shows that it is the duplicate entry. We can then find the missing entry by forming the XOR of $(011)_2$ with all entries in the array, and XORing that result with the XOR of all numbers from 0 to 5, which yields $(100)_2$, i.e., 4.

```
struct DuplicateAndMissing {
  int duplicate, missing;
};


DuplicateAndMissing FindDuplicateMissing(const vector<int>& A) {
  // Compute the XOR of all numbers from 0 to |A| - 1 and all entries in A.
  int miss_XOR_dup = 0;
  for (int i = 0; i < A.size(); ++i) {
    miss_XOR_dup ^= i ^ A[i];
  }

  // We need to find a bit that's set to 1 in miss_XOR_dup. Such a bit
  // must exist if there is a single missing number and a single duplicated
  // number in A.
  //
  // The bit-fiddling assignment below sets all of bits in differ_bit to 0
  // except for the least significant bit in miss_XOR_dup that's 1.
  int differ_bit = miss_XOR_dup & (~(miss_XOR_dup - 1));
  int miss_or_dup = 0;
  for (int i = 0; i < A.size(); ++i) {
    // Focus on entries and numbers in which the differ_bit-th bit is 1.
    if (i & differ_bit) {
      miss_or_dup ^= i;
    }
    if (A[i] & differ_bit) {
      miss_or_dup ^= A[i];
    }
  }

  // miss_or_dup is either the missing value or the duplicated entry.
  for (int A_i : A) {
```

201

```
    if (A_i == miss_or_dup) {  // miss_or_dup is the duplicate.
      return {miss_or_dup, miss_or_dup ^ miss_XOR_dup};
    }
  }
  // miss_or_dup is the missing value.
  return {miss_or_dup ^ miss_XOR_dup, miss_or_dup};
}
```

The time complexity is $O(n)$ and the space complexity is $O(1)$.

13

Hash Tables

The new methods are intended to reduce the amount of space required to contain the hash-coded information from that associated with conventional methods. The reduction in space is accomplished by exploiting the possibility that a small fraction of errors of commission may be tolerable in some applications.

— *"Space/time trade-offs in hash coding with allowable errors,"*
B. H. BLOOM, 1970

The idea underlying a *hash table* is to store objects according to their key field in an array. Objects are stored in array locations based on the "hash code" of the key. The hash code is an integer computed from the key by a hash function. If the hash function is chosen well, the objects are distributed uniformly across the array locations.

If two keys map to the same location, a "collision" is said to occur. The standard mechanism to deal with collisions is to maintain a linked list of objects at each array location. If the hash function does a good job of spreading objects across the underlying array and take $O(1)$ time to compute, on average, lookups, insertions, and deletions have $O(1 + n/m)$ time complexity, where n is the number of objects and m is the length of the array. If the "load" n/m grows large, rehashing can be applied to the hash table. A new array with a larger number of locations is allocated, and the objects are moved to the new array. Rehashing is expensive ($O(n + m)$ time) but if it is done infrequently (for example, whenever the number of entries doubles), its amortized cost is low.

A hash table is qualitatively different from a sorted array—keys do not have to appear in order, and randomization (specifically, the hash function) plays a central role. Compared to binary search trees (discussed in Chapter 15), inserting and deleting in a hash table is more efficient (assuming rehashing is infrequent). One disadvantage of hash tables is the need for a good hash function but this is rarely an issue in practice. Similarly, rehashing is not a problem outside of realtime systems and even for such systems, a separate thread can do the rehashing.

A hash function has one hard requirement—equal keys should have equal hash codes. This may seem obvious, but is easy to get wrong, e.g., by writing a hash function that is based on address rather than contents, or by including profiling data.

A softer requirement is that the hash function should "spread" keys, i.e., the hash codes for a subset of objects should be uniformly distributed across the underlying array. In addition, a hash function should be efficient to compute.

Now we illustrate the steps in designing a hash function suitable for strings. First, the hash function should examine all the characters in the string. It should give a large range of values, and should not let one character dominate (e.g., if we simply cast characters to integers and multiplied them, a single 0 would result in a hash code of 0). We would also like a rolling hash function, one in which if a character is deleted from the front of the string, and another added to the end, the new hash code can be computed in $O(1)$ time (see Solution 7.14 on Page 107). The following function has these properties:

```
int StringHash(const string& str, int modulus) {
  const int kMult = 997;
  int val = 0;
  for (char c : str) {
    val = (val * kMult + c) % modulus;
  }
  return val;
}
```

A hash table is a good data structure to represent a dictionary, i.e., a set of strings. In some applications, a trie, which is a tree data structure that is used to store a dynamic set of strings, has computational advantages. Unlike a BST, nodes in the tree do not store a key. Instead, the node's position in the tree defines the key which it is associated with. See Problem 22.23 on Page 437 for an example of trie construction and application.

13.1 PARTITION INTO ANAGRAMS

Anagrams are popular word play puzzles, where by rearranging letters of one set of words, you get another set of words. For example, "eleven plus two" is an anagram for "twelve plus one". Crossword puzzle enthusiasts and Scrabble players benefit from the ability to view all possible anagrams of a given set of letters.

Write a program that takes as input a set of words and returns groups of anagrams for those words. Each group must contain at least two words.

For example, if the input is "debitcard", "elvis", "silent", "badcredit", "lives", "freedom", "listen", "levis", "money" then there are three groups of anagrams: (1.) "debitcard", "badcredit"; (2.) "elvis", "lives", "levis"; (3.) "silent", "listen". (Note that "money" does not appear in any group, since it has no anagrams in the set.)

Hint: Map strings to strings so that strings which are anagrams map to the same string.

Solution: Let's begin by considering the problem of testing whether one word is an anagram of another. Since anagrams do not depend on the ordering of characters in the strings, we can perform the test by sorting the characters in the string. Two words are anagrams if and only if they result in equal strings after sorting. For example, sort("logarithmic") and sort("algorithmic") are both "acghiilmort", so "logarithmic" and "algorithmic" are anagrams.

We can form the described grouping of strings by iterating through all strings, and comparing each string with all other remaining strings. If two strings are anagrams, we do not consider the second string again. This leads to an $O(n^2 m \log m)$ algorithm, where n is the number of strings and m is the maximum string length.

Looking more carefully at the above computation, note that the key idea is to map strings to a representative. Given any string, its sorted version can be used as a unique identifier for the anagram group it belongs to. What we want is a map from a sorted string to the anagrams it corresponds to. Anytime you need to store a set of strings, a hash table is an excellent choice. Our final algorithm proceeds by adding sort(s) for each string s in the dictionary to a hash table. The sorted strings are keys, and the values are arrays of the corresponding strings from the original input.

```
vector<vector<string>> FindAnagrams(const vector<string>& dictionary) {
  unordered_map<string, vector<string>> sorted_string_to_anagrams;
  for (const string& s : dictionary) {
    // Sorts the string, uses it as a key, and then appends
    // the original string as another value into hash table.
    string sorted_str(s);
    sort(sorted_str.begin(), sorted_str.end());
    sorted_string_to_anagrams[sorted_str].emplace_back(s);
  }

  vector<vector<string>> anagram_groups;
  for (const auto& p : sorted_string_to_anagrams) {
    if (p.second.size() >= 2) {  // Found anagrams.
      anagram_groups.emplace_back(p.second);
    }
  }
  return anagram_groups;
}
```

The computation consists of n calls to sort and n insertions into the hash table. Sorting all the keys has time complexity $O(nm \log m)$. The insertions add a time complexity of $O(nm)$, yielding $O(nm \log m)$ time complexity in total.

13.2 TEST FOR PALINDROMIC PERMUTATIONS

A palindrome is a string that reads the same forwards and backwards, e.g., "level", "rotator", and "foobaraboof".

Write a program to test whether the letters forming a string can be permuted to form a palindrome. For example, "edified" can be permuted to form "deified".

Hint: Find a simple characterization of strings that can be permuted to form a palindrome.

Solution: A brute-force approach is to compute all permutations of the string, and test each one for palindromicity. This has a very high time complexity. Examining the approach in more detail, one thing to note is that if a string begins with say 'a', then we only need consider permutations that end with 'a'. This observation

205

can be used to prune the permutation-based algorithm. However, a more powerful conclusion is that all characters must occur in pairs for a string to be permutable into a palindrome, with one exception, if the string is of odd length. For example, for the string "edified", which is of odd length (7) there are two 'e', two 'f's, two 'i's, and one 'd'—this is enough to guarantee that "edified" can be permuted into a palindrome.

More formally, if the string is of even length, a necessary and sufficient condition for it to be a palindrome is that each character in the string appear an even number of times. If the length is odd, all but one character should appear an even number of times. Both these cases are covered by testing that at most one character appears an odd number of times, which can be checked using a hash table mapping characters to frequencies.

```cpp
bool CanFormPalindrome(const string& s) {
  unordered_map<char, int> char_frequencies;
  // Compute the frequency of each char in s.
  for (char c : s) {
    ++char_frequencies[c];
  }

  // A string can be permuted as a palindrome if and only if the number of
  // chars whose frequencies is odd is at most 1.
  int odd_frequency_count = 0;
  for (const auto& p : char_frequencies) {
    if ((p.second % 2) && ++odd_frequency_count > 1) {
      return false;
    }
  }
  return true;
}
```

The time complexity is $O(n)$, where n is the length of the string. The space complexity is $O(c)$, where c is the number of distinct characters appearing in the string.

13.3 IS AN ANONYMOUS LETTER CONSTRUCTIBLE?

Write a program which takes text for an anonymous letter and text for a magazine and determines if it is possible to write the anonymous letter using the magazine. The anonymous letter can be written using the magazine if for each character in the anonymous letter, the number of times it appears in the anonymous letter is no more than the number of times it appears in the magazine.

Hint: Count the number of distinct characters appearing in the letter.

Solution: A brute force approach is to count for each character in the character set the number of times it appears in the letter and in the magazine. If any character occurs more often in the letter than the magazine we return false, otherwise we return true. This approach is potentially slow because it iterates over all characters, including those that do not occur in the letter or magazine. It also makes multiple passes over both the letter and the magazine—as many passes as there are characters in the character set.

A better approach is to make a single pass over the letter, storing the character counts for the letter in a single hash table—keys are characters, and values are the number of times that character appears. Next, we make a pass over the magazine. When processing a character c, if c appears in the hash table, we reduce its count by 1; we remove it from the hash when its count goes to zero. If the hash becomes empty, we return true. If we reach the end of the letter and the hash is nonempty, we return false—each of the characters remaining in the hash occurs more times in the letter than the magazine.

```cpp
bool IsLetterConstructibleFromMagazine(const string& letter_text,
                                       const string& magazine_text) {
  unordered_map<char, int> char_frequency_for_letter;
  // Compute the frequencies for all chars in letter_text.
  for (char c : letter_text) {
    ++char_frequency_for_letter[c];
  }

  // Check if the characters in magazine_text can cover characters
  // in char_frequency_for_letter.
  for (char c : magazine_text) {
    auto it = char_frequency_for_letter.find(c);
    if (it != char_frequency_for_letter.cend()) {
      --it->second;
      if (it->second == 0) {
        char_frequency_for_letter.erase(it);
        if (char_frequency_for_letter.empty()) {
          // All characters for letter_text are matched.
          break;
        }
      }
    }
  }
  // Empty char_frequency_for_letter means every char in letter_text can be
  // covered by a character in magazine_text.
  return char_frequency_for_letter.empty();
}
```

In the worst-case, the letter is not constructible or the last character of the magazine is essentially required. Therefore, the time complexity is $O(m + n)$ where m and n are the number of characters in the letter and magazine, respectively. The space complexity is the size of the hash table constructed in the pass over the letter, i.e., $O(L)$, where L is the number of distinct characters appearing in the letter.

If the characters are coded in ASCII, we could do away with the hash table and use a 256 entry integer array A, with $A[i]$ being set to the number of times the character i appears in the letter.

The International Standard Book Number (ISBN) is a unique commercial book identifier. It is a string of length 10. The first 9 characters are digits; the last character is a check character. The check character is the sum of the first 9 digits, modulo 11, with 10 represented by 'X'. (Modern ISBNs use 13 digits, and the check digit is taken modulo 10; this problem is concerned with 10-digit ISBNs.)

Create a cache for looking up prices of books identified by their ISBN. You implement support lookup, insert, and remove methods. Use the Least Recently Used (LRU) policy for cache eviction. If an ISBN is already present, insert should not change the price, but it should update that entry to be the most recently used entry. Lookup should also update that entry to be the most recently used entry.

Hint: Amortize the cost of deletion. Alternatively, use an auxiliary data structure.

Solution: Hash tables are ideally suited for fast lookups. We can use a hash table to quickly lookup price by using ISBNs as keys. Along with each key, we store a value, which is the price and the most recent time a lookup was done on that key.

This yields $O(1)$ lookup times on cache hits. Inserts into the cache are also $O(1)$ time, until the cache is full. Once the cache fills up, to add a new entry we have to find the LRU entry, which will be evicted to make place for the new entry. Finding this entry takes $O(n)$ time, where n is the cache size.

One way to improve performance is to use lazy garbage collection. Specifically, let's say we want the cache to be of size n. We do not delete any entries from the hash table until it grows to $2n$ entries. At this point we iterate through the entire hash table, and find the median age of items. Subsequently we discard everything below the median. The worst-case time to delete becomes $O(n)$ but it will happen at most once every n operations. Therefore, the amortized time to delete is $O(1)$. The drawback of this approach is the $O(n)$ time needed for some lookups that miss on a full cache, and the $O(n)$ increase in memory.

An alternative is to maintain a separate queue of keys. In the hash table we store for each key a reference to its location in the queue. Each time an ISBN is looked up and is found in the hash table, it is moved to the front of the queue. (This requires us to use a linked list implementation of the queue, so that items in the middle of the queue can be moved to the head.) When the length of the queue exceeds n, when a new element is added to the cache, the item at the tail of the queue is deleted from the cache, i.e., from the queue and the hash table.

```
template <size_t capacity>
class LRUCache {
 public:
  bool Lookup(int isbn, int* price) {
    auto it = isbn_price_table_.find(isbn);
    if (it == isbn_price_table_.end()) {
      return false;
    }
```

```
      *price = it->second.second;
      // Since key has just been accessed, move it to the front.
      MoveToFront(isbn, it);
      return true;
  }

  void Insert(int isbn, int price) {
      auto it = isbn_price_table_.find(isbn);
      // We add the value for key only if key is not present - we don't update
      // existing values.
      if (it != isbn_price_table_.end()) {
          // Specification says we should make isbn the most recently used.
          MoveToFront(isbn, it);
      } else {
          if (isbn_price_table_.size() == capacity) {
              // Removes the least recently used ISBN to get space.
              isbn_price_table_.erase(lru_queue_.back());
              lru_queue_.pop_back();
          }

          lru_queue_.emplace_front(isbn);
          isbn_price_table_[isbn] = {lru_queue_.begin(), price};
      }
  }

  bool Erase(int isbn) {
      auto it = isbn_price_table_.find(isbn);
      if (it == isbn_price_table_.end()) {
          return false;
      }

      lru_queue_.erase(it->second.first);
      isbn_price_table_.erase(it);
      return true;
  }

 private:
  typedef unordered_map<int, pair<list<int>::iterator, int>> Table;

  // Forces this key-value pair to move to the front.
  void MoveToFront(int isbn, const Table::iterator& it) {
      lru_queue_.erase(it->second.first);
      lru_queue_.emplace_front(isbn);
      it->second.first = lru_queue_.begin();
  }

  Table isbn_price_table_;
  list<int> lru_queue_;
};
```

The time complexity for each lookup is $O(1)$ for the hash table lookup and $O(1)$ for updating the queue, i.e., $O(1)$ overall.

Problem 10.4 on Page 152 is concerned with computing the LCA in a binary tree with parent pointers in time proportional to the height of the tree. The algorithm presented in Solution 10.4 on Page 152 entails traversing all the way to the root even if the nodes whose LCA is being computed are very close to their LCA.

Design an algorithm for computing the LCA of two nodes in a binary tree. The algorithm's time complexity should depend only on the distance from the nodes to the LCA.

Hint: Focus on the extreme case described in the problem introduction.

Solution: The brute-force approach is to traverse upwards from the one node to the root, recording the nodes on the search path, and then traversing upwards from the other node, stopping as soon as we see a node on the path from the first node. The problem with this approach is that if the two nodes are far from the root, we end up traversing all the way to the root, even if the LCA is the parent of the two nodes, i.e., they are siblings. This is illustrated in by L and N in Figure 10.1 on Page 146.

Intuitively, the brute-force approach is suboptimal because it potentially processes nodes well above the LCA. We can avoid this by alternating moving upwards from the two nodes and storing the nodes visited as we move up in a hash table. Each time we visit a node we check to see if it has been visited before.

```
BinaryTreeNode<int>* LCA(const unique_ptr<BinaryTreeNode<int>>& node_0,
                         const unique_ptr<BinaryTreeNode<int>>& node_1) {
  auto *iter_0 = node_0.get(), *iter_1 = node_1.get();
  unordered_set<const BinaryTreeNode<int>*> nodes_on_path_to_root;
  while (iter_0 || iter_1) {
    // Ascend tree in tandem for these two nodes.
    if (iter_0) {
      if (nodes_on_path_to_root.emplace(iter_0).second == false) {
        return iter_0;
      }
      iter_0 = iter_0->parent;
    }
    if (iter_1) {
      if (nodes_on_path_to_root.emplace(iter_1).second == false) {
        return iter_1;
      }
      iter_1 = iter_1->parent;
    }
  }
  throw invalid_argument("node_0 and node_1 are not in the same tree");
}
```

Note that we are trading space for time. The algorithm for Solution 10.4 on Page 152 used $O(1)$ space and $O(h)$ time, whereas the algorithm presented above uses $O(D0+D1)$ space and time, where $D0$ is the distance from the LCA to the first node, and $D1$ is the distance from the LCA to the second node. In the worst-case, the nodes are leaves whose LCA is the root, and we end up using $O(h)$ space and time, where h is the height of the tree.

13.6 COMPUTE THE k MOST FREQUENT QUERIES

You are given a log file containing search queries. Each query is a string, and queries are separated by newlines. Diverse applications, such as autocompletion and trend analysis, require computing the most frequent queries. In the abstract, you are to solve the following problem.

You are given an array of strings. Compute the k strings that appear most frequently in the array.

Hint: Consider extreme values for k, as well as scenarios where there are a relatively small number of distinct strings.

Solution: The brute-force approach is to first find the distinct strings and how often each one of them occurs using a hash table—keys are strings and values are frequencies. After building the hash table, we create a new array on the unique strings and sort the new array, using a custom comparator in which strings are ordered by their frequency (which we get via a lookup in the hash table). The k top entries in the new array after sorting are the result. The time complexity is $O(n + m \log m)$, where n is the number of strings the original array, and m is the number of distinct strings. The first term comes from building the hash table, and the second comes from the complexity to sort the array. The space complexity is $O(m)$.

Since all that is required is the k most frequent strings, the sort phase in above algorithm is overkill because it tells us about the relative frequencies of strings that are infrequent too. We can achieve a time complexity of $O(n + m \log k)$. This approach is superior when m is large, i.e., comparable to n, and k is small. We do this by maintaining a min-heap of the k most frequent strings. We add the first k strings to the hash table. We compare the frequency of each subsequent string with the frequency of the string at the root of the min-heap. If the new string's frequency is greater than the root's frequency, we delete the root and add the new string to the min-heap. The k strings in the min-heap at the end of the iteration are the result. In the worst-case, each iterative step entails a heap delete and insert, so the time complexity is $O(n + m \log k)$. The space complexity is dominated by the hash table, i.e., $O(m)$.

We can improve the time complexity to almost certain $O(n + m) = O(n)$ by using the algorithm in Solution 12.9 on Page 195 to compute the k largest elements in the array of unique strings, again comparing strings on their frequencies. The space complexity is $O(m)$.

13.7 FIND THE NEAREST REPEATED ENTRIES IN AN ARRAY

People do not like reading text in which a word is used multiple times in a short paragraph. You are to write a program which helps identify such a problem.

Write a program which takes as input an array and finds the distance between a closest pair of equal entries. For example, if s = ⟨"All", "work", "and", "no", "play", "makes", "for", "no", "work", "no", "fun", "and", "no", "results"⟩, then the second and third occurrences of "no" is the closest pair.

Hint: Each entry in the array is a candidate.

Solution: The brute-force approach is to iterate over all pairs of entries, check if they are the same, and if so, if the distance between them is less than the smallest such distance seen so far. The time complexity is $O(n^2)$, where n is the array length.

We can improve upon the brute-force algorithm by noting that when examining an entry, we do not need to look at every other entry—we only care about entries which are the same. We can store the set of indices corresponding to a given value using a hash table and iterate over all such sets. However, there is a better approach—when processing an entry, all we care about is the closest previous equal entry. Specifically, as we scan through the array, we record for each value seen so far, we store in a hash table the latest index at which it appears. When processing the element, we use the hash table to see the latest index less than the current index holding the same value.

For the given example, when processing the element at index 9, which is "no", the hash table tells us the most recent previous occurrence of "no" is at index 7, so we update the distance of the closest pair of equal entries seen so far to 2.

```
int FindNearestRepetition(const vector<string>& paragraph) {
  unordered_map<string, int> word_to_latest_index;
  int nearest_repeated_distance = numeric_limits<int>::max();
  for (int i = 0; i < paragraph.size(); ++i) {
    auto latest_equal_word = word_to_latest_index.find(paragraph[i]);
    if (latest_equal_word != word_to_latest_index.end()) {
      nearest_repeated_distance =
          min(nearest_repeated_distance, i - latest_equal_word->second);
    }
    word_to_latest_index[paragraph[i]] = i;
  }
  return nearest_repeated_distance;
}
```

The time complexity is $O(n)$, since we perform a constant amount of work per entry. The space complexity is $O(d)$, where d is the number of distinct entries in the array.

13.8 FIND THE SMALLEST SUBARRAY COVERING ALL VALUES

When you type keywords in a search engine, the search engine will return results, and each result contains a digest of the web page, i.e., a highlighting within that page of the keywords that you searched for. For example, a search for the keywords "Union" and "save" on a page with the text of the Emancipation Proclamation should return the result shown in Figure 13.1 on the next page.

> My paramount object in this struggle is to **save** the **Union**, and is not either to save or to destroy slavery. If I could save the Union without freeing any slave I would do it, and if I could save it by freeing all the slaves I would do it; and if I could save it by freeing some and leaving others alone I would also do that.

Figure 13.1: Search result with digest in boldface and search keywords underlined.

The digest for this page is the text in boldface, with the keywords underlined for emphasis. It is the shortest substring of the page which contains all the keywords in the search. The problem of computing the digest is abstracted as follows.

Write a program which takes an array of strings and a set of strings, and return the indices of the starting and ending index of a shortest subarray of the given array that "covers" the set, i.e., contains all strings in the set.

Hint: What is the maximum number of minimal subarrays that can cover the query?

Solution: The brute force approach is to iterate over all subarrays, testing if the subarray contains all strings in the set. If the array length is n, there are $O(n^2)$ subarrays. Testing whether the subarray contains each string in the set is an $O(n)$ operation using a hash table to record which strings are present in the subarray. The overall time complexity is $O(n^3)$.

We can improve the time complexity to $O(n^2)$ by growing the subarrays incrementally. Specifically, we can consider all subarrays starting at i in order of increasing length, stopping as soon as the set is covered. We use a hash table to record which strings in the set remain to be covered. Each time we increment the subarray length, we need $O(1)$ time to update the set of remaining strings.

We can further improve the algorithm by noting that when we move from i to $i + 1$ we can reuse the work performed from i. Specifically, let's say the smallest subarray starting at i covering the set ends at j. There is no point in considering subarrays starting at $i + 1$ and ending before j, since we know they cannot cover the set. When we advance to $i + 1$, either we still cover the set, or we have to advance j to cover the set. We continuously advance one of i or j, which implies an $O(n)$ time complexity.

As a concrete example, consider the array ⟨*apple, banana, apple, apple, dog, cat, apple, dog, banana, apple, cat, dog*⟩ and the set {*banana, cat*}. The smallest subarray covering the set starting at 0 ends at 5. Next, we advance to 1. Since the element at 0 is not in the set, the smallest subarray covering the set still ends at 5. Next, we advance to 2. Now we do not cover the set, so we advance from 5 to 8—now the subarray from 2 to 8 covers the set. We update the start index from 2 to 3 to 4 to 5 and continue to cover the set. When we advance to 6, we no longer cover the set, so we advance the end index till we get to 10. We can advance the start index to 8 and still cover the set. After we move past 8, we cannot cover the set. The shortest subarray covering the set is from 8 to 10.

```
struct Subarray {
```

```
    int start, end;
};

Subarray FindSmallestSubarrayCoveringSet(
    const vector<string> &paragraph, const unordered_set<string> &keywords) {
  unordered_map<string, int> keywords_to_count;
  Subarray result = Subarray{-1, -1};
  for (int left = 0, right = 0; right < paragraph.size();) {
    // Keeps advancing right until it reaches end or keywords_to_count has
    // all keywords.
    for (; right < paragraph.size() &&
           keywords_to_count.size() < keywords.size();
         ++right) {
      if (keywords.find(paragraph[right]) != keywords.end()) {
        ++keywords_to_count[paragraph[right]];
      }
    }

    // Keeps advancing left until it reaches end or keywords_to_count does not
    // have all keywords.
    for (; left < right && keywords_to_count.size() == keywords.size();
         ++left) {
      if (keywords.find(paragraph[left]) != keywords.end()) {
        auto keyword_count = keywords_to_count.find(paragraph[left]);
        --keyword_count->second;
        if (keyword_count->second == 0) {
          keywords_to_count.erase(keyword_count);
          if ((result.start == -1 && result.end == -1) ||
              right - 1 - left < result.end - result.start) {
            result = {left, right - 1};
          }
        }
      }
    }
  }
  return result;
}
```

The complexity is $O(n)$, where n is the length of the array, since for each of the two indices we spend $O(1)$ time per advance, and each is advanced at most $n - 1$ times.

The disadvantage of this approach is that we need to keep the subarrays in memory. We can achieve a streaming algorithm by keeping track of latest occurrences of query keywords as we process A. We use a doubly linked list L to store the last occurrence (index) of each keyword in Q, and hash table H to map each keyword in Q to the corresponding node in L. Each time a word in Q is encountered, we remove its node from L (which we find by using H), create a new node which records the current index in A, and append the new node to the end of L. We also update H. By doing this, each keyword in L is ordered by its order in A; therefore, if L has n_Q words (i.e., all keywords are shown) and the current index minus the index stored in the first node in L is less than current best, we update current best. The complexity is still $O(n)$.

```
Subarray FindSmallestSubarrayCoveringSubset(
    istringstream* sin, const vector<string>& query_strings) {
  // Tracks the last occurrence (index) of each string in query_strings.
  list<int> loc;
  unordered_map<string, list<int>::iterator> dict;
  for (const string& s : query_strings) {
    dict.emplace(s, loc.end());
  }

  Subarray res = Subarray{-1, -1};
  int idx = 0;
  string s;
  while (*sin >> s) {
    auto it = dict.find(s);
    if (it != dict.end()) {  // s is in query_strings.
      if (it->second != loc.end()) {
        // Explicitly remove s so that when we add it, it's the string most
        // recently added to loc.
        loc.erase(it->second);
      }
      loc.emplace_back(idx);
      it->second = --loc.end();
    }

    if (loc.size() == query_strings.size()) {
      // We have seen all strings in query_strings, let's get to work.
      if ((res.start == -1 && res.end == -1) ||
          idx - loc.front() < res.end - res.start) {
        res = {loc.front(), idx};
      }
    }
    ++idx;
  }
  return res;
}
```

Variant: Suppose that the input is presented in streaming fashion, i.e., elements are read one at a time, and you cannot read earlier entries. The set of strings is much smaller, and can be stored in RAM. How would you modify your solution for this case?

Variant: Given an array A, find a shortest subarray $A[i : j]$ such that each distinct value present in A is also present in the subarray.

Variant: Given an array A, rearrange the elements so that the shortest subarray containing all the distinct values in A has maximum possible length.

Variant: Given an array A and a positive integer k, rearrange the elements so that no two equal elements are k or less apart.

Variant: Given an array A, find a longest subarray $A[i : j]$ such that all elements in $A[i : j]$ are distinct.

In Problem 13.8 on Page 213 we did not differentiate between the order in which keywords appeared. If the digest has to include the keywords in the order in which they appear in the search textbox, we may get a different digest. For example, for the search keywords "Union" and "save", in that order, the digest would be "**Union, and is not either to save**".

Write a program that takes two arrays of strings, and return the indices of the starting and ending index of a shortest subarray of the first array (the "paragraph" array) that "sequentially covers", i.e., contains all the strings in the second array (the "keywords" array), in the order in which they appear in the keywords array. You can assume all keywords are distinct. For example, let the paragraph array be ⟨apple, banana, cat, apple⟩, and the keywords array be ⟨banana, apple⟩. The paragraph subarray starting at index 0 and ending at index 1 does not fulfill the specification, even though it contains all the keywords, since they do not appear in the specified order. On the other hand, the subarray starting at index 1 and ending at index 3 does fulfill the specification.

Hint: For each index in the paragraph array, compute the shortest subarray ending at that index which fulfills the specification.

Solution: The brute-force approach is to iterate over all subarrays of the paragraph array. To check whether a subarray of the paragraph array sequentially covers the keyword array, we search for the first occurrence of the first keyword. We never need to consider a later occurrence of the first keyword, since subsequent occurrences do not give us any additional power to cover the keywords. Next we search for the first occurrence of the second keyword that appears after the first occurrence of the first keyword. No earlier occurrence of the second keyword is relevant, since those occurrences can never appear in the correct order. This observation leads to an $O(n)$ time algorithm for testing whether a subarray fulfills the specification, where n is the length of the paragraph array. Since there are $O(n^2)$ subarrays of the paragraph array, the overall time complexity is $O(n^3)$.

The brute-force algorithm repeats work. We can improve the time complexity to $O(n^2)$ by computing for each index, the shortest subarray starting at that index which sequentially covers the keyword array. The idea is that we can compute the desired subarray by advancing from the start index and marking off the keywords in order.

The improved algorithm still repeats work—as we advance through the paragraph array, we can reuse our computation of the earliest occurrences of keywords. To do this, we need auxiliary data structures to record previous results.

Specifically, we use a hash table to map keywords to their most recent occurrences in the paragraph array as we iterate through it, and a hash table mapping each keyword to the length of the shortest subarray ending at the most recent occurrence of that keyword.

These two hash tables give us is the ability to determine the shortest subarray sequentially covering the first k keywords given the shortest subarray sequentially covering the first $k - 1$ keywords.

When processing the ith string in the paragraph array, if that string is the jth keyword, we update the most recent occurrence of that keyword to i. The shortest subarray ending at i which sequentially covers the first j keywords consists of the shortest subarray ending at the most recent occurrence of the first $j - 1$ keywords plus the elements from the most recent occurrence of the $(j - 1)$th keyword to i. This computation is implemented below.

```cpp
struct Subarray {
  // Represent subarray by starting and ending indices, inclusive.
  int start, end;
};

Subarray FindSmallestSequentiallyCoveringSubset(
    const vector<string>& paragraph, const vector<string>& keywords) {
  // Maps each keyword to its index in the keywords array.
  unordered_map<string, int> keyword_to_idx;
  // Initializes keyword_to_idx.
  for (int i = 0; i < keywords.size(); ++i) {
    keyword_to_idx.emplace(keywords[i], i);
  }

  // Since keywords are uniquely identified by their indices in keywords
  // array, we can use those indices as keys to lookup in a vector.
  vector<int> latest_occurrence(keywords.size(), -1);
  // For each keyword (identified by its index in keywords array), stores the
  // length of the shortest subarray ending at the most recent occurrence of
  // that keyword that sequentially cover all keywords up to that keyword.
  vector<int> shortest_subarray_length(keywords.size(),
                                       numeric_limits<int>::max());

  int shortest_distance = numeric_limits<int>::max();
  Subarray result = Subarray{-1, -1};
  for (int i = 0; i < paragraph.size(); ++i) {
    if (keyword_to_idx.count(paragraph[i])) {
      int keyword_idx = keyword_to_idx.find(paragraph[i])->second;
      if (keyword_idx == 0) {  // First keyword.
        shortest_subarray_length[keyword_idx] = 1;
      } else if (shortest_subarray_length[keyword_idx - 1] !=
                 numeric_limits<int>::max()) {
        int distance_to_previous_keyword =
            i - latest_occurrence[keyword_idx - 1];
        shortest_subarray_length[keyword_idx] =
            distance_to_previous_keyword +
            shortest_subarray_length[keyword_idx - 1];
      }
      latest_occurrence[keyword_idx] = i;

      // Last keyword, look for improved subarray.
      if (keyword_idx == keywords.size() - 1 &&
          shortest_subarray_length.back() < shortest_distance) {
```

```
        shortest_distance = shortest_subarray_length.back();
        result = {i - shortest_subarray_length.back() + 1, i};
      }
    }
  }
  return result;
}
```

Processing each entry of the paragraph array entails a constant number of lookups and updates, leading to an $O(n)$ time complexity, where n is the length of the paragraph array. The additional space complexity is dominated by the three hash tables, i.e., $O(m)$, where m is the number of keywords.

13.10 FIND THE LONGEST SUBARRAY WITH DISTINCT ENTRIES

Write a program that takes an array and returns the length of a longest subarray with the property that all its elements are distinct. For example, if the array is $\langle f, s, f, e, t, w, e, n, w, e \rangle$ then a longest subarray all of whose elements are distinct is $\langle s, f, e, t, w \rangle$.

Hint: What should you do if the subarray from indices i to j satisfies the property, but the subarray from i to $j + 1$ does not?

Solution: We begin with a brute-force approach. For each subarray, we test if all its elements are distinct using a hash table. The time complexity is $O(n^3)$, where n is the array length since there are $O(n^2)$ subarrays, and their average length is $O(n)$.

We can improve on the brute-force algorithm by noting that if a subarray contains duplicates, every array containing that subarray will also contain duplicates. Therefore, for any given starting index, we can compute the longest subarray starting at that index containing no duplicates in time $O(n)$, since we can incrementally add elements to the hash table of elements from the starting index. This leads to an $O(n^2)$ algorithm. As soon as we get a duplicate, we cannot find a longer beginning at the same initial index that is duplicate-free.

We can improve the time complexity by reusing previous computation as we iterate through the array. Suppose we know the longest duplicate-free subarray ending at a given index. The longest duplicate-free subarray ending at the next index is either the previous subarray appended with the element at the next index, if that element does not appear in the longest duplicate-free subarray at the current index. Otherwise it is the subarray beginning at the most recent occurrence of the element at the next index to the next index. To perform this case analysis as we iterate, all we need is a hash table storing the most recent occurrence of each element, and the longest duplicate-free subarray ending at the current element.

For the given example, $\langle f, s, f, e, t, w, e, n, w, e \rangle$, when we process the element at index 2, the longest duplicate-free subarray ending at index 1 is from 0 to 1. The hash table tells us that the element at index 2, namely f, appears in that subarray, so we update the longest subarray ending at index 2 to being from index 1 to 2. Indices 3–5 introduce fresh elements. Index 6 holds a repeated value, e, which appears within the longest subarray ending at index 5; specifically, it appears at index 3. Therefore, the longest subarray ending at index 6 to start at index 4.

```
int LongestSubarrayWithDistinctEntries(const vector<int>& A) {
  // Records the most recent occurrences of each entry.
  unordered_map<int, size_t> most_recent_occurrence;
  size_t longest_dup_free_subarray_start_idx = 0, result = 0;
  for (size_t i = 0; i < A.size(); ++i) {
    auto dup_idx = most_recent_occurrence.emplace(A[i], i);
    // Defer updating dup_idx until we see a duplicate.
    if (!dup_idx.second) {
      // A[i] appeared before. Did it appear in the longest current subarray?
      if (dup_idx.first->second >= longest_dup_free_subarray_start_idx) {
        result = max(result, i - longest_dup_free_subarray_start_idx);
        longest_dup_free_subarray_start_idx = dup_idx.first->second + 1;
      }
      dup_idx.first->second = i;
    }
  }
  result = max(result, A.size() - longest_dup_free_subarray_start_idx);
  return result;
}
```

The time complexity is $O(n)$, since we perform a constant number of operations per element.

13.11 FIND THE LENGTH OF A LONGEST CONTAINED INTERVAL

Write a program which takes as input a set of integers represented by an array, and returns the size of a largest subset of integers in the array having the property that if two integers are in the subset, then so are all integers between them. For example, if the input is $\langle 3, -2, 7, 9, 8, 1, 2, 0, -1, 5, 8 \rangle$, the largest such subset is $\{-2, -1, 0, 1, 2, 3\}$, so you should return 6.

Hint: Do you really need a total ordering on the input?

Solution: The brute-force algorithm is to sort the array and then iterate through it, recording for each entry the largest subset with the desired property ending at that entry.

On closer inspection we see that sorting is not essential to the functioning of the algorithm. We do not need the total ordering—all we care are about is whether the integers adjacent to a given value are present. This suggests using a hash table to store the entries. Now we iterate over the entries in the array. If an entry e is present in the hash table, we compute the largest interval including e such that all values in the interval are contained in the hash table. We do this by iteratively searching entries in the hash table of the form $e + 1, e + 2, \ldots$, and $e - 1, e - 2, \ldots$. When we are done, to avoid doing duplicated computation we remove all the entries in the computed interval from the hash table, since all these entries are in the same largest contained interval.

As a concrete example, consider $A = \langle 10, 5, 3, 11, 6, 100, 4 \rangle$. We initialize the hash table to $\{6, 10, 3, 11, 5, 100, 4\}$. The first entry in A is 10, and we find the largest interval contained in A including 10 by expanding from 10 in each direction by doing lookups in the hash table. The largest set is $\{10, 11\}$ and is of size 2. This computation updates the hash table to $\{6, 3, 5, 100, 4\}$. The next entry in A is 6. Since it is contained in the hash table, we know that the largest interval contained in A including 6 has not been computed yet. Expanding from 5, we see that 3, 4, 6 are all in the hash table, and 2 and 7 are not in the hash table, so the largest set containing 6 is $\{3, 4, 5, 6\}$, which is of size 4. We update the hash table to $\{100\}$. The three entries after 5, namely 3, 11, 6 are not present in the hash table, so we know we have already computed the longest intervals in A containing each of these. Then we get to 100, which cannot be extended, so the largest set containing it is $\{100\}$, which is of size 1. We update the hash table to $\{\}$. Since 4 is not in the hash table, we can skip it. The largest of the three sets is $\{3, 4, 5, 6\}$, i.e., the size of the largest contained interval is 4.

```
int LongestContainedRange(const vector<int>& A) {
  // unprocessed_entries records the existence of each entry in A.
  unordered_set<int> unprocessed_entries(A.begin(), A.end());

  int max_interval_size = 0;
  while (!unprocessed_entries.empty()) {
    int a = *unprocessed_entries.begin();
    unprocessed_entries.erase(a);

    // Finds the lower bound of the largest range containing a.
    int lower_bound = a - 1;
    while (unprocessed_entries.count(lower_bound)) {
      unprocessed_entries.erase(lower_bound);
      --lower_bound;
    }

    // Finds the upper bound of the largest range containing a.
    int upper_bound = a + 1;
    while (unprocessed_entries.count(upper_bound)) {
      unprocessed_entries.erase(upper_bound);
      ++upper_bound;
    }

    max_interval_size = max(max_interval_size, upper_bound - lower_bound - 1);
  }
  return max_interval_size;
}
```

The time complexity of this approach is $O(n)$, where n is the array length, since we add and remove array elements in the hash table no more than once.

Student test scores are recorded in a file. Each line consists of a student ID, which is an alphanumeric string, and an integer between 0 and 100, inclusive.

Write a program which takes as input a file containing test scores and returns the student who has the maximum score averaged across his or her top three tests. If the student has fewer than three test scores, ignore that student.

Hint: Generalize to computing the top k scores.

Solution: A straightforward approach would be to find the scores for each student, sort those scores, and average the top three. More specifically, we can find the scores for each student in a single pass, recording them using a map which takes a student id and stores scores for that student in a dynamic array. When all lines have been processed, we iterate through the map, sort each corresponding array, and average the top three scores for each student, skipping students with fewer than three scores. We track the student with the maximum average score as we iterate through the map.

The time complexity of this approach is $O(n \log n)$, where n is the number of lines in the input file. The worst-case corresponds to an input in which there is a single student, since we have to sort that student's score array. The space complexity is $O(n)$, regardless of the input.

Storing the entire set of scores for a student is wasteful, since we use only the top three scores. We can use a dynamic data structure to track just the top three scores seen so far. If three scores already have been seen for a student, and then a score is read for that student which is better than the lowest score of these three scores, we evict the lowest score, and add the new score. A min-heap is a natural candidate for holding the top three scores for each student. Note that scores can be repeated, so we need to use a data structure that supports duplicate entries.

For example, suppose the first three scores seen for Adam are 97, 91, and 96, in that order. The min-heap for Adam contains 97 after the first of his scores is read, 91, 97 after the second of his scores is read, and 91, 96, 97 after the third of his scores is read. Suppose the next score for Adam in the file is 88. Since 88 is less than 91 we do not update his top three scores. Then if the next score for Adam is 97, which is greater than 91, we remove the 91 and add 97, updating his top three scores to 96, 97, 97.

```
string FindStudentWithHighestBestOfThreeScores(ifstream* ifs) {
  // Use a multset to handle duplicated test scores.
  unordered_map<string, priority_queue<int, vector<int>, greater<int>>>
      student_scores;
  string name;
  int score;
  while (*ifs >> name >> score) {
    student_scores[name].emplace(score);
    if (student_scores[name].size() > 3) {
      student_scores[name].pop();  // Only keep the top 3 scores.
    }
  }
```

```
  string top_student = "no such student";
  int current_top_three_scores_sum = 0;
  for (const auto& scores : student_scores) {
    if (scores.second.size() == 3) {
      int current_scores_sum = GetTopThreeScoresSum(scores.second);
      if (current_scores_sum > current_top_three_scores_sum) {
        current_top_three_scores_sum = current_scores_sum;
        top_student = scores.first;
      }
    }
  }
  return top_student;
}

// Returns the sum of top three scores.
int GetTopThreeScoresSum(
    priority_queue<int, vector<int>, greater<int>> scores) {
  int sum = 0;
  while (!scores.empty()) {
    sum += scores.top();
    scores.pop();
  }
  return sum;
}
```

Since we track at most three scores for a student, updating takes constant-time operation. Therefore, the algorithm spends $O(1)$ time per test score, yielding an $O(n)$ time bound. The space complexity is $O(m)$, where m is the number of distinct students. In the worst-case, $m = O(n)$, but in the best-case it can be much better, e.g., if there are only few students but lots of test scores.

13.13 COMPUTE ALL STRING DECOMPOSITIONS

This problem is concerned with taking a string (the "sentence" string) and a set of strings (the "words"), and finding the substrings of the sentence which are the concatenation of all the words (in any order). For example, if the sentence string is "amanaplanacanal" and the set of words is {"can", "apl", "ana"}, "aplanacan" is a substring of the sentence that is the concatenation of all words.

Write a program which takes as input a string (the "sentence") and an array of strings (the "words"), and returns the starting indices of substrings of the sentence string which are the concatenation of all the strings in the words array. Each string must appear exactly once, and their ordering is immaterial. Assume all strings in the words array have equal length. It is possible for the words array to contain duplicates.

Hint: Exploit the fact that the words have the same length.

Solution: Let's begin by considering the problem of checking whether a string is the concatenation strings in words. We can solve this problem recursively—we find a string from words that is a prefix of the given string, and recurse with the remaining words and the remaining suffix.

When all strings in words have equal length, say n, only one distinct string in words can be a prefix of the given string. So we can directly check the first n characters of the string to see if they are in words. If not, the string cannot be the concatenation of words. If it is, we remove that string from words and continue with the remainder of the string and the remaining words.

To find substrings in the sentence string that are the concatenation of the strings in words, we can use the above process for each index in the sentence as the starting index.

```
vector<int> FindAllSubstrings(const string& s, const vector<string>& words) {
  unordered_map<string, int> word_to_freq;
  for (const string& word : words) {
    ++word_to_freq[word];
  }

  int unit_size = words.front().size();
  vector<int> result;
  for (int i = 0; i + unit_size * words.size() <= s.size(); ++i) {
    if (MatchAllWordsInDict(s, word_to_freq, i, words.size(), unit_size)) {
      result.emplace_back(i);
    }
  }
  return result;
}

bool MatchAllWordsInDict(const string& s,
                         const unordered_map<string, int>& word_to_freq,
                         int start, int num_words, int unit_size) {
  unordered_map<string, int> curr_string_to_freq;
  for (int i = 0; i < num_words; ++i) {
    string curr_word = s.substr(start + i * unit_size, unit_size);
    auto iter = word_to_freq.find(curr_word);
    if (iter == word_to_freq.end()) {
      return false;
    }
    ++curr_string_to_freq[curr_word];
    if (curr_string_to_freq[curr_word] > iter->second) {
      // curr_word occurs too many times for a match to be possible.
      return false;
    }
  }
  return true;
}
```

We analyze the time complexity as follows. Let m be the number of words and n the length of each word. Let N be the length of the sentence. For any fixed i, to check if the string of length nm starting at an offset of i in the sentence is the concatenation of all words has time complexity $O(nm)$, assuming a hash table is used to store the set of words. This implies the overall time complexity is $O(Nnm)$. In practice, the individual checks are likely to be much faster because we can stop as soon as a mismatch is detected.

The problem is made easier, complexity-wise and implementation-wise, by the fact that the words are all the same length—it makes testing if a substring equals the concatenation of words straightforward.

13.14 FIND A HIGHEST AFFINITY PAIR

A web server logs page views in a log file. The log file consists of a line per page view. A page view consists of a page id and a user id, separated by a comma. The affinity of a pair of pages is the number of distinct users who viewed both. For example, in the log file below, the affinity of ayhoo and oogleg is 2.

```
ayhoo,ap42
oogleg,ap42
tweeter,thl
oogleg,aa314
oogleg,aa314
oogleg,thl
tweeter,aa314
tweeter,ap42
ayhoo,aa314
```

Write a program which takes as input a log file and returns a pair of pages which have the highest affinity.

Hint: Choose your data structure carefully.

Solution: A natural approach is to iterate over all pairs of pages. To avoid multiple passes over the log file, we first make a pass over the log files and record for each distinct page, the set of users who viewed that page. A hash table with pages as keys and sets of users as values is a natural data structure for this purpose.

Next we iterate over all pairs of pages, compute the number of users who viewed both, and compare it with the maximum affinity seen so far. The code implementing for this is as follows.

```
struct PagePair {
  string page_a, page_b;
};

PagePair HighestAffinityPair(ifstream* ifs) {
  // Creates a mapping from pages to distinct users.
  unordered_map<string, set<string>> page_users_map;
  string page, user;
  while (*ifs >> page >> user) {
    page_users_map[page].emplace(user);
  }
```

```
PagePair result;
int max_count = 0;
// Compares all pairs of pages to users maps.
for (auto a = page_users_map.begin(); a != page_users_map.end(); ++a) {
  auto b = a;
  for (advance(b, 1); b != page_users_map.end(); ++b) {
    vector<string> intersect_users;
    set_intersection(a->second.begin(), a->second.end(), b->second.begin(),
                     b->second.end(), back_inserter(intersect_users));

    // Updates result if we find larger intersection.
    if (intersect_users.size() > max_count) {
      max_count = intersect_users.size();
      result = {a->first, b->first};
    }
  }
}
return result;
}
```

Let P be the number of pages, and V the number of views. The space complexity is dominated by the page-to-user map, which is $O(P + V) = O(V)$, since $V \geq P$. The time complexity to build the map is $O(V)$. There are P pages and V page views, and the set of users who viewed a page can be as high as V. Therefore, the time complexity to iterate over all pairs of pages and form pair-wise intersections is $O(P^2 V)$. However, this bound is pessimistic, since it is predicated on each of the P pages being associated with each of the V views. In fact, there are only V^2 possible pair-wise intersections, which bounds the time complexity to compute intersections to the smaller of $O(P^2 V)$ and $O(V^2)$.

13.15 TEST THE COLLATZ CONJECTURE

The Collatz conjecture is the following: Take any natural number. If it is odd, triple it and add one; if it is even, halve it. Repeat the process indefinitely. No matter what number you begin with, you will eventually arrive at 1.

As an example, if we start with 11 we get the sequence $11, 34, 17, 52, 26, 13, 40,$ $20, 10, 5, 16, 8, 4, 2, 1$. Despite intense efforts, the Collatz conjecture has not been proved or disproved.

Suppose you were given the task of checking the Collatz conjecture for the first billion integers. A direct approach would be to compute the convergence sequence for each number in this set.

Test the Collatz conjecture for the first n positive integers.

Hint: How would you efficiently check the conjecture for n assuming it holds for all $m < n$?

Solution: Often interview questions are open-ended with no definite good solution— all you can do is provide a good heuristic and code it well.

The Collatz hypothesis can fail in two ways—a sequence returns to a previous number in the sequence, which implies it will loop forever, or a sequence goes to infinity. The latter cannot be tested with a fixed integer word length, so we simply flag overflows.

The general idea is to iterate through all numbers and for each number repeatedly apply the rules till you reach 1. Here are some of the ideas that you can try to accelerate the check:

- Reuse computation by storing all the numbers you have already proved to converge to 1; that way, as soon as you reach such a number, you can assume it would reach 1.
- To save time, skip even numbers (since they are immediately halved, and the resulting number must have already been checked).
- If you have tested every number up to k, you can stop the chain as soon as you reach a number that is less than or equal to k. You do not need to store the numbers below k in the hash table.
- If multiplication and division are expensive, use bit shifting and addition.
- Partition the search set and use many computers in parallel to explore the subsets, as show in Solution 20.9 on Page 380.

Since the numbers in a sequence may grow beyond 32 bits, you should use 64-bit integer and keep testing for overflow; alternately, you can use arbitrary precision integers.

```cpp
bool TestCollatzConjecture(int n) {
  // Stores odd numbers already tested to converge to 1.
  unordered_set<long> verified_numbers;

  // Starts from 3, since hypothesis holds trivially for 1 and 2.
  for (int i = 3; i <= n; i += 2) {
    unordered_set<long> sequence;
    long test_i = i;
    while (test_i >= i) {
      if (!sequence.emplace(test_i).second) {
        // We previously encountered test_i, so the Collatz sequence
        // has fallen into a loop. This disproves the hypothesis, so
        // we short-circuit, returning false.
        return false;
      }

      if (test_i % 2) {  // Odd number.
        if (!verified_numbers.emplace(test_i).second) {
          break;  // test_i has already been verified to converge to 1.
        }
        long next_test_i = 3 * test_i + 1;  // Multiply by 3 and add 1.
        if (next_test_i <= test_i) {
          throw overflow_error("Collatz sequence overflow for " +
                               to_string(i));
        }
        test_i = next_test_i;
      } else {
```

```
        test_i /= 2;  // Even number, halve it.
      }
    }
  }
  return true;
}
```

We cannot say much about time complexity beyond the obvious, namely that it is at least proportional to n.

13.16 IMPLEMENT A HASH FUNCTION FOR CHESS

The state of a game of chess is determined by what piece is present on each square, as illustrated in Figure 13.2. Each square may be empty, or have one of six classes of pieces; each piece may be black or white. Thus $\lceil \lg(1 + 6 \times 2) \rceil = 4$ bits suffice per square, which means that a total of $64 \times 4 = 256$ bits can represent the state of the chessboard. (The actual state of the game is slightly more complex, as it needs to capture which side is to move, castling rights, *en passant*, etc., but we will use the simpler model for this question.)

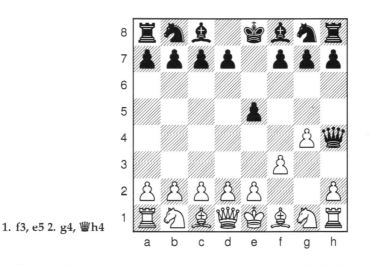

1. f3, e5 2. g4, ♛h4

Figure 13.2: Chessboard corresponding to the fastest checkmate, *Fool's Mate*.

Chess playing computers need to store sets of states, e.g., to determine if a particular state has been evaluated before, or is known to be a winning state. To reduce storage, it is natural to apply a hash function to the 256 bits of state, and ignore collisions. The hash code can be computed by a conventional hash function for strings. However, since the computer repeatedly explores nearby states, it is advantageous to consider hash functions that can be efficiently computed based on incremental changes to the board.

227

Design a hash function for chess game states. Your function should take a state and the hash code for that state, and a move, and efficiently compute the hash code for the updated state.

Hint: XOR is associative, commutative, and fast to compute. Additionally, $a \oplus a = 0$.

Solution: A straightforward hash function is to treat the board as a sequence of 64 base 13 digits. There is one digit per square, with the squares numbered from 0 to 63. Each digit encodes the state of a square: blank, white pawn, white rook,. . . ,white king, black pawn, . . . , black king. We use the hash function $\sum_{i=0}^{63} c_i p^i$, where c_i is the digit in location i, and p is a prime (see on Page 204 for more details).

Note that this hash function has some ability to be updated incrementally. If, for example, a black knight taken by a white bishop the new hash code can be computed by subtracting the terms corresponding to the initial location of the knight and bishop, and adding a term for a blank at the initial location of the bishop and a term for the bishop at the knight's original position.

Now we describe a hash function which is much faster to update. It is based on creating a random 64-bit integer code for each of the 13 states that each of the 64 squares can be in. These $13 \times 64 = 832$ random codes are constants in the program. The hash code for the state of the chessboard is the XOR of the code for each location. Updates are very fast—for the example above, we XOR the code for black knight on i_1, white bishop on i_2, white bishop on i_1, and blank on i_2.

Incremental updates to the first hash function entail computing terms like p^i which is more expensive than computing an XOR, which is why the second hash function is preferable. The maximum number of word-level XORs performed is 4, for a capture or a castling.

As an example, consider a simpler game played on a 2×2 board, with at most two pieces, P and Q present on the board. At most one piece can be present at a board position. Denote the board positions by $(0,0)$, $(0,1)$, $(1,0)$, and $(1,1)$. We use the following random 7-bit codes for each individual position:

- For $(0,0)$: $(1100111)_2$ for blank, $(1011000)_2$ for P, $(1100010)_2$ for Q.
- For $(0,1)$: $(1111100)_2$ for blank, $(1000001)_2$ for P, $(0001111)_2$ for Q.
- For $(1,0)$: $(1100101)_2$ for blank, $(1101101)_2$ for P, $(0011101)_2$ for Q.
- For $(1,1)$: $(0100001)_2$ for blank, $(0101100)_2$ for P, $(1001011)_2$ for Q.

Consider the following state: P is present at $(0,0)$ and Q at $(1,1)$, with the remaining positions blank. The hash code for this state is $(1011000)_2 \oplus (1111100)_2 \oplus (1100101)_2 \oplus (1001011)_2 = (0001010)_2$. Now to compute the code for the state where Q moves to $(0,1)$, we XOR the code for the current state with $(1001011)_2$ (removes Q from $(1,1)$), $(0100001)_2$ (adds blank at $(1,1)$), $(1111100)_2$ (removes blank from $(0,1)$), and $(0001111)_2$ (adds Q at $(0,1)$). Note that, regardless of the size of the board and the number of pieces, this approach uses four XORs to get the updated state.

Variant: How can you include castling rights and *en passant* information in the state?

228

14

Sorting

PROBLEM 14 *(Meshing).* *Two monotone sequences S, T, of lengths n, m, respectively, are stored in two systems of $n(p + 1)$, $m(p + 1)$ consecutive memory locations, respectively: $s, s + 1, \ldots, s + n(p + 1) - 1$ and $t, t + 1, \ldots, t + m(p + 1) - 1$. ... It is desired to find a monotone permutation R of the sum $[S, T]$, and place it at the locations $r, r + 1, \ldots, r + (n + m)(p + 1) - 1$.*

— *"Planning And Coding Of Problems For An Electronic Computing Instrument,"*
H. H. GOLDSTINE AND J. VON NEUMANN, 1948

Sorting—rearranging a collection of items into increasing or decreasing order—is a common problem in computing. Sorting is used to preprocess the collection to make searching faster (as we saw with binary search through an array), as well as identify items that are similar (e.g., students are sorted on test scores).

Naive sorting algorithms run in $O(n^2)$ time. A number of sorting algorithms run in $O(n \log n)$ time—heapsort, merge sort, and quicksort are examples. Each has its advantages and disadvantages: for example, heapsort is in-place but not stable; merge sort is stable but not in-place; quicksort runs $O(n^2)$ time in worst-case. (An in-place sort is one which uses $O(1)$ space; a stable sort is one where entries which are equal appear in their original order.)

A well-implemented quicksort is usually the best choice for sorting. We briefly outline alternatives that are better in specific circumstances.

For short arrays, e.g., 10 or fewer elements, insertion sort is easier to code and faster than asymptotically superior sorting algorithms. If every element is known to be at most k places from its final location, a min-heap can be used to get an $O(n \log k)$ algorithm (Solution 11.3 on Page 174). If there are a small number of distinct keys, e.g., integers in the range $[0..255]$, counting sort, which records for each element, the number of elements less than it, works well. This count can be kept in an array (if the largest number is comparable in value to the size of the set being sorted) or a BST, where the keys are the numbers and the values are their frequencies. If there are many duplicate keys we can add the keys to a BST, with linked lists for elements which have the same key; the sorted result can be derived from an in-order traversal of the BST.

Most sorting algorithms are not stable. Merge sort, carefully implemented, can be made stable. Another solution is to add the index as an integer rank to the keys to break ties.

Most sorting routines are based on a compare function that takes two items as input and returns −1 if the first item is smaller than the second item, 0 if they are equal and 1 otherwise. However, it is also possible to use numerical attributes directly, e.g., in radix sort.

The heap data structure is discussed in detail in Chapter 11. Briefly, a max-heap (min-heap) stores keys drawn from an ordered set. It supports $O(\log n)$ inserts and $O(1)$ time lookup for the maximum (minimum) element; the maximum (minimum) key can be deleted in $O(\log n)$ time. Heaps can be helpful in sorting problems, as illustrated by Problems 11.1 on Page 171, 11.2 on Page 173, and 11.3 on Page 174.

14.1 COMPUTE THE INTERSECTION OF TWO SORTED ARRAYS

A natural implementation for a search engine is to retrieve documents that match the set of words in a query by maintaining an inverted index. Each page is assigned an integer identifier, its *document-ID*. An inverted index is a mapping that takes a word w and returns a sorted array of page-ids which contain w—the sort order could be, for example, the page rank in descending order. When a query contains multiple words, the search engine finds the sorted array for each word and then computes the intersection of these arrays—these are the pages containing all the words in the query. The most computationally intensive step of doing this is finding the intersection of the sorted arrays.

Write a program which takes as input two sorted arrays, and returns a new array containing elements that are present in both of the input arrays. The input arrays may have duplicate entries, but the returned array should be free of duplicates. For example, the input is $\langle 2, 3, 3, 5, 5, 6, 7, 7, 8, 12 \rangle$ and $\langle 5, 5, 6, 8, 8, 9, 10, 10 \rangle$, your output should be $\langle 5, 6, 8 \rangle$.

Hint: Solve the problem if the input array lengths differ by orders of magnitude. What if they are approximately equal?

Solution: The brute-force algorithm is a "loop join", i.e., traversing through all the elements of one array and comparing them to the elements of the other array. Let m and n be the lengths of the two input arrays.

```
vector<int> IntersectTwoSortedArrays(const vector<int>& A,
                                     const vector<int>& B) {
  vector<int> insersection_A_B;
  for (int i = 0; i < A.size(); ++i) {
    if (i == 0 || A[i] != A[i - 1]) {
      for (int b : B) {
        if (A[i] == b) {
          insersection_A_B.emplace_back(A[i]);
          break;
        }
      }
    }
  }
}
```

```
    return insersection_A_B;
}
```

The brute-force algorithm has $O(mn)$ time complexity.

Since both the arrays are sorted, we can make some optimizations. First, we can iterate through the first array and use binary search in array to test if the element is present in the second array.

```
vector<int> IntersectTwoSortedArrays(const vector<int>& A,
                                     const vector<int>& B) {
  vector<int> intersection_A_B;
  for (int i = 0; i < A.size(); ++i) {
    if ((i == 0 || A[i] != A[i - 1]) &&
        binary_search(B.cbegin(), B.cend(), A[i])) {
      intersection_A_B.emplace_back(A[i]);
    }
  }
  return intersection_A_B;
}
```

The time complexity is $O(m \log n)$, where m is the length of the array being iterated over. We can further improve our run time by choosing the shorter array for the outer loop since if n is much smaller than m, then $n \log(m)$ is much smaller than $m \log(n)$.

This is the best solution if one set is much smaller than the other. However, it is not the best when the array lengths are similar because we are not exploiting the fact that both arrays are sorted. We can achieve linear runtime by simultaneously advancing through the two input arrays in increasing order. At each iteration, if the array elements differ, the smaller one can be eliminated. If they are equal, we add that value to the intersection and advance both. (We handle duplicates by comparing the current element with the previous one.) For example, if the arrays are $A = \langle 2, 3, 3, 5, 7, 11 \rangle$ and $B = \langle 3, 3, 7, 15, 31 \rangle$, then we know by inspecting the first element of each that 2 cannot belong to the intersection, so we advance to the second element of A. Now we have a common element, 3, which we add to the result, and then we advance in both arrays. Now we are at 3 in both arrays, but we know 3 has already been added to the result since the previous element in A is also 3. We advance in both again without adding to the intersection. Comparing 5 to 7, we can eliminate 5 and advance to the fourth element in A, which is 7, and equal to the element that B's iterator holds, so it is added to the result. We then eliminate 11, and since no elements remain in A, we return $\langle 3, 7 \rangle$.

```
vector<int> IntersectTwoSortedArrays(const vector<int>& A,
                                     const vector<int>& B) {
  vector<int> intersection_A_B;
  int i = 0, j = 0;
  while (i < A.size() && j < B.size()) {
    if (A[i] == B[j] && (i == 0 || A[i] != A[i - 1])) {
      intersection_A_B.emplace_back(A[i]);
      ++i, ++j;
```

```
    } else if (A[i] < B[j]) {
      ++i;
    } else {   // A[i] > B[j].
      ++j;
    }
  }
  return intersection_A_B;
}
```

Since we spend $O(1)$ time per input array element, the time complexity for the entire algorithm is $O(m + n)$.

14.2 IMPLEMENT MERGESORT IN-PLACE

Suppose you are given two sorted arrays of integers. If one array has enough empty entries at its end, it can be used to store the combined entries of the two arrays in sorted order. For example, consider $\langle 5, 13, 17, \_, \_, \_, \_, \_ \rangle$ and $\langle 3, 7, 11, 19 \rangle$, where $\_$ denotes an empty entry. Then the combined sorted entries can be stored in the first array as $\langle 3, 5, 7, 11, 13, 17, 19, \_ \rangle$.

Write a program which takes as input two sorted arrays of integers, and updates the first to the combined entries of the two arrays in sorted order. Assume the first array has enough empty entries at its end to hold the result.

Hint: Avoid repeatedly moving entries.

Solution: The challenge in this problem lies in writing the result back into the first array—if we had a third array to store the result it, we could solve by iterating through the two input arrays in tandem, writing the smaller of the entries into the result. The time complexity is $O(m + n)$, where m and n are the number of entries initially in the first and second arrays.

We cannot use the above approach with the first array playing the role of the result and still keep the time complexity $O(m + n)$. The reason is that if an entry in the second array is smaller than some entry in the first array, we will have to shift that and all subsequent entries in the first array to the right by 1. In the worst-case, each entry in the second array is smaller than every entry in the first array, and the time complexity is $O(mn)$.

We do have spare space at the end of the first array. We take advantage of this by filling the first array from its end. The last element in the result will be written to index $m + n - 1$. For example, if $A = \langle 5, 13, 17, \_, \_, \_, \_, \_ \rangle$ and $B = \langle 3, 7, 11, 19 \rangle$, then A is updated in the following manner: $\langle 5, 13, 17, \_, \_, \_, 19, \_ \rangle$, $\langle 5, 13, 17, \_, \_, 17, 19, \_ \rangle$, $\langle 5, 13, 17, \_, 13, 17, 19, \_ \rangle$, $\langle 5, 13, 17, 11, 13, 17, 19, \_ \rangle$, $\langle 5, 13, 7, 11, 13, 17, 19, \_ \rangle$, $\langle 5, 5, 7, 11, 13, 17, 19, \_ \rangle$, $\langle 3, 5, 7, 11, 13, 17, 19, \_ \rangle$.

Note that we will never overwrite an entry in the first array that has not already been processed. The reason is that even if every entry of the second array is larger than each element of the first array, all elements of the second array will fill up indices

m to $m + n - 1$ inclusive, which does not conflict with entries stored in the first array. This idea is implemented in the program below. Note the resemblance to Solution 7.4 on Page 95, where we also filled values from the end.

```
void MergeTwoSortedArrays(int A[], int m, int B[], int n) {
  int a = m - 1, b = n - 1, write_idx = m + n - 1;
  while (a >= 0 && b >= 0) {
    A[write_idx--] = A[a] > B[b] ? A[a--] : B[b--];
  }
  while (b >= 0) {
    A[write_idx--] = B[b--];
  }
}
```

The time complexity is $O(m + n)$. It uses $O(1)$ additional space.

14.3 COUNT THE FREQUENCIES OF CHARACTERS IN A SENTENCE

Computers are ideally suited to taking a large amount of data and summarizing it, e.g., as gross statistics.

Given a string, print in alphabetical order each character that appears in the string, and the number of times that it appears. For example, if the string is "bcdacebe", output "(a, 1), (b, 2), (c, 2), (d, 1), (e, 2)".

Hint: Exploit the fact that the keys are drawn from a small set.

Solution: A brute-force solution is to create a hash table which we use to count the number of occurrences of each character. Subsequently, we add the distinct characters to an array and sort it to obtain the set of distinct character in order. A drawback of this approach is the additional space needed for the auxiliary hash table.

We can solve the problem without any additional storage by treating the string as an array of characters and sorting that array. For example, sorting "bcdacebe" yields "abbccdee". The effect of this is to order characters. It also brings equal characters together, which allows us to compute the number of times a character appears in-place. Specifically, we iterate through the sorted array and count the number of occurrences of each character.

```
void CountOccurrences(string S) {
  sort(S.begin(), S.end());

  int current_character_count = 1;
  for (int i = 1; i < S.size(); ++i) {
    if (S[i] == S[i - 1]) {
      ++current_character_count;
    } else {
      cout << '(' << S[i - 1] << ',' << current_character_count << "),";
      current_character_count = 1;
    }
  }
}
```

233

```
  cout << '(' << S.back() << ',' << current_character_count << ')' << endl;
}
```

The time complexity is that of sorting, namely $O(n \log n)$, where n is the length of the string.

As an alternative, we could use an auxiliary array of integers indexed by characters, which counts the number of occurrences of each character. This is similar to the hash table approach above, but avoids the sorting step. When the number of distinct characters in the string is comparable to the total number of characters, this approach is very fast without much space overhead. This is likely to hold for a language like English, which has 26 distinct characters, but less so for Chinese, which has over 8000 distinct characters.

Variant: A person object has an age field, which is an integer in the range $[0, 200]$, and a name field, which is a string. Array A is an array of person objects, which is to be sorted on the age field. The sort must be stable. Design an $O(n)$ time algorithm for sorting A. Is it possible to sort in $O(n)$ time if ties are to be broken on the name field?

14.4 REMOVE FIRST-NAME DUPLICATES

Design an efficient algorithm for removing all first-name duplicates from an array. For example, if the input is ⟨(Ian, Botham), (David, Gower), (Ian, Bell), (Ian, Chappell)⟩, one result could be ⟨(Ian, Bell), (David, Gower)⟩; ⟨(David, Gower), (Ian, Botham)⟩ would also be acceptable.

Hint: Bring equal items close together.

Solution: A brute-force approach is to use a hash table. For the names example, we would need a hash function and an equals function which use the first name only. We first create the hash table and then iterate over it to write entries to the result array. The time complexity is $O(n)$, where n is the number of items. The hash table has a worst-case space complexity of $O(n)$.

We can avoid the additional space complexity if we can reuse the input array for storing the final result. First we sort the array, which brings equal elements together. Sorting can be done in $O(n \log n)$ time. The subsequent elimination of duplicates takes $O(n)$ time. Note that sorting an array requires that its elements are comparable.

```
struct Name {
  bool operator==(const Name& that) const {
    return first_name == that.first_name;
  }

  bool operator<(const Name& that) const {
    if (first_name != that.first_name) {
      return first_name < that.first_name;
    }
    return last_name < that.last_name;
```

```
    }

    string first_name, last_name;
};

void EliminateDuplicate(vector<Name>* A) {
    sort(A->begin(), A->end());  // Makes identical elements become neighbors.
    // unique() removes adjacent duplicates and returns an iterator to the
    // element the follows the last element not removed. The effect of erase()
    // is to restrict A to the distinct elements.
    A->erase(unique(A->begin(), A->end()), A->end());
}
```

The time complexity is $O(n \log n)$ and the space complexity is $O(1)$.

14.5 RENDER A CALENDAR

Consider the problem of designing an online calendaring application. One component of the design is to render the calendar, i.e., display it visually.

Suppose each day consists of a number of events, where an event is specified as a start time and a finish time. Individual events for a day are to be rendered as nonoverlapping rectangular regions whose sides are parallel to the X- and Y-axes. Let the X-axis correspond to time. If an event starts at time b and ends at time e, the upper and lower sides of its corresponding rectangle must be at b and e, respectively. Figure 14.1 represents a set of events.

Suppose the Y-coordinates for each day's events must lie between 0 and L (a pre-specified constant), and each event's rectangle must have the same "height" (distance between the sides parallel to the X-axis). Your task is to compute the maximum height an event rectangle can have. In essence, this is equivalent to the following problem.

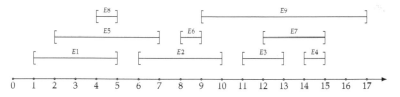

Figure 14.1: A set of nine events. The earliest starting event begins at time 1; the latest ending event ends at time 17. The maximum number of concurrent events is 3, e.g., $\{E1, E5, E8\}$ as well as others.

Write a program that takes a set of events, and determines the maximum number of events that take place concurrently.

Hint: Focus on endpoints.

Solution: The number of events scheduled for a given time changes only at times that are start or end times of an event. This leads the following brute-force algorithm. For each endpoint, compute the number of events that contain it. The maximum number

235

of concurrent events is the maximum of this quantity over all endpoints. If there are n intervals, the total number of endpoints is $2n$. Computing the number of events containing an endpoint takes $O(n)$ time, since checking whether an interval contains a point takes $O(1)$ time. Therefore, the overall time complexity is $O(2n \times n) = O(n^2)$.

The inefficiency in the brute-force algorithm lies in the fact that it does not take advantage of locality, i.e., as we move from one endpoint to another. Intuitively, we can improve the run time by sorting the set of all the endpoints in ascending order. (If two endpoints have equal times, and one is a start time and the other is an end time, the one corresponding to a start time comes first. If both are start or finish times, we break ties arbitrarily.)

Now as we proceed through endpoints we can incrementally track the number of events taking place at that endpoint using a counter. For each endpoint that is the start of an interval, we increment the counter by 1, and for each endpoint that is the end of an interval, we decrement the counter by 1. The maximum value attained by the counter is maximum number of overlapping intervals.

For the example in Figure 14.1 on the facing page, the first seven endpoints are 1(start), 2(start), 4(start), 5(end), 5(end), 6(start), 7(end). The counter values are updated to 1, 2, 3, 2, 1, 2, 1.

```
struct Event {
  int start, finish;
};


struct Endpoint {
  bool operator<(const Endpoint& e) const {
    // If times are equal, an endpoint that starts an interval comes first.
    return time != e.time ? time < e.time : (isStart && !e.isStart);
  }

  int time;
  bool isStart;
};


int FindMaxSimultaneousEvents(const vector<Event>& A) {
  // Builds an array of all endpoints.
  vector<Endpoint> E;
  for (const Event& event : A) {
    E.emplace_back(Endpoint{event.start, true});
    E.emplace_back(Endpoint{event.finish, false});
  }
  // Sorts the endpoint array according to the time, breaking ties
  // by putting start times before end times.
  sort(E.begin(), E.end());

  // Track the number of simultaneous events, and record the maximum
  // number of simultaneous events.
  int max_num_simultaneous_events = 0, num_simultaneous_events = 0;
  for (const Endpoint& endpoint : E) {
    if (endpoint.isStart) {
```

```
    ++num_simultaneous_events;
    max_num_simultaneous_events =
        max(num_simultaneous_events, max_num_simultaneous_events);
  } else {
    --num_simultaneous_events;
  }
}
return max_num_simultaneous_events;
}
```

Sorting the endpoint array takes $O(n \log n)$ time; iterating through the sorted array takes $O(n)$ time, yielding an $O(n \log n)$ time complexity. The space complexity is $O(n)$, which is the size of the endpoint array.

Variant: Users $1, 2, \ldots, n$ share an Internet connection. User i uses b_i bandwidth from time s_i to f_i, inclusive. What is the peak bandwidth usage?

14.6 MERGING INTERVALS

Suppose the time during the day that a person is busy is stored as a set of disjoint time intervals. If an event is added to the person's calendar, the set of busy times may need to be updated.

In the abstract, we want a way to add an interval to a set of disjoint intervals and represent the new set as a set of disjoint intervals. For example, if the initial set of intervals is $[-4, -1], [0, 2], [3, 6], [7, 9], [11, 12], [14, 17]$, and the added interval is $[1, 8]$, the result is $[-4, -1], [0, 9], [11, 12], [14, 17]$.

Write a program which takes as input an array of disjoint closed intervals with integer endpoints, sorted by increasing order of left endpoint, and an interval to be added, and returns the union of the intervals in the array and the added interval. Your result should be expressed as a union of disjoint intervals sorted by left endpoint.

Hint: What is the union of two closed intervals?

Solution: A brute-force approach is to find the smallest left endpoint and the largest right endpoint in the set of intervals in the array and the added interval. We then form the result by testing every integer between these two values for membership in an interval. The time complexity is $O(Dn)$, where D is the difference between the two extreme values and n is the number of intervals. Note that D may be much larger than n. For example, the brute-force approach will iterate over all integers from 0 to 1000000 if the array is $\langle [0, 1], [999999, 1000000] \rangle$ and the added interval is $[10, 20]$.

The brute-force approach examines values that are not endpoints, which is wasteful, since if an integer point p is not an endpoint, it must lie in the same interval as $p - 1$ does. A better approach is to focus on endpoints, and use the sorted property to quickly process intervals in the array.

Specifically, processing an interval in the array takes place in three stages:

(1.) First, we iterate through intervals which appear completely before the interval to be added—all these intervals are added directly to the result.

(2.) As soon as we encounter an interval that intersects the interval to be added, we compute its union with the interval to be added. This union is itself an interval. We iterate through subsequent intervals, as long as they intersect with the union we are forming. This single union is added to the result.

(3.) Finally, we iterate through the remaining intervals. Because the array was originally sorted, none of these can intersect with the interval to be added, so we add these intervals to the result.

Suppose the sorted array of intervals is $[-4, -1], [0, 2], [3, 6], [7, 9], [11, 12], [14, 17]$, and the added interval is $[1, 8]$. We begin in Stage 1. Interval $[-4, -1]$ does not intersect $[1, 8]$, so we add it directly to the result. Next we proceed to $[0, 2]$. Since $[0, 2]$ intersects $[1, 8]$, we are now in Stage 2 of the algorithm. We add the union of the two, $[0, 8]$, to the result. Now we process $[3, 6]$—it lies completely in $[0, 8]$, so we proceed to $[7, 9]$. It intersects $[1, 8]$ but is not completely contained in it, so we update the most recently added interval to the result, $[1, 8]$ to $[0, 9]$. Next we proceed to $[11, 12]$. It does not intersect the most recently added interval to the result, $[0, 9]$, so we are in Stage 3. We add it and all subsequent intervals to the result, which is now $[-4, -1], [0, 9]$, $[11, 12], [14, 17]$. Note how the algorithm operates "locally"—sortedness guarantees that we do not miss any combinations of intervals.

The program implementing this idea is given below.

```
struct Interval {
  int left, right;
};

vector<Interval> AddInterval(const vector<Interval>& disjoint_intervals,
                             Interval new_interval) {
  size_t i = 0;
  vector<Interval> result;

  // Processes intervals in disjoint_intervals which come before new_interval.
  while (i < disjoint_intervals.size() &&
         new_interval.left > disjoint_intervals[i].right) {
    result.emplace_back(disjoint_intervals[i++]);
  }

  // Processes intervals in disjoint_intervals which overlap with
  // new_interval.
  while (i < disjoint_intervals.size() &&
         new_interval.right >= disjoint_intervals[i].left) {
    // If [a, b] and [c, d] overlap, their union is [min(a, c),max(b, d)].
    new_interval = {min(new_interval.left, disjoint_intervals[i].left),
                    max(new_interval.right, disjoint_intervals[i].right)};
    ++i;
  }
  result.emplace_back(new_interval);
```

```
// Processes intervals in disjoint_intervals which come after new_interval.
result.insert(result.end(), disjoint_intervals.begin() + i,
              disjoint_intervals.end());
return result;
}
```

Since the program spends $O(1)$ time per entry, its time complexity is $O(n)$.

14.7 COMPUTE THE UNION OF INTERVALS

In this problem we consider sets of intervals with integer endpoints; the intervals may be open or closed at either end. We want to compute the union of the intervals in such sets. A concrete example is given in Figure 14.2.

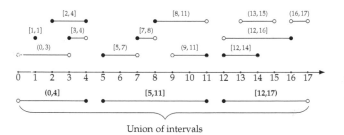

Union of intervals

Figure 14.2: A set of intervals and their union.

Design an algorithm that takes as input a set of intervals, and outputs their union expressed as a set of disjoint intervals.

Hint: Do a case analysis.

Solution: The brute-force approach of considering every number from the minimum left endpoint to the maximum right endpoint described at the start of Solution 14.6 on Page 238 will work for this problem too. As before, its time complexity is $O(Dn)$, where D is the difference between the two extreme values and n is the number of intervals, which is unacceptable when D is large.

We can improve the run time by focusing on intervals instead of individual values. We perform the following iteratively: select an interval arbitrarily, and find all intervals it intersects with. If it does not intersect any interval, remove it from the set and add it to the result. Otherwise, take its union with all the intervals it intersects with (the union must itself be an interval), remove it and all the intervals it intersects with from the result, and add the union to the set. Since we remove at least one interval from the set each time, and the time to process each interval (test intersection and form unions) is $O(n)$, the time complexity is $O(n^2)$.

A faster implementation of the above approach is to process the intervals in sorted order, so that we can limit our attention to a subset of intervals as we proceed. Specifically, we begin by sorting the intervals on their left endpoints. The idea is

239

that this allows us to not have to revisit intervals which are entirely to the left of the interval currently being processed.

We refer to an interval which does not include its left endpoint as being left-open. Left-closed, right-open, and right-closed are defined similarly. When sorting, if two intervals have the same left endpoint, we put intervals which are left-closed first. We break ties arbitrarily.

As we iterate through the sorted array of intervals, we have the following cases:

- The interval most recently added to the result does not intersect the current interval, nor does its right endpoint equal the left endpoint of the current interval. In this case, we simply add the current interval to the end of the result array as a new interval.
- The interval most recently added to the result intersects the current interval. In this case, we update the most recently added interval to the union of it with the current interval.
- The interval most recently added to the result has its right endpoint equal to the left endpoint of the current interval, and one (or both) of these endpoints are closed. In this case too, we update the most recently added interval to the union of it with the current interval.

For the example in Figure 14.2 on the preceding page, the result array updates in the following way: $\langle(0,3)\rangle$, $\langle(0,4]\rangle$, $\langle(0,4],[5,7)\rangle$, $\langle(0,4],[5,8)\rangle$, $\langle(0,4],[5,11)\rangle$, $\langle(0,4],[5,11]\rangle$, $\langle(0,4],[5,11],[12,14)\rangle$, $\langle(0,4],[5,11],[12,16)\rangle$, $\langle(0,4],[5,11],[12,17)\rangle$.

```
struct Interval {
 private:
  struct Endpoint {
    bool isClosed;
    int val;
  };

 public:
  bool operator<(const Interval& i) const {
    if (left.val != i.left.val) {
      return left.val < i.left.val;
    }
    // Left endpoints are equal, so now see if one is closed and the other open
    // - closed intervals should appear first.
    return left.isClosed && !i.left.isClosed;
  }

  Endpoint left, right;
};

vector<Interval> UnionOfIntervals(vector<Interval> intervals) {
  // Empty input.
  if (intervals.empty()) {
    return {};
  }
```

```
    // Sort intervals according to left endpoints of intervals.
    sort(intervals.begin(), intervals.end());
    Interval curr(intervals.front());
    vector<Interval> result;
    for (int i = 1; i < intervals.size(); ++i) {
      if (intervals[i].left.val < curr.right.val ||
          (intervals[i].left.val == curr.right.val &&
           (intervals[i].left.isClosed || curr.right.isClosed))) {
        if (intervals[i].right.val > curr.right.val ||
            (intervals[i].right.val == curr.right.val &&
             intervals[i].right.isClosed)) {
          curr.right = intervals[i].right;
        }
      } else {
        result.emplace_back(curr);
        curr = intervals[i];
      }
    }
    result.emplace back(curr);
    return result;
}
```

The time complexity is dominated by the sort step, i.e., $O(n \log n)$.

14.8 PARTITIONING AND SORTING AN ARRAY WITH MANY REPEATED ENTRIES

Suppose you need to reorder the elements of a very large array so that equal elements appear together. For example, if the array is $\langle b, a, c, b, d, a, b, d \rangle$ then $\langle a, a, b, b, b, c, d, d \rangle$ is an acceptable reordering, as is $\langle d, d, c, a, a, b, b, b \rangle$.

If the entries are integers, this reordering can be achieved by sorting the array. If the number of distinct integers is very small relative to the size of the array, an efficient approach to sorting the array is to count the number of occurrences of each distinct integer and write the appropriate number of each integer, in sorted order, to the array. When array entries are objects, with multiple fields, only one of which is to be used as a key, the problem is harder to solve.

You are given an array of student objects. Each student has an integer-valued age field that is to be treated as a key. Rearrange the elements of the array so that students of equal age appear together. The order in which different ages appear is not important. How would your solution change if ages have to appear in sorted order?

Hint: Count the number of students for each age.

Solution: The brute-force approach is to sort the array, comparing on age. If the array length is n, the time complexity is $O(n \log n)$ and space complexity is $O(1)$. The inefficiency in this approach stems from the fact that it does more than is required—the specification simply asks for students of equal age to be adjacent.

241

We use the approach described in the introduction to the problem. However, we cannot apply it directly, since we need to write objects, not integers—two students may have the same age but still be different.

For example, consider the array $\langle$(Greg, 14), (John, 12), (Andy, 11), (Jim, 13), (Phil, 12), (Bob, 13), (Chip, 13), (Tim, 14)$\rangle$. We can iterate through the array and record the number of students of each age in a hash. Specifically, keys are ages, and values are the corresponding counts. For the given example, on completion of the iteration, the hash is (14, 2), (12, 2), (11, 1), (13, 3). This tells us that we need to write two students of age 14, two students of age 12, one student of age 11 and three students of age 13. We can write these students in any order, as long as we keep students of equal age adjacent.

If we had a new array to write to, we can write the two students of age 14 starting at index 0, the two students of age 12 starting at index $0 + 2 = 2$, the one student of age 11 at index $2 + 2 = 4$, and the three students of age 13 starting at index $4 + 1 = 5$. We would iterate through the original array, and write each entry into the new array according to these offsets. For example, after the first four iterations, the new array would be $\langle$(Greg, 14), ␣, (John, 12), ␣, (Andy, 11), (Jim, 13), ␣, ␣$\rangle$.

The time complexity of this approach is $O(n)$, but it entails $O(n)$ additional space for the result array. We can avoid having to allocate a new array by performing the updates in-place. The idea is to maintain a subarray for each of the different types of elements. Each subarray marks out entries which have not yet been assigned elements of that type. We swap elements across these subarrays to move them to their correct position.

In the program below, we use two hash tables to track the subarrays. One is the starting offset of the subarray, the other its size. As soon as the subarray becomes empty, we remove it.

```
struct Person {
  int age;
  string name;
};


void GroupByAge(vector<Person>* person_array) {
  unordered_map<int, int> age_to_count;
  for (const Person& p : *person_array) {
    ++age_to_count[p.age];
  }
  unordered_map<int, int> age_to_offset;
  int offset = 0;
  for (const auto& p : age_to_count) {
    age_to_offset[p.first] = offset;
    offset += p.second;
  }

  while (age_to_offset.size()) {
    auto from = age_to_offset.begin();
    auto to = age_to_offset.find((*person_array)[from->second].age);
```

```
  swap((*person_array)[from->second], (*person_array)[to->second]);
  // Use age_to_count to see when we are finished with a particular age.
  --age_to_count[to->first];
  if (age_to_count[to->first] > 0) {
    ++to->second;
  } else {
    age_to_offset.erase(to);
  }
  }
}
```

The time complexity is $O(n)$, since the first pass entails n hash table inserts, and the second pass spends $O(1)$ time to move one element to its proper location. The additional space complexity is dictated by the hash table, i.e., $O(m)$, where m is the number of distinct ages.

If the entries are additionally required to appear sorted by age, we can use a BST-based map (Chapter 15) to map ages to counts, since the BST-based map keeps ages in sorted order. For our example, the age-count pairs would appear in the order $(11, 1), (12, 2), (13, 3), (14, 2)$. The time complexity becomes $O(n + m \log m)$, since BST insertion takes time $O(\log m)$. Such a sort is often referred to as a counting sort.

14.9 TEAM PHOTO DAY—1

You are a photographer for a soccer meet. You will be taking pictures of pairs of opposing teams. All teams have the same number of players. A team photo consists of a front row of players and a back row of players. A player in the back row must be taller than the player in front of him, as illustrated in Figure 14.3. All players in a row must be from the same team.

Back row

Front row

Figure 14.3: A team photo. Each team has 10 players, and each player in the back row is taller than the corresponding player in the front row.

Design an algorithm that takes as input two teams and the heights of the players in the teams and checks if it is possible to place players to take the photo subject to the placement constraint.

Hint: First try some concrete inputs, then make a general conclusion.

Solution: A brute-force approach is to consider every permutation of one array, and compare it against the other array, element by element. Suppose there are n players in each team. It takes $O(n!)$ time to enumerate every possible permutation of a team, and testing if a permutation leads to a satisfactory arrangement takes $O(n)$ time. Therefore, the time complexity is $O(n! \times n)$, clearly unacceptable.

Intuitively, we should narrow the search by focusing on the hardest to place players. Suppose we want to place Team A behind Team B. If A's tallest player is not taller than the tallest player in B, then it's not possible to place Team A behind Team B and satisfy the placement constraint. Conversely, if Team A's tallest player is taller than the tallest player in B, we should place him in front of the tallest player in B, since the tallest player in B is the hardest to place. Applying the same logic to the remaining players, the second tallest player in A should be taller than the second tallest player in B, and so on.

We can efficiently check whether A's tallest, second tallest, etc. players are each taller than B's tallest, second tallest, etc. players by first sorting the arrays of player heights. Figure 14.4 shows the teams in Figure 14.3 on the facing page sorted by their heights.

Back row

Front row

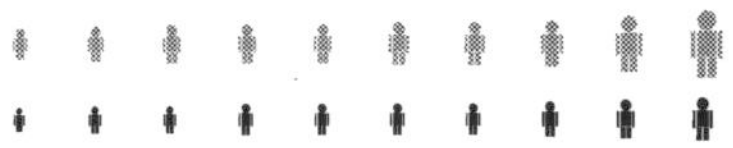

Figure 14.4: The teams from Figure 14.3 on the facing page in sorted order.

The program below uses this idea to test if a given team can be placed in front of another team.

```cpp
struct Player {
  bool operator<(const Player& that) const { return height < that.height; }

  int height;
};

class Team {
 public:
  explicit Team(const vector<int>& height) {
    for (int h : height) {
      players_.emplace_back(Player{h});
    }
  }

  // Checks if A can be placed in front of B.
  static bool valid_placement_exists(const Team& A, const Team& B) {
    vector<Player> A_sorted(A.SortPlayersByHeight());
    vector<Player> B_sorted(B.SortPlayersByHeight());
    for (int i = 0; i < A_sorted.size() && i < B_sorted.size(); ++i) {
      if (B_sorted[i] < A_sorted[i]) {
        return false;
      }
    }
    return true;
  }

 private:
  vector<Player> SortPlayersByHeight() const {
```

```
    vector<Player> sorted_players(players_);
    sort(sorted_players.begin(), sorted_players.end());
    return sorted_players;
  }

  vector<Player> players_;
};
```

The time complexity is that of sorting, i.e., $O(n \log n)$.

14.10 IMPLEMENT A FAST SORTING ALGORITHM FOR LISTS

Implement a routine which sorts lists efficiently. It should be a stable sort, i.e., the relative positions of equal elements must remain unchanged.

Hint: In what respects are lists superior to arrays?

Solution: The brute-force approach is to repeatedly delete the smallest element in the list and add it to the end of a new list. The time complexity is $O(n^2)$ and the additional space complexity is $O(n)$, where n is the number of nodes in the list. We can refine the simple algorithm to run in $O(1)$ space by reordering the nodes, instead of creating new ones.

```
shared_ptr<ListNode<int>> InsertionSort(const shared_ptr<ListNode<int>>& L) {
  auto dummy_head = make_shared<ListNode<int>>(ListNode<int>{0, L});
  auto iter = L;
  // The sublist consisting of nodes up to and including iter is sorted in
  // increasing order. We need to ensure that after we move to iter->next
  // this property continues to hold. We do this by swapping iter->next
  // with its predecessors in the list till it's in the right place.
  while (iter && iter->next) {
    if (iter->data > iter->next->data) {
      auto target = iter->next, pre = dummy_head;
      while (pre->next->data < target->data) {
        pre = pre->next;
      }
      auto temp = pre->next;
      pre->next = target;
      iter->next = target->next;
      target->next = temp;
    } else {
      iter = iter->next;
    }
  }
  return dummy_head->next;
}
```

The time complexity is $O(n^2)$, which corresponds to the case where the list is reverse-sorted to begin with. The space complexity is $O(1)$.

To improve on runtime, we can gain intuition from considering arrays. Quicksort is the best all round sorting algorithm for arrays—it runs in time $O(n \log n)$, and is in-place. However, it is not stable. Mergesort applied to arrays is a stable $O(n \log n)$ algorithm. However, it is not in-place, since there is no way to merge two sorted halves of an array in-place in linear time.

Unlike arrays, lists can be merged in-place—conceptually, this is because insertion into the middle of a list is an $O(1)$ operation. The following program implements a mergesort on lists. We decompose the list into two equal-sized sublists around the node in the middle of the list. We find this node by advancing two iterators through the list, one twice as fast as the other. When the fast iterator reaches the end of the list, the slow iterator is at the middle of the list. We recurse on the sublists, and use Solution 8.1 on Page 110 (merge two sorted lists) to combine the sorted sublists.

```
shared_ptr<ListNode<int>> StableSortList(shared_ptr<ListNode<int>> L) {
  // Base cases: L is empty or a single node, nothing to do.
  if (L == nullptr || L->next == nullptr) {
    return L;
  }

  // Find the midpoint of L using a slow and a fast pointer.
  shared_ptr<ListNode<int>> pre_slow = nullptr, slow = L, fast = L;
  while (fast && fast->next) {
    pre_slow = slow;
    fast = fast->next->next, slow = slow->next;
  }

  pre_slow->next = nullptr;  // Splits the list into two equal-sized lists.

  return MergeTwoSortedLists(StableSortList(L), StableSortList(slow));
}
```

The time complexity is the same as that of mergesort, i.e., $O(n \log n)$. Though no memory is explicitly allocated, the space complexity is $O(\log n)$. This is the maximum function call stack depth, since each recursive call is with an argument that is half as long.

14.11 COMPUTE A SALARY THRESHOLD

You are working in the finance office for ABC corporation. ABC needs to cut payroll expenses to a specified target. The chief executive officer wants to do this by putting a cap on last year's salaries. Every employee who earned more than the cap last year will be paid the cap this year; employees who earned no more than the cap will see no change in their salary.

For example, if there were five employees with salaries last year were $90, $30, $100, $40, and $20, and the target payroll this year is $210, then 60 is a suitable salary cap, since $60 + 30 + 60 + 40 + 20 = 210$.

Design an algorithm for computing the salary cap, given existing salaries and the target payroll.

Hint: How does the payroll vary with the cap?

Solution: Brute-force is not much use—there are an infinite number of possibilities for the cap.

The cap lies between 0 and the maximum current salary. The payroll increases with the cap, which suggests using binary search in this range—if a cap is too high, no higher cap will work; the same is true if the cap is too low.

Suppose there are n employees. Let the array holding salary data be A. The payroll, $P(c)$, implied by a cap of c is $\sum_{i=0}^{n-1} \min(A[i], c)$. Each step of the binary search evaluating $P(c)$ which takes time $O(n)$. As in Solution 12.6 on Page 191, the number of binary search steps depends on the largest salary and the desired accuracy.

We can use a slightly more analytical method to avoid the need for a specified tolerance. The intuition is that as we increase the cap, as long as it does not exceed someone's salary, the payroll increases linearly. This suggests iterating through the salaries in increasing order. Assume the salaries are given by an array A, which is sorted. Suppose the cap for a total payroll of T is known to lie between the kth and $(k + 1)$th salaries. We want $\sum_{i=0}^{k-1} A[i] + (n - k)c$ to equal $= T$, which solves to $c = (T - \sum_{i=0}^{k-1} A[i])/(n - k)$.

For the given example, $A = \langle 20, 30, 40, 90, 100 \rangle$, and $T = 210$. The payrolls for caps equal to the salaries in A are $\langle 100, 140, 190, 270, 280 \rangle$. Since $T = 210$ lies between 190 and 270, the cap lies between the 40 and 90. For any cap c between 40 and 90, the implied payroll is $20 + 30 + 40 + 2c$. We want this to be 210, so we solve $20 + 30 + 40 + 2c = 210$ for c, yielding $c = 60$.

```
double FindSalaryCap(double target_payroll, vector<double> current_salaries) {
  sort(current_salaries.begin(), current_salaries.end());
  double unadjusted_salary_sum = 0.0;
  for (int i = 0; i < current_salaries.size(); ++i) {
    const double adjusted_salary_sum =
        current_salaries[i] * (current_salaries.size() - i);
    if (unadjusted_salary_sum + adjusted_salary_sum >= target_payroll) {
      return (target_payroll - unadjusted_salary_sum) /
          (current_salaries.size() - i);
    }
    unadjusted_salary_sum += current_salaries[i];
  }
  // No solution, since target_payroll > existing payroll.
  return -1.0;
}
```

The most expensive operation for this entire solution is sorting A, hence the run time is $O(n \log n)$. Once we have A sorted, we simply iterate through its entries looking for the first entry which implies a payroll that exceeds the target, and then solve for the cap using an arithmetical expression.

If we are given the salary array sorted in advance as well as its prefix sums, then for a given value of T, we can use binary search to get the cap in $O(\log n)$ time.

Variant: Solve the same problem using only $O(1)$ space.

15

Binary Search Trees

The number of trees which can be formed with
$n + 1$ *given knots* $\alpha, \beta, \gamma, \ldots = (n + 1)^{n-1}$.

— *"A Theorem on Trees,"*
A. CAYLEY, 1889

Adding and deleting elements to an array is computationally expensive, when the array needs to stay sorted. BSTs are similar to arrays in that the stored values (the "keys") are stored in a sorted order. BSTs offer the ability to search for a key as well as find the *min* and *max* elements, look for the successor or predecessor of a search key (which itself need not be present in the BST), and enumerate the keys in a range in sorted order. However, unlike with a sorted array, keys can be added to and deleted from a BST efficiently.

A BST is a binary tree as defined in Chapter 10 in which the nodes store keys that are comparable, e.g., integers or strings. The keys stored at nodes have to respect the BST property—the key stored at a node is greater than or equal to the keys stored at the nodes of its left subtree and less than or equal to the keys stored in the nodes of its right subtree. Figure 15.1 on the next page shows a BST whose keys are the first 16 prime numbers.

Key lookup, insertion, and deletion take time proportional to the height of the tree, which can in worst-case be $O(n)$, if insertions and deletions are naively implemented. However, there are implementations of insert and delete which guarantee the tree remains "height-balanced", i.e., has height $O(\log n)$. These require storing and updating additional data at the tree nodes. Red-black trees are an example of height-balanced BSTs and are widely used in data structure libraries.

The BST prototype is as follows:

```
template <typename T>
struct BSTNode {
  T data;
  unique_ptr<BSTNode<T>> left, right;
};
```

15.1 TEST IF A BINARY TREE SATISFIES THE BST PROPERTY

Write a program that takes as input a binary tree and checks if the tree satisfies the BST property.

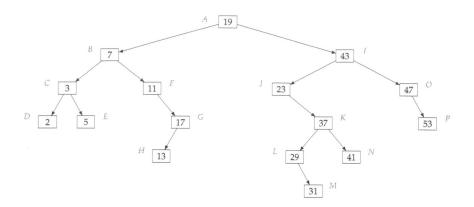

Figure 15.1: An example BST.

Hint: Is it correct to check for each node that its key is greater than or equal to the key at its left child and less than or equal to the key at its right child?

Solution: A direct approach, based on the definition of a BST, is to begin with the root, and compute the maximum key stored in the root's left subtree, and the minimum key in the root's right subtree. We check that the key at the root is greater than or equal to the maximum from the left subtree and less than or equal to the minimum from the right subtree. If both these checks pass, we recursively check the root's left and right subtrees. If either check fails, we return false.

Computing the minimum key in a binary tree is straightforward: we take the minimum of the key stored at its root, the minimum key of the left subtree, and the minimum key of the right subtree. The maximum key is computed similarly. Note that the minimum can be in either subtree, since a general binary tree may not satisfy the BST property.

The problem with this approach is that it will repeatedly traverse subtrees. In the worst-case, when the tree is a BST and each node's left child is empty, the complexity is $O(n^2)$, where n is the number of nodes. The complexity can be improved to $O(n)$ by caching the largest and smallest keys at each node; this requires $O(n)$ additional storage for the cache.

We now present two approaches which have $O(n)$ time complexity and $O(h)$ additional space complexity, where h is the height of the tree.

The first approach is to check constraints on the values for each subtree. The initial constraint comes from the root. Every node in its left (right) subtree must have a key less than or equal (greater than or equal) to the key at the root. This idea generalizes: if all nodes in a tree must have keys in the range $[l, u]$, and the key at the root is w (which itself must be between $[l, u]$, otherwise the requirement is violated at the root itself), then all keys in the left subtree must be in the range $[l, w]$, and all keys stored in the right subtree must be in the range $[w, u]$.

As a concrete example, when applied to the BST in Figure 15.1, the initial range is

$[-\infty, \infty]$. For the recursive call on the subtree rooted at B, the constraint is $[-\infty, 19]$; the 19 is the upper bound required by A on its left subtree. For the recursive call starting at the subtree rooted at F, the constraint is $[7, 19]$. For the recursive call starting at the subtree rooted at K, the constraint is $[23, 43]$. The binary tree in Figure 10.1 on Page 146 is identified as not being a BST when the recursive call reaches C—the constraint is $[-\infty, 6]$, but the key at F is 271, so the tree cannot satisfy the BST property.

```
bool IsBinaryTreeBST(const unique_ptr<BinaryTreeNode<int>>& tree) {
  return AreKeysInRange(tree, numeric_limits<int>::min(),
                        numeric_limits<int>::max());
}


bool AreKeysInRange(const unique_ptr<BinaryTreeNode<int>>& tree, int low_range,
                    int high_range) {
  if (tree == nullptr) {
    return true;
  } else if (tree->data < low_range || tree->data > high_range) {
    return false;
  }

  return AreKeysInRange(tree->left, low_range, tree->data) &&
         AreKeysInRange(tree->right, tree->data, high_range);
}
```

Alternatively, we can use the fact that an inorder traversal visits keys in sorted order. Furthermore, if an inorder traversal of a binary tree visits keys in sorted order, then that binary tree must be a BST. (This follows directly from the definition of a BST and the definition of an inorder walk.) Thus we can check the BST property by performing an inorder traversal, recording the key stored at the last visited node. Each time a new node is visited, its key is compared with the key of the previously visited node. If at any step in the walk, the key at the previously visited node is greater than the node currently being visited, we have a violation of the BST property.

All these approaches explore the left subtree first. Therefore, even if the BST property does not hold at a node which is close to the root (e.g., the key stored at the right child is less than the key stored at the root), their time complexity is still $O(n)$.

We can search for violations of the BST property in a BFS manner, thereby reducing the time complexity when the property is violated at a node whose depth is small.

Specifically, we use a queue, where each queue entry contains a node, as well as an upper and a lower bound on the keys stored at the subtree rooted at that node. The queue is initialized to the root, with lower bound $-\infty$ and upper bound ∞. We iteratively check the constraint on each node. If it violates the constraint we stop— the BST property has been violated. Otherwise, we add its children along with the corresponding constraint.

For the example in Figure 15.1 on the preceding page, we initialize the queue with $(A, [-\infty, \infty])$. Each time we pop a node, we first check the constraint. We pop the first entry, $(A, [-\infty, \infty])$, and add its children, with the corresponding constraints, i.e., $(B, [-\infty, 19])$ and $(I, [19, \infty])$. Next we pop $(B, [-\infty, 19])$, and add its children, i.e.,

$(C, [-\infty, 7])$ and $(D, [7, 19])$. Continuing through the nodes, we check that all nodes satisfy their constraints, and thus verify the tree is a BST.

If the BST property is violated in a subtree consisting of nodes within a particular depth, the violation will be discovered without visiting any nodes at a greater depth. This is because each time we enqueue an entry, the lower and upper bounds on the node's key are the tightest possible.

```cpp
struct QueueEntry {
  const unique_ptr<BinaryTreeNode<int>>& tree_node;
  int lower_bound, upper_bound;
};

bool IsBinaryTreeBST(const unique_ptr<BinaryTreeNode<int>>& tree) {
  queue<QueueEntry> BFS_queue;
  BFS_queue.emplace(QueueEntry{tree, numeric_limits<int>::min(),
                               numeric_limits<int>::max()});

  while (!BFS_queue.empty()) {
    if (BFS_queue.front().tree_node.get()) {
      if (BFS_queue.front().tree_node->data < BFS_queue.front().lower_bound ||
          BFS_queue.front().tree_node->data > BFS_queue.front().upper_bound) {
        return false;
      }

      BFS_queue.emplace(QueueEntry{BFS_queue.front().tree_node->left,
                                   BFS_queue.front().lower_bound,
                                   BFS_queue.front().tree_node->data});
      BFS_queue.emplace(QueueEntry{BFS_queue.front().tree_node->right,
                                   BFS_queue.front().tree_node->data,
                                   BFS_queue.front().upper_bound});
    }
    BFS_queue.pop();
  }
  return true;
}
```

15.2 Find the first occurrence of a key in a BST

Searching for a key in a BST is very similar to binary search in a sorted array. Many variants of the basic search problem can be posed for BSTs.

Write a program that takes as input a BST and a value, and returns the node whose key equals the input value and appears first in an inorder traversal of the BST. For example, when applied to the BST in Figure 15.2 on the next page, your program should return Node B for 108, Node G for 285, and null for 143. Your initial attempt can use recursion, but your final solution cannot.

Hint: Make use of the divide and conquer principle.

Solution: The brute-force approach is to do an inorder traversal, and stop at the first node whose key equals the input value. The time complexity is $O(n)$, where n is the

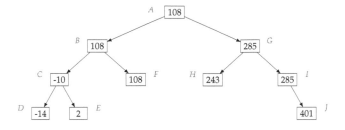

Figure 15.2: A BST with duplicate keys.

number of nodes. A major drawback of this approach is that it does not exploit the BST property.

The idiomatic way to search for a value in a BST is to first check if the tree is empty; if so, return null. If the root stores the specified key, return the root. If neither of these cases holds, recurse on the left or right child of the root, depending on whether the input value is less than or greater than the key at the root, thereby using the BST property to focus on only one subtree. This approach may not return the first node with the specified input value.

Note the similarity to Problem 12.1 on Page 184 which asks for the first occurrence of a value in a sorted array. We can solve the current problem in an analogous fashion. Specifically, modify the idiomatic search as follows—if the input value equals the root's key, also check to see if it appears in the root's left subtree, in which case we return the node returned by that call. Correctness follows from the fact that the nodes in the root's left subtree all appear before the root in an inorder traversal.

As a concrete example, for the BST in Figure 15.2 and input value 108, the function recurses on nodes A, B, C, E, in that order. Specifically, since A holds 108 and B holds 108 we update the first seen occurrence of 108 to A and then to B. Since the key at C is smaller than 108, we check its right child E. Node E's key, 2, is less than 108, and E has no right child. Therefore, B has to be the first occurrence of 108. For the input value 285, the function recurses on nodes A, G, H in that order. Since G holds 285, and H's key is smaller than 285, we know that G is the first occurrence of 285. For the input value 143, the function recurses on nodes A, G, H in that order; since no node holds 143, it is not present.

```
BSTNode<int>* FindFirstEqualK(const unique_ptr<BSTNode<int>>& tree, int k) {
  if (!tree) {
    return nullptr;  // No match.
  } else if (tree->data == k) {
    // Recursively search the left subtree for first node containing k.
    auto* node = FindFirstEqualK(tree->left, k);
    return node ? node : tree.get();
  }
  // Search the left or right subtree based on relative values of tree->data
  // and k.
  return FindFirstEqualK(tree->data < k ? tree->right : tree->left, k);
```

253

}

Since we descend one level with each call, the time complexity is $O(h)$, where h is the height of the tree. The space complexity is also $O(h)$—this is the maximum depth of the function call stack.

The straightforward implementation of the standard BST search is tail recursive, and can mechanically be converted to iterative code. However, the recursive version for finding the first occurrence of a value is not tail recursive, and needs to be written from scratch. The iterative code below descends the tree iteratively, eliminating one subtree at each iteration.

```
BSTNode<int>* FindFirstEqualK(const unique_ptr<BSTNode<int>>& tree, int k) {
  BSTNode<int> *first_so_far = nullptr, *curr = tree.get();
  while (curr) {
    if (curr->data < k) {
      curr = curr->right.get();
    } else if (curr->data > k) {
      curr = curr->left.get();
    } else {  // curr->data == k.
      // Record this node, and search for the first node in the left subtree.
      first_so_far = curr;
      curr = curr->left.get();
    }
  }
  return first_so_far;
}
```

The time complexity is $O(h)$, and the space complexity is $O(1)$.

15.3 FIND THE FIRST KEY LARGER THAN A GIVEN VALUE IN A BST

Write a program that takes as input a BST and a value, and returns the first key that would appear in an inorder traversal which is greater than the input value. For example, when applied to the BST in Figure 15.1 on Page 251 you should return 29 for input 23.

Hint: Perform binary search, keeping some additional state.

Solution: We can find the desired node in $O(n)$ time, where n is the number of nodes in the BST, by doing an inorder walk. This approach does not use the BST property.

A better approach is to use the BST search idiom. We store the best candidate for the result and update that candidate as we iteratively descend the tree, eliminating subtrees by comparing the keys stored at nodes with the input value. Specifically, if the current subtree's root holds a value less than or equal to the input value, we search the right subtree. If the current subtree's root stores a key that is greater than the input value, we search in the left subtree, updating the candidate to the current root. Correctness follows from the fact that whenever we first set the candidate, the desired result must be within the tree rooted at that node. This approach is conceptually similar to Solution 12.2 on Page 186.

254

For example, when searching for the first node whose key is greater than 23 in the BST in Figure 15.1 on Page 251, the node sequence is A, I, J, K, L. Since L has no left child, its key, 29, is the result.

```
BSTNode<int>* FindFirstGreaterThanK(const unique_ptr<BSTNode<int>>& tree,
                                    int k) {
  BSTNode<int> *subtree = tree.get(), *first_so_far = nullptr;
  while (subtree) {
    if (subtree->data > k) {
      first_so_far = subtree;
      subtree = subtree->left.get();
    } else {  // Root and all keys in left subtree are <= k, so skip them.
      subtree = subtree->right.get();
    }
  }
  return first_so_far;
}
```

The time complexity is $O(h)$, where h is the height of the tree. The space complexity is $O(1)$.

15.4 FIND THE k LARGEST ELEMENTS IN A BST

A BST is a sorted data structure, which suggests that it should be possible to find the k largest keys easily.

Write a program that takes as input a BST and an integer k, and returns the k largest elements in the BST in decreasing order. For example, if the input is the BST in Figure 15.1 on Page 251 and $k = 3$, your program should return $\langle 53, 47, 43 \rangle$.

Hint: What does an inorder traversal yield?

Solution: The brute-force approach is to do an inorder traversal, which enumerates keys in ascending order, and return the last k visited nodes. A queue is ideal for storing visited nodes, since it makes it easy to evict nodes visited more than k steps previously. A drawback of this approach is that it potentially processes many nodes that cannot possibly be in the result, e.g., if k is small and the left subtree is large.

A better approach is to begin with the desired nodes, and work backwards. We do this by recursing first on the right subtree and then on the left subtree. This amounts to a reverse-inorder traversal. For the BST in Figure 15.1 on Page 251, the reverse inorder visit sequence is $\langle P, O, I, N, K, M, L, J, A, G, H, F, B, E, C, D \rangle$.

As soon as we visit k nodes, we can halt. The code below uses a dynamic array to store the desired keys. As soon as the array has k elements, we return. We store newer nodes at the end of the array, as per the problem specification.

To find the five biggest keys in the tree in Figure 15.1 on Page 251, we would recurse on A, I, O, P, in that order. Returning from recursive calls, we would visit P, O, I, in that order, and add their keys to the result. Then we would recurse on J, K, N, in that order. Finally, we would visit N and then K, adding their keys to the result. Then we would stop, since we have five keys in the array.

```
vector<int> FindKLargestInBST(const unique_ptr<BSTNode<int>>& tree, int k) {
  vector<int> k_largest_elements;
  FindKLargestInBSTHelper(tree, k, &k_largest_elements);
  return k_largest_elements;
}

void FindKLargestInBSTHelper(const unique_ptr<BSTNode<int>>& tree, int k,
                             vector<int>* k_largest_elements) {
  // Perform reverse inorder traversal.
  if (tree && k_largest_elements->size() < k) {
    FindKLargestInBSTHelper(tree->right, k, k_largest_elements);
    if (k_largest_elements->size() < k) {
      k_largest_elements->emplace_back(tree->data);
      FindKLargestInBSTHelper(tree->left, k, k_largest_elements);
    }
  }
}
```

The time complexity is $O(h + k)$, which can be much better than performing a conventional inorder walk, e.g., when the tree is balanced and k is small. The complexity bound comes from the observation that the number of times the program descends in the tree can be at most h more than the number of times it ascends the tree, and each ascent happens after we visit a node in the result. After k nodes have been added to the result, the program stops.

15.5 COMPUTE THE LCA IN A BST

Since a BST is a specialized binary tree, the notion of lowest common ancestor, as expressed in Problem 10.4 on Page 152, holds for BSTs too.

In general, computing the LCA of two nodes in a BST is no easier than computing the LCA in a binary tree, since structurally a binary tree can be viewed as a BST where all the keys are equal. However, when the keys are distinct, it is possible to improve on the LCA algorithms for binary trees.

Design an algorithm that takes as input a BST and two nodes, and returns the LCA of the two nodes. For example, for the BST in Figure 15.1 on Page 251, and nodes C and G, your algorithm should return B. Assume all keys are distinct. Nodes do not have references to their parents.

Hint: Take advantage of the BST property.

Solution: In Solution 10.3 on Page 151 we presented an algorithm for this problem in the context of binary trees. The idea underlying that algorithm was to do a postorder traversal—the LCA is the first node visited after the two nodes whose LCA we are to compute have been visited. The time complexity was $O(n)$, where n is the number of nodes in the tree.

This approach can be improved upon when operating on BSTs with distinct keys. Consider the BST in Figure 15.1 on Page 251 and nodes C and G. Since both C and

G holds keys that are smaller than A's key, their LCA must lie in A's left subtree. Examining B, since C's key is less than B's key, and B's key is less than G's key. B must be the LCA of C and G.

Let s and b be the two nodes whose LCA we are to compute, and without loss of generality assume the key at s is smaller. (Since the problem specified keys are distinct, it cannot be that s and b hold equal keys.) Consider the key stored at the root of the BST. There are four possibilities:

- If the root's key is the same as that stored at s or at b, we are done—the root is the LCA.
- If the key at s is smaller than the key at the root, and the key at b is greater than the key at the root, the root is the LCA.
- If the keys at s and b are both smaller than that at the root, the LCA must lie in the left subtree of the root.
- If both keys are larger than that at the root, then the LCA must lie in the right subtree of the root.

```
// Input nodes are not nonempty and the key at s is less than or equal to that
// at b.
BSTNode<int>* FindLCA(const unique_ptr<BSTNode<int>>& tree,
                      const unique_ptr<BSTNode<int>>& s,
                      const unique_ptr<BSTNode<int>>& b) {
  auto* p = tree.get();
  while (p->data < s->data || p->data > b->data) {
    // Keep searching since p is outside of [s, b].
    while (p->data < s->data) {
      p = p->right.get();  // LCA must be in p's right child.
    }
    while (p->data > b->data) {
      p = p->left.get();  // LCA must be in p's left child.
    }
  }
  // Now, s->data <= p->data && p->data <= b->data.
  return p;
}
```

Since we descend one level with each iteration, the time complexity is $O(h)$, where h is the height of the tree.

15.6 Reconstruct a BST from traversal data

As discussed in Problem 10.10 on Page 159 there are many different binary trees that yield the same sequence of visited nodes in an inorder traversal. This is also true for preorder and postorder traversals. Given the sequence of nodes that an inorder traversal sequence visits and either of the other two traversal sequences, there exists a unique binary tree that yields those sequences. Here we study if it is possible to reconstruct the tree with less traversal information when the tree is known to be a BST.

It is critical that the elements stored in the tree be unique. If the root contains key v and the tree contains more occurrences of v, we cannot always identify from the sequence whether the subsequent vs are in the left subtree or the right subtree. For example, for the tree rooted at G in Figure 15.2 on Page 254 the preorder traversal sequence is $285, 243, 285, 401$. The same preorder traversal sequence is seen if 285 appears in the left subtree as the right child of the node with key 243 and 401 is at the root's right child.

Suppose you are given the sequence in which keys are visited in an inorder traversal of a BST, and all keys are distinct. Can you reconstruct the BST from the sequence? If so, write a program to do so. Solve the same problem for preorder and postorder traversal sequences.

Hint: Draw the five BSTs on the keys $1, 2, 3$, and the corresponding traversal orders.

Solution: First, with some experimentation, we see the sequence of keys generated by an inorder traversal is not enough to reconstruct the tree. For example, the key sequence $\langle 1, 2, 3 \rangle$ corresponds to five distinct BSTs as shown in Figure 15.3.

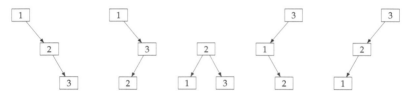

Figure 15.3: Five distinct BSTs for the traversal sequence $\langle 1, 2, 3 \rangle$.

However, the story for a preorder sequence is different. As an example, consider the preorder key sequence $\langle 43, 23, 37, 29, 31, 41, 47, 53 \rangle$. The root must hold 43, since it's the first visited node. The left subtree contains keys less than 43, i.e., $23, 37, 29, 31, 41$, and the right subtree contains keys greater than 43, i.e., $47, 53$. Furthermore, $\langle 23, 37, 29, 31, 41 \rangle$ is exactly the preorder sequence for the left subtree and $\langle 47, 53 \rangle$ is exactly the preorder sequence for the right subtree. We can recursively reason that 23 and 47 are the roots of the left and right subtree, and continue to build the entire tree, which is exactly the subtree rooted at Node I in Figure 15.1 on Page 251.

Generalizing, in any preorder traversal sequence, the first key corresponds to the root. The subsequence which begins at the second element and ends at the last key less than the root, corresponds to the preorder traversal of the root's left subtree. The final subsequence, consisting of keys greater than the root corresponds to the preorder traversal of the root's right subtree. We recursively reconstruct the BST by recursively reconstructing the left and right subtrees from the two subsequences then adding them to the root.

```
unique_ptr<BSTNode<int>> RebuildBSTFromPreorder(
    const vector<int>& preorder_sequence) {
  return RebuildBSTFromPreorderHelper(preorder_sequence, 0,
                                      preorder_sequence.size());
}

// Builds a BST from preorder_sequence[start : end - 1].
```

```
unique_ptr<BSTNode<int>> RebuildBSTFromPreorderHelper(
    const vector<int>& preorder_sequence, int start, int end) {
  if (start >= end) {
    return nullptr;
  }
  int transition_point = start + 1;
  while (transition_point < end &&
         preorder_sequence[transition_point] < preorder_sequence[start]) {
    ++transition_point;
  }
  return make_unique<BSTNode<int>>(BSTNode<int>{
      preorder_sequence[start],
      RebuildBSTFromPreorderHelper(preorder_sequence, start + 1,
                                   transition_point),
      RebuildBSTFromPreorderHelper(preorder_sequence, transition_point, end)});
}
```

The worst-case input for this algorithm is the pre-order sequence corresponding to a left-skewed tree. The worst-case time complexity satisfies the recurrence $W(n) = W(n-1) + O(n)$, which solves to $O(n^2)$. The best-case input is a sequence corresponding to a right-skewed tree, and the corresponding time complexity is $O(n)$. When the sequence corresponds to a balanced BST, the time complexity is given by $B(n) = 2B(n/2) + O(n)$, which solves to $O(n \log n)$.

The implementation above potentially iterates over nodes multiple times, which is wasteful. A better approach is to reconstruct the left subtree in the same iteration as identifying the nodes which lie in it. The code shown below takes this approach. The intuition is that we do not want to iterate from first entry after the root to the last entry smaller than the root, only to go back and partially repeat this process for the root's left subtree. We can avoid repeated passes over nodes by including the range of keys we want to reconstruct the subtrees over. For example, looking at the preorder key sequence $\langle 43, 23, 37, 29, 31, 41, 47, 53 \rangle$, instead of recursing on $\langle 23, 37, 29, 31, 41 \rangle$ (which would involve an iteration to get the last element in this sequence). We can directly recur on $\langle 23, 37, 29, 31, 41, 47, 53 \rangle$, with the constraint that we are building the subtree on nodes whose keys are less than 43.

```
unique_ptr<BSTNode<int>> RebuildBSTFromPreorder(
    const vector<int>& preorder_sequence) {
  int root_idx = 0;
  return RebuildBSTFromPreorderOnValueRange(
      preorder_sequence, numeric_limits<int>::min(),
      numeric_limits<int>::max(), &root_idx);
}

// Builds a BST on the subtree rooted at root_idx from preorder_sequence on
// keys in (lower_bound, upper_bound).
unique_ptr<BSTNode<int>> RebuildBSTFromPreorderOnValueRange(
    const vector<int>& preorder_sequence, int lower_bound, int upper_bound,
    int* root_idx_pointer) {
  int& root_idx = *root_idx_pointer;
  if (root_idx == preorder_sequence.size()) {
    return nullptr;
```

```
    }

    int root = preorder_sequence[root_idx];
    if (root < lower_bound || root > upper_bound) {
      return nullptr;
    }
    ++root_idx;
    // Note that RebuildBSTFromPreorderOnValueRange updates root_idx. So the
    // order of following two calls are critical.
    auto left_subtree = RebuildBSTFromPreorderOnValueRange(
        preorder_sequence, lower_bound, root, root_idx_pointer);
    auto right_subtree = RebuildBSTFromPreorderOnValueRange(
        preorder_sequence, root, upper_bound, root_idx_pointer);
    return make_unique<BSTNode<int>>(
        BSTNode<int>{root, move(left_subtree), move(right_subtree)});
}
```

The worst-case time complexity is $O(n)$, since it performs a constant amount of work per node. Note the similarity to Solution 22.26 on Page 442.

A postorder traversal sequence also uniquely specifies the BST, and the algorithm for reconstructing the BST is very similar to that for the preorder case.

15.7 FIND THE CLOSEST ENTRIES IN THREE SORTED ARRAYS

Design an algorithm that takes three sorted arrays and returns one entry from each such that the minimum interval containing these three entries is as small as possible. For example, if the three arrays are $\langle 5, 10, 15 \rangle$, $\langle 3, 6, 9, 12, 15 \rangle$, and $\langle 8, 16, 24 \rangle$, then $15, 15, 16$ lie in the smallest possible interval.

Hint: How would you proceed if you needed to pick three entries in a single sorted array?

Solution: The brute-force approach is to try all possible triples, e.g., with three nested for loops. The length of the minimum interval containing a set of numbers is simply the difference of the maximum and the minimum values in the triple. The time complexity is $O(lmn)$, where l, m, n are the lengths of each of the three arrays.

The brute-force approach does not take advantage of the sortedness of the input arrays. For the example in the problem description, the smallest intervals containing $(5, 3, 16)$ and $(5, 3, 24)$ must be larger than the smallest interval containing $(5, 3, 8)$ (since 8 is the maximum of $5, 3, 8$, and $8 < 16 < 24$).

Let's suppose we begin with the triple consisting of the smallest entries in each array. Let s be the minimum value in the triple and t the maximum value in the triple. Then the smallest interval with left endpoint s containing elements from each array must be $[s, t]$, since the remaining two values are the minimum possible.

Now remove s from the triple and bring the next smallest element from the array it belongs to into the triple. Let s' and t' be the next minimum and maximum values in the new triple. Observe $[s', t']$ must be the smallest interval whose left endpoint is s': the other two values are the smallest values in the corresponding arrays that are greater than or equal to s'. By iteratively examining and removing the smallest element from the triple, we compute the minimum interval starting at that element. Since the minimum interval containing elements from each array must begin with the element of *some* array, we are guaranteed to encounter the minimum element.

For example, we begin with $(5, 3, 8)$. The smallest interval whose left endpoint is 3 has length $8 - 3 = 5$. The element after 3 is 6, so we continue with the triple $(5, 6, 8)$. The smallest interval whose left endpoint is 5 has length $8 - 5 = 3$. The element after 5 is 10, so we continue with the triple $(10, 6, 8)$. The smallest interval whose left endpoint is 6 has length $10 - 6 = 4$. The element after 6 is 9, so we continue with the triple $(10, 9, 8)$. Proceeding in this way, we obtain the triples $(10, 9, 16)$, $(10, 12, 16)$, $(15, 12, 16)$, $(15, 15, 16)$. Out of all these triples, the one contained in a minimum length interval is $(15, 15, 16)$.

In the following code, we implement a general purpose function which finds the closest entries in k sorted arrays. Since we need to repeatedly insert, delete, find the minimum, and find the maximum amongst a collection of k elements, a BST is the natural choice.

```cpp
int FindClosestElementsInSortedArrays(
    const vector<vector<int>>& sorted_arrays) {
  int min_distance_so_far = numeric_limits<int>::max();

  struct IterTail {
    vector<int>::const_iterator iter, tail;
  };
  // Stores two iterators in each entry. One for traversing, and the other to
  // check we reach the end.
  multimap<int, IterTail> iter_and_tail;
  for (const vector<int>& sorted_array : sorted_arrays) {
    iter_and_tail.emplace(sorted_array.front(), IterTail{sorted_array.cbegin(),
                                                sorted_array.cend()});
  }

  while (true) {
    int min_value = iter_and_tail.cbegin()->first,
        max_value = iter_and_tail.crbegin()->first;
    min_distance_so_far = min(max_value - min_value, min_distance_so_far);
    const auto next_min = next(iter_and_tail.cbegin()->second.iter),
               next_end = iter_and_tail.cbegin()->second.tail;
    // Return if some array has no remaining elements.
    if (next_min == next_end) {
      return min_distance_so_far;
    }
    iter_and_tail.emplace(*next_min, IterTail{next_min, next_end});
    iter_and_tail.erase(iter_and_tail.cbegin());
  }
}
```

The time complexity is $O(n \log k)$, where n is the total number of elements in the k arrays. For the special case $k = 3$ specified in the problem statement, the time complexity is $O(n \log 3) = O(n)$.

Numbers of the form $a + b\sqrt{q}$, where a and b are nonnegative integers, and q is an integer which is not the square of another integer, have special properties, e.g., they are closed under addition and multiplication. Some of the first few numbers of this form are given in Figure 15.4.

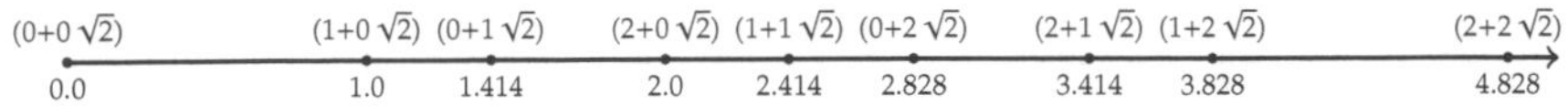

Figure 15.4: Some points of the form $a + b\sqrt{2}$. (For typographical reasons, this figure does not include all numbers of the form $a + b\sqrt{2}$ between 0 and $2 + 2\sqrt{2}$, e.g., $3 + 0\sqrt{2}, 4 + 0\sqrt{2}, 0 + 3\sqrt{2}, 3 + 1\sqrt{2}$ lie in the interval but are not included.)

Design an algorithm for efficiently computing the k smallest numbers of the form $a + b\sqrt{2}$ for nonnegative integers a and b.

Hint: Systematically enumerate points.

Solution: A key fact about $\sqrt{2}$ is that it is irrational, i.e., it cannot equal to $\frac{a}{b}$ for any integers a, b. This implies that if $x + y\sqrt{2} = x' + y'\sqrt{2}$, where x and y are integers, then $x = x'$ and $y = y'$ (since otherwise $\sqrt{2} = \frac{x - x'}{y - y'}$).

Here is a brute-force solution. Generate all numbers of the form $a + b\sqrt{2}$ where a and b are integers, $0 \le a, b \le k - 1$. This yields exactly k^2 numbers and the k smallest numbers must lie in this collection. We can sort these numbers and return the k smallest ones. The time complexity is $O(k^2 \log(k^2)) = O(k^2 \log k)$.

Intuitively, it is wasteful to generate k^2 numbers, since we only care about a small fraction of them.

We know the smallest number is $0 + 0\sqrt{2}$. The candidates for next smallest number are $1 + 0\sqrt{2}$ and $0 + 1\sqrt{2}$. From this, we can deduce the following algorithm. We want to maintain a collection of real numbers, initialized to $0 + 0\sqrt{2}$. We perform k extractions of the smallest element, call it $a + b\sqrt{2}$, followed by insertion of $(a+1) + b\sqrt{2}$ and $a + (b + 1)\sqrt{2}$ to the collection.

The operations on this collection are extract the minimum and insert. Since it is possible that the same number may be inserted more than once, we need to ensure the collection does not create duplicates when the same item is inserted twice. A BST satisfies these operations efficiently, and is used in the implementation below. It is initialized to contain $0 + 0\sqrt{2}$. We extract the minimum from the BST, which is $0 + 0\sqrt{2}$, and insert $1 + 0\sqrt{2}$ and $0 + 1\sqrt{2}$ to the BST. We extract the minimum from the BST, which is $1 + 0\sqrt{2}$, and insert $2 + 0\sqrt{2}$ and $1 + 1\sqrt{2}$ to the BST, which now consists of $0 + 1\sqrt{2} = 1.414, 2 + 0\sqrt{2} = 2, 1 + 1\sqrt{2} = 2.414$. We extract the minimum from the BST, which is $0 + 1\sqrt{2}$, and insert $1 + 1\sqrt{2}$ and $0 + 2\sqrt{2}$. The first value is already present, so the BST updates to $2 + 0\sqrt{2} = 2, 1 + 1\sqrt{2} = 2.414, 0 + 2\sqrt{2} = 2.828$. (Although it's not apparent from this small example, the values we add back to the BST may be smaller than values already present in it, so we really need the BST to hold values.)

```cpp
struct ABSqrt2 {
  ABSqrt2(int a, int b) : a(a), b(b), val(a + b * sqrt(2)) {}

  bool operator<(const ABSqrt2& that) const { return val < that.val; }

  int a, b;
  double val;
};

vector<ABSqrt2> GenerateFirstKABSqrt2(int k) {
  set<ABSqrt2> candidates;
  // Initial for 0 + 0 * sqrt(2).
  candidates.emplace(0, 0);

  vector<ABSqrt2> result;
  while (result.size() < k) {
    auto next_smallest = candidates.cbegin();
    result.emplace_back(*next_smallest);

    // Adds the next two numbers derived from next_smallest.
    candidates.emplace(next_smallest->a + 1, next_smallest->b);
    candidates.emplace(next_smallest->a, next_smallest->b + 1);
    candidates.erase(next_smallest);
  }
  return result;
}
```

In each iteration we perform a deletion and two insertions. There are k such insertions, so the time complexity is $O(k \log k)$. The space complexity is $O(k)$, since there are not more than $2k$ insertions.

Now we describe an $O(n)$ time solution. It is simple to implement, but is less easy to understand than the one based on BST. The idea is that the $(n + 1)$th value will be the sum of 1 or $\sqrt{2}$ with a previous value. We could iterate through all the entries in the result and track the smallest such value which is greater than nth value. However, this takes time $O(n)$ to compute the $(n + 1)$th element.

Intuitively, there is no need to examine all prior values entries when computing $(n+1)$th value. Let's say we are storing the result in an array A. Then we need to track just two entries—i, the smallest index such that $A[i] + 1 > A[n - 1]$, and j, smallest index such that $A[j] + \sqrt{2} > A[n - 1]$. Clearly, the $(n + 1)$th entry will be the smaller of $A[i] + 1$ and $A[j] + \sqrt{2}$. After obtaining the $(n + 1)$th entry, if it is $A[i] + 1$, we increment i. If it is $A[j] + \sqrt{2}$, we increment j. If $A[i] + 1$ equals $A[j] + \sqrt{2}$, we increment both i and j.

To illustrate, suppose A is initialized to $\langle 0 \rangle$, and i and j are 0. The computation proceeds as follows:

1. Since $A[0] + 1 = 1 < A[0] + \sqrt{2} = 1.414$, we push 1 into A and increment i. Now $A = \langle 0, 1 \rangle$, $i = 1, j = 0$.
2. Since $A[1] + 1 = 2 > A[0] + \sqrt{2} = 1.414$, we push 1.414 into A and increment j. Now $A = \langle 0, 1, 1.414 \rangle$, $i = 1, j = 1$.

3. Since $A[1] + 1 = 2 < A[1] + \sqrt{2} = 2.414$, we push 2 into A and increment i. Now $A = \langle 0, 1, 1.414, 2 \rangle$, $i = 2, j = 1$.
4. Since $A[2] + 1 = 2.414 = A[1] + \sqrt{2} = 2.414$, we push 2.414 into A and increment both i and j. Now $A = \langle 0, 1, 1.414, 2, 2.414 \rangle$, $i = 3, j = 2$.
5. Since $A[3] + 1 = 3 > A[2] + \sqrt{2} = 2.828$, we push 2.828 into A and increment j. Now $A = \langle 0, 1, 1.414, 2, 2.828 \rangle$, $i = 3, j = 3$.
6. Since $A[3] + 1 = 3 < A[3] + \sqrt{2} = 3.414$, we push 3 into A and increment i. Now $A = \langle 0, 1, 1.414, 2, 2.828, 3 \rangle$, $i = 4, j = 3$.

```
struct ABSqrt2 {
  ABSqrt2(int a, int b) : a(a), b(b), val(a + b * sqrt(2)) {}

  int a, b;
  double val;
};


vector<ABSqrt2> GenerateFirstKABSqrt2(int k) {
  // Will store the first k numbers of the form a + b sqrt(2).
  vector<ABSqrt2> result;
  result.emplace_back(0, 0);
  int i = 0, j = 0;
  for (int n = 1; n < k; ++n) {
    ABSqrt2 result_i_plus_1(result[i].a + 1, result[i].b);
    ABSqrt2 result_j_plus_sqrt2(result[j].a, result[j].b + 1);
    if (result_i_plus_1.val < result_j_plus_sqrt2.val) {
      ++i;
      result.emplace_back(result_i_plus_1);
    } else if (result_i_plus_1.val > result_j_plus_sqrt2.val) {
      ++j;
      result.emplace_back(result_j_plus_sqrt2);
    } else {  // result_i_plus_1 == result_j_plus_sqrt2.
      ++i, ++j;
      result.emplace_back(result_i_plus_1);
    }
  }
  return result;
}
```

Each additional element takes $O(1)$ time to compute, implying an $O(n)$ time complexity to compute the first n values of the form $a + b\sqrt{2}$.

15.9 THE MOST VISITED PAGES PROBLEM

You are given a server log file containing billions of lines. Each line contains a number of fields. For this problem, the relevant field is an id denoting the page that was accessed.

Write a function to read a log file line, and a function to find the k most visited pages, where k is an input to the function. Optimize performance for the situation where calls to the two functions are interleaved. You can assume the set of distinct pages is small enough to fit in RAM.

As a concrete example, suppose the log file ids appear in the following order: $g, a, t, t, a, a, a, g, t, c, t, a, t$, i.e., there are four pages with ids a, c, g, t. After the first 10 lines have been read, the most common page is a with a count of 4, and the next most common page is t with a count of 3.

Hint: For each page, count of the number of times it has been visited.

Solution: A brute-force approach is to have the read function add the page on the line to the end of a dynamic array. For the find function, the number of times each page has been visited can be obtained by sorting the array, and iterating through it. The space complexity is $O(n)$, where n is the number of lines.

Alternatively, we can store the page-to-visit-count data in a hash table. The k most visited pages are the k pages with the highest counts, and can be computed using the algorithm for computing the kth smallest entry in an array given in Solution 12.9 on Page 195. (We would need to reverse the comparator to get the k pages with highest counts.) Reading a log file entry takes $O(1)$ time, regardless of whether we keep pages in an array or store (page,visit-count) pairs in a hash table. The time to compute the k most visited pages is $O(m)$, where m is the number of distinct pages processed up to that point.

Intuitively, the brute-force algorithm performs poorly when there are many calls to computing the k most visited pages. The reason is that it does not take advantage of incrementality—processing a few more lines does not change the page-to-visit-counts drastically.

Height-balanced BSTs are a good choice when performing many incremental updates while preserving sortedness. Adding and removing an entry in a height-balanced BST on N nodes takes time $O(\log N)$. Therefore it makes sense to store the page-to-visit-counts in a balanced BST. The BST nodes store (page,visit-count) pairs. These pairs are ordered by visit-count, with ties broken on page.

Updating the tree after reading a line from the log file is slightly challenging because we cannot easily update the corresponding (page,visit-count). The reason is that the BST is ordered by visit-counts, not pages. The solution is to use an additional data structure, namely a hash table, which maps pages to (page,visit-count) pairs in the BST. If the pair is present, the visit-count in the pair in the BST is updated. Note that directly changing the pair does not automatically update the BST it lies in. The simplest way to update the BST is to delete the pair from the BST, update the pair, and then insert the updated pair back into the BST. (Library implementations of height-balanced BSTs ensure that inserts and deletes preserve balance.)

To find the k most visited pages we find the maximum element in the BST and make $k-1$ calls to the predecessor function. If the tree is balanced, the time complexity of $k-1$ calls to predecessor is $O(k + \log m)$. For $k \ll m$ this compares very favorably with having to iterate through the entire collection lines or pages as we did in brute-force approaches.

The time complexity of adding a log file entry is dominated by the BST update, which is $O(\log m)$. This is higher than in the brute-force approach, and is the price we pay for fast queries.

For the given example, after the first four entries have been read, the BST contains the following (visit-count, page) pairs $(1, a), (1, g), (2, t)$ in this order, and the hash table maps a, g, t to $(1, a), (1, g), (2, t)$, respectively. After we read the fifth entry, a, we use the hash table to find the corresponding entry $(1, a)$ and update it to $(2, a)$, yielding the tree $(1, g), (2, a), (2, t)$. After the first ten entries, the tree consists of $(1, c), (2, g), (3, t), (4, a)$. The most visited page at this point is a, with a visit count of 4.

Variant: Write a program for the same problem with $O(1)$ time complexity for the read function and $O(k)$ time complexity for the find function.

15.10 BUILD A MINIMUM HEIGHT BST FROM A SORTED ARRAY

Given a sorted array, the number of BSTs that can be built on the entries in the array grows enormously with its size. Some of these trees are skewed, and are closer to lists; others are more balanced. See Figure 15.3 on Page 259 for an example.

How would you build a BST of minimum possible height from a sorted array?

Hint: Which element should be the root?

Solution: Brute-force is not much help here—enumerating all possible BSTs for the given array in search of the minimum height one requires a nontrivial recursion, not to mention enormous time complexity.

Intuitively, to make a minimum height BST, we want the subtrees to be as balanced as possible—there's no point in one subtree being shorter than the other, since the height is determined by the taller one. More formally, balance can be achieved by keeping the number of nodes in both subtrees as close as possible.

Let n be the length of the array. To achieve optimum balance we can make the element in the middle of the array, i.e., the $\lfloor \frac{n}{2} \rfloor$th entry, the root, and recursively compute minimum height BSTs for the subarrays on either side of this entry.

As a concrete example, if the array is $\langle 2, 3, 5, 7, 11, 13, 17, 19, 23 \rangle$, the root's key will be the middle element, i.e., 11. This implies the left subtree is to be built from $\langle 2, 3, 5, 7 \rangle$, and the right subtree is to be built from $\langle 13, 17, 19, 23 \rangle$. To make both of these minimum height, we call the procedure recursively.

```
unique_ptr<BSTNode<int>> BuildMinHeightBSTFromSortedArray(
    const vector<int>& A) {
  return BuildMinHeightBSTFromSortedArrayHelper(A, 0, A.size());
}

// Build a min-height BST over the entries in A[start : end - 1].
unique_ptr<BSTNode<int>> BuildMinHeightBSTFromSortedArrayHelper(
    const vector<int>& A, int start, int end) {
  if (start >= end) {
    return nullptr;
  }
  int mid = start + ((end - start) / 2);
  return make_unique<BSTNode<int>>(BSTNode<int>{
      A[mid], BuildMinHeightBSTFromSortedArrayHelper(A, start, mid),
```

```
        BuildMinHeightBSTFromSortedArrayHelper(A, mid + 1, end)});
}
```

The time complexity $T(n)$ satisfies the recurrence $T(n) = 2T(n/2) + O(1)$, which solves to $T(n) = O(n)$. Another explanation for the time complexity is that we make exactly n calls to the recursive function and spend $O(1)$ within each call.

15.11   INSERTION AND DELETION IN A BST

A BST is a dynamic data structure—in particular, if implemented carefully, key insertion and deletion can be made very fast.

Design efficient functions for inserting and removing keys in a BST. Assume that all elements in the BST are unique, and that your insertion method must preserve this property.

Hint: Deleting leaves is easy. Pay attention to the children of internal nodes when you delete it.

Solution: A brute-force approach to insertion might be to traverse the entire tree looking for the place to add the new key, and then reconstruct the new tree from the new ordering. Deletion can be done in the same way. The time complexity is $O(n)$, where n is the number of nodes in the tree. In principle, the space complexity can be reduced to $O(h)$, where h is the height of the tree, using the techniques in Solution 22.27 on Page 443 and 22.26 on Page 442.

For linear data structures like lists and arrays, we cannot improve upon the $O(n)$ time complexity. However, for BSTs we can use the BST property to quickly find the part of the tree to update, and the linked nature of the data structure to efficiently add or remove keys. The way to achieve efficiency, both in terms of runtime complexity and coding effort, is to minimize the number of links to be updated.

We begin with insertion. Inserting a value into a tree that is empty is trivial: we create a node holding the value to be inserted, setting the node's left and right children to empty subtrees.

For a nonempty tree, we insert by searching for the input value. If it exists, we return, since duplicates are disallowed. Otherwise we must have reached an empty subtree, so we create a node whose key is the input value, and update the node whose child was the empty subtree according to the relative value of that node's key and the input value.

For example, if we were to insert the key 9 to the tree in Figure 15.1 on Page 251, we would compare 9 with 19, 7, and 11 in that order. Since $9 < 11$, and Node F has an empty left subtree, we add a new node containing 9 and set F's left subtree to the new node.

Deletion begins with first identifying the node containing the key to be deleted. Suppose the node to be deleted has no children. Then we remove the corresponding child field in the parent of the node to be deleted. For example, to delete N from the tree in Figure 15.1 on Page 251, we set K's right child to null. If the node to be deleted has a single child, we update the parent of the node to be deleted to have that child in place of the node to be deleted. For example, to delete G in the example, we would set F's right child to H.

Now we consider the case where the node to be deleted has two children, e.g., Node A. We can effectively delete the node by replacing its contents with the contents of its successor (which must appear in the right subchild), and then deleting the successor (which is relatively straightforward since it cannot have a left child). For example, to delete A, we would replace its content by 23 (J's content), and then delete J (by setting the left subchild of J's parent I to the right subchild of J, i.e., K).

```cpp
class BinarySearchTree {
public:
  bool Insert(int key) {
    if (root_ == nullptr) {
      root_ = make_unique<TreeNode>(TreeNode{key, nullptr, nullptr});
    } else {
      TreeNode *curr = root_.get(), *parent = nullptr;
      while (curr) {
        parent = curr;
        if (key == curr->data) {
          return false;  // key already present, no duplicates to be added.
        } else if (key < curr->data) {
          curr = curr->left.get();
        } else {  // key > curr->data.
          curr = curr->right.get();
        }
      }

      // Inserts key according to key and parent.
      if (key < parent->data) {
        parent->left.reset(new TreeNode{key});
      } else {
        parent->right.reset(new TreeNode{key});
      }
    }
    return true;
  }

  bool Delete(int key) {
    // Find the node with key.
    TreeNode *curr = root_.get(), *parent = nullptr;
    while (curr && curr->data != key) {
      parent = curr;
      curr = key < curr->data ? curr->left.get() : curr->right.get();
    }

    if (!curr) {
      // There's no node with key in this tree.
      return false;
    }

    TreeNode *key_node = curr;
    if (key_node->right) {
      // Finds the minimum of the right subtree.
```

268

```
      TreeNode *r_key_node = key_node->right.get(), *r_parent = key_node;
      while (r_key_node->left) {
        r_parent = r_key_node;
        r_key_node = r_key_node->left.get();
      }
      key_node->data = r_key_node->data;
      // Moves links to erase the node.
      if (r_parent->left.get() == r_key_node) {
        r_parent->left.reset(r_key_node->right.release());
      } else {  // r_parent->right.get() == r_key_node.
        r_parent->right.reset(r_key_node->right.release());
      }
    } else {
      // Updates root_ link if needed.
      if (root_.get() == key_node) {
        root_.reset(key_node->left.release());
      } else {
        if (parent->left.get() == key_node) {
          parent->left.reset(key_node->left.release());
        } else {  // parent->right.get() == key_node.
          parent->right.reset(key_node->left.release());
        }
      }
    }
    return true;
  }

 private:
  struct TreeNode {
    int data;
    unique_ptr<TreeNode> left, right;
  };

  unique_ptr<TreeNode> root_ = nullptr;
};
```

Both insertion and deletion times are dominated by the time to search for a key and to find the minimum element in a subtree. Both of these times are proportional to the height of the tree.

In the worst-case, the BST can grow to be skewed. For example, if the initial tree is empty, and n successive insertions are done, where each key inserted is larger than the previous one, the height of the resulting tree is n. A red-black tree is a BST with fast specialized insertion and deletion routines that keep the tree height-balanced, i.e., $O(\log n)$ height.

Variant: Solve the same problem with the added constraint that you can only change links. (In particular, you cannot change the key stored at any node.)

15.12 TEST IF THREE BST NODES ARE TOTALLY ORDERED

Write a program which takes two nodes in a BST and a third node, the "middle" node, and determines if one of the two nodes is a proper ancestor and the other a proper descendant of the middle. (A proper ancestor of a node is an ancestor that is not equal to the node; a proper descendant is defined similarly.) For example, in Figure 15.1 on Page 251, if the middle is Node J, your function should return true if the two nodes are $\{A, K\}$ or $\{I, M\}$. It should return false if the two nodes are $\{I, P\}$ or $\{J, K\}$. You can assume that all keys are unique. Nodes do not have pointers to their parents

Hint: For what specific arrangements of the three nodes does the check pass?

Solution: A brute-force approach would be to check if the first node is a proper ancestor of the middle and the second node is a proper descendant of the middle. If this check returns true, we return true. Otherwise, we return the result of the same check, swapping the roles of the first and second nodes. For the BST in Figure 15.1 on Page 251, with the two nodes being $\{L, I\}$ and middle K, searching for K from L would be unsuccessful, but searching for K from I would succeed. We would then search for L from K, which would succeed, so we would return true.

Searching has time complexity $O(h)$, where h is the height of the tree, since we can use the BST property to prune one of the two children at each node. Since we perform a maximum of three searches, the total time complexity is $O(h)$.

One disadvantage of trying the two input nodes for being the middle's ancestor one-after-another is that even when the three nodes are very close, e.g., if the two nodes are $\{A, J\}$ and middle node is I in Figure 15.1 on Page 251, if we begin the search for the middle from the lower of the two nodes, e.g., from J, we incur the full $O(h)$ time complexity.

We can prevent this by performing the searches for the middle from both alternatives in an interleaved fashion. If we encounter the middle from one node, we subsequently search for the second node from the middle. This way we avoid performing an unsuccessful search on a large subtree. For the example of $\{A, J\}$ and middle I in Figure 15.1 on Page 251, we would search for I from both A and J, stopping as soon as we get to I from A, thereby avoiding a wasteful search from J. (We would still have to search for J from I to complete the computation.)

```
bool PairIncludesAncestorAndDescendantOfM(
    const unique_ptr<BSTNode<int>>& possible_anc_or_desc_0,
    const unique_ptr<BSTNode<int>>& possible_anc_or_desc_1,
    const unique_ptr<BSTNode<int>>& middle) {
  auto* search_0 = possible_anc_or_desc_0.get();
  auto* search_1 = possible_anc_or_desc_1.get();

  // Perform interleaved searching from possible_anc_or_desc_0 and
  // possible_anc_or_desc_1 for middle.
  while (search_0 != possible_anc_or_desc_1.get() &&
         search_0 != middle.get() &&
         search_1 != possible_anc_or_desc_0.get() &&
         search_1 != middle.get() && (search_0 || search_1)) {
    if (search_0) {
      search_0 = search_0->data > middle->data ? search_0->left.get()
                                               : search_0->right.get();
    }
```

270

```
        if (search_1) {
            search_1 = search_1->data > middle->data ? search_1->left.get()
                                                      : search_1->right.get();
        }
    }

    // If both searches were unsuccessful, or we got from
    // possible_anc_or_desc_0 to possible_anc_or_desc_1 without seeing middle,
    // or from possible_anc_or_desc_1 to possible_anc_or_desc_0 without seeing
    // middle, middle cannot lie between possible_anc_or_desc_0 and
    // possible_anc_or_desc_1.
    if ((search_0 != middle.get() && search_1 != middle.get()) ||
        search_0 == possible_anc_or_desc_1.get() ||
        search_1 == possible_anc_or_desc_0.get()) {
        return false;
    }

    // If we get here, we already know one of possible_anc_or_desc_0 or
    // possible_anc_or_desc_1 has a path to middle. Check if middle has a path
    // to possible_anc_or_desc_1 or to possible_anc_or_desc_0.
    return search_0 == middle.get()
               ? SearchTarget(middle, possible_anc_or_desc_1)
               : SearchTarget(middle, possible_anc_or_desc_0);
}

bool SearchTarget(const unique_ptr<BSTNode<int>>& from,
                  const unique_ptr<BSTNode<int>>& target) {
    auto* iter = from.get();
    while (iter && iter != target.get()) {
        iter = iter->data > target->data ? iter->left.get() : iter->right.get();
    }
    return iter == target.get();
}
```

When the middle node does have an ancestor and descendant in the pair, the time complexity is $O(d)$, where d is the difference between the depths of the ancestor and descendant. The reason is that the interleaved search will stop when the ancestor reaches the middle node, i.e., after $O(d)$ iterations. The search from the middle node to the descendant then takes $O(d)$ steps to succeed. When the middle node does not have an ancestor and descendant in the pair, the time complexity is $O(h)$, which corresponds to a worst-case search in a BST.

15.13 THE RANGE LOOKUP PROBLEM

Consider the problem of developing a web-service that takes a geographical location, and returns the nearest restaurant. The service starts with a set of restaurant locations—each location includes X and Y-coordinates. A query consists of a location, and should return the nearest restaurant (ties can be broken arbitrarily).

One approach is to build two BSTs on the restaurant locations: T_X sorted on the X coordinates, and T_Y sorted on the Y coordinates. A query on location (p, q) can be performed by finding all the restaurants whose X coordinate is in the interval

$[p-D, p+D]$, and all the restaurants whose Y coordinate is in the interval $[q-D, q+D]$, taking the intersection of these two sets, and finding the restaurant in the intersection which is closest to (p, q). Heuristically, if D is chosen correctly, the subsets are small and a brute-force search for the closest point is fast. One approach is to start with a small value for D and keep doubling it until the final intersection is nonempty.

There are other data structures which are more robust, e.g., Quadtrees and k-d trees, but the approach outlined above works well in practice.

Write a program that takes as input a BST and an interval and returns the BST keys that lie in the interval. For example, for the tree in Figure 15.1 on Page 251, and interval $[16, 31]$, you should return $17, 19, 23, 29, 31$.

Hint: How many edges are traversed when the successor function is repeatedly called m times?

Solution: A brute-force approach would be to perform a traversal (inorder, postorder, or preorder) of the BST and record the keys in the specified interval. The time complexity is that of the traversal, i.e., $O(n)$, where n is the number of nodes in the tree.

The brute-force approach does not exploit the BST property—it would work unchanged for an arbitrary binary tree.

We can use the BST property to prune the traversal as follows:
- If the root of the tree holds a key that is less than the left endpoint of the interval, the left subtree cannot contain any node whose key lies in the interval.
- If the root of the tree holds a key that is greater than the right endpoint of the interval, the right subtree cannot contain any node whose key lies in the interval.
- Otherwise, the root of the tree holds a key that lies within the interval, and it is possible for both the left and right subtrees to contain nodes whose keys lie in the interval.

For example, for the tree in Figure 15.1 on Page 251, and interval $[16, 42]$, we begin the traversal at A, which contains 19. Since 19 lies in $[16, 42]$, we explore both of A's children, namely B and I. Continuing with B, we see B's key 7 is less than 16, so no nodes in B's left subtree can lie in the interval $[16, 42]$. Similarly, when we get to I, since $43 > 42$, we need not explore I's right subtree.

```
struct Interval {
  int left, right;
};

vector<int> RangeLookupInBST(const unique_ptr<BSTNode<int>>& tree,
                             const Interval& interval) {
  vector<int> result;
  RangeLookupInBSTHelper(tree, interval, &result);
  return result;
}

void RangeLookupInBSTHelper(const unique_ptr<BSTNode<int>>& tree,
                            const Interval& interval, vector<int>* result) {
  if (tree == nullptr) {
```

```
    return;
  }
  if (interval.left <= tree->data && tree->data <= interval.right) {
    // tree->data lies in the interval.
    RangeLookupInBSTHelper(tree->left, interval, result);
    result->emplace_back(tree->data);
    RangeLookupInBSTHelper(tree->right, interval, result);
  } else if (interval.left > tree->data) {
    RangeLookupInBSTHelper(tree->right, interval, result);
  } else {  // interval.right > tree->data
    RangeLookupInBSTHelper(tree->left, interval, result);
  }
}
```

The time complexity is tricky to analyze. It makes sense to reason about time complexity in terms of the number of keys m that lie in the specified interval. We partition the nodes into two categories—those that the program recurses on and those that it does not. For our working example, the program recurses on $A, B, F, G, H, I, J, K, L, M, N$. Not all of these have keys in the specified interval, but no nodes outside of this set can have keys in the interval. Looking more carefully at the nodes we recurse on, we see these nodes can be partitioned into three subsets—nodes on the search path to 16, nodes on the search path to 42, and the rest. All nodes in the third subset must lie in the result, but some of the nodes in the first two subsets may or may not lie in the result. The traversal spends $O(h)$ time visiting the first two subsets, and $O(m)$ time traversing the third subset—each edge is visited twice, once downwards, once upwards. Therefore the total time complexity is $O(m + h)$, which is much better than $O(n)$ brute-force approach when the tree is balanced, and very few keys lie in the specified range.

Augmented BSTs

Thus far we have considered BSTs in which each node stores a key, a left child, a right child, and, possibly, the parent. Adding fields to the nodes can speed up certain queries, as the following problems illustrate.

15.14 ADD CREDITS

Consider a server that a large number of clients connect to. Each client is identified by a string. Each client has a "credit", which is a nonnegative integer value. The server needs to maintain a data structure to which clients can be added, removed, queried, or updated. In addition, the server needs to be able to add a specified number of credits to all clients simultaneously.

Design a data structure that implements the following methods:
- Insert: add a client with specified credit, replacing any existing entry for the client.
- Remove: delete the specified client.
- Lookup: return the number of credits associated with the specified client.

- Add-to-all: increment the credit count for all current clients by the specified amount.
- Max: return a client with the highest number of credits.

Hint: Use additional global state.

Solution: A hash table is a natural data structure for this application. However, it does not support efficient max operations, nor is there an obvious way to perform the simultaneous increment, short traversing all entries. A BST does have efficient max operation, but it too does not natively support the global increment.

A general principle when adding behaviors to an object is to wrap the object, and add functions in the wrapper, which add behaviors before or after delegating to the object. In our context, this suggests storing the clients in a BST, and having the wrapper track the total increment amount.

For example, if we have clients A, B, C, with credits $1, 2, 3$, respectively, and want to add 5 credits to each, the wrapper sets the total increment amount to 5. A lookup on B then is performed by looking up in the BST, which returns 2, and then adding 5 before returning. If we want to add 4 more credits to each, we simply update the total increment amount to 9.

One issue to watch out for is what happens to clients inserted after a call to the add-to-all function. Continuing with the given example, if we were to now add D with a credit of 6, the lookup would return $6 + 9$, which is an error.

The solution is simple—subtract the increment from the credit, i.e., add D with a credit of $6 - 9 = -3$ to the BST. Now a lookup for D will return $-3 + 9$, which is the correct amount.

More specifically, the BST keys are credits, and the corresponding values are the clients with that credit. This makes for fast max-queries. However, to perform lookups and removes by client quickly, the BST by itself is not enough (since it is ordered by credit, not client id). We can solve this by maintaining an additional hash table in which keys are clients, and values are credits. Lookup is trivial. Removes entails a lookup in the hash to get the credit, and then a search into the BST to get the set of clients with that credit, and finally a delete on that set.

```
class ClientsCreditsInfo {
 public:
  void Insert(const string& client_id, int c) {
    Remove(client_id);
    client_to_credit_.emplace(client_id, c - offset_);
    credit_to_clients_[c - offset_].emplace(client_id);
  }

  bool Remove(const string& client_id) {
    auto credit_iter = client_to_credit_.find(client_id);
    if (credit_iter != client_to_credit_.end()) {
      credit_to_clients_[credit_iter->second].erase(client_id);
      if (credit_to_clients_[credit_iter->second].empty()) {
        credit_to_clients_.erase(credit_iter->second);
      }
```

```
      client_to_credit_.erase(credit_iter);
      return true;
    }
    return false;
  }

  int Lookup(const string& client_id) const {
    auto credit_iter = client_to_credit_.find(client_id);
    return credit_iter == client_to_credit_.cend() ? -1 : credit_iter->second +
                                                           offset_;
  }

  void AddAll(int C) { offset_ += C; }

  string Max() const {
    auto iter = credit_to_clients_.crbegin();
    return iter == credit_to_clients_.crend() || iter->second.empty()
           ? ""
           : *iter->second.cbegin();
  }

 private:
  int offset_ = 0;
  unordered_map<string, int> client_to_credit_;
  map<int, unordered_set<string>> credit_to_clients_;
};
```

The time complexity to insert and remove is dominated by the BST, i.e., $O(\log n)$, where n is the number of clients in the data structure. Lookup and add-to-all operate only on the hash table, and have $O(1)$ time complexity. Library BST implementations uses caching to perform max in $O(1)$ time.

15.15   COUNT THE NUMBER OF ENTRIES IN AN INTERVAL

One problem with the approach to the restaurant problem outlined in Problem 15.13 on Page 272 is that the number of entries in the interval along the X-axis could be much larger than the number of entries in the interval along the Y-axis, or vice versa. One way to address this is to first compute the number of entries that lie in a interval.

Suppose each node in a BST has a size field, which denotes the number of nodes at the subtree rooted at that node, inclusive of the node. How would you efficiently compute the number of keys that lie in a given interval? Your solution should work in the presence of duplicate keys.

Hint: How would you count the number of entries that are less than a given value? How does that relate to the question?

Solution: We can find the number of nodes whose entries lie in a specified interval using the approach of Solution 15.13 on Page 273, and counting nodes, rather than inserting them into a list. This leads to the same time complexity, i.e., $O(h + m)$, where

275

h is the height of the tree and m is the number of nodes with keys within the interval. However, we can potentially do much better by exploiting the size field.

For simplicity, suppose we want to find the number of entries that are less than a specified value. As an example, say we want to count the number of keys less than 40 in the BST in Figure 15.1 on Page 251, and that each node has a size field. Since the root A's key, 19, is less than 40, the BST property tells us that all keys in A's left subtree are less than 40. Therefore we can add 7 (which we get from the left child's size field) and 1 (for A itself) to the running count, and recurse with A's right child.

Generalizing, let's say we want to count all entries less than v. We initialize count to 0. Since there can be duplicate keys in the tree, we search for the first occurrence of v in an inorder traversal using Solution 15.3 on Page 255. (If v is not present, we stop when we have determined this.) Each time we take a left child, we leave count unchanged; each time we take a right child, we add one plus the size of the corresponding left child. If v is present, when we reach the first occurrence of v, we add the size of v's left child, The same approach can be used to find the number of entries that are greater than v, less than or equal to v, and greater than or equal to v.

For example, to count the number of less than 40 in the BST in Figure 15.1 on Page 251 we would search for 40. Since A's key, 19 is less than 40, we update count to $7 + 1 = 8$ and continue from I. Since I's key, 43 is greater than 40, we move to I's left child, J. Since J's key, 23 is less than 40, update count to $8 + 1 = 9$, and continue from K. Since K's key, 37 is less than 40, we update count to $9 + 2 + 1 = 12$, and continue from N. Since N's key, 41, is greater than 40, we move to N's left child, which is empty. No other keys can be less than 40, so we return count, i.e., 12. Note how we avoided exploring A and K's left subtrees.

The time bound for these computations is $O(h)$, since the search always descends the tree. When m is large, e.g., comparable to the total number of nodes in the tree, and the tree is balanced, this is much faster than the $O(h + m)$ pruned inorder traversal in Solution 15.13 on Page 273.

To compute the number of nodes with keys in the interval $[L, U]$, first compute the number of nodes with keys less than L and the number of nodes with keys greater than U, and subtract that from the total number of nodes (which is the size stored at the root).

Variant: Define the "Markowitz bullet" of a set of points P in the upper right quadrant of the Cartesian plane to be those points which are not below and to the right of any other point in P. Design a data structure for representing the Markowitz bullet. Specifically, it should be possible to efficiently check if a new point is below and to the right of some point in the Markowitz bullet, and to add a point to the Markowitz bullet (which may result in other points being removed from the bullet).

16

Recursion

The power of recursion evidently lies in the possibility of defining an infinite set of objects by a finite statement. In the same manner, an infinite number of computations can be described by a finite recursive program, even if this program contains no explicit repetitions.

— *"Algorithms + Data Structures = Programs,"*
N. E. Wirth, 1976

Recursion is a method where the solution to a problem depends partially on solutions to smaller instances of related problems. Two key ingredients to a successful use of recursion are identifying the base cases, which are to be solved directly, and ensuring progress, that is the recursion converges to the solution.

A divide-and-conquer algorithm works by repeatedly decomposing a problem into two or more smaller independent subproblems of the same kind, until it gets to instances that are simple enough to be solved directly. The solutions to the subproblems are then combined to give a solution to the original problem. Merge sort and quicksort are classical examples of divide-and-conquer.

Divide-and-conquer is not synonymous with recursion. In divide-and-conquer, the problem is divided into two or more independent smaller problems that are of the same type as the original problem. Recursion is more general—there may be a single subproblem, e.g., binary search, the subproblems may not be independent, e.g., dynamic programming, and they may not be of the same type as the original, e.g., regular expression matching. In addition, sometimes to improve runtime, and occasionally to reduce space complexity, a divide-and-conquer algorithm is implemented using iteration instead of recursion.

16.1 THE TOWER OF HANOI PROBLEM

A peg contains rings in sorted order, with the largest ring being the lowest. You are to transfer these rings to another peg, which is initially empty. This is illustrated in Figure 16.1 on the facing page.

Write a program which prints a sequence of operations that transfers n rings from one peg to another. You have a third peg, which is initially empty. The only operation you can perform is taking a single ring from the top of one peg and placing it on the top of another peg. You must never place a larger ring above a smaller ring.

Hint: If you know how to transfer the top $n - 1$ rings, how does that help move the nth ring?

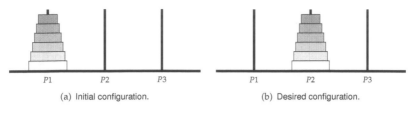

(a) Initial configuration.   (b) Desired configuration.

Figure 16.1: Tower of Hanoi with 6 pegs.

Solution: The insight to solving this problem can be gained by trying examples. The three ring transfer can be achieved by moving the top two rings to the third peg, then moving the lowest ring (which is the largest) to the second peg, and then transferring the two rings on the third peg to the second peg, using the first peg as the intermediary. To transfer four rings, move the top three rings to the third peg, then moving the lowest ring (which is the largest) to the second peg, and then transfer the three rings on the third peg to the second peg, using the first peg as an intermediary. For both the three ring and four ring transfers, the first and third steps are instances of the same problem, which suggests the use of recursion. This approach is illustrated in Figure 16.2. Code implementing this idea is given below.

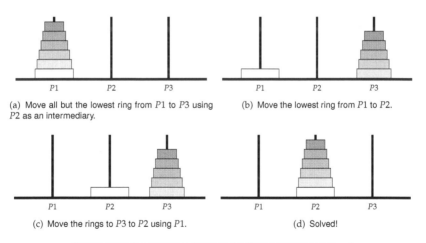

(a) Move all but the lowest ring from $P1$ to $P3$ using $P2$ as an intermediary.
     (b) Move the lowest ring from $P1$ to $P2$.

(c) Move the rings to $P3$ to $P2$ using $P1$.
     (d) Solved!

Figure 16.2: A recursive solution to the Tower of Hanoi for $n = 6$.

```
const int kNumPegs = 3;

void ComputeTowerHanoi(int num_rings) {
  array<stack<int>, kNumPegs> pegs;
  // Initialize pegs.
  for (int i = num_rings; i >= 1; --i) {
    pegs[0].push(i);
  }

  ComputeTowerHanoiSteps(num_rings, pegs, 0, 1, 2);
```

```
}

void ComputeTowerHanoiSteps(int num_rings_to_move,
                            array<stack<int>, kNumPegs>& pegs, int from_peg,
                            int to_peg, int use_peg) {
  if (num_rings_to_move > 0) {
    ComputeTowerHanoiSteps(num_rings_to_move - 1, pegs, from_peg, use_peg,
                           to_peg);
    pegs[to_peg].push(pegs[from_peg].top());
    pegs[from_peg].pop();
    cout << "Move from peg " << from_peg << " to peg " << to_peg << endl;
    ComputeTowerHanoiSteps(num_rings_to_move - 1, pegs, use_peg, to_peg,
                           from_peg);
  }
}
```

The number of moves, $T(n)$, satisfies the following recurrence: $T(n) = T(n-1) + 1 + T(n-1) = 1 + 2T(n-1)$. The first $T(n-1)$ corresponds to the transfer of the top $n-1$ rings from $P1$ to $P3$, and the second $T(n-1)$ corresponds to the transfer from $P3$ to $P2$. This recurrence solves to $T(n) = 2^n - 1$. One way to see this is to "unwrap" the recurrence: $T(n) = 1 + 2 + 4 + \cdots + 2^k T(n-k)$. Printing a single move takes $O(1)$ time, so the time complexity is $O(2^n)$.

Variant: Solve the same problem without using recursion.

Variant: Find the minimum number of operations subject to the constraint that each operation must involve $P3$.

Variant: Find the minimum number of operations subject to the constraint that each transfer must be from $P1$ to $P2$, $P2$ to $P3$, or $P3$ to $P1$.

Variant: Find the minimum number of operations subject to the constraint that a ring can never be transferred directly from $P1$ to $P2$ (transfers from $P2$ to $P1$ are allowed).

Variant: Find the minimum number of operations when the stacking constraint is relaxed to the following—the largest ring on a peg must be the lowest ring on the peg. (The remaining rings on the peg can be in any order, e.g., it is fine to have the second-largest ring above the third-largest ring.)

Variant: You have $2n$ disks of n different sizes, two of each size. You cannot place a larger disk on a smaller disk, but can place a disk of equal size on top of the other. Compute the minimum number of moves to transfer the $2n$ disks from $P1$ to $P2$.

Variant: You have $2n$ disks which are colored black or white. You cannot place a white disk directly on top of a black disk. Compute the minimum number of moves to transfer the $2n$ disks from $P1$ to $P2$.

Variant: Find the minimum number of operations if you have a fourth peg, $P4$.

A nonattacking placement of queens is one in which no two queens are in the same row, column, or diagonal. See Figure 16.3 for an example.

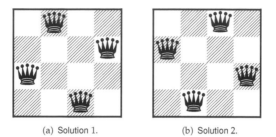

(a) Solution 1.   (b) Solution 2.

Figure 16.3: The only two ways in which four queens can be placed on a 4 × 4 chessboard.

Write a program which returns all distinct nonattacking placements of n queens on an $n \times n$ chessboard, where n is an input to the program.

Hint: If the first queen is placed at (i, j), where can the remaining queens definitely not be placed?

Solution: A brute-force approach is to consider all possible placements of the n queens—there are $\binom{n^2}{n}$ possible placements which grows very large with n.

Since we never would place two queens on the same row, a much faster solution is to enumerate placements that use distinct rows. Such a placement cannot lead to conflicts on rows, but it may lead to conflicts on columns and diagonals. It can be represented by an array of length n, where the ith entry is the location of the queen on Row i.

As an example, if $n = 4$, begin by placing the first row's queen at Column 0. Now we enumerate all placements of the form $(0, \_, \_, \_)$. Placing the second row's queen at Column 0 leads to a column conflict, so we skip all placements of the form $(0, 0, \_, \_)$. Placing the second row's queen at Column 1 leads to a diagonal conflict, so we skip all placements of the form $(0, 1, \_, \_)$. Now we turn to placements of the form $(0, 2, 0, \_)$. Such placements are conflicting because of the conflict on Column 0. Now we turn to placements of the form $(0, 2, 1, \_)$ and $(0, 2, 2, \_)$. Such placements are conflicting because of the diagonal conflict between the queens at Row 1 and Column 2 and Row 2 and Column 1, and the column conflict between the queens at Row 1 and Column 2 and Row 2 and Column 2, respectively, so we move on to $(0, 2, 3, \_)$, which also violates a diagonal constraint. Now we advance to placements of the form $(0, 3, \_, \_)$. Both $(0, 3, 1, \_)$ and $(0, 3, 2, \_)$ lead to conflicts, implying there is no nonattacking placement possible with a queen placed at Row 0 and Column 0. The first nonattacking placement is $(1, 3, 0, 2)$; the only other nonattacking placement is $(2, 0, 3, 1)$.

```
vector<vector<int>> NQueens(int n) {
  vector<int> placement;
  vector<vector<int>> result;
```

```
  SolveNQueens(n, 0, &placement, &result);
  return result;
}

void SolveNQueens(int n, int row, vector<int>* col_placement,
                  vector<vector<int>>* result) {
  if (row == n) {
    // All queens are legally placed.
    result->emplace_back(*col_placement);
  } else {
    for (int col = 0; col < n; ++col) {
      col_placement->emplace_back(col);
      if (IsValid(*col_placement)) {
        SolveNQueens(n, row + 1, col_placement, result);
      }
      col_placement->pop_back();
    }
  }
}

// Test if a newly placed queen will conflict any earlier queens
// placed before.
bool IsValid(const vector<int>& col_placement) {
  int row_id = col_placement.size() - 1;
  for (int i = 0; i < row_id; ++i) {
    int diff = abs(col_placement[i] - col_placement[row_id]);
    if (diff == 0 || diff == row_id - i) {
      // A column or diagonal constraint is violated.
      return false;
    }
  }
  return true;
}
```

The time complexity is lower bounded by the number of nonattacking placements. No exact form is known for this quantity as a function of n, but it is conjectured to tend to $n!/c^n$, where $c \approx 2.54$, which is super-exponential.

Variant: Compute the number of nonattacking placements of n queens on an $n \times n$ chessboard.

Variant: Compute the smallest number of queens that can be placed to attack each uncovered square.

Variant: Compute a placement of 32 knights, or 14 bishops, 16 kings or 8 rooks on an 8×8 chessboard in which no two pieces attack each other.

16.3 GENERATE PERMUTATIONS

This problem is concerned with computing all permutations of an array. For example, if the array is $\langle 2, 3, 5, 7 \rangle$ one output could be $\langle 2, 3, 5, 7 \rangle$, $\langle 2, 3, 7, 5 \rangle$, $\langle 2, 5, 3, 7 \rangle$, $\langle 2, 5, 7, 3 \rangle$, $\langle 2, 7, 3, 5 \rangle$, $\langle 2, 7, 5, 3 \rangle$, $\langle 3, 2, 5, 7 \rangle$, $\langle 3, 2, 7, 5 \rangle$, $\langle 3, 5, 2, 7 \rangle$, $\langle 3, 5, 7, 2 \rangle$, $\langle 3, 7, 2, 5 \rangle$, $\langle 3, 7, 5, 2 \rangle$,

$\langle 5,2,3,7 \rangle$, $\langle 5,2,7,3 \rangle$, $\langle 5,3,2,7 \rangle$, $\langle 5,3,7,2 \rangle$, $\langle 5,7,2,3 \rangle$, $\langle 5,7,2,3 \rangle$, $\langle 7,2,3,5 \rangle$, $\langle 7,2,5,3 \rangle$, $\langle 7,3,2,5 \rangle$, $\langle 7,3,5,2 \rangle$, $\langle 7,5,2,3 \rangle$, $\langle 7,5,3,2 \rangle$. (Any other ordering is acceptable too.)

Write a program which takes as input an array of distinct integers and generates all permutations of that array. No permutation of the array may appear more than once.

Hint: How many possible values are there for the first element?

Solution: Let the input array be A. Suppose its length is n. A truly brute-force approach would be to enumerate all arrays of length n whose entries are from A, and check each such array for being a permutation. This enumeration can be performed recursively, e.g., enumerate all arrays of length $n - 1$ whose entries are from A, and then for each array, consider the n arrays of length n which is formed by adding a single entry to the end of that array. Since the number of possible arrays is n^n, the time and space complexity are staggering.

A better approach is to recognize that once a value has been chosen for an entry, we do not want to repeat it. Specifically, every permutation of A begins with one of $A[0], A[1], \ldots, A[n-1]$. The idea is to generate all permutations that begin with $A[0]$, then all permutations that begin with $A[1]$, and so on. Computing all permutations beginning with $A[0]$ entails computing all permutations of $A[1 : n-1]$, which suggests the use of recursion. To compute all permutations beginning with $A[1]$ we swap $A[0]$ with $A[1]$ and compute all permutations of the updated $A[1 : n - 1]$. We then restore the original state before embarking on computing all permutations beginning with $A[2]$, and so on.

For example, for the array $\langle 7,3,5 \rangle$, we would first generate all permutations starting with 7. This entails generating all permutations of $\langle 3,5 \rangle$, which we do by finding all permutations of $\langle 3,5 \rangle$ beginning with 3. Since $\langle 5 \rangle$ is an array of length 1, it has a single permutation. This implies $\langle 3,5 \rangle$ has a single permutation beginning with 3. Next we look for permutations of $\langle 3,5 \rangle$ beginning with 5. To do this, we swap 3 and 5, and find, as before, there is a single permutation of $\langle 3,5 \rangle$ beginning with 5, namely, $\langle 5,3 \rangle$. Hence, there are two permutations of A beginning with 7, namely $\langle 7,3,5 \rangle$ and $\langle 7,5,3 \rangle$. We swap 7 with 3 to find all permutations beginning with 3, namely $\langle 3,7,5 \rangle$ and $\langle 3,5,7 \rangle$. The last two permutations we add are $\langle 5,3,7 \rangle$ and $\langle 5,7,3 \rangle$.

```cpp
vector<vector<int>> Permutations(vector<int> A) {
  vector<vector<int>> result;
  DirectedPermutations(0, &A, &result);
  return result;
}

void DirectedPermutations(int i, vector<int> *A_ptr,
                          vector<vector<int>> *result) {
  vector<int> &A = *A_ptr;
  if (i == A.size() - 1) {
    result->emplace_back(A);
    return;
  }

  // Try every possibility for A[i].
  for (int j = i; j < A.size(); ++j) {
```

```
    swap(A[i], A[j]);
    // Generate all permutations for A[i + 1 : A.size() - 1].
    DirectedPermutations(i + 1, A_ptr, result);
    swap(A[i], A[j]);
  }
}
```

The time complexity is determined by the number of recursive calls, since within each function the time spent is $O(1)$, not including the time in the subcalls. The number of function calls, $C(n)$ satisfies the recurrence $C(n) = 1 + nC(n - 1)$ for $n \geq 1$, with $C(0) = 1$. Expanding this, we see $C(n) = 1 + n + n(n - 1) + n(n - 1)(n - 2) + \cdots + n! = n!(1/n! + 1/(n - 1)! + 1/(n - 2)! + \cdots + 1/1!)$. The sum $(1 + 1/1! + 1/2! + \cdots + 1/n!)$ tends to Euler's number e, so $C(n)$ tends to $(e - 1)n!$, i.e., $O(n!)$. The time complexity $T(n)$ is $O(n \times n!)$, since we do $O(n)$ computation per call outside of the recursive calls.

Now we describe a qualitatively different algorithm for this problem. In Solution 6.11 on Page 74 we showed how to efficiently compute the permutation that follows a given permutation, e.g., $\langle 2, 3, 1, 4 \rangle$ is followed by $\langle 2, 3, 4, 1 \rangle$. We can extend that algorithm to solve the current problem. The idea is that the n distinct entries in the array can be mapped to $1, 2, 3, \ldots$, with 1 corresponding to the smallest entry. For example, if the array is $\langle 7, 3, 5 \rangle$, we first sort it to obtain, $\langle 3, 5, 7 \rangle$. Using the approach of Solution 6.11 on Page 74, the next array will be $\langle 3, 7, 5 \rangle$, followed by $\langle 5, 3, 7 \rangle$, $\langle 5, 7, 3 \rangle$, $\langle 7, 3, 5 \rangle$, $\langle 7, 5, 3 \rangle$. This is the approach in the program below.

```
vector<vector<int>> Permutations(vector<int> A) {
  vector<vector<int>> result;
  // Generate the first permutation in dictionary order.
  sort(A.begin(), A.end());
  do {
    result.emplace_back(A);
  } while (next_permutation(A.begin(), A.end()));
  return result;
}
```

The time complexity is $O(n \times n!)$, since there are $n!$ permutations and we spend $O(n)$ time to store each one.

Variant: Solve Problem 16.3 on Page 282 when the input array may have duplicates. You should not repeat any permutations. For example, if $A = \langle 2, 2, 3, 0 \rangle$ then the output should be $\langle 2, 2, 0, 3 \rangle$, $\langle 2, 2, 3, 0 \rangle$, $\langle 2, 0, 2, 3 \rangle$, $\langle 2, 0, 3, 2 \rangle$, $\langle 2, 3, 2, 0 \rangle$, $\langle 2, 3, 0, 2 \rangle$, $\langle 0, 2, 2, 3 \rangle$, $\langle 0, 2, 3, 2 \rangle$, $\langle 0, 3, 2, 2 \rangle$, $\langle 3, 2, 2, 0 \rangle$, $\langle 3, 2, 0, 2 \rangle$, $\langle 3, 0, 2, 2 \rangle$.

16.4 GENERATE THE POWER SET

The power set of a set S is the set of all subsets of S, including both the empty set $\emptyset$ and S itself. The power set of $\{0, 1, 2\}$ is graphically illustrated in Figure 16.4 on the facing page.

Write a function that takes as input a set and returns its power set.

Hint: There are 2^n subsets for a given set S of size n. There are 2^k k-bit words.

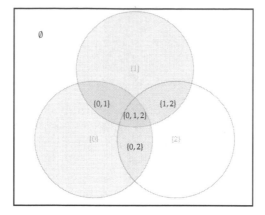

Figure 16.4: The power set of $\{0, 1, 2\}$ is $\{\emptyset, \{0\}, \{1\}, \{2\}, \{0, 1\}, \{1, 2\}, \{0, 2\}, \{0, 1, 2\}\}$.

Solution: A brute-force way is to compute all subsets U that do not include a particular element (which could be any single element). Then we compute all subsets V which do include that element. Each subset set must appear in U or in V, so the final result is just $U \cup V$. The construction is recursive, and the base case is when the input set is empty, in which case we return $\{\{\}\}$.

As an example, let $S = \{0, 1, 2\}$. Pick any element, e.g., 0. First, we recursively compute all subsets of $\{1, 2\}$. To do this, we select 1. This leaves us with $\{2\}$. Now we pick 2, and get to a base case. So the set of subsets of $\{2\}$ is $\{\}$ union with $\{2\}$, i.e., $\{\{\}, \{2\}\}$. The set of subsets of $\{1, 2\}$ then is $\{\{\}, \{2\}\}$ union with $\{\{1\}, \{1, 2\}\}$, i.e., $\{\{\}, \{2\}, \{1\}, \{1, 2\}\}$. The set of subsets of $\{0, 1, 2\}$ then is $\{\{\}, \{2\}, \{1\}, \{1, 2\}\}$ union with $\{\{0\}, \{0, 2\}, \{0, 1\}, \{0, 1, 2\}\}$, i.e., $\{\{\}, \{2\}, \{1\}, \{1, 2\}, \{0\}, \{0, 2\}, \{0, 1\}, \{0, 1, 2\}\}$,

```cpp
vector<vector<int>> GeneratePowerSet(const vector<int>& input_set) {
  vector<vector<int>> power_set;
  vector<int> selected_so_far;
  DirectedPowerSet(input_set, 0, &selected_so_far, &power_set);
  return power_set;
}

// Generate all subsets whose intersection with input_set[0], ...,
// input_set[to_be_selected - 1] is exactly selected_so_far.
void DirectedPowerSet(const vector<int>& input_set, int to_be_selected,
                      vector<int>* selected_so_far,
                      vector<vector<int>>* power_set) {
  if (to_be_selected == input_set.size()) {
    power_set->emplace_back(*selected_so_far);
    return;
  }
  // Generate all subsets that contain input_set[to_be_selected].
  selected_so_far->emplace_back(input_set[to_be_selected]);
  DirectedPowerSet(input_set, to_be_selected + 1, selected_so_far, power_set);
  // Generate all subsets that do not contain input_set[to_be_selected].
  selected_so_far->pop_back();
  DirectedPowerSet(input_set, to_be_selected + 1, selected_so_far, power_set);
```

}

The number of recursive calls, $C(n)$ satisfies the recurrence $C(n) = 2C(n-1)$, which solves to $C(n) = O(2^n)$. Since we spend $O(n)$ time within a call, the time complexity is $O(n2^n)$.

A drawback of the above approach is that its space complexity is $O(2^n)$, even if we just want to print the subsets, rather than returning all of them. A more incremental way to enumerate the subsets is to recognize that for a given ordering of the elements of S, there exists a one-to-one correspondence between the 2^n bit arrays of length n and the set of all subsets of S—the 1s in the n-length bit array v indicate the elements of S in the subset corresponding to v. For example, if $S = \{a, b, c, d\}$, the bit array $\langle 1, 0, 1, 1 \rangle$ denotes the subset $\{a, c, d\}$.

If n is less than or equal to the width of an integer on the architecture (or language) we are working on, we can enumerate bit arrays by enumerating integers in $[0, 2^n - 1]$ and examining the indices of bits set in these integers. These indices are determined by first isolating the lowest set bit by computing $y = x \& \sim(x - 1)$, which is described on Page 24, and then getting the index by computing $\lg y$.

```cpp
vector<vector<int>> GeneratePowerSet(const vector<int>& input_set) {
  vector<vector<int>> power_set;
  for (int int_for_subset = 0; int_for_subset < (1 << input_set.size());
       ++int_for_subset) {
    int bit_array = int_for_subset;
    vector<int> subset;
    while (bit_array) {
      subset.emplace_back(input_set[log2(bit_array & ~(bit_array - 1))]);
      bit_array &= bit_array - 1;
    }
    power_set.emplace_back(subset);
  }
  return power_set;
}
```

Since each set takes $O(n)$ time to compute, the time complexity is $O(n2^n)$. In practice, this approach is very fast. Furthermore, its space complexity is $O(n)$ when we want to just enumerate subsets, e.g., to print them, rather that to return a list of all subsets.

Variant: Solve this problem when the input array may have duplicates, i.e., denotes a multiset. You should not repeat any multiset. For example, if $A = \langle 1, 2, 3, 2 \rangle$, then you should return $\langle \langle \rangle, \langle 1 \rangle, \langle 2 \rangle, \langle 3 \rangle, \langle 1, 2 \rangle, \langle 1, 3 \rangle, \langle 2, 2 \rangle, \langle 2, 3 \rangle, \langle 1, 2, 2 \rangle, \langle 1, 2, 3 \rangle, \langle 2, 2, 3 \rangle, \langle 1, 2, 2, 3 \rangle \rangle$.

16.5 GENERATE ALL SUBSETS OF SIZE k

There are a number of testing applications in which it is required to compute all subsets of a given size for a specified set.

Write a program which computes all size k subsets of $\{1, 2, \ldots, n\}$, where k and n are program inputs. For example, if $k = 2$ and $n = 5$, then the result is the following: $\{\{1, 2\}, \{1, 3\}, \{1, 4\}, \{1, 5\}, \{2, 3\}, \{2, 4\}, \{2, 5\}, \{3, 4\}, \{3, 5\}, \{4, 5\}\}$

Hint: Think of the right function signature.

Solution: One brute-force approach is to compute all subsets of $\{1, 2, \ldots, n\}$, and then restrict the result to subsets of size k. A convenient aspect of this approach is that we can use Solution 16.4 on Page 285 to compute all subsets. The time complexity is $O(n2^n)$, regardless of k. When k is much smaller than n, or nearly equal to n, it ends up computing many subsets which cannot possibly be of the right size.

To gain efficiency, we use a more focused approach. In particular, we can make nice use of case analysis. There are two possibilities for a subset—it does not contain 1, or it does contain 1. In the first case, we return all subsets of size k of $\{2, 3, \ldots, n\}$; in the second case, we compute all $k - 1$ sized subsets of $\{2, 3, \ldots, n\}$ and add 1 to each of them.

For example, if $n = 4$ and $k = 2$, then we compute all subsets of size 2 from $\{2, 3, 4\}$, and all subsets of size 1 from $\{2, 3, 4\}$. We add 1 to each of the latter, and the result is the union of the two sets of subsets, i.e., $\{\{2, 3\}, \{2, 4\}, \{3, 4\}\} \cup \{\{1, 2\}, \{1, 3\}, \{1, 4\}\}$.

```cpp
vector<vector<int>> Combinations(int n, int k) {
  vector<vector<int>> result;
  vector<int> partial_combination;
  DirectedCombinations(n, k, 1, &partial_combination, &result);
  return result;
}

void DirectedCombinations(int n, int k, int offset,
                          vector<int>* partial_combination,
                          vector<vector<int>>* result) {
  if (partial_combination->size() == k) {
    result->emplace_back(*partial_combination);
    return;
  }

  // Generate remaining combinations over {offset, ..., n - 1} of size
  // num_remaining.
  const int num_remaining = k - partial_combination->size();
  for (int i = offset; i <= n && num_remaining <= n - i + 1; ++i) {
    partial_combination->emplace_back(i);
    DirectedCombinations(n, k, i + 1, partial_combination, result);
    partial_combination->pop_back();
  }
}
```

The time complexity is $O(n\binom{n}{k})$; the reasoning is analogous to that for the recursive solution enumerating the powerset (Page 286).

16.6 GENERATE STRINGS OF MATCHED PARENS

Strings in which parens are matched are defined by the following three rules:
- The empty string, "", is a string in which parens are matched.
- The addition of a leading left parens and a trailing right parens to a string in which parens are matched results in a string in which parens are matched. For example, since "(())()" is a string with matched parens, so is "((())())".

- The concatenation of two strings in which parens are matched is itself a string in which parens are matched. For example, since "(())()" and "()" are strings with matched parens, so is "(())()()".

For example, the set of strings containing two pairs of matched parens is {(()), ()()}, and the set of strings with three pairs of matched parens is {((())), (()()), (())(), ()(()), ()()()}.

Write a program that takes as input a number and returns all the strings with that number of matched pairs of parens.

Hint: Think about what the prefix of a string of matched parens must look like.

Solution: A brute-force approach would be to enumerate all strings on $2k$ parentheses. To test if the parens in a string are matched, we use Solution 9.3 on Page 132, specialized to one type of parentheses. There are 2^{2k} possible strings, which is a lower bound on the time complexity. Even if we restrict the enumeration to strings with an equal number of left and right parens, there are $\binom{2k}{k}$ strings to consider.

We can greatly improve upon the time complexity by enumerating in a more directed fashion. For example, some strings can never be completed to a string with k pairs of matched parens, e.g., if a string begins with). Therefore, one way to be more directed is to build strings incrementally. We will ensure that as each additional character is added, the resulting string has the potential to be completed to a string with k pairs of matched parens.

Suppose we have a string whose length is less than $2k$, and we know that string can be completed to a string with k pairs of matched parens. How can we extend that string with an additional character so that the resulting string can still be completed to a string with k pairs of matched parens?

There are two possibilities: we add a left parens, or we add a right parens.
- If we add a left parens, and still want to complete the string to a string with k pairs of matched parens, it must be that the number of left parens we need is greater than 0.
- If we add a right parens, and still want to complete the string to a string with k pairs of matched parens, it must be that the number of left parens we need is less than the number of right parens (i.e., there are unmatched left parens in the string).

As a concrete example, if $k = 2$, we would go through the following sequence of strings: "", "(", "((", "(()", "(())", "()", "()(", "()()". Of these, "(())" and "()()" are complete, and we would add them to the result.

```
vector<string> GenerateBalancedParentheses(int num_pairs) {
  vector<string> result;
  DirectedGenerateBalancedParentheses(num_pairs, num_pairs, "", &result);
  return result;
}

void DirectedGenerateBalancedParentheses(int num_left_parens_needed,
                                         int num_right_parens_needed,
                                         const string& valid_prefix,
                                         vector<string>* result) {
```

```
if (!num_left_parens_needed && !num_right_parens_needed) {
  result->emplace_back(valid_prefix);
  return;
}

if (num_left_parens_needed > 0) {   // Able to insert '('.
  DirectedGenerateBalancedParentheses(num_left_parens_needed - 1,
                                      num_right_parens_needed,
                                      valid_prefix + '(', result);
}
if (num_left_parens_needed < num_right_parens_needed) {
  // Able to insert ')'.
  DirectedGenerateBalancedParentheses(num_left_parens_needed,
                                      num_right_parens_needed - 1,
                                      valid_prefix + ')', result);
}
}
```

The number $C(k)$ of strings with k pairs of matched parens grows very rapidly with k. Specifically, it can be shown that $C(k + 1) = \sum_{i=0}^{k} \binom{k}{i}/(k + 1)$, which solves to $(2k)!/((k!(k + 1)!))$.

16.7 GENERATE PALINDROMIC DECOMPOSITIONS

A string is said to be palindromic if it reads the same backwards and forwards. A decomposition of a string is a set of strings whose concatenation is the string. For example, "611116" is palindromic, and "611", "11", "6" is one decomposition for it.

Compute all palindromic decompositions of a given string. For example, if the string is "0204451881", then the decomposition "020", "44", "5", "1881" is palindromic, as is "020", "44", "5", "1", "88", "1". However, "02044, "5", "1881" is not a palindromic decomposition.

Hint: Focus on the first palindromic string in a palindromic decomposition.

Solution: We can brute-force compute all palindromic decompositions by first computing all decompositions, and then checking which ones are palindromic. To compute all decompositions, we use prefixes of length $1, 2 \ldots$ for the first string in the decomposition, and recursively compute the decomposition of the corresponding suffix. The number of such decompositions is 2^{n-1}, where n is the length of the string. (One way to understand this is from the fact that every n-bit vector corresponds to a unique decomposition—the 1s in the bit vector denote the starting point of a substring.)

Clearly, the brute-force approach is inefficient because it continues with decompositions that cannot possibly be palindromic, e.g., it will recursively compute decompositions that begin with "02" for "0204451881". We need a more directed approach—specifically, we should enumerate decompositions that begin with a palindrome.

For the given example, "0204451881", we would recursively compute palindromic sequences for "204451881" (since "0" is a palindrome), and for "4451881" (since "020" is a palindrome). To compute palindromic decompositions for "204451881", we would recursively compute palindromic sequences for "04451881" (since "2" is the only prefix that is a palindrome). To compute palindromic decompositions for "04451881", we would recursively compute palindromic sequences for "4451991" (since "0" is the only prefix that is a palindrome). To compute palindromic decompositions for "4451991", we would recursively compute palindromic sequences for "451991" (since "4" is a palindrome) and for "51991" (since "44' is a palindrome).

```cpp
vector<vector<string>> PalindromePartitioning(const string& input) {
  vector<vector<string>> result;
  vector<string> partial_partition;
  DirectedPalindromePartitioning(input, 0, &partial_partition, &result);
  return result;
}


void DirectedPalindromePartitioning(const string& input, int offset,
                                    vector<string>* partial_partition,
                                    vector<vector<string>>* result) {
  if (offset == input.size()) {
    result->emplace_back(*partial_partition);
    return;
  }

  for (int i = offset + 1; i <= input.size(); ++i) {
    string prefix = input.substr(offset, i - offset);
    if (IsPalindrome(prefix)) {
      partial_partition->emplace_back(prefix);
      DirectedPalindromePartitioning(input, i, partial_partition, result);
      partial_partition->pop_back();
    }
  }
}

bool IsPalindrome(const string& prefix) {
  for (int i = 0, j = prefix.size() - 1; i < j; ++i, --j) {
    if (prefix[i] != prefix[j]) {
      return false;
    }
  }
  return true;
}
```

The worst-case time complexity is still $O(n \times 2^n)$, e.g., if the input string consists of n repetitions of a single character. However, our program has much better best-case time complexity than the brute-force approach, e.g., when there are very few palindromic decompositions.

16.8 GENERATE BINARY TREES

Write a program which returns all distinct binary trees with a specified number of nodes. For example, if the number of nodes is specified to be three, return the trees in Figure 16.5 on the facing page.

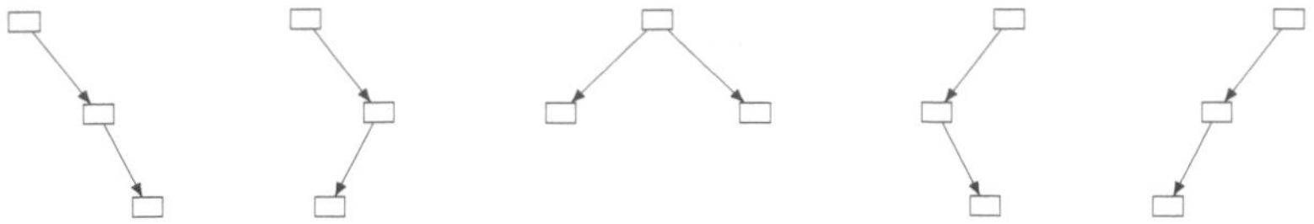

Figure 16.5: The five binary trees on three nodes.

Hint: Can two binary trees whose left subtrees differ in size be the same?

Solution: A brute-force approach to generate all binary trees on n nodes would be to generate all binary trees on $n - 1$ or fewer nodes. Afterwards, form all binary trees with a root and a left child with $n - 1$ or fewer nodes, and a right child with $n - 1$ or fewer nodes. The resulting trees would all be distinct, since no two would have the same left and right child. However, some will have fewer than $n - 1$ nodes, and some will have more.

The key to efficiency is to direct the search. If the left child has k nodes, we should only use right children with $n - 1 - k$ nodes, to get binary trees with n nodes that have that left child. Specifically, we get all binary trees on n nodes by getting all left subtrees on i nodes, and right subtrees on $n - 1 - i$ nodes, for i between 0 and $n - 1$.

Looking carefully at Figure 16.5, you will see the first two trees correspond to the trees on three nodes which have a left subtree of size 0 and a right subtree of size 2. The third tree is the only tree on three nodes which has a left subtree of size 1 and a right subtree of size 1. The last two trees correspond to the trees on three nodes which have a left subtree of size 2 and a right subtree of size 0. The set of two trees on two nodes is itself computed recursively: there is a single binary tree on one node, and it may be on either side of the root.

```cpp
vector<unique_ptr<BinaryTreeNode<int>>> GenerateAllBinaryTrees(int num_nodes) {
  vector<unique_ptr<BinaryTreeNode<int>>> result;
  if (num_nodes == 0) {  // Empty tree, add as an nullptr.
    result.emplace_back(nullptr);
  }

  for (int num_left_tree_nodes = 0; num_left_tree_nodes < num_nodes;
       ++num_left_tree_nodes) {
    int num_right_tree_nodes = num_nodes - 1 - num_left_tree_nodes;
    auto left_subtrees = GenerateAllBinaryTrees(num_left_tree_nodes);
    auto right_subtrees = GenerateAllBinaryTrees(num_right_tree_nodes);
    // Generates all combinations of left_subtrees and right_subtrees.
    for (auto& left : left_subtrees) {
      for (auto& right : right_subtrees) {
        result.emplace_back(
            new BinaryTreeNode<int>{0, move(left), move(right)});
      }
    }
  }
  return result;
}
```

The number of calls $C(n)$ to the recursive function satisfies the recurrence $C(n) = \sum_{i=1}^{n} C(n-i)C(i-1)$. The quantity $C(n)$ is called the nth Catalan number. It is known to be equal to $\frac{(2n)!}{n!(n+1)!}$. Comparing Solution 16.6 on Page 288 to this solution, you will see considerable similarity—the Catalan numbers appear in numerous types of combinatorial problems.

16.9 IMPLEMENT A SUDOKU SOLVER

Implement a Sudoku solver. See Problem 6.17 on Page 83 for a definition of Sudoku.

Hint: Apply the constraints to speed up a brute-force algorithm.

Solution: A brute-force approach would be to try every possible assignment to empty entries, and then check if that assignment leads to a valid solution using Solution 6.17 on Page 83. This is wasteful, since if setting a value early on leads to a constraint violation, there is no point in continuing. Therefore, we should apply the backtracking principle.

Specifically, we traverse the 2D array entries one at a time. If the entry is empty, we try each value for the entry, and see if the updated 2D array is still valid; if it is, we recurse. If all the entries have been filled, the search is successful. The naive approach to testing validity is calling Solution 6.17 on Page 83. However, we can reduce runtime considerably by making use of the fact that we are adding a value to an array that already satisfies the constraints. This means that we need to check just the row, column, and subgrid of the added entry.

For example, suppose we begin with the lower-left entry for the configuration in Figure 6.2(a) on Page 83. Adding a 1 to entry does not violate any row, column, or subgrid constraint, so we move on to the next entry in that row. We cannot put a 1, since that would now violate a row constraint; however, a 2 is acceptable.

```
const int kEmptyEntry = 0;

bool SolveSudoku(vector<vector<int>>* partial_assignment) {
  return SolvePartialSudoku(0, 0, partial_assignment);
}

bool SolvePartialSudoku(int i, int j,
                        vector<vector<int>>* partial_assignment) {
  if (i == partial_assignment->size()) {
    i = 0;  // Starts a new row.
    if (++j == (*partial_assignment)[i].size()) {
      return true;  // Entire matrix has been filled without conflict.
    }
  }

  // Skips nonempty entries.
  if ((*partial_assignment)[i][j] != kEmptyEntry) {
    return SolvePartialSudoku(i + 1, j, partial_assignment);
  }

  for (int val = 1; val <= partial_assignment->size(); ++val) {
```

```
    // It's substantially quicker to check if entry val conflicts
    // with any of the constraints if we add it at (i,j) before
    // adding it, rather than adding it and then checking all constraints.
    // The reason is that we know we are starting with a valid configuration,
    // and the only entry which can cause a problem is entryval at (i,j).
    if (ValidToAddVal(*partial_assignment, i, j, val)) {
      (*partial_assignment)[i][j] = val;
      if (SolvePartialSudoku(i + 1, j, partial_assignment)) {
        return true;
      }
    }
  }

  (*partial_assignment)[i][j] = kEmptyEntry;  // Undo assignment.
  return false;
}

bool ValidToAddVal(const vector<vector<int>>& partial_assignment, int i, int j,
                   int val) {
  // Check row constraints.
  for (int k = 0; k < partial_assignment.size(); ++k) {
    if (val == partial_assignment[k][j]) {
      return false;
    }
  }

  // Check column constraints.
  for (int k = 0; k < partial_assignment.size(); ++k) {
    if (val == partial_assignment[i][k]) {
      return false;
    }
  }

  // Check region constraints.
  int region_size = sqrt(partial_assignment.size());
  int I = i / region_size, J = j / region_size;
  for (int a = 0; a < region_size; ++a) {
    for (int b = 0; b < region_size; ++b) {
      if (val ==
          partial_assignment[region_size * I + a][region_size * J + b]) {
        return false;
      }
    }
  }
  return true;
}
```

Because the program is specialized to 9×9 grids, it does not make sense to speak of its time complexity, since there is no notion of scaling with a size parameter. However, since the problem of solving Sudoku generalized to $n \times n$ grids is NP-complete, it should not be difficult to prove that the generalization of this algorithm to $n \times n$ grids has exponential time complexity.

An n-bit Gray code is a permutation of $\{0, 1, 2, \ldots, 2^n - 1\}$ such that the binary representations of successive integers in the sequence differ in only one place. (This is with wraparound, i.e., the last and first elements must also differ in only one place.) For example, both $\langle (000)_2, (100)_2, (101)_2, (111)_2, (110)_2, (010)_2, (011)_2, (001)_2 \rangle =$ $\langle 0, 4, 5, 7, 6, 2, 3, 1 \rangle$ and $\langle 0, 1, 3, 2, 6, 7, 5, 4 \rangle$ are Gray codes for $n = 3$.

Write a program which takes n as input and returns an n-bit Gray code.

Hint: Write out Gray codes for $n = 2, 3, 4$.

Solution: A brute-force approach would be to enumerate sequences of length 2^n whose entries are n bit integers. We would test if the sequence is a Gray code, and stop as soon as we find one. The complexity is astronomical—there are $2^{n \times 2^n}$ sequences. We can improve complexity by enumerating permutations of $0, 1, 2, \ldots, 2^n - 1$, since we want distinct entries, but this is still a very high complexity.

We can do much better by directing the enumeration. Specifically, we build the sequence incrementally, adding a value only if it is distinct from all values currently in the sequence, and differs in exactly one place with the previous value. (For the last value, we have to check that it differs in one place from the first value.) This is the approach shown below. For $n = 4$, we begin with $(0000)_2$. Next we try changing bits in $(0000)_2$, one-at-a-time to get a value not currently present in the sequence, which yields $(0001)_2$, which we append to the sequence. Changing bits in $(0001)_2$, one-at-a-time, we get $(0000)_2$ (which is already present), and then $(0011)_2$, which is not, so we append it to the sequence, which is now $\langle (0000)_2, (0001)_2, (0011)_2 \rangle$. The next few values are $(0010)_2, (0011)_2, (0111)_2$.

```
vector<int> GrayCode(int num_bits) {
  unordered_set<int> history;
  history.emplace(0);
  vector<int> result;
  result.emplace_back(0);
  DirectedGrayCode(num_bits, &history, &result);
  return result;
}

bool DirectedGrayCode(int num_bits, unordered_set<int>* history,
                      vector<int>* result) {
  if (result->size() == (1 << num_bits)) {
    // Check if the first and last codes differ by one bit.
    return DiffersByOneBit(result->front(), result->back());
  }

  for (int i = 0; i < num_bits; ++i) {
    int previous_code = result->back();
    int candidate_next_code = previous_code ^ (1 << i);
    if (!history->count(candidate_next_code)) {
      history->emplace(candidate_next_code);
      result->emplace_back(candidate_next_code);
      if (DirectedGrayCode(num_bits, history, result)) {
        return true;
```

```
        }
        history->erase(candidate_next_code);
        result->pop_back();
      }
    }
    return false;
}

bool DiffersByOneBit(int x, int y) {
    int bit_difference = x ^ y;
    return bit_difference && !(bit_difference & (bit_difference - 1));
}
```

Now we present a more analytical solution. The inspiration comes from small case analysis. The sequence $\langle (00)_2, (01)_2, (11)_2, (10)_2 \rangle$ is a 2-bit Gray code. To get to $n = 3$, we cannot just prepend 0 to each elements of $\langle (00)_2, (01)_2, (11)_2, (10)_2 \rangle$, 1 to $\langle (00)_2, (01)_2, (11)_2, (10)_2 \rangle$ and concatenate the two sequences—that leads to the Gray code property being violated from $(010)_2$ to $(100)_2$. However, it is preserved everywhere else.

Since Gray codes differ in one place on wrapping around, prepending 1 to the reverse of $\langle (00)_2, (01)_2, (11)_2, (10)_2 \rangle$ solves the problem when transitioning from a leading 0 to a leading 1. For $n = 3$ this leads to the sequence $\langle (000)_2, (001)_2, (011)_2, (010)_2, (110)_2, (111)_2, (101)_2, (100)_2 \rangle$. The general solution uses recursion in conjunction with this reversing, and is presented below.

```
vector<int> GrayCode(int num_bits) {
    if (num_bits == 0) {
      return {0};
    }
    if (num_bits == 1) {
      return {0, 1};
    }

    // These implicitly begin with 0 at bit-index (num_bits - 1).
    auto gray_code_num_bits_minus_1 = GrayCode(num_bits - 1);
    // Now, add a 1 at bit-index (num_bits - 1) to all entries in
    // grayCodeNumBitsMinus1.
    int leading_bit_one = 1 << (num_bits - 1);
    vector<int> reflection;
    // Process in reverse order to achieve reflection of
    // gray_code_num_bits_minus_1.
    for (int i = gray_code_num_bits_minus_1.size() - 1; i >= 0; --i) {
      reflection.emplace_back(leading_bit_one | gray_code_num_bits_minus_1[i]);
    }
    vector<int> result = gray_code_num_bits_minus_1;
    result.insert(result.end(), reflection.begin(), reflection.end());
    return result;
}
```

Since integer shift and add take constant time, the time complexity is $O(n2^n)$.

Packets in Ethernet local area networks (LANs) are routed according to the unique path in a tree whose leaves correspond to clients, internal nodes to switches, and edges to physical connection. In this problem, we want to design an algorithm for finding the "worst-case" route, i.e., the two clients that are furthest apart.

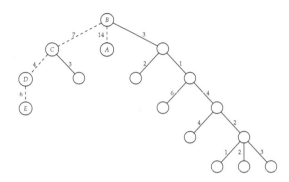

Figure 16.6: The diameter for the above tree is 31. The corresponding path is $\langle A, B, C, D, E \rangle$, which is depicted by the dashed edges.

The diameter of a tree is defined to be the length of a longest path in the tree. Figure 16.6 illustrates the diameter concept. Design an efficient algorithm to compute the diameter of a tree.

Hint: The longest path may or may not pass through the root.

Solution: We can compute the diameter with a brute-force approach. Specifically, we can run BFS, described on Page 350, from each node, recording the maximum value of the shortest path distances computed. BFS in a graph with n vertices and m edges has time complexity $O(m+n)$. Therefore, the brute-force algorithm has $O(n(m \mid n)) = O(n^2)$ time complexity since the number of edges in a tree is one less than the number of vertices.

The above approach is inefficient, since it repeatedly processes the same vertices and edges. We can achieve better time complexity by using divide-and-conquer. Consider a longest path in the tree. Either it passes through the root or it does not pass through the root.

- If the longest path does not pass through the root, it must be entirely within one of the subtrees. Therefore, in this case, the longest path length in the tree is the maximum of the diameters of the subtrees.
- If the longest path does pass through the root, it must be between a pair of nodes in distinct subtrees that are furthest from the root. The distance from the root to the node in the ith subtree T_i that is furthest from it is $f_i = h_i + l_i$, where h_i is the height of T_i and l_i is the length of the edge from the root to the root of T_i.

Since one of the two cases must hold, the longest length path is the larger of the maximum of the subtree diameters and the sum of the two largest f_is.

The base cases correspond to a tree that has no children, in which case the length of the longest path is 0.

For the tree in Figure 16.6 on the preceding page, the subtree diameters, computed recursively, are 13, 0, and 15 (from left to right). The heights are 10, 0, and 10 (from left to right). The distance from the root to the furthest node of the first subtree is $7 + 10 = 17$, the distance from the root to the furthest node of the second subtree is $14 + 0 = 14$, and the distance from the root to the furthest node of the third subtree is $3 + 10 = 13$. The largest diameter in a subtree is 15, which is less than the sum of the two greatest distances ($17 + 14 = 31$), so the diameter of the tree is 31.

```cpp
struct TreeNode {
  struct Edge {
    unique_ptr<TreeNode> root;
    double length;
  };

  vector<Edge> edges;
};

struct HeightAndDiameter {
  double height, diameter;
};

double ComputeDiameter(const unique_ptr<TreeNode>& T) {
  return T ? ComputeHeightAndDiameter(T).diameter : 0.0;
}

HeightAndDiameter ComputeHeightAndDiameter(const unique_ptr<TreeNode>& r) {
  double diameter = numeric_limits<double>::min();
  array<double, 2> heights = {{0.0, 0.0}};  // Stores the max two heights.
  for (const auto& e : r->edges) {
    HeightAndDiameter h_d = ComputeHeightAndDiameter(e.root);
    if (h_d.height + e.length > heights[0]) {
      heights[1] = heights[0];
      heights[0] = h_d.height + e.length;
    } else if (h_d.height + e.length > heights[1]) {
      heights[1] = h_d.height + e.length;
    }
    diameter = max(diameter, h_d.diameter);
  }
  return {heights[0], max(diameter, heights[0] + heights[1])};
}
```

Since the time spent at each node is proportional to the number of its children, the time complexity is proportional to the size of the tree, i.e., $O(n)$.

Variant: Consider a computer network organized as a rooted tree. A node can send a message to only one child at a time, and it takes one second for the child to receive the message. The root periodically receives a message from an external source. It needs to send this message to all the nodes in the tree. The root has complete knowledge of how the network is organized. Design an algorithm that computes the sequence of transfers that minimizes the time taken to transfer a message from the root to all the nodes in the tree.

CHAPTER

17

Dynamic Programming

> *The important fact to observe is that we have attempted to solve a maximization problem involving a particular value of x and a particular value of N by first solving the general problem involving an arbitrary value of x and an arbitrary value of N.*

> — *"Dynamic Programming,"*
> R. E. BELLMAN, 1957

DP is a general technique for solving optimization, search, and counting problems that can be decomposed into subproblems. Like divide-and-conquer, DP solves the problem by combining the solutions of multiple smaller problems, but what makes DP different is that the same subproblem may reoccur. Therefore, a key to making DP efficient is caching the results of intermediate computations. Problems whose solutions use DP are a popular choice for hard interview questions.

To illustrate the idea underlying DP, consider the problem of computing Fibonacci numbers. The first two Fibonacci numbers are 0 and 1. Successive numbers are the sums of the two previous numbers. The first few Fibonacci numbers are $0, 1, 1, 2, 3, 5, 8, 13, 21, \ldots$. The Fibonacci numbers arise in many diverse applications— biology, data structure analysis, and parallel computing are some examples.

Mathematically, the nth Fibonacci number $F(n)$ is given by the equation $F(n) = F(n-1) + F(n-2)$, with $F(0) = 0$ and $F(1) = 1$. A function to compute $F(n)$ that recursively invokes itself has a time complexity that is exponential in n. This is because the recursive function computes some $F(i)$s repeatedly. Figure 17.1 on the following page graphically illustrates how the function is repeatedly called with the same arguments.

Caching intermediate results makes the time complexity for computing the nth Fibonacci number linear in n, albeit at the expense of $O(n)$ storage. The program below computes $F(n)$ via iteration in $O(n)$ time. Compared to a recursive program with caching, the iterative program fills in the cache in a bottom-up fashion, and reuses storage to reduce space complexity to $O(1)$.

```
int Fibonacci(int n) {
  if (n <= 1) {
    return n;
  }
  int prev_prev = 0, prev = 1;
  for (int i = 2; i <= n; ++i) {
    int next = prev + prev_prev;
```

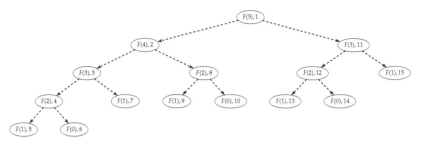

Figure 17.1: Tree of recursive calls when naively computing the 5th Fibonacci number, $F(5)$. Each node is a call: $F(x)$ indicates a call with argument x, and the italicized numbers on the right are the sequence in which calls take place. The children of a node are the subcalls made by that call. Note how there are 2 calls to $F(3)$, and 3 calls to each of $F(2)$, $F(1)$, and $F(0)$.

```
    prev_prev = prev;
    prev = next;
  }
  return prev;
}
```

The key to solving a DP problem efficiently is finding a way to break the problem into subproblems such that

- the original problem can be solved relatively easily once solutions to the subproblems are available, and
- these subproblem solutions are cached.

Usually, but not always, the subproblems are easy to identify.

Here is a more sophisticated application of DP. Consider the following problem: find a subarray of a given array of integers whose sum is maximum. As a concrete example, the maximum subarray for the array in Figure 17.2 starts at index 0 and ends at index 3.

904	40	523	12	-335	-385	-124	481	-31
$A[0]$	$A[1]$	$A[2]$	$A[3]$	$A[4]$	$A[5]$	$A[6]$	$A[7]$	$A[8]$

Figure 17.2: An array with a maximum subarray sum of 1479.

The brute-force algorithm, which computes each subarray sum, has $O(n^3)$ time complexity—there are $\frac{n(n+1)}{2}$ subarrays, and each subarray sum takes $O(n)$ time to compute. The brute-force algorithm can be improved to $O(n^2)$, at the cost of $O(n)$ additional storage, by first computing $S[k] = \sum A[0:k]$ for all k. The sum for $A[i:j]$ is then $S[j] - S[i-1]$, where $S[-1]$ is taken to be 0.

Here is a natural divide-and-conquer algorithm. Take $m = \lfloor \frac{n}{2} \rfloor$ to be the middle index of A. Solve the problem for the subarrays $L = A[0:m]$ and $R = A[m+1:n-1]$. In addition to the answers for each, we also return the maximum subarray sum l for a subarray ending at the last entry in L, and the maximum subarray sum r for a subarray

299

starting at the first entry of R. The maximum subarray sum for A is the maximum of $l + r$, the answer for L, and the answer for R. The time complexity analysis is similar to that for quicksort, and the time complexity is $O(n \log n)$. Because of off-by-one errors, it takes some time to get the program just right.

Now we will solve this problem by using DP. A natural thought is to assume we have the solution for the subarray $A[0 : n - 2]$. However, even if we knew the largest sum subarray for subarray $A[0 : n - 2]$, it does not help us solve the problem for $A[0 : n - 1]$. Instead we need to know the subarray amongst all subarrays $A[0 : i]$, $i < n - 1$, with the smallest subarray sum. The desired value is $S[n - 1]$ minus this subarray's sum. We compute this subarray by iterating through the array. For each index j, the maximum subarray ending at j is equal to $S[j] - \min_{k \le j} S[k]$. During the iteration, we track the minimum $S[k]$ we have seen so far and compute the maximum subarray for each index. The time spent per index is constant, leading to an $O(n)$ time and $O(1)$ space solution. The code below returns a pair of indices (i, j) such that $A[i : j - 1]$ is a maximum subarray. It is legal for all array entries to be negative, or the array to be empty. The algorithm handles these input cases correctly. Specifically, it returns equal indices, which denote an empty subarray.

```
// Used to represent subarry consisting of elements from index start
// (inclusive) to index end (exclusive)
struct Subarray {
  int start = 0, end = 0;
};

Subarray FindMaximumSubarray(const vector<int>& A) {
  // A[range.start : range.end - 1] will be the maximum subarray.
  Subarray range;
  int min_idx = -1, min_sum = 0, sum = 0, max_sum = 0;
  for (int i = 0; i < A.size(); ++i) {
    sum += A[i];
    if (sum < min_sum) {
      min_sum = sum, min_idx = i;
    }
    if (sum - min_sum > max_sum) {
      max_sum = sum - min_sum, range = {min_idx + 1, i + 1};
    }
  }
  return range;
}
```

17.1 COUNT THE NUMBER OF SCORE COMBINATIONS

In an American football game, a play can lead to 2 points (safety), 3 points (field goal), or 7 points (touchdown, assuming the extra point). Many different combinations of 2, 3, and 7 point plays can make up a final score. For example, four combinations of plays yield a score of 12:

- 6 safeties ($2 \times 6 = 12$),
- 3 safeties and 2 field goals ($2 \times 3 + 3 \times 2 = 12$),

- 1 safety, 1 field goal and 1 touchdown ($2 \times 1 + 3 \times 1 + 7 \times 1 = 12$), and
- 4 field goals ($3 \times 4 = 12$).

Write a program that takes a final score and scores for individual plays, and returns the number of combinations of plays that result in the final score.

Hint: Count the number of combinations in which there are 0 w_0 plays, then 1 w_0 plays, etc.

Solution: We can gain some intuition by considering small scores. For example, a 9 point score can be achieved in the following ways:
- scoring 7 points, followed by a 2 point play,
- scoring 6 points, followed by a 3 point play, and
- scoring 2 points, followed by a 7 point play.

Generalizing, an s point score can be achieved by an $s - 2$ point score, followed by a 2 point play, an $s - 3$ point score, followed by a 3 point play, or an $s - 7$ point score, followed by a 7 point play. This gives us a mechanism for recursively enumerating all possible scoring sequences which lead to a given score. Note that different sequences may lead to the same score combination, e.g., a 2 point play followed by a 7 point play and a 7 point play followed by a 2 point play both lead to a final score of 9. A brute-force approach might be to enumerate these sequences, and count the distinct combinations within these sequences, e.g., by sorting each sequence and inserting into a hash table, similar to Solution 13.1 on Page 205.

The time complexity is very high, since there may be a very large number of scoring sequences. Since all we care about are the combinations, a better approach is to focus on the number of combinations for each possible number of plays of a single type.

For example, if the final score is 12 and we are only allowed 2 point plays, there is exactly one way to get 12. Now suppose we are allowed both 2 and 3 point plays. Since all we care about are combinations, assume the 2 point plays come before the 3 point plays. We could have zero 2 point plays, for which there is one combination of 3 point plays, one 2 point play, for which there no combination of 3 point plays (since 3 does not evenly divide $12 - 2$, two 2 point plays, for which there no combination of 3 point plays (since 3 does not evenly $12 - 2 \times 2$), three 2 point plays, for which there is one combination of 3 point plays (since 3 evenly divides $12 - 2 \times 3$), etc. To count combinations when we add 7 point plays to the mix, we add the number of combinations of 2 and 3 that lead to 12 and to 5—these are the only scores from which 7 point plays can lead to 12.

Naively implemented, for the general case, i.e., individual play scores are $W[0], W[1], \ldots, W[n-1]$, and s the final score, the approach outlined above has exponential complexity because it repeatedly solves the same problems. We can use DP to reduce its complexity. Let the 2D array $A[i][j]$ store the number of score combinations that result in a total of j, using individual plays of scores $W[0], W[1], \ldots, W[i-1]$. For example, $A[1][12]$ is the number of ways in which we can achieve a total of 12 points, using 2 and/or 3 point plays. Then $A[i+1][j]$ is simply $A[i][j]$ (no $W[i+1]$ point plays used to get to j), plus $A[i][j - W[i+1]]$ (one $W[i+1]$ point play), plus $A[i][j - 2W[i+1]]$ (two $W[i+1]$ point plays), etc.

The algorithm directly based on the above discussion consists of three nested loops. The outer loop is over the total range of scores, the next is over scores for individual plays, and the third is over the number of plays possible for the current individual play and score combination. Its complexity is $O(sn^2)$ (first loop is to n, second is to s, third is bounded by n).

Looking more carefully at the computation for the row $A[i+1]$, it becomes apparent that it is not as efficient as it could be. As an example, suppose we are working with 2 and 3 point plays. Suppose we are done with 2 point plays. Let $A[0]$ be the row holding the result for just 2 point plays, i.e., $A[0][j]$ is the number of combinations of 2 point plays that result in a final score of j. The number of score combinations to get a final score of 12 when we include 3 point plays in addition to 2 point plays is $A[0][0] + A[0][3] + A[0][6] + A[0][9] + A[0][12]$. The number of score combinations to get a final score of 15 when we include 3 point plays in addition to 2 point plays is $A[0][0] + A[0][3] + A[0][6] + A[0][9] + A[0][12] + A[0][15]$. Clearly this repeats computation—$A[0][0] + A[0][3] + A[0][6] + A[0][9] + A[0][12]$ was computed when considering the final score of 12.

Note that $A[1][15] = A[0][15] + A[1][12]$. Therefore a better way to fill in $A[1]$ is as follows: $A[1][0] = A[0][0], A[1][1] = A[0][1], A[1][2] = A[0][2], A[1][3] = A[0][3] + A[1][0], A[1][4] = A[0][4] + A[1][1], A[1][5] = A[0][5] + A[1][2], \ldots$. Observe that $A[1][i]$ takes $O(1)$ time to compute—it's just $A[0][i] + A[1][i-3]$. See Figure 17.3 for an example table.

	0	1	2	3	4	5	6	7	8	9	10	11	12
2	1	0	1	0	1	0	1	0	1	0	1	0	1
2,3	1	0	1	1	1	1	2	1	2	2	2	2	3
2,3,7	1	0	1	1	1	1	1	2	2	3	3	3	4

Figure 17.3: DP table for $2, 3, 7$ point plays (rows) and final scores from 0 to 12 (columns). As an example, for $2, 3, 7$ point plays and a total of 9, the entry is the sum of the entry for $2, 3$ point plays and a total of 9 (no 7 point plays) and the entry for $2, 3, 7$ point plays and a total of 2 (one additional 7 point play).

The code below implements the generalization of this approach.

```
int NumCombinationsForFinalScore(int final_score,
                                 const vector<int>& individual_play_scores) {
  vector<vector<int>> num_combinations_for_score(
      individual_play_scores.size(), vector<int>(final_score + 1, 0));
  for (int i = 0; i < individual_play_scores.size(); ++i) {
    num_combinations_for_score[i][0] = 1;  // One way to reach 0.
    for (int j = 1; j <= final_score; ++j) {
      int without_this_play =
          i >= 1 ? num_combinations_for_score[i - 1][j] : 0;
      int with_this_play =
          j >= individual_play_scores[i]
              ? num_combinations_for_score[i][j - individual_play_scores[i]]
              : 0;
```

```
        num_combinations_for_score[i][j] = without_this_play + with_this_play;
    }
  }
  return num_combinations_for_score.back().back();
}
```

The time complexity is $O(sn)$ (two loops, one to s, the other to n) and the space complexity is $O(sn)$ (the size of the 2D array).

Variant: Solve the same problem using $O(s)$ space.

Variant: Write a program that takes a final score and scores for individual plays, and returns the number of sequences of plays that result in the final score. For example, 18 sequences of plays yield a score of 12. Some examples are $\langle 2, 2, 2, 3, 3 \rangle$, $\langle 2, 3, 2, 2, 3 \rangle$, $\langle 2, 3, 7 \rangle$, $\langle 7, 3, 2 \rangle$.

Variant: Suppose the final score is given in the form (s, s'), i.e., Team 1 scored s points and Team 2 scored s' points. How would you compute the number of distinct scoring sequences which result in this score? For example, if the final score is $(6, 3)$ then Team 1 scores 3, Team 2 scores 3, Team 1 scores 3 is a scoring sequence which results in this score.

Variant: Suppose the final score is (s, s'). How would you compute the maximum number of times the team that lead could have changed? For example, if $s = 10$ and $s' = 6$, the lead could have changed 4 times: Team 1 scores 2, then Team 2 scores 3 (lead change), then Team 1 scores 2 (lead change), then Team 2 scores 3 (lead change), then Team 1 scores 3 (lead change) followed by 3.

17.2 Compute the Levenshtein distance

Spell checkers make suggestions for misspelled words. Given a misspelled string, a spell checker should return words in the dictionary which are close to the misspelled string.

In 1965, Vladimir Levenshtein defined the distance between two words as the minimum number of "edits" it would take to transform the misspelled word into a correct word, where a single edit is the *insertion, deletion,* or *substitution* of a single character. For example, the Levenshtein distance between "Saturday" and "Sundays" is 4—delete the first 'a' and 't', substitute 'r' by 'n' and insert the trailing 's'.

Write a program that takes two strings and computes the minimum number of edits needed to transform the first string into the second string.

Hint: Consider the same problem for prefixes of the two strings.

Solution: A brute-force approach would be to enumerate all strings that are distance $1, 2, 3, \ldots$ from the first string, stopping when we reach the second string. The number of strings may grow enormously, e.g., if the first string is n 0s and the second is n 1s we will visit all of the 2^n possible bit strings from the first string before we reach the second string.

A better approach is to "prune" the search. For example, if the last character of the first string equals the last character of the second string, we can ignore this character. If they are different, we can focus on the initial portion of each string and perform a final edit step. (As we will soon see, this final edit step may be an insertion, deletion, or substitution.)

Let a and b be the length of strings A and B, respectively. Let $E(A[0 : a-1], B[0 : b-1])$ be the Levenshtein distance between the strings A and B. (Note that $A[0 : a - 1]$ is just A, but we prefer to write A using the subarray notation for exposition; we do the same for B.)

We now make some observations:

- If the last character of A equals the last character of B, then $E(A[0 : a - 1], B[0 : b - 1]) = E(A[0 : a - 2], B[0 : b - 2])$.
- If the last character of A is not equal to the last character of B then

$$E(A[0 : a - 1], B[0 : b - 1]) = 1 + \min \left(\begin{array}{l} E(A[0 : a - 2], B[0 : b - 2]), \\ E(A[0 : a - 1], B[0 : b - 2]), \\ E(A[0 : a - 2], B[0 : b - 1]) \end{array} \right)$$

The three terms correspond to transforming A to B by the following three ways:

- Transforming $A[0 : a - 1]$ to $B[0 : b - 1]$ by transforming $A[0 : a - 2]$ to $B[0 : b - 2]$ and then substituting A's last character with B's last character.
- Transforming $A[0 : a - 1]$ to $B[0 : b - 1]$ by transforming $A[0 : a - 1]$ to $B[0 : b - 2]$ and then adding B's last character at the end.
- Transforming $A[0 : a - 1]$ to $B[0 : b - 1]$ by transforming $A[0 : a - 2]$ to $B[0 : b - 1]$ and then deleting A's last character.

These observations are quite intuitive. Their rigorous proof, which we do not give, is based on reordering steps in an arbitrary optimum solution for the original problem.

DP is a great way to solve this recurrence relation: cache intermediate results on the way to computing $E(A[0 : a - 1], B[0 : b - 1])$.

We illustrate the approach in Figure 17.4 on Page 307. This shows the E values for "Carthorse" and "Orchestra". Uppercase and lowercase characters are treated as being different. The Levenshtein distance for these two strings is 8.

```
int LevenshteinDistance(const string& A, const string& B) {
  vector<vector<int>> distance_between_prefixes(A.size(),
                                    vector<int>(B.size(), -1));
  return ComputeDistanceBetweenPrefixes(A, A.size() - 1, B, B.size() - 1,
                      &distance_between_prefixes);
}

int ComputeDistanceBetweenPrefixes(
    const string& A, int A_idx, const string& B, int B_idx,
    vector<vector<int>>* distance_between_prefixes_ptr) {
```

```
vector<vector<int>>& distance_between_prefixes =
    *distance_between_prefixes_ptr;
if (A_idx < 0) {
  // A is empty so add all of B's characters.
  return B_idx + 1;
} else if (B_idx < 0) {
  // B is empty so delete all of A's characters.
  return A_idx + 1;
}
if (distance_between_prefixes[A_idx][B_idx] == -1) {
  if (A[A_idx] == B[B_idx]) {
    distance_between_prefixes[A_idx][B_idx] = ComputeDistanceBetweenPrefixes(
        A, A_idx - 1, B, B_idx - 1, distance_between_prefixes_ptr);
  } else {
    int substitute_last = ComputeDistanceBetweenPrefixes(
        A, A_idx - 1, B, B_idx - 1, distance_between_prefixes_ptr);
    int add_last = ComputeDistanceBetweenPrefixes(
        A, A_idx - 1, B, B_idx, distance_between_prefixes_ptr);
    int delete_last = ComputeDistanceBetweenPrefixes(
        A, A_idx, B, B_idx - 1, distance_between_prefixes_ptr);
    distance_between_prefixes[A_idx][B_idx] =
        1 + min({substitute_last, add_last, delete_last});
  }
}
return distance_between_prefixes[A_idx][B_idx];
}
```

The value $E(A[0 : a-1], B[0 : b-1])$ takes time $O(1)$ to compute once $E(A[0 : k], B[0 : l])$ is known for all $k < a$ and $l < b$. This implies $O(ab)$ time complexity for the algorithm. Our implementation uses $O(ab)$ space.

Variant: Compute the Levenshtein distance using $O(\min(a, b))$ space and $O(ab)$ time.

Variant: Given A and B as above, compute a longest sequence of characters that is a subsequence of A and of B. For example, the longest subsequence which is present in both strings in Figure 17.4 on the next page is $\langle r, h, s \rangle$.

Variant: Given a string A, compute the minimum number of characters you need to delete from A to make the resulting string a palindrome.

Variant: Given a string A and a regular expression r, what is the string in the language of the regular expression r that is closest to A? The distance between strings is the Levenshtein distance specified above.

Variant: Define a string t to be an interleaving of strings s_1 and s_2 if there is a way to interleave the characters of s_1 and s_2, keeping the left-to-right order of each, to obtain t. For example, if s_1 is "gtaa" and s_2 is "atc", then "gattaca" and "gtataac" can be formed by interleaving s_1 and s_2 but "gatacta" cannot. Design an algorithm that takes as input strings s_1, s_2 and t, and determines if t is an interleaving of s_1 and s_2.

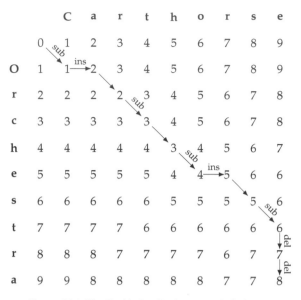

Figure 17.4: The E table for "Carthorse" and "Orchestra".

17.3 COUNT THE NUMBER OF WAYS TO TRAVERSE A 2D ARRAY

In this problem you are to count the number of ways of starting at the top-left corner of a 2D array and getting to the bottom-right corner. All moves must either go right or down. For example, we show three ways in a 5×5 2D array in Figure 17.5. (As we will see, there are a total of 70 possible ways for this example.)

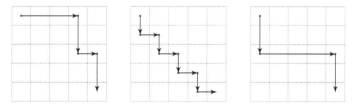

Figure 17.5: Paths through a 2D array.

Write a program that counts how many ways you can go from the top-left to the bottom-right in a 2D array.

Hint: If $i > 0$ and $j > 0$, you can get to (i, j) from $(i - 1, j)$ or $(j - 1, i)$.

Solution: A brute-force approach is to enumerate all possible paths. This can be done using recursion. However, there is a combinatorial explosion in the number of paths, which leads to huge time complexity.

The problem statement asks for the number of paths, so we focus our attention on that. A key observation is that because paths must advance down or right, the number of ways to get to the bottom-right entry is the number of ways to get to the entry immediately above it, plus the number of ways to get to the entry immediately to its left. Let's treat the origin $(0, 0)$ as the top-left entry. Generalizing, the number of ways to get to (i, j) is the number of ways to get to $(i - 1, j)$ plus the number of ways to get to $(i, j - 1)$. (If $i = 0$ or $j = 0$, there is only one way to get to (i, j) from the origin.) This is the basis for a recursive algorithm to count the number of paths. Implemented naively, the algorithm has exponential time complexity—it repeatedly recurses on the same locations. The solution is to cache results. For example, the number of ways to get to (i, j) for the configuration in Figure 17.5 on the previous page is cached in a matrix as shown in Figure 17.6.

```
int NumberOfWays(int n, int m) {
  vector<vector<int>> number_of_ways(n, vector<int>(m, 0));
  return ComputeNumberOfWaysToXY(n - 1, m - 1, &number_of_ways);
}


int ComputeNumberOfWaysToXY(int x, int y,
                            vector<vector<int>>* number_of_ways_ptr) {
  if (x == 0 && y == 0) {
    return 1;
  }

  vector<vector<int>>& number_of_ways = *number_of_ways_ptr;
  if (number_of_ways[x][y] == 0) {
    int ways_top =
        x == 0 ? 0 : ComputeNumberOfWaysToXY(x - 1, y, number_of_ways_ptr);
    int ways_left =
        y == 0 ? 0 : ComputeNumberOfWaysToXY(x, y - 1, number_of_ways_ptr);
    number_of_ways[x][y] = ways_top + ways_left;
  }
  return number_of_ways[x][y];
}
```

The time complexity is $O(nm)$, and the space complexity is $O(nm)$, where n is the number of rows and m is the number of columns.

1	1	1	1	1
1	2	3	4	5
1	3	6	10	15
1	4	10	20	35
1	5	15	35	70

Figure 17.6: The number of ways to get from $(0, 0)$ to (i, j) for $0 \le i, j \le 4$.

A more analytical way of solving this problem is to use the fact that each path from $(0, 0)$ to $(n - 1, m - 1)$ is a sequence of $m - 1$ horizontal steps and $n - 1$ vertical steps. There are $\binom{n+m-2}{n-1} = \binom{n+m-2}{m-1} = \frac{(n+m-2)!}{(n-1)!(m-1)!}$ such paths.

Variant: Solve the same problem using $O(\min(n, m))$ space.

307

Variant: Solve the same problem in the presence of obstacles, specified by a Boolean 2D array, where a true represents an obstacle.

Variant: A fisherman is in a rectangular sea. The value of the fish at point (i, j) in the sea is specified by an $n \times m$ 2D array A. Write a program that computes the maximum value of fish a fisherman can catch on a path from the upper leftmost point to the lower rightmost point. The fisherman can only move down or right, as illustrated in Figure 17.7.

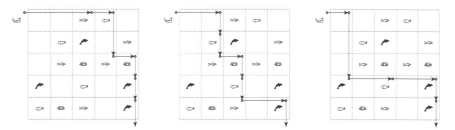

Figure 17.7: Alternate paths for a fisherman. Different types of fish have different values, which are known to the fisherman.

Variant: Solve the same problem when the fisherman can begin and end at any point. He must still move down or right. (Note that the value at (i, j) may be negative.)

Variant: A decimal number is a sequence of digits, i.e., a sequence over $\{0, 1, 2, \ldots, 9\}$. The sequence has to be of length 1 or more, and the first element in the sequence cannot be 0. Call a decimal number D *monotone* if $D[i] \le D[i + 1], 0 \le i < |D|$. Write a program which takes as input a positive integer k and computes the number of decimal numbers of length k that are monotone.

Variant: Call a decimal number D, as defined above, *strictly monotone* if $D[i] < D[i + 1], 0 \le i < |D|$. Write a program which takes as input a positive integer k and computes the number of decimal numbers of length k that are strictly monotone.

17.4 COMPUTE THE BINOMIAL COEFFICIENTS

The symbol $\binom{n}{k}$ is the short form for the expression $\frac{n(n-1)\cdots(n-k+1)}{k(k-1)\cdots(3)(2)(1)}$. It is the number of ways to choose a k-element subset from an n-element set. It is not obvious that the expression defining $\binom{n}{k}$ always yields an integer. Furthermore, direct computation of $\binom{n}{k}$ from this expression quickly results in the numerator or denominator overflowing if integer types are used, even if the final result fits in a 32-bit integer. If floats are used, the expression may not yield a 32-bit integer.

Design an efficient algorithm for computing $\binom{n}{k}$ which has theproperty that it never overflows if the final result fits in the integer word size.

Hint: Write an equation.

Solution: A brute-force approach would be to compute $n(n-1)\cdots(n-k+1)$, then $k(k-1)\cdots(3)(2)(1)$, and finally divide the former by the latter. As pointed out in the problem introduction, this can lead to overflows, even when the final result fits in the integer word size.

It is tempting to proceed by pairing terms in the numerator and denominator that have common factors and cancel them out. This approach is unsatisfactory because of the need to factor numbers, which itself is challenging.

A better approach is to avoid multiplications and divisions entirely. Fundamentally, the binomial coefficient counts the number of subsets of size k in a set of size n. We could enumerate k-sized subsets of $\{0, 1, 2, \ldots, n-1\}$ sets using recursion, as in Solution 16.5 on Page 286. The idea is as follows. Consider the nth element in the initial set. A subset of size k will either contain this element, or not contain it. This is the basis for a recursive enumeration—find all subsets of size $k-1$ amongst the first $n-1$ elements and add the nth element these sets, and then find all subsets of size k amongst the first $n-1$ elements. The union of these two sets of subsets is all subsets of size k.

However, since all we care about is the *number* of such subsets, we can do much better complexity-wise. The recursive enumeration also implies that the binomial coefficient must satisfy the following formula:

$$\binom{n}{k} = \binom{n-1}{k} + \binom{n-1}{k-1}$$

This identity yields a straightforward recursion for $\binom{n}{k}$. The base cases are $\binom{r}{r}$ and $\binom{r}{0}$, both of which are 1. The individual results from the subcalls are 32-bit integers and if $\binom{n}{k}$ can be represented by a 32-bit integer, they can too, so it is not possible for intermediate results to overflow.

For example, $\binom{5}{2} = \binom{4}{2} + \binom{4}{1}$. Expanding $\binom{4}{2}$, we get $\binom{4}{2} = \binom{3}{2} + \binom{3}{1}$. Expanding $\binom{3}{2}$, we get $\binom{3}{2} = \binom{2}{2} + \binom{2}{1}$. Note that $\binom{2}{2}$ is a base case, returning 1. Continuing this way, we get $\binom{4}{2}$, which is 6 and $\binom{4}{1}$, which is 4, so $\binom{5}{2} = 6 + 4 = 10$.

Naively implemented, the above recursion will have repeated subcalls with identical arguments and exponential time complexity. This can be avoided by caching intermediate results.

```
int ComputeBinomialCoefficient(int n, int k) {
  vector<vector<int>> x_choose_y(n + 1, vector<int>(k + 1, 0));
  return ComputeXChooseY(n, k, &x_choose_y);
}


int ComputeXChooseY(int x, int y, vector<vector<int>>* x_choose_y_ptr) {
  if (y == 0 || x == y) {
    return 1;
  }

  vector<vector<int>>& x_choose_y = *x_choose_y_ptr;
  if (x_choose_y[x][y] == 0) {
    int without_y = ComputeXChooseY(x - 1, y, x_choose_y_ptr);
```

```
    int with_y = ComputeXChooseY(x - 1, y - 1, x_choose_y_ptr);
    x_choose_y[x][y] = without_y + with_y;
  }
  return x_choose_y[x][y];
}
```

The number of subproblems is $O(nk)$ and once $\binom{n-1}{k}$ and $\binom{n-1}{k-1}$ are known, $\binom{n}{k}$ can be computed in $O(1)$ time, yielding an $O(nk)$ time complexity. The space complexity is also $O(nk)$; it can easily be reduced to $O(k)$.

17.5 SEARCH FOR A SEQUENCE IN A 2D ARRAY

Suppose you are given a 2D array of integers (the "grid"), and a 1D array of integers (the "pattern"). We say the pattern is said to occur in the grid if it is possible to start from some entry in the grid and traverse adjacent entries in the order specified by the pattern till all entries in the pattern have been visited. The entries adjacent to an entry are the ones directly above, below, to the left, and to the right, assuming they exist. For example, the entries adjacent to $(3,4)$ are $(3,3)$, $(3,5)$, $(4,4)$ and $(5,4)$. It is acceptable to visit an entry in the grid more than once.

As an example, if the grid is

$$\begin{bmatrix} 1 & 2 & 3 \\ 3 & 4 & 5 \\ 5 & 6 & 7 \end{bmatrix}$$

and the pattern is $\langle 1, 3, 4, 6 \rangle$, then the pattern occurs in the grid—consider the entries $\langle (0,0), (1,0), (1,1), (2,1) \rangle$. However, $\langle 1, 2, 3, 4 \rangle$ does not occur in the grid.

Write a program that takes as arguments a 2D array and a 1D array, and checks whether the 1D array appears in the 2D array.

Hint: Start with length 1 prefixes of the 1D array, then move on to length $2, 3, \ldots$ prefixes.

Solution: A brute-force approach might be to enumerate all 1D subarrays of the 2D subarray. This has very high time complexity, since there are many possible subarrays. Its inefficiency stems from not using the target 1D subarray to guide the search.

Let the 2D array be A, and the 1D array be S. Here is a guided way to search for matches. Let's say we have a suffix of S to match, and a starting point to match from. If the suffix is empty, we are done. Otherwise, for the suffix to occur from the starting point, the first entry of the suffix must equal the entry at the starting point, and the remainder of the suffix must occur starting at a point adjacent to the starting point.

For example, when searching for $\langle 1, 3, 4, 6 \rangle$ starting at $(0,0)$, since we match 1 with $A[0][0]$, we would continue searching for $\langle 3, 4, 6 \rangle$ from $(0,1)$ (which fails immediately, since $A[0][1] \neq 3$) and from $(1,0)$. Since $A[0][1] = 3$, we would continue searching for $\langle 4, 6 \rangle$ from $(0,1)$'s neighbors, i.e., from $(0,0)$ (which fails immediately), then from $(1,1)$ (which eventually leads to success).

In the program below, we cache intermediate results to avoid repeated calls to the recursion with identical arguments.

```
struct HashTuple {
  size_t operator()(const tuple<int, int, int>& t) {
    return hash<int>()(get<0>(t)) ^ hash<int>()(get<1>(t)) ^
           hash<int>()(get<2>(t));
  }
};


bool IsPatternContainedInGrid(const vector<vector<int>>& grid,
                              const vector<int>& pattern) {
  // Each entry in previous_attempts is a point in the grid and suffix of
  // pattern (identified by its offset). Presence in previousAttempts indicates
  // the suffix is not contained in the grid starting from that point.
  unordered_set<tuple<int, int, int>, HashTuple> previous_attempts;
  for (int i = 0; i < grid.size(); ++i) {
    for (int j = 0; j < grid[i].size(); ++j) {
      if (IsPatternSuffixContainedStartingAtXY(grid, i, j, pattern, 0,
                                               &previous_attempts)) {
        return true;
      }
    }
  }
  return false;
}


bool IsPatternSuffixContainedStartingAtXY(
    const vector<vector<int>>& grid, int x, int y, const vector<int>& pattern,
    int offset,
    unordered_set<tuple<int, int, int>, HashTuple>* previous_attempts) {
  if (pattern.size() == offset) {
    // Nothing left to complete.
    return true;
  }
  // Check if (x, y) lies within grid.
  if (x < 0 || x >= grid.size() || y < 0 || y >= grid[x].size() ||
      previous_attempts->find({x, y, offset}) != previous_attempts->cend()) {
    return false;
  }

  if (grid[x][y] == pattern[offset] &&
      (IsPatternSuffixContainedStartingAtXY(grid, x - 1, y, pattern,
                                            offset + 1, previous_attempts) ||
       IsPatternSuffixContainedStartingAtXY(grid, x + 1, y, pattern,
                                            offset + 1, previous_attempts) ||
       IsPatternSuffixContainedStartingAtXY(grid, x, y - 1, pattern,
                                            offset + 1, previous_attempts) ||
       IsPatternSuffixContainedStartingAtXY(grid, x, y + 1, pattern,
                                            offset + 1, previous_attempts))) {
    return true;
  }
  previous_attempts->emplace(x, y, offset);
  return false;
}
```

The complexity is $O(nm|S|)$, where n and m are the dimensions of A—we do a constant amount of work within each call to the match function, except for the recursive calls, and the number of calls is not more than the number of entries in the 2D array.

Variant: Solve the same problem when you cannot visit an entry in A more than once.

Variant: Enumerate all solutions when you cannot visit an entry in A more than once.

17.6 THE KNAPSACK PROBLEM

A thief breaks into a clock store. Each clock has a weight and a value, which are known to the thief. His knapsack cannot hold more than a specified combined weight. His intention is to take clocks whose total value is maximum subject to the knapsack's weight constraint.

His problem is illustrated in Figure 17.8. If the knapsack can hold at most 130 ounces, he cannot take all the clocks. If he greedily chooses clocks, in decreasing order of value-to-weight ratio, he will choose P, H, O, B, I, and L in that order for a total value of \$669. However, $\{H, J, O\}$ is the optimum selection, yielding a total value of \$695.

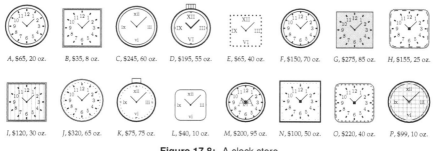

Figure 17.8: A clock store.

Write a program for the knapsack problem that selects a subset of items that has maximum value and satisfies the weight constraint. All items have integer weights and values.

Hint: Greedy approaches are doomed.

Solution: Greedy strategies such as picking the most valuable clock, or picking the clock with maximum value-to-weight ratio, do not always give the optimum solution.

We can always get the optimum solution by considering all subsets, e.g., using Solution 16.4 on Page 286. This has exponential time complexity in the number of clocks. However, brute-force enumeration is wasteful because it ignores the weight constraint. For example, no subset that includes Clocks F and G can satisfy the weight constraint.

The better approach is to simultaneously consider the weight constraint. For example, what is the optimum solution if a given clock is chosen, and what is the optimum solution if that clock is not chosen? Each of these can be solved recursively with the implied weight constraint. For the given example, if we choose the Clock A, we need to find the maximum value of clocks from Clocks B–P with a capacity of $130 - 20$ and add \$65 to that value. If we do not choose Clock A, we need to find the maximum value of clocks from Clocks B–P with a capacity of 130. The larger of these two values is the optimum solution.

More formally, let the clocks be numbered from 0 to $n - 1$, with the weight and the value of the ith clock denoted by w_i and v_i. Denote by $V[i][w]$ the optimum solution when we are restricted to Clocks $0, 1, 2, \ldots, i - 1$ and can carry w weight. Then $V[i][w]$ satisfies the following recurrence:

$$V[i][w] = \begin{cases} \max\left(V[i-1][w], V[i-1][w-w_i] + v_i\right), & \text{if } w_i \leq w; \\ V[i-1][w], & \text{otherwise.} \end{cases}$$

We take $i = 0$ or $w = 0$ as bases cases—for these, $V[i][w] = 0$.

We demonstrate the above algorithm in Figure 17.9. Suppose there are four items, 🕐,🔔,💎,🦆 whose value and weight are given in Figure 17.9(a). Then the corresponding V table is given in Figure 17.9(b). As an example, the extreme lower right entry is the maximum of the entry above (70) and 30 plus the entry for 🕐,🔔,💎 with capacity $5 - 2$ (50), i.e., 80.

Item	Value	Weight
🕐	\$60	5 oz.
🔔	\$50	3 oz.
💎	\$70	4 oz.
🦆	\$30	2 oz.

(a) Value-weight table.

	0	1	2	3	4	5
🕐	0	0	0	0	0	60
🕐🔔	0	0	0	50	50	60
🕐🔔💎	0	0	0	50	70	70
🕐🔔💎🦆	0	0	0	50	70	80

(b) Knapsack table for the items in (a). The columns correspond to capacities from 0 to 5.

Figure 17.9: A small example of the knapsack problem. The knapsack capacity is 5 oz.

```
struct Item {
  int weight, value;
};

int OptimumSubjecToCapacity(const vector<Item>& items, int capacity) {
  // V[i][j] holds the optimum value when we choose from the first i items and
  // have a capacity of j.
  vector<vector<int>> V(items.size(), vector<int>(capacity + 1, -1));
  return OptimumSubjectToItemAndCapacity(items, items.size() - 1, capacity,
                                         &V);
}

// Returns the optimum value when we choose from the first k items and have a
// capacity of available_capacity.
int OptimumSubjectToItemAndCapacity(const vector<Item>& items, int k,
```

313

```
                        int available_capacity,
                        vector<vector<int>>* V_ptr) {
  if (k < 0) {
    // No items can be chosen.
    return 0;
  }

  vector<vector<int>>& V = *V_ptr;
  if (V[k][available_capacity] == -1) {
    int without_curr_item = OptimumSubjectToItemAndCapacity(
        items, k - 1, available_capacity, V_ptr);
    int with_curr_item =
        available_capacity < items[k].weight
            ? 0
            : items[k].value + OptimumSubjectToItemAndCapacity(
                                   items, k - 1,
                                   available_capacity - items[k].weight,
                                   V_ptr);
    V[k][available_capacity] = max(without_curr_item, with_curr_item);
  }
  return V[k][available_capacity];
}
```

The algorithm computes $V[n-1][w]$ in $O(nw)$ time, and uses $O(nw)$ space.

Variant: Solve the same problem using $O(w)$ space.

Variant: Solve the fractional knapsack problem. In this formulation, the thief can take a fractional part of an item, e.g., by breaking it. Assume the value of a fraction of an item is that fraction times the value of the item.

Variant: In the "divide-the-spoils-fairly" problem, two thieves who have successfully completed a burglary want to know how to divide the stolen items into two groups such that the difference between the value of these two groups is minimized. For example, they may have stolen the clocks in Figure 17.8 on Page 313, and would like to divide the clocks between them so that the difference of the dollar value of the two sets is minimized. For this instance, an optimum split is $\{A, G, J, M, O, P\}$ to one thief and the remaining to the other thief. The first set has value \$1179, and the second has value \$1180. An equal split is impossible, since the sum of the values of all the clocks is odd. Write a program to solve the divide-the-spoils-fairly problem.

Variant: Solve the divide-the-spoils-fairly problem with the additional constraint that the thieves have the same number of items.

Variant: The US President is elected by the members of the Electoral College. The number of electors per state and Washington, D.C., are given in Table 17.1 on the next page. All electors from each state as well as Washington, D.C., cast their vote for the same candidate. Write a program to determine if a tie is possible in a presidential election with two candidates.

314

Table 17.1: Electoral college votes.

State	Electors	State	Electors	State	Electors
Alabama	9	Louisiana	8	Ohio	18
Alaska	3	Maine	4	Oklahoma	7
Arizona	11	Maryland	10	Oregon	7
Arkansas	6	Massachusetts	11	Pennsylvania	20
California	55	Michigan	16	Rhode Island	4
Colorado	9	Minnesota	10	South Carolina	9
Connecticut	7	Mississippi	6	South Dakota	3
Delaware	3	Missouri	10	Tennessee	11
Florida	29	Montana	3	Texas	38
Georgia	16	Nebraska	5	Utah	6
Hawaii	4	Nevada	6	Vermont	3
Idaho	4	New Hampshire	4	Virginia	13
Illinois	20	New Jersey	14	Washington	12
Indiana	11	New Mexico	5	West Virginia	5
Iowa	6	New York	29	Wisconsin	10
Kansas	6	North Carolina	15	Wyoming	3
Kentucky	8	North Dakota	3	Washington, D.C.	3

17.7 THE BEDBATHANDBEYOND.COM PROBLEM

Suppose you are designing a search engine. In addition to getting keywords from a page's content, you would like to get keywords from Uniform Resource Locators (URLs). For example, bedbathandbeyond.com yields the keywords "bed, bath, beyond, bat, hand": the first two coming from the decomposition "bed bath beyond" and the latter two coming from the decomposition "bed bat hand beyond".

Given a dictionary, i.e., a set of strings, and a name, design an efficient algorithm that checks whether the name is the concatenation of a sequence of dictionary words. If such a concatenation exists, return it. A dictionary word may appear more than once in the sequence. e.g., "a", "man", "a", "plan", "a", "canal" is a valid sequence for "amanaplanacanal".

Hint: Solve the generalized problem, i.e., determine for each prefix of the name whether it is the concatenation of dictionary words.

Solution: The natural approach is to use recursion, i.e., find dictionary words that begin the name, and solve the problem recursively on the remainder of the name. Implemented naively, this approach has very high time complexity on some input cases, e.g., if the name is N repetitions of "AB" followed by "C" and the dictionary words are "A", "B", and "AB" the time complexity is exponential in N. For example, for the string "ABABC", then we recurse on the substring "ABC" twice (once from the sequence "A", "B" and once from "AB").

The solution is straightforward—cache intermediate results. The cache keys are prefixes of the string. The corresponding value is a Boolean denoting whether the prefix can be decomposed into a sequence of valid words.

It's easy to determine if a string is a valid word—we simply store the dictionary in a hash table. A prefix of the given string can be decomposed into a sequence of dictionary words exactly if it is a dictionary word, or there exists a shorter prefix which can be decomposed into a sequence of dictionary words and the difference of the shorter prefix and the current prefix is a dictionary word.

For example, for "amanaplanacanal":

1. the prefix "a" has a valid decomposition (since "a" is a dictionary word),
2. the prefix "am" has a valid decomposition (since "am" is a dictionary word),
3. the prefix "ama" has a valid decomposition (since "a" has a valid decomposition, and "am" is a dictionary word), and
4. "aman" has a valid decomposition (since "am" has a valid decomposition and "an" is a dictionary word).

Skipping ahead,

5. "amanapl" does not have a valid decomposition (since none of "l", "pl", apl", etc. are dictionary words), and
6. "amanapla" does not have a valid decomposition (since the only dictionary word ending the string is "a" and "amanapl" does not have a valid decomposition).

The algorithm tells us if we can break a given string into dictionary words, but does not yield the words themselves. We can obtain the words with a little more book-keeping. Specifically, if a prefix has a valid decomposition, we record the length of the last dictionary word in the decomposition.

```
vector<string> DecomposeIntoDictionaryWords(
    const string& domain, const unordered_set<string>& dictionary) {
  // When the algorithm finishes, last_length[i] != -1 indicates
  // domain.substr(0, i + 1) has a valid decomposition, and the length of the
  // last string in the decomposition is last_length[i].
  vector<int> last_length(domain.size(), -1);
  for (int i = 0; i < domain.size(); ++i) {
    // If domain.substr(0, i + 1) is a dictionary word, set last_length[i] to
    // the length of that word.
    if (dictionary.find(domain.substr(0, i + 1)) != dictionary.cend()) {
      last_length[i] = i + 1;
    }

    // If last_length[i] = -1 look for j < i such that domain.substr(0, j + 1)
    // has a valid decomposition and domain.substring(j + 1, i + 1) is a
    // dictionary word. If so, record the length of that word in
    // last_length[i].
    if (last_length[i] == -1) {
      for (int j = 0; j < i; ++j) {
        if (last_length[j] != -1 &&
            dictionary.find(domain.substr(j + 1, i - j)) !=
                dictionary.cend()) {
          last_length[i] = i - j;
          break;
        }
      }
    }
  }

  vector<string> decompositions;
```

```
  if (last_length.back() != -1) {
    // domain can be assembled by dictionary words.
    int idx = domain.size() - 1;
    while (idx >= 0) {
      decompositions.emplace_back(
          domain.substr(idx + 1 - last_length[idx], last_length[idx]));
      idx -= last_length[idx];
    }
    reverse(decompositions.begin(), decompositions.end());
  }
  return decompositions;
}
```

Let n be the length of the input string s. For each $k < n$ we check for each $j < k$ whether the substring $s[j + 1 : k]$ is a dictionary word, and each such check requires $O(k - j)$ time. This implies the time complexity is $O(n^3)$. We can improve the time complexity as follows. Let W be the length of the longest dictionary word. We can restrict j to range from $k - W$ to $k - 1$ without losing any decompositions, so the time complexity improves to $O(n^2W)$.

If we want all possible decompositions, we can store all possible values of j that gives us a correct break with each position. Note that the number of possible decompositions can be exponential here. This is illustrated by the string "itsitsitsits...".

Variant: Palindromic decompositions were described in Problem 16.7 on Page 289. Observe every string s has at least one palindromic decomposition, which is the trivial one consisting of the individual characters. For example, if s is "0204451881" then "0", "2", "0", "4", "4", "5", "1", "8", "8", "1" is such a trivial decomposition. The minimum decomposition of s is "020", "44", "5", "1881". How would you compute a palindromic decomposition of a string s that uses a minimum number of substrings?

17.8 FIND THE MINIMUM WEIGHT PATH IN A TRIANGLE

A sequence of integer arrays in which the nth array consists of n entries naturally corresponds to a triangle of numbers. See Figure 17.10 for an example.

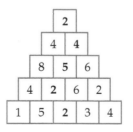

Figure 17.10: A number triangle.

Define a path in the triangle to be a sequence of entries in the triangle in which adjacent entries in the sequence correspond to entries that are adjacent in the triangle.

The path must start at the top, descend the triangle continuously, and end with an entry on the bottom row. The weight of a path is the sum of the entries.

Write a program that takes as input a triangle of numbers and returns the weight of a minimum weight path. For example, the minimum weight path for the number triangle in Figure 17.10 on the facing page is shown in bold face, and its weight is 15.

Hint: What property does the prefix of a minimum weight path have?

Solution: A brute-force approach is to enumerate all possible paths. Although these paths are quite easy to enumerate, there are 2^{n-1} such paths in a number triangle with n rows.

A far better way is to consider entries in the ith row. For any such entry, if you look at the minimum weight path ending at it, the part of the path that ends at the previous row must also be a minimum weight path. This gives us a DP solution. We iteratively compute the minimum weight of a path ending at each entry in Row i. Since after we complete processing Row i, we do not need the results for Row $i - 1$ to process Row $i + 1$, we can reuse storage.

```
int MinimumPathWeight(const vector<vector<int>>& triangle) {
  if (triangle.empty()) {
    return 0;
  }

  // As we iterate, prev_row stores the minimum path sum to each entry in
  // triangle[i - 1].
  vector<int> prev_row(triangle.front());
  for (int i = 1; i < triangle.size(); ++i) {
    // Stores the minimum path sum to each entry in triangle[i].
    vector<int> curr_row(triangle[i]);
    curr_row.front() += prev_row.front();  // For the first element.
    for (int j = 1; j < curr_row.size() - 1; ++j) {
      curr_row[j] += min(prev_row[j - 1], prev_row[j]);
    }
    curr_row.back() += prev_row.back();  // For the last element.

    // Uses swap to assign curr_row's content to prev_row in O(1) time.
    prev_row.swap(curr_row);
  }
  return *min_element(prev_row.cbegin(), prev_row.cend());
}
```

The time spent per element is $O(1)$ and there are $1 + 2 + \cdots + n = n(n + 1)/2$ elements, implying an $O(n^2)$ time complexity. The space complexity is $O(n)$.

17.9 PICK UP COINS FOR MAXIMUM GAIN

In the pick-up-coins game, an even number of coins are placed in a line, as in Figure 17.11 on the next page. Two players take turns at choosing one coin each—they can only choose from the two coins at the ends of the line. The game ends when all the coins have been picked up. The player whose coins have the higher total value wins. A player cannot pass his turn.

Figure 17.11: A row of coins.

Design an efficient algorithm for computing the maximum total value for the starting player in the pick-up-coins game.

Hint: Relate the best play for the first player to the best play for the second player.

Solution: First of all, note that greedily selecting the maximum of the two end coins, does not yield the best solution. If the coins are $5, 25, 10, 1$, if the first player is greedy and chooses 5, the second player can pick up the 25. Now the first player will choose the 10, and the second player gets the 1, so the first player has a total of 15 and the second player has a total of 26. A better move for the first player is picking up 1. Now the second player is forced to expose the 25, so the first player will achieve 26.

The drawback of greedy selection is that it does not consider the opportunities created for the second player. Intuitively, the first player wants to balance selecting high coins with minimizing the coins available to the second player.

The second player is assumed to play the best move he possibly can. Therefore, the second player will choose the coin that maximizes *his* revenue. Call the sum of the coins selected by a player his revenue. Let $R(a, b)$ be the maximum revenue a player can get when it is his turn to play, and the coins remaining on the table are at indices a to b, inclusive. Let C be an array representing the line of coins, i.e., $C[i]$ is the value of the ith coin. If the first player selects the coin at a, since the second player plays optimally, the first player will end up with a total revenue of $C[a] + S(a+1, b) - R(a+1, b)$, where $S(a, b)$ is the sum of the coins from positions a to b, inclusive. If he selects the coin at b, he will end up with a total revenue of $C[b] + S(a, b - 1) - R(a, b - 1)$. Since the first player wants to maximize revenue, he chooses the greater of the two, i.e., $R(a, b) = \max(C[a] + S(a+1, b) - R(a+1, b), C[b] + S(a, b-1) - R(a, b-1))$. This recursion for R can be solved easily using DP.

Now we present a slightly different recurrence for R. Since the second player seeks to maximize his revenue, and the total revenue is a constant, it is equivalent for the the second player to move so as to minimize the first player's revenue. Therefore, $R(a, b)$ satisfies the following equations:

$$
R(a, b) = \begin{cases} \max \left(\begin{array}{l} C[a] + \min \left(\begin{array}{l} R(a+2, b), \\ R(a+1, b-1) \end{array} \right), \\ C[b] + \min \left(\begin{array}{l} R(a+1, b-1), \\ R(a, b-2) \end{array} \right) \end{array} \right), & \text{if } a \le b; \\ 0, & \text{otherwise.} \end{cases}
$$

319

In essence, the strategy is to minimize the maximum revenue the opponent can gain. The benefit of this "min-max" recurrence for $R(a, b)$, compared to our first formulation, is that it does not require computing $S(a + 1, b)$ and $S(a, b - 1)$.

For the coins $\langle 10, 25, 5, 1, 10, 5\rangle$, the optimum revenue for the first player is 31. Some of subproblems encountered include computing the optimum revenue for $\langle 10, 25\rangle$ (which is 25), $\langle 5, 1\rangle$ (which is 5), and $\langle 5, 1, 10, 5\rangle$ (which is 15).

For the coins in Figure 17.11 on the facing page, the maximum revenue for the first player is 140¢, i.e., whatever strategy the second player uses, the first player can guarantee a revenue of at least 140¢. In contrast, if both players always pick the more valuable of the two coins available to them, the first player will get only 120¢.

In the program below, we solve for R using DP.

```
int MaximumRevenue(const vector<int>& coins) {
  vector<vector<int>> maximum_revenue_for_range(coins.size(),
                                      vector<int>(coins.size(), 0));
  return ComputeMaximumRevenueForRange(coins, 0, coins.size() - 1,
                                  &maximum_revenue_for_range);
}


int ComputeMaximumRevenueForRange(
    const vector<int>& coins, int a, int b,
    vector<vector<int>>* maximum_revenue_for_range_ptr) {
  if (a > b) {
    // No coins left.
    return 0;
  }

  vector<vector<int>>& maximum_revenue_for_range =
      *maximum_revenue_for_range_ptr;
  if (maximum_revenue_for_range[a][b] == 0) {
    int max_revenue_a =
        coins[a] +
        min(ComputeMaximumRevenueForRange(coins, a + 2, b,
                                      maximum_revenue_for_range_ptr),
            ComputeMaximumRevenueForRange(coins, a + 1, b - 1,
                                      maximum_revenue_for_range_ptr));
    int max_revenue_b =
        coins[b] + min(ComputeMaximumRevenueForRange(
                           coins, a + 1, b - 1, maximum_revenue_for_range_ptr),
                       ComputeMaximumRevenueForRange(
                           coins, a, b - 2, maximum_revenue_for_range_ptr));
    maximum_revenue_for_range[a][b] = max(max_revenue_a, max_revenue_b);
  }
  return maximum_revenue_for_range[a][b];
}
```

There are $O(n^2)$ possible arguments for $R(a, b)$, where n is the number of coins, and the time spent to compute R from previously computed values is $O(1)$. Hence, R can be computed in $O(n^2)$ time.

You are climbing stairs. You can advance 1 to k steps at a time. Your destination is exactly n steps up.

Write a program which takes as inputs n and k returns the number of ways in which you can get to your destination. For example, if $n = 4$ and $k = 2$, there are five ways in which to get to the destination:
- four single stair advances,
- two single stair advances followed by a double stair advance,
- a single stair advance followed by a double stair advance followed by a single stair advance,
- a double stair advance followed by two single stairs advances, and
- two double stair advances.

Hint: How many ways are there in which you can you take the last step?

Solution: A brute-force enumerative solution does not make sense, since there are an exponential number of possibilities to consider.

Since the first advance can be one step, two steps,..., k steps, and all of these lead to different ways to get to the top, we can write the following equation for the number of steps $F(n, k)$:

$$F(n,k) = \sum_{i=1}^{k} F(n - i, k)$$

For the working example, $F(4, 2) = F(4 - 2, 2) + F(4 - 1, 2)$. Recursing, $F(4 - 2, 2) = F(4 - 2 - 2, 2) + F(4 - 2 - 1, 2)$. Both $F(0, 2)$ and $F(1, 2)$ are base-cases, with a value of 1, so $F(4 - 2, 2) = 2$. Continuing with $F(4 - 1, 2)$, $F(4 - 1, 2) = F(4 - 1 - 2, 2) + F(4 - 1 - 1, 2)$. The first term is a base-case, with a value of 1. The second term has already been computed—its value is 2. Therefore, $F(4 - 1, 2) = 3$, and $F(4, 2) = 3 + 2$.

In the program below, we cache values of $F(i, k)$, $0 \le i \le n$ to improve time complexity.

```
int NumberOfWaysToTop(int top, int maximum_step) {
  vector<int> number_of_ways_to_h(top + 1, 0);
  return ComputeNumberOfWaysToH(top, maximum_step, &number_of_ways_to_h);
}

int ComputeNumberOfWaysToH(int h, int maximum_step,
                           vector<int>* number_of_ways_to_h_ptr) {
  if (h <= 1) {
    return 1;
  }

  vector<int>& number_of_ways_to_h = *number_of_ways_to_h_ptr;
  if (number_of_ways_to_h[h] == 0) {
    for (int i = 1; i <= maximum_step && h - i >= 0; ++i) {
      number_of_ways_to_h[h] +=
          ComputeNumberOfWaysToH(h - i, maximum_step, number_of_ways_to_h_ptr);
    }
```

```
    }
    return number_of_ways_to_h[h];
}
```

We take $O(k)$ time to fill in each entry, so the total time complexity is $O(kn)$. The space complexity is $O(n)$.

17.11 THE PRETTY PRINTING PROBLEM

Consider the problem of laying out text using a fixed width font. Each line can hold no more than a fixed number of characters. Words on a line are to be separated by exactly one blank. Therefore, we may be left with whitespace at the end of a line (since the next word will not fit in the remaining space). This whitespace is visually unappealing.

Define the *messiness* of the end-of-line whitespace as follows. The messiness of a single line ending with b blank characters is b^2. The total messiness of a sequence of lines is the sum of the messinesses of all the lines. A sequence of words can be split across lines in different ways with different messiness, as illustrated in Figure 17.12.

```
I have inserted a large number of␣␣␣␣        I have inserted a large number␣␣␣␣␣␣␣
new examples from the papers for the         of new examples from the papers␣␣␣␣␣␣
Mathematical Tripos during the last␣         for the Mathematical Tripos during␣␣
twenty years, which should be useful         the last twenty years, which should␣
to Cambridge students.␣␣␣␣␣␣␣␣␣␣␣␣␣␣         be useful to Cambridge students.␣␣␣␣␣
```

(a) Messiness = $3^2 + 0^2 + 1^2 + 0^2 + 14^2 = 206$.   (b) Messiness = $6^2 + 5^2 + 2^2 + 1^2 + 4^2 = 82$.

Figure 17.12: Two layouts for the same sequence of words; the line length L is 36.

Given text, i.e., a string of words separated by single blanks, decompose the text into lines such that no word is split across lines and the messiness of the decomposition is minimized. Each line can hold no more than a specified number of characters.

Hint: Focus on the last word and the last line.

Solution: A greedy approach is to fit as many words as possible in each line. However, some experimentation shows this is suboptimal. See Figure 17.13 on the following page for an example. In essence, the greedy algorithm does not spread words uniformly across the lines, which is the key requirement of the problem. Adding a new word may necessitate moving earlier words.

Suppose we want to find the optimum placement for the ith word. As we have just seen, we cannot trivially extend the optimum placement for the first $i-1$ words to an optimum placement for the ith word. Put another way, the placement that results by removing the ith word from an optimum placement for the first i words is not an always an optimum placement for the first $i - 1$ words. However, what we can say is that if in the optimum placement for the ith word the last line consists of words $j, j + 1, \ldots, i$, then in this placement, the first $j - 1$ words must be placed optimally.

322

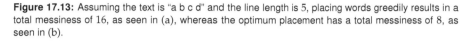

(a) Greedy placement: Line 1 has a messiness of 0^2, and Line 2 has a messiness of 4^2.

(b) Optimum placement: Line 1 has a messiness of 2^2, and Line 2 has a messiness of 2^2.

Figure 17.13: Assuming the text is "a b c d" and the line length is 5, placing words greedily results in a total messiness of 16, as seen in (a), whereas the optimum placement has a total messiness of 8, as seen in (b).

In an optimum placement of the first i words, the last line consists of *some* subset of words ending in the ith word. Furthermore, since the first i words are assumed to be optimally placed, the placement of words on the lines prior to the last one must be optimum. Therefore, we can write a recursive formula for the minimum messiness, $M(i)$, when placing the first i words. Specifically, $M(i)$, equals $\min_{j \le i} f(j, i) + M(j - 1)$, where $f(j, i)$ is the messiness of a single line consisting of words j to i inclusive.

We give an example of this approach in Figure 17.14. The optimum placement of "aaa bbb c d ee" is shown in Figure 17.14(a). The optimum placement of "aaa bbb c d ee ff" is shown in Figure 17.14(b).

To determine the optimum placement for "aaa bbb c d ee ff gggggg", we consider two cases—the final line is "ff gggggg", and the final line is "gggggg". (No more cases are possible, since we cannot fit "ee ff gggggg" on a single line.)

If the final line is "ff gggggg", then the "aaa bb c d ee" must be placed as in Figure 17.14(a); in the second case, "aaa bbb c d ee ff" must be placed as in Figure 17.14(b). These two cases are shown in Figure 17.14(c) and Figure 17.14(d), respectively. Comparing the two, we see Figure 17.14(d) has the lower messiness and is therefore optimum.

(a) Optimum placement for "aaa bbb c d ee".

(b) Optimum placement for "aaa bbb c d ee ff".

(c) Optimum placement for "aaa bbb c d ee ff gggggg" when the final line is "gggggg".

(d) Optimum placement for "aaa bbb c d ee ff gggggg" when the final line is "ff gggggg".

Figure 17.14: Solving the pretty printing problem for text "aaa bb c d ee ff gggggg" and line length 11.

The recursive computation has exponential complexity, because it visits identical subproblems repeatedly. The solution is to cache the values for M.

```
int MinimumMessiness(const vector<string>& words, int line_length) {
  // minimum_messiness[i] is the minimum messiness when placing words[0 : i].
  vector<int> minimum_messiness(words.size(), numeric_limits<int>::max());
  int num_remaining_blanks = line_length - words[0].size();
  minimum_messiness[0] = num_remaining_blanks * num_remaining_blanks;
  for (int i = 1; i < words.size(); ++i) {
    num_remaining_blanks = line_length - words[i].size();
    minimum_messiness[i] =
        minimum_messiness[i - 1] + num_remaining_blanks * num_remaining_blanks;
    // Try adding words[i - 1], words[i - 2], ...
    for (int j = i - 1; j >= 0; --j) {
      num_remaining_blanks -= (words[j].size() + 1);
      if (num_remaining_blanks < 0) {
        // Not enough space to add more words.
        break;
      }
      int first_j_messiness = j - 1 < 0 ? 0 : minimum_messiness[j - 1];
      int current_line_messiness = num_remaining_blanks * num_remaining_blanks;
      minimum_messiness[i] = min(minimum_messiness[i],
                                 first_j_messiness + current_line_messiness);
    }
  }
  return minimum_messiness.back();
}
```

Let L be the line length. Then there can certainly be no more than L words on a line, so the amount of time spent processing each word is $O(L)$. Therefore, if there are n words, the time complexity is $O(nL)$. The space complexity is $O(n)$ for the cache.

Variant: Solve the same problem when the messiness is the sum of the messinesses of all but the last line.

Variant: Suppose the messiness of a line ending with b blank characters is defined to be b. Can you solve the messiness minimization problem in $O(n)$ time and $O(1)$ space?

17.12 FIND THE LONGEST NONDECREASING SUBSEQUENCE

The problem of finding the longest nondecreasing subsequence in a sequence of integers has implications to many disciplines, including string matching and analyzing card games. As a concrete instance, the length of a longest nondecreasing subsequence for the array in Figure 17.15 on the next page is 4. There are multiple longest nondecreasing subsequences, e.g., $\langle 0, 4, 10, 14 \rangle$ and $\langle 0, 2, 6, 9 \rangle$.

Write a program that takes as input an array of numbers and returns the length of a longest subsequence in the array.

Hint: Express the longest nondecreasing subsequence ending at an entry in terms of the longest nondecreasing subsequence appearing in the subarray consisting of preceding elements.

0	8	4	12	2	10	6	14	1	9
$A[0]$	$A[1]$	$A[2]$	$A[3]$	$A[4]$	$A[5]$	$A[6]$	$A[7]$	$A[8]$	$A[9]$

Figure 17.15: An array whose longest nondecreasing subsequences are of length 4.

Solution: A brute-force approach would be to enumerate all possible subsequences, testing each one for being nondecreasing. Since there are 2^n subsequences of an array of length n, the time complexity would be huge. Some heuristic pruning can be applied, but the program grows very cumbersome.

If we have processed the initial set of entries of the input array, intuitively this should help us when processing the next entry. For the given example, if we know the lengths of the longest nondecreasing subsequences that end at Entries $0, 1, \ldots, 5$ and we want to know the longest nondecreasing subsequence that ends at Entry 6, we simply look for the longest subsequence ending at an entry in $A[0:5]$ whose value is less than or equal to $A[6]$. For Entry 6 in the example in Figure 17.15, there are two such longest subsequences, namely the ones ending at 2 and 4, both of which yield nondecreasing subsequences of length 3 ending at $A[6]$.

Generalizing, define $L[i]$ to be the length of the longest nondecreasing subsequence of A that ends at and includes $A[i]$. The longest nondecreasing subsequence that ends at i is of length 1 (if $A[i]$ is smaller than all preceding entries) or has some element, call it $A[j]$, as its penultimate entry, in which case the subsequence restricted to j and before must be the longest subsequence ending at j. Based on this, $L[i]$ is either 1 (if $A[i]$ is less than all previous entries), or $1 + \max\{L[j] | j < i \text{ and } A[j] < A[i]\}$.

We can use this relationship to compute L, recursively or iteratively. If we want the sequence as well, for each i, in addition to storing the length of the sequence nondecreasing sequence ending at i, we store the index of the last element of the subsequence that we extended to get the value assigned to $L[i]$.

Applying this algorithm to the example in Figure 17.15, we compute L as follows:

1. $L[0] = 1$ (since there are no entries before Entry 0)
2. $L[1] = 1 + \max(L[0]) = 2$ (since $A[0] \le A[1]$)
3. $L[2] = 1 + \max(L[0]) = 2$ (since $A[0] \le A[2]$ and $A[1] > A[2]$)
4. $L[3] = 1 + \max(L[0], L[1], L[2]) = 3$ (since $A[0], A[1]$ and $A[2] \le A[3]$)
5. $L[4] = 1 + \max(L[0]) = 2$ (since $A[0] \le A[4], A[1], A[2]$ and $A[3] > A[4]$)
6. $L[5] = 1 + \max(L[0], L[1], L[2], L[4]) = 3$ (since $A[0], A[1], A[2], A[4] \le A[5]$ and $A[3] > A[5]$)
7. $L[6] = 1 + \max(L[0], L[2], L[4]) = 3$ (since $A[0], A[2], A[4] \le A[6]$ and $A[1], A[3], A[5] > A[6]$)
8. $L[7] = 1 + \max(L[0], L[1], L[2], L[3], L[4], L[5], L[6]) = 4$ (since $A[0], A[1], A[2], A[3], A[4], A[5], A[6] \le A[7]$)
9. $L[8] = 1 + \max(L[0]) = 2$ (since $A[0] \le A[8]$ and $A[1], A[2], A[3], A[4], A[5], A[6], A[7] > A[8]$)

10. $L[9] = 1 + \max(L[0], L[1], L[2], L[4], L[6], L[8]) = 4$ (since $A[0], A[1], A[2], A[4], A[6], A[8] \le A[9]$ and $A[3], A[5], A[7] > A[9]$)

Therefore the maximum length of a longest nondecreasing subsequence is 4. There are two possible sequences, one ending at $A[7]$ and the other ending at $A[9]$.

Here is an iterative implementation of the algorithm.

```
int LongestNondecreasingSubsequenceLength(const vector<int>& A) {
  // max_length[i] holds the length of the longest nondecreasing subsequence of
  // A[0 : i].
  vector<int> max_length(A.size(), 1);
  for (int i = 1; i < A.size(); ++i) {
    for (int j = 0; j < i; ++j) {
      if (A[i] >= A[j]) {
        max_length[i] = max(max_length[i], max_length[j] + 1);
      }
    }
  }
  return *max_element(max_length.begin(), max_length.end());
}
```

The time complexity is $O(n^2)$ (each $L[i]$ takes $O(n)$ time to compute), and the space complexity is $O(n)$ (to store L).

Variant: Write a program that takes as input an array of numbers and returns a longest nondecreasing subsequence in the array.

Variant: Define a sequence of numbers $\langle a_0, a_1, \ldots, a_{n-1} \rangle$ to be *alternating* if $a_i < a_{i+1}$ for even i and $a_i > a_{i+1}$ for odd i. Given an array of numbers A of length n, find a longest subsequence $\langle i_0, \ldots, i_{k-1} \rangle$ such that $\langle A[i_0], A[i_1], \ldots, A[i_{k-1}] \rangle$ is alternating.

Variant: Define a sequence of numbers $\langle a_0, a_1, \ldots, a_{n-1} \rangle$ to be *weakly alternating* if no three consecutive terms in the sequence are increasing or decreasing. Given an array of numbers A of length n, find a longest subsequence $\langle i_0, \ldots, i_{k-1} \rangle$ such that $\langle A[i_0], A[i_1], \ldots, A[i_{k-1}] \rangle$ is weakly alternating.

Variant: Define a sequence of numbers $\langle a_0, a_1, \ldots, a_{n-1} \rangle$ to be *convex* if $a_i < \frac{a_{i-1} + a_{i+1}}{2}$, for $1 \le i \le n - 2$. Given an array of numbers A of length n, find a longest subsequence $\langle i_0, \ldots, i_{k-1} \rangle$ such that $\langle A[i_0], A[i_1], \ldots, A[i_{k-1}] \rangle$ is convex.

Variant: Define a sequence of numbers $\langle a_0, a_1, \ldots, a_{n-1} \rangle$ to be *bitonic* if there exists k such that $a_i < a_{i+1}$, for $0 \le i < k$ and $a_i > a_{i+1}$, for $k \le i < n - 1$. Given an array of numbers A of length n, find a longest subsequence $\langle i_0, \ldots, i_{k-1} \rangle$ such that $\langle A[i_0], A[i_1], \ldots, A[i_{k-1}] \rangle$ is bitonic.

Variant: Define a sequence of points in the plane to be *ascending* if each point is above and to the right of the previous point. How would you find a maximum ascending subset of a set of points in the plane?

Variant: Compute the longest nondecreasing subsequence in $O(n \log n)$ time.

18

Greedy Algorithms and Invariants

> *The intended function of a program, or part of a program, can be specified by making general assertions about the values which the relevant variables will take after execution of the program.*
>
> — *"An Axiomatic Basis for Computer Programming,"*
> C. A. R. HOARE, 1969

Greedy algorithms

A greedy algorithm is an algorithm that computes a solution in steps; at each step the algorithm makes a decision that is locally optimum, and it never changes that decision.

The example on Page 38 illustrates how different greedy algorithms for the same problem can differ in terms of optimality. As another example, consider making change for 48 pence in the old British currency where the coins came in 30, 24, 12, 6, 3, and 1 pence denominations. Suppose our goal is to make change using the smallest number of coins. The natural greedy algorithm iteratively chooses the largest denomination coin that is less than or equal to the amount of change that remains to be made. If we try this for 48 pence, we get three coins—30 + 12 + 6. However, the optimum answer would be two coins—24 + 24.

In its most general form, the coin changing problem is NP-hard on Page 40, but for some coinages, the greedy algorithm is optimum—e.g., if the denominations are of the form $\{1, r, r^2, r^3\}$. (An *ad hoc* argument can be applied to show that the greedy algorithm is also optimum for US coinage.) The general problem can be solved in pseudo-polynomial time using DP in a manner similar to Problem 17.6 on Page 313.

As another example of how greedy reasoning can fail, consider the following problem: Four travelers need to cross a river as quickly as possible in a small boat. Only two people can cross at one time. The time to cross the river is dictated by the slower person in the boat (if there is just one person, that is his time). The four travelers have times of 5, 10, 20, and 25 minutes. The greedy schedule would entail having the two fastest travelers cross initially (10), with the fastest returning (5), picking up the faster of the two remaining and crossing again (20), and with the fastest returning for the slowest traveler (5 + 25). The total time taken would be 10 + 5 + 20 + 5 + 25 = 65 minutes. However, a better approach would be for the fastest two to cross (10), with the faster traveler returning (5), and then having the two slowest travelers cross (25), with the second fastest returning (10) to pick up the fastest traveler (10). The total time for this schedule is 10 + 5 + 25 + 10 + 10 = 60 minutes.

One way to compress text is by building a code book which maps each character to a bit string, referred to as its code word. Compression consists of concatenating the bit strings for each character to form a bit string for the entire text. (The codebook, i.e., the mapping from characters to corresponding bit strings is stored separately, e.g., in a preamble.)

When decompressing the string, we read bits until we find a string that is in the code book and then repeat this process until the entire text is decoded. For the compression to be reversible, it is sufficient that the code words have the property that no code word is a prefix of another. For example, 011 is a prefix of 0110 but not a prefix of 1100.

Since our objective is to compress the text, we would like to assign the shorter bit strings to more common characters and the longer bit strings to less common characters. We will restrict our attention to individual characters. (We may achieve better compression if we examine common sequences of characters, but this increases the time complexity.)

The intuitive notion of commonness is formalized by the *frequency* of a character which is a number between zero and one. The sum of the frequencies of all the characters is 1. The average code length is defined to be the sum of the product of the length of each character's code word with that character's frequency. Table 18.1 shows the frequencies of letters of the English alphabet.

Table 18.1: English characters and their frequencies, expressed as percentages, in everyday documents.

Character	Frequency	Character	Frequency	Character	Frequency
a	8.17	j	0.15	s	6.33
b	1.49	k	0.77	t	9.06
c	2.78	l	4.03	u	2.76
d	4.25	m	2.41	v	0.98
e	12.70	n	6.75	w	2.36
f	2.23	o	7.51	x	0.15
g	2.02	p	1.93	y	1.97
h	6.09	q	0.10	z	0.07
i	6.97	r	5.99		

Given a set of characters with corresponding frequencies, find a code book that has the smallest average code length.

Hint: Reduce the problem from n characters to one on $n - 1$ characters.

Solution: The trivial solution is to used fixed length bit strings for each character. To be precise, if there are n distinct characters, we can use $\lceil \lg n \rceil$ bits per character. If all characters are equally likely, this is optimum, but when there is large variation in frequencies, we can do much better.

A natural heuristic is to split the set of characters into two subsets, which have approximately equal aggregate frequencies, solve the problem for each subset, and then add a 0 to the codes from the first set and a 1 to the codes from the second set to differentiate the codes from the two subsets. This approach does not always result in the optimum coding, e.g., when the characters are A, B, C, D with frequencies $\{0.4, 0.35, 0.2, 0.05\}$, it forms the code words $00, 10, 11, 01$, where as the optimum coding is $0, 10, 110, 111$. It also requires being able to partition the characters into two subsets whose aggregate frequencies are close, which is computationally challenging.

Another strategy is to assign 0 to the character with highest frequency, solve the same problem on the remaining characters, and then prefix those codes with a 1. This approach fares very poorly when characters have the same frequency, e.g., if A, B, C, D all have frequency 0.25, the resulting coding is $0, 10, 100, 111$, whereas $00, 01, 10, 11$ is the optimum coding. Intuitively, this strategy fails because it does not take into account the relative frequencies.

Huffman coding yields an optimum solution to this problem. (There may be other optimum codes as well.) It is based on the idea that you should focus on the least frequent characters, rather than the most frequent ones. Specifically, combine the two least frequent characters into a new character, recursively solve the problem on the resulting $n - 1$ characters; then create codes for the two combined characters from the code for their combined character by adding a 0 for one and a 1 for the other.

More precisely, Huffman coding proceeds in three steps:

(1.) Sort characters in increasing order of frequencies and create a binary tree node for each character. Denote the set just created by S.

(2.) Create a new node u whose children are the two nodes with smallest frequencies and assign u's frequency to be the sum of the frequencies of its children.

(3.) Remove the children from S and add u to S. Repeat from Step (2.) till S consists of a single node, which is the root.

Mark all the left edges with 0 and the right edges with 1. The path from the root to a leaf node yields the bit string encoding the corresponding character.

Applying this algorithm to the frequencies for English characters presented in Table 18.1 on the previous page yields the Huffman tree in Figure 18.1 on the facing page. The path from root to leaf yields that character's Huffman code, which is listed in Table 18.2. For example, the codes for t, e, and z are $000, 100$, and 001001000, respectively.

Table 18.2: Huffman codes for English characters, assuming the frequencies given in Table 18.1 on the previous page.

Character	Huffman code	Character	Huffman code	Character	Huffman code
a	1110	j	001001011	s	0111
b	110000	k	0010011	t	000
c	01001	l	11110	u	01000
d	11111	m	00111	v	001000
e	100	n	1010	w	00110
f	00101	o	1101	x	001001010
g	110011	p	110001	y	110010
h	0110	q	001001001	z	001001000
i	1011	r	0101		

The codebook is explicitly given in Table 18.2. The average code length for this coding is 4.205. In contrast, the trivial coding takes $\lceil \log 26 \rceil = 5$ bits for each character.

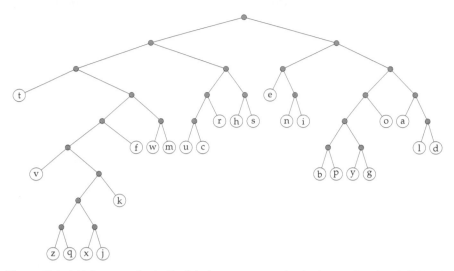

Figure 18.1: A Huffman tree for the English characters, assuming the frequencies given in Table 18.1 on Page 329.

In the implementation below, we use a min-heap of candidate nodes to represent *S*.

```
struct CharWithFrequency {
  char c;
  double freq;
};

struct BinaryTreeNode {
  double aggregate_freq;
  CharWithFrequency* s;
  shared_ptr<BinaryTreeNode> left, right;
};

unordered_map<char, string> HuffmanEncoding(
    vector<CharWithFrequency>* symbols) {
  // Initially assigns each symbol into candidates.
  priority_queue<
      shared_ptr<BinaryTreeNode>, vector<shared_ptr<BinaryTreeNode>>,
      function<bool(shared_ptr<BinaryTreeNode>, shared_ptr<BinaryTreeNode>)>>
  candidates([](const shared_ptr<BinaryTreeNode>& lhs,
                const shared_ptr<BinaryTreeNode>& rhs) -> bool {
    return lhs->aggregate_freq > rhs->aggregate_freq;
  });
  for (auto& s : *symbols) {
    candidates.emplace(new BinaryTreeNode{s.freq, &s, nullptr, nullptr});
  }

  // Keeps combining two nodes until there is one node left.
  while (candidates.size() > 1) {
    shared_ptr<BinaryTreeNode> left = candidates.top();
    candidates.pop();
```

```
    shared_ptr<BinaryTreeNode> right = candidates.top();
    candidates.pop();
    candidates.emplace(new BinaryTreeNode{
        left->aggregate_freq + right->aggregate_freq, nullptr, left, right});
  }

  unordered_map<char, string> huffman_encoding;
  // Traverses the binary tree, assigning codes to nodes.
  AssignHuffmanCode(candidates.top(), new string, &huffman_encoding);
  return huffman_encoding;
}

void AssignHuffmanCode(const shared_ptr<BinaryTreeNode>& tree, string* code,
                       unordered_map<char, string>* huffman_encoding) {
  if (tree) {
    if (tree->s) {
      // This node is a leaf.
      (*huffman_encoding)[tree->s->c] = *code;
    } else {  // Non-leaf node.
      code->push_back('0');
      AssignHuffmanCode(tree->left, code, huffman_encoding);
      code->pop_back();
      code->push_back('1');
      AssignHuffmanCode(tree->right, code, huffman_encoding);
      code->pop_back();
    }
  }
}
```

Since each invocation of Steps (2.) on Page 330 and (3.) on Page 330 requires two *extract-min* and one *insert* operation, it takes $O(n \log n)$ time to build the Huffman tree, where n is the number of characters.

It is exceedingly unlikely that you would be asked for a rigorous proof of optimality in an interview setting. The proof that the Huffman algorithm yields the minimum average code length uses induction on the number of characters. The induction step itself makes use of proof by contradiction, with the two leaves in the Huffman tree corresponding to the rarest characters playing a central role.

18.2 COMPUTE AN OPTIMUM ASSIGNMENT OF TASKS

We consider the problem of assigning tasks to workers. Each worker must be assigned exactly two tasks. Each task takes a fixed amount of time. Tasks are independent, i.e., there are no constraints of the form "Task 4 cannot start before Task 3 is completed." Any task can be assigned to any worker.

We want to assign tasks to workers so as to minimize how long it takes before all tasks are completed. For example, if there are 6 tasks whose durations are 5, 2, 1, 6, 4, 4 hours, then an optimum assignment is to give the first two tasks (i.e., the tasks with duration 5 and 2) to one worker, the next two (1 and 6) to another worker, and the last two (4 and 4) to the last worker. For this assignment, all tasks will finish after $\max(5 + 2, 1 + 6, 4 + 4) = 8$ hours.

Design an algorithm that takes as input a set of tasks and returns an optimum assignment.

Hint: What additional task should be assigned to the worker who is assigned the longest task?

Solution: Simply enumerating all possible sets of pairs of tasks is not feasible—there are too many of them. (The precise number assignments is $\binom{n}{2}\binom{n-2}{2}\binom{n-4}{2}\ldots\binom{4}{2}\binom{2}{2} = n!/2^{n/2}$, where n is the number of tasks.)

Instead we should look more carefully at the structure of the problem. Extremal values are important—the task that takes the longest needs the most help. In particular, it makes sense to pair the task with longest duration with the task of shortest duration. This intuitive observation can be understood by looking at any assignment in which a longest task is not paired with a shortest task. By swapping the task that the longest task is currently paired with with the shortest task, we get an assignment which is as good.

Note that we are not claiming that the time taken for the optimum assignment is the sum of the maximum and minimum task durations. Indeed this may not even be the case, e.g., if the two longest duration tasks are close to each other in duration and the shortest duration task takes much less time than the second shortest task. As a concrete example if the task durations are $1, 8, 9, 10$ the optimum delay is $8 + 9 = 17$, not $1 + 10$.

In summary, we sort the set of task durations, and pair the shortest, second shortest, third shortest, etc. tasks with the longest, second longest, third longest, etc. tasks. For example, if the durations are $5, 2, 1, 6, 4, 4$, then on sorting we get $1, 2, 4, 4, 5, 6$, and the pairings are $(1, 6), (2, 5),$ and $(4, 4)$.

```
struct PairedTasks {
  int task_1, task_2;
};


vector<PairedTasks> OptimumTaskAssignment(vector<int> task_durations) {
  sort(task_durations.begin(), task_durations.end());
  vector<PairedTasks> optimum_assignments;
  for (int i = 0, j = task_durations.size() - 1; i < j; ++i, --j) {
    optimum_assignments.emplace_back(
        PairedTasks{task_durations[i], task_durations[j]});
  }
  return optimum_assignments;
}
```

The time complexity is dominated by the time to sort, i.e., $O(n \log n)$.

18.3 SCHEDULE TO MINIMIZE WAITING TIME

A database has to respond to a set of client SQL queries. The service time required for each query is known in advance. For this application, the queries must be processed by the database one at a time, but can be done in any order. The time a query waits before its turn comes is called its waiting time.

Given service times for a set of queries, compute a schedule in which to process queries that minimizes the total waiting time. For example, if the service times are $\langle 2, 5, 1, 3 \rangle$, if we schedule in the given order, the total waiting time is $0 + (2) + (2+5) + (2+5+1) = 17$. If however, we schedule queries in order of decreasing service times, the total waiting time is $0 + (5) + (5+3) + (5+3+2) = 23$.

Hint: Focus on extreme values.

Solution: We can solve this problem by enumerating all schedules and picking the best one. The complexity is very high—$O(n!)$ to be precise, where n is the number of queries.

Intuitively, it makes sense to serve the short queries first. The justification is as follows. Since the service time of each query adds to the waiting time of all queries remaining to be processed, if we put a slow query before a fast one, by swapping the two we improve the waiting time for all queries between the slow and fast query, and do not change the waiting time for the other queries. We do increase the waiting time of the slow query, but this cancels out with the decrease in the waiting time of the fast query. Hence, we should sort the queries by their service time and then process them in the order of nondecreasing service time.

For the given example, the best schedule processes queries in increasing order of service times. It has a total waiting time of $0 + (1) + (1+2) + (1+2+3) = 10$. Note that scheduling queries with longer service times, which we gave as an earlier example, is the worst approach.

```
int MinimumTotalWaitingTime(vector<int> service_times) {
  // Sort the service times in increasing order.
  sort(service_times.begin(), service_times.end());

  int total_waiting_time = 0;
  for (int i = 0; i < service_times.size(); ++i) {
    int num_remaining_queries = service_times.size() - (i + 1);
    total_waiting_time += service_times[i] * num_remaining_queries;
  }
  return total_waiting_time;
}
```

The time complexity is dominated by the time to sort, i.e., $O(n \log n)$.

18.4 THE INTERVAL COVERING PROBLEM

Consider a foreman responsible for a number of tasks on the factory floor. Each task starts at a fixed time and ends at a fixed time. The foreman wants to visit the floor to check on the tasks. Your job is to help him minimize the number of visits he makes. In each visit, he can check on all the tasks taking place at the time of the visit. A visit takes place at a fixed time, and he can only check on tasks taking place at exactly that time. For example, if there are tasks at times $[0, 3], [2, 6], [3, 4], [6, 9]$, then visit times $0, 2, 3, 6$ cover all tasks. A smaller set of visit times that also cover all tasks is $3, 6$. In the abstract, you are to solve the following problem.

You are given a set of closed intervals. Design an efficient algorithm for finding a minimum sized set of numbers that covers all the intervals.

Hint: Think about extremal points.

Solution: Note that we can restrict our attention to numbers which are endpoints without losing optimality. A brute-force approach might be to enumerate every possible subset of endpoints, checking for each one if it covers all intervals, and if so, determining if it has a smaller size than any previous such subset. Since a set of size k has 2^k subsets, the time complexity is very high.

We could simply return the left end point of each interval, which is fast to compute but, as the example in the problem statement showed, may not be the minimum number of visit times. Similarly, always greedily picking an endpoint which covers the most intervals may also lead to suboptimum results, e.g., consider the six intervals $[1, 2], [2, 3], [3, 4], [2, 3], [3, 4], [4, 5]$. The point 3 appears in four intervals, more than any other point. However, if we choose 3, we do not cover $[1, 2]$ and $[4, 5]$, so we need two additional points to cover all six intervals. If we pick 2 and 4, each individually covers just three intervals, but combined they cover all six.

It is a good idea to focus on extreme cases. In particular, consider the interval that ends first, i.e., the interval whose right endpoint is minimum. To cover it, we must pick a number that appears in it. Furthermore, we should pick its right endpoint, since any other intervals covered by a number in the interval will continue to be covered if we pick the right endpoint. (Otherwise the interval we began with cannot be the interval that ends first.) Once we choose that endpoint, we can remove all other covered intervals, and continue with the remaining set.

The above observation leads to the following algorithm. First sort all the endpoints. As we iterate through the endpoints in sorted order, we record intervals that have been visited but are not yet covered. Each time a right endpoint is encountered whose interval has not already been covered, that right endpoint is added to the result. This right endpoint covers all intervals that have been visited but not covered so far.

For the given example, the leftmost right endpoint is 2. Therefore, we choose 2, and $[1, 2], [2, 3], [2, 3]$ to the visited set. Now the next right endpoint is 3. Since 3 is a right endpoint for $[2, 3]$, which has already been selected, we can move ahead to 4, which is a right endpoint. We add $[3, 4], [3, 4], [4, 5]$ to the visited set, and are done—no intervals remain.

It is relatively straightforward to write a program that processes endpoints one at a time. The program below is slightly different from the one described above. It is shorter (it does not require a separate endpoint type), slicker, but its operation is more subtle. Specifically, it sorts intervals in order of increasing left endpoint. Then it iteratively intersects intervals as long as the intersection is nonempty. We claim the right endpoint of the last nonempty intersection must be the leftmost right endpoint.

The reasoning is as follows. Let the right endpoint of the computed intersection be r. Suppose for contradiction that r is not the leftmost right endpoint. Let the interval that has the leftmost right endpoint be $[l', r']$, with $r' < r$.

To show a contradiction we can show that $[l', r']$ must have already been inter-

334

sected. Consider the interval $[l, r]$ that r is the right endpoint of. Suppose $l' < l$. Since intervals were sorted by left endpoint, we must have processed $[l', r']$ before we got to $[l, r]$. Now suppose $l' \geq l$. For the intersection to become empty before we get to $[l', r']$, it must be that some interval $[l'', r'']$ appears after $[l, r]$ and before $[l', r']$ which makes the intersection empty. Since intervals are sorted by left endpoint, we must have $l'' \geq l$. Furthermore, since the intersection becomes empty, as soon as we intersect $[l'', r'']$, r'' must be less then some left endpoint of an interval that was already intersected. This means r'' must be less than r', contradicting the hypothesis that r' was the leftmost right endpoint.

After computing the leftmost right endpoint, the algorithm starts intersecting from the next interval to get the next leftmost right endpoint amongst uncovered intervals.

```
struct Interval {
  bool operator<(const Interval& that) const { return left < that.left; }

  int left, right;
};

vector<int> FindMinimumVisits(vector<Interval> intervals) {
  sort(intervals.begin(), intervals.end());
  vector<int> result;
  int idx = 0;
  while (idx < intervals.size()) {
    Interval intersection = intervals[idx];
    while (idx < intervals.size() &&
           AreIntersecting(intervals[idx], intersection)) {
      intersection = ComputeIntersection(intervals[idx], intersection);
      ++idx;
    }
    result.emplace_back(intersection.right);
  }
  return result;
}

bool AreIntersecting(const Interval& a, const Interval& b) {
  return !(a.left > b.right || b.left > a.right);
}

Interval ComputeIntersection(const Interval& a, const Interval& b) {
  return {max(a.left, b.left), min(a.right, b.right)};
}
```

Since we spend $O(1)$ time per index, the time complexity after the initial sort is $O(n)$, where n is the number of intervals Therefore, the time taken is dominated by the initial sort, i.e., $O(n \log n)$.

Variant: You are responsible for the security of a castle. The castle has a circular perimeter. A total of n robots patrol the perimeter—each robot is responsible for a closed connected subset of the perimeter, i.e., an arc. (The arcs for different robots may overlap.) You want to monitor the robots by installing cameras at the center of the castle that look out to the perimeter. Each camera can look along a ray. To

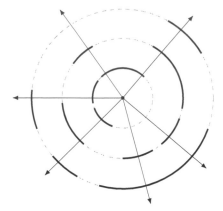

Figure 18.2: An instance of the minimum ray covering problem, with 12 partially overlapping arcs. Arcs have been drawn at different distances for illustration. For this instance, six cameras are sufficient, corresponding to the six rays.

save cost, you would like to minimize the number of cameras. See Figure 18.2 for an example.

Variant: There are a number of points in the plane that you want to observe. You are located at the point $(0, 0)$. You can rotate about this point, and your field-of-view is a fixed angle. Where direction should you face to maximize the number of visible points?

Invariants

An invariant is a condition that is true during execution of a program. Invariants can be used to design algorithms as well as reason about their correctness. For example, binary search, maintains the invariant that the space of candidate solutions contains all possible solutions as the algorithm executes.

Sorting algorithms nicely illustrate algorithm design using invariants. For example, intuitively, selection sort is based on finding the smallest element, the next smallest element, etc. and moving them to their right place. More precisely, we work with successively larger subarrays beginning at index 0, and preserve the invariant that these subarrays are sorted, their elements are less than or equal to the remaining elements, and the entire array remains a permutation of the original array.

As a more sophisticated example, consider Solution 15.8 on Page 263, specifically the $O(k)$ algorithm for generating the first k numbers of the form $a + b\sqrt{2}$. The key idea there is to process these numbers in sorted order. The queues in that code maintain multiple invariants: queues are sorted, duplicates are never present, and the separation between elements is bounded.

18.5 THE 3-SUM PROBLEM

Design an algorithm that takes as input an array and a number, and determines if there are three entries in the array (not necessarily distinct) which add up to the specified number. For example, if the array is $\langle 11, 2, 5, 7, 3 \rangle$ then there are three entries in the array which add up to 21 (3, 7, 11 and 5, 5, 11). (Note that we can use 5 twice, since the problem statement said we can use the same entry more than once.) However, no three entries add up to 22.

Hint: How would you check if a given array entry can be added to two more entries to get the specified number?

Solution: The brute-force algorithm is to consider all possible triples, e.g., by three nested for-loops iterating over all entries. The time complexity is $O(n^3)$, where n is the length of the array, and the space complexity is $O(1)$.

Let A be the input array and t the specified number. We can improve the time complexity to $O(n^2)$ by storing the array entries in a hash table first. Then we iterate over pairs of entries, and for each $A[i] + A[j]$ we look for $t - (A[i] + A[j])$ in the hash table. The space complexity now is $O(n)$.

We can avoid the additional space complexity by first sorting the input. Specifically, sort A and for each $A[i]$, search for indices j and k such that $A[j] + A[k] = t - A[i]$. We can do each such search in $O(n \log n)$ time by iterating over $A[j]$ values and doing binary search for $A[k]$.

We can improve the time complexity to $O(n)$ by starting with $A[0] + A[n - 1]$. If this equals $t - A[i]$, we're done. Otherwise, if $A[0] + A[n - 1] < t - A[i]$, we move to $A[1] + A[n - 1]$—there is no chance of $A[0]$ pairing with any other entry to get $t - A[i]$ (since $A[n-1]$ is the largest value in A). Similarly, if $A[0] + A[n-1] > t - A[i]$, we move to $A[0] + A[n - 2]$. This approach eliminates an entry in each iteration, and spends $O(1)$ time in each iteration, yielding an $O(n)$ time bound to find $A[j]$ and $A[k]$ such that $A[j] + A[k] = t - A[i]$, if such entries exist. The invariant is that if two elements which sum to the desired value exist, they must lie within the subarray currently under consideration.

For the given example, after sorting the array is $\langle 2, 3, 5, 7, 11 \rangle$. For entry $A[0] = 2$, to see if there are $A[j]$ and $A[k]$ such that $A[0] + A[j] + A[k] = 21$, we search for two entries that add up to $21 - 2 = 19$.

The code for this approach is shown below.

```
bool HasThreeSum(vector<int> A, int t) {
  sort(A.begin(), A.end());

  for (int a : A) {
    // Finds if the sum of two numbers in A equals to t - a.
    if (HasTwoSum(A, t - a)) {
      return true;
    }
  }
  return false;
}
```

The additional space needed is $O(1)$, and the time complexity is the sum of the time taken to sort, $O(n \log n)$, and then to run the $O(n)$ algorithm to find a pair in a sorted array that sums to a specified value, which is $O(n^2)$ overall.

337

Variant: Solve the same problem when the three elements must be distinct. For example, if $A = \langle 5, 2, 3, 4, 3 \rangle$ and $t = 9$, then $A[2] + A[2] + A[2]$ is not acceptable, $A[2] + A[2] + A[4]$ is not acceptable, but $A[1] + A[2] + A[3]$ and $A[1] + A[3] + A[4]$ are acceptable.

Variant: Solve the same problem when k, the number of elements to sum, is an additional input.

Variant: Write a program that takes as input an array of integers A and an integer T, and returns a 3-tuple $(A[p], A[q], A[r])$ where p, q, r are all distinct, minimizing $|T - (A[p] + A[q] + A[r])|$, and $A[p] \leq A[r] \leq A[s]$.

Variant: Write a program that takes as input an array of integers A and an integer T, and returns the number of 3-tuples (p, q, r) such that $A[p] + A[q] + A[r] \leq T$ and $p < q < r$.

18.6 FIND THE MAJORITY ELEMENT

Several applications require identification of elements in a sequence which occur more than a specified fraction of the total number of elements in the sequence. For example, we may want to identify the users using excessive network bandwidth or IP addresses originating the most Hypertext Transfer Protocol (HTTP) requests. Here we consider a simplified version of this problem.

You are reading a sequence of strings. You know *a priori* that more than half the strings are repetitions of a single string (the "majority element") but the positions where the majority element occurs are unknown. Write a program that makes a single pass over the sequence and identifies the majority element. For example, if the input is $\langle b, a, c, a, a, b, a, a, c, a \rangle$, then a is the majority element (it appears in 6 out of the 10 places).

Hint: Take advantage of the existence of a majority element to perform elimination.

Solution: The brute-force approach is to use a hash table to record the repetition count for each distinct element. The time complexity is $O(n)$, where n is the number of elements in the input, but the space complexity is also $O(n)$.

Randomized sampling can be used to identify a majority element with high probability using less storage, but is not exact.

The intuition for a better algorithm is as follows. We can group entries into two subgroups—those containing the majority element, and those that do not hold the majority element. Since the first subgroup is given to be larger in size than the second, if we see two entries that are different, at most one can be the majority element. By discarding both, the difference in size of the first subgroup and second subgroup remains the same, so the majority of the remaining entries remains unchanged.

The algorithm then is as follows. We have a candidate for the majority element, and track its count. It is initialized to the first entry. We iterate through remaining entries. Each time we see an entry equal to the candidate, we increment the count. If the entry is different, we decrement the count. If the count becomes zero, we set the next entry to be the candidate.

Here is a mathematical justification of the approach. Let's say the majority element occurred m times out of n entries. By the definition of majority element, $\frac{m}{n} > \frac{1}{2}$. At most one of the two distinct entries that are discarded can be the majority element. Hence, after discarding them, the ratio of the number of remaining majority elements to the total number of remaining elements is either $\frac{m}{(n-2)}$ (neither discarded element was the majority element) or $\frac{(m-1)}{(n-2)}$ (one discarded element was the majority element). It is simple to verify that if $\frac{m}{n} > \frac{1}{2}$, then both $\frac{m}{(n-2)} > \frac{1}{2}$ and $\frac{(m-1)}{(n-2)} > \frac{1}{2}$.

For the given example, $\langle b, a, c, a, a, b, a, a, c, a \rangle$, we initialize the candidate to b. The next element, a is different from the candidate, so the candidate's count goes to 0. Therefore, we pick the next element c to be the candidate, and its count is 1. The next element, a, is different so the count goes back to 0. The next element is a, which is the new candidate. The subsequent b decrements the count to 0. Therefore the next element, a, is the new candidate, and it has a nonzero count till the end.

```
string MajoritySearch(istringstream* input_stream) {
  string candidate, iter;
  int candidate_count = 0;
  while (*input_stream >> iter) {
    if (candidate_count == 0) {
      candidate = iter;
      candidate_count = 1;
    } else if (candidate == iter) {
      ++candidate_count;
    } else {
      --candidate_count;
    }
  }
  return candidate;
}
```

Since we spend $O(1)$ time per entry, the time complexity is $O(n)$. The additional space complexity is $O(1)$.

The code above assumes a majority word exists in the sequence. If no word has a strict majority, it still returns a word from the stream, albeit without any meaningful guarantees on how common that word is. We could check with a second pass whether the returned word was a majority. Similar ideas can be used to identify words that appear more than n/k times in the sequence, as discussed in Problem 22.45 on Page 481.

18.7 THE GASUP PROBLEM

In the gasup problem, a number of cities are arranged on a circular road. You need to visit all the cities and come back to the starting city. A certain amount of gas is available at each city. The amount of gas summed up over all cities is equal to the amount of gas required to go around the road once. Your gas tank has unlimited capacity. Call a city *ample* if you can begin at that city with an empty tank, refill at it,

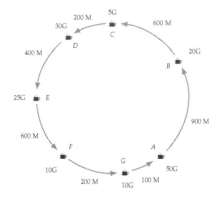

Figure 18.3: The length of the circular road is 3000 miles, and your vehicle gets 20 miles per gallon. The distance noted at each city is how far it is from the next city. For this configuration, we can begin with no gas at City D, and complete the circuit successfully, so D is an ample city.

then travel through all the remaining cities, refilling at each, and return to the ample city, without running out of gas at any point. See Figure 18.3 for an example.

Given an instance of the gasup problem, how would you efficiently compute an ample city, if one exists?

Hint: Think about starting with more than enough gas to complete the circuit without gassing up. Track the amount of gas as you perform the circuit, gassing up at each city.

Solution: The brute-force approach is to simulate the traversal from each city. This approach has time $O(n^2)$ time complexity, where n is the number of cities.

Greedy approaches, e.g., finding the city with the most gas, the city closest to the next city, or the city with best distance-to-gas ratio, do not work. For the given example, A has the most gas, but you cannot get to C starting from A. The city G is closest to the next city (A), and has the lowest distance-to-gas ratio (100/10) but it cannot get to D.

We can gain insight by looking at the graph of the amount of gas as we perform the traversal. See Figure 18.4 on the next page for an example. The amount of gas in the tank could become negative, but we ignore the physical impossibility of that for now. These graphs are the same up to a translation about the Y-axis and a cyclic shift about the X-axis.

In particular, consider a city where the amount of gas in the tank is minimum when we enter that city. Observe that it does not depend where we begin from—because graphs are the same up to translation and shifting, a city that is minimum for one graph will be a minimum city for all graphs. Let c be a city where the amount of gas in the tank before we refuel at that city is minimum. Now suppose we pick c as the starting point, with the gas present at c. Since we never have less gas than we started with at c, and when we return to c we have 0 gas (since it's given that the total amount of gas is just enough to complete the traversal) it means we can complete the journey without running out of gas. Note that the reasoning given above demonstrates that there always exists an ample city.

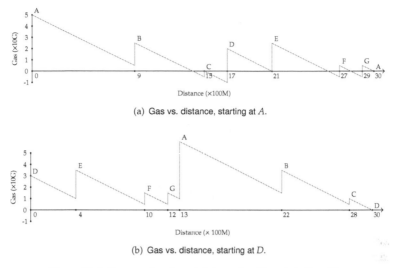

(a) Gas vs. distance, starting at A.

(b) Gas vs. distance, starting at D.

Figure 18.4: Gas as a function of distance for different starting cities.

The computation to determine c can be easily performed with a single pass over all the cities simulating the changes to amount of gas as we advance.

```
const int kMPG = 20;

// gallons[i] is the amount of gas in city i, and distances[i] is the distance
// city i to the next city.
size_t FindAmpleCity(const vector<int>& gallons,
                     const vector<int>& distances) {
  int remaining_gallons = 0;
  struct CityAndRemainingGas {
    int city = 0, remaining_gallons - 0;
  };
  CityAndRemainingGas city_remaining_gallons_pair;
  int num_cities = gallons.size();
  for (int i = 1; i < num_cities; ++i) {
    remaining_gallons += gallons[i - 1] - distances[i - 1] / kMPG;
    if (remaining_gallons < city_remaining_gallons_pair.remaining_gallons) {
      city_remaining_gallons_pair = {i, remaining_gallons};
    }
  }
  return city_remaining_gallons_pair.city;
}
```

The time complexity is $O(n)$, and the space complexity is $O(1)$.

18.8 COMPUTE THE MAXIMUM WATER TRAPPED BY A PAIR OF VERTICAL LINES

An array of integers naturally defines a set of lines parallel to the Y-axis, starting from $x = 0$ as illustrated in Figure 18.5(a) on the facing page. The goal of this problem is to find the pair of lines that together with the X-axis "trap" the most water. See Figure 18.5(b) for an example.

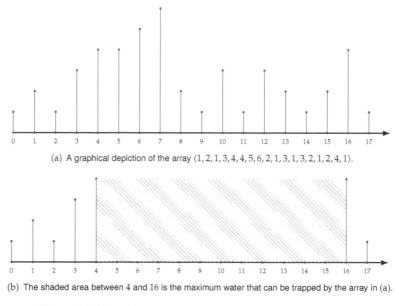

(a) A graphical depiction of the array $\langle 1, 2, 1, 3, 4, 4, 5, 6, 2, 1, 3, 1, 3, 2, 1, 2, 4, 1 \rangle$.

(b) The shaded area between 4 and 16 is the maximum water that can be trapped by the array in (a).

Figure 18.5: Example of maximum water trapped by a pair of vertical lines.

Write a program which takes as input an integer array and returns the pair of entries that trap the maximum amount of water.

Hint: Start with 0 and $n - 1$ and work your way in.

Solution: Let A be the array, and n its length. There is a straightforward $O(n^3)$ brute-force solution—for each pair of indices $(i, j), i < j$, the water trapped by the corresponding lines is $(j - i) \times \min(A[i], A[j])$, which can easily be computed in $O(n)$ time. The maximum of all these is the desired quantity. This algorithm can easily be improved to $O(n^2)$ time by keeping the running minimum as we iterate over j.

In an attempt to achieve a better time complexity, we can try divide-and-conquer. We find the maximum water that can be trapped by the left half of A, the right half of A, and across the center of A. Finding the maximum water trapped by an element on the left half and the right half entails considering combinations of the $n/2$ entries from left half and $n/2$ entries on the right half. Therefore, the time complexity $T(n)$ of this divide-and-conquer approach satisfies $T(n) = 2T(n/2) + O(n^2/4)$ which solves to $T(n) = O(n^2)$. This is no better than the brute-force solution, and considerably trickier to code.

A good starting point is to consider the widest pair, i.e., 0 and $n - 1$. We record the corresponding amount of trapped water, i.e., $((n-1)-0) \times \min(A[0], A[n-1])$. Suppose $A[0] < A[n - 1]$. Then for any k, the water trapped between 0 and k is less than the water trapped between 0 and $n - 1$, so we focus our attention on the maximum water that can be trapped between 1 and $n - 1$. The converse is true if $A[0] > A[n - 1]$—we need never consider $n - 1$ again. If $A[0] = A[n - 1]$, we can eliminate both 0 and $n - 1$ from further consideration. We use this approach iteratively to continuously reduce the subarray that must be explored, while recording the most water trapped so far. In essence, we are exploring the best way in which to trade-off width for height.

For the given example, we begin with $(0, 17)$, which has a capacity of $1 \times 17 = 17$. Since the left and right lines have the same height, namely 1, we can advance both, so now we consider $(1, 16)$. The capacity is $2 \times 15 = 30$. Since $2 < 4$, we move to $(2, 16)$. The capacity is $1 \times 14 = 14$. Since $1 < 4$, we move to $(3, 16)$. The capacity is $3 \times 13 = 39$. Since $3 < 4$, we move to $(4, 16)$. The capacity is $4 \times 12 = 48$. Future iterations, which we do not show, do not surpass 48, which is the result.

```
int GetMaxTrappedWater(const vector<int>& heights) {
  int i = 0, j = heights.size() - 1, max_water = 0;
  while (i < j) {
    int width = j - i;
    max_water = max(max_water, width * min(heights[i], heights[j]));
    if (heights[i] > heights[j]) {
      --j;
    } else if (heights[i] < heights[j]) {
      ++i;
    } else {  // heights[i] == heights[j].
      ++i, --j;
    }
  }
  return max_water;
}
```

We iteratively eliminate one line at a time, and we spend $O(1)$ time per iteration, so the time complexity is $O(n)$.

18.9 COMPUTE THE LARGEST RECTANGLE UNDER THE SKYLINE

You are given a sequence of adjacent buildings. Each has unit width and an integer height. These buildings form the skyline of a city. An architect wants to know the area of a largest rectangle contained in this skyline. See Figure 18.6 for an example.

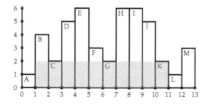

Figure 18.6: A collection of unit-width buildings, and the largest contained rectangle. The text label identifying the building is just below and to the right of its upper left-hand corner. The shaded area is the largest rectangle under the skyline. Its area is $2 \times (11 - 1)$. Note that the tallest rectangle is from 7 to 9, and the widest rectangle is from 0 to 1, but neither of these are the largest rectangle under the skyline.

Let A be an array representing the heights of adjacent buildings of unit width. Design an algorithm to compute the area of the largest rectangle contained in this skyline.

Hint: How would you efficiently find the largest rectangle which includes the ith building, and has height $A[i]$?

Solution: A brute-force approach is to take each (i, j) pair, find the minimum of subarray $A[i : j]$, and multiply that by $j - i + 1$. This has time complexity $O(n^3)$, where n is the length of A. This can be improved to $O(n^2)$ by iterating over i and then $j \geq i$ and tracking the minimum height of buildings from i to j, inclusive. However, there is no reasonable way to further refine this algorithm to get the time complexity below $O(n^2)$.

Another brute-force solution is to consider for each i the furthest left and right we can go without dropping below $A[i]$ in height. In essence, we want to know the largest rectangle that is "supported" by Building i, which can be viewed as acting like a "pillar" of that rectangle. For the given example, the largest rectangle supported by G extends from 1 to 11, and the largest rectangle supported by F extends from 3 to 6.

We can easily determine the largest rectangle supported by Building i with a single forward and a single backward iteration from i. Since i ranges from 0 to $n - 1$, the time complexity of this approach is $O(n^2)$.

This brute-force solution can be refined to get a much better time complexity. Specifically, suppose we iterate over buildings from left to right. When we process Building i, we do not know how far to the right the largest rectangle it supports goes. However, we do know that the largest rectangles supported by earlier buildings whose height is greater than $A[i]$ cannot extend past i, since Building i "blocks" these rectangles. For example, when we get to F in Figure 18.6 on the preceding page, we know that the largest rectangles supported by Buildings B, D, and E (whose heights are greater than F's height) cannot extend past 5.

Looking more carefully at the example, we see that there's no need to consider B when examining F, since C has already blocked the largest rectangle supported by B. In addition, there's no reason to consider C: since G's height is the same as C's height, and C has not been blocked yet, G and C will have the same largest supported rectangle. Generalizing, as we advance through the buildings, all we really need is to keep track of is buildings that have not been blocked yet. Additionally, we can replace existing buildings whose height equals that of the current building with the current building. Call these buildings the set of active pillars.

Initially there are no buildings in the active pillar set. As we iterate from 0 to 12, the active pillar sets are $\{A\}$, $\{A, B\}$, $\{A, C\}$, $\{A, C, D\}$, $\{A, C, D, E\}$, $\{A, C, F\}$, $\{A, G\}$, $\{A, G, H\}$, $\{A, G, H\}$, $\{A, G, I\}$, $\{A, G, J\}$, $\{A, K\}$, $\{A\}$, and $\{A, M\}$.

Whenever a building is removed from the active pillar set, we know exactly how far to the right the largest rectangle that it supports goes to. For example, when we reach C we know B's supported rectangle ends at 2, and when we reach F, we know that D and E's largest supported rectangles end at 5.

When we remove a blocked building from the active pillar set, to find how far to the left its largest supported rectangle extends we simply look for the closest active pillar that has a lower height. For example, when we reach F, the active pillars are $\{A, C, D, E\}$. We remove E and D from the set, since both are taller than F. The largest rectangle supported by E has height 6 and begins after D, i.e., at 4; its area is $6 \times (5 - 4) = 6$. The largest rectangle supported by D has height 5 and begins after C, i.e., at 3; its area is $5 \times (5 - 3) = 10$.

There are a number of data structures that can be used to store the active pillars and the right data structure is key to making the above algorithm efficient. When we process a new building we need to find the buildings in the active pillar set that are blocked. Because insertion and deletion into the active pillar set take place in last-in first-out order, a stack is a reasonable choice for maintaining the set. Specifically, the rightmost building in the active pillar set appears at the top. Using a stack also makes it easy to find how far to the left the largest rectangle that's supported by a building in the active pillar set extends—we simply look at the building below it in the stack. For example, when we process F, the stack is A, C, D, E, with E at the top. Comparing F's height with E, we see E is blocked so the largest rectangle under E ends at where F begins, i.e., at 5. Since the next building in the stack is D, we know that the largest rectangle under E begins where D ends, i.e., at 4.

The algorithm described above is almost complete. The missing piece is what to do when we get to the end of the iteration. The stack will not by empty when we reach the end—at the very least it will contain the last building. We deal with these elements just as we did before, the only difference being that the largest rectangle supported by each building in the stack ends at n, where n is the number of elements in the array. For the given example, the stack contains A and M when we get to the end, and the largest supported rectangles for both of these end at 13.

```cpp
int CalculateLargestRectangle(const vector<int>& heights) {
  stack<int> pillar_indices;
  int max_rectangle_area = 0;
  for (int i = 0; i <= heights.size(); ++i) {
    if (!pillar_indices.empty() && i < heights.size() &&
        heights[i] == heights[pillar_indices.top()]) {
      // Replace earlier building with same height by current building. This
      // ensures the later buildings have the correct left endpoint.
      pillar_indices.pop();
      pillar_indices.emplace(i);
    }
    // By iterating to heights.size() instead of heights.size() - 1, we can
    // uniformly handle the computation for rectangle area here.
    while (!pillar_indices.empty() &&
           IsNewPillarOrReachEnd(heights, i, pillar_indices.top())) {
      int height = heights[pillar_indices.top()];
      pillar_indices.pop();
      int width = pillar_indices.empty() ? i : i - pillar_indices.top() - 1;
      max_rectangle_area = max(max_rectangle_area, height * width);
    }
    pillar_indices.emplace(i);
  }
  return max_rectangle_area;
}
```

```
bool IsNewPillarOrReachEnd(const vector<int>& heights, int curr_idx,
                           int last_pillar_idx) {
  return curr_idx < heights.size()
             ? heights[curr_idx] < heights[last_pillar_idx]
             : true;
}
```

The time complexity is $O(n)$. When advancing through buildings, the time spent for building is proportional to the number of pushes and pops performed when processing it. Although for some buildings, we may perform multiple pops, in total we perform at most n pushes and at most n pops. This is because in the advancing phase, an entry i is added at most once to the stack and cannot be popped more than once. The time complexity of processing remaining stack elements after the advancing is complete is also $O(n)$ since there are at most n elements in the stack, and the time to process each one is $O(1)$. Thus, the overall time complexity is $O(n)$. The space complexity is $O(n)$, which is the largest the stack can grow to, e.g., if buildings appear in sorted in ascending order.

Variant: Find the largest square under the skyline.

19

Graphs

Concerning these bridges, it was asked whether anyone could arrange a route in such a way that he would cross each bridge once and only once.

— "*The solution of a problem relating to the geometry of position,*"
L. EULER, 1741

Informally, a graph is a set of vertices and connected by edges. Formally, a directed graph is a set V of *vertices* and a set $E \subset V \times V$ of edges. Given an edge $e = (u, v)$, the vertex u is its *source*, and v is its *sink*. Graphs are often decorated, e.g., by adding lengths to edges, weights to vertices, a start vertex, etc. A directed graph can be depicted pictorially as in Figure 19.1.

A *path* in a directed graph from u to vertex v is a sequence of vertices $\langle v_0, v_1, \ldots, v_{n-1} \rangle$ where $v_0 = u$, $v_{n-1} = v$, and each (v_i, v_{i+1}) is an edge. The sequence may consist of a single vertex. The *length* of the path $\langle v_0, v_1, \ldots, v_{n-1} \rangle$ is $n - 1$. Intuitively, the length of a path is the number of edges it traverses. If there exists a path from u to v, v is said to be *reachable* from u. For example, the sequence $\langle a, c, e, d, h \rangle$ is a path in the graph represented in Figure 19.1.

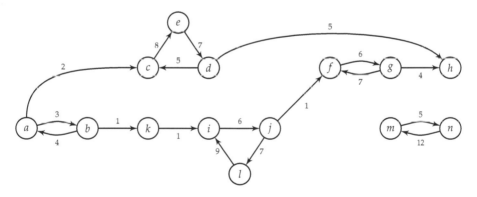

Figure 19.1: A directed graph with weights on edges.

A *directed acyclic graph* (DAG) is a directed graph in which there are no *cycles*, i.e., paths which contain one or more edges and which begin and end at the same vertex. See Figure 19.2 on the facing page for an example of a directed acyclic graph. Vertices in a DAG which have no incoming edges are referred to as *sources*; vertices which have no outgoing edges are referred to as *sinks*. A *topological ordering* of the vertices in a DAG is an ordering of the vertices in which each edge is from a vertex earlier in the ordering to a vertex later in the ordering. Solution 19.9 on Page 365 uses the notion of topological ordering.

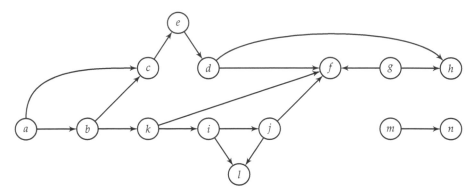

Figure 19.2: A directed acyclic graph. Vertices a, g, m are sources and vertices l, f, h, n are sinks. The ordering $\langle a, b, c, e, d, g, h, k, i, j, f, l, m, n \rangle$ is a topological ordering of the vertices.

An undirected graph is also a tuple (V, E); however, E is a set of unordered pairs of vertices. Graphically, this is captured by drawing arrowless connections between vertices, as in Figure 19.3.

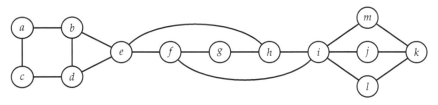

Figure 19.3: An undirected graph.

If G is an undirected graph, vertices u and v are said to be *connected* if G contains a path from u to v; otherwise, u and v are said to be *disconnected*. A graph is said to be connected if every pair of vertices in the graph is connected. A *connected component* is a maximal set of vertices C such that each pair of vertices in C is connected in G. Every vertex belongs to exactly one connected component.

For example, the graph in Figure 19.3 is connected, and it has a single connected component. If edge (h, i) is removed, it remains connected. If additionally (f, i) is removed, it becomes disconnected and there are two connected components.

A directed graph is called *weakly connected* if replacing all of its directed edges with undirected edges produces an undirected graph that is connected. It is *connected* if it contains a directed path from u to v or a directed path from v to u for every pair of vertices u and v. It is *strongly connected* if it contains a directed path from u to v and a directed path from v to u for every pair of vertices u and v.

Graphs naturally arise when modeling geometric problems, such as determining connected cities. However, they are more general, and can be used to model many kinds of relationships.

A graph can be implemented in two ways—using *adjacency lists* or an *adjacency matrix*. In the adjacency list representation, each vertex v, has a list of vertices to which it has an edge. The adjacency matrix representation uses a $|V| \times |V|$ Boolean-valued matrix indexed by vertices, with a 1 indicating the presence of an edge. The time and space complexities of a graph algorithm are usually expressed as a function of the number of vertices and edges.

A *tree* (sometimes called a free tree) is a special sort of graph—it is an undirected graph that is connected but has no cycles. (Many equivalent definitions exist, e.g., a graph is a free tree if and only if there exists a unique path between every pair of vertices.) There are a number of variants on the basic idea of a tree. A rooted tree is one where a designated vertex is called the root, which leads to a parent-child relationship on the nodes. An ordered tree is a rooted tree in which each vertex has an ordering on its children. Binary trees, which are the subject of Chapter 10, differ from ordered trees since a node may have only one child in a binary tree, but that node may be a left or a right child, whereas in an ordered tree no analogous notion exists for a node with a single child. Specifically, in a binary tree, there is position as well as order associated with the children of nodes.

As an example, the graph in Figure 19.4 is a tree. Note that its edge set is a subset of the edge set of the undirected graph in Figure 19.3 on the previous page. Given a graph $G = (V, E)$, if the graph $G' = (V, E')$ where $E' \subset E$, is a tree, then G' is referred to as a spanning tree of G.

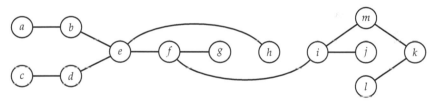

Figure 19.4: A tree.

Graph search

Computing vertices which are reachable from other vertices is a fundamental operation which can be performed in one of two idiomatic ways, namely depth-first search (DFS) and breadth-first search (BFS). Both have linear time complexity—$O(|V| + |E|)$ to be precise. In the worst-case there is a path from the initial vertex covering all vertices without any repeats, and the DFS edges selected correspond to this path, so the space complexity of DFS is $O(|V|)$ (this space is implicitly allocated on the function call stack). The space complexity of BFS is also $O(|V|)$, since in a worst-case there is an edge from the initial vertex to all remaining vertices, implying that they will all be in the BFS queue simultaneously at some point.

DFS and BFS differ from each other in terms of the additional information they provide, e.g., BFS can be used to compute distances from the start vertex and DFS can be used to check for the presence of cycles. Key notions in DFS include the concept of *discovery time* and *finishing time* for vertices.

19.1 SEARCH A MAZE

It is natural to apply graph models and algorithms to spatial problems. Consider a black and white digitized image of a maze—white pixels represent open areas and black spaces are walls. There are two special white pixels: one is designated the entrance and the other is the exit. The goal in this problem is to find a way of getting from the entrance to the exit, as illustrated in Figure 19.5.

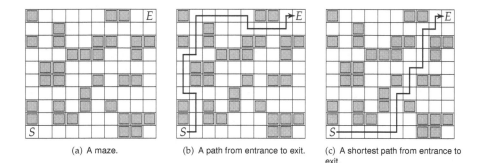

(a) A maze.　　(b) A path from entrance to exit.　　(c) A shortest path from entrance to exit.

Figure 19.5: An instance of the maze search problem, with two solutions, where S and E denote the entrance and exit, respectively.

Given a 2D array of black and white entries representing a maze with designated entrance and exit points, find a path from the entrance to the exit, if one exists.

Hint: Model the maze as a graph.

Solution: A brute-force approach would be to enumerate every possible path from entry to exit. However, we know from Solution 17.3 on Page 307 that the number of paths is astronomical. Of course, pruning helps, since we can stop as soon as a path hits a black pixel, but the worse-case behavior of enumerative approaches is still very bad.

Another approach is to perform a random walk moving from a white pixel to a random adjacent white pixel. Given enough time this will find a path, if one exists. However, it repeats visits, which retards the progress. The random walk does suggest the right way—we should keep track of pixels that we have already visited. This is exactly what DFS and BFS do to ensure progress.

This suggests modeling the maze as a graph. Each vertex corresponds to a white pixel. We will index the vertices based on the coordinates of the corresponding pixel, i.e., vertex $v_{i,j}$ corresponds to the white entry at (i, j) in the 2D array. Edges model adjacent white pixels.

Now, run a DFS starting from the vertex corresponding to the entrance. If at some point, we discover the exit vertex in the DFS, then there exists a path from the entrance to the exit. If we implement recursive DFS then the path would consist of all the vertices in the call stack corresponding to previous recursive calls to the DFS routine.

This problem can also be solved using BFS from the entrance vertex on the same graph model. The BFS tree has the property that the computed path will be a shortest path from the entrance. However BFS is more difficult to implement than DFS since in DFS, the compiler implicitly handles the DFS stack, whereas in BFS, the queue has to be explicitly coded. Since the problem did not call for a shortest path, it is better to use DFS.

```cpp
typedef enum { WHITE, BLACK } Color;
struct Coordinate {
  bool operator==(const Coordinate& that) const {
    return x == that.x && y == that.y;
  }

  int x, y;
};

vector<Coordinate> SearchMaze(vector<vector<Color>> maze, const Coordinate& s,
                              const Coordinate& e) {
  vector<Coordinate> path;
  maze[s.x][s.y] = BLACK;
  path.emplace_back(s);
  if (!SearchMazeHelper(s, e, &maze, &path)) {
    path.pop_back();
  }
  return path;  // Empty path means no path between s and e.
}

// Perform DFS to find a feasible path.
bool SearchMazeHelper(const Coordinate& cur, const Coordinate& e,
                      vector<vector<Color>>* maze, vector<Coordinate>* path) {
  if (cur == e) {
    return true;
  }

  const array<array<int, 2>, 4> kShift = {{{0, 1}, {0, -1}, {1, 0}, {-1, 0}}};
  for (const array<int, 2>& s : kShift) {
    Coordinate next{cur.x + s[0], cur.y + s[1]};
    if (IsFeasible(next, *maze)) {
      (*maze)[next.x][next.y] = BLACK;
      path->emplace_back(next);
      if (SearchMazeHelper(next, e, maze, path)) {
        return true;
      }
      path->pop_back();
    }
  }
  return false;
```

```
}
```

```
// Checks cur is within maze and is a white pixel.
bool IsFeasible(const Coordinate& cur, const vector<vector<Color>>& maze) {
    return cur.x >= 0 && cur.x < maze.size() && cur.y >= 0 &&
           cur.y < maze[cur.x].size() && maze[cur.x][cur.y] == WHITE;
}
```

The time complexity is the same as that for DFS, namely $O(|V| + |E|)$.

19.2 PAINT A BOOLEAN MATRIX

Let A be a Boolean 2D array encoding a black-and-white image. The entry $A(a, b)$ can be viewed as encoding the color at entry (a, b). Call two entries adjacent if one is to the left, right, above or below the other. Note that the definition implies that an entry can be adjacent to at most four other entries, and that adjacency is symmetric, i.e., if $e0$ is adjacent to entry $e1$, then $e1$ is adjacent to $e0$.

Define a path from entry $e0$ to entry $e1$ to be a sequence of adjacent entries, starting at $e0$, ending at $e1$, with successive entries being adjacent. Define the region associated with a point (i, j) to be all points (i', j') such that there exists a path from (i, j) to (i', j') in which all entries are the same color. In particular this implies (i, j) and (i', j') must be the same color.

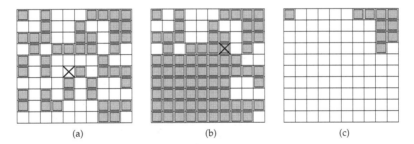

Figure 19.6: The color of all squares associated with the first square marked with a × in (a) have been recolored to yield the coloring in (b). The same process yields the coloring in (c).

Implement a routine that takes an $n \times m$ Boolean array A together with an entry (x, y) and flips the color of the region associated with (x, y). See Figure 19.6 for an example of flipping.

Hint: Solve this conceptually, then think about implementation optimizations.

Solution: As with Solution 19.1 on Page 351, graph search can overcome the complexity of enumerative and random search solutions. Specifically, entries can be viewed as vertices, with vertices corresponding to adjacent entries begin connected by edges.

For the current problem, we are searching for all vertices whose color is the same as that of (x, y) that are reachable from (x, y). Breadth-first search is natural when starting with a set of vertices. Specifically, we can use a queue to store such vertices. The queue is initialized to (x, y). The queue is popped iteratively. Call the popped point p. First, we record p's initial color, and then flip its color. Next we examine p neighbors. Any neighbor which is the same color as p's initial color is added to the queue. The computation ends when the queue is empty. Correctness follows from the fact that any point that is added to the queue is reachable from (x, y) via a path consisting of points of the same color, and all points reachable from (x, y) via points of the same color will eventually be added to the queue.

```
void FlipColor(int x, int y, vector<deque<bool>>* A_ptr) {
  vector<deque<bool>>& A = *A_ptr;
  const array<array<int, 2>, 4> kDirs = {
      {{{0, 1}}, {{0, -1}}, {{1, 0}}, {{-1, 0}}}};
  const bool color = A[x][y];

  struct Coordinate {
    int x, y;
  };
  queue<Coordinate> q;
  A[x][y] = !color;  // Flips.
  q.emplace(Coordinate{x, y});
  while (!q.empty()) {
    Coordinate curr = q.front();
    for (const array<int, 2>& dir : kDirs) {
      const int next_x = curr.x + dir[0], next_y = curr.y + dir[1];
      if (next_x >= 0 && next_x < A.size() && next_y >= 0 &&
          next_y < A[next_x].size() && A[next_x][next_y] == color) {
        // Flips the color.
        A[next_x][next_y] = !color;
        q.emplace(Coordinate{next_x, next_y});
      }
    }
    q.pop();
  }
}
```

The time complexity is the same as that of BFS, i.e., $O(mn)$. The space complexity is a little better than the worst-case for BFS, since there are at most $O(m + n)$ vertices that are at the same distance from a given entry.

We also provide a recursive solution which is in the spirit of DFS. It does not need a queue but implicitly uses a stack, namely the function call stack.

```
void FlipColor(int x, int y, vector<deque<bool>>* A_ptr) {
  vector<deque<bool>>& A = *A_ptr;
  const array<array<int, 2>, 4> kDirs = {
      {{{0, 1}}, {{0, -1}}, {{1, 0}}, {{-1, 0}}}};
  const bool color = A[x][y];

  A[x][y] = !color;  // Flips.
  for (const array<int, 2>& dir : kDirs) {
    const int next_x = x + dir[0], next_y = y + dir[1];
    if (next_x >= 0 && next_x < A.size() && next_y >= 0 &&
```

353

```
        next_y < A[next_x].size() && A[next_x][next_y] == color) {
      FlipColor(next_x, next_y, A_ptr);
    }
  }
}
```

The time complexity is the same as that of DFS.

Both the algorithms given above differ slightly from traditional BFS and DFS algorithms. The reason is that we have a color field already available, and hence do not need the auxiliary color field traditionally associated with vertices BFS and DFS. Furthermore, since we are simply determining reachability, we only need two colors, whereas BFS and DFS traditionally use three colors to track state. (The use of an additional color makes it possible, for example, to answer questions about cycles in directed graphs, but that is not relevant here.)

Variant: Design an algorithm for computing the black region that contains the most points.

Variant: Design an algorithm that takes a point (a, b), sets $A(a, b)$ to black, and returns the size of the black region that contains the most points. Assume this algorithm will be called multiple times, and you want to keep the aggregate run time as low as possible.

19.3 COMPUTE ENCLOSED REGIONS

This problem is concerned with computing regions within a 2D grid that are enclosed. See Figure 19.7 for an illustration of the problem.

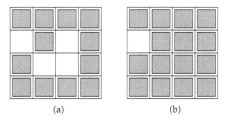

(a)   (b)

Figure 19.7: Three of the four white squares in (a) are *enclosed*, i.e., there is no path from any of them to the boundary that only passes through white squares. (b) shows the white squares that are not enclosed.

The computational problem can be formalized using 2D arrays of Bs (blacks) and Ws (whites). Figure 19.7(a) is encoded by

$$A = \begin{bmatrix} B & B & B & B \\ W & B & W & B \\ B & W & W & B \\ B & B & B & B \end{bmatrix}.$$

Figure 19.7(b) on the preceding page is encoded by

$$\begin{bmatrix} B & B & B & B \\ W & B & B & B \\ B & B & B & B \\ B & B & B & B \end{bmatrix}.$$

Let A be a 2D array whose entries are either W or B. Write a program that takes A, and replaces all Ws that cannot reach the boundary with a B.

Hint: It is easier to compute the complement of the desired result.

Solution: It is easier to focus on the inverse problem, namely identifying Ws that can reach the boundary. The reason that the inverse is simpler is that if a W is adjacent to a W that is can reach the boundary, then the first W can reach it too. The Ws on the boundary are the initial set. Subsequently, we find Ws neighboring the boundary Ws, and iteratively grow the set. Whenever we find a new W that can reach the boundary, we need to record it, and at some stage search for new Ws from it. A queue is a reasonable data structure to track Ws to be processed. The approach amounts to breadth-first search starting with a set of vertices rather than a single vertex.

```cpp
void FillSurroundedRegions(vector<vector<char>>* board) {
  if (board->empty()) {
    return;
  }

  vector<deque<bool>> visited(board->size(),
                    deque<bool>(board->front().size(), false));
  for (size_t i = 1; i < board->size() - 1; ++i) {
    for (size_t j = 1; j < (*board)[i].size() - 1; ++j) {
      if ((*board)[i][j] == 'W' && !visited[i][j]) {
        MarkRegionIfSurrounded(i, j, board, &visited);
      }
    }
  }
}


void MarkRegionIfSurrounded(int i, int j, vector<vector<char>>* board,
                    vector<deque<bool>>* visited) {
  struct Coordinate {
    int x, y;
  };
  vector<Coordinate> q;  // Uses it as an queue.
  q.emplace_back(Coordinate{i, j}), (*visited)[i][j] = true;
  bool is_surrounded = true;
  size_t idx = 0;
  // Uses BFS to traverse this region.
  while (idx < q.size()) {
    const auto curr = q[idx++];
    // A 'W' on the border means this region is not surrounded.
    if (curr.x == 0 || curr.x == board->size() - 1 || curr.y == 0 ||
```

```
        curr.y == (*board)[curr.x].size() - 1) {
      is_surrounded = false;
    } else {
      const static array<array<int, 2>, 4> kDirs = {
          {{0, 1}, {0, -1}, {1, 0}, {-1, 0}}};
      for (const array<int, 2>& d : kDirs) {
        const Coordinate next = Coordinate{curr.x + d[0], curr.y + d[1]};
        if ((*board)[next.x][next.y] == 'W' && !(*visited)[next.x][next.y]) {
          (*visited)[next.x][next.y] = true;
          q.emplace_back(next);
        }
      }
    }
  }

  if (is_surrounded) {
    // Marks surrounded regions in q.
    for (const Coordinate& p : q) {
      (*board)[p.x][p.y] = 'B';
    }
  }
}
```

The time and space complexity are the same as those for BFS, namely $O(mn)$, where m and n are the number of rows and columns in A.

19.4 DEGREES OF CONNECTEDNESS—1

A *connected graph* is one in which for any two vertices u and v there exists a path from u to v. The notion of connectedness holds for both directed and undirected graphs—for undirected graphs, we sometimes simply say there exists a path between u and v.

Intuitively, some graphs are more connected than others—e.g., a clique (an undirected graph in which every two vertices are connected by an edge) is more connected than a tree. To be more quantitative, a graph is defined to be minimally-connected if it is connected and there is no edge that can be removed while still leaving the graph connected. For example, the undirected graph in Figure 19.4 on Page 350 is minimally-connected.

Write a program that takes as input an undirected graph, which you can assume to be connected, and checks if the graph is minimally-connected.

Hint: Think about cycles.

Solution: Let the input graph be $G = (V, E)$, and assume G is undirected and connected. Since DFS or BFS can be easily used to see if a graph is connected, a brute-force approach would be to test for each edge whether its removal leaves a connected graph. The time complexity is $O(|E|(|V| + |E|))$—we make $|E|$ calls to graph search in the worst case.

Looking at the problem more carefully, note that if the graph remains connected after we remove the edge (u, v) it means that it must be that there is path between

u and v in the original graph that does not use (u, v). This is possible if and only if u and v lie on a cycle in G. Thus we have reduced the problem of checking if G is minimally-connected to the checking if there exists a cycle in G.

We can check for the existence of a cycle in G by running DFS on G. Recall DFS maintains a color for each vertex. Initially, all vertices are white. When a vertex is first discovered, it is colored gray. When DFS finishes processing a vertex, that vertex is colored black.

As soon as we discover an edge from a gray vertex back to a gray vertex which is not its immediate predecessor in the search, a cycle exists in G and we can stop.

```cpp
struct GraphVertex {
  enum Color { white, gray, black } color;
  vector<GraphVertex*> edges;
};

bool IsGraphMinimallyConnected(vector<GraphVertex>* G) {
  return G->empty() || !HasCycle(&G->front(), nullptr);
}

bool HasCycle(GraphVertex* cur, const GraphVertex* pre) {
  // Visiting a gray vertex means a cycle.
  if (cur->color == GraphVertex::gray) {
    return true;
  }

  cur->color = GraphVertex::gray;  // marks current vertex as a gray one.
  // Traverse the neighbor vertices.
  for (GraphVertex*& next : cur->edges) {
    if (next != pre && next->color != GraphVertex::black) {
      if (HasCycle(next, cur)) {
        return true;
      }
    }
  }
  cur->color = GraphVertex::black;  // marks current vertex as black.
  return false;
}
```

In general, the time complexity of DFS is $O(|V|+|E|)$. However, the algorithm described above has time complexity $O(|V|)$. This is because an undirected graph with no cycles can have at most $|V| - 1$ edges.

Variant: Solve the minimally-connected problem for an undirected graph using only two colors per vertex. (Do not use auxiliary data structures such as hash tables to mimic the third color.)

19.5 CLONE A GRAPH

Consider a vertex type for a directed graph in which there are two fields: an integer label and a list of references to other vertices. Design an algorithm that takes a reference to a vertex u, and creates a copy of the graph on the vertices reachable from u. Return the copy of u.

Hint: Maintain a map from vertices in the original graph to their counterparts in the clone.

Solution: We traverse the graph starting from u. Each time we encounter a vertex or an edge that is not yet in the clone, we add it to the clone. We recognize new vertices by maintaining a hash table mapping vertices in the original graph to their counterparts in the new graph. Any standard graph traversal algorithm works—the code below uses breadth first search.

```
struct GraphVertex {
  int label;
  vector<GraphVertex*> edges;
};

GraphVertex* CloneGraph(GraphVertex* G) {
  if (!G) {
    return nullptr;
  }

  unordered_map<GraphVertex*, GraphVertex*> vertex_map;
  queue<GraphVertex*> q;
  q.emplace(G);
  vertex_map.emplace(G, new GraphVertex({G->label}));
  while (!q.empty()) {
    auto v = q.front();
    q.pop();
    for (GraphVertex* e : v->edges) {
      // Try to copy vertex e.
      if (vertex_map.find(e) == vertex_map.end()) {
        vertex_map.emplace(e, new GraphVertex({e->label}));
        q.emplace(e);
      }
      // Copy edge v->e.
      vertex_map[v]->edges.emplace_back(vertex_map[e]);
    }
  }
  return vertex_map[G];
}
```

The space complexity is $O(|V| + |E|)$, which is the space taken by the result. Excluding the space for the result, the space complexity is $O(|V|)$—this comes from the hash table, as well as the BFS queue.

19.6 MAKING WIRED CONNECTIONS

Consider a collection of electrical pins on a printed circuit board (PCB). For each pair of pins, there may or may not be a wire joining them. This is shown in Figure 19.8 on the following page, where vertices correspond to pins, and edges indicate the presence of a wire between pins. (The significance of the colors is explained later.)

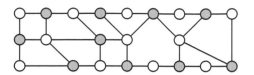

Figure 19.8: A set of pins and wires between them.

Design an algorithm that takes a set of pins and a set of wires connecting pairs of pins, and determines if it is possible to place some pins on the left half of a PCB, and the remainder on the right half, such that each wire is between left and right halves. Return such a division, if one exists. For example, the light vertices and dark vertices in Figure 19.8 are such division.

Hint: Model as a graph and think about the implication of an odd length cycle.

Solution: A brute-force approach might be to try all partitions of the pins into two sets. However, the number of such partitions is very high.

A better approach is to use connectivity information to guide the partitioning. Assume the pins are numbered from 0 to $p - 1$. Create an undirected graph G whose vertices are the pins. Add an edge between pairs of vertices if the corresponding pins are connected by a wire. For simplicity, assume G is connected; if not, the connected components can be analyzed independently.

Run BFS on G beginning with any vertex v_0. Assign v_0 arbitrarily to lie on the left half. All vertices at an odd distance from v_0 are assigned to the right half.

When performing BFS on an undirected graph, all newly discovered edges will either be from vertices which are at a distance d from v_0 to undiscovered vertices (which will then be at a distance $d + 1$ from v_0) or from vertices which are at a distance d to vertices which are also at a distance d. First, assume we never encounter an edge from a distance k vertex to a distance k vertex. In this case, each wire is from a distance k vertex to a distance $k + 1$ vertex, so all wires are between the left and right halves.

If any edge is from a distance k vertex to a distance k vertex, we stop—the pins cannot be partitioned into left and right halves as desired. The reason is as follows. Let u and v be such vertices. Consider the first common ancestor a in the BFS tree of u and v (such an ancestor must exist since the search started at v_0). The paths p_u and p_v in the BFS tree from a to u and v are of equal length; therefore, the cycle formed by going from a to u via p_u, then through the edge (u, v), and then back to a from v via p_v has an odd length. A cycle in which the vertices can be partitioned into two sets must have an even number of edges—it has to go back and forth between the sets and terminate at the starting vertex, and each back and forth adds two edges. Therefore, the vertices in an odd length cycle cannot be partitioned into two sets such that all edges are between the sets.

```
struct GraphVertex {
    int d = -1;
    vector<GraphVertex*> edges;
```

```
};

bool IsAnyPlacementFeasible(vector<GraphVertex>* G) {
  for (GraphVertex& v : *G) {
    if (v.d == -1) {  // Unvisited vertex.
      v.d = 0;
      if (!BFS(&v)) {
        return false;
      }
    }
  }
  return true;
}

bool BFS(GraphVertex* s) {
  queue<GraphVertex*> q;
  q.emplace(s);

  while (!q.empty()) {
    for (GraphVertex*& t : q.front()->edges) {
      if (t->d == -1) {  // Unvisited vertex.
        t->d = q.front()->d + 1;
        q.emplace(t);
      } else if (t->d == q.front()->d) {
        return false;
      }
    }
    q.pop();
  }
  return true;
}
```

The complexity is the same as for BFS, i.e., $O(p + w)$ time complexity, where w is the number of wires, and $O(p)$ space complexity.

Graphs that can be partitioned as described above are known as bipartite graphs. Another term for such graphs is 2-colorable (since the vertices can be assigned one of two colors without neighboring vertices having the same color).

19.7 TRANSFORM ONE STRING TO ANOTHER

Let s and t be strings and D a dictionary, i.e., a set of strings. Define s to *produce* t if there exists a sequence of strings from the dictionary $P = \langle s_0, s_1, \ldots, s_{n-1} \rangle$ such that the first string is s, the last string is t, and adjacent strings have the same length and differ in exactly one character. The sequence P is called a *production sequence*. For example, if the dictionary is {bat, cot, dog, dag, dot, cat}, then $\langle$cat, cot, dot, dog$\rangle$ is production sequence.

Given a dictionary D and two strings s and t, write a program to determine if s produces t. Assume that all characters are lowercase alphabets. If s does produce t, output the length of a shortest production sequence; otherwise, output -1.

360

Hint: Treat strings as vertices in an undirected graph, with an edge between *u* and *v* if and only if the corresponding strings differ in one character.

Solution: A brute-force approach may be to explore all strings that differ in one character from the starting string, then two characters from the starting string, etc. The problem with this approach is that it may explore lots of strings that are outside the dictionary.

A better approach is to be more focused on dictionary words. In particular, it's natural to model this problem using graphs. The vertices correspond to strings from the dictionary and the edge (u, v) indicates that the strings corresponding to *u* and *v* differ in exactly one character. Note that the relation "differs in one character" is symmetric, so the graph is undirected.

For the given example, the vertices would be {bat, cot, dog, dag, dot, cat}, and the edges would be {(bat, cat), (cot, dot), (cot, cat), (dog, dag), (dog, dot)}.

A production sequence is simply a path in *G*, so what we need is a shortest path from *s* to *t* in *G*. Shortest paths in an undirected graph are naturally computed using BFS.

```cpp
// Uses BFS to find the least steps of transformation.
int TransformString(unordered_set<string> D, const string& s,
                    const string& t) {
  struct StringWithDistance {
    string candidate_string;
    int distance;
  };
  queue<StringWithDistance> q;
  D.erase(s);   // Marks s as visited by erasing it in D.
  q.emplace(StringWithDistance{s, 0});

  while (!q.empty()) {
    StringWithDistance f(q.front());
    // Returns if we find a match.
    if (f.candidate_string == t) {
      return f.distance;   // Number of steps reaches t.
    }

    // Tries all possible transformations of f.candidate_string.
    string str = f.candidate_string;
    for (int i = 0; i < str.size(); ++i) {
      for (int j = 0; j < 26; ++j) {  // Iterates through 'a' ~ 'z'.
        str[i] = 'a' + j;
        auto it(D.find(str));
        if (it != D.end()) {
          D.erase(it);
          q.emplace(StringWithDistance{str, f.distance + 1});
        }
      }
      str[i] = f.candidate_string[i];   // Reverts the change of str.
    }
    q.pop();
  }
```

361

```
        return -1;   // Cannot find a possible transformations.
}
```

The number of vertices is the number d of words in the dictionary. The number of edges is, in the worst-case, $O(d^2)$. The time complexity is that of BFS, namely $O(d + d^2) = O(d^2)$. If the string length n is less than d then the maximum number of edges out of a vertex is $O(n)$, implying an $O(nd)$ bound.

19.8 ADDITION CHAIN EXPONENTIATION

An addition chain exponentiation program for computing x^n is a finite sequence $\langle x, x^{i_1}, x^{i_2}, \ldots, x^n \rangle$ where each element after the first is either the square of some previous element or the product of any two previous elements. For example, the term x^{15} can be computed by the following two addition chain exponentiation programs.

$$P1 \quad = \quad \langle x, x^2 = (x)^2, x^4 = (x^2)^2, x^8 = (x^4)^2, x^{12} = x^8 x^4, x^{14} = x^{12} x^2, x^{15} = x^{14} x \rangle$$
$$P2 \quad = \quad \langle x, x^2 = (x)^2, x^3 = x^2 x, x^5 = x^3 x^2, x^{10} = (x^5)^2, x^{15} = x^{10} x^5 \rangle$$

It is not obvious, but the second program, P2, is the shortest addition chain exponentiation program for computing x^{15}.

Given a positive integer n, how would you compute a shortest addition chain exponentiation program to evaluate x^n?

Hint: Find a shortest addition chain exponentiation program for x^k given shortest programs for x^i, for all $i < k$.

Solution: Here is a brute-force approach that is surprisingly fast. Compute all addition chain exponentiation programs of length k, in increasing order of k. For $k = 1$, there is only one shortest program, namely, $\langle x \rangle$. We maintain a queue of programs ordered by length. We iteratively pop the queue. Suppose we pop a program D of length k. We try all combinations of elements in D to get length $k + 1$ programs, which we add to the back of the queue.

Note that this process yields addition chain exponentiation programs that are not necessarily optimum. However, since we are systematically exploring programs in order of length, the *first* time we encounter an addition chain exponentiation program yielding n, it must be a shortest addition chain exponentiation program.

Code implementing this idea is presented below. Note the close resemblance to breadth-first search. Indeed, the algorithm can be viewed as BFS on the graph of all programs, where an edge exists from D to D' if D' is D followed by an element which derived from previous elements of D.

```
vector<int> ShortestAdditionChain(int n) {
  if (n == 1) {
    return {1};
  }
```

```
queue<vector<int>> addition_chains;
// Constructs the initial addition_chain with one node whose value is 1.
addition_chains.emplace(1, 1);
while (!addition_chains.empty()) {
  vector<int> candidate_addition_chain = addition_chains.front();
  addition_chains.pop();
  // Tries all possible combinations in candidate_addition_chain.
  for (int a : candidate_addition_chain) {
    int power = a + candidate_addition_chain.back();
    if (power > n) {
      break;  // No possible solution for candidate_addition_chain.
    }
    vector<int> new_addition_chain(candidate_addition_chain);
    new_addition_chain.emplace_back(power);

    if (power == n) {
      return new_addition_chain;
    }
    addition_chains.emplace(new_addition_chain);
  }
}
}
```

This program is heuristic, and we cannot give a nontrivial bound on its time complexity. No efficient optimal methods are currently known for arbitrary exponents, and the related problem of finding a shortest addition chain for a given set of exponents is known to be NP-complete.

Advanced graph algorithms

Up to this point we looked at basic search and combinatorial properties of graphs. The algorithms we considered were all linear time complexity and relatively straightforward—the major challenge was in modeling the problem appropriately.

There are four classes of complex graph problems that can be solved efficiently, i.e., in polynomial time. Most other problems on graphs are either variants of these or, very likely, not solvable by polynomial time algorithms. These four classes are:

- *Shortest path*—given a graph, directed or undirected, with costs on the edges, find the minimum cost path from a given vertex to all vertices. Variants include computing the shortest paths for all pairs of vertices, and the case where costs are all nonnegative.
- *Minimum spanning tree*—given an undirected graph $G = (V, E)$, assumed to be connected, with weights on each edge, find a subset E' of the edges with minimum total weight such that the subgraph $G' = (V, E')$ is connected.
- *Matching*—given an undirected graph, find a maximum collection of edges subject to the constraint that every vertex is incident to at most one edge. The matching problem for bipartite graphs is especially common and the algorithm for this problem is much simpler than for the general case. A common variant

is the maximum weighted matching problem in which edges have weights and a maximum weight edge set is sought, subject to the matching constraint.

- *Maximum flow*—given a directed graph with a capacity for each edge, find the maximum flow from a given source to a given sink, where a flow is a function mapping edges to numbers satisfying conservation (flow into a vertex equals the flow out of it) and the edge capacities. The minimum cost circulation problem generalizes the maximum flow problem by adding lower bounds on edge capacities, and for each edge, a cost per unit flow.

These four problem classes have polynomial time algorithms and can be solved efficiently in practice for very large graphs. Algorithms for these problems tend to be specialized, and the natural approach does not always work best. For example, it is natural to apply divide-and-conquer to compute the MST as follows. Partition the vertex set into two subsets, compute MSTs for the subsets independently, and then join these two MSTs with an edge of minimum weight between them. Figure 19.9 shows how this algorithm can lead to suboptimal results.

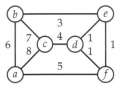 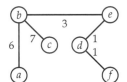 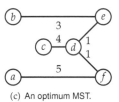

| (a) A weighted undirected graph. | (b) An MST built by divide-and-conquer from the MSTs on $\{a, b, c\}$ and $\{d, e, f\}$. The edge (b, e) is the lightest edge connecting the two MSTs. | (c) An optimum MST. |

Figure 19.9: Divide-and-conquer applied to the MST problem is suboptimum—the MST in (b) has weight 18, but the MST in (c) has weight 14.

In this chapter we restrict our attention to shortest-path problems.

19.9 TEAM PHOTO DAY—2

How would you generalize your solution to Problem 14.9 on Page 244, to determine the largest number of teams that can be photographed simultaneously subject to the same constraints?

Hint: Form a DAG in which paths correspond to valid placements.

Solution: Let G be the DAG with vertices corresponding to the teams as follows and edges from vertex X to Y iff Team X can be placed behind Team Y.

Every sequence of teams where a team can be placed behind its predecessor corresponds to a path in G. To find the longest such sequence, we simply need to find the longest path in the DAG G. We can do this, for example, by topologically ordering the vertices in G; the longest path terminating at vertex v is the maximum of the longest paths terminating at v's fan-ins concatenated with v itself.

```
struct GraphVertex {
  vector<GraphVertex*> edges;
  int max_distance = 1;
  bool visited = false;
};


int FindLargestNumberTeams(vector<GraphVertex>* G) {
  stack<GraphVertex*> vertex_order(BuildTopologicalOrdering(G));
  return FindLongestPath(&vertex_order);
}

stack<GraphVertex*> BuildTopologicalOrdering(vector<GraphVertex>* G) {
  stack<GraphVertex*> vertex_order;
  for (auto& g : *G) {
    if (!g.visited) {
      DFS(&g, &vertex_order);
    }
  }
  return vertex_order;
}


int FindLongestPath(stack<GraphVertex*>* vertex_order) {
  int max_distance = 0;
  while (!vertex_order->empty()) {
    GraphVertex* u = vertex_order->top();
    max_distance = max(max_distance, u->max_distance);
    for (GraphVertex*& v : u->edges) {
      v->max_distance = max(v->max_distance, u->max_distance + 1);
    }
    vertex_order->pop();
  }
  return max_distance;
}

void DFS(GraphVertex* cur, stack<GraphVertex*>* vertex_order) {
  cur->visited = true;
  for (GraphVertex* next : cur->edges) {
    if (!next->visited) {
      DFS(next, vertex_order);
    }
  }
  vertex_order->emplace(cur);
}
```

The topological ordering computation is $O(|V| + |E|)$ and dominates the computation time. Clearly $|V|$ is the number of teams. The number of edges E depends on the heights, but can be as high as $O(|V|^2)$, e.g., when there is a path of length $|V| - 1$.

19.10 COMPUTE A SHORTEST PATH WITH FEWEST EDGES

In the usual formulation of the shortest path problem, the number of edges in the path is not a consideration. For example, considering the shortest path problem from *a* to *h* in Figure 19.1 on Page 348, the sum of the edge costs on the path $\langle a, c, e, d, h \rangle$ is 22, which is the same as for path $\langle a, b, k, i, j, f, g, h \rangle$. Both are shortest paths, but the latter has three more edges.

Heuristically, if we did want to avoid paths with a large number of edges, we can add a small amount to the cost of each edge. However, depending on the structure of the graph and the edge costs, this may not result in the shortest path.

Design an algorithm which takes as input a graph $G = (V, E)$, directed or undirected, a nonnegative cost function on E, and vertices s and t; your algorithm should output a path with the fewest edges amongst all shortest paths from s to t.

Hint: Change the edge cost and cast it as an instance of the standard shortest path problem.

Solution: Dijkstra's shortest path algorithm uses scalar values for edge length. However, it can easily be modified to the case where the edge weight is a pair if *addition* and *comparison* can be defined over these pairs. In this case, if the edge cost is c, we say the length of the edge is given by the pair $(c, 1)$. We define addition to be just component-wise addition. Hence, if we sum up the edge lengths over a path, we essentially get the total cost and the number of edges in the path. The compare function first compares the total cost, and breaks ties on the number of edges. We can run Dijkstra's shortest path algorithm with this compare function and find the shortest path that requires the least number of edges.

Since a heap does not support efficient updates, it is more convenient to use a BST than a heap to implement the algorithm.

```
struct GraphVertex {
  struct DistanceWithFewestEdges {
    int distance, min_num_edges;
  };
  DistanceWithFewestEdges distance_with_fewest_edges =
      DistanceWithFewestEdges{numeric_limits<int>::max(), 0};

  struct VertexWithDistance {
    GraphVertex& vertex;
    int distance;
  };
  vector<VertexWithDistance> edges;
  int id;  // The id of this vertex.
  const GraphVertex* pred = nullptr;  // The predecessor in the shortest path.
};

struct Comp {
  bool operator()(const GraphVertex* lhs, const GraphVertex* rhs) {
    return lhs->distance_with_fewest_edges.distance <
              rhs->distance_with_fewest_edges.distance ||
          (lhs->distance_with_fewest_edges.distance ==
              rhs->distance_with_fewest_edges.distance &&
            lhs->distance_with_fewest_edges.min_num_edges <
              rhs->distance_with_fewest_edges.min_num_edges);
  }
};
```

```
void DijkstraShortestPath(GraphVertex* s, const GraphVertex* t) {
  // Initialization of the distance of starting point.
  s->distance_with_fewest_edges = {0, 0};
  set<GraphVertex*, Comp> node_set;
  node_set.emplace(s);

  while (!node_set.empty()) {
    // Extracts the minimum distance vertex from heap.
    GraphVertex* u = *node_set.cbegin();
    if (u->id == t->id) {
      break;
    }
    node_set.erase(node_set.cbegin());

    // Relax neighboring vertices of u.
    for (const GraphVertex::VertexWithDistance& v : u->edges) {
      int v_distance = u->distance_with_fewest_edges.distance + v.distance;
      int v_num_edges = u->distance_with_fewest_edges.min_num_edges + 1;
      if (v.vertex.distance_with_fewest_edges.distance > v_distance ||
          (v.vertex.distance_with_fewest_edges.distance == v_distance &&
             v.vertex.distance_with_fewest_edges.min_num_edges > v_num_edges)) {
        node_set.erase(&v.vertex);
        v.vertex.pred = u;
        v.vertex.distance_with_fewest_edges = {v_distance, v_num_edges};
        node_set.emplace(&v.vertex);
      }
    }
  }

  // Outputs the shortest path with fewest edges.
  OutputShortestPath(t);
}

void OutputShortestPath(const GraphVertex* v) {
  if (v) {
    OutputShortestPath(v->pred);
    cout << v >id << " ";
  }
}
```

The time complexity is that of the basic implementation of Dijkstra's algorithm, i.e., $O((|E| + |V|) \log |V|)$.

Variant: A flight is specified by a start-time, originating city, destination city, and arrival-time (possibly on a later day). A time-table is a set of flights. Given a time-table, a starting city, a starting time, and a destination city, how would you compute the soonest you could get to the destination city? Assume all flights start and end on time, that you need 60 minutes between flights, and a flight departing from A to B cannot arrive earlier at B than another flight from A to B which departed earlier.

20

Parallel Computing

> *The activity of a computer must include the proper reacting to a possibly great variety of messages that can be sent to it at unpredictable moments, a situation which occurs in all information systems in which a number of computers are coupled to each other.*
>
> — *"Cooperating sequential processes,"*
> E. W. DIJKSTRA, 1965

Parallel computation has become increasingly common. For example, laptops and desktops come with multiple processors which communicate through shared memory. High-end computation is often done using clusters consisting of individual computers communicating through a network.

Parallelism provides a number of benefits:

- High performance—more processors working on a task (usually) means it is completed faster.
- Better use of resources—a program can execute while another waits on the disk or network.
- Fairness—letting different users or programs share a machine rather than have one program run at a time to completion.
- Convenience—it is often conceptually more straightforward to do a task using a set of concurrent programs for the subtasks rather than have a single program manage all the subtasks.
- Fault tolerance—if a machine fails in a cluster that is serving web pages, the others can take over.

Concrete applications of parallel computing include graphical user interfaces (GUI) (a dedicated thread handles UI actions while other threads are, for example, busy doing network communication and passing results to the UI thread, resulting in increased responsiveness), Java virtual machines (a separate thread handles garbage collection which would otherwise lead to blocking, while another thread is busy running the user code), web servers (a single logical thread handles a single client request), scientific computing (a large matrix multiplication can be split across a cluster), and web search (multiple machines crawl, index, and retrieve web pages).

The two primary models for parallel computation are the shared memory model, in which each processor can access any location in memory, and the distributed memory model, in which a processor must explicitly send a message to another processor to access its memory. The former is more appropriate in the multicore setting and the latter is more accurate for a cluster. The questions in this chapter are mostly focused on the shared memory model. We cover a few problems related to the distributed memory model, such as leader election and sorting large data sets, at the end of the chapter.

Writing correct parallel programs is challenging because of the subtle interactions between parallel components. One of the key challenges is races—two concurrent instruction sequences access the same address in memory and at least one of them writes to that address. Other challenges to correctness are

- starvation (a processor needs a resource but never gets it; e.g., Problem 20.7 on Page 378),
- deadlock (Thread A acquires Lock $L1$ and Thread B acquires Lock $L2$, following which A tries to acquire $L2$ and B tries to acquire $L1$), and
- livelock (a processor keeps retrying an operation that always fails).

Bugs caused by these issues are difficult to find using testing. Debugging them is also difficult because they may not be reproducible since they are usually load dependent. It is also often true that it is not possible to realize the performance implied by parallelism—sometimes a critical task cannot be parallelized, making it impossible to improve performance, regardless of the number of processors added. Similarly, the overhead of communicating intermediate results between processors can exceed the performance benefits.

20.1 IMPLEMENT CACHING FOR A MULTITHREADED DICTIONARY

The program below is part of an online spell correction service. Clients send as input a string, and the service returns an array of strings in its dictionary that are closest to the input string (this array could be computed, for example, using Solution 17.2 on Page 304). The service caches results to improve performance. Critique the implementation and provide a solution that overcomes its limitations.

```
public static class UnsafeSpellCheckService extends SpellCheckService {
  private static final int MAX_ENTRIES = 3;

  private static LinkedHashMap<String, String[]> cachedClosestStrings
      = new LinkedHashMap<String, String[]>() {
        protected boolean removeEldestEntry(Map.Entry eldest) {
          return size() > MAX_ENTRIES;
        }
      };

  public static void service(ServiceRequest req, ServiceResponse resp) {
    String w = req.extractWordToCheckFromRequest();
    if (cachedClosestStrings.containsKey(w)) {
      resp.encodeIntoResponse(cachedClosestStrings.get(w));
      return;
    }
    String[] closestToLastWord = Spell.closestInDictionary(w);
    cachedClosestStrings.put(w, closestToLastWord);
  }
}
```

Hint: Look for races, and lock as little as possible to avoid reducing throughput.

Solution: The solution has a race condition. Suppose clients *A* and *B* make concurrent requests, and the service launches a thread per request. Suppose the thread for request *A* finds that the input string is present in the cache, and then, immediately after that check, the thread for request *B* is scheduled. Suppose this thread's lookup fails, so it computes the result, and adds it to the cache. If the cache is full, an entry will be evicted, and this may be the result for the string passed in request *A*. Now when request *A* is scheduled back, it does a lookup for the value corresponding to its input string, expecting it to be present (since it checked that that string is a key in the cache). However, the cache will return null.

A thread-safe solution would be to synchronize every call to the service. In this case, only one thread could be executing the method and there is no races between cache reads and writes. However, it also leads to poor performance—only one thread can execute the service call at a time.

The solution is to lock just the part of the code that operates on the cached values—specifically, the check on the cached value and the updates to the cached values:

In the program below, multiple threads can be concurrently computing closest strings. This is good because the calls take a long time (this is why they are cached). Locking ensures that the read assignment on a hit and write assignment on completion are atomic.

```
public static class SafeSpellCheckService extends SpellCheckService {
  private static final int MAX_ENTRIES = 3;

  private static LinkedHashMap<String, String[]> cachedClosestStrings
    = new LinkedHashMap<String, String[]>() {
        protected boolean removeEldestEntry(Map.Entry eldest) {
          return size() > MAX_ENTRIES;
        }
      };

  public static void service(ServiceRequest req, ServiceResponse resp) {
    String w = req.extractWordToCheckFromRequest();
    synchronized (S2Alternative.class) {
      if (cachedClosestStrings.containsKey(w)) {
        resp.encodeIntoResponse(cachedClosestStrings.get(w));
        return;
      }
    }
    String[] closestToLastWord = Spell.closestInDictionary(w);
    synchronized (S2Alternative.class) {
      cachedClosestStrings.put(w, closestToLastWord);
    }
  }
}
```

Variant: Threads 1 to *n* execute a method called `critical`. Before this, they execute a method called `rendezvous`. The synchronization constraint is that only one thread

370

can execute `critical` at a time, and all threads must have completed executing `rendezvous` before `critical` can be called. You can assume n is stored in a variable n that is accessible from all threads. Design a synchronization mechanism for the threads. All threads must execute the same code. Threads may call `critical` multiple times, and you should ensure that a thread cannot call `critical` a $(k+1)$th time until all other threads have completed their kth calls to `critical`.

20.2 ANALYZE TWO UNSYNCHRONIZED INTERLEAVED THREADS

Threads $t1$ and $t2$ each increment an integer variable `counter` N times, as show in the code below. This program yields nondeterministic results. Usually, it prints $2N$ but sometimes it prints a smaller value. The problem is more pronounced for large N. As a concrete example, on one run the program output 1320209 when $N = 1000000$ was specified at the command line.

```
public static class IncrementThread implements Runnable {
  public void run() {
    for (int i = 0; i < TwoThreadIncrementDriver.N; i++) {
      TwoThreadIncrementDriver.counter++;
    }
  }
}

public static class TwoThreadIncrementDriver {
  public static int counter;
  public static int N;

  public static void main(String[] args) throws Exception {
    N = (args.length > 0) ? new Integer(args[0]) : 100;

    Thread t1 = new Thread(new IncrementThread());
    Thread t2 = new Thread(new IncrementThread());

    t1.start();
    t2.start();
    t1.join();
    t2.join();

    System.out.println(counter);
  }
}
```

What are the maximum and minimum values that could be printed by `TwoThreadIncrement` as a function of N?

Hint: Be as perverse as you can when scheduling the threads.

Solution: First, note that `TwoThreadIncrement.counter` is unguarded, which opens up the possibility of its value being determined by the order in which threads that write to it are scheduled by the thread scheduler.

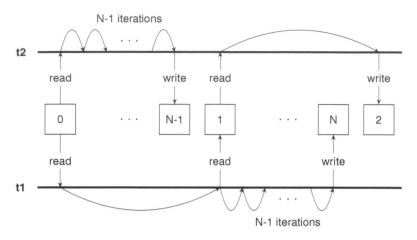

Figure 20.1: Worst-case schedule for two unsynchronized threads.

The maximum value is $2N$. This occurs when the thread scheduler runs one thread to completion, followed by the other thread.

When $N = 1$, the minimum value of `TwoThreadIncrement.counter` is 1: $t1$ reads, $t2$ reads, $t1$ increments and writes, then $t2$ increments and writes. When $N > 1$, the final value of `TwoThreadIncrement.counter` must be at least 2. The reasoning is as follows. There are two possibilities. A thread, call it T, performs a read-increment-write-read-increment-write without the other thread writing between reads, in which case the written value is at least 2. If the other thread now writes a 1, it has not yet completed, so it will increment at least once more. Otherwise, T's second read returns a value of 1 or more (since the other thread has performed at least one write).

The lower bound of 2 is achieved according to the following thread schedule:

- $t1$ loads the value of `TwoThreadIncrement.counter`, which is 0.
- $t2$ executes the loop $N - 1$ times.
- $t1$ doesn't know that the value of `TwoThreadIncrement.counter` has changed and writes 1 to `TwoThreadIncrement.counter`.
- $t2$ loads the value of `TwoThreadIncrement.counter`, which is 1.
- $t1$ executes the loop for the remaining $N - 1$ iterations.
- $t2$ doesn't know that the value of `TwoThreadIncrement.counter` has changed, and writes 2 to `TwoThreadIncrement.counter`.

This schedule is depicted in Figure 20.1.

20.3 IMPLEMENT SYNCHRONIZATION FOR TWO INTERLEAVING THREADS

Thread $t1$ prints odd numbers from 1 to 100; Thread $t2$ prints even numbers from 1 to 100.

Write Java code in which the two threads, running concurrently, print the numbers from 1 to 100 in order.

Hint: The two threads need to notify each other when they are done.

Solution: A brute-force solution is to use a lock which is repeatedly captured by the threads. A single variable, protected by the lock, indicates who went last. The drawback of this approach is that it employs the busy waiting antipattern: processor time that could be used to execute a different task is instead wasted on useless activity.

Below we present a solution based on the same idea, but one that avoids busy locking by using wait() and notify() primitives.

```java
public static class OddEvenMonitor {
  public static final boolean ODD_TURN = true;
  public static final boolean EVEN_TURN = false;
  private boolean turn = ODD_TURN;

  // Need synchronized in order to call wait(), see
  // http://stackoverflow.com/questions/2779484 for discussion
  public synchronized void waitTurn(boolean oldTurn) {
    while (turn != oldTurn) {
      try {
        wait();
      } catch (InterruptedException e) {
        System.out.println("InterruptedException in wait(): " + e);
      }
    }
    // Move on, it's our turn.
  }

  // Need synchronized in order to call notify()
  public synchronized void toggleTurn() {
    turn ^= true;
    notify();
  }
}

public static class OddThread extends Thread {
  private final OddEvenMonitor monitor;

  public OddThread(OddEvenMonitor monitor) { this.monitor = monitor; }
  @Override
  public void run() {
    for (int i = 1; i <= 100; i += 2) {
      monitor.waitTurn(OddEvenMonitor.ODD_TURN);
      System.out.println("i = " + i);
      monitor.toggleTurn();
    }
  }
}

public static class EvenThread extends Thread {
  private final OddEvenMonitor monitor;

  public EvenThread(OddEvenMonitor monitor) { this.monitor = monitor; }
  @Override
```

```
  public void run() {
    for (int i = 2; i <= 100; i += 2) {
      monitor.waitTurn(OddEvenMonitor.EVEN_TURN);
      System.out.println("i = " + i);
      monitor.toggleTurn();
    }
  }
}

public static void main(String[] args) throws InterruptedException {
  OddEvenMonitor monitor = new OddEvenMonitor();
  Thread t1 = new OddThread(monitor);
  Thread t2 = new EvenThread(monitor);
  t1.start();
  t2.start();
  t1.join();
  t2.join();
}
```

20.4 IMPLEMENT A THREAD POOL

The following program, implements part of a simple HTTP server:

```
public static class SingleThreadWebServer {
  public static final int PORT = 8080;
  public static void main(String[] args) throws IOException {
    ServerSocket serversock = new ServerSocket(PORT);
    for (;;) {
      Socket sock = serversock.accept();
      processReq(sock);
    }
  }
}
```

Suppose you find that the program has poor performance because it frequently blocks on I/O. What steps could you take to improve the program's performance? Feel free to use any utilities from the standard library, including concurrency classes.

Hint: Use multithreading, but control the number of threads.

Solution: The first attempt to solve this problem might be to have main launch a new thread per request rather than process the request itself:

```
public static class ConcurrentWebServer {
  private static final int SERVERPORT = 8080;
  public static void main(String[] args) throws IOException {
    final ServerSocket serversocket = new ServerSocket(SERVERPORT);
    while (true) {
      final Socket connection = serversocket.accept();
      Runnable task = new Runnable() {
        public void run() { Worker.handleRequest(connection); }
      };
```

```
    new Thread(task).start();
    }
  }
}
```

The problem with this approach is that we do not control the number of threads
launched. A thread consumes a nontrivial amount of resources, such as the time taken
to start and end the thread and the memory used by the thread. For a lightly-loaded
server, this may not be an issue but under load, it can result in exceptions that are
challenging, if not impossible, to handle.

The right trade-off is to use a *thread pool*. As the name implies, this is a collection of
threads, the size of which is bounded. A thread pool can be implemented relatively
easily using a blocking queue, i.e., a queue which blocks the writing thread on a put
until the queue is empty. However, since the problem statement explicitly allows us
to use library routines, we can use the thread pool implementation provided in the
Executor framework, which is the approach used below.

```
public static class ThreadPoolWebServer {
  private static final int NTHREADS = 100;
  private static final int SERVERPORT = 8080;
  private static final Executor exec = Executors.newFixedThreadPool(NTHREADS);

  public static void main(String[] args) throws IOException {
    ServerSocket serversocket = new ServerSocket(SERVERPORT);
    while (true) {
      final Socket connection = serversocket.accept();
      Runnable task = new Runnable() {
        public void run() { Worker.handleRequest(connection); }
      };
      exec.execute(task);
    }
  }
}
```

20.5 DEADLOCK

When threads need to acquire multiple locks to enter a critical section, deadlock can
result. As an example, suppose both $T1$ and $T2$ need to acquire locks L and M. If
$T1$ first acquires L, and then $T2$ then acquires M, they end up waiting on each other
forever.

Identify a concurrency bug in the program below, and modify the code to resolve the
issue.

```
static class Account {
  private int balance;
  private int id;
  private static int globalId;

  Account(int balance) {
```

```
    this.balance = balance;
    this.id = ++globalId;
  }

  private boolean move(Account to, int amount) {
    synchronized (this) {
      synchronized (to) {
        if (amount > balance) {
          return false;
        }
        to.balance += amount;
        this.balance -= amount;
        System.out.println("returning true");
        return true;
      }
    }
  }

  public static void transfer(final Account from, final Account to,
                              final int amount) {
    Thread transfer = new Thread(new Runnable() {
      public void run() { from.move(to, amount); }
    });
    transfer.start();
  }
}
```

Solution: Suppose $U1$ initiates a transfer to $U2$, and immediately afterwards, $U2$ initiates a transfer to $U1$. Since each transfer takes place in a separate thread, it's possible for the first thread to lock $U1$ and then the second thread to be scheduled in and take the lock $U2$. The program is now deadlocked—each of the two threads is waiting for the lock held by the other thread.

One solution is to have a global lock which is acquired by the transfer method. The drawback is that it blocks transfers that are unrelated, e.g., $U3$ cannot transfer to $U4$ if there is a pending transfer from $U5$ to $U6$.

The canonical way to avoid deadlock is to have a global ordering on locks and acquire them in that order. Since accounts have a unique integer id, the update below is all that is needed to solve the deadlock.

```
Account lock1 = (id < to.id) ? this : to;
Account lock2 = (id < to.id) ? to : this;
synchronized (lock1) {
  // Does not matter if lock1 equals lock2: since Java locks are
  // reentrant, we will re-acquire lock2.
  synchronized (lock2) {
```

20.6 IMPLEMENT A TIMER CLASS

Consider a web-based calendar in which the server hosting the calendar has to perform a task when the next calendar event takes place. (The task could be sending an email or a Short Message Service (SMS).) Your job is to design a facility that manages the execution of such tasks.

Develop a Timer class that manages the execution of deferred tasks. The Timer constructor takes as its argument an object which includes a Run method and a name field, which is a string. Timer must support—(1.) starting a thread, identified by name, at a given time in the future; and (2.) canceling a thread, identified by name (the cancel request is to be ignored if the thread has already started).

Hint: There are two aspects—data structure design and concurrency.

Solution: The two aspects to the design are the data structures and the locking mechanism.

We use two data structures. The first is a min-heap in which we insert key-value pairs: the keys are run times and the values are the thread to run at that time. A dispatch thread runs these threads; it sleeps from call to call and may be woken up if a thread is added to or deleted from the pool. If woken up, it advances or retards its remaining sleep time based on the top of the min-heap. On waking up, it looks for the thread at the top of the min-heap—if its launch time is the current time, the dispatch thread deletes it from the min-heap and executes it. It then sleeps till the launch time for the next thread in the min-heap. (Because of deletions, it may happen that the dispatch thread wakes up and finds nothing to do.)

The second data structure is a hash table with thread ids as keys and entries in the min-heap as values. If we need to cancel a thread, we go to the min-heap and delete it. Each time a thread is added, we add it to the min-heap; if the insertion is to the top of the min-heap, we interrupt the dispatch thread so that it can adjust its wake up time.

Since the min-heap is shared by the update methods and the dispatch thread, we need to lock it. The simplest solution is to have a single lock that is used for all read and writes into the min-heap and the hash table.

20.7 The readers-writers problem

Consider an object s which is read from and written to by many threads. (For example, s could be the cache from Problem 20.1 on Page 370.) You need to ensure that no thread may access s for reading or writing while another thread is writing to s. (Two or more readers may access s at the same time.)

One way to achieve this is by protecting s with a mutex that ensures that two threads cannot access s at the same time. However, this solution is suboptimal because it is possible that a reader R1 has locked s and another reader R2 wants to access s. Reader R2 does not have to wait until R1 is done reading; instead, R2 should start reading right away.

This motivates the first readers-writers problem: protect s with the added constraint that no reader is to be kept waiting if s is currently opened for reading.

Implement a synchronization mechanism for the first readers-writers problem.

Hint: Track the number of readers.

Solution: We want to keep track of whether the string is being read from, as well as whether the string is being written to. Additionally, if the string is being read from, we want to know the number of concurrent readers. We achieve this with a pair of locks—LR and LW—and a read counter locked by LR.

A reader proceeds as follows. It locks LR, increments the counter, and releases LR. After it performs its reads, it locks LR, decrements the counter, and releases LR. A writer locks LW, then performs the following in an infinite loop. It locks LR, checks to see if the read counter is 0; if so, it performs its write, releases LR, and breaks out of the loop. Finally, it releases LW. In the code below we use the Java wait() and notify() primitives to avoid the CPU cycles wasted in a busy wait.

```
// LR and LW are static members of type Object in the RW class.
// They serve as read and write locks. The static integer
// field readCount in RW tracks the number of readers.
public static class Reader extends Thread {
  public void run() {
    while (true) {
      synchronized (RW.LR) { RW.readCount++; }
      System.out.println(RW.data);
      synchronized (RW.LR) {
        RW.readCount--;
        RW.LR.notify();
      }
      Task.doSomeThingElse();
    }
  }
}

public static class Writer extends Thread {
  public void run() {
    while (true) {
      synchronized (RW.LW) {
        boolean done = false;
        while (!done) {
          synchronized (RW.LR) {
            if (RW.readCount == 0) {
              RW.data = new Date().toString();
              done = true;
            } else {
              // Use wait/notify to avoid busy waiting.
              try {
                // Protect against spurious notify, see
                // stackoverflow.com do-spurious-wakeups-actually-happen.
                while (RW.readCount != 0) {
                  RW.LR.wait();
                }
              } catch (InterruptedException e) {
                System.out.println("InterruptedException in Writer wait");
              }
            }
          }
```

```
            }
          }
        }
      Task.doSomeThingElse();
    }
  }
}
```

20.8 THE READERS-WRITERS PROBLEM WITH WRITE PREFERENCE

Suppose we have an object s as in Problem 20.7 on Page 378. In the solution to Problem 20.7 on Page 378, a reader $R1$ may have the lock; if a writer W is waiting for the lock and then a reader $R2$ requests access, $R2$ will be given priority over W. If this happens often enough, W will starve. Instead, suppose we want W to start as soon as possible.

This motivates the second readers-writers problem: protect s with "writer-preference", i.e., no writer, once added to the queue, is to be kept waiting longer than absolutely necessary.

Implement a synchronization mechanism for the second readers-writers problem.

Hint: Force readers to acquire a write lock.

Solution: We want to give writers the preference. We achieve this by modifying Solution 20.7 on the previous page to have a reader start by locking LW and then immediately releasing LW. In this way, a writer who acquires the LW lock is guaranteed to be ahead of the subsequent readers.

20.9 TEST THE COLLATZ CONJECTURE IN PARALLEL

In Problem 13.15 on Page 226 and its solution we introduced the Collatz conjecture and heuristics for checking it. In this problem, you are to build a parallel checker for the Collatz conjecture. Specifically, assume your program will run on a multicore machine, and threads in your program will be distributed across the cores. Your program should check the Collatz conjecture for every integer in $[1, U]$ where U is an input to your program.

Design a multi-threaded program for checking the Collatz conjecture. Make full use of the cores available to you. To keep your program from overloading the system, you should not have more than n threads running at a time.

Hint: Use multithreading for performance—take care to minimize threading overhead.

Solution: Heuristics for pruning checks on individual integers are discussed in Solution 13.15 on Page 226. The aim of this problem is implementing a multi-threaded checker. We could have a master thread launch n threads, one per number, starting with $1, 2, \ldots, x$. The master thread would keep track of what number needs to be processed next, and when a thread returned, it could re-assign it the next unchecked number.

The problem with this approach is that the time spent executing the check in an individual thread is very small compared to the overhead of communicating with the thread. The natural solution is to have each thread process a subrange of $[1, U]$. We could do this by dividing $[1, U]$ into n equal sized subranges, and having Thread i handle the ith subrange.

The heuristics for checking the Collatz conjecture take longer on some integers than others, and in the strategy above there is the potential of a situation arising where one thread takes much longer to complete than the others, which leads to most of the cores being idle.

A good compromise is to have threads handle smaller intervals, which are still large enough to offset the thread overhead. We can maintain a work-queue consisting of unprocessed intervals, and assigning these to returning threads. The Java Executor framework is ideally suited to implementing this, and an implementation is given in the code below:

```java
// Performs basic unit of work, i.e., checking CH for an interval
public static class MyRunnable implements Runnable {
  public int lower;
  public int upper;

  MyRunnable(int lower, int upper) {
    this.lower = lower;
    this.upper = upper;
  }

  @Override
  public void run() {
    for (int i = lower; i <= upper; ++i) {
      Collatz.CollatzCheck(i, new HashSet<BigInteger>());
    }
  }
}

// Checks an individual number
public static boolean CollatzCheck(BigInteger aNum, Set<BigInteger> visited) {
  if (aNum.equals(BigInteger.ONE)) {
    return true;
  } else if (visited.contains(aNum)) {
    return false;
  }
  visited.add(aNum);
  if (aNum.getLowestSetBit() == 1) { // Odd number.
    return CollatzCheck(
        new BigInteger("3").multiply(aNum).add(BigInteger.ONE), visited);
  } else { // Even number.
    return CollatzCheck(aNum.shiftRight(1), visited); // Divide by 2.
  }
}
```

```
public static boolean CollatzCheck(int aNum, Set<BigInteger> visited) {
  BigInteger b = new BigInteger(new Integer(aNum).toString());
  return CollatzCheck(b, visited);
}

public static ExecutorService execute() {
  // Uses the Executor framework for task assignment and load balancing
  List<Thread> threads = new ArrayList<Thread>();
  ExecutorService executor = Executors.newFixedThreadPool(NTHREADS);
  for (int i = 0; i < (N / RANGESIZE); ++i) {
    Runnable worker = new MyRunnable(i * RANGESIZE + 1, (i + 1) * RANGESIZE);
    executor.execute(worker);
  }
  executor.shutdown();
  return executor;
}
```

20.10 DESIGN TERASORT AND PETASORT

Modern datasets are huge. For example, it is estimated that a popular social network contains over two trillion distinct items.

How would you sort a billion 1000 byte strings? How about a trillion 1000 byte strings?

Hint: Can a trillion 1000 byte strings fit on one machine?

Solution: A billion 1000 byte strings cannot fit in the RAM of a single machine, but can fit on the hard drive of a single machine. Therefore, one approach is to partition the data into smaller blocks that fit in RAM, sort each block individually, write the sorted block to disk, and then combine the sorted blocks. The sorted blocks can be merged using for example Solution 11.1 on Page 171. The UNIX sort program uses these principles when sorting very large files, and is faster than direct implementations of the merge-based algorithm just described.

If the data consists of a trillion 1000 byte strings, it cannot fit on a single machine— it must be distributed across a cluster of machines. The most natural interpretation of sorting in this scenario is to organize the data so that lookups can be performed via binary search. Sorting the individual datasets is not sufficient, since it does not achieve a global ordering—lookups entail a binary search on each machine. The straightforward solution is to have one machine merge the sorted datasets, but then that machine will become the bottleneck.

A solution which does away with the bottleneck is to first reorder the data so that the ith machine stores strings in a range, e.g., Machine 3 is responsible for strings that lie between *daily* and *ending*. The range-to-machine mapping R can be computed by sampling the individual files and sorting the sampled values. If the sampled subset is small enough, it can be sorted by a single machine. The techniques in Solution 12.9 on Page 195 can be used to determine the ranges assigned to each machine. Specifically, let A be the sorted array of sampled strings. Suppose there are M machines. Define $r_i = iA[n/M]$, where n is the length of A. Then Machine i is responsible for strings in the range $[r_i, r_{i+1})$. If the distribution of the data is known *a priori*, e.g., it is uniform, the sampling step can be skipped.

The reordering can be performed in a completely distributed fashion by having each machine route the strings it begins with to the responsible machines.

After reordering, each machine sorts the strings it stores. Consequently queries such as lookups can be performed by using R to determine which individual machine to forward the lookup to.

20.11 IMPLEMENT DISTRIBUTED THROTTLING

You have n machines ("crawlers") for downloading the entire web. The responsibility for a given URL is assigned to the crawler whose ID is Hash(URL) mod n. Downloading a web page takes away bandwidth from the web server hosting it.

Implement crawling under the constraint that in any given minute your crawlers do not request more than b bytes from any website.

Hint: Use a server to coordinate the crawl.

Solution: This problem, as posed, is ambiguous.
- Since we usually download one file in one request, if a file is greater than b bytes, there is no way we can meet the constraint of serving fewer than b bytes every minute, unless we can work with the lower layers of the network stack such as the transport layer or the network layer. Often the system designer could look at the distribution of file sizes and conclude that this problem happens so infrequently that we do not care. Alternatively, we may choose to download no more than the first b bytes of any file.
- Given that the host's bandwidth is a resource for which there could be contention, one important design choice to be made is how to resolve a contention. Do we let requests get served in first-come first-served order or is there a notion of priority? Often crawlers have a built-in notion of priority based on how important the document is to the users or how fresh the current copy is.

One way of doing this could be to maintain a permission server with which each crawler checks to see if it is okay to hit a particular host. The server can keep an account of how many bytes have been downloaded from the server in the last minute and not permit any crawler to hit the server if we are already close to the quota. If we do not care about priority, then we can keep the interface synchronous where a server requests permission to download a file and it immediately gets approved or denied. If we care about priorities, then the server may enqueue the request and inform the crawler when the file is available for download. The queues at the permission server may be based on priorities.

If the permission server becomes a bottleneck, we can use multiple permission servers such that the responsibility of a given host is decided by applying a hash function to the host name and assigning it to a particular server based on the hash code.

21

Design Problems

We have described a simple but very powerful and flexible protocol which provides for variation in individual network packet sizes, transmission failures, sequencing, flow control, and the creation and destruction of process-to-process associations.

— *"A Protocol for Packet Network Intercommunication,"*
V. G. CERF AND R. E. KAHN, 1974

You may be asked in an interview how to go about creating a set of services or a larger system, possibly on top of an algorithm that you have designed. These problems are fairly open-ended, and many can be the starting point for a large software project.

In an interview setting when someone asks such a question, you should have a conversation in which you demonstrate an ability to think creatively, understand design trade-offs, and attack unfamiliar problems. You should sketch key data structures and algorithms, as well as the technology stack (programming language, libraries, OS, hardware, and services) that you would use to solve the problem.

The answers in this chapter are presented in this context—they are meant to be examples of good responses in an interview and are not comprehensive state-of-the-art solutions.

We review patterns that are useful for designing systems in Table 21.1. Some other things to keep in mind when designing a system are implementation time, extensibility, scalability, testability, security, internationalization, and IP issues.

Table 21.1: System design patterns.

Design principle	Key points
Decomposition	Split the functionality, architecture, and code into manageable, reusable components.
Parallelism	Decompose the problem into subproblems that can be solved independently on different machines.
Caching	Store computation and later look it up to save work.

DECOMPOSITION

Good decompositions are critical to successfully solving system-level design problems. Functionality, architecture, and code all benefit from decomposition.

For example, in our solution to designing a system for online advertising (Problem 21.13 on Page 397), we decompose the goals into categories based on the stake holders. We decompose the architecture itself into a front-end and a back-end. The front-end is divided into user management, web page design, reporting functionality, etc. The back-end is made up of middleware, storage, database, cron services, and algorithms for ranking ads. The design of TEX (Problem 21.6 on Page 391) and Connexus (Problem 21.12 on Page 397) also illustrate such decompositions.

Decomposing code is a hallmark of object-oriented programming. The subject of design patterns is concerned with finding good ways to achieve code-reuse. Broadly speaking, design patterns are grouped into creational, structural, and behavioral patterns. Many specific patterns are very natural—strategy objects, adapters, builders, etc., appear in a number of places in our codebase. Freeman *et al.*'s *"Head First Design Patterns"* is, in our opinion, the right place to study design patterns.

Parallelism

PARALLELISM

In the context of interview questions parallelism is useful when dealing with scale, i.e., when the problem is too large to fit on a single machine or would take an unacceptably long time on a single machine. The key insight you need to display is that you know how to decompose the problem so that

- each subproblem can be solved relatively independently, and
- the solution to the original problem can be efficiently constructed from solutions to the subproblems.

Efficiency is typically measured in terms of central processing unit (CPU) time, random access memory (RAM), network bandwidth, number of memory and database accesses, etc.

Consider the problem of sorting a petascale integer array. If we know the distribution of the numbers, the best approach would be to define equal-sized ranges of integers and send one range to one machine for sorting. The sorted numbers would just need to be concatenated in the correct order. If the distribution is not known then we can send equal-sized arbitrary subsets to each machine and then merge the sorted results, e.g., using a min-heap. Details are given in Solution 20.10 on Page 382.

The solutions to Problems 21.8 on Page 393 and 21.15 on Page 399 also illustrate the use of parallelism.

CACHING

Caching is a great tool whenever computations are repeated. For example, the central idea behind dynamic programming is caching results from intermediate computations. Caching is also extremely useful when implementing a service that is expected to respond to many requests over time, and many requests are repeated. Workloads on web services exhibit this property. Solution 20.1 on Page 371 sketches the design of an online spell correction service; one of the key issues is performing cache updates in the presence of concurrent requests. Solution 20.9 on Page 380 shows how multithreading combines with caching in code which tests the Collatz hypothesis.

Designing a good spelling correction system can be challenging. We discussed spelling correction in the context of edit distance (Problem 17.2 on Page 304). However, in that problem, we only computed the Levenshtein distance between a pair of strings. A spell checker must find a set of words that are closest to a given word from the entire dictionary. Furthermore, the Levenshtein distance may not be the right distance function when performing spelling correction—it does not take into account the commonly misspelled words or the proximity of letters on a keyboard.

How would you build a spelling correction system?

Hint: Start with an appropriate notion of distance between words.

Solution: The basic idea behind most spelling correction systems is that the misspelled word's Levenshtein distance from the intended word tends to be very small (one or two edits). Hence, if we keep a hash table for all the words in the dictionary and look for all the words that have a Levenshtein distance of 2 from the text, it is likely that the intended word will be found in this set. If the alphabet has m characters and the search text has n characters, we need to perform $O(n^2 m^2)$ hash table lookups. More precisely, for a word of length n, we can pick any two characters and change them to any other character in the alphabet. The total number of ways of selecting any two characters is $n(n - 1)/2$, and each character can be changed to one of $(m - 1)$ other chars. Therefore, the number of lookups is $n(n - 1)(m - 1)^2/2$.

The intersection of the set of all strings at a distance of two or less from a word and the set of dictionary words may be large. It is important to provide a ranked list of suggestions to the users, with the most likely candidates are at the beginning of the list. There are several ways to achieve this:

- Typing errors model—often spelling mistakes are a result of typing errors. Typing errors can be modeled based on keyboard layouts.
- Phonetic modeling—a big class of spelling errors happen when the person spelling it knows how the words sounds but does not know the exact spelling. In such cases, it helps to map the text to phonemes and then find all the words that map to the same phonetic sequence.
- History of refinements—often users themselves provide a great amount of data about the most likely misspellings by first entering a misspelled word and then correcting it. This historic data is often immensely valuable for spelling correction.
- Stemming—often the size of a dictionary can be reduced by keeping only the stemmed version of each word. (This entails stemming the query text.)

21.2 Design a solution to the stemming problem

When a user submits the query "computation" to a search engine, it is quite possible he might be interested in documents containing the words "computers", "compute", and "computing" also. If you have several keywords in a query, it becomes difficult to search for all combinations of all variants of the words in the query.

Stemming is the process of reducing all variants of a given word to one common root, both in the query string and in the documents. An example of stemming would be mapping {*computers, computer, compute*} to *compute*. It is almost impossible to succinctly capture all possible variants of all words in the English language but a few simple rules can get us most cases.

Design a stemming algorithm that is fast and effective.

Hint: The examples are suggestive of general rules.

Solution: Stemming is a large topic. Here we mention some basic ideas related to stemming—this is in no way a comprehensive discussion on stemming approaches.

Most stemming systems are based on simple rewrite rules, e.g., remove suffixes of the form "es", "s", and "ation". Suffix removal does not always work. For example, wolves should be stemmed to wolf. To cover this case, we may have a rule that replaces the suffix "ves" with "f".

Most rules amount to matching a set of suffixes and applying the corresponding transformation to the string. One way of efficiently performing this is to build a finite state machine based on all the rules.

A more sophisticated system might have exceptions to the broad rules based on the stem matching some patterns. The Porter stemmer, developed by Martin Porter, is considered to be one of the most authoritative stemming algorithms in the English language. It defines several rules based on patterns of vowels and consonants.

Other approaches include the use of stochastic methods to learn rewrite rules and n-gram based approaches where we look at the surrounding words to determine the correct stemming for a word.

21.3 PLAGIARISM DETECTOR

Design an efficient algorithm that takes as input a set of text files and returns pairs of files which have substantial commonality.

Hint: Design a hash function which can incrementally hash $S[i : i + k - 1]$ for $i = 0, 1, 2, \ldots$.

Solution: We will treat each file as a string. We take a pair of files as having substantial commonality if they have a substring of length k in common, where k is a measure of commonality. (Later, we will have a deeper discussion as to the validity of this model.)

Let l_i be the length of the string corresponding to the ith file. For each such string we can compute $l_i - k + 1$ hash codes, one for *each* k length substring.

We insert these hash codes in a hash table G, recording which file each code corresponds to, and the offset the corresponding substring appears at. A collision indicates that the two length-k substrings are potentially the same.

Since we are computing hash code for each k length substring, it is important for efficiency to have a hash function which can be updated incrementally when we delete one character and add another. Solution 7.14 on Page 107 describes such a hash function.

In addition, it is important to have many slots in G, so that collisions of unequal strings is rare. A total of $\sum_{i=1}^{|S|}(l_i - k + 1)$ strings are added to the hash table. If k is small relative to the string length and G has significantly fewer slots than the total number of characters in the strings, then we are certain to have collisions.

If it is not essential to return an exact answer, we can save storage by only considering a subset of substrings, e.g., those whose hash codes have 0s in the last b bits. This means that on average we consider $\frac{1}{2^b}$ of the total set of substrings (assuming the hash function does a reasonable job of spreading keys).

The solution presented above can lead to many false positives. For example, if each file corresponds to an HTML page, all pages with a common embedded script of length k or longer will show up as having substantial overlap. We can account for this through preprocessing, e.g., parsing the documents and removing headers. (This may require multiple passes with some manual inspection driving the process.) This solution will also not work if, for example, the files are similar in that they are the exact same program, but with ids renamed. (It is however, resilient to code blocks being moved around.) By normalizing ids, we can cast the problem back into one of finding common substrings.

The approach we have just described is especially effective when the number of files is very large and the files are spread over many servers. In particular, the map-reduce framework can be used to achieve the effect of a single G spread over many servers.

21.4 Pair users by attributes

You are building a social network where each user specifies a set of attributes. You would like to pair each user with another unpaired user that specified the same set of attributes.

You are given a sequence of users where each user has a unique 32-bit integer key and a set of attributes specified as strings. When you read a user, you should pair that user with another previously read user with identical attributes who is currently unpaired, if such a user exists. If the user cannot be paired, you should add him to the unpaired set.

Hint: Map sets of attributes to strings.

Solution: A brute-force approach is to compare each new user's attributes with the attributes of users in the unpaired set. This leads to $O(n^2)$ time complexity, where n is the number of users.

To improve the time complexity, we need a way to find users who have the same attributes as the new user. A hash table whose keys are subsets of attributes and values are users is the perfect choice. This leaves us with the problem of designing a hash function which is suitable for subsets of attributes.

If the total number of possible attributes is small, we can represent a subset of attributes with a bit array, where each index represents a specific attribute. Specifically, we store a 1 at an index if that attribute is present. We can then use any hash function for bit arrays. The time complexity to process the n users is a hash lookup per user, i.e., $O(nm)$, where m is the number of distinct attributes. The space complexity is also $O(nm)$—n entries, each of size m.

If the set of possible attributes is large, and most users have a small subset of those attributes, the bit vector representation for subsets is inefficient from both a time and space perspective. A better approach to represent sparse subsets is directly record the elements. To ensure equal subsets have equal hash codes, we need to represent the subsets in a unique way. One approach is to sort the elements. We can view the sorted sequence of attributes as a single string, namely the concatenation the individual elements. We then use a hash function for strings. For example, if the possible attributes are {USA, Senior, Income, Prime Customer}, and a user has attributes {USA, Income}, we represent his set of attributes as the string "Income,USA".

The time complexity of this approach is $O(M)$, where M is the sum of the sizes of the attribute sets for all users.

21.5 Design a system for detecting copyright infringement

YouTV.com is a successful online video sharing site. Hollywood studios complain that much of the material uploaded to the site violates copyright.

Design a feature that allows a studio to enter a set V of videos that belong to it, and to determine which videos in the YouTV.com database match videos in V.

Hint: Normalize the video format and create signatures.

Solution: If we replaced videos everywhere with documents, we could use the techniques in Solution 21.3 on Page 388, where we looked for near duplicate documents by computing hash codes for each length-k substring.

Videos differ from documents in that the same content may be encoded in many different formats, with different resolutions, and levels of compression.

One way to reduce the duplicate video problem to the duplicate document problem is to re-encode all videos to a common format, resolution, and compression level. This in itself does not mean that two videos of the same content get reduced to identical files—the initial settings affect the resulting videos. However, we can now "signature" the normalized video.

A trivial signature would be to assign a 0 or a 1 to each frame based on whether it has more or less brightness than average. A more sophisticated signature would be a 3 bit measure of the red, green, and blue intensities for each frame. Even more sophisticated signatures can be developed, e.g., by taking into account the regions on individual frames. The motivation for better signatures is to reduce the number of false matches returned by the system, and thereby reduce the amount of time needed to review the matches.

The solution proposed above is algorithmic. However, there are alternative approaches that could be effective: letting users flag videos that infringe copyright (and possibly rewarding them for their effort), checking for videos that are identical to

389

videos that have previously been identified as infringing, looking at meta-information in the video header, etc.

Variant: Design an online music identification service.

21.6 DESIGN TEX

The TEX system for typesetting beautiful documents was designed by Don Knuth. Unlike GUI based document editing programs, TEX relies on a markup language, which is compiled into a device independent intermediate representation. TEX formats text, lists, tables, and embedded figures; supports a very rich set of fonts and mathematical symbols; automates section numbering, cross-referencing, index generation; exports an API; and much more.

How would you implement TEX?

Hint: There are two aspects—building blocks (e.g., fonts, symbols) and hierarchical layout.

Solution: Note that the problem does not ask for the design of TEX, which itself is a complex problem involving feature selection, and language design. There are a number of issues common to implementing any such program: programming language selection, lexing and parsing input, error handling, macros, and scripting.

Two key implementation issues specific to TEX are a specifying fonts and symbols (e.g., $A, b, f, \Sigma, \oint, \text{ש}$), and assembling a document out of components.

Focusing on the second aspect, a reasonable abstraction is to use a rectangular bounding box to describe components. The description is hierarchical: each individual symbol is a rectangle, lines and paragraphs are made out of these rectangles and are themselves rectangles, as are section titles, tables and table entries, and included images. A key algorithmic problem is to assemble these rectangles, while preserving hard constraints on layout, and soft constraints on aesthetics. See also Problem 17.11 on Page 323 for an example of the latter.

Turning our attention to symbol specification, the obvious approach is to use a 2D array of bits to represent each symbol. This is referred to as a bit-mapped representation. The problem with bit-mapped fonts is that the resolution required to achieve acceptable quality is very high, which leads to huge documents and font-libraries. Different sizes of the same symbol need to be individually mapped, as do italicized and bold-face versions.

A better approach is to define symbols using mathematical functions. A reasonable approach is to use a language that supports quadratic and cubic functions, and elementary graphics transformations (rotation, interpolation, and scaling). This approach overcomes the limitations of bit-mapped fonts—parameters such as aspect ratio, font slant, stroke width, serif size, etc. can be programmed.

Other implementation issues include enabling cross-referencing, automatically creating indices, supporting colors, and outputting standard page description formats (e.g., PDF)).

Donald Knuth's book *"Digital Typography"* describes in great detail the design and implementation of TEX.

Keyword-based search engines maintain a collection of several billion documents. One of the key computations performed by a search engine is to retrieve all the documents that contain the keywords contained in a query. This is a nontrivial task in part because it must be performed in a few tens of milliseconds.

Here we consider a smaller version of the problem where the collection of documents can fit within the RAM of a single computer.

Given a million documents with an average size of 10 kilobytes, design a program that can efficiently return the subset of documents containing a given set of words.

Hint: Build on the idea of a book's index.

Solution: The predominant way of doing this is to build inverted indices. In an inverted index, for each word, we store a sequence of locations where the word occurs. The sequence itself could be represented as an array or a linked list. Location is defined to be the document ID and the offset in the document. The sequence is stored in sorted order of locations (first ordered by document ID, then by offset). When we are looking for documents that contain a set of words, what we need to do is find the intersection of sequences for each word. Since the sequences are already sorted, the intersection can be done in time proportional to the aggregate length of the sequences. We list a few optimizations below.

- *Compression*—compressing the inverted index helps both with the ability to index more documents as well as memory locality (fewer cache misses). Since we are storing sorted sequences, one way of compressing is to use delta compression where we only store the difference between the successive entries. The deltas can be represented in fewer bits.
- *Caching*—the distribution of queries is usually fairly skewed and it helps a great deal to cache the results of some of the most frequent queries.
- *Frequency-based optimization*—since search results often do not need to return every document that matches (only top ten or so), only a fraction of highest quality documents can be used to answer most of the queries. This means that we can make two inverted indices, one with the high quality documents that stays in RAM and one with the remaining documents that stays on disk. This way if we can keep the number of queries that require the secondary index to a small enough number, then we can still maintain a reasonable throughput and latency.
- *Intersection order*—since the total intersection time depends on the total size of sequences, it would make sense to intersect the words with smaller sets first. For example, if we are looking for "USA GDP 2009", it would make sense to intersect the lists for GDP and 2009 before trying to intersect the sequence for USA.

We could also build a multilevel index to improve accuracy on documents. For a high priority web page, we can decompose the page into paragraphs and sentences, which are indexed individually. That way the intersections for the words might be within the same context. We can pick results with closer index values from these sequences.

See the sorted array intersection problem 14.1 on Page 231 and digest problem 13.8 on Page 213 for related issues.

21.8 IMPLEMENT PAGERANK

The PageRank algorithm assigns a rank to a web page based on the number of "important" pages that link to it. The algorithm essentially amounts to the following:

(1.) Build a matrix A based on the hyperlink structure of the web. Specifically, $A_{ij} = \frac{1}{d_j}$ if page j links to page i; here d_j is the number of distinct pages linked from page j.

(2.) Find X satisfying $X = \epsilon[1] + (1 - \epsilon)AX$. Here ϵ is a constant, e.g., $\frac{1}{7}$, and $[1]$ represents a column vector of 1s. The value $X[i]$ is the rank of the ith page.

The most commonly used approach to solving the above equation is to start with a value of X, where each component is $\frac{1}{n}$ (where n is the number of pages) and then perform the following iteration: $X_k = \epsilon[1] + (1 - \epsilon)AX_{k-1}$.

Design a system that can compute the ranks of ten billion web pages in a reasonable amount of time.

Hint: This must be performed on an ensemble of machines. The right data structures will simplify the computation.

Solution: Since the web graph can have billions of vertices and it is mostly a sparse graph, it is best to represent the graph as an adjacency list. Building the adjacency list representation of the graph may require a significant amount of computation, depending upon how the information is collected. Usually, the graph is constructed by downloading the pages on the web and extracting the hyperlink information from the pages. Since the URL of a page can vary in length, it is often a good idea to represent the URL by a hash code.

The most expensive part of the PageRank algorithm is the repeated matrix multiplication. Usually, it is not possible to keep the entire graph information in a single machine's RAM. Two approaches to solving this problem are described below.

- Disk-based sorting—we keep the column vector X in memory and load rows one at a time. Processing Row i simply requires adding $A_{i,j}X_j$ to X_j for each j such that $A_{i,j}$ is not zero. The advantage of this approach is that if the column vector fits in RAM, the entire computation can be performed on a single machine. This approach is slow because it uses a single machine and relies on the disk.

- Partitioned graph—we use n servers and partition the vertices (web pages) into n sets. This partition can be computed by partitioning the set of hash codes in such a way that it is easy to determine which vertex maps to which machine. Given this partitioning, each machine loads its vertices and their outgoing edges into RAM. Each machine also loads the portion of the PageRank vector corresponding to the vertices it is responsible for. Then each machine does a local matrix multiplication. Some of the edges on each machine may correspond to vertices that are owned by other machines. Hence the result vector contains nonzero entries for vertices that are not owned by the local machine. At the end of the local multiplication it needs to send updates to other hosts so that these values can be correctly added up. The advantage of this approach is that it can process arbitrarily large graphs.

PageRank runs in minutes on a single machine on the graph consisting of the six million pages that constitute Wikipedia. It takes roughly 70 iterations to converge on this graph. Anecdotally, PageRank takes roughly 200 iterations to converge on the web graph.

21.9 DESIGN A SCALABLE PRIORITY SYSTEM

Maintaining a set of prioritized jobs in a distributed system can be tricky. Applications include a search engine crawling web pages in some prioritized order, as well as event-driven simulation in molecular dynamics. In both cases the number of jobs is in the billions and each has its own priority.

Design a system for maintaining a set of prioritized jobs that implements the following API: (1.) insert a new job with a given priority; (2.) delete a job; (3.) find the highest priority job. Each job has a unique ID. Assume the set cannot fit into a single machine's memory.

Hint: How would you partition jobs across machines? Is it always essential to operate on the highest priority job?

Solution: If we have enough RAM on a single machine, the most simple solution would be to maintain a min-heap where entries are ordered by their priority. An additional hash table can be used to map jobs to their corresponding entry in the min-heap to make deletions fast.

A more scalable solution entails partitioning the problem across multiple machines. One approach is to apply a hash function to the job ids and partition the resulting hash codes into ranges, one per machine. Insert as well as delete require communication with just one server. To do extract-min, we send a lookup minimum message to all the machines, infer the min from their responses, and then delete it.

At a given time many clients may be interested in the highest priority event, and it is challenging to distribute this problem well. If many clients are trying to do this operation at the same time, we may run into a situation where most clients will find that the min event they are trying to extract has already been deleted. If the throughput of this service can be handled by a single machine, we can make one server solely responsible for responding to all the requests. This server can prefetch the top hundred or so events from each of the machines and keep them in a heap.

In many applications, we do not need strong consistency guarantees. We want to spend most of our resources taking care of the highest priority jobs. In this setting, a client could pick one of the machines at random, and request the highest priority job. This would work well for the distributed crawler application. It is not suited to event-driven simulation because of dependencies.

A photomosaic is built from a collection of images called "tiles" and a target image. The photomosaic is another image which approximates the target image and is built by juxtaposing the tiles. Quality is defined by human perception.

Design a program that produces high quality mosaics with minimal compute time.

Hint: How would you define the distance between two images?

Solution: A good way to begin is to partition the image into $s \times s$-sized squares, compute the average color of each such image square, and then find the tile that is closest to it in the color space. Distance in the color space can be the $L2$-distance over the Red-Green-Blue (RGB) intensities for the color. As you look more carefully at the problem, you might conclude that it would be better to match each tile with an image square that has a similar structure. One way could be to perform a coarse pixelization (2×2 or 3×3) of each image square and finding the tile that is "closest" to the image square under a distance function defined over all pixel colors. In essence, the problem reduces to finding the closest point from a set of points in a k-dimensional space.

Given m tiles and an image partitioned into n squares, then a brute-force approach would have $O(mn)$ time complexity. You could improve on this by first indexing the tiles using an appropriate search tree. You can also run the matching in parallel by partitioning the original image into subimages and searching for matches on the subimages independently.

21.11   IMPLEMENT MILEAGE RUN

Airlines often give customers who fly frequently with them a "status". This status allows them early boarding, more baggage, upgrades to executive class, etc. Typically, status is a function of miles flown in the past twelve months. People who travel frequently by air sometimes want to take a round trip flight simply to maintain their status. The destination is immaterial—the goal is to minimize the cost-per-mile (cpm), i.e., the ratio of dollars spent to miles flown.

Design a system that will help its users find mileage runs.

Hint: Partition the implied features into independent tasks.

Solution: There are two distinct aspects to the design. The first is the user-facing portion of the system. The second is the server backend that gets flight-price-distance information and combines it with user input to generate the alerts.

We begin with the user-facing portion. For simplicity, we illustrate it with a web-app, with the realization that the web-app could also be written as a desktop or mobile app. The web-app has the following components: a login page, a manage alerts page, a create an alert page, and a results page. For such a system we would like defer to a single-sign-on login service such as that provided by Google or Facebook. The management page would present login information, a list of alerts, and the ability to create an alert.

One reasonable formulation of an alert is that it is an origin city, a target cpm, and optionally, a date or range of travel dates. The results page would show flights satisfying the constraints. Note that other formulations are also possible, such as how frequently to check for flights, a set of destinations, a set of origins, etc.

The classical approach to implement the web-app front end is through dynamically generated HTML on the server, e.g., through Java Server Pages. It can be made more visually appealing and intuitive by making appropriate use of cascaded style sheets, which are used for fonts, colors, and placements. The UI can be made more efficient through the use of Javascript to autocomplete common fields, and make attractive date pickers.

Modern practice is to eschew server-side HTML generation, and instead have a single-page application, in which Javascript reads and writes JavaScript Object Notation (JSON) objects to the server, and incrementally updates the single-page based. The AngularJS framework supports this approach.

The web-app backend server has four components: gathering flight data, matching user-generated alerts to this data, persisting data and alerts, and generating the responses to browser initiated requests.

Flight data can be gathered via "scraping" or by subscribing to a flight data service. Scraping refers to extraction of data from a website. It can be quite involved—some of the issues are parsing the results from the website, filling in form data, and running the Javascript that often populates the actual results on a page. Selenium is a Java library that can programmatically interface to the Firefox browser, and is appropriate for scraping sites that are rich in Javascript. Most flight data services are paid. ITA software provides a very widely used paid aggregated flight data feed service. The popular Kayak site provides an Extensible Markup Language (XML) feed of recently discovered fares, which can be a good free alternative. Flight data does not include the distance between airports, but there are websites which return the distance between airport codes which can be used to generate the cpm for a flight.

There are a number of common web application frameworks—essentially libraries that handle many common tasks—that can be used to generate the server. Java and Python are very commonly used for writing the backend for web applications.

Persistence of data can be implemented through a database. Most web application frameworks provide support for automating the process of reading and writing objects from and to a database. Finally, web application frameworks can route incoming HTTP requests to appropriate code—this is through a configuration file matching URLs to methods. The framework provides convenience methods for accessing HTTP fields and writing results. Frameworks also provide HTTP templating mechanisms, wherein developers intersperse HTML with snippets of code that dynamically add content to the HTML.

Web application frameworks typically implement cron functionality, wherein specified functions are executed at a regular interval. This can be used to periodically scrape data and check if the condition of an alert is matched by the data.

Finally, the web app can be deployed via a platform-as-a-service such as Amazon Web Services and Google App Engine.

How would you design Connexus, a system by which users can share pictures? Address issues around access control (public, private), picture upload, organizing pictures, summarizing sets of pictures, allowing feedback, and displaying geographical and temporal information for pictures.

Hint: Think about the UI, in particular UI widgets that make for an engaging product.

Solution: There are three aspects to Connexus. The first is the server backend, used to store images, and meta-data, such as author, comments, hashtags, GPS coordinates, etc., as well as run cron jobs to identify trending streams. The technology for this is similar to Mileage Run (Solution 21.11 on Page 395), with the caveat that a database is not suitable for storing large binary objects such as images.

The web UI is also similar to Mileage Run, with a login page, a management page, and pages for displaying images. Images can be grouped based on a concept of a stream, with comment boxes annotating streams. Facebook integration would make it easier to share links to streams, and post new images as status updates. Search capability and discussion boards also enhance the user experience.

Some UI features that are especially appealing are displaying images by location on a zoomable map, slider UI controls to show subsets of images in a stream based on the selected time intervals, a file upload dialog with progress measures, support for multiple simultaneous uploads, and drag-and-drop upload. All these UI widgets are provided by, for example, the jQuery-UI Javascript library. (This library also makes the process of creating autocompletion on text entry fields trivial.)

Connexus is an application that begs for a mobile client. A smartphone provides a camera, location information, and push notifications. These can be used to make it easier to create and immediately upload geo-tagged images, find nearby images, and be immediately notified on updates and comments. The two most popular mobile platforms, iOS and Android, have APIs rich in UI widgets and media access. Both can use serialization formats such as JSON or protocol buffers to communicate with the server via remote procedure calls layered over HTTP.

21.13   DESIGN AN ONLINE ADVERTISING SYSTEM

Jingle, a search engine startup, has been very successful at providing a high-quality Internet search service. A large number of customers have approached Jingle and asked it to display paid advertisements for their products and services alongside search results.

Design an advertising system for Jingle.

Hint: Consider the stakeholders separately.

Solution: Reasonable goals for such a system include
- providing users with the most relevant ads,
- providing advertisers the best possible return on their investment, and
- minimizing the cost and maximizing the revenue to Jingle.

Two key components for such a system are:

- The front-facing component, which advertisers use to create advertisements, organize campaigns, limit when and where ads are shown, set budgets, and create performance reports.
- The ad-serving system, which selects which ads to show on the searches.

The front-facing system can be a fairly conventional web application, i.e., a set of web pages, middleware that responds to user requests, and a database. Key features include:

- User authentication—a way for users to create accounts and authenticate themselves. Alternatively, use an existing single sign-on login service, e.g., Facebook or Google.
- User input—a set of form elements to let advertisers specify ads, advertising budget, and search keywords to bid on.
- Performance reports—a way to generate reports on how the advertiser's money is being spent.
- Customer service—even the best of automated systems require occasional human interaction, e.g., ways to override limits on keywords. This requires an interface for advertisers to contact customer service representatives, and an interface for those representatives to interact with the system.

The whole front-end system can be built using, for example, HyperText Markup Language (HTML) and JavaScript. A commonly used approach is to use a LAMP stack on the server-side: Linux as the OS, Apache as the HTTP server, MySQL as the database software, and PHP for the application logic.

The ad-serving system is less conventional. The ad-serving system would build a specialized data structure, such as a decision tree, from the ads database. It chooses ads from the database of ads based on their "relevance" to the search. In addition to keywords, the ad-serving systems can use knowledge of the user's search history, how much the advertiser is willing to pay, the time of day, user locale, and type of browser. Many strategies can be envisioned here for estimating relevance, such as, using information retrieval or machine learning techniques that learn from past user interactions.

The ads could be added to the search results by embedding JavaScript in the results page. This JavaScript pulls in the ads from the ad-serving system directly. This helps isolate the latency of serving search results from the latency of serving ad results.

21.14 Design a recommendation system

Jingle wants to generate more page views on its news site. A product manager has the idea to add to each article a sidebar of clickable snippets from articles that are likely to be of interest to someone reading the current article.

Design a system that automatically generates a sidebar of related articles.

Hint: This problem can be solved with various degrees of algorithmic sophistication: none at all, simple frequency analysis, or machine learning.

Solution: The key technical challenge in this problem is to come up with the list of articles—the code for adding these to a sidebar is trivial.

One suggestion might be to add articles that have proved to be popular recently. Another is to have links to recent news articles. A human reader at Jingle could tag articles which he believes to be significant. He could also add tags such as finance, sports, and politics, to the articles. These tags could also come from the HTML meta-tags or the page title.

We could also provide randomly selected articles to a random subset of readers and see how popular these articles prove to be. The popular articles could then be shown more frequently.

On a more sophisticated level, Jingle could use automatic textual analysis, where a similarity is defined between pairs of articles—this similarity is a real number and measures how many words are common to the two. Several issues come up, such as the fact that frequently occurring words such as "for" and "the" should be ignored and that having rare words such as "arbitrage" and "diesel" in common is more significant than having say, "sale" and "international".

Textual analysis has problems, such as the fact that two words may have the same spelling but completely different meanings (anti-virus means different things in the context of articles on acquired immune deficiency syndrome (AIDS) and computer security). One way to augment textual analysis is to use collaborative filtering—using information gleaned from many users. For example, by examining cookies and timestamps in the web server's log files, we can tell what articles individual users have read. If we see many users have read both A and B in a single session, we might want to recommend B to anyone reading A. For collaborative filtering to work, we need to have many users.

21.15   Design an optimized way of distributing large files

Jingle is developing a search feature for breaking news. New articles are collected from a variety of online news sources such as newspapers, bulletin boards, and blogs, by a single lab machine at Jingle. Every minute, roughly one thousand articles are posted and each article is 100 kilobytes.

Jingle would like to serve these articles from a data center consisting of a 1000 servers. For performance reasons, each server should have its own copy of articles that were recently added. The data center is far away from the lab machine.

Design an efficient way of copying one thousand files each 100 kilobytes in size from a single lab server to each of 1000 servers in a distant data center.

Hint: Exploit the data center.

Solution: Assume that the bandwidth from the lab machine is a limiting factor. It is reasonable to first do trivial optimizations, such as combining the articles into a single file and compressing this file.

Opening 1000 connections from the lab server to the 1000 machines in the data center and transferring the latest news articles is not feasible since the total data transferred will be approximately 100 gigabytes (without compression).

Since the bandwidth between machines in a data center is very high, we can copy the file from the lab machine to a single machine in the data center and have the machines in the data center complete the copy. Instead of having just one machine serve the file to the remaining 999 machines, we can have each machine that has received the file initiate copies to the machines that have not yet received the file. In theory, this leads to an exponential reduction in the time taken to do the copy.

Several additional issues have to be dealt with. Should a machine initiate further copies before it has received the entire file? (This is tricky because of link or server failures.) How should the knowledge of machines which do not yet have copies of the file be shared? (There can be a central repository or servers can simply check others by random selection.) If the bandwidth between machines in a data center is not a constant, how should the selections be made? (Servers close to each other, e.g., in the same rack, should prefer communicating with each other.)

Finally, it should be mentioned that there are open source solutions to this problem, e.g., Unison and BitTorrent, which would be a good place to start.

21.16 Design the World Wide Web

Design the World Wide Web. Specifically, describe what happens when you enter a URL in a browser address bar, and press return.

Hint: Follow the flow of information.

Solution: At the network level, the browser extracts the domain name component of the URL, and determines the IP address of the server, e.g., through a call to a Domain Name Server (DNS), or a cache lookup. It then communicates using the HTTP protocol with the server. HTTP itself is built on top of TCP/IP, which is responsible for routing, reassembling, and resending packets, as well as controlling the transmission rate.

The server determines what the client is asking for by looking at the portion of the URL that comes after the domain name, and possibly also the body of the HTTP request. The request may be for something as simple a file, which is returned by the webserver; HTTP spells out a format by which the type of the returned file is specified. For example, the URL http://go.com/imgs/abc.png may encode a request for the file whose hierarchical name is imgs/abc.png relative to a base directory specified at configuration to the web server.

The URL may also encode a request to a service provided by the web server. For example, http://go.com/lookup/flight?num=UA37,city=AUS is a request to the lookup/flight service, with an argument consisting of two attribute-value pair. The service could be implemented in many ways, e.g., Java code within the server, or a Common Gateway Interface (CGI) script written in Perl. The service generates a HTTP response, typically HTML, which is then returned to the browser. This response could encode data which

399

is used by scripts running in the browser. Common data formats include JSON and XML.

The browser is responsible for taking the returned HTML and displaying it on the client. The rendering is done in two parts. First, a parse tree (the DOM) is generated from the HTML, and then a rendering library "paints" the screen. The returned HTML may include scripts written in JavaScript. These are executed by the browser, and they can perform actions like making requests and updating the DOM based on the responses—this is how a live stock ticker is implemented. Styling attributes (CSS) are commonly used to customize the look of a page.

Many more issues exist on both the client and server side: security, cookies, HTML form elements, HTML styling, and handlers for multi-media content, to name a few.

21.17 ESTIMATE THE HARDWARE COST OF A PHOTO SHARING APP

Estimate the hardware cost of the server hardware needed to build a photo sharing app used by every person on the earth.

Hint: Use variables to denote quantities and costs, and relate them with equations. Then fill in reasonable values.

Solution: The cost is a function of server CPU and RAM resources, storage, and bandwidth, as well as the number and size of the images that are uploaded each day. We will create an estimate based on unit costs for each of these. We assume a distributed architecture in which images are spread ("sharded") across servers.

Assume each user uploads i images each day with an average size of s bytes, and that each image is viewed v times. After d days, the storage requirement is $isdN$, where N is the number of users. Assuming $v \gg 1$, i.e., most images are seen many times, the server cost is dominated by the time to serve the images. The servers are required to serve up Niv images and $Nivs$ bytes each day. Assuming a server can handle h HTTP requests per second and has an outgoing bandwidth of b bytes per second, the number of required servers is $\max(Niv/Th, Nivs/Tb)$, where T is the number of seconds in a day.

Reasonable values for N, i, s, and v are 10^{10}, 10, 10^5, and 100. Reasonable values for h and b are 10^4 and 10^8. There are approximately 10^5 seconds in a day. Therefore the number of servers required is $\max((10^{10} \times 10 \times 100)/(10^5 \times 10^4), (10^{10} \times 10 \times 100 \times 10^5)/(10^5 \times 10^8)) = 10^5$. Each server would cost \$1000, so the total cost would be of the order of 100 million dollars.

Storage costs are approximately \$0.1 per gigabyte, and we add $Nis = 10^{10} \times 10 \times 10^5$ bytes each day, so each day we need to add a million dollars worth of storage.

The above calculation leaves out many costs, such as electricity, cooling, and network. It also neglects computations such as computing trending data and spam analysis. Furthermore, there is no measure of the cost of redundancy, such as replicated storage, or the ability to handle nonuniform loads. Nevertheless, it is a decent starting point. What is remarkable is the fact that the entire world can be connected through images at a very low cost—pennies per person.

Honors Class

The supply of problems in mathematics is inexhaustible, and as soon as one problem is solved numerous others come forth in its place.

— *"Mathematical Problems,"*
D. HILBERT, 1900

This chapter contains problems that are more difficult to solve than the ones presented earlier. Many of them are commonly asked at interviews, albeit with the expectation that the candidate will not deliver the best solution.

There are several reasons why we included these problems:

- Although mastering these problems is not essential to your success, if you do solve them, you will have put yourself into a very strong position, similar to training for a race with ankle weights.
- If you are asked one of these questions or a variant thereof, and you successfully derive the best solution, you will have strongly impressed your interviewer. The implications of this go beyond being made an offer—your salary, position, and status will all go up.
- Some of the problems are appropriate for candidates interviewing for specialized positions, e.g., optimizing large scale distributed systems, machine learning for computational finance, etc. They are also commonly asked of candidates with advanced degrees.
- Finally, if you love a good challenge, these problems will provide it!

You should be happy if your interviewer asks you a hard question—it implies high expectations, and is an opportunity to shine, compared, for example, to being asked to write a program that tests if a string is palindromic.

Problems roughly follow the sequence of topics of the previous chapters, i.e., we begin with primitive types, and end with graphs. We recommend you solve these problems in a randomized order. The following problems are a good place to begin with: Problems 22.1, 22.6, 22.8, 22.10, 22.14, 22.15, 22.22, 22.26, 22.30, 22.32, 22.41, 22.48, 22.51. White ninja (👁️) problems are though challenging, should be solvable by a good candidate given enough time. Black ninja (🥷) problems are exceptionally difficult, and are suitable for testing a candidate's response to stress, as described on Page17.

The greatest common divisor (GCD) of positive integers x and y is the largest integer d such that d divides x evenly, and d divides y evenly, i.e., x mod $d = 0$ and y mod $d = 0$.

Design an efficient algorithm for computing the GCD of two numbers without using multiplication, division or the modulus operators.

Hint: Use case analysis: both even; both odd; one even and one odd.

Solution: The straightforward algorithm is based on recursion. If $x = y$, GCD$(x, y) = x$; otherwise, assume without loss of generality, that $x > y$. Then GCD(x, y) is the GCD$(x - y, y)$.

The recursive algorithm based on the above does not use multiplication, division or modulus, but for some inputs it is very slow. As an example, if the input is $x = 2^n$, $y = 2$, the algorithm makes 2^{n-1} recursive calls. The time complexity can be improved by observing that the repeated subtraction amounts to division, i.e., when $x > y$, GCD$(x, y) =$ GCD$(y, x$ mod $y)$, but this approach uses integer division which was explicitly disallowed in the problem statement.

Here is a fast solution, which is also based on recursion, but does not use general multiplication or division. Instead it special-cases division to division by 2.

An example is illustrative. Suppose we were to compute the GCD of 24 and 300. Instead of repeatedly subtracting 24 from 300, we can observe that since both are even, the result is $2 \times$ GCD$(12, 150)$. Dividing by 2 is a right shift by 1, so we do not need a general division operation. Since 12 and 150 are both even, GCD$(12, 150) = 2 \times$ GCD$(6, 75)$. Since 75 is odd, the GCD of 6 and 75 is the same as the GCD of 3 and 75, since 2 cannot divide 75. The GCD of 3 and 75 is the GCD of 3 and $75 - 3 = 72$. Repeatedly applying the same logic, GCD$(3, 72) =$ GCD$(3, 36) =$ GCD$(3, 18) =$ GCD$(3, 9) =$ GCD$(3, 6) =$ GCD$(3, 3) = 3$. This implies GCD$(24, 300) = 2 \times 2 \times 3 = 12$.

More generally, the base case is when the two arguments are equal. Otherwise, we check if none, one, or both numbers are even. If both are even, we compute the GCD of the halves of the original numbers, and return that result times 2; if exactly one is even, we half it, and return the GCD of the resulting pair; if both are odd, we subtract the smaller from the larger and return the GCD of the resulting pair. Multiplication by 2 is trivially implemented with a single left shift. Division by 2 is done with a single right shift.

```
long long GCD(long long x, long long y) {
  if (x == y) {
    return x;
  } else if (!(x & 1) && !(y & 1)) {  // x and y are even.
    return GCD(x >> 1, y >> 1) << 1;
  } else if (!(x & 1) && y & 1) {  // x is even, and y is odd.
    return GCD(x >> 1, y);
  } else if (x & 1 && !(y & 1)) {  // x is odd, and y is even.
    return GCD(x, y >> 1);
  } else if (x > y) {  // Both x and y are odd, and x > y.
    return GCD(x - y, y);
  }
  return GCD(x, y - x);  // Both x and y are odd, and x <= y.
```

}

Note that the last step leads to a recursive call with one even and one odd number. Consequently, in every two calls, we reduce the combined bit length of the two numbers by at least one, meaning that the time complexity is proportional to the sum of the number of bits in x and y, i.e., $O(\log x + \log y))$.

22.2 FIND THE FIRST MISSING POSITIVE ENTRY ☺

Let A be an array of length n. Design an algorithm to find the smallest positive integer which is not present in A. You do not need to preserve the contents of A. For example, if $A = \langle 3, 5, 4, -1, 5, 1, -1 \rangle$, the smallest positive integer not present in A is 2.

Hint: First, find an upper bound for x.

Solution: A brute-force approach is to sort A and iterate through it looking for the first gap in the entries after we see an entry equal to 0. The time complexity is that of sorting, i.e., $O(n \log n)$.

Since all we want is the smallest positive number in A, we explore other algorithms that do not rely on sorting. We could store the entries in A in a hash table S (Chapter 13), and then iterate through the positive integers $1, 2, 3, \ldots$ looking for the first one that is not in S. The time complexity is $O(n)$ to create S, and then $O(n)$ to perform the lookups, since we must find a missing entry by the time we get to $n + 1$ as there are only n entries. Therefore the time complexity is $O(n)$. The space complexity is $O(n)$, e.g., if the entries from A are all distinct positive integers.

The problem statement gives us a hint which we can use to reduce the space complexity. Instead of using an external hash table to store the set of positive integers, we can use A itself. Specifically, if A contains k between 1 and n, we set $A[k-1]$ to k. (We use $k - 1$ because we need to use all n entries, including the entry at index 0, which will be used to record the presence of 1.) Note that we need to save the presence of the existing entry in $A[k-1]$ if it is between 1 and n. Because A contains n entries, the smallest positive number that is missing in A cannot be greater than $n + 1$.

For example, let $A = \langle 3, 4, 0, 2 \rangle$, $n = 4$. we begin by recording the presence of 3 by writing it in $A[3 - 1]$; we save the current entry at index 2 by writing it to $A[0]$. Now $A = \langle 0, 4, 3, 2 \rangle$. Since 0 is outside the range of interest, we advance to $A[1]$, i.e., 4, which is within the range of interest. We write 4 in $A[4 - 1]$, and save the value at that location to index 1, and A becomes $\langle 0, 2, 3, 4 \rangle$. The value at $A[1]$ already indicates that a 2 is present, so we advance. The same holds for $A[2]$ and $A[3]$.

Now we make a pass through A looking for the first index i such that $A[i] \neq i + 1$; this is the smallest missing positive entry, which is 1 for our example.

```
// A is passed by value argument, since we change it.
int FindFirstMissingPositive(vector<int> A) {
  // Record which values are present by writing A[i] to index A[i] - 1 if A[i]
  // is between 1 and A.size(), inclusive. We save the value at index
  // A[i] - 1 by swapping it with the entry at i. If A[i] is negative or
  // greater than n, we just advance i.
  size_t i = 0;
```

```
while (i < A.size()) {
    if (A[i] > 0 && A[i] <= A.size() && A[A[i] - 1] != A[i]) {
        swap(A[i], A[A[i] - 1]);
    } else {
        ++i;
    }
}

// Second pass through A to search for the first index i such that
// A[i] != i+1, indicating that i + 1 is absent. If all numbers between 1
// and A.size() are present, the smallest missing positive is A.size() + 1.
for (size_t i = 0; i < A.size(); ++i) {
    if (A[i] != i + 1) {
        return i + 1;
    }
}
return A.size() + 1;
}
```

The time complexity is $O(n)$, since we perform a constant amount of work per entry. Because we reuse A, the space complexity is $O(1)$.

22.3 Buy and sell a stock k times 🥷

This problem generalizes the buy and sell problem introduced on Page 1.

Write a program to compute the maximum profit that can be made by buying and selling a share k times over a given day range. Your program takes k and an array of daily stock prices as input.

Solution: Here is a straightforward algorithm. Iterate over j from 1 to k and iterate through A, recording for each index i the best solution for $A[0 : i]$ with j pairs. We store these solutions in an auxiliary array of length n. The overall time complexity will be $O(kn^2)$; by reusing the arrays, we can reduce the additional space complexity to $O(n)$.

We can improve the time complexity to $O(kn)$, and the additional space complexity to $O(k)$ as follows. Define B_i^j to be the most money you can have if you must make $j - 1$ buy-sell transactions prior to i and buy at i. Define S_i^j to be the maximum profit achievable with j buys and sells with the jth sell taking place at i. Then the following mutual recurrence holds:

$$S_i^j = A[i] + \max_{i' < i} B_{i'}^j$$
$$B_i^j = \max_{i' < i} S_{i'}^{j-1} - A[i]$$

The key to achieving an $O(kn)$ time bound is the observation that computing B and S requires computing $\max_{i' < i} B_{i'}^{j-1}$ and $\max_{i' < i} S_{i'}^{j-1}$. These two quantities can be computed in constant time for each i and j with a conditional update. In code:

```
double MaxKPairsProfits(const vector<double> &A, int k) {
    vector<double> k_sum(2 * k, numeric_limits<double>::lowest());
```

404

```
for (int i = 0; i < A.size(); ++i) {
  vector<double> pre_k_sum(k_sum);
  for (int j = 0, sign = -1; j < k_sum.size() && j <= i; ++j, sign *= -1) {
    double diff = sign * A[i] + (j == 0 ? 0 : pre_k_sum[j - 1]);
    k_sum[j] = max(diff, pre_k_sum[j]);
  }
}
return k_sum.back();  // Returns the last selling profits as the answer.
}
```

22.4 COMPUTE THE MAXIMUM PRODUCT OF ALL ENTRIES BUT ONE

Suppose you are given an array A of integers, and are asked to find the largest product that can be made by multiplying all but one of the entries in A. (You cannot use an entry more than once.) For example, if $A = \langle 3, 2, 5, 4 \rangle$, the result is $3 \times 5 \times 4 = 60$, if $A = \langle 3, 2, -1, 4 \rangle$, the result is $3 \times 2 \times 4 = 24$, and if $A = \langle 3, 2, -1, 4, -1, 6 \rangle$, the result is $3 \times -1 \times 4 \times -1 \times 6 = 72$.

One approach is to form the product P of all the elements, and then find the maximum of $P/A[i]$ over all i. This takes $n - 1$ multiplications (to form P) and n divisions (to compute each $P/A[i]$). Suppose because of finite precision considerations we cannot use a division-based approach; we can only use multiplications. The brute-force solution entails computing all n products of $n - 1$ elements; each such product takes $n - 2$ multiplications, i.e., $O(n^2)$ time complexity.

Given an array A of length n whose entries are integers, compute the largest product that can be made using $n - 1$ entries in A. You cannot use an entry more than once. Array entries may be positive, negative, or 0. Your algorithm cannot use the division operator, explicitly or implicitly.

Hint: Consider the products of the first $i - 1$ and the last $n - i$ elements. Alternatively, count the number of negative entries and zero entries.

Solution: The brute-force approach to compute $P/A[i]$ is to multiplying the entries appearing before i with those that appear after i. This leads to $n(n - 2)$ multiplications, since for each term $P/A[i]$ we need $n - 2$ multiplications.

Note that there is substantial overlap in computation when computing $P/A[i]$ and $P/A[i + 1]$. In particular, the product of the entries appearing before $i + 1$ is $A[i]$ times the product of the entries appearing before i. We can compute all products of entries before i with $n - 1$ multiplications, and all products of entries after i with $n - 1$ multiplications, and store these values in arrays L and R, respectively. The desired result then is the maximum over all i of $L[i] \times R[i]$.

```
int FindBiggestNMinusOneProduct(const vector<int>& A) {
  // Builds forward product L, and backward product R.
  vector<int> L, R(A.size());
  partial_sum(A.cbegin(), A.cend(), back_inserter(L), multiplies<int>());
  partial_sum(A.crbegin(), A.crend(), R.rbegin(), multiplies<int>());

  // Finds the biggest product of (n - 1) numbers.
```

```
  int max_product = numeric_limits<int>::min();
  for (int i = 0; i < A.size(); ++i) {
    int forward = i > 0 ? L[i - 1] : 1;
    int backward = i + 1 < A.size() ? R[i + 1] : 1;
    max_product = max(max_product, forward * backward);
  }
  return max_product;
}
```

The time complexity is $O(n)$; the space complexity is $O(n)$, since the solution uses two arrays, each of length n.

We now solve this problem in $O(n)$ time and $O(1)$ additional storage. The insight comes from the fact that if there are no negative entries, the maximum product comes from using all but the smallest element. (Note that this result is correct if the number of 0 entries is zero, one, or more.)

If the number of negative entries is odd, regardless of how many 0 entries and positive entries, the maximum product uses all entries except for the negative entry with the smallest absolute value, i.e., the greatest negative entry.

Going further, if the number of negative entries is even, the maximum product again uses all but the smallest nonnegative element, assuming the number of nonnegative entries is greater than zero. (This is correct, even in the presence of 0 entries.)

If the number of negative entries is even, and there are no nonnegative entries, the result must be negative. Since we want the largest product, we leave out the entry whose magnitude is largest, i.e., the least negative entry.

This analysis yields a two-stage algorithm. First, determine the applicable scenario, e.g., are there an even number of negative entries? Consequently, perform the actual multiplication to get the result.

```
int FindBiggestNMinusOneProduct(const vector<int>& A) {
  int least_nonnegative_idx = -1;
  int number_of_negatives = 0, greatest_negative_idx = -1,
      least_negative_idx = -1;

  // Identify the least negative, greatest negative, and least nonnegative
  // entries.
  for (int i = 0; i < A.size(); ++i) {
    if (A[i] < 0) {
      ++number_of_negatives;
      if (least_negative_idx == -1 || A[least_negative_idx] < A[i]) {
        least_negative_idx = i;
      }
      if (greatest_negative_idx == -1 || A[i] < A[greatest_negative_idx]) {
        greatest_negative_idx = i;
      }
    } else {  // A[i] >= 0.
      if (least_nonnegative_idx == -1 || A[i] < A[least_nonnegative_idx]) {
        least_nonnegative_idx = i;
      }
    }
  }

  int product = 1;
```

```
int idx_to_skip =
    number_of_negatives % 2
        ? least_negative_idx
        // Check if there are any nonnegative entry.
        : (least_nonnegative_idx != -1 ? least_nonnegative_idx
                                       : greatest_negative_idx);
for (int i = 0; i < A.size(); ++i) {
    if (i != idx_to_skip) {
        product *= A[i];
    }
}
return product;
}
```

The algorithm performs a traversal of the array, with a constant amount of computation per entry, a nested conditional, followed by another traversal of the array, with a constant amount of computation per entry. Hence, the time complexity is $O(n) + O(1) + O(n) = O(n)$. The additional space complexity is $O(1)$, corresponding to the local variables.

Variant: Let A be as above. Compute an array B where $B[i]$ is the product of all elements in A except $A[i]$. You cannot use division. Your time complexity should be $O(n)$, and you can only use $O(1)$ additional space.

Variant: Let A be as above. Compute the maximum over the product of all triples of distinct elements of A.

22.5 COMPUTE THE LONGEST CONTIGUOUS INCREASING SUBARRAY

An array is increasing if each element is less than its succeeding element except for the last element.

Implement an algorithm that takes as input an array A of n elements, and returns the beginning and ending indices of a longest increasing subarray of A. For example, if $A = \langle 2, 11, 3, 5, 13, 7, 19, 17, 23 \rangle$, the longest increasing subarray is $\langle 3, 5, 13 \rangle$, and you should return $(2, 4)$.

Hint: If $A[i] \geq A[i + 1]$, instead of checking $A[i + 1] \leq A[i + 2]$, go further out in the array.

Solution: The brute-force algorithm is to test every subarray: two nested loops iterate through the starting and ending index of the subarray, an inner loop to test if the subarray is increasing, and some logic to track the longest subarray. The time complexity is $O(n^3)$, e.g., for the array $\langle 0, 1, 2, 3, \ldots, n - 1 \rangle$. The time complexity can easily be improved to $O(n^2)$ by caching whether the subarray $A[i : j]$ is increasing when examining $A[i : j + 1]$.

Looking more carefully at the example, the longest subarray ending at 3 is $A[2 : 2]$, because $3 < 11$. Conversely, since $13 > 5$, the longest subarray ending at 13 is the longest subarray ending at 5 (which is $A[2 : 3]$) together with 13, i.e., $A[2 : 4]$. In general, the longest increasing subarray ending at index $j + 1$ inclusive is

1. the single entry $A[j + 1]$, if $A[j + 1] \leq A[j]$, or

2. the longest increasing subarray ending at index j together with $A[j + 1]$, if $A[j + 1] > A[j]$.

This fact can be used directly to improve the brute-force algorithm to one whose time complexity is $O(n)$.

The additional space complexity is $O(1)$, since all we need is the length of the longest subarray ending at j when processing $j + 1$. Two additional variables can be used to hold the length and ending index of the longest increasing subarray seen so far.

We can heuristically improve upon the $O(n)$ algorithm by observing that if $A[i-1] \not< A[i]$ (i.e., we are starting to look for a new subarray starting at i) and the longest contiguous subarray seen up to index i has length L, we can move on to index $i + L$ and work backwards towards i. Specifically, if for any $j, i < j \le i + L$ we have $A[j - 1] \not< A[j]$, we can skip the earlier indices. For example, after processing 13, we work our way back from the entry at index $4 + 3 = 7$, i.e., 13's index plus the length of the longest increasing subarray seen so far (3). Since $A[7] = 17 < A[6] = 19$, we do not need to examine prior entries—no increasing array ending at $A[7]$ can be longer than the current best.

```
struct Subarray {
  int start = 0, end = 0;
};

Subarray FindLongestIncreasingSubarray(const vector<int> &A) {
  int max_length = 1;
  Subarray ans;
  int i = 0;
  while (i < A.size() - max_length) {
    // Backward check and skip if A[j - 1] >= A[j].
    bool is_skippable = false;
    for (int j = i + max_length; j > i; --j) {
      if (A[j - 1] >= A[j]) {
        i = j;
        is_skippable = true;
        break;
      }
    }

    // Forward check if it is not skippable.
    if (!is_skippable) {
      i += max_length;
      while (i < A.size() && A[i - 1] < A[i]) {
        ++i, ++max_length;
      }
      ans = {i - max_length, i - 1};
    }
  }
  return ans;
}
```

Skipping is a heuristic in that it does not improve the worst-case complexity. If the array consists of alternating 0s and 1s, we still examine each element, implying an

408

$O(n)$ time bound, but the best-case complexity reduces to $O(\max(n/L, L))$, where L is the length of the longest increasing subarray.

22.6 ROTATE AN ARRAY 🐟

Let A be an array of n elements. If memory is not a concern, rotating A by i positions is trivial; we create a new array B of length n, and set $B[j] = A[(i + j) \bmod n]$ for each j. If all we have is additional storage for c elements, we can repeatedly rotate the array by c a total of $\lceil i/c \rceil$ times; this increases the time complexity to $O(n \lceil i/c \rceil)$.

Design an algorithm for rotating an array A of n elements to the right by i positions. Do not use library functions implementing rotate.

Hint: Use concrete examples to form a hypothesis relating n, i, and the number of cycles.

Solution: There are two brute-force algorithms: perform shift-by-one i times, which has $O(ni)$ time complexity and $O(1)$ space complexity. The other is to use an additional array of length i as a buffer to move elements i at a time. This has $O(n)$ time complexity and $O(i)$ space complexity.

The key to achieving both $O(n)$ time complexity and $O(1)$ space complexity is to use the fact that a permutation can be applied using constant additional storage (Problem 6.10 on Page 71) with the permutation corresponding to a rotation.

A rotation by itself is not a cyclic permutation. However, a rotation is a permutation, and as such can be decomposed to a set of cyclic permutations. For example, for the case where $n = 6$ and $i = 2$, the rotation corresponds to the permutation $\langle 4, 5, 1, 2, 3, 4 \rangle$. This permutation can be achieved by the cyclic permutations $(0, 2, 4)$ and $(1, 3, 5)$. Similarly, when $n = 15$ and $i = 6$, the cycles are $\langle 0, 6, 12, 3, 9 \rangle$, $\langle 1, 7, 13, 4, 10 \rangle$, and $\langle 2, 8, 14, 5, 11 \rangle$.

The examples lead us to conjecture the following:

(1.) All cycles have the same length, and are a shifted version of the cycle $\langle 0, i \bmod n, 2i \bmod n, \ldots, (l - 1)i \bmod n \rangle$.

(2.) The number of cycles is the GCD of n and i.

These conjectures can be justified on heuristic grounds. (A formal proof requires looking at the prime factorizations for i and n.)

Assuming these conjectures to be correct, we can apply the rotation one cycle at a time, as follows. The first elements of the different cyclic permutations are at indices $0, 1, 2, \ldots, \text{GCD}(n, i) - 1$. For each cycle, we apply it by shifting elements in the cycle one-at-a-time.

```
void RotateArray(int rotate_amount, vector<int>* A_ptr) {
  rotate_amount %= A_ptr->size();
  int num_cycles = GCD(A_ptr->size(), rotate_amount);
  int cycle_length = A_ptr->size() / num_cycles;

  for (int c = 0; c < num_cycles; ++c) {
    ApplyCyclicPermutation(rotate_amount, c, cycle_length, A_ptr);
  }
}
```

```
void ApplyCyclicPermutation(int rotate_amount, int offset, int cycle_length,
                            vector<int>* A_ptr) {
  vector<int>& A = *A_ptr;
  int temp = A[offset];
  for (int i = 1; i < cycle_length; ++i) {
    swap(A[(offset + i * rotate_amount) % A.size()], temp);
  }
  A[offset] = temp;
}
```

The time complexity is $O(n)$, since we perform a constant amount of work per entry. The space complexity is $O(1)$.

We now provide an alternative to the permutation approach. The new solution works well in practice and is considerably simpler. Assume that $A = \langle 1, 2, 3, 4, a, b \rangle$, and $i = 2$. Then in the rotated A there are two subarrays, $\langle 1, 2, 3, 4 \rangle$ and $\langle a, b \rangle$ that keep their original orders. Therefore, rotation can be seen as the exchanges of the two subarrays of A. It is easy to perform these exchanges in $O(n)$ time. To implement these exchanges to use $O(1)$ space we use an array-reverse function. Using A and i as an example, we first reverse A to get A' ($\langle 1, 2, 3, 4, a, b \rangle$ becomes $\langle b, a, 4, 3, 2, 1 \rangle$), then reverse the first i elements of A' ($\langle b, a, 4, 3, 2, 1 \rangle$ becomes $\langle a, b, 4, 3, 2, 1 \rangle$), and reverse the remaining elements starting from the ith element of A' ($\langle a, b, 4, 3, 2, 1 \rangle$ becomes $\langle a, b, 1, 2, 3, 4 \rangle$) which yields the rotated A.

```
void RotateArray(int i, vector<int>* A) {
  i %= A->size();
  reverse(A->begin(), A->end());
  reverse(A->begin(), A->begin() + i);
  reverse(A->begin() + i, A->end());
}
```

We note in passing that a completely different approach is to perform the rotation in blocks of k, reusing freed space for temporary storage. It can be made to work, but the final rotation has to be performed very carefully, and the resulting code is complex.

22.7 IDENTIFY POSITIONS ATTACKED BY ROOKS 🥷

This problem is concerned with computing squares in a chessboard which can be attacked by rooks that have been placed at arbitrary locations. The scenario is illustrated in Figure 22.1(a) on the following page.

Write a program which takes as input a 2D array A of 1s and 0s, where the 0s encode the positions of rooks on an $n \times m$ chessboard, as show in Figure 22.1(b) on the next page and updates the array to contain 0s at all locations which can be attacked by rooks, as shown in Figure 22.1(c) on the following page.

Hint: Make use of the first row and the first column.

Solution: This problem is trivial with an additional n-bit array R and an additional m-bit array C. We simply initialize R and C to 1s. Then we iterate through all entries

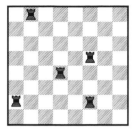

1	0	1	1	1	1	1	1
1	1	1	1	1	1	1	1
1	1	1	1	1	1	1	1
1	1	1	1	1	0	1	1
1	1	1	0	1	1	1	1
1	1	1	1	1	1	1	1
0	1	1	1	1	0	1	1
1	1	1	1	1	1	1	1

0	0	0	0	0	0	0	0
0	0	1	0	1	0	1	1
0	0	1	0	1	0	1	1
0	0	0	0	0	0	0	0
0	0	0	0	0	0	0	0
0	0	1	0	1	0	1	1
0	0	0	0	0	0	0	0
0	0	1	0	1	0	1	1

(a) Initial placement of 5 rooks on an 8 × 8 chessboard.

(b) Rook placement from (a) encoded using an 8 × 8 2D array—a 0 indicates a rook is placed at that position.

(c) 2D array encoding positions that can be attacked by rooks placed as in (a)—a 0 indicates an attacked position.

Figure 22.1: Rook attack.

of A, and for each (i, j) such that $A[i][j] = 0$, we set $R[i]$ and $C[j]$ to 0. Consequently, a 0 in $R[i]$ indicates that Row i should be set to 0; columns are analogous. A second iteration through all entries can be used to set the 0s in A.

The drawback with the above approach is the use of $O(n + m)$ additional storage. The solution is to use storage in A itself. The reason we can do this is because if a single 0 appears in a row, the entire row is cleared. Consequently, we can store a single extra bit r denoting whether Row 0 has a 0 within it. Now Row 0 can play the role of C in the algorithm in the previous paragraph. If we record a 0 in $R[i]$, that is the value we would be writing at that location, so the original entry is not lost. If $R[i]$ holds a 1 after the first pass, it retains that value, unless r indicates Row 0 is to be cleared. Columns are handled in exactly the same way.

```
void RookAttack(vector<vector<int>>* A_ptr) {
  vector<vector<int>>& A = *A_ptr;
  size_t m = A.size(), n = A[0].size();
  bool has_first_row_zero = false;
  for (size_t j = 0; j < n; ++j) {
    if (!A[0][j]) {
      has_first_row_zero = true;
      break;
    }
  }
  bool has_first_column_zero = false;
  for (size_t i = 0; i < m; ++i) {
    if (!A[i][0]) {
      has_first_column_zero = true;
      break;
    }
  }

  for (size_t i = 1; i < m; ++i) {
    for (size_t j = 1; j < n; ++j) {
      if (!A[i][j]) {
        A[i][0] = A[0][j] = 0;
      }
    }
  }
```

```
    }
    for (size_t i = 1; i < m; ++i) {
      if (!A[i][0]) {
        for (size_t j = 1; j < n; ++j) {
          A[i][j] = 0;
        }
      }
    }

    for (size_t j = 1; j < n; ++j) {
      if (!A[0][j]) {
        for (size_t i = 1; i < m; ++i) {
          A[i][j] = 0;
        }
      }
    }

    if (has_first_row_zero) {
      for (size_t j = 0; j < n; ++j) {
        A[0][j] = 0;
      }
    }
    if (has_first_column_zero) {
      for (size_t i = 0; i < m; ++i) {
        A[i][0] = 0;
      }
    }
  }
```

The time complexity is $O(nm)$ since we perform $O(1)$ computation per entry. The space complexity is $O(1)$.

22.8 JUSTIFY TEXT

This problem is concerned with justifying text. It abstracts a problem arising in typesetting. The input is specified as a sequence of words, and the target line length. After justification, each individual line must begin with a word, and each subsequent word must be separated from prior words with at least one blank. If a line contains more than one word, it should not end in a blank. The sequences of blanks within each line should be as close to equal in length as possible, with the longer blank sequences, if any, appearing at the initial part of the line. As an exception, the very last line should use single blanks as separators, with additional blanks appearing at its end.

For example, if A = ⟨"The", "quick", "brown", "fox", "jumped", "over", "the", "lazy", "dogs."⟩ and the line length L is 11, then the returned result should be "The␣␣␣quick", "brown␣␣␣fox", "jumped␣over", "the␣␣␣␣lazy", "dogs.␣␣␣␣␣␣". The symbol ␣ denotes a blank.

Write a program which takes as input an array A of strings and a positive integer L, and computes the justification of the text specified by A.

Hint: Solve it on a line-by-line basis, assuming a single space between pairs of words. Then figure out how to distribute excess blanks.

Solution: The challenge in solving this problem is that it requires lookahead. Specifically, the number of spaces between words in a line cannot be computed till complete set of words in that line is known.

We solve the problem on a line-by-line basis. First, we compute the words that go into each line, assuming a single space between words. After we know the words in a line, we compute the number of blanks in that line and distribute the blanks evenly. The final line is special-cased.

```
vector<string> JustifyText(const vector<string>& words, size_t L) {
  size_t curr_line_start = 0, num_words_curr_line = 0, curr_line_length - 0;
  vector<string> result;
  for (size_t i = 0; i < words.size(); ++i) {
    // curr_line_start is the first word in the current line, and i is used to
    // identify the last word.
    ++num_words_curr_line;
    size_t lookahead_line_length =
        curr_line_length + words[i].size() + (num_words_curr_line - 1);
    if (lookahead_line_length == L) {
      result.emplace_back(
          JoinALineWithSpace(words, curr_line_start, i, i - curr_line_start));
      curr_line_start = i + 1, num_words_curr_line = 0, curr_line_length = 0;
    } else if (lookahead_line_length > L) {
      result.emplace_back(JoinALineWithSpace(words, curr_line_start, i - 1,
                                             L - curr_line_length));
      curr_line_start = i, num_words_curr_line = 1;
      curr_line_length = words[i].size();
    } else {  // lookahead_line_length < L.
      curr_line_length += words[i].size();
    }
  }

  // Handles the last line. Last line is to be left-aligned.
  if (num_words_curr_line > 0) {
    string line - JoinALineWithSpace(words, curr_line_start, words.size() - 1,
                                     num_words_curr_line - 1);
    line.append(L - curr_line_length - (num_words_curr_line - 1), ' ');
    result.emplace_back(line);
  }
  return result;
}

// Joins strings in words[start : end] with num_spaces spaces spread evenly.
string JoinALineWithSpace(const vector<string>& words, size_t start,
                          size_t end, size_t num_spaces) {
  size_t num_words_curr_line = end - start + 1;
  string line;
  for (size_t i = start; i < end; ++i) {
    line += words[i];
    --num_words_curr_line;
    size_t num_curr_space =
        ceil(static_cast<double>(num_spaces) / num_words_curr_line);
```

413

```
    line.append(num_curr_space, ' ');
    num_spaces -= num_curr_space;
  }
  line += words[end];
  line.append(num_spaces, ' ');
  return line;
}
```

Let n be the sum of the lengths of the strings in A. We spend $O(1)$ time per character in the first pass as well as the second pass, yielding an $O(n)$ time complexity.

22.9 Reverse sublists k at a time 🥷

This problem entails reversing sublists of a given singly linked list k at a time. For example, the result of reversing sublists of size 3 in the list in Figure 8.8(a) on Page 120 is shown in Figure 8.11(a) on Page 124.

Write a program which takes as input a singly linked list L and a nonnegative integer k, and reverses the list k nodes at a time. If the number of nodes n in the list is not a multiple of k, leave the last n mod k nodes unchanged. Do not change the data stored within a node.

Hint: Perform a case analysis.

Solution: The basic idea is straightforward—we use Solution 8.2 on Page 111 to reverse the sublist consisting of the first k nodes, then the sublist of the next k nodes, etc. The new head of the reversed sublist must be made the successor of the tail of the previous sublist. We use two iterators, one for the head and one for the tail of sublist being reversed. The implementation requires additional variables to record the nodes adjacent to the sublist.

```
shared_ptr<ListNode<int>> ReverseK(shared_ptr<ListNode<int>> L, int k) {
  auto dummy_head = make_shared<ListNode<int>>(ListNode<int>{0, L});
  shared_ptr<ListNode<int>> sublist_predecessor = dummy_head,
                            sublist_head = dummy_head->next,
                            sublist_successor = dummy_head,
                            sublist_tail = dummy_head->next;
  while (sublist_head) {
    // Identify the tail of sublist of k nodes to be reversed.
    int num_remaining = k;
    while (num_remaining) {
      sublist_successor = sublist_tail;
      sublist_tail = sublist_tail->next;
      --num_remaining;
      if (!sublist_tail) {
        break;
      }
    }
    if (num_remaining > 0) {
      // Specification says not to reverse.
      return dummy_head->next;
    }
```

```
    sublist_successor->next = nullptr;
    ReverseLinkedList(sublist_head);

    // Splice the reversed sublist.
    sublist_predecessor->next = sublist_successor;
    // Go on to the head of next sublist.
    sublist_predecessor = sublist_head, sublist_head->next = sublist_tail;
    sublist_head = sublist_tail, sublist_successor = nullptr;
  }
  return dummy_head->next;
}
```

There are n/k sublists, each of which takes $O(k)$ time to reverse, yielding a time complexity of $O(n)$.

22.10 IMPLEMENT LIST ZIPPING 👁

Let L be a singly linked list. Assume its nodes are numbered starting at 0. Define the zip of L to be the list consisting of the interleaving of the nodes numbered $0, 1, 2, \ldots$ with the nodes numbered $n - 1, n - 2, n - 3, \ldots$, where n is the number of nodes in the list. The zipping function is illustrated in Figure 4.1 on Page 27.

Implement the zip function.

Hint: Consider traversing the list in reverse order.

Solution: A brute-force approach is to iteratively identify the head and tail, remove them from the original list, and append the pair to the result. The time complexity is $O(n) + O(n - 2) + O(n - 4) + \cdots = O(n^2)$, where n is the number of nodes. The space complexity is $O(1)$.

The $O(n^2)$ complexity comes from having to repeatedly traverse the list to identify the tail. Note that getting the head of a singly linked list is an $O(1)$ time operation. This suggests paying a one-time cost of $O(n)$ to reverse the second half of the original list. Now all we need to do is interleave this with the first half of the original list.

```
shared_ptr<ListNode<int>> ZippingLinkedList(
    const shared_ptr<ListNode<int>>& L) {
  if (!L || !L->next) {
    return L;
  }

  // Finds the second half of L.
  auto slow = L, fast = L;
  while (fast && fast->next) {
    fast = fast->next->next, slow = slow->next;
  }

  auto first_half_head = L, second_half_head = slow->next;
  slow->next = nullptr;  // Splits the list into two lists.

  second_half_head = ReverseLinkedList(second_half_head);

  // Interleave the first half and the reversed of the second half.
```

415

```
  auto first_half_iter = first_half_head, second_half_iter = second_half_head;
  while (second_half_iter) {
    auto temp = second_half_iter->next;
    second_half_iter->next = first_half_iter->next;
    first_half_iter->next = second_half_iter;
    first_half_iter = first_half_iter->next->next;
    second_half_iter = temp;
  }
  return first_half_head;
}
```

The time complexity is $O(n)$. The space complexity is $O(1)$.

22.11 COPY A POSTINGS LIST 👁

Postings lists are described in Problem 9.6 on Page 135. Implement a function which takes a postings list and returns a copy of it. You can modify the original list, but must restore it to its initial state before returning.

Hint: Copy the jump field and then copy the next field.

Solution: Here is a brute-force algorithm. First, create a copy of the postings list, without assigning values to the jump field. Next, use a hash table to store the mapping from nodes in the original postings list to nodes in the copied list. Finally, traverse the original list and the new list in tandem, using the mapping to assign each jump field. The time and space complexity are $O(n)$, where n is the number of nodes in the original postings list.

The key to improving space complexity is to use the next field for each node in the original list to record the mapping from the original node to its copy. To avoid losing the structure of the original list, we use the next field in each copied node to point to the successor of its original node. See Figure 22.2(b) on the following page for an example. Now we can proceed like we did in the brute-force algorithm. We assign the jump field in the copied nodes, using the next field in the original list to get the corresponding nodes in the copy. See Figure 22.2(c) on the next page. Finally, we undo the changes made to the original list and update the next fields of the copied list, as in Figure 22.2(d) on the following page for an example.

```
shared_ptr<PostingListNode> CopyPostingsList(
    const shared_ptr<PostingListNode>& L) {
  if (L == nullptr) {
    return nullptr;
  }

  // Stage 1: Makes a copy of the original list without assigning the jump
  //          field, and creates the mapping for each node in the original
  //          list to the copied list.
  auto iter = L;
  while (iter) {
    auto new_node = make_shared<PostingListNode>(
        PostingListNode{iter->order, iter->next, nullptr});
    iter->next = new_node;
```

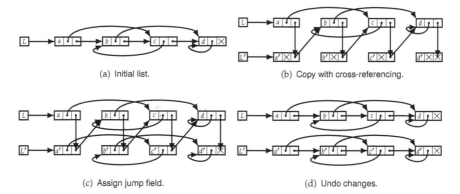

(a) Initial list.

(b) Copy with cross-referencing.

(c) Assign jump field.

(d) Undo changes.

Figure 22.2: Duplicating a postings list.

```
    iter = new_node->next;
}

// Stage 2: Assigns the jump field in the copied list.
iter = L;
while (iter) {
  if (iter->jump) {
    iter->next->jump = iter->jump->next;
  }
  iter = iter->next->next;
}

// Stage 3: Reverts the original list, and assigns the next field of
//          the copied list.
iter = L;
auto new_list_head = iter->next;
while (iter->next) {
  auto temp = iter->next;
  iter->next = temp->next;
  iter = temp;
}
return new_list_head;
}
```

The time complexity is $O(n)$. The space complexity is $O(1)$.

22.12 COMPUTE THE MEDIAN OF A SORTED CIRCULAR LINKED LIST

It is relatively straightforward to find the median of a sorted linked list. Here we consider the same problem for a sorted circular linked list, illustrated in Figure 22.3 on the next page.

Write a program that takes a pointer to an arbitrary node in a sorted circular linked list, and returns the median of the linked list.

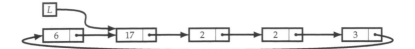

Figure 22.3: Example of a sorted circular linked list.

Hint: Use two iterators—when one reaches the end, the other should be at the middle.

Solution: A brute-force approach is to first add the elements to an array. Consequently, we can sort the array to find the median, or use the algorithm in Solution 12.9 on Page 195. Both approaches need $O(n)$ additional space, where n is the number of nodes.

A key observation is that the median is $n/2$ steps from the smallest element in the list. Therefore, a better approach is to find the smallest element (the first such if there are duplicates) and compute n.

```
double FindMedianSortedCircularLinkedList(
    const shared_ptr<ListNode<int>>& arbitrary_node) {
  // Checks if all nodes are identical and identifies the first smallest node.
  auto iter = arbitrary_node, first_smallest_node = arbitrary_node;
  int n = 0;
  do {
    if (iter->data > iter->next->data) {
      first_smallest_node = iter->next;
    }
    ++n, iter = iter->next;
  } while (iter != arbitrary_node);

  // Advances to the middle of the list.
  for (int i = 0; i < ((n - 1) / 2); ++i) {
    first_smallest_node = first_smallest_node->next;
  }
  return n % 2 ? first_smallest_node->data
               : 0.5 * (first_smallest_node->data +
                        first_smallest_node->next->data);
}
```

The time complexity is $O(n)$ and the space complexity is $O(1)$.

22.13 COMPUTE THE LONGEST SUBSTRING WITH MATCHING PARENS

Problem 9.3 on Page 132 defines matched strings of parens, brackets, and braces. This problem is restricted to strings of parens. Specifically, this problem is concerned with a long substrings of matched parens. As an example, if s is "((()()(()(", then "(())()" is a longest substring of matched parens.

Write a program that takes as input a string made up of the characters '(' and ')', and returns the size of a maximum length substring in which the parens are matched.

418

Hint: Start with a brute-force algorithm and then refine it by considering cases in which you can advance more quickly.

Solution: One approach would be to run the algorithm in Solution 9.3 on Page 132 on all substrings. The time complexity is $O(n^3)$, where n is the length of the string—there are $\binom{n}{2} = \frac{n(n-1)}{2}$ substrings, and the matching algorithm runs in time $O(n)$.

Note that if a prefix of a string fails the matched test because of an unmatched right parens, no extension of that prefix can be matched. Therefore, a faster approach is for each i to find the longest substring starting at the ith character that is matched. This leads to an $O(n^2)$ algorithm.

Finally, if a substring ends in an unmatched right parens, but all of that substring's prefixes ending in right parens are matched, then no nonempty suffix of the prefix can be the prefix of a matched string, since any such suffix has fewer left parens. Therefore, as soon as a prefix has an unmatched right parens, we can continue with the next character after that prefix. We store the left parentheses' indices in a stack. At the same time, when we process a right parens for the given prefix, if it matched, we use the index at the top of the stack to update the longest matched string seen for this prefix.

For the given example, "((())()(()(", we push left parentheses and pop on right parentheses. Before the first pop, the stack is $\langle 0, 1, 2 \rangle$, where the first array element is the bottom of the stack. The corresponding matched substring length is $3 - 1 = 2$. Before the second pop, the stack is $\langle 0, 1 \rangle$. The corresponding matched substring length is $4 - 0 = 4$. Before the third pop, the stack is $\langle 0, 5 \rangle$. The corresponding matched substring length is $6 - 0 = 6$. Before the last pop, the stack is $\langle 0, 7, 8 \rangle$. The corresponding matched substring length is $9 - 7 = 2$.

```
int LongestValidParentheses(const string& s) {
  int max_length = 0, end = -1;
  stack<int> left_parentheses_indices;
  for (int i = 0; i < s.size(); ++i) {
    if (s[i] == '(') {
      left_parentheses_indices.emplace(i);
    } else if (left_parentheses_indices.empty()) {
      end = i;
    } else {
      left_parentheses_indices.pop();
      int start = left_parentheses_indices.empty()
                    ? end
                    : left_parentheses_indices.top();
      max_length = max(max_length, i - start);
    }
  }
  return max_length;
}
```

The time and space complexity are $O(n)$.

Network traffic control sometimes requires studying traffic volume over time. This problem explores the development of an efficient algorithm for computing the traffic volumes.

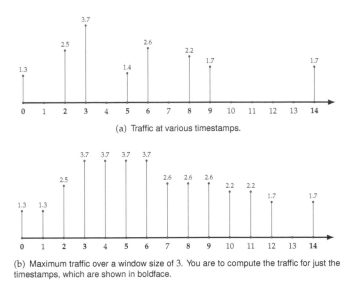

(a) Traffic at various timestamps.

(b) Maximum traffic over a window size of 3. You are to compute the traffic for just the timestamps, which are shown in boldface.

Figure 22.4: Traffic profile before and after windowing.

You are given traffic at various timestamps and a window length. Compute for each timestamp, the maximum traffic over the window length time interval which ends at that timestamp. See Figure 22.4 for an example.

Hint: You need to be able to identify the maximum element in a queue quickly.

Solution: Assume the input is specified by window length w and an array A of pairs consisting of integer timestamp and corresponding traffic volume. If A is not sorted by timestamp, we sort it. For example, the traffic in 22.4(a) corresponds to the array $\langle (0, 1.3), (2, 2.5), (3, 3.7), (5, 1.4), (6, 2.6), (8, 2.2), (9, 1.7), (14, 1.1) \rangle$.

The brute-force algorithm entails finding for each i, the maximum in the subarray consisting of elements whose timestamps lie in the window ending at $A[i]$'s timestamp. The time complexity is $O(nw)$, where n is the length of A. The reason is that every window may have up to $w + 1$ elements.

The intuition for improving the time complexity of the brute-force approach stems from noting that as we advance the window only the boundary changes. Specifically, some older elements fall out of the window, and a new element is added. Therefore a queue is a perfect representation for the window. We need the maximum traffic within each window, which suggests using Solution 9.12 on Page 143. queue with maximum

Initialize Q to an empty queue with maximum. Iteratively enqueue (t_i, t_i) in order of increasing i. For each i, iteratively dequeue Q until the difference of the timestamp at Q's head and t_i is less than or equal to w. The sequence of maximum values in the queue for each i is the desired result.

```cpp
struct TrafficElement {
  // Following operators are needed for QueueWithMax with maximum.
  bool operator>(const TrafficElement& that) const {
    return volume > that.volume || (volume == that.volume && time > that.time);
  }

  bool operator==(const TrafficElement& that) const {
    return time == that.time && volume == that.volume;
  }

  bool operator>=(const TrafficElement& that) const {
    return *this > that || *this == that;
  }

  int time;
  double volume;
};

vector<TrafficElement> CalculateTrafficVolumes(const vector<TrafficElement>& A,
                                               int w) {
  QueueWithMax<TrafficElement> sliding_window;
  vector<TrafficElement> maximum_volumes;
  for (const auto traffic_info : A) {
    sliding_window.Enqueue(traffic_info);
    while (traffic_info.time - sliding_window.Head().time > w) {
      sliding_window.Dequeue();
    }
    maximum_volumes.emplace_back(
        TrafficElement{traffic_info.time, sliding_window.Max().volume});
  }
  return maximum_volumes;
}
```

Each element is enqueued once. Each element is dequeued at most once. Since the queue with maximum data structure has an $O(1)$ amortized time complexity per operation, the overall time complexity is $O(n)$. The additional space complexity is $O(w)$.

22.15 IMPLEMENT PREORDER AND POSTORDER TRAVERSALS WITHOUT RECURSION

This problem is concerned with traversing nodes in a binary tree in postorder and in preorder. See Page 147 for details and examples of these traversals. Generally speaking, a traversal computation is easy to implement if recursion is allowed.

Write a program which takes as input a binary tree and performs a preorder traversal of the tree. Do not use recursion. Nodes do not contain parent references. Do the same for a postorder traversal.

Hint: Study the function call stack for the recursive versions.

Solution: The brute-force approach to remove recursion from a function is to mimic the function call stack with an explicit stack. One of the challenges with this approach is to determine where to return to.

We can get intuition as to the best way to perform a preorder traversal without recursion by noting that a preorder traversal visits nodes in a last in, first out order. We can perform the preorder traversal using a stack of tree nodes. The stack is initialized to contain the root. We visit a node by popping it, adding first its right child, and then its left child to the stack. (We add the left child after the right child, since we want to continue with the left child.)

For the binary tree in Figure 10.1 on Page 146, the first few stack states are $\langle A \rangle$, $\langle I, B \rangle$, $\langle I, F, C \rangle$, $\langle I, F, E, D \rangle$, $\langle I, F, E \rangle$, $\langle I, F \rangle$, $\langle I, G \rangle$, $\langle I, H \rangle$, and $\langle I \rangle$. (The top of the stack is the rightmost node in the sequences.)

```
vector<int> PreorderTraversal(const unique_ptr<BinaryTreeNode<int>>& tree) {
  stack<BinaryTreeNode<int>*> path;
  path.emplace(tree.get());
  vector<int> result;
  while (!path.empty()) {
    auto curr = path.top();
    path.pop();
    if (curr == nullptr) {
      continue;
    }
    result.emplace_back(curr->data);
    path.emplace(curr->right.get());
    path.emplace(curr->left.get());
  }
  return result;
}
```

Since we push and pop each node exactly once, the time complexity is $O(n)$, where n is the number of nodes. The space complexity is $O(h)$, where h is the height of the tree, since, with the possible exception of the top of the stack, the nodes in the stack correspond to the right children of the nodes on a path beginning at the root.

Now we address the problem of implementing a postorder traversal without recursion. First we discuss a roundabout way of doing this. An inverted preorder traversal is the following: visit root, inverted preorder traverse the right subtree, then inverted preorder traverse the left subtree. For example, the inverted preorder traversal of the tree in Figure 10.1 on Page 146 visits nodes in the following order: $\langle A, I, O, P, J, K, N, L, M, B, F, G, H, C, E, D \rangle$.

Intuitively, since the inverted preorder traversal is visit root, traverse right, traverse left, its reverse is traverse left, traverse right, visit root, i.e., the postorder traversal. Therefore, one way to compute the postorder traversal visit sequence without using recursion is to perform an inverted preorder traversal and instead of outputting nodes, we store them. When the inverted preorder traversal is complete, we iterate through the nodes in last-in, first-out order, which gives the postorder traversal sequence.

The inverted preorder traversal itself can be performed nonrecursively using the solution to the first part of this problem, with the order in which the left and right children are pushed swapped. This algorithm is implemented in the code below.

```
vector<int> PostorderTraversal(const unique_ptr<BinaryTreeNode<int>>& tree) {
  vector<int> sequence = InvertedPreorderTraversal(tree);
  reverse(sequence.begin(), sequence.end());
  return sequence;
}

vector<int> InvertedPreorderTraversal(
    const unique_ptr<BinaryTreeNode<int>>& tree) {
  stack<BinaryTreeNode<int>*> path;
  path.emplace(tree.get());
  vector<int> result;
  while (!path.empty()) {
    auto* curr = path.top();
    path.pop();
    if (curr == nullptr) {
      continue;
    }
    result.emplace_back(curr->data);
    path.emplace(curr->left.get());
    path.emplace(curr->right.get());
  }
  return result;
}
```

The time and space complexity are both $O(n)$, where n is the number of nodes in the tree.

In addition to its being unintuitive, a more technical limitation of the approach given above is that it requires $O(n)$ additional space. If the result is to be returned as an array, this is unavoidable. However, if we are simply required to print the nodes, it is possible to reduce the space complexity to $O(h)$ where h is the height of the tree.

We know that a recursive implementation of a postorder traversal takes $O(n)$ and $O(h)$ space, so we should be able to achieve this complexity by using a stack to mimic the function call stack. One challenge is keeping track of where to return to, since there are two recursive calls. The function call stack keeps a return address, but instruction addresses are not accessible from user code. We can determine where to continue from by inspecting where the last visited node is relative to the current node. This is explained in more detail below.

We maintain a stack of nodes which evolves exactly as the sequence of nodes that the recursive algorithm makes calls from.

To determine when a nonleaf at the top of the stack is ready for visiting, we need to know if we are moving back up the tree, and if so, which side of this nonleaf we are returning from. If we are coming back up from the left, we do not want to push the left child again, but do want to push the right child, since we still need to mimic the second recursive call. If we are coming up from the right child both children have been visited, so we want to pop the stack and visit the nonleaf node.

```
// We use stack and previous node pointer to simulate postorder traversal.
```

```
vector<int> PostorderTraversal(const unique_ptr<BinaryTreeNode<int>>& tree) {
  if (tree == nullptr) {  // Empty tree.
    return {};
  }

  stack<BinaryTreeNode<int>*> path;
  BinaryTreeNode<int>* prev = nullptr;
  path.emplace(tree.get());
  vector<int> postorder_sequence;
  while (!path.empty()) {
    auto curr = path.top();
    if (prev == nullptr || prev->left.get() == curr ||
        prev->right.get() == curr) {
      // We came down to curr from prev.
      if (curr->left != nullptr) {  // Traverse left.
        path.emplace(curr->left.get());
      } else if (curr->right != nullptr) {  // Traverse right.
        path.emplace(curr->right.get());
      } else {  // Leaf node, so visit current node.
        postorder_sequence.emplace_back(curr->data);
        path.pop();
      }
    } else if (curr->left.get() == prev) {
      // Done with left, so now traverse right.
      if (curr->right != nullptr) {
        path.emplace(curr->right.get());
      } else {  // No right child, so visit curr.
        postorder_sequence.emplace_back(curr->data);
        path.pop();
      }
    } else {
      // Finished traversing left and right, so visit curr.
      postorder_sequence.emplace_back(curr->data);
      path.pop();
    }
    prev = curr;
  }
  return postorder_sequence;
}
```

The time complexity is $O(n)$, since we perform a constant amount of work per node (a push and a pop). The space complexity is $O(h)$, since the stack corresponds to a path starting at the root.

Variant: Implement an inorder traversal of a binary tree without recursion.

22.16 Compute fair bonuses 😎

You manage a team of developers. You have to give concert tickets as a bonus to the developers. For each developer, you know how many lines of code he wrote the previous week, and you want to reward more productive developers.

The developers sit in a row. Each developer, save for the first and last, has two neighbors. You must give each developer one or more tickets in such a way that if a developer has written more lines of code than a neighbor, then he receives more tickets than his neighbor.

Your task is to develop an algorithm that computes the minimum number of tickets you need to buy to satisfy the constraint. For example, if Andy, Bob, Charlie, and David sit in a row from left to right, and they wrote 300, 400, 500, and 200 lines of code, respectively, the previous week, then Andy and David should receive one ticket each, Bob should receive two tickets, and Charlie should receive three tickets, for a total of seven tickets.

Write a program for computing the minimum number of tickets to distribute to the developers, while ensuring that if a developer has written more lines of code than a neighbor, then he receives more tickets than his neighbor.

Hint: Consider iteratively improving an assignment that may not satisfy the constraint.

Solution: A brute-force approach is to start by giving each developer a ticket. Next we perform the following iteration. We check if all developers are satisfied. If they are all satisfied, we are done. Otherwise, if some developer is not satisfied, i.e., he has written more lines of code than a neighbor, but does not have more tickets than that neighbor, we give him one more ticket than his neighbor. This approach uses the minimum number of tickets initially, and every additional ticket that is given is necessary. The time complexity is $O(kn^2)$, where k is the maximum number of tickets given to any single developer, and n is the number of developers.

The key insight to a better algorithm is the observation that the least productive developer never needs to be given more than a single ticket. We can propagate this observation by processing developers in increasing order of productivity. Subsequently, when we process a developer if his neighbors have been processed, he must be at least as productive as them. If a developer is more productive than a neighbor, he must be given at a minimum one more ticket than that neighbor. If a developer is only as productive as his neighbors, we only need give him the same number of tickets, as per the problem specification.

For the given example, our algorithm starts by giving 1 ticket to David. Andy is next in order of productivity, so we give him 1 ticket, since he has only one neighbor, who is more productive than him. Next we process Bob. He is more productive than Andy, so we give him $1 + 1 = 2$ tickets. Then comes Charlie. He is a neighbor of Charlie and David, and is more productive than both, so we give him $\max(2, 1) + 1 = 3$ tickets, for a total of 7 tickets.

This approach yields the correct result because once a developer is processed, we only process developers who are at least as productive in the future, meaning that once his bonus is assigned, it will never need updating in the future. Furthermore, any bonus that we assign is forced upon us by the problem constraints.

A min-heap is a suitable data structure for processing the developers, and is used in the following program.

```
vector<int> CalculateBonus(const vector<int>& productivity) {
  struct EmployeeData {
    int productivity, index;
  };
```

```
priority_queue<EmployeeData, vector<EmployeeData>,
                function<bool(EmployeeData, EmployeeData)>>
    min_heap([](const EmployeeData& lhs, const EmployeeData& rhs) -> bool {
        return lhs.index > rhs.index;
    });
for (int i = 0; i < productivity.size(); ++i) {
    min_heap.emplace(EmployeeData{i, productivity[i]});
}

// Initially assigns one ticket to everyone.
vector<int> tickets(productivity.size(), 1);
// Fills tickets from lowest rating to highest rating.
while (!min_heap.empty()) {
    int next_dev = min_heap.top().productivity;
    // Handles the left neighbor.
    if (next_dev > 0) {
        if (productivity[next_dev] > productivity[next_dev - 1]) {
            tickets[next_dev] = tickets[next_dev - 1] + 1;
        }
    }
    // Handles the right neighbor.
    if (next_dev + 1 < tickets.size()) {
        if (productivity[next_dev] > productivity[next_dev + 1]) {
            tickets[next_dev] = max(tickets[next_dev], tickets[next_dev + 1] + 1);
        }
    }
    min_heap.pop();
}
return tickets;
}
```

Since each extraction from a min-heap takes time $O(\log n)$, the time complexity is $O(n \log n)$.

The approach presented above is in the spirit of a brute-force solution. On some reflection, a total ordering on the developers is overkill, since the specified constraint is very local. Indeed, we can improve the time complexity to $O(n)$ by making two passes over the array.

We start by giving each developer a single ticket. Then we make a left-to-right pass in which we give each developer who has more productivity than the developer on his left one ticket more than the developer on his left. We then do the same in a right-to-left pass.

Any amount added is required, so we cannot get by with fewer tickets. Note that every developer who is more productive than his right neighbor has more tickets than that neighbor. Furthermore, if a developer is more productive than his left neighbor, in the left-to-right pass we already give him more tickets than his left neighbor, and we can only increase his ticket count in the right-to-left pass.

```
vector<int> CalculateBonus(const vector<int>& productivity) {
    // Initially assigns one ticket to everyone.
    vector<int> tickets(productivity.size(), 1);
    // From left to right.
    for (int i = 1; i < productivity.size(); ++i) {
        if (productivity[i] > productivity[i - 1]) {
```

```
      tickets[i] = tickets[i - 1] + 1;
    }
  }
  // From right to left.
  for (int i = productivity.size() - 2; i >= 0; --i) {
    if (productivity[i] > productivity[i + 1]) {
      tickets[i] = max(tickets[i], tickets[i + 1] + 1);
    }
  }
  return tickets;
}
```

22.17 FIND k ELEMENTS CLOSEST TO THE MEDIAN 👁

Suppose you have an array and you want to find the k items in the array which are closest to the median. For example, for the array $\langle 7, 14, 10, 12, 2, 11, 29, 3, 4 \rangle$, if $k = 5$, then the median is 10 and the result is $\{7, 14, 10, 12, 11\}$.

Design an algorithm to compute the k elements closest to the median of an array.

Hint: Would it help to find the k largest items that are less than the median?

Solution: A brute-force approach is to sort the array, get the median, and then inspect the k elements on either side of the median. The time complexity is $O(n \log n)$, where n is the length of the array.

The key insight to a better solution is that we do not need to sort the whole array to compute the median. We described an almost certain $O(n)$ time, $O(1)$ space algorithm for computing the ith smallest element in an array in Solution 12.9 on Page 195. By setting $k = n/2$, we can use it to compute the median of the array.

Assuming that we have computed the median M in $O(n)$ time, we can compute the k elements closest to M by maintaining a max-heap of elements of the array. The value associated with the ith element of the array A is its distance to the median, i.e., $|M - A[i]|$.

We start by adding the first k elements of the array to the max-heap. Now we process the remaining elements. For $j = k$ to $n - 1$, if $|M - A[j]|$ is larger than the maximum value stored in the max-heap, we ignore it; otherwise, we remove the maximum element of the max-heap, and insert $A[j]$ in its place. When all elements are processed, the max-heap contains the k elements closest to the median. The time complexity is $O(n \log k)$—$O(n)$ extract-max and add operations on a max-heap containing no more than k elements. The space complexity is $O(k)$, which is the size of the max-heap.

A better approach, is to use the algorithm for computing the kth smallest entry in an array given in Solution 12.9 on Page 195. This algorithm reorders the array so that the k smallest elements appear at the beginning of the array.

Let the array B be defined by $B[j] = |A[j] - M|$. Run the algorithm in Solution 12.9 on Page 195 on B to move the k smallest elements to the start of B; these elements are the result. We do not need to explicitly create B—we can instead use a custom comparator on A's elements.

```
class Comp {
 public:
  explicit Comp(double median) : median_(median){};

  bool operator()(int a, int b) const {
    return fabs(a - median_) < fabs(b - median_);
  }

 private:
  const double median_;
};

vector<int> FindKClosestToMedian(vector<int> A, int k) {
  nth_element(A.begin(), A.begin() + k - 1, A.end(), Comp{FindMedian(&A)});
  // Since nth_element reordered A so that elements closest in absolute value
  // to median have been moved to the front of A, the first k entries are the
  // result.
  return {A.begin(), A.begin() + k};
}

// Promote the return value to double to prevent precision error.
double FindMedian(vector<int>* A) {
  auto target = A->begin() + A->size() / 2;
  nth_element(A->begin(), target, A->end());
  if (A->size() % 2 == 1) {  // A has odd number of elements.
    return *target;
  } else {  // A has even number of elements.
    int x = *target;
    nth_element(A->begin(), target - 1, A->end());
    return (x + *(target - 1)) / 2.0;
  }
}
```

The time complexity is almost certainly $O(n)$, and the additional space complexity is $O(1)$.

22.18 SEARCH A SORTED ARRAY OF UNKNOWN LENGTH

Binary search is usually applied to an array of known length. Sometimes, the array is "virtual", i.e., it is an abstraction of data that is spread across multiple machines. In such cases, the length is not known in advance; accessing elements beyond the end results in an exception.

Design an algorithm that takes a sorted array whose length is not known, and a key, and returns an index of an array element which is equal to the key. Assume that an out-of-bounds access throws an exception.

Hint: Can divide and conquer be used to find the end of the array?

Solution: The brute-force approach is to iterate through the array, one element at a time, stopping when either the key is found or an exception is thrown (in which case the key is not present). The time complexity is $O(n)$, where n is the length of the input array.

A better approach is to take advantage of sortedness. If we know the array length, we can use binary search to search for the key. We can compute the array length by testing whether indices $0, 1, 3, 7, 15, \ldots$ are valid. As soon as we find an invalid index, say $2^i - 1$, we can use binary search over the interval $[2^{i-1}, 2^i - 2]$ to find the first invalid index, which is the length of the array.

We can improve on the above approach by comparing the value of the element at index $2^i - 1$ with the key, since if it is greater than the key, we can do binary search over indices $[2^{i-1}, 2^i - 2]$ for the key. Conceptually, we can treat out-of-bounds indices in the same way as valid indices by treating an out-of-bounds index as holding infinity.

For example, consider the array in Figure 12.1 on Page 184. Suppose we are searching for the key 243. We examine indices 0, 1, 3, 7. Since $A[7] = 285 > 243$, we now perform conventional binary search over the interval $[4, 6]$ for 243. If instead, we were searching for the key 400, we would examine indices 0, 1, 3, 7, 15. Since 15 is not a valid index, we would stop, and perform conventional binary search over the interval $[8, 14]$. The first midpoint is 11, which is out-of-bounds and treated as holding infinity, so we update the interval to $[8, 10]$. The next interval is $[8, 8]$, followed by $[8, 7]$ which is empty, indicating that the key 400 is not present.

```cpp
int BinarySearchUnknownLength(const vector<int>& A, int k) {
  // Find the possible range where k exists.
  int p = 0;
  while (true) {
    try {
      int idx = (1 << p) - 1;  // 2^p - 1.
      if (A.at(idx) == k) {
        return idx;
      } else if (A.at(idx) > k) {
        break;
      }
    } catch (const exception& e) {
      break;
    }
    ++p;
  }

  // Binary search between indices 2^(p - 1) and 2^p - 2, inclusive.
  int left = max(0, 1 << (p - 1)), right = (1 << p) - 2;
  while (left <= right) {
    int mid = left + ((right - left) / 2);
    try {
      if (A.at(mid) == k) {
        return mid;
      } else if (A.at(mid) > k) {
        right = mid - 1;
      } else {  // A.at(mid) < k
        left = mid + 1;
      }
    } catch (const exception& e) {
      right = mid - 1;  // Search the left part if out-of-bound.
    }
  }
  return -1;  // Nothing matched k.
```

}

The run time of the first loop is $O(\log n)$, since we double the tested index with each iteration. The second loop is conventional binary search, i.e., $O(\log n)$, so the total time complexity is $O(\log n)$.

22.19 SEARCH IN TWO SORTED ARRAYS ⬤

You are given two sorted arrays and a positive integer k. Design an algorithm for computing the kth smallest element in an array consisting of the elements of the initial two arrays arranged in sorted order. Array elements may be duplicated within and across the input arrays.

Hint: The first k elements of the first array together with the first k elements of the second array are initial candidates. Iteratively eliminates a constant fraction of the candidates.

Solution: You could merge the two arrays into a third sorted array and then look for the answer—the merge would take $O(m + n)$ time, where m and n are the lengths of the input arrays.

You can optimize somewhat by building the merged array on the first k elements, which would be an $O(k)$ operation—this is faster than forming the combined array when k is small, but when k is comparable to m and n, the time complexity is $O(m+n)$.

What we really need is some form of binary search that takes advantage of the sortedness of A and B. Intuitively, if we focus on finding the indices in A and B that correspond to the first k elements, we stand a good chance of using binary search. Specifically, suppose the first k elements of the union of A and B consist of the first x elements of A and the first $k - x$ elements of B. We'll now see how to use binary search to determine x.

Let's maintain an interval $[b, t]$ that contains x. The iteration continues as long as $b < t$. We will contract this interval by half in each iteration. At each iteration consider the midpoint, $x = b + \lfloor \frac{t-b}{2} \rfloor$. If $A[x] < B[(k - x) - 1]$, then $A[x]$ must be in the first $k - 1$ elements of the union, so we update b to $x + 1$ and continue. Similarly, if $A[x-1] > B[k-x]$, then $A[x-1]$ cannot be in the first k elements, so we can update t to $x - 1$. Otherwise, we must have $B[(k - x) - 1] \le A[x]$ and $A[x - 1] \le B[k - x]$, in which case the result is the larger of $A[x - 1]$ and $B[(k - x) - 1]$, since the first x elements of A and the first $k - x$ elements of B when sorted end in $A[x - 1]$ or $B[(k - x) - 1]$.

If the iteration ends without returning, it must be that $b = t$. Clearly, $x = b = t$. We simply return the larger of $A[x - 1]$ and $B[(k - x) - 1]$. (If $A[x - 1] = B[(k - x) - 1]$, we arbitrarily return either.)

The initial values for b and t need to be chosen carefully. Naively setting $b = 0, t = k$ does not work, since this choice may lead to array indices in the search lying outside the range of valid indices. The indexing constraints for A and B can be resolved by initializing b to $\max(0, k - n)$ and t to $\min(m, k)$.

```
int FindKthInTwoSortedArrays(const vector<int>& A, const vector<int>& B,
                             int k) {
  // Lower bound of elements we will choose in A.
```

```
int b = max(0, static_cast<int>(k - B.size()));
// Upper bound of elements we will choose in A.
int t = min(static_cast<int>(A.size()), k);

while (b < t) {
  int x = b + ((t - b) / 2);
  int A_x_1 = (x <= 0 ? numeric_limits<int>::min() : A[x - 1]);
  int A_x = (x >= A.size() ? numeric_limits<int>::max() : A[x]);
  int B_k_x_1 = (k - x <= 0 ? numeric_limits<int>::min() : B[k - x - 1]);
  int B_k_x = (k - x >= B.size() ? numeric_limits<int>::max() : B[k - x]);

  if (A_x < B_k_x_1) {
    b = x + 1;
  } else if (A_x_1 > B_k_x) {
    t = x - 1;
  } else {
    // B[k - x - 1] <= A[x] && A[x - 1] < B[k - x].
    return max(A_x_1, B_k_x_1);
  }
}

int A_b_1 = b <= 0 ? numeric_limits<int>::min() : A[b - 1];
int B_k_b_1 = k - b - 1 < 0 ? numeric_limits<int>::min() : B[k - b - 1];
return max(A_b_1, B_k_b_1);
}
```

Since in each iteration we halve the length of $[b, t]$ the time complexity is $O(\log k)$.

22.20 FIND THE kTH LARGEST ELEMENT—LARGE n, SMALL k ⊘

The goal of this problem is to design an algorithm for computing the kth largest element in a sequence of elements that is presented one element at a time. The length of the sequence is not known in advance, and could be very large.

Design an algorithm for computing the kth largest element in a sequence of elements.

Hint: Track the k largest elements, but don't update the collection immediately after each new element is read.

Solution: The natural approach is to use a min-heap containing the k largest elements seen thus far, just as in Solution 11.4 on Page 175. When the last element in the sequence is read, the desired value is the element at the root of the min-heap. This approach has time complexity $O(n \log k)$, where n is the total number of elements in the sequence.

We know of a very fast algorithm for finding the kth largest element in an array of fixed size (Solution 12.9 on Page 195). We cannot directly apply that here without allocating $O(n)$ space. However, we can break our input into fixed size arrays and run Solution 12.9 on Page 195 over those arrays to eliminate all but the k largest elements from each array. These elements are added over to the next array.

```
int FindKthLargestUnknownLength(istringstream* sin, int k) {
  vector<int> candidates;
```

```
  int x;
  while (*sin >> x) {
    candidates.emplace_back(x);
    if (candidates.size() == 2 * k - 1) {
      // Reorders elements about median with larger elements appearing before
      // the median.
      nth_element(candidates.begin(), candidates.begin() + k - 1,
                  candidates.end(), greater<int>());
      // Reset idx to keep just the k largest elements seen so far.
      candidates.resize(k);
    }
  }
  // Finds the k-th largest element in candidates.
  nth_element(candidates.begin(), candidates.begin() + k - 1, candidates.end(),
              greater<int>());
  return candidates[k - 1];
}
```

By using $2k - 1$ as the array size, the time complexity to find the kth largest element is almost certain $O(k)$. It is run every $k - 1$ elements, implying an $O(n)$ time complexity.

Note that we could use less storage, e.g., an array of length $3k/2$, and still achieve $O(n)$ time complexity. The actual run time would be higher with an array of length $3k/2$ since we only discard $k/2$ elements for each call to finding the kth largest element. This is a classic space-time trade-off. If we used a $4k$ long array, we could discard $3k$ elements for one call to Solution 12.9 on Page 195. The time complexity of Solution 12.9 on Page 195 is proportional to the length of the array, so using a length $4k$ array compared to a length $3k/2$ array yields a speed-up of $\frac{(3/2)}{(1/2)/(4/3)} = 2.25$. Clearly more storage leads to faster run times (in the extreme we read all n and do a single call to Solution 12.9 on Page 195), so there is a trade-off with respect to how much storage we want.

22.21 FIND AN ELEMENT THAT APPEARS ONLY ONCE

Given an integer array of length n, where each element except for one appears twice, with the remaining element appearing only once, we can use $O(n)$ space and $O(n)$ time to find the element that appears exactly once, e.g., using a hash table. However, there is a better solution: compute the bitwise-XOR ($\oplus$) of all the elements in the array. Because $x \oplus x = 0$, all elements that appear an even number of times cancel out, and the element that appears exactly once remains. Therefore, this problem can be solved using $O(1)$ space.

Given an integer array, in which each entry but one appears in triplicate, with the remaining element appearing once, find the element appearing once. For example, if the array is $\langle 2, 4, 2, 5, 2, 5, 5 \rangle$, you should return 4.

Hint: Count the number of 1s at each index.

Solution: The brute-force solutions in Solution 22.21, namely using a hash table or sorting will work for this problem too, with the same time and space complexities.

One way to view Solution 12.12 on Page 201 is that it counts modulo 2 for each bit-position the number of entries in which the bit in that position is 1. Specifically, the XOR of elements at indices $[0, i-1]$, determines exactly which bit-positions have been odd number of times in elements of the input array whose indices are in $[0, i-1]$.

The analogous approach for the current problem is to count modulo 3 for each bit-position the number of times the bit in that position has been 1. The effect of counting modulo 3 is to eliminate the elements that appear three times, and so the bit-positions which have a count of 1 are precisely those bit-positions in the count which are set to 1.

The example array, $\langle 2, 4, 2, 5, 2, 5, 5 \rangle$, expressed in binary is $\langle (010)_2, (100)_2, (010)_2, (101)_2, (010)_2, (101)_2, (101)_2 \rangle$. The number of bits set to 1 in position 0 (the LSB) across all 7 array entries is 3; the number of bits set to 1 in position 1 is 3, and the number of bits set to 1 in position 2 is 4. By taking each of these quantities modulo 3 we cast out the contributions of elements that appear exactly three times, which leaves us with a 1 in the MSB and 0 in the remaining two positions, i.e., the element which only appeared once.

We can implement the above idea using an array C of integers whose length equals the integer word size. Entry $C[i]$ will be used to count the number of 1s in bit-position i, across all the inputs. By the above argument, after the entire input is processed, $C[i]$ mod 3 will be 1 at exactly those bit-positions where the input that appears once has a 1.

```
int FindElementAppearsOnce(const vector<int> &A) {
  array<int, 32> counts = {};
  for (int x : A) {
    for (int i = 0; i < 32; ++i) {
      if (x & (1 << i)) {
        ++counts[i];
      }
    }
  }

  int result = 0;
  for (int i = 0; i < 32; ++i) {
    result |= (counts[i] % 3) * (1 << i);
  }
  return result;
}
```

The time complexity is $O(n)$ and space complexity is $O(1)$.

Variant: Solve the same problem when one entry appears twice and the rest appear three times.

22.22 FIND THE LINE THROUGH THE MOST POINTS 👓

You are given a set of points in the plane. Each point has integer coordinates. Design an algorithm for computing a line that contains the maximum number of points in the set.

Hint: A line can be uniquely represented by two numbers.

Solution: This problem may seem daunting at first—there are literally infinitely many lines. The only lines we care about are those that pass through points in the set, and, more specifically, lines that pass through at least two points in the set.

A brute-force approach then is to compute all such lines, and for each such line, count exactly how many points from the set lie on it. We can use a hash table to represent the set of lines. The set of points corresponding to a line could itself be stored using a hash table. If there are n points in the set, there are $n(n-1)/2$ pairs of points. Naively, we would compute the set of lines defined by pairs of points, and then iterate over all points, checking for each line if that point belongs to that line. The time complexity is dominated by the iteration over points and lines, which is $O(n \times n(n-1)/2) = O(n^3)$.

A better approach is to add the pair of points to the set of points on the line they define immediately. for each pair we have to do a lookup, an insert into the hash table if the defined line is not already present, and two inserts into the corresponding set of points. The hash table operations are $O(1)$ time, leading to an $O(n^2)$ time complexity for this part of the computation. The space complexity is also $O(n^2)$. This is a consequence of the time complexity. At a first glance, it seems like the space complexity might be higher, since there are $O(n^2)$ pairs of lines, and each can have up to $O(n)$ points. However, there is an inverse relationship between the number of lines and the number of points per line.

We finish by finding the line with the maximum number of points with a simple iteration through the hash table searching for the line with the most points in its corresponding set. There are at most $n(n-1)/2$ lines, so the iteration takes $O(n^2)$ time, yielding an overall time bound of $O(n^2)$.

The design of a hash function appropriate for lines is more challenging than it may seem at first. The equation of the line through (x_1, y_1) and (x_2, y_2) is

$$y = \frac{y_2 - y_1}{x_2 - x_1}x + \frac{x_2 y_1 - x_1 y_2}{x_2 - x_1}.$$

One idea would be to compute a hash code from the slope and the Y-intercept of this line as an ordered pair of floating-point numbers. However, because of finite precision arithmetic, we may have three points that are collinear map to distinct buckets.

A more robust hash function treats the slope and the Y-intercept as rationals. A rational is an ordered pair of integers: the numerator and the denominator. We need to bring the rational into a canonical form before applying the hash function. One canonical form is to make the denominator always nonnegative, and relatively prime to the numerator. Lines parallel to the Y-axis are a special case. For such lines, we use the X-intercept in place of the Y-intercept, and use $\frac{1}{0}$ as the slope.

```
struct Point {
    // Equal function for hash.
    bool operator==(const Point& that) const {
        return x == that.x && y == that.y;
```

```
  }

  int x, y;
};

// Hash function for Point.
struct HashPoint {
  size_t operator()(const Point& p) const {
    return hash<int>()(p.x) ^ hash<int>()(p.y);
  }
};

struct Rational {
  bool operator==(const Rational& that) const {
    return numerator == that.numerator && denominator == that.denominator;
  }

  int numerator, denominator;
};

Rational GetCanonicalForm(int a, int b) {
  int gcd = GCD(abs(a), abs(b));
  a /= gcd, b /= gcd;
  return b < 0 ? Rational{-a, -b} : Rational{a, b};
}

// Line function of two points, a and b, and the equation is
// y = x(b.y - a.y) / (b.x - a.x) + (b.x * a.y - a.x * b.y) / (b.x - a.x).
struct Line {
  Line(const Point& a, const Point& b) {
    slope =
        a.x != b.x ? GetCanonicalForm(b.y - a.y, b.x - a.x) : Rational{1, 0};
    intercept = a.x != b.x ? GetCanonicalForm(b.x * a.y - a.x * b.y, b.x - a.x)
                           : Rational{a.x, 1};
  }

  // Equal function for Line.
  bool operator==(const Line& that) const {
    return slope == that.slope && intercept == that.intercept;
  }

  // slope is a rational number. Note that if the line is parallel to y-axis
  // that we store 1/0.
  Rational slope;
  // intercept is a rational number for the y-intercept unless
  // the line is parallel to y-axis in which case it is the x-intercept.
  Rational intercept;
};

// Hash function for Line.
struct HashLine {
  size_t operator()(const Line& l) const {
    return hash<int>()(l.slope.numerator) ^ hash<int>()(l.slope.denominator) ^
           hash<int>()(l.intercept.numerator) ^
           hash<int>()(l.intercept.denominator);
  }
```

```
};

Line FindLineWithMostPoints(const vector<Point>& P) {
  // Add all possible lines into hash table.
  unordered_map<Line, unordered_set<Point, HashPoint>, HashLine> table;
  for (int i = 0; i < P.size(); ++i) {
    for (int j = i + 1; j < P.size(); ++j) {
      Line l(P[i], P[j]);
      table[l].emplace(P[i]), table[l].emplace(P[j]);
    }
  }

  // Return the line with most points have passed.
  return max_element(table.cbegin(), table.cend(),
                     [](const auto& a, const auto& b) {
                       return a.second.size() < b.second.size();
                     })
      ->first;
}
```

22.23 FIND THE SHORTEST UNIQUE PREFIX

It is natural to speak of prefixes and suffixes of strings. For example, the prefixes of "banana" are "" (the empty string), "b", "ba", "ban", "bana", "banan", "banana". The suffixes of "banana" are "banana", "anana", "nana", "ana", "na", "a", "".

This problem is concerned with finding the shortest prefix of a string (the query string) that is not in a set of strings (the dictionary strings). If all prefixes of the string are present, return the empty string. For example:

- The query is "cat", the dictionary is {"dog", "be", "cut"}: return "ca" since the prefixes of "cat" are "c", "ca", and "cat", and "c" is a prefix of a word in the dictionary, but "ca" is not.
- The query is "cat", the dictionary is {"dog", "be", "cut", "car"}: return "cat" "c" and "ca" are prefixes of words in the dictionary, but "cat" is not.

Write a program that takes as input a query string and a dictionary, i.e., a nonempty set of strings, and returns the shortest prefix of the query string which is not a prefix of any string in the dictionary. Assume all strings are nonempty. Return the empty string if all prefixes of the query are prefixes of some string in the dictionary. For example, if the query string is "cat", the dictionary is {"dog", "be", "cut", "car", "catsnip", "category"}, your program should return "", since all prefixes of "cat" are prefixes of words in the dictionary.

Hint: How would you represent a set of strings as a rooted tree?

Solution: First, note that this problem only makes sense if the function is called many times with different query strings and an unchanging set of dictionary strings. Otherwise, there is nothing that can improve upon the brute-force approach of comparing the query string with each dictionary string.

If the dictionary is fixed, we can improve upon the brute-force approach by pre-processing the dictionary strings into bins, which are subsets of the dictionary strings based on their initial character. This way, we do not need to compare the query string with all dictionary strings, just those that begin with the same character. If there are no dictionary words starting with the initial character of the query string, the length-1 prefix of the query string is the desired string. Otherwise, we need to solve the same problem with the suffix of the query string and the suffixes of the dictionary strings in the corresponding bucket.

For example, if the query string is "cat" and the {"dog", "be", "cut", "car"}, the bins are {"be"}, {"car", "cut"}, and {"dog"}. We focus on the set {"car", "cur"}, and look for the longest prefix of "at" not in {"ar", "ur"}.

Generalizing this idea, we can recursively bin the subsets, which leads us to the idea of the trie. This is a data structure for storing a set of strings based on positional trees. To be concrete, suppose the strings are over the alphabet {"a", "b", ..., "z"}. Each node has a hash table mapping each character in the alphabet to the corresponding child pointer. Some or all of the children may be null. A path of length l starting from the root naturally corresponds to a string of l characters. Each node has a Boolean field indicating whether the string corresponding to the path from the root is a string in the set.

Finding a shortest prefix of s that is not a prefix of any string in the represented set is simply a matter of finding the first node m on the search path from the root that does not have a child corresponding to the next character in s.

```
class Trie {
public:
  bool Insert(const string& s) {
    auto* p = root_.get();
    for (char c : s) {
      if (p->leaves.find(c) == p->leaves.cend()) {
        p->leaves[c] = make_unique<TrieNode>(TrieNode());
      }
      p = p->leaves[c].get();
    }

    // s already existed in this trie.
    if (p->isString) {
      return false;
    } else {  // p->isString == false.
      p->isString = true;  // Inserts s into this trie.
      return true;
    }
  }

  string GetShortestUniquePrefix(const string& s) {
    auto* p = root_.get();
    string prefix;
    for (char c : s) {
      prefix += c;
      if (p->leaves.find(c) == p->leaves.cend()) {
        return prefix;
      }
      p = p->leaves[c].get();
    }
```

```
    return {};
  }

private:
  struct TrieNode {
    bool isString = false;
    unordered_map<char, unique_ptr<TrieNode>> leaves;
  };

  unique_ptr<TrieNode> root_ = make_unique<TrieNode>(TrieNode());
};

string FindShortestPrefix(const string& s, const unordered_set<string>& D) {
  // Builds a trie according to given dictionary D.
  Trie T;
  for (const string& word : D) {
    T.Insert(word);
  }
  return T.GetShortestUniquePrefix(s);
}
```

The time complexity to construct the trie is $O(|D|L)$ where L is the length of the longest string in D. The query time takes $O(\min(L, n)))$, where n is the length of s.

Variant: How would you find the shortest string that is not a prefix of any string in D?

22.24 COMPUTE THE SMALLEST NONCONSTRUCTIBLE CHANGE

Suppose you have some coins. There are some amounts of change that you may not be able to make with these coins, e.g., you cannot create a change amount greater than the sum of the coin's denominations. For example, if your coins have denomination $1, 1, 1, 1, 1, 5, 10, 25$, then the smallest value of change which cannot be made is 21.

Write a program which takes an array of positive integers and returns the smallest number which is not to the sum of a subset of elements of the array.

Hint: Small examples should lead you to a general hypothesis.

Solution: A brute-force approach would be to enumerate all possible values, starting from 1, testing each value to see if it is the sum of array elements. However, there is no simple efficient algorithm for checking if a given number is the sum of a subset of entries in the array. Heuristics may be employed, but the program will be unwieldy.

It is instructive to begin with some small concrete examples. Observe that $\langle 1, 2 \rangle$ produces $1, 2, 3$, and $\langle 1, 3 \rangle$ produces $1, 3, 4$. A trivial observation is that the smallest element in the array sets a lower bound on the change amount that can be constructed from that array, so if the array does not contain a 1, it cannot produce 1. However, it may be possible to produce 2 without a 2 being present, since there can be 2 or more 1s present.

Continuing with a larger example, $\langle 1, 2, 4 \rangle$ produces $1, 2, 3, 4, 5, 6, 7$, and $\langle 1, 2, 5 \rangle$ produces $1, 2, 3, 5, 6, 7, 8$. Generalizing, suppose a collection of numbers can produce

438

every value up to and including V, but not $V + 1$. Now consider the effect of adding a new element u to the collection. If $u \le V + 1$, we can still produce every value up to and including $V + u$ and we cannot produce $V + u + 1$. On the other hand, if $u > V + 1$, then even by adding u to the collection we cannot produce $V + 1$.

Another observation is that the order of the elements within the array makes no difference to the amounts that are constructible. However, by sorting the array allows us to stop when we reach a value that is too large to help, since all subsequent values are at least as large as that value. Specifically, let $M[i-1]$ be the maximum constructible amount from the first i elements of the sorted array. If the next array element x is greater than $M[i-1] + 1$, $M[i-1]$ is still the maximum constructible amount, so we stop and return $M[i-1] + 1$ as the result. Otherwise, we set $M[i] = M[i-1] + x$ and continue with element $(i + 1)$.

As a concrete example, suppose we are given $\langle 12, 2, 1, 15, 2, 4 \rangle$. This sorts to $\langle 1, 2, 2, 4, 12, 15 \rangle$. The maximum constructible amount we can make with the first element is 1. The second element, 2, is less than or equal to $1 + 1$, so we can produce all values up to and including 3 now. The third element, 2, allows us to produce all values up to and including 5. The fourth element, 4, allows us to produce all values up to 9. The fifth element, 12 is greater than $9 + 1$, so we cannot produce 10. We stop—10 is the smallest number that cannot be constructed.

The code implementing this approach is shown below.

```
int SmallestNonconstructibleValue(vector<int> A) {
  sort(A.begin(), A.end());
  int max_constructible_value = 0;
  for (int a : A) {
    if (a > max_constructible_value + 1) {
      break;
    }
    max_constructible_value += a;
  }
  return max_constructible_value + 1;
}
```

The time complexity as a function of n, the length of the array, is $O(n \log n)$ to sort and $O(n)$ to iterate, i.e., $O(n \log n)$.

22.25 FIND THE MOST VISITED PAGES IN A WINDOW

This problem is a continuation of Problem 15.9 on Page 265. The difference is that each line includes a visit-time and only pages whose visit-times are no older than a specified duration (the "window size") of the visit-time of the most recently read page are to be considered. The window size is specified at the beginning, and never changes.

Implement the API in Problem 15.9 on Page 265, with the following update: compute the k most visited pages from the pages whose visit-time is within W of the most recent page's visit-time. Here W, the window size, is an input parameter fixed for a given log file. You can assume visit-times increase as you process the file.

Hint: Use a federation of data structures.

Solution: A brute-force approach would be to store all (page,visit-time) pairs and restrict the query to the pairs whose visit time is no more than W less than the most recent visit-time.

We can reduce RAM usage by noting that once a line in the log file has a visit-time that is too old, we do not need to return to that entry ever again. The natural way to "age out" (page,visit-time) pairs is to store them in a queue. Whenever we add a new (page,visit-time) pair, it goes to the head of the queue, and we pop entries which are more than W delayed with respect to the visit-time.

The rest of the algorithm is very similar to Solution 15.9 on Page 266. We use a BST to store (page,visit-count) pairs, ordered by visit-counts, breaking ties on pages. We keep a hash table mapping pages to their (page,visit-count) pair. Each time a page visit is evicted from the queue, we decrement that page's visit-count, updating the BST.

The time complexity for adding pages is dominated by updates to the BST. In the worst-case, every page is unique and all appear in the window, leading to an $O(n \log n)$ time complexity, where n is the number of log entries. The space complexity is $O(n)$.

In practical settings, the maximum number of pages in a window, and hence in the BST, will likely be much less than n. If the number of entries in a window is no more than c, then the time complexity for n calls to the add function is $O(n \log c)$—the $\log c$ term corresponds to the time needed to perform BST updates. The space complexity is $O(c)$.

As a concrete example, let the log file contain the entries $(g, 1), (a, 2), (t, 3), (t, 6), (a, 7), (a, 11), (a, 11), (g, 15), (t, 16), (t, 17), (a, 18), (t, 21)$. Let the window duration be 4. Then after the first five entries have been read, the BST contains the following keys, in this order: $(1, a), (2, t)$. If $k = 1$, i.e., we want the most common page in the window, we simply return t. The queue contains $(t, 3), (t, 6), (a, 7)$, from tail to head. After the next entry, $(a, 11)$ is read, the elements $(t, 3)$ and $(t, 6)$ are popped (since the visit-times 3 and 6 are earlier than $11 - 4 = 7$. Entry $(a, 11)$ is added to the queue. The BST now contains just $(2, a)$.

Variant: Solve the same problem when the logfile can contain multiple visits to a page at the same time, and entries can be out-of-order with respect to visit-time.

Variant: Write a program for the same problem with $O(1)$ time complexity for the read function and $O(k)$ time complexity for the find function.

22.26 CONVERT A SORTED DOUBLY LINKED LIST INTO A BST

Lists and BSTs are both examples of "linked" data structures, i.e., some fields are references to other objects of the same type. Since nodes in a doubly linked list and in a BST both have a key field and two references, it's natural to consider the following problem.

Write a program that takes as input a doubly linked list of sorted numbers and builds a height-balanced BST on the entries in the list. Reuse the nodes of the list for the

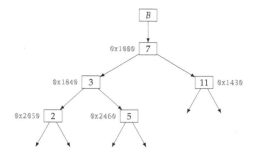

(a) A BST on five nodes—edges that do not terminate in nodes denote empty subtrees. The number in hex adjacent to each node represents its address in memory.

(b) The sorted doubly linked list corresponding to the BST in (a). Note how the tree nodes have been used for the list nodes.

Figure 22.5: BST and sorted doubly linked list interconversion.

BST, using the previous and next fields for the left and right children, respectively. See Figure 22.5(b) for an example of a doubly linked list, and Figure 22.5(a) for the BST on the same nodes.

Hint: Update reference fields, not node contents.

Solution: If the list nodes were in an array, we could index directly into the array to obtain the midpoint, and the time complexity would satisfy $T(n) = O(1) + 2T(\frac{n}{2})$, where n is the number of nodes in the list, which solves to $T(n) = O(n)$. This is the approach of Solution 15.10 on Page 267. We can recycle the list nodes, but creating the array entails $O(n)$ additional space.

A direct approach to the construction which does not allocate new nodes is to find the midpoint of the list, and use it as the root, recursing on the first half and the second half of the list. The time complexity satisfies the recurrence $T(n) = O(n) + 2T(\frac{n}{2})$—the $O(n)$ term comes from the traversal required to find the midpoint of the list, which itself entails computing the length of the list. This solves to $T(n) = O(n \log n)$. The added time complexity compared to the array-based approach comes from the inability to find a midpoint in a list in $O(1)$ time.

The key insight to improving the time complexity without adding to the space complexity is noting that since we have to spend $O(n)$ time to find the midpoint, we should do more than just get the midpoint. Specifically, we can first create a balanced BST on the first $\lfloor \frac{n}{2} \rfloor$ nodes. Then we use the $(\lfloor \frac{n}{2} \rfloor + 1)$th node as the root of the final BST and set its left child to the BST just created.

Since we are changing the links in the list, we need to be careful to ensure we can recover the root. We can do this by keeping a reference to the head of the list being processed, and advancing this reference inside the recursive calls. This allows us to compute the root while computing the left subtree.

Finally we create a balanced BST on the remaining $n - \lfloor \frac{n}{2} \rfloor - 1$ nodes, and set it as the root's right child.

```
// Returns the root of the corresponding BST. The prev and next fields of the
// list nodes are used as the BST nodes left and right fields, respectively.
// The length of the list is given.
shared_ptr<ListNode<int>> BuildBSTFromSortedDoublyList(
    shared_ptr<ListNode<int>> L, int length) {
  return BuildBSTFromSortedDoublyListHelper(&L, 0, length);
}

// Builds a BST from the (start + 1)-th to the end-th node, inclusive, in L,
// and returns the root.
shared_ptr<ListNode<int>> BuildBSTFromSortedDoublyListHelper(
    shared_ptr<ListNode<int>>* L_ref, int start, int end) {
  if (start >= end) {
    return nullptr;
  }

  int mid = start + ((end - start) / 2);
  auto left = BuildBSTFromSortedDoublyListHelper(L_ref, start, mid);
  // The last function call sets L_ref to the successor of the maximum node in
  // the tree rooted at left.
  auto curr = *L_ref;
  *L_ref = (*L_ref)->next;
  curr->prev = left;
  curr->next = BuildBSTFromSortedDoublyListHelper(L_ref, mid + 1, end);
  return curr;
}
```

The algorithms spends $O(1)$ time per node, leading to an $O(n)$ time complexity. No dynamic memory allocation is required. The maximum number of call frames in the function call stack is $\lceil \lg n \rceil$, yielding an $O(\log n)$ space complexity.

22.27 CONVERT A BST TO A SORTED DOUBLY LINKED LIST 👓

A BST node has two references, left and right. A doubly linked list node has two references, previous and next. If we interpret the BST's left pointer as previous and the BST's right pointer as next, a BST's node can be used as a node in a doubly linked list. Also, the inorder traversal of a BST represents an ordered set just like a doubly linked list. Therefore it is natural to ask if is possible to take a BST and rewrite its node reference fields so that it represents a doubly linked list such that the resulting list represents the inorder traversal sequence of the tree.

Design an algorithm that takes as input a BST and returns a sorted doubly linked list on the same elements. Your algorithm should not do any dynamic allocation. The original BST does not have to be preserved; use its nodes as the nodes of the resulting list, as shown in Figure 22.5 on the facing page.

Hint: The tricky part is attaching the root to its subtrees.

Solution: In the absence of the allocation constraint, the problem can be easily solved using a dynamic array to write nodes to a list as we perform an inorder traversal. The time complexity is $O(n)$, where n is the number of nodes, but the space complexity is also $O(n)$.

Speaking generally, a key benefit of lists is that we can easily append one list to another. In particular, if we have lists for the left and right subtrees, we can easily splice them in with the root in $O(1)$ time.

```
struct HeadAndTail {
  shared_ptr<BSTNode<int>> head, tail;
};

shared_ptr<BSTNode<int>> BSTToDoublyLinkedList(
    const shared_ptr<BSTNode<int>>& tree) {
  return BSTToDoublyLinkedListHelper(tree).head;
}

// Transforms a BST into a sorted doubly linked list in-place,
// and return the head and tail of the list.
HeadAndTail BSTToDoublyLinkedListHelper(const shared_ptr<BSTNode<int>>& tree) {
  // Empty subtree.
  if (!tree) {
    return {nullptr, nullptr};
  }

  // Recursively builds the list from left and right subtrees.
  HeadAndTail left = BSTToDoublyLinkedListHelper(tree->left);
  HeadAndTail right = BSTToDoublyLinkedListHelper(tree->right);

  // Appends tree to the list from left subtree.
  if (left.tail) {
    left.tail->right = tree;
  }
  tree->left = left.tail;

  // Appends the list from right subtree to tree.
  tree->right = right.head;
  if (right.head) {
    right.head->left = tree;
  }

  return {left.head ? left.head : tree, right.tail ? right.tail : tree};
}
```

Since we do a constant amount of work per tree node, the time complexity is $O(n)$. The space complexity is the maximum depth of the function call stack, i.e., $O(h)$, where h is the height of the BST. The worst-case is for a skewed tree—n activation records are pushed on the stack.

22.28 Merge two BSTs

Given two BSTs, it is straightforward to create a BST containing the union of their keys: traverse one, and insert its keys into the other.

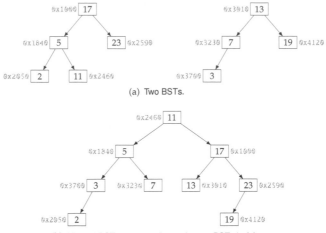

(a) Two BSTs.

(b) Merged BST corresponding to the two BSTs in (a).

Figure 22.6: Example of merging two BSTs. The number in hex adjacent to each node represents its address in memory.

Design an algorithm that takes as input two BSTs and merges them to form a balanced BST. For any node, you can update its left and right subtree fields, but cannot change its key. See Figure 22.6 for an example. Your solution can dynamically allocate no more than a few bytes.

Hint: Can you relate this problem to Problems 22.27 on Page 443 and 22.26 on Page 441?

Solution: A brute-force approach is to traverse one tree and add its keys to the second tree. The time complexity depends on how balanced the second tree is, and how we perform the insert. In the best-case, we start with the second tree being balanced, and preserve balance as we perform additions, yielding a time complexity of $O(n \log n)$, where n is the total number of nodes. Performing the updates while reusing existing nodes is tricky if we do an inorder walk since the links change. However, it is fairly simple if we do a post-order walk, since when we visit the node, we do not need any information from its original left and right subtrees. Note that adding nodes while preserving balance is nontrivial to implement, see Solution 15.11 on Page 268 for details.

Looking more carefully at the brute-force approach, it is apparent that it does not exploit the fact that both the sources of data being merged are sorted. In particular, if memory was not a constraint, we could perform an inorder walk on each tree, writing the result of each to a sorted array. Then we could put the union of the two arrays into a third sorted array. Finally, we could build a balanced BST from the union array using recursion, e.g., using Solution 15.10 on Page 267. The time complexity would be $O(n)$, but the additional space complexity is $O(n)$.

It is good to remember that a list can be viewed as a tree in which each node's left child is empty. It is relatively simple to create a list of the same nodes as a tree

(Solution 22.27 on Page 443). We can take these two lists and form a new list on the same nodes which is the union of the keys in sorted order (Solution 8.1 on Page 110). This new list can be viewed as a tree holding the union of the keys of the original trees. The time complexity is $O(n)$, and space complexity is $O(h)$, where h is the maximum of the heights of the two initial trees.

The problem with this approach is that while it meets the time and space constraints, it returns a tree that is completely unbalanced. However, we can convert this tree to a balanced one using Solution 22.26 on Page 442, completing the desired construction.

```
shared_ptr<BSTNode<int>> MergeTwoBSTs(shared_ptr<BSTNode<int>> A,
                                      shared_ptr<BSTNode<int>> B) {
  A = BSTToDoublyList(A), B = BSTToDoublyList(B);
  int A_length = CountLength(A), B_length = CountLength(B);
  return BuildBSTFromSortedDoublyList(MergeTwoSortedLists(A, B),
                                      A_length + B_length);
}
```

The time complexity of each stage is $O(n)$, and since we recycle storage, the additional space complexity is dominated by the time to convert a BST to a list, which is $O(h)$.

22.29 TEST IF A BINARY TREE IS AN ALMOST BST

Define a binary tree with integer keys at the nodes to be an *almost BST* if it does not satisfy the BST property, but there exists a pair of nodes such that swapping the keys at those nodes makes the resulting binary tree a BST. See Figure 22.7 for an example of an almost BST.

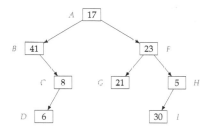

Figure 22.7: An example of a binary tree that is an almost BST—swapping the keys at Nodes B and H results in a BST.

Write a program that takes as input a binary tree with integer keys, and determines if it is an almost BST. If it is an almost BST, reconstruct the corresponding BST.

Hint: This problem is easy to solve if you use $O(n)$ additional space. However, most of that space is wasted.

Solution: A brute-force approach is to create an array of nodes as they appear in an inorder traversal. We then traverse this array. If it is already sorted according to the key at each node, the binary tree is already a BST. Otherwise, for it to be an almost BST, there must be a *single* pair of array entries which on swapping results in a sorted array. Such a pair can be identified via a pair of nested for-loops with $O(n^2)$ time complexity, where n is the number of nodes in the tree. As an example, the array for the almost BST in Figure 22.7 on the facing page is $\langle 41, 6, 8, 17, 21, 23, 30, 5 \rangle$. Swapping 5 and 41 results in a sorted array.

A better approach is to traverse the array with a single for loop and find nodes that are out of order. Specifically, if the pair that needs to be swapped is adjacent in the array, there will be a single entry which is smaller than its predecessor. Otherwise there are two such entries. In either case, we perform a swap. This improves the time complexity to $O(n)$.

We can circumvent the $O(n)$ additional space for the array by performing an inorder traversal and implicitly searching for the out-of-order nodes. By the earlier argument, a binary tree is an almost BST if there is a pair of keys which must be swapped to get a sorted order. The corresponding BST for the binary tree is derived by swapping these keys. If the two keys that must be swapped correspond to a node and its successor, we exchange these. Otherwise there must be two inverted node pairs. In this case, we swap the key at the first node of the first inverted node pair with the key at the second node of the second inverted node pair. For example, in Figure 22.7 on the preceding page the pairs (B, C) and (F, H) are the inverted pairs, so we swap the key at B (41) with the key at H (5).

The code below uses an explicit variable to track the predecessor of the first node that is out of place through the traversal.

```
struct Inversion {
  BinaryTreeNode<int> *prev, *next;
};

void ReconstructBST(unique_ptr<BinaryTreeNode<int>>* almost_BST) {
  Inversion inversion_0 = {nullptr, nullptr};
  Inversion inversion_1 = {nullptr, nullptr};
  BinaryTreeNode<int>* prev = nullptr;
  ReconstructBSTHelper(almost_BST->get(), &inversion_0, &inversion_1, &prev);
  if (inversion_1.next) {  // Swaps the out of order nodes.
    swap(inversion_0.prev->data, inversion_1.next->data);
  } else {
    swap(inversion_0.prev->data, inversion_0.next->data);
  }
}


void ReconstructBSTHelper(BinaryTreeNode<int>* almost_BST,
                          Inversion* inversion_0, Inversion* inversion_1,
                          BinaryTreeNode<int>** prev) {
  if (almost_BST == nullptr) {
    return;
  }

  ReconstructBSTHelper(almost_BST->left.get(), inversion_0, inversion_1, prev);
  if (*prev && (*prev)->data > almost_BST->data) {
    // Inversion detected.
    if (inversion_0->prev == nullptr && inversion_0->next == nullptr) {
```

```
      *inversion_0 = {*prev, almost_BST};
    } else {
      *inversion_1 = {*prev, almost_BST};
    }
  }
  *prev = almost_BST;   // Records the previous node as the current node.
  ReconstructBSTHelper(almost_BST->right.get(), inversion_0, inversion_1,
                       prev);
}
```

The time and space complexities are that of an inorder traversal, i.e., $O(n)$ and $O(h)$, respectively, where h is the height of the tree.

Variant: Solve the same problem without changing the contents of nodes, i.e., by updating links.

22.30 THE VIEW FROM ABOVE

This is a simplified version of a problem that often comes up in computer graphics.

You are given a set of line segments. Each segment consists of a closed interval of the X-axis, a color, and a height. When viewed from above, the color at point x on the X-axis is the color of the highest segment that includes x. This is illustrated in Figure 22.8.

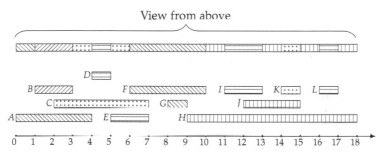

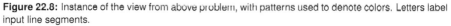

Figure 22.8: Instance of the view from above problem, with patterns used to denote colors. Letters label input line segments.

Write a program that takes lines segments as input, and outputs the view from above for these segments. You can assume no two segments whose intervals overlap have the same height.

Hint: First organize the individual line segments.

Solution: A key observation is that, viewed from above, the color can change at most at an endpoint. This discretizes the problem—we only need to consider the endpoints, of which there are at most twice as many as line segments.

A brute-force algorithm then is to take these endpoints, and for each endpoint, find the highest line segment containing it. To express the result as line segments, we need to sort endpoints

Finding the highest line segment containing an endpoint has time complexity $O(n)$, where n is the number of line segments, leading to an $O(n^2)$ overall time bound.

We can improve the time complexity by recognizing that it is grossly inefficient to test each endpoint against all line segments. Instead, we should track just the line segments that contain the endpoint being processed, and to get the color efficiently we should keep these line segments sorted by height

Specifically, we scan endpoints, maintaining the set of line segments that intersect the current endpoint. This set is stored in a BST with the height being the key. The color is determined by the highest line segment. When we encounter a left endpoint, we add the corresponding line segment in a BST. When we encounter a right endpoint, we remove the corresponding line segment from the BST.

As a concrete example, consider Figure 22.8 on the preceding page. When we are processing J's left endpoint, the BST consists of H and I, with H appearing first (since it is lower than I). We add J to the BST, in between H and I. The next endpoint processed is I's right endpoint, at which stage we remove I from the BST. Now J is the highest line segment. From J's left endpoint to I's right endpoint, the view from above will be I.

```
struct LineSegment {
  int left, right;  // Specifies the interval.
  int color;
  int height;
};

class Endpoint {
 public:
  bool operator<(const Endpoint& that) const { return Value() < that.Value(); }

  int Value() const { return isLeft_ ? line_->left : line_->right; }

  bool isLeft_;
  const LineSegment* line_;
};

void CalculateViewFromAbove(const vector<LineSegment>& A) {
  vector<Endpoint> sorted_endpoints;
  for (const LineSegment& a : A) {
    sorted_endpoints.emplace_back(Endpoint{true, &a});
    sorted_endpoints.emplace_back(Endpoint{false, &a});
  }
  sort(sorted_endpoints.begin(), sorted_endpoints.end());

  int prev_xaxis = sorted_endpoints.front().Value();  // Leftmost end point.
  unique_ptr<LineSegment> prev = nullptr;
  map<int, const LineSegment*> active_line_segments;
  for (const Endpoint& endpoint : sorted_endpoints) {
    if (!active_line_segments.empty() && prev_xaxis != endpoint.Value()) {
      if (prev == nullptr) {  // Found first segment.
        prev = make_unique<LineSegment>(
            LineSegment{prev_xaxis, endpoint.Value(),
                        active_line_segments.crbegin()->second->color,
                        active_line_segments.crbegin()->second->height});
```

```
      } else {
        if (prev->height == active_line_segments.crbegin()->second->height &&
            prev->color == active_line_segments.crbegin()->second->color &&
            prev_xaxis == prev->right) {
          prev->right = endpoint.Value();
        } else {
          cout << "[" << prev->left << ", " << prev->right << "]"
               << ", color = " << prev->color << ", height = " << prev->height
               << endl;
          *prev = {prev_xaxis, endpoint.Value(),
                   active_line_segments.crbegin()->second->color,
                   active_line_segments.crbegin()->second->height};
        }
      }
    }
    prev_xaxis = endpoint.Value();

    if (endpoint.isLeft_ == true) {  // Left end point.
      active_line_segments.emplace(endpoint.line_->height, endpoint.line_);
    } else {  // Right end point.
      active_line_segments.erase(endpoint.line_->height);
    }
  }

  // Output the remaining segment (if any).
  if (prev) {
    cout << "[" << prev->left << ", " << prev->right << "]"
         << ", color = " << prev->color << ", height - " << prev->height
         << endl;
  }
}
```

The time to sort is $O(n \log n)$. Assuming that the BST library implementation is height-balanced, processing each endpoint takes $O(\log n)$ time. Therefore, the time complexity is $O(n \log n)$.

Variant: Solve the same problem when multiple segments may have the same height. Break ties arbitrarily.

Variant: Design an efficient algorithm for computing the length of the union of a set of closed intervals.

Variant: Design an efficient algorithm for computing the area of a set of rectangles whose sides are aligned with the X and Y axes.

Variant: Runners $R_1, R_2, \ldots, R_n$ race on a track of length L. Runner R_i begins at an offset s_i from the start of the track, and runs at speed v_i. Compute the set of runners who lead the race at some time.

Variant: Given a set H of nonintersecting horizontal line segments in the 2D plane, and a set V of nonintersecting vertical line segments in the 2D plane, determine if any pair of line segments intersect.

A *min-first* BST is one in which the minimum key is stored at the root. Additionally, each key in the left subtree is less than every key in the right subtree. The subtrees themselves are min-first BSTs. See Figure 22.9 for an example.

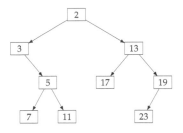

Figure 22.9: A min-first BST.

Write a program that takes a min-first BST and a value as input, and checks whether the tree contains the value.

Hint: Can the min-first property help prune the search?

Solution: A brute-force approach is to perform an inorder walk, testing each node to see if it contains the given input value. The time complexity is $O(n)$, where n is the number of nodes. This approach makes no use of the properties of min-first BSTs.

We now look at some concrete inputs to see how we can make use of the properties of min-first BSTs. For example, for the min-first BST in Figure 22.9, we know that 1 cannot be present simply by examining the root—in a min-first BST, all keys are greater than or equal to the key at the root, which itself holds a key (2) which is greater than 1.

Consider searching for a large value, e.g., 100. Since the root's left child holds a key that is less than 100, we cannot eliminate the left subtree. Similarly, comparing 100 to the key at the root's right child, we cannot eliminate the right subtree. At first it would seem we are now obliged to explore both subtrees. However, min-first BSTs have another property that we have not yet exploited—each key in the left subtree is less than every key in the right subtree. In particular, since 100 is greater than 13, the key at the right child, we know that 100 cannot appear in the left subtree (since every key in the left subtree is smaller than 13). Generalizing, if the given key is greater than the key at the root's right child, it cannot appear in the left child. Furthermore, if the given key is less than the key at the root's right child, e.g., 11, it cannot appear in the right child. Therefore, the recursion explores only one child for each node.

As a concrete example, consider searching for 17 in the min-first BST in Figure 22.9. Noting that 17 > 2, we compare with the right subtree's key, 13. Since 17 > 13, we know that it is impossible for 17 to appear in the subtree whose root has key 3. Continuing with the right subtree, since 17 < 19, we know it is impossible for 17 to appear in the subtree whose root has key 19. When we turn to the left subtree of the tree whose root has key 13, we find a match and return true. If instead we were searching for 10, we would traverse left (since 10 < 13 and 10 > 3), then right (since 10 > 5), then left (since 10 < 11). Since the node with key 7 has no children, there is not match, and we return false.

```
bool SearchMinFirstBST(const unique_ptr<BinaryTreeNode<int>>& min_first_BST,
                       int k) {
  // First handle the base cases.
  if (!min_first_BST || min_first_BST->data > k) {
    return false;
  } else if (min_first_BST->data == k) {
    return true;
  }

  // Recursively search just the right subtree if the smallest key in the
  // right subtree is greater than or equal to k.
  if (min_first_BST->right && k >= min_first_BST->right->data) {
    return SearchMinFirstBST(min_first_BST->right, k);
  }
  return SearchMinFirstBST(min_first_BST->left, k);
}
```

Since each recursive step entails visiting a deeper node, the time complexity is $O(h)$ where h is the height of the tree.

Variant: Print the keys in a min-first BST in sorted order.

Variant: A max-first BST is defined analogously to the min-first BST, the difference being that the largest key is stored at the root. Design an algorithm that takes an n node min-BST and converts it to a max-BST in $O(n)$ time. Use as little additional space as possible.

Variant: Implement insert and delete functions for a min-first BST.

22.32 IMPLEMENT REGULAR EXPRESSION MATCHING

A regular expression is a sequence of characters that forms a search pattern. For this problem we define a simple subset of a full regular expression language. We describe regular expressions by examples, rather than a formal syntax and semantics.

A regular expression is a string made up of the following characters: alphanumeric, . (dot), * (star), ^, and $. Examples of regular expressions are a, aW, aW.9, aW.9*, aW.*9*, ^a, aW$, and ^aW.9*$. Not all strings are valid regular expressions. For example, if ^ appears, it must be the first character, if $ appears, it must be the last character, and star must follow an alphanumeric character or dot. Beyond the base cases—a single alphanumeric character, dot, a single alphanumeric character followed by a star, dot followed by star—regular expressions are concatenations of shorter regular expressions.

Now we describe what it means for a regular expression to match a string. Intuitively, an alphanumeric character matches itself, dot matches any single character, and star matches zero or more occurrences of the preceding character.

In the absence of ^ and $, there is no concept of an "anchor". In particular, if the string contains any substring matched by the regular expression, the regular expression matches the string itself.

The following examples illustrate the concept of a regular expression matching a string. More than one substring may be matched. If a match exists, we underline a matched substring.

- aW9 matches any string containing aW9 as a substring. For example, <u>aW9</u>, <u>aW9</u>bcW, ab8<u>aW9</u>, and cc2<u>aW9</u>raW9z are all matched by aW9, but aW8, bcd8, and xy are not.
- a.9. matches any string containing a substring of length 4 whose first and third characters are a and 9, respectively. For example, <u>ab9w</u>, <u>ac9bc</u>W, ab8<u>a999</u>, and cc2<u>aW9r</u> are all matched by a.9., but az9, a989a, and bac9 are not.
- aW*9 matches any string containing a substring beginning with a, ending with 9, with zero or more Ws in between. For example, <u>a9</u>, <u>aW9</u>, <u>aWW9</u>b9cW, aU9<u>aWW9</u>, ab8<u>aWWW9</u>W9aa, and cc2a9r<u>aW9z</u>WW9ac are all matched by aW*9, but aWWU9, baX9, and aXW9Wa are not.
- a.*9 matches any string containing a substring beginning with a ending with 9, with zero or more characters between. For example, <u>a9</u>, <u>aZ9</u>, <u>aZW9</u>b9cW, <u>aU9</u>a9, b8<u>aWUW9</u>W, and cc2<u>a9</u>raU9z are all matched by a.*9, but 9UWaW8, b9aaaX, and XUq8 are not.
- aW9*.b3 matches any string containing a substring beginning with aW, followed by zero or more 9s, followed by a single character, followed by b3. For example, ce<u>aW999zb34</u>b3az, ce<u>aW9b34</u>, and pq<u>aWzb38</u>q are matched by aW9*.b3, but ceaW98zb34 and pqaW988b38q are not.

If the regular expression begins with ^, that indicates the match must begin at the start of the string. If the regular expression ends with $, the match must end at the end of the string.

- ^aW.9 matches strings which begin with a substring consisting of a, followed by W, followed by any character, followed by 9. For example, <u>aW99</u>zer, <u>aWW9</u>, and <u>aWP9</u>GA are all matched by ^aW.9, but baWx9, aW9, and aWcc90 are not.
- aW.9$ matches strings whose last character is 9, third last character is W and fourth last character is a. (The second last character can be anything.) For example, <u>aWW9</u>, aWW9abc<u>aWz9</u>, ba<u>aWX9</u>, and abc<u>aWP9</u>, are all matched by aW.9$, but aWW99, aW, and aWcc90 are not.
- ^aW9$ is matched by <u>aW9</u> and nothing else.

Design an algorithm that takes a regular expression and a string, and checks if the regular expression matches the string.

Hint: Regular expressions are defined recursively.

Solution: The key insight is that regular expressions are defined recursively, both in terms of their syntax (what strings are valid regular expressions), as well as their semantics (when does a regular expression match a string). This suggests the use of recursion to do matching.

452

First, some notation: s^k denotes the kth suffix of string s, i.e., the string resulting from deleting the first k characters from s. For example, if s = aWaW9W9, then s^0 = aWaW9W9, and s^2 = aW9W9.

Let r be a regular expression and s a string. If r starts with $\wedge$, then for r to match s, the remainder of r must match a prefix of s. If r ends with a \$, then for r to match s, some suffix of s must be matched by r without the trailing \$. If r does not begin with $\wedge$, or end with \$, r matches s if it matches some substring of s.

A function that checks whether a regular expression matches a string at its beginning has to check the following cases:

(1.) Length-0 regular expressions.

(2.) A regular expression starting with $\wedge$ or ending with \$.

(3.) A regular expression starting with a * match, e.g., a*wXY or .*Wa.

(4.) A regular expression starting with an alphanumeric character or dot.

Case (1.) is trivial, we just return true. Case (2.) entails a single call to the match function for a regular expression beginning with $\wedge$, and some checking logic for a regular expression ending with \$. Case (3.) is handled by a traversal down the string checking that the prefix of the string thus far matches the alphanumeric character or dot until some suffix is matched by the remainder of the regular expression. Each suffix check is a call to the match function. Case (4.) involves examining a character, possibly followed by a call to the match function.

As an example, consider the regular expression ab.c*d. To check if it matches s = caeabbedeabacccde, we iterate over the string. Since $s[0]$ = c, we cannot match the regular expression at the start of s. Next we try s^1. Since $s[1]$ = a, we recursively continue checking with s^1 and b.c*d. However $s[2] \neq$ b, so we return false from this call. Continuing, s^2 is immediately eliminated. With s^3, since $s[3]$ = a, we continue recursively checking with s^4 and b.c*d. Since $s[4]$ = b, we continue checking with .c*d. Since dot matches any single character, it matches $s[5]$, so we continue checking with c*d. Since $s[6]$ = e, the only prefix of s^6 which matches c*d is the empty one. However, when we continue checking with d, since $s[6] \neq$ d, we return false for this call. Skipping some unsuccessful checks, we get to s^9. Similar to before, we continue to s^{17}, and c*d. The string beginning at offset 12 matches c* with prefixes of length $0, 1, 2, 3$. After the first three, we do not match with the remaining d. However, after the prefix ccc, the following string does end in d, so we return true.

```
bool IsMatch(const string &regex, const string &s) {
  // Case (2.): regex starts with '^'.
  if (regex.front() == '^') {
    return IsMatchHere(regex, 1, s, 0);
  }

  for (int i = 0; i <= s.size(); ++i) {
    if (IsMatchHere(regex, 0, s, i)) {
      return true;
    }
  }
  return false;
}
```

```
bool IsMatchHere(const string &regex, int regex_offset, const string &s,
                 int s_offset) {
  if (regex_offset == regex.size()) {
    // Case (1.): Empty regex matches all strings.
    return true;
  }

  if (regex_offset == regex.size() - 1 && regex[regex_offset] == '$') {
    // Case (2.): Reach the end of regex, and last char is '$'.
    return s_offset == s.size();
  }

  if (regex.size() - regex_offset >= 2 && regex[regex_offset + 1] == '*') {
    // Case (3.): A '*' match.
    // Iterate through s, checking '*' condition, if '*' condition holds,
    // performs the remaining checks.
    for (int i = s_offset + 1;
             i < s.size() &&
             (regex[regex_offset] == '.' || regex[regex_offset] == s[i - 1]);
             ++i) {
      if (IsMatchHere(regex, regex_offset + 2, s, i)) {
        return true;
      }
    }
    // See '*' matches zero character in s[s_offset : s.size() - 1].
    return IsMatchHere(regex, regex_offset + 2, s, s_offset);
  }

  // Case (4.): regex begins with single character match.
  return s_offset < s.size() &&
         (regex[regex_offset] == '.' || regex[regex_offset] == s[s_offset]) &&
         IsMatchHere(regex, regex_offset + 1, s, s_offset + 1);
}
```

Let $C(x, k)$ be k copies of the string x concatenated together. For the regular expression $C(a.*, k)$ and string $C(ab, k-1)$ the algorithm presented above takes time exponential in k. We cannot give a more precise bound on the time complexity.

Variant: Solve the same problem for regular expressions without the $\wedge$ and $ \$ $ operators.

22.33 Synthesize an expression 🔒

Consider an expression of the form $\langle 3 \odot 1 \odot 4 \odot 1 \odot 5 \rangle$, where each $\odot$ is an operator, e.g., $+, -, \times, \div$. The expression takes different values based on what the operators are. Some examples are 14 (if all operators are $+$), 60 (if all operators are $\times$), and 22 $(3 - 1 + 4 \times 1 \times 5)$.

Determining an operator assignment such that the resulting expression takes a specified value is, in general, a difficult computational problem. For example, suppose the operators are $+$ and $-$, and we want to know whether we can select each $\odot$ such that the resulting expression evaluates to 0. The problem of partitioning a set of integers into two subsets which sum up to the same value, which is a famous NP-complete problem, directly reduces to our problem.

Write a program that takes an array of digits and a target value, and returns true if it is possible to intersperse multiplies (×) and adds (+) with the digits of the array such that the resulting expression evaluates to the target value. For example, if the array is $\langle 1, 2, 3, 2, 5, 3, 7, 8, 5, 9 \rangle$ and the target value is 995, then the target value can be realized by the expression $123 + 2 + 5 \times 3 \times 7 + 85 \times 9$, so your program should return true.

Hint: Build the assignment incrementally.

Solution: Let A be the array of digits and k the target value. We want to intersperse × and + operations among these digits in such a way that the resulting expression equals k.

For each pair of characters, $(A[i], A[i + 1])$, we can choose to insert a ×, a +, or no operator. If the length of A is n, the number of such locations is $n - 1$, implying we can encode the choice with an array of length $n - 1$. Each entry is one of three values—×, +, and ␣ (which indicates no operator is added at that location). There are exactly 3^{n-1} such arrays, so a brute-force solution is to systematically enumerate all arrays. For each enumerated array, we compute the resulting expression, and return as soon as we evaluate to k. The time complexity is $O(n \times 3^n)$, since each expression takes time $O(n)$ to evaluate.

To improve runtime, we use a more focused enumeration. Specifically, the first operator can appear after the first, second, third, etc. digit, and it can be a + or ×. For + to be a possibility, it must be that the sum of the value given by the initial operator assignment plus the value encoded by the remaining digits is greater than or equal to the target value. This is because the maximum value is achieved when there are no operators. For example, for $\langle 1, 2, 3, 4, 5 \rangle$, we can never achieve a target value of 1107 if the first operator is a + placed after the 3 (since $123 + 45 < 1107$). This gives us a heuristic for pruning the search.

```
bool ExpressionSynthesis(const vector<int>& digits, int target) {
  vector<char> operators;
  vector<int> operands;
  return DirectedExpressionSynthesis(digits, target, 0, 0, &operands,
                                     &operators);
}

bool DirectedExpressionSynthesis(const vector<int>& digits, int target,
                                 int current_term, int offset,
                                 vector<int>* operands,
                                 vector<char>* operators) {
  current_term = current_term * 10 + digits[offset];
  if (offset == digits.size() - 1) {
    operands->emplace_back(current_term);
    if (Evaluate(*operands, *operators) == target) {  // Found a match.
      return true;
    }
    operands->pop_back();
    return false;
  }
```

```cpp
      // No operator.
      if (DirectedExpressionSynthesis(digits, target, current_term, offset + 1,
                                      operands, operators)) {
        return true;
      }
      // Tries multiplication operator '*'.
      operands->emplace_back(current_term), operators->emplace_back('*');
      if (DirectedExpressionSynthesis(digits, target, 0, offset + 1, operands,
                                      operators)) {
        return true;
      }
      operands->pop_back(), operators->pop_back();
      // Tries addition operator '+'.
      operands->emplace_back(current_term);
      // First check feasibility of plus operator.
      if (target - Evaluate(*operands, *operators) <=
          RemainingInt(digits, offset + 1)) {
        operators->emplace_back('+');
        if (DirectedExpressionSynthesis(digits, target, 0, offset + 1, operands,
                                        operators)) {
          return true;
        }
        operators->pop_back();
      }
      operands->pop_back();
      return false;
    }

    // Calculates the int represented by digits[idx : digits.size() - 1].
    int RemainingInt(const vector<int>& digits, int idx) {
      int val = 0;
      for (int i = idx; i < digits.size(); ++i) {
        val = val * 10 + digits[i];
      }
      return val;
    }

    int Evaluate(const vector<int>& operands, const vector<char>& operators) {
      stack<int> intermediate_operands;
      int operand_idx = 0;
      intermediate_operands.push(operands[operand_idx++]);
      // Evaluates '*' first.
      for (char oper : operators) {
        if (oper == '*') {
          int product = intermediate_operands.top() * operands[operand_idx++];
          intermediate_operands.pop();
          intermediate_operands.push(product);
        } else {  // oper == '+'.
          intermediate_operands.push(operands[operand_idx++]);
        }
      }

      // Evaluates '+' second.
      int sum = 0;
      while (!intermediate_operands.empty()) {
```

```
        sum += intermediate_operands.top();
        intermediate_operands.pop();
    }
    return sum;
}
```

Despite the heuristics helping in some cases, we cannot prove a better bound for the worst-case time complexity than the original $O(n3^n)$.

22.34 COUNT INVERSIONS ☻

Let A be an array of integers. Call the pair of indices (i, j) inverted if $i < j$ and $A[i] > A[j]$. For example, if $A = \langle 4, 1, 2, 3 \rangle$, then the pair of indices $(0, 3)$ is inverted. Intuitively, the number of inverted pairs in an array is a measure of how unsorted it is.

Design an efficient algorithm that takes an array of integers and returns the number of inverted pairs of indices.

Hint: Let A and B be arrays. How would you count the number of inversions where one element is from A and the other from B in the array consisting of elements from A and B?

Solution: The brute-force algorithm examines all pairs of indices (i, j), where $i < j$. has an $O(n^2)$ complexity, where n is the length of the array.

One way to recognize that the brute-force algorithm is inefficient is to consider how we would check if an array is sorted. We would not test for every element if all subsequent elements are greater than or equal to it—we just test the next element, since greater than or equal is transitive.

This suggests the use of sorting to speed up counting the number of inverted pairs. In particular, if we sort the second half of the array, then to see how many inversions exist with an element in the first half, we could do a binary search for that element in the second half. The elements before its location in the second half are the ones inverted with respect to it.

Elaborating, suppose we have counted the number of inversions in the left half L and the right half R of A. What are the inversions that remain to be counted? Sorting L and R makes it possible to efficiently obtain this number. For any (i, j) pair where i is an index in L and j is an index in R, if $L[i] > R[j]$, then for all $j' < j$ we must have $L[i] > R[j']$.

For example, if $A = \langle 3, 6, 4, 2, 5, 1 \rangle$, then $L = \langle 3, 6, 4 \rangle$, and $R = \langle 2, 5, 1 \rangle$. After sorting, $L = \langle 3, 4, 6 \rangle$, and $R = \langle 1, 2, 5 \rangle$. The inversion counts for L and R are 1 and 2, respectively. When merging to form their sorted union, since $1 < 3$, we know $4, 6$ are also inverted with respect to 1, so we add $|L| - 0 = 3$ to the inversion count. Next we process 2. Since $2 < 3$, we know $4, 6$ are also inverted with respect to 2, so we add $|L| - 0 = 3$ to the inversion count. Next we process 3. Since $5 > 3$, 3 does not add any more inversions. Next we process 4. Since $5 > 4$, 4 does not add any more inversions. Next we process 5. Since $5 < 6$, we add $|L| - 2$ (which is the index of 6) $= 1$ to the inversion count. In all we add $3 + 3 + 1 = 7$ to inversion counts for L and R (which were 1 and 2, respectively) to get the total number of inversions, 10.

```
int CountInversions(vector<int> A) {
  return CountSubarrayInversions(0, A.size(), &A);
}

// Return the number of inversions in (*A_ptr)[start : end - 1].
int CountSubarrayInversions(int start, int end, vector<int>* A_ptr) {
  if (end - start <= 1) {
    return 0;
  }

  int mid = start + ((end - start) / 2);
  return CountSubarrayInversions(start, mid, A_ptr) +
         CountSubarrayInversions(mid, end, A_ptr) +
         MergeSortAndCountInversionsAcrossSubarrays(start, mid, end, A_ptr);
}

// Merge two sorted subarrays (*A_ptr)[start : mid - 1] and (*A_ptr)[mid : end
// - 1] into (*A_ptr)[start : end - 1] and return the number of inversions
// across (*A_ptr)[start : mid - 1] and (*A_ptr)[mid : end - 1].
int MergeSortAndCountInversionsAcrossSubarrays(int start, int mid, int end,
                                               vector<int>* A_ptr) {
  vector<int> sorted_A;
  int left_start = start, right_start = mid, inversion_count = 0;

  vector<int>& A = *A_ptr;
  while (left_start < mid && right_start < end) {
    if (A[left_start] <= A[right_start]) {
      sorted_A.emplace_back(A[left_start++]);
    } else {
      // A[left_start : mid - 1] are the inversions of A[right_start].
      inversion_count += mid - left_start;
      sorted_A.emplace_back(A[right_start++]);
    }
  }
  copy(A.begin() + left_start, A.begin() + mid, back_inserter(sorted_A));
  copy(A.begin() + right_start, A.begin() + end, back_inserter(sorted_A));

  // Updates A with sorted_A.
  copy(sorted_A.begin(), sorted_A.end(), A.begin() + start);
  return inversion_count;
}
```

The time complexity satisfies $T(n) = O(n) + 2T(n-1)$, which solves to $O(n \log n)$, where n is the length of the array.

Variant: Runners numbered from 0 to $n - 1$ race on a straight one-way road to a common finish line. The runners have different (constant) speeds and start at different distances from the finish line. Specifically, Runner i has a speed s_i and begins at a distance d_i from the finish line. Each runner stops at the finish line, and the race ends when all runners have reached the finish line. How many times does one runner pass another?

A number of buildings are visible from a point. A building appears as a rectangle, with the bottom of each building lying on a fixed horizontal line. A building is specified using its left and right coordinates, and its height. One building may partly obstruct another, as shown in Figure 22.10(a). The skyline is the list of coordinates and corresponding heights of what is visible.

For example, the skyline corresponding to the buildings in Figure 22.10(a) is given in Figure 22.10(b). (The patterned rectangles within the skyline are used to describe Problem 18.9 on Page 344; they are not relevant to the current problem.)

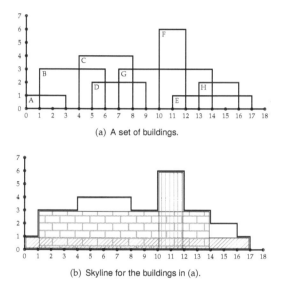

(a) A set of buildings.

(b) Skyline for the buildings in (a).

Figure 22.10: Buildings, their skyline, and the largest contained rectangle. The text label identifying the building is just below and to the right of its upper left-hand corner.

Design an efficient algorithm for computing the skyline.

Hint: Think of an efficient way of merging skylines.

Solution: The simplest solution is to compute the skyline incrementally. For one building, the skyline is trivial. Suppose we know the skyline for some buildings, and need to compute the skyline when another building is added. Let the new building's left and right coordinates be L and R, and its height H. To add it, we iterate through the existing skyline from left to right to see where L should be added. Then we move through the existing skyline until we pass R, increasing any heights that are less than H to H.

This algorithm is simple, but has $O(n^2)$ complexity if there are n buildings, since adding the nth building may entail $O(n)$ comparisons. The key to improving efficiency is the observation that it takes linear time to merge two skylines (if they are represented in left-to-right order), which is the same as the time to merge a single skyline, but gets much more done.

This suggests the use of divide-and-conquer: compute skylines for one half of the buildings, the other half of the buildings, and then merge the results. The merge is similar to the procedure for adding a single building, described above, and can be performed in $O(n)$ time. We iterate through the two skylines together from left-to-right, matching their X coordinates, and updating heights appropriately.

As an example, consider merging the skyline for Buildings A, B, C, D with the skyline for Buildings E, F, G, H. From 0 to 7, the skyline for A, B, C, D determines the height, because these are the only buildings present. At 7, since the skyline for A, B, C, D is taller, than that for E, F, G, H, we use its height, 4, going forward. At 8, since the skyline for E, F, G, H is taller, so we use its height, 3, going forward. After 9, the skyline for E, F, G, H determines the height, because these are the only buildings going forward.

```cpp
struct Rectangle {
  int left, right, height;
};
typedef vector<Rectangle> Skyline;

Skyline ComputeSkyline(const vector<Rectangle>& buildings) {
  return ComputeSkylineInInterval(buildings, 0, buildings.size());
}


Skyline ComputeSkylineInInterval(const vector<Rectangle>& buildings,
                                 int left_endpoint, int right_endpoint) {
  if (right_endpoint - left_endpoint <= 1) { // 0 or 1 skyline, just copy it.
    return {buildings.cbegin() + left_endpoint,
            buildings.cbegin() + right_endpoint};
  }
  int mid = left_endpoint + ((right_endpoint - left_endpoint) / 2);
  auto left_skyline = ComputeSkylineInInterval(buildings, left_endpoint, mid);
  auto right_skyline =
      ComputeSkylineInInterval(buildings, mid, right_endpoint);
  return MergeSkylines(&left_skyline, &right_skyline);
}

Skyline MergeSkylines(Skyline* left_skyline, Skyline* right_skyline) {
  int i = 0, j = 0;
  Skyline merged;

  while (i < left_skyline->size() && j < right_skyline->size()) {
    if ((*left_skyline)[i].right < (*right_skyline)[j].left) {
      merged.emplace_back((*left_skyline)[i++]);
    } else if ((*right_skyline)[j].right < (*left_skyline)[i].left) {
      merged.emplace_back((*right_skyline)[j++]);
    } else if ((*left_skyline)[i].left <= (*right_skyline)[j].left) {
      MergeIntersectSkylines(&merged, &(*left_skyline)[i], &i,
                             &(*right_skyline)[j], &j);
    } else { // left_skyline[i].left > right_skyline[j].left.
      MergeIntersectSkylines(&merged, &(*right_skyline)[j], &j,
                             &(*left_skyline)[i], &i);
    }
  }
```

```
    }
    merged.insert(merged.end(), left_skyline->begin() + i, left_skyline->end());
    merged.insert(merged.end(), right_skyline->begin() + j,
                  right_skyline->end());
    return merged;
}

void MergeIntersectSkylines(Skyline* merged, Rectangle* a, int* a_idx,
                            Rectangle* b, int* b_idx) {
    if (a->right <= b->right) {
        if (a->height > b->height) {
            if (b->right != a->right) {
                merged->emplace_back(*a), ++*a_idx;
                b->left = a->right;
            } else {
                ++*b_idx;
            }
        } else if (a->height == b->height) {
            b->left = a->left, ++*a_idx;
        } else {  // a->height < b->height.
            if (a->left != b->left) {
                merged->emplace_back(Rectangle{a->left, b->left, a->height});
            }
            ++*a_idx;
        }
    } else {  // a->right > b->right.
        if (a->height >= b->height) {
            ++*b_idx;
        } else {
            if (a->left != b->left) {
                merged->emplace_back(Rectangle{a->left, b->left, a->height});
            }
            a->left = b->right;
            merged->emplace_back(*b), ++*b_idx;
        }
    }
}
```

The time complexity $T(n)$ satisfies the recurrence $T(n) = 2T(n/2) + O(n)$, where the latter term comes from the merge step. This solves to $T(n) = O(n \log n)$.

The answer presented above is the way a textbook would present it. Here is an alternative to the textbook solution that is much simpler, and, except for degenerate inputs, performs much better. It is based on "digitizing" the problem. Let's say the left-most coordinate for any building is l and the right-most coordinate for any building is r. Then the final skyline will start at l and end at r. We draw the the skyline building by building as follows. We represent the skyline with an array, where the ith element of the array hold the height of coordinate i of the current skyline. This array is initialized to 0s. For each building, we iterate over the coordinates, and update the skyline—if the current skyline's height at coordinate i is less than the height of the building, we update the skyline at i to the building's height.

```
struct Rectangle {
```

```
  int left, right, height;
};
typedef vector<Rectangle> Skyline;

Skyline ComputeSkyline(const vector<Rectangle>& buildings) {
  int min_left = numeric_limits<int>::max(),
      max_right = numeric_limits<int>::min();
  for (const Rectangle& building : buildings) {
    min_left = min(min_left, building.left);
    max_right = max(max_right, building.right);
  }

  vector<int> heights(max_right - min_left + 1, 0);
  for (const Rectangle& building : buildings) {
    for (int i = building.left; i <= building.right; ++i) {
      heights[i - min_left] = max(heights[i - min_left], building.height);
    }
  }

  Skyline result;
  int left = 0;
  for (int i = 1; i < heights.size(); ++i) {
    if (heights[i] != heights[i - 1]) {
      result.emplace_back(
          Rectangle{left + min_left, i - 1 + min_left, heights[i - 1]});
      left = i;
    }
  }
  result.emplace_back(Rectangle{left + min_left, max_right, heights.back()});
  return result;
}
```

The time complexity is $O(nW)$, where W is the width of the widest building. In theory, W could be very large, making this approach much worse than the textbook solution. In practice, W will be a constant, and the digitized solution will be much faster. It is also vastly simpler to code and to understand.

Variant: Solve the skyline problem when each building has the shape of an isosceles triangle with a 90 degree angle at its apex.

22.36 FIND THE TWO CLOSEST POINTS 🐦

Suppose you were asked to design a collision warning program for a ship control system. Specifically, your program receives coordinates for the different ships, and has to compute the pair of ships that is at greatest risk of collision. Assuming that the pair with the greatest risk is the pair that is closest, your problem then becomes the following.

You are given a list of points in the 2D Cartesian plane. Each point has integer X and Y coordinates. How would you find the two closest points?

Hint: Start with the one dimensional case.

Solution: The brute-force solution is to consider all pairs of points: this yields an $O(n^2)$ algorithm, where n is the number of points.

To improve upon the brute-force solution, it is instructive to consider the one-dimensional case. The obvious solution for the one-dimensional case is to iterate through the points in sorted order, comparing the distance between successive points with the running minimum. However, this does not generalize to the 2D case, since there is no natural total ordering of the points. Another approach for the one-dimensional case is divide-and-conquer: partition the set about the median, solve the problem for the left and right partitions, and combine the results. The last step entails finding points closest to the median from the left and right partitions.

The complexity of the partitioning approach is the same as that of the approach based on sorting—$O(n \log n)$, where n is the number of points. However, the partitioning approach is applicable in more than one dimension. Specifically, we can split the points into two equal-sized sets using a line $x = P$ parallel to the Y-axis. (Such a line can be found by computing the median of the values for the X coordinates using Solution 12.9 on Page 195.)

We can then compute the closest pair of points recursively on the two sets; let the closest pair of points on the left of P be d_l apart and the closest pair of points to the right of P be d_r apart. Let $d = \min(d_l, d_r)$.

Now, all we need to look at is points which are in the band $[P - d, P + d]$. In degenerate situations, all points may be within this band. If we compare all the pairs, the complexity becomes quadratic again. However, we can sort the points in the band on their Y coordinates and iterate through the sorted list, looking for points d or less distance from the point being processed.

The recursion can be sped up by switching to brute-force when a small number of points remain.

```
struct Point {
  int x, y;
};
const int kBruteForceThreshold = 50;

struct PairOfPoints {
  Point p1, p2;
};

struct PairOfPointsWithDistance {
  Point p1, p2;
  double distance;
};

PairOfPoints FindClosestPairPoints(vector<Point> points) {
  sort(points.begin(), points.end(),
       [](const Point& a, const Point& b) -> bool { return a.x < b.x; });
  auto closest_two_points_with_distance =
      FindClosestPairPointsInSubarray(points, 0, points.size());
  return {closest_two_points_with_distance.p1,
          closest_two_points_with_distance.p2};
}
```

```
// Returns the closest two points and their distance as a tuple in
// points[begin : end - 1].
PairOfPointsWithDistance FindClosestPairPointsInSubarray(
    const vector<Point>& points, int begin, int end) {
  if (end - begin <= kBruteForceThreshold) {  // Switch to brute-force.
    return SolveByEnumerateAllPairs(points, begin, end);
  }

  int mid = begin + (end - begin) / 2;
  auto result0 = FindClosestPairPointsInSubarray(points, begin, mid);
  auto result1 = FindClosestPairPointsInSubarray(points, mid, end);
  auto best_result_in_subsets =
      result0.distance < result1.distance ? result0 : result1;
  // Stores the points whose separation along the X-axis is less than min_d.
  vector<Point> remain;
  for (const Point& p : points) {
    if (abs(p.x - points[mid].x) < best_result_in_subsets.distance) {
      remain.emplace_back(p);
    }
  }

  auto mid_ret =
      FindClosestPairInRemain(&remain, best_result_in_subsets.distance);
  return mid_ret.distance < best_result_in_subsets.distance
             ? mid_ret
             : best_result_in_subsets;
}

// Returns the closest two points and the distance between them.
PairOfPointsWithDistance SolveByEnumerateAllPairs(const vector<Point>& points,
                                                  int begin, int end) {
  PairOfPointsWithDistance ret;
  ret.distance = numeric_limits<double>::max();
  for (int i = begin; i < end; ++i) {
    for (int j = i + 1; j < end; ++j) {
      double dis = Distance(points[i], points[j]);
      if (dis < ret.distance) {
        ret = {points[i], points[j], dis};
      }
    }
  }
  return ret;
}

// Returns the closest two points and its distance as a tuple.
PairOfPointsWithDistance FindClosestPairInRemain(vector<Point>* remain,
                                                 double d) {
  sort(remain->begin(), remain->end(),
       [](const Point& a, const Point& b) -> bool { return a.y < b.y; });

  // At most six points in remain.
  PairOfPointsWithDistance ret;
  ret.distance = numeric_limits<double>::max();
  for (int i = 0; i < remain->size(); ++i) {
    for (int j = i + 1;
         j < remain->size() && (*remain)[j].y - (*remain)[i].y < d; ++j) {
```

464

```
    double dis = Distance((*remain)[i], (*remain)[j]);
    if (dis < ret.distance) {
      ret = {(*remain)[i], (*remain)[j], dis};
    }
  }
}
  return ret;
}

double Distance(const Point& a, const Point& b) {
  return sqrt((a.x - b.x) * (a.x - b.x) + (a.y - b.y) * (a.y - b.y));
}
```

Intuitively, there cannot be many such points to consider in the band, since otherwise the closest pair in the left and right partitions would have to be less than d apart. This intuition can be analytically justified—Shamos and Hoey's famous 1975 paper *"Closest-point problems"* shows that no more than six points can be within d distance of any point, which leads to a $O(n \log n)$ time complexity. (The time complexity is dominated by the sort step.)

22.37 MEASURE WITH DEFECTIVE JUGS 🥷

You have three measuring jugs, A, B, and C. The measuring marks have worn out, making it impossible to measure exact volumes. Specifically, each time you measure with A, all you can be sure of is that you have a volume that is in the range $[230, 240]$ mL. (The next time you use A, you may get a different volume—all that you know with certainty is that the quantity will be in $[230, 240]$ mL.) Jugs B and C can be used to measure a volume in $[290, 310]$ mL and in $[500, 515]$ mL, respectively. Your recipe for chocolate chip cookies calls for at least 2100 mL and no more than 2300 mL of milk.

Write a program that determines if there exists a sequence of steps by which the required amount of milk can be obtained using the worn-out jugs. The milk is being added to a large mixing bowl, and hence cannot be removed from the bowl. Furthermore, it is not possible to pour one jug's contents into another. Your scheme should always work, i.e., return between 2100 and 2300 mL of milk, independent of how much is chosen in each individual step, as long as that quantity satisfies the given constraints.

Hint: Solve the n jugs case.

Solution: It is natural to solve this problem using recursion—if we use jug A for the last step, we need to correctly measure a volume of milk that is at least $2100 - 230 = 1870$ mL—the last measurement may be as little as 230 mL, and anything less than 1870 mL runs the risk of being too little. Similarly, the volume must be at most $2300 - 240 = 2060$ mL. The volume is not achievable if it is not achievable with any of the three jugs as ending points. We cache intermediate computations to reduce the number of recursive calls.

465

In the following code, we implement a general purpose function which finds the feasibility among n jugs.

```
struct Jug {
  int low, high;
};

struct VolumeRange {
  int low, high;

  bool operator==(const VolumeRange& that) const {
    return low == that.low && high == that.high;
  }
};

struct HashVolumeRange {
  size_t operator()(const VolumeRange& p) const {
    return hash<int>()(p.low) ^ hash<int>()(p.high);
  }
};

bool CheckFeasible(const vector<Jug>& jugs, int L, int H) {
  unordered_set<VolumeRange, HashVolumeRange> cache;
  return CheckFeasibleHelper(jugs, L, H, &cache);
}

bool CheckFeasibleHelper(const vector<Jug>& jugs, int L, int H,
                         unordered_set<VolumeRange, HashVolumeRange>* c) {
  if (L > H || c->find({L, H}) != c->cend() || (L < 0 && H < 0)) {
    return false;
  }

  // Checks the volume for each jug to see if it is possible.
  for (const Jug& j : jugs) {
    if ((L <= j.low && j.high <= H) ||  // Base case: j is contained in [L, H]
        CheckFeasibleHelper(jugs, L - j.low, H - j.high, c)) {
      return true;
    }
  }
  c->emplace(VolumeRange{L, H});  // Marks this as impossible.
  return false;
}
```

The time complexity is $O((L+1)(H+1)n)$. The time directly spent within each call to CheckFeasibleHelper, except for the recursive calls, is $O(n)$, and because of the cache, there are at most $(L+1)(H+1)$ calls to CheckFeasibleHelper. The space complexity is $O((L+1)(H+1))$, which is the upper bound on the size of the cache.

Note that it is possible to formulate this problem using Integer Linear Programming (ILP). However, typically interviewers will not be satisfied with a reduction to ILP since such a solution does not demonstrate any programming skills.

Variant: Suppose Jug i can be used to measure any quantity in $[l_i, u_i]$ exactly. Determine if it is possible to measure a quantity of milk between L and U.

Finding the maximum subarray sum in an array can be solved in linear time, as described on Page 300. However, if the given array A is circular, which means the first and last elements of the array are to be treated as being adjacent to each other, the algorithm yields suboptimum solutions. For example, if A is the array in Figure 17.2 on Page 300, the maximum subarray sum starts at index 7 and ends at index 3, but the algorithm described on Page 301 returns the subarray from index 0 to index 3.

Given a circular array A, compute its maximum subarray sum in $O(n)$ time, where n is the length of A. Can you devise an algorithm that takes $O(n)$ time and $O(1)$ space?

Hint: The maximum subarray may or may not wrap around.

Solution: First recall the standard algorithm for the conventional maximum subarray sum problem. This proceeds by computing the maximum subarray sum $S[i]$ when the subarray ends at i, which is $\max(S[i-1] + A[i], A[i])$. Its time complexity is $O(n)$, where n is the length of the array, and space complexity is $O(1)$.

One approach for the maximum circular subarray is to break the problem into two separate instances. The first instance is the noncircular one, and is solved as described above.

The second instance entails looking for the maximum subarray that cycles around. Naively, this entails finding the maximum subarray that starts at index 0, the maximum subarray ending at index $n-1$, and adding their sums. However, these two subarrays may overlap, and simply subtracting out the overlap does not always give the right result (consider the array $\langle 10, -4, 5, -4, 10 \rangle$).

Instead, we compute for each i the maximum subarray sum S_i for the subarray that starts at 0 and ends at or before i, and the maximum subarray E_i for the subarray that starts after i and ends at the last element. Then the maximum subarray sum for a subarray that cycles around is the maximum over all i of $S_i + E_i$.

```
int MaxSubarraySumInCircular(const vector<int>& A) {
  return max(FindMaxSubarray(A), FindCircularMaxSubarray(A));
}

// Calculates the non-circular solution.
int FindMaxSubarray(const vector<int>& A) {
  int maximum_till = 0, maximum = 0;
  for (int a : A) {
    maximum_till = max(a, a + maximum_till);
    maximum = max(maximum, maximum_till);
  }
  return maximum;
}

// Calculates the solution which is circular.
int FindCircularMaxSubarray(const vector<int>& A) {
  // Maximum subarray sum starts at index 0 and ends at or before index i.
  vector<int> maximum_begin;
  int sum = A.front();
  maximum_begin.emplace_back(sum);
```

```
    for (int i = 1; i < A.size(); ++i) {
      sum += A[i];
      maximum_begin.emplace_back(max(maximum_begin.back(), sum));
    }

    // Maximum subarray sum starts at index i + 1 and ends at the last element.
    vector<int> maximum_end(A.size());
    maximum_end.back() = 0;
    sum = 0;
    for (int i = A.size() - 2; i >= 0; --i) {
      sum += A[i + 1];
      maximum_end[i] = max(maximum_end[i + 1], sum);
    }

    // Calculates the maximum subarray which is circular.
    int circular_max = 0;
    for (int i = 0; i < A.size(); ++i) {
      circular_max = max(circular_max, maximum_begin[i] + maximum_end[i]);
    }
    return circular_max;
}
```

The time complexity and space complexity are both $O(n)$.

Alternatively, the maximum subarray that cycles around can be determined by computing the minimum subarray—the remaining elements yield a subarray that cycles around. (One or both of the first and last elements may not be included in this subarray, but that is fine.) This approach uses $O(1)$ space and $O(n)$ time; code for it is given below.

```
int MaxSubarraySumInCircular(const vector<int>& A) {
  // Finds the max in non-circular case and circular case.
  return max(FindOptimumSubarrayUsingComp(A, max),  // Non-circular case.
             accumulate(A.cbegin(), A.cend(), 0) -
                 FindOptimumSubarrayUsingComp(A, min));  // Circular case.
}

int FindOptimumSubarrayUsingComp(const vector<int>& A,
                                 const int& (*comp)(const int&, const int&)) {
  int till = 0, overall = 0;
  for (int a : A) {
    till = comp(a, a + till);
    overall = comp(overall, till);
  }
  return overall;
}
```

22.39 Determine the critical height ☺

You need to test the design of a protective case. Specifically, the case can protect the enclosed device from a fall from up to some number of floors, and you want to determine what that number of floors is. You can assume the following:

- All cases have identical physical properties. In particular, if one breaks when falling from a particular level, all of them will break when falling from that level.
- A case that survives a fall can be used again, and a broken case must be discarded.
- If a case breaks when dropped, then it would break if dropped from a higher floor, and if a case survives a fall, then it would survive a shorter fall.

It is not ruled out that the first-floor windows break eggs, nor is it ruled out that eggs can survive the 36th-floor windows.

You know that there exists a floor such that the case will break if it is dropped from any floor at or above that floor, will remain intact if dropped from a lower floor. The ground floor is numbered zero, and it is given that the case will not break if dropped from the ground floor.

An additional constraint is that you can perform only a fixed number of drops before the building supervisor stops you.

Note that if we have a single case and are allowed only 5 drops, then the highest we can measure to is 5 floors, testing from 1, 2, 3, 4, and 5. We cannot skip a floor, since the case may break immediately after the skipped floor, and we would have no way to know if the critical floor was the last one tested or a skipped floor. If the case does not break, we know it is able to last to a fifth floor drop.

If we have two cases and are allowed 5 drops, we can do better. For example, we could test by dropping from floors 2, 4, 6, 8, 9. If a case breaks on the first four drops, we have narrowed the critical floor to that floor or the one below it. We can test the one below it with the second case. If the case breaks on the fifth drop, we know the critical floor is 9. If the case does not break, we know it is able to last to a ninth floor drop. Clearly having two cases is better than one.

Given c cases and a maximum of d allowable drops, what is the maximum number of floors that you can test in the worst-case?

Hint: Write a recurrence relation.

Solution: Let $F(c, d)$ be the maximum number of floors we can test with c identical cases and at most d drops. We know that $F(1, d) = d$. Suppose we know the value of $F(i, j)$ for all $i \leq c$ and $j \leq d$.

If we are given $c + 1$ cases and d drops we can start at floor $F(c, d - 1) + 1$ and drop a case. If the case breaks, then we can use the remaining c cases and $d - 1$ drops to determine the floor exactly, since it must be in the range $[1, F(c, d - 1)]$. If the case did not break, we proceed to floor $F(c, d - 1) + 1 + F(c + 1, d - 1)$.

Therefore, F satisfies the recurrence

$$F(c + 1, d) = F(c, d - 1) + 1 + F(c + 1, d - 1).$$

We can compute F using DP as below:

```
int GetHeight(int cases, int drops) {
  vector<vector<int>> F(cases + 1, vector<int>(drops + 1, -1));
  return GetHeightHelper(cases, drops, &F);
```

```
}

int GetHeightHelper(int cases, int drops, vector<vector<int>>* F) {
  if (cases == 0 || drops == 0) {
    return 0;
  } else if (cases == 1) {
    return drops;
  } else {
    if ((*F)[cases][drops] == -1) {
      (*F)[cases][drops] = GetHeightHelper(cases, drops - 1, F) +
                           GetHeightHelper(cases - 1, drops - 1, F) + 1;
    }
    return (*F)[cases][drops];
  }
}
```

The time and space complexity are $O((c + 1)(d + 1))$.

Variant: Solve the same problem with $O(c)$ space.

Variant: How would you compute the minimum number of drops needed to find the breaking point from 1 to F floors using c cases?

Variant: Men numbered from 1 to n are arranged in a circle in clockwise order. Every kth man is removed, until only one man remains. What is the number of the last man?

22.40 VOLTAGE SELECTION IN A LOGIC CIRCUIT

A logic circuit is an ensemble of logic gates operating on a set of external inputs. The gates implement basic Boolean operations such as AND, OR and NOT. Formally, a logic circuit can be modeled as a directed acyclic graph (DAG)—the external inputs are the sources of the DAG and gates are the remaining nodes.

In this problem we consider the special case where the DAG is a rooted tree. Each node can use either a high voltage or a low voltage. A low voltage node consumes less power, but has a weaker signal. It is a design constraint that a low voltage node should never be input to another low voltage node. If a node is assigned a low voltage, its power consumption is the number of its children plus one; if it is assigned a high voltage, its power consumption is twice that. For example, the topmost node in Figure 22.11(a) on the next page has two children, and it is assigned a high voltage. Therefore, the power it uses is $2 \times (2 + 1) = 6$. The same node in Figure 22.11(c) on the following page is assigned a low voltage, so the power it uses is $2 + 1 = 3$.

Figure 22.11 on the next page shows three voltage assignments for the same logic circuit. All assignments satisfy the design constraint. Figure 22.11(a) on the following page proceeds greedily in a bottom up fashion, assigning leaves to L. Figure 22.11(b) on the next page proceeds greedily in a top-down fashion, assigning the root to H, its children to L, and continuing downwards. Figure 22.11(c) on the following page is the optimal assignment.

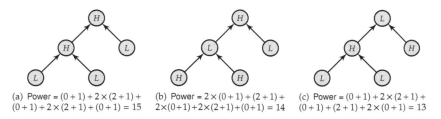

(a) Power = $(0+1) + 2 \times (2+1) +$
$(0+1) + 2 \times (2+1) + (0+1) = 15$

(b) Power = $2 \times (0+1) + (2+1) +$
$2 \times (0+1) + 2 \times (2+1) + (0+1) = 14$

(c) Power = $(0+1) + 2 \times (2+1) +$
$(0+1) + (2+1) + 2 \times (0+1) = 13$

Figure 22.11: The node labels L or H indicating a high or low voltage node, respectively.

Design an algorithm for minimizing power that takes as input a rooted tree and assigns each node to a low or high voltage, subject to the design constraint.

Hint: There are two possibilities for each node—find the optimum minimum power for each.

Solution: Let $l(r)$ and $h(r)$ be the power consumption of node r under low and high voltages, respectively. Let $L(r)$ be the minimum possible power that can be achieved when we assign a low voltage to r. Let $H(r)$ be the minimum possible power that can be achieved when r is assigned a high voltage.

Denote the set of all nodes that are inputs to r by $I(r)$. Then the following recurrence relationships must hold for L and H:

$$L(r) = l(r) + \sum_{c \in I(r)} H(c),$$

$$H(r) = h(r) + \sum_{c \in I(r)} \min\left(L(c), H(c)\right).$$

Using these equations, we can tabulate the values of L and H for all nodes. The desired solution is the minimum of the values of L and H for the root of the tree. Since we do a constant number of operations per node, the overall complexity is $O(n)$, where n is the number of nodes.

22.41 FIND THE MAXIMUM 2D SUBARRAY ⚅

The following problem has applications to image processing.

Let A be an $n \times m$ Boolean 2D array. Design efficient algorithms for the following two problems:

- What is the largest 2D subarray containing only 1s?
- What is the largest square 2D subarray containing only 1s?

What are the time and space complexities of your algorithms as a function of n and m?

Hint: How would you efficiently check if $A[i : i + a][j : j + b]$ satisfies the constraints, assuming you have already performed similar checks?

Solution: A brute-force approach is to examine all 2D subarrays. Since a 2D subarray is characterized by two diagonally opposite corners the total number of such arrays is

471

$O(m^2n^2)$. Each 2D subarray can be checked by examining the corresponding entries, so the overall complexity is $O(m^3n^3)$. This can be easily reduced to $O(m^2n^2)$ by processing 2D subarrays by size, and reusing results—the 2D subarray $A[i : i + a][j : j + b]$ is feasible if and only if the 2D subarrays $A[i : i+a-1][j : j+b-1]$, $A[i+a : i+a][j : j+b-1]$, $A[i : i+a-1][j+b : j+b]$, and $A[i+a : i+a][j+b : j+b]$ are feasible. This is an $O(1)$ time operation, assuming that feasibility of the smaller 2D subarrays has already been computed and stored. (Note that this solution requires $O(m^2n^2)$ storage.)

The following approach lowers the time and space complexity. For each feasible entry $A[i][j]$ we record $(h_{i,j}, w_{i,j})$, where $h_{i,j}$ is the largest L such that all the entries in $A[i : i + L - 1][j : j]$ are feasible, and $w_{i,j}$ is the largest L such that all the entries in $A[i : i][j : j + L - 1]$ are feasible. This computation can be performed in $O(mn)$ time, and requires $O(mn)$ storage.

Now for each feasible entry $A[i][j]$ we calculate the largest 2D subarray that has $A[i][j]$ as its bottom-left corner. We do this by processing each entry in $A[i : i+h_{i,j}-1][j : j]$. As we iterate through the entries in vertical order, we update w to the smallest $w_{i,j}$ amongst the entries processed so far. The largest 2D subarray that has $A[i][j]$ as its bottom-left corner and $A[i'][j]$ as its top-left corner has area $(i' - i + 1)w$. We track the largest 2D subarray seen so far across all $A[i][j]$ processed.

```
struct MaxHW {
  int h, w;
};

int MaxRectangleSubmatrix(const vector<deque<bool>>& A) {
  // DP table stores (h, w) for each (i, j).
  vector<vector<MaxHW>> table(A.size(), vector<MaxHW>(A.front().size()));

  for (int i = A.size() - 1; i >= 0; --i) {
    for (int j = A[i].size() - 1; j >= 0; --j) {
      // Find the largest h such that (i, j) to (i + h - 1, j) are feasible.
      // Find the largest w such that (i, j) to (i, j + w - 1) are feasible.
      table[i][j] =
          A[i][j] ? MaxHW{i + 1 < A.size() ? table[i + 1][j].h + 1 : 1,
                          j + 1 < A[i].size() ? table[i][j + 1].w + 1 : 1}
                  : MaxHW{0, 0};
    }
  }

  int max_rect_area = 0;
  for (int i = 0; i < A.size(); ++i) {
    for (int j = 0; j < A[i].size(); ++j) {
      // Process (i, j) if it is feasible and is possible to update
      // max_rect_area.
      if (A[i][j] && table[i][j].w * table[i][j].h > max_rect_area) {
        int min_width = numeric_limits<int>::max();
        for (int a = 0; a < table[i][j].h; ++a) {
          min_width = min(min_width, table[i + a][j].w);
          max_rect_area = max(max_rect_area, min_width * (a + 1));
        }
      }
    }
  }
}
```

```
    return max_rect_area;
}
```

The time complexity per $A[i][j]$ is proportional to the number of rows, i.e., $O(n)$, yielding an overall time complexity of $O(mn^2)$, and space complexity of $O(mn)$.

If we are looking for the largest feasible square region, we can improve the complexity as follows—we compute the $(h_{i,j}, w_{i,j})$ values as before. Suppose we know the length s of the largest square region that has $A[i+1][j+1]$ as its bottom-left corner. Then the length of the side of the largest square with $A[i][j]$ as its bottom-left corner is at most $s+1$, which occurs if and only if $h_{i,j} \geq s+1$ and $w_{i,j} \geq s+1$. The general expression for the length is $\min(s+1, h_{i,j}, w_{i,j})$. Note that this is an $O(1)$ time computation. In total, the run time is $O(mn)$, a factor of n better than before.

The calculations above can be sped up by intelligent pruning. For example, if we already have a feasible 2D subarray of dimensions $H \times W$, there is no reason to process an entry $A[i][j]$ for which $h_{i,j} \leq H$ and $w_{i,j} \leq W$.

```
struct MaxHW {
  int h, w;
};

int MaxSquareSubmatrix(const vector<deque<bool>>& A) {
  // DP table stores (h, w) for each (i, j).
  vector<vector<MaxHW>> table(A.size(), vector<MaxHW>(A.front().size()));

  for (int i = A.size() - 1; i >= 0; --i) {
    for (int j = A[i].size() - 1; j >= 0; --j) {
      // Finds the largest h such that (i, j) to (i + h - 1, j) are feasible.
      // Finds the largest w such that (i, j) to (i, j + w - 1) are feasible.
      table[i][j] =
          A[i][j] ? MaxHW{i + 1 < A.size() ? table[i + 1][j].h + 1 : 1,
                          j + 1 < A[i].size() ? table[i][j + 1].w + 1 : 1}
                  : MaxHW{0, 0};
    }
  }

  // A table stores the length of the largest square for each (i, j).
  vector<vector<int>> s(A.size(), vector<int>(A.front().size(), 0));
  int max_square_area = 0;
  for (int i = A.size() - 1; i >= 0; --i) {
    for (int j = A[i].size() - 1; j >= 0; --j) {
      int side = min(table[i][j].h, table[i][j].w);
      if (A[i][j]) {
        // Gets the length of largest square with bottom-left corner (i, j).
        if (i + 1 < A.size() && j + 1 < A[i + 1].size()) {
          side = min(s[i + 1][j + 1] + 1, side);
        }
        s[i][j] = side;
        max_square_area = max(max_square_area, side * side);
      }
    }
  }
  return max_square_area;
}
```

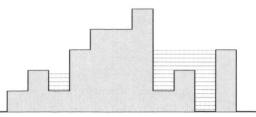

Figure 22.12: The area of the horizontal lines is the maximum amount of water that can be trapped by the solid region. For this container, it is $1 + 2 + 1 + 3 = 7$.

The largest 2D subarray can be found in $O(nm)$ time using a qualitatively different approach. Essentially, we reduce our problem to n instances of the largest rectangle under the skyline problem described in Problem 18.9 on Page 344. First, for each $A[i][j]$ we determine the largest $h_{i,j}$ such that $A[i : i + h_{i,j} - 1][j : j]$ is feasible. (If $A[i][j] = 0$ then $h_{i,j} = 0$.) Then for each of the n rows, starting with the topmost one, we compute the largest 2D subarray whose bottom edge is on that row in time $O(m)$, using Solution 18.9 on Page 345. This computation can be performed in time $O(n)$ once the $h_{i,j}$ values have been computed. The final solution is the maximum of the n instances.

The time complexity for each row is $O(m)$ for computing the h values, assuming we record the h values for the previous row, and $O(m)$ for computing the largest rectangle under the skyline, i.e., $O(m)$ in total per row. Therefore the total time complexity is $O(mn)$. The additional space complexity is $O(m)$—this is the space for recording the h values and running the largest rectangle under the skyline computation.

```
int MaxRectangleSubmatrix(const vector<deque<bool>>& A) {
  vector<int> table(A.front().size(), 0);
  int max_rect_area = 0;
  // Find the maximum among all instances of the largest rectangle.
  for (int i = A.size() - 1; i >= 0; --i) {
    for (int j = 0; j < A[i].size(); ++j) {
      table[j] = A[i][j] ? i + 1 < A.size() ? table[j] + 1 : 1 : 0;
    }
    max_rect_area = max(max_rect_area, CalculateLargestRectangle(table));
  }
  return max_rect_area;
}
```

The largest square 2D subarray containing only 1s can be computed similarly, with a minor variant on the algorithm in Solution 18.9 on Page 345.

22.42 TRAPPING WATER ☜

The goal of this problem is to compute the capacity of a type of one-dimensional container. The computation is illustrated in Figure 22.12.

A one-dimensional container is specified by an array of n nonnegative integers, specifying the height of each unit-width rectangle. Design an algorithm for computing the capacity of the container.

Hint: Draw pictures, and focus on the extremes.

Solution: We can get a great deal of insight by visualizing pouring water into the container. When the maximum capacity is achieved, the cross-section consists of a region in which the water level is nondecreasing, followed by a region in which the water level is nonincreasing. The transition from nondecreasing to nonincreasing takes place around a maximum entry in A. Let $A[m]$ be a maximum value entry. Then we compute the capacity of $A[0 : m - 1]$ and $A[m : n - 1]$ independently. These capacities are determined via an iteration. For each entry in $A[0 : m - 1]$ we compute the difference between its value entry and the running maximum, and add that to the total capacity. We handle $A[m : n - 1]$ analogously. The time complexity is $O(n)$ to find a maximum, and then $O(n)$ for each of the two iterations, i.e., the total time complexity is $O(n)$. The space complexity is $O(1)$—all that is needed is to record several variables.

```
int CalculateTrappingWater(const vector<int> &A) {
  if (A.empty()) {
    return 0;
  }

  // Finds the index with maximum height.
  int max_h = distance(A.cbegin(), max_element(A.cbegin(), A.cend()));

  // Calculates the water within [1 : max_h - 1].
  int sum = 0, left = A.front();
  for (int i = 1; i < max_h; ++i) {
    if (A[i] >= left) {
      left = A[i];
    } else {
      sum += left - A[i];
    }
  }

  // Calculates the water within [max_h + 1 : A.size() - 2].
  int right = A.back();
  for (int i = A.size() - 2; i > max_h; --i) {
    if (A[i] >= right) {
      right = A[i];
    } else {
      sum += right - A[i];
    }
  }
  return sum;
}
```

Variant: Solve the water filling problem with an algorithm that accesses A's elements in order and can read an element only once. Use minimum additional space.

Suppose you want to build a large distributed storage system on the web. Millions of users will store terabytes of data on your servers. One way to design the system would be to compute a hash code for each user's login ID, partition the hash codes across equal-sized buckets, and store the data for each bucket of users on one server. For this scheme, mapping a user to his server entails evaluating a hash function.

However, if a small number of users occupy a large fraction of the storage space, this scheme will not achieve a balanced partition. One way to solve this problem is to use a nonuniform partitioning.

You have n users with unique hash codes h_0 through h_{n-1}, and m servers. The hash codes are ordered by index, i.e., $h_i < h_{i+1}$ for $i \in [0, n-2]$. User i requires b_i bytes of storage. The values $k_0 < k_1 < \cdots < k_{m-2}$ are used to assign users to servers. Specifically, the user with hash code c gets assigned to the server with the lowest ID i such that $c \le k_i$, or to Server $m-1$ if no such i exists. This restricted mapping of users to servers means that the user-to-server lookup can be implemented with a BST on $m-1$ nodes, rather than a hash table on n users. The load on a server is the sum of the bytes of storage of all users assigned to that server. Compute values for $k_0, k_1, \ldots, k_{m-2}$ that minimizes the load on the most heavily loaded server.

Hint: Consider the problem of determining if it is feasible to implement the storage using no more than M bytes per server.

Solution: Let $L(p, q)$ be the maximum load on a server when users with hash codes h_0 through h_p are assigned to Servers 0 through q in an optimum way, i.e., when the maximum load is minimized. Then the following recurrence holds:

$$L(p, q) = \min_{x \in [0, p]} \left(\max \left(L(x, q-1), \sum_{i=x+1}^{p} b_i \right) \right)$$

In other words, to find the optimum assignment of users with hash codes $\{h_0, h_1, \ldots, h_p\}$ to q servers, we find x such that if we assign the first $x+1$ users optimally to $q-1$ servers and the remainder to Server q, the maximum load on a given server is minimized.

We can use the recurrence to tabulate the values in L till we get $L(n-1, m-1)$. The base case corresponds to entries of the form $L(p, 0)$, in which case the maximum load is $\sum_{i=0}^{p} b_i$. The time complexity to compute each $L(i, j)$ is $O(n)$, so the overall complexity to compute $L(n-1, m-1)$ is $O(n^2 m)$.

A qualitatively different approach, based on a greedy algorithm, is to check whether $k_0, k_1, \ldots, k_{m-2}$ can be chosen so as to ensure that no server stores more than b bytes. For a given b, this can easily be done—iterate through the n users in the order of their hash codes, and assign them to the servers greedily, i.e., assign users to servers, moving on the next server when the capacity of the current server is exceeded.

```
vector<int> DecideLoadBalancing(vector<int> user_file_size, int server_num) {
    // Uses binary search to find the assignment with minimized maximum load.
```

```
int l = 0, r = accumulate(user_file_size.cbegin(), user_file_size.cend(), 0);
vector<int> feasible_assignment;
while (l <= r) {
  int m = l + ((r - l) / 2);
  vector<int> assign_res(server_num, 0);
  bool is_feasible =
      GreedyAssignment(user_file_size, server_num, m, &assign_res);
  if (is_feasible) {
    feasible_assignment = assign_res;
    r = m - 1;
  } else {
    l = m + 1;
  }
}
  return feasible_assignment;
}

bool GreedyAssignment(const vector<int>& user_file_size, int server_num,
                      int limit, vector<int>* assign_res) {
  int server_idx = 0;
  for (int file : user_file_size) {
    while (server_idx < server_num &&
           file + (*assign_res)[server_idx] > limit) {
      ++server_idx;
    }

    if (server_idx >= server_num) {
      return false;
    } else {
      (*assign_res)[server_idx] += file;
    }
  }
  return true;
}
```

We perform binary search to get the minimum b, and the corresponding values for $k_0, k_1, \ldots, k_{m-2}$. The time complexity of the approach is $O(n \log W)$, where W is the total number of bytes that are to be stored, i.e., $W = \sum_{i=0}^{m-1} b_i$. This approach is much faster in practice: when $n = 10000$, $m = 100$, and loads are uniform integer random variables in the range $[1, 100]$, the $O(n^2 m)$ DP algorithm takes over an hour on our machine. In contrast, binary search for w took 0.1 seconds. Furthermore, binary search requires no additional storage beyond that needed to store the final result. The complexity of the code is also greatly reduced compared to the DP algorithm.

The takeaway is that there may be qualitatively different ways to search for a solution, and that it is important to look for ways in which to eliminate candidates.

22.44 SEARCH FOR A PAIR-SUM IN AN ABS-SORTED ARRAY ✏

An abs-sorted array is an array of numbers in which $|A[i]| \leq |A[j]|$ whenever $i < j$. For example, the array in Figure 22.13 on the next page, though not sorted in the standard sense, is abs-sorted.

-49	75	103	-147	164	-197	-238	314	348	-422
$A[0]$	$A[1]$	$A[2]$	$A[3]$	$A[4]$	$A[5]$	$A[6]$	$A[7]$	$A[8]$	$A[9]$

Figure 22.13: An abs-sorted array.

Design an algorithm that takes an abs-sorted array A and a number K, and returns a pair of indices of elements in A that sum up to K. For example, if the input to your algorithm is the array in Figure 22.13 and $K = 167$, your algorithm should output $(3, 7)$. Output $(-1, -1)$ if there is no such pair.

Hint: This problem easy to solve with $O(n)$ additional space—why? To solve it with $O(1)$ additional space, first assume all elements are positive.

Solution: First consider the case where the array is sorted in the conventional sense. In this case we can start with the pair consisting of the first element and the last element: $(A[0], A[n-1])$. Let $s = A[0] + A[n-1]$. If $s = K$, we are done. If $s < K$, we increase the sum by moving to pair $(A[1], A[n-1])$. We need never consider $A[0]$; since the array is sorted, for all $i, A[0] + A[i] \leq A[0] + A[n-1] = K < s$. If $s > K$, we can decrease the sum by considering the pair $(A[0], A[n-2])$; by analogous reasoning, we need never consider $A[n-1]$ again. We iteratively continue this process till we have found a pair that sums up to K or the indices meet, in which case the search ends. This solution works in $O(n)$ time and $O(1)$ space in addition to the space needed to store A.

This approach will not work when the array entries are sorted by absolute value. In this instance, we need to consider three cases:

(1.) Both the numbers in the pair are negative.

(2.) Both the numbers in the pair are positive.

(3.) One is negative and the other is positive.

For Cases (1.) and (2.), we can run the above algorithm separately by just limiting ourselves to either positive or negative numbers. For Case (3.), we can use the same approach where we have one index for positive numbers, one index for negative numbers, and they both start from the highest possible index and then go down.

```cpp
struct IndexPair {
  int index_1, index_2;
};

IndexPair FindPairSumK(const vector<int>& A, int k) {
  IndexPair result = FindPositiveNegativePair(A, k);
  if (result.index_1 == -1 && result.index_2 == -1) {
    return k >= 0 ? FindPairUsingCompare(A, k, less<int>())
                  : FindPairUsingCompare(A, k, greater_equal<int>());
  }
  return result;
}

template <typename Compare>
IndexPair FindPairUsingCompare(const vector<int>& A, int k, Compare comp) {
```

```
IndexPair result = IndexPair{0, static_cast<int>(A.size() - 1)};
while (result.index_1 < result.index_2 && comp(A[result.index_1], 0)) {
  ++result.index_1;
}
while (result.index_1 < result.index_2 && comp(A[result.index_2], 0)) {
  --result.index_2;
}

while (result.index_1 < result.index_2) {
  if (A[result.index_1] + A[result.index_2] == k) {
    return result;
  } else if (comp(A[result.index_1] + A[result.index_2], k)) {
    do {
      ++result.index 1;
    } while (result.index_1 < result.index_2 && comp(A[result.index_1], 0));
  } else {
    do {
      --result.index_2;
    } while (result.index_1 < result.index_2 && comp(A[result.index_2], 0));
  }
}
  return {-1, -1};  // No answer.
}

IndexPair FindPositiveNegativePair(const vector<int>& A, int k) {
  // result.index_1 for positive, and result.index_2 for negative.
  IndexPair result = IndexPair{static_cast<int>(A.size() - 1),
                               static_cast<int>(A.size() - 1)};
  // Find the last positive or zero.
  while (result.index_1 >= 0 && A[result.index_1] < 0) {
    --result.index_1;
  }

  // Find the last negative.
  while (result.index_2 >= 0 && A[result.index_2] >= 0) {
    --result.index_2;
  }

  while (result.index_1 >= 0 && result.index_2 >= 0) {
    if (A[result.index_1] + A[result.index_2] == k) {
      return result;
    } else if (A[result.index_1] + A[result.index_2] > k) {
      do {
        --result.index_1;
      } while (result.index_1 >= 0 && A[result.index_1] < 0);
    } else {  // A[result.index_1] + A[result.index_2] < k.
      do {
        --result.index_2;
      } while (result.index_2 >= 0 && A[result.index_2] >= 0);
    }
  }
  return {-1, -1};  // No answer.
}
```

Since the computation entails three passes through the array, each of which takes $O(n)$

479

time, its time complexity is $O(n)$. No memory is allocated, so the space complexity is $O(1)$.

A much simpler solution is based on a hash table (Chapter 13) to store all the numbers and then for each number x in the array, lookup $K - x$ in the hash table. If the hash function does a good job of spreading the keys, the time complexity for this approach is $O(n)$. However, it requires $O(n)$ additional storage.

If the array is sorted on elements (and not absolute values), for each $A[i]$ we can use binary search to find $K - A[i]$. This approach uses $O(1)$ additional space and has time complexity $O(n \log n)$. However, it is strictly inferior to the two pointer technique described at the beginning of the solution.

Variant: Design an algorithm that takes as input an array of integers A, and an integer K, and returns a pair of indices i and j such that $A[j] - A[i] = K$, if such a pair exists.

22.45 THE HEAVY HITTER PROBLEM

This problem is a generalization of Problem 18.6 on Page 339. In practice we may not be interested in a majority token but all tokens whose count exceeds say 1% of the total token count. It is fairly straightforward to show that it is impossible to compute such tokens in a single pass when you have limited memory. However, if you are allowed to pass through the sequence twice, it is possible to identify the common tokens.

You are reading a sequence of strings separated by whitespace. You are allowed to read the sequence twice. Devise an algorithm that uses $O(k)$ memory to identify the words that occur more than $\frac{n}{k}$ times, where n is the length of the sequence.

Hint: Maintain a list of k candidates.

Solution: This is essentially a generalization of Problem 18.6 on Page 339. Here instead of discarding two distinct words, we discard k distinct words at any given time and we are guaranteed that all the words that occurred more than $\frac{1}{k}$ times the length of the sequence prior to discarding continue to appear more than $\frac{1}{k}$ times in the remaining sequence. To implement this strategy, we need a hash table of the current candidates.

```
// Finds the candidates which may occur > n / k times.
vector<string> SearchFrequentItems(int k, istringstream* sin) {
  string buf;
  unordered_map<string, int> hash;
  int n = 0;   // Count the number of strings.

  while (*sin >> buf) {
    ++hash[buf], ++n;
    // Detecting k items in hash, at least one of them must have exactly
    // one in it. We will discard those k items by one for each.
    if (hash.size() == k) {
      auto it = hash.begin();
      while (it != hash.end()) {
        if (--(it->second) == 0) {
```

480

```
          hash.erase(it++);
        } else {
          ++it;
        }
      }
    }
  }
}

// Resets hash for the following counting.
for (auto& it : hash) {
  it.second = 0;
}

// Resets the stream and read it again.
sin->clear();
sin->seekg(0, ios::beg);
// Counts the occurrence of each candidate word.
while (*sin >> buf) {
  auto it = hash.find(buf);
  if (it != hash.end()) {
    ++it->second;
  }
}

// Selects the word which occurs > n / k times.
vector<string> ret;
for (const auto& it : hash) {
  if (it.second > static_cast<double>(n) / k) {
    ret.emplace_back(it.first);
  }
}
return ret;
}
```

The code may appear to take $O(nk)$ time since the inner loop may take k steps (decrementing count for all k entries) and the outer loop is called n times. However each word in the sequence can be erased only once, so the total time spent erasing is $O(n)$ and the rest of the steps inside the outer loop run in $O(1)$ time.

The first step yields a set S of not more than k words; set S is a superset of the words that occur greater than $\frac{n}{k}$ times. To get the exact set, we need to make another pass over the sequence and count the number of times each word in S actually occurs. We return the words in S which occur more than $\frac{n}{k}$ times.

22.46 FIND THE LONGEST SUBARRAY WHOSE SUM $\leq k$ 🥷

Here we consider finding the longest subarray subject to a constraint on the subarray sum. For example, for the array in Figure 22.14 on the facing page, the longest subarray whose subarray sum is no more than 184 is $A[3:6]$.

Design an algorithm that takes as input an array A of n numbers and a key k, and returns the length of a longest subarray of A for which the subarray sum is less than or equal to k.

431	-15	639	342	-14	565	-924	635	167	-70
A[0]	A[1]	A[2]	A[3]	A[4]	A[5]	A[6]	A[7]	A[8]	A[9]

Figure 22.14: An array for the longest subarray whose sum $\leq k$ problem.

Hint: When can you be sure that an index i cannot be the starting point of a subarray with the desired property, without looking past i?

Solution: The brute-force solution entails computing $\sum_{k=i}^{j} A[k]$, i.e., the sum of the element in $A[i:j]$, for all $0 \leq i \leq j \leq n-1$, where n is the length of A. Let P be the prefix sum array for A, i.e., $P[i] = \sum_{k=0}^{i} A[k]$; P can be computed in a single iteration over A in $O(n)$ time. Note that the sum of the elements in the subarray $A[i:j]$ is $P[j] - P[i-1]$ (for convenience, take $P[-1] = 0$). The time complexity of the brute-force solution is $O(n^2)$, and the additional space complexity is $O(n)$ (the size of P).

The trick to improving the time complexity to $O(n)$ comes from the following observation. Suppose $u < v$ and $P[u] \geq P[v]$. Then u will never be the ending point of a solution. The reason is that for any $w \leq u$, $A[w:v]$ is longer than $A[w:u]$ and if $A[w:u]$ satisfies the sum constraint, so must $A[w:v]$. This motivates the definition of the array Q: set $Q[i] = \min(P[i], Q[i+1])$ for $i < n-1$, and $Q[n-1] = P[n-1]$.

Let $a \leq b$ be indices of elements in A. Define $M_{a,b}$ to be the minimum possible sum of a subarray beginning at a and extending to b or beyond. Note that $M_{0,b} = Q[b]$, and $M_{a,b} = Q[b] - P[a-1]$, when $a > 0$. If $M_{a,b} > k$, no subarray starting at a that includes b can satisfy the sum constraint, so we can increment a. If $M_{a,b} \leq k$, then we are assured there exists a subarray of length $b - a + 1$ satisfying the sum constraint, so we compare the length of the longest subarray satisfying the sum constraint identified so far to $b - a + 1$ and conditionally update it. Consequently, we can increment b.

Suppose we initialize a and b to 0 and iteratively perform the increments to a and b described above until $b = n$. Then we will discover the length of a maximum length subarray that satisfies the sum constraint. We justify this claim after presenting an implementation of these ideas below.

```
int FindLongestSubarrayLessEqualK(const vector<int> &A, int k) {
  // Builds the prefix sum according to A.
  vector<int> prefix_sum;
  partial_sum(A.cbegin(), A.cend(), back_inserter(prefix_sum));

  // Early returns if the sum of A is smaller than or equal to k.
  if (prefix_sum.back() <= k) {
    return A.size();
  }

  // Builds min_prefix_sum.
  vector<int> min_prefix_sum(A.size());
  min_prefix_sum.back() = prefix_sum.back();
  for (int i = min_prefix_sum.size() - 2; i >= 0; --i) {
    min_prefix_sum[i] = min(prefix_sum[i], min_prefix_sum[i + 1]);
  }
}
```

```
int a = 0, b = 0, max_length = 0;
while (a < A.size() && b < A.size()) {
  int min_curr_sum =
      a > 0 ? min_prefix_sum[b] - prefix_sum[a - 1] : min_prefix_sum[b];
  if (min_curr_sum <= k) {
    int curr_length = b - a + 1;
    if (curr_length > max_length) {
      max_length = curr_length;
    }
    ++b;
  } else {  // min_curr_sum > k.
    ++a;
  }
}
return max_length;
}
```

Now we argue the correctness of the program. Let $A[a^* : b^*]$ be a maximum length subarray that satisfies the sum constraint. Note that we increment b until $M_{a,b} > k$. In particular, when we increment a to $a + 1$, $A[a : b - 1]$ does satisfy the sum constraint, but $A[a : b]$ does not. This implies $A[a : b - 1]$ is the longest subarray starting at a that satisfies the sum constraint.

The iteration ends when $b = n$. At this point, we claim $a \geq a^*$. If not, then $A[a : n-1]$ satisfies the sum constraint, since we incremented b to n, and $(n-1)-a+1 > b^* - a^* +1$, contradicting the optimality of $A[a^* : b^*]$. Therefore, a must be assigned to a^* at some iteration. At this point, $b \leq b^*$ since $A[a^* - 1 : b - 1]$ satisfies the sum constraint. For, if $b > b^*$, then $(b - 1) - (a^* - 1) + 1 = b - a^* + 1 > b^* - a^* + 1$, violating the maximality of $A[a^* : b^*]$. Since $b \leq b^*$ and $a = a^*$, the algorithm will increment b till it becomes b^* (since $A[a^* : b^*]$ satisfies the sum constraint), and thus will identify $b^* - a^* + 1$ as the optimum solution.

Variant: Design an algorithm for finding the longest subarray of a given array such that the average of the subarray elements is $\leq k$.

22.47   DEGREES OF CONNECTEDNESS—2 🥷

Suppose you are given a set of data centers connected through a set of dedicated point-to-point links. You want to reach from any data center to any other data center through a combination of these dedicated links. Sometimes, one of these links can become temporarily out of service and you want to ensure that your network is fault-tolerant, i.e., can sustain up to one out of service link.

The notion of fault-tolerance can be formalized as follows. Define an undirected graph to be fault-tolerant if it is connected and it remains connected even when any single edge is removed. As an illustration, the undirected graph in Figure 19.3 on Page 349 is fault-tolerant: any single edge can be removed, and there will still exist a path from any vertex to any other vertex. However, if the edge (h, i) is removed, then the remaining graph, though connected, is not fault-tolerant, since the subsequent removal of edge (f, i) results in an unconnected graph. For example, there will be no path from a to m, since all paths in the original graph pass through either (h, i) or (f, i).

Write a program that takes as input an undirected graph, which you can assume to be connected, and checks if the graph is fault-tolerant.

Hint: When is a graph not fault-tolerant?

Solution: Let the input graph be $G = (V, E)$. Clearly, G is not fault-tolerant if and only if there exists a "bridge", i.e., an edge e such that $G' = (V, E \setminus \{e\})$ is disconnected. The latter condition holds if and only if no cycle includes edge e.

We can find an edge (u, v) that is not on a cycle with DFS. Without loss of generality, assume u is discovered first. Observe that the removal of (u, v) disconnects G if and only if no back edges exist between v or v's descendants and u or u's ancestors. Define $l(v)$ to be the minimum of the discovery time $d(v)$ of v and $d(w)$ of w such that (t, w) is a back edge from t, where t is a descendant of v, and w is an ancestor of v.

We claim $l(v) < d(v)$ if and only if a back edge exists between v or one of v's descendants to u or one of u's ancestors. If $l(v) < d(v)$, then there exists a path from v through one of its descendants to an ancestor of v, i.e., v lies on a cycle. For every vertex v, except the root, if $l(v) = d(v)$, it is not possible to get from v back to u; hence removal of (u, v) disconnects u and v. If the root is connected to an edge whose removal disconnects G, the other vertex on that edge will be identified by the technique above, meaning we do not need to consider the root at all.

To compute $l(v)$, note that once we have processed all of v's children, then $l(v) = \min(d(v), \min_{x \in \text{children}(v)} l(x))$.

```cpp
struct GraphVertex {
    int d, l;  // Discovery and leaving time.
    vector<GraphVertex*> edges;
};

bool IsGraphFaultTolerant(vector<GraphVertex>* G) {
    if (!G->empty()) {
        return HasBridge(&G->front(), nullptr, 0);
    }
    return true;
}

bool HasBridge(GraphVertex* cur, GraphVertex* pre, int time) {
    cur->d = ++time, cur->l = numeric_limits<int>::max();
    for (GraphVertex*& next : cur->edges) {
        if (next != pre) {
            if (next->d != 0) {  // Back edge.
                cur->l = min(cur->l, next->d);
            } else {  // Forward edge.
                if (!HasBridge(next, cur, time)) {
                    return false;
                }
                cur->l = min(cur->l, next->l);
            }
        }
    }
}
```

```
    return (pre == nullptr || cur->l < cur->d);
}
```

The program's time complexity is that of DFS—computing $l(v)$ does not add to the asymptotic complexity of DFS since it is just constant additional work per edge, so we can check fault-tolerance in $O(|V| + |E|)$ time.

Variant: Let G be a connected undirected graph. A vertex of G is an *articulation point* if its removal disconnects G. An edge of G is a *bridge* if its removal disconnects G. A *biconnected component* (BCC) of G is a maximal set of edges having the property that any two edges in the set lie on common simple cycle. Design algorithms for computing articulation points, bridges, and BCCs.

22.48 COMPUTE A MINIMUM DELAY SCHEDULE, UNLIMITED RESOURCES 😈

Let $\mathcal{T} = \{T_0, T_1, \ldots, T_{n-1}\}$ be a set of tasks. Each task runs on a single generic server. Task T_i has a duration τ_i, and a set P_i (possibly empty) of tasks that must be completed before T_i can be started. The set is *feasible* if there does not exist a sequence of tasks $\langle T_0, T_1, \ldots, T_{n-1}, T_0 \rangle$ starting and ending at the same task such that for each consecutive pair of tasks, the first task must be completed before the second task can begin.

Given an instance of the task scheduling problem, compute the least amount of time in which all the tasks can be performed, assuming an unlimited number of servers. Explicitly check that the system is feasible.

Hint: What property does a minimal set of infeasible tasks have?

Solution: This problem is naturally modeled using a directed graph. Vertices correspond to tasks, and an edge from u to v indicates that u must be completed before v. The system is infeasible if and only if a cycle is present in the derived graph.

We can check the presence of a cycle by performing a DFS. If no cycle is present, the DFS numbering yields a topological ordering of the graph, i.e., an ordering of the vertices such that v follows u whenever an edge is present from u to v. Specifically, the DFS finishing time gives a topological ordering in reverse order. Therefore, both testing for a cycle and computing a topological ordering can be performed in $O(n+m)$ time, where n and m are the number of vertices and edges in the graph, respectively.

Since the number of servers is unlimited, T_i can be completed τ_i time after all the tasks it depends on have completed. Therefore, we can compute the soonest each task can complete by processing tasks in topological order, starting from the tasks that depend on no other tasks. If no such tasks exist, there must be a sequence of tasks starting and ending at the same task, such that each task requires the previous task to be completed before it can be started, i.e., the system is infeasible.

When the number of servers is limited, the problem becomes NP-complete.

22.49 ROAD NETWORK 😈

The California Department of Transportation is considering adding a new section of highway to the California Highway System. Each highway section connects two cities. City officials have submitted proposals for the new highway—each proposal includes the pair of cities being connected and the length of the section.

Write a program which takes the existing highway network (specified as a set of highway sections between pairs of cities) and proposals for new highway sections, and returns the proposed highway section which leads to the most improvement in the total driving distance. The total driving distance is defined to be the sum of the shortest path distances between all pairs of cities. All sections, existing and proposed, allow for bi-directional traffic, and the original network is connected.

Hint: Suppose we add a new section from b_s to b_f. If the shortest path from u to v passes through this section, what must be true of the part of the path from u to b_s?

Solution: Note that we cannot add more than one proposal to the existing network and run a shortest path algorithm—we may end up with a shortest path which uses multiple proposals.

The brute-force approach would be to first compute the shortest path distances for all pairs in the original network. Then consider the new sections, one-at-a-time, and then compute the new shortest path distances for all pairs, recording the total improvement. The all-pairs shortest path problem can be solved in time $O(n^3)$ using the Floyd-Warshall algorithm, leading to an overall $O(kn^3)$ time complexity.

We can improve upon this by running the all pairs shortest paths algorithm just once. Let $S(u, v)$ be the 2D array of shortest path distances for each pair of cities. Each proposal p is a pair of cities (x, y). For the pair of cities (a, b), the best we can do by using proposal p is $\min(S(a, b), S(a, x) + d(x, y) + S(y, b), S(a, y) + d(y, x) + S(x, b))$ where $d(x, y)$ is the distance of the proposed highway p between x and y. This computation is $O(1)$ time, so we can evaluate all the proposals in time proportional to the number of proposals times the number of pairs after we have computed the shortest path between each pair of cities. This results in an $O(n^3 + kn^2)$ time complexity, which improves substantially on the brute-force approach.

```
struct HighwaySection {
  int x, y;
  double distance;
};


HighwaySection FindBestProposals(const vector<HighwaySection>& H,
                                 const vector<HighwaySection>& P, int n) {
  // G stores the shortest path distances between all pairs of vertices.
  vector<vector<double>> G(n,
                           vector<double>(n, numeric_limits<double>::max()));
  for (int i = 0; i < n; ++i) {
    G[i][i] = 0;
  }
  // Builds an undirected graph G based on existing highway sections H.
  for (const HighwaySection& h : H) {
    G[h.x][h.y] = G[h.y][h.x] = h.distance;
  }

  // Performs Floyd Warshall to build the shortest path between vertices.
  FloydWarshall(&G);
```

486

```
// Examines each proposal for shorter distance for all pairs.
double best_distance_saving = numeric_limits<double>::min();
HighwaySection best_proposal = {-1, -1, 0.0};  // Default.
for (const HighwaySection& p : P) {
  double proposal_saving = 0.0;
  for (int a = 0; a < n; ++a) {
    for (int b = 0; b < n; ++b) {
      double saving = G[a][b] - (G[a][p.x] + p.distance + G[p.y][b]);
      proposal_saving += saving > 0.0 ? saving : 0.0;
    }
  }
  if (proposal_saving > best_distance_saving) {
    best_distance_saving = proposal_saving;
    best_proposal = p;
  }
}
return best_proposal;
}


void FloydWarshall(vector<vector<double>>* G) {
  for (int k = 0; k < G->size(); ++k) {
    for (int i = 0; i < G->size(); ++i) {
      for (int j = 0; j < G->size(); ++j) {
        if ((*G)[i][k] != numeric_limits<double>::max() &&
            (*G)[k][j] != numeric_limits<double>::max() &&
            (*G)[i][j] > (*G)[i][k] + (*G)[k][j]) {
          (*G)[i][j] = (*G)[i][k] + (*G)[k][j];
        }
      }
    }
  }
}
```

22.50 Test if arbitrage is possible

You are exploring the remote valleys of Papua New Guinea, one of the last uncharted places in the world. You come across a tribe that does not have money—instead it relies on the barter system. A total of n commodities are traded and the exchange rates are specified by a 2D array. For example, three sheep can be exchanged for seven goats and four goats can be exchanged for 200 pounds of wheat.

Transaction costs are zero, exchange rates do not fluctuate, fractional quantities of items can be sold, and the exchange rate between each pair of commodities is finite. Table 4.4 on Page 34 shows exchange rates for currency trades, which is similar in spirit to the current problem.

Design an efficient algorithm to determine whether there exists an arbitrage—a way to start with a single unit of some commodity C and convert it back to more than one unit of C through a sequence of exchanges.

Hint: The effect of a sequence of conversions is multiplicative. Can you recast the problem so that it can be calculated additively?

Solution: We define a weighted directed graph $G = (V, E = V \times V)$, where V corresponds to the set of commodities. The weight $w(e)$ of edge $e = (u, v)$ is the amount of commodity v we can buy with one unit of commodity u. Observe that an arbitrage exists if and only if there exists a cycle in G whose edge weights multiply out to more than 1.

Create a new graph $G' = (V, E)$ with weight function $w'(e) = -\lg w(e)$. Since $\lg(a \times b) = \lg a + \lg b$, there exists a cycle in G whose edge weights multiply out to more than 1 if and only if there exists a cycle in G' whose edge weights sum up to less than $\lg 1 = 0$. (This property is true for logarithms to any base, so if it is more efficient for example to use base-e, we can do so.)

The Bellman-Ford algorithm detects negative-weight cycles. Usually, finding a negative-weight cycle is done by adding a dummy vertex s with 0-weight edges to each vertex in the given graph and running the Bellman-Ford single-source shortest path algorithm from s. However, for the arbitrage problem, the graph is complete. Hence, we can run Bellman-Ford algorithm from any single vertex, and get the right result.

```cpp
bool IsArbitrageExist(vector<vector<double>> G) {
  // Transforms each edge in G.
  for (vector<double>& edge_list : G) {
    for (double& edge : edge_list) {
      edge = -log10(edge);
    }
  }

  // Uses Bellman-Ford to find negative weight cycle.
  return BellmanFord(G, 0);
}

bool BellmanFord(const vector<vector<double>>& G, int source) {
  vector<double> dis_to_source(G.size(), numeric_limits<double>::max());
  dis_to_source[source] = 0;

  for (size_t times = 1; times < G.size(); ++times) {
    bool have_update = false;
    for (size_t i = 0; i < G.size(); ++i) {
      for (size_t j = 0; j < G[i].size(); ++j) {
        if (dis_to_source[i] != numeric_limits<double>::max() &&
            dis_to_source[j] > dis_to_source[i] + G[i][j]) {
          have_update = true;
          dis_to_source[j] = dis_to_source[i] + G[i][j];
        }
      }
    }

    // No update in this iteration means no negative cycle.
    if (have_update == false) {
      return false;
    }
  }

  // Detects cycle if there is any further update.
```

```
  for (size_t i = 0; i < G.size(); ++i) {
    for (size_t j = 0; j < G[i].size(); ++j) {
      if (dis_to_source[i] != numeric_limits<double>::max() &&
          dis_to_source[j] > dis_to_source[i] + G[i][j]) {
        return true;
      }
    }
  }
  return false;
}
```

The time complexity of the general Bellman-Ford algorithm is $O(|V||E|)$. Here, $|E| = O(|V|^2)$ and $|V| = n$, so the time complexity is $O(n^3)$.

22.51 THE READERS-WRITERS PROBLEM WITH FAIRNESS 🥷

The specifications to Problems 20.7 on Page 378 and 20.8 on Page 380 allow starvation—the first may starve writers, the second may starve readers. The third readers-writers problem adds the constraint that neither readers nor writers should starve.

Implement a synchronization mechanism for the third readers-writers problem.

Hint: Introduce additional state.

Solution: We can achieve fairness by having a bit indicating whether the last operation performed was a read or a write. If the last operation done was a read, a reader on acquiring a lock must release the lock and retry—this gives writers priority in acquiring the lock. A similar operation is done by writers.

Note that this solution entails readers and writers having to wait longer than is absolutely necessary. Specifically, readers may wait even if s is opened for read and writers may wait even if no one else has a lock on s.

Variant: Categorical starvation refers to a phenomenon in which one category of threads makes another category of threads wait indefinitely. Both Solutions 20.7 on Page 379 and 20.8 on Page 380 exhibit categorical starvation, with the readers and writers constituting the categories. Solution 22.51 guarantees no categorical starvation. Thread starvation refers to a phenomenon in which a specific thread waits indefinitely while others proceed. Solve Problem 22.51 with the added constraint that it is free of thread starvation.

22.52 IMPLEMENT A PRODUCER-CONSUMER QUEUE 🥷

Two threads, the producer P and the consumer C, share a fixed length array of strings. The producer generates strings one at a time which it writes into the array; the consumer removes strings from the array, one at a time.

Design a synchronization mechanism which ensures that P does not try to add a string into the array if it is full and C does not try to remove data from an empty buffer.

Hint: Use `wait` and `notify` judiciously.

Solution: This problem can be solved for a single producer and a single consumer with a pair of semaphores—*fillCount* is incremented and *emptyCount* is decremented whenever an item is added to the buffer. If the producer wants to decrement *emptyCount* when its count is zero, the producer sleeps. The next time an item is consumed, *emptyCount* is incremented and the producer is woken up. The consumer operates analogously. The Java methods, `wait` and `notify`, can be used to implement the desired functionality.

In the presence of multiple producers and consumers, the solution above has two races—two producers can try writing to the same slot and two consumers can read from the same slot. These races can be removed by adding mutexes around the insert and delete calls.

Part III

Notation, Language, and Index

Notation

To speak about notation as the only way that you can guarantee structure of course is already very suspect.

— E. S. Parker

We use the following convention for symbols, unless the surrounding text specifies otherwise:

A	k-dimensional array
L	linked list or doubly linked list
S	set
T	tree
G	graph
V	set of vertices of a graph
E	set of edges of a graph

Symbolism	Meaning
$(d_{k-1} \ldots d_0)_r$	radix-r representation of a number, e.g., $(1011)_2$
$\log_b x$	logarithm of x to the base b
$\lg x$	logarithm of x to the base 2
$\|S\|$	cardinality of set S
$S \setminus T$	set difference, i.e., $S \cap T'$, sometimes written as $S - T$
$\|x\|$	absolute value of x
$\lfloor x \rfloor$	greatest integer less than or equal to x
$\lceil x \rceil$	smallest integer greater than or equal to x
$\langle a_0, a_1, \ldots, a_{n-1} \rangle$	sequence of n elements
$\sum_{R(k)} f(k)$	sum of all $f(k)$ such that relation $R(k)$ is true
$\min_{R(k)} f(k)$	minimum of all $f(k)$ such that relation $R(k)$ is true
$\max_{R(k)} f(k)$	maximum of all $f(k)$ such that relation $R(k)$ is true
$\sum_{k=a}^{b} f(k)$	shorthand for $\sum_{a \leq k \leq b} f(k)$
$\{a \mid R(a)\}$	set of all a such that the relation $R(a)$ = true
$[l, r]$	closed interval: $\{x \mid l \leq x \leq r\}$
$[l, r)$	left-closed, right-open interval: $\{x \mid l \leq x < r\}$
$\{a, b, \ldots\}$	well-defined collection of elements, i.e., a set
A_i or $A[i]$	the ith element of one-dimensional array A

$A[i:j]$	subarray of one-dimensional array A consisting of elements at indices i to j inclusive
$A[i][j]$ or $A[i,j]$	the element in ith row and jth column of 2D array A
$A[i_1:i_2][j_1:j_2]$	2D subarray of 2D array A consisting of elements from i_1th to i_2th rows and from j_1th to j_2th column, inclusive
$\binom{n}{k}$	binomial coefficient: number of ways of choosing k elements from a set of n items
$n!$	n-factorial, the product of the integers from 1 to n, inclusive
$O\big(f(n)\big)$	big-oh complexity of $f(n)$, asymptotic upper bound
$x \bmod y$	mod function
$x \oplus y$	bitwise-XOR function
$x \approx y$	x is approximately equal to y
null	pointer value reserved for indicating that the pointer does not refer to a valid address
$\emptyset$	empty set
∞	infinity: Informally, a number larger than any number.
$x \ll y$	much less than
$x \gg y$	much greater than
$\Rightarrow$	logical implication

C++11, and C++ for Java developers

The limits of my language means the limits of my world.

— L. WITTGENSTEIN

C++ best practices

We use a number of C++ best practices. These are largely drawn from Google's C++ programming style guide (which is freely available) and from Scott Meyer's wonderful book "Effective Modern C++". The following are examples of practices that you may not appreciate without a short explanation:

- We use deque<bool> for Boolean arrays, rather than vector<bool>. The latter is not an STL container, and does not really hold bools. For example, bool *pb =&A[0]; will not compile if *A* is of type vector<bool>.
- Input arguments to functions are either values or const references. We never allow non-const references, except when required by convention, e.g., swap(). We use pointers to pass output arguments to functions. (This is motivated by not wanting readers to have to go to the function source code to see if an argument is updated by the called function.)

C++11 constructs

C++11 adds a number of features to C++ that make for elegant and efficient code. The C++11 constructs used in the solution code are as follows:

- The auto attribute assigns the type of a variable based on the initializer expression.
- The enhanced range-based for-loop allows for easy iteration over a list of elements.
- The emplace_front and emplace_back methods add new elements to the beginning and end of the container. They are more efficient than push_front and push_back, and are variadic, i.e., takes a variable number arguments. The emplace method is similar and applicable to containers where there is only one way to insert (e.g., a stack or a map).
- The array type is similar to ordinary arrays, but supports .size() and boundary checking. (It does not support automatic and dynamic resizing.)
- The tuple type implements an ordered set.

494

- Anonymous functions ("lambdas") can be written via the [] notation. See Solution 22.44 on Page 478 for an example.
- An initializer list uses the {} notation to avoid having to make explicit calls to constructors when building list-like objects.

C++ for Java developers

C++ is an order of magnitude more complex than Java. Here are some facts about C++ that can help Java programmers better understand the solution code:

- Operators in C++ can be overloaded. For example, < can be applied to comparing BigNumber objects. The array indexing operator ([]) is often overloaded for unordered maps and tree maps, e.g., map[k] returns the value associated with key k.
- Java's HashMap and HashSet correspond to C++'s unordered_map and unordered_set, respectively. Java's TreeSet and TreeMap correspond to C++'s set and map.
- For set, the comparator is the second argument to the template specification. For map, the comparator is the third argument to the template specification. (If < is overloaded, the comparator is optional in both cases.)
- For unordered_map the first argument is the key type, the second is the value type, and the third (optional) is the hash function. For unordered_set the first argument is the key type, the second (optional) is the hash function, the third (optional) is the equals function. The class may simply overload ==, i.e., implement the method operator==. See Solution 22.22 on Page 435 for an example.
- C++ uses streams for input-output. The overloaded operators « and » are used to read and write primitive types and objects from and to streams.
- The :: notation is used to invoke a static member function or refer to a static field.
- C++ has a built-in pair class used to represent arbitrary pairs.
- A static_cast is used to cast primitive types, e.g., int to double, as well as an object to a derived class. The latter is not checked at run time. The compiler checks obvious incompatibilities at compile time.
- A unique_ptr is a smart pointer that retains sole ownership of an object through a pointer and destroys that object when the unique_ptr goes out of scope.
- A shared_ptr is a smart pointer with a reference count which the runtime system uses to implement automatic garbage collection.

Index of Terms

Acknowledgments

Several of our friends, colleagues, and readers gave feedback. We would like to thank Taras Bobrovytsky, Senthil Chellappan, Yi-Ting Chen, Monica Farkash, Dongbo Hu, Jing-Tang Keith Jang, Matthieu Jeanson, Gerson Kurz, Danyu Liu, Hari Mony, Shaun Phillips, Gayatri Ramachandran, Ulises Reyes, Kumud Sanwal, Tom Shiple, Ian Varley, Shaohua Wan, Don Wong, and Xiang Wu for their input.

I, Adnan Aziz, thank my teachers, friends, and students from IIT Kanpur, UC Berkeley, and UT Austin for having nurtured my passion for programming. I especially thank my friends Vineet Gupta, Tom Shiple, and Vigyan Singhal, and my teachers Robert Solovay, Robert Brayton, Richard Karp, Raimund Seidel, and Somenath Biswas, for all that they taught me. My coauthor, Tsung-Hsien Lee, brought a passion that was infectious and inspirational. My coauthor, Amit Prakash, has been a wonderful collaborator for many years—this book is a testament to his intellect, creativity, and enthusiasm. I look forward to a lifelong collaboration with both of them.

I, Tsung-Hsien Lee, would like to thank my coauthors, Adnan Aziz and Amit Prakash, who give me this once-in-a-life-time opportunity. I also thank my teachers Wen-Lian Hsu, Ren-Song Tsay, Biing-Feng Wang, and Ting-Chi Wang for having initiated and nurtured my passion for computer science in general, and algorithms in particular. I would like to thank my friends Cheng-Yi He, Da-Cheng Juan, Chien-Hsin Lin, and Chih-Chiang Yu, who accompanied me on the road of savoring the joy of programming contests; and Kuan-Chieh Chen, Chun-Cheng Chou, Ray Chuang, Wilson Hong, Wei-Lun Hung, Nigel Liang, and Huan-Kai Peng, who give me valuable feedback on this book. Last, I would like to thank all my friends and colleagues at Google, Facebook, National Tsing Hua University, and UT Austin for the brainstorming on puzzles; it is indeed my greatest honor to have known all of you.

I, Amit Prakash, have my coauthor and mentor, Adnan Aziz, to thank the most for this book. To a great extent, my problem solving skills have been shaped by Adnan. There have been occasions in life when I would not have made it through without his help. He is also the best possible collaborator I can think of for any intellectual endeavor. I have come to know Tsung-Hsien through working on this book. He has been a great coauthor. His passion and commitment to excellence can be seen everywhere in this book. Over the years, I have been fortunate to have had great teachers at IIT Kanpur and UT Austin. I would especially like to thank my teachers Scott Nettles, Vijaya Ramachandran, and Gustavo de Veciana. I would also like to thank my friends and colleagues at Google, Microsoft, IIT Kanpur, and UT Austin for many stimulating conversations and problem solving sessions. Finally, and most importantly, I want to thank my family who have been a constant source of support, excitement, and joy all my life and especially during the process of writing this book.

ADNAN AZIZ
TSUNG-HSIEN LEE
AMIT PRAKASH
October, 2012

Austin, Texas
Mountain View, California
Belmont, California

Made in the USA
San Bernardino, CA
12 March 2016